DATA SCIENCE FOR MIGRATION AND MOBILITY

For over 100 years the *Proceedings of the British Academy* series has provided a unique record of British scholarship in the humanities and social sciences. Each themed volume drives scholarship forward and are landmarks in their field. For more information about the series and guidance on submitting a proposal for publication, please visit www.thebritishacademy.ac.uk/proceedings

PROCEEDINGS OF THE BRITISH ACADEMY • 251

DATA SCIENCE FOR MIGRATION AND MOBILITY

Edited by
ALBERT A. SALAH, EMRE E. KORKMAZ,
AND TUBA BIRCAN

Published for THE BRITISH ACADEMY
by OXFORD UNIVERSITY PRESS

Oxford University Press, Great Clarendon Street, Oxford OX2 6DP

© *The British Academy 2022*

Database right The British Academy (maker)

First edition published in 2022

All rights reserved. No part of this publication may be reproduced, stored in a retrieval system, or transmitted, in any form or by any means, without the prior permission in writing of the British Academy, or as expressly permitted by law, by licence, or under terms agreed with the appropriate reprographics rights organisation. Enquiries concerning reproduction outside the scope of the above should be sent to the Publications Department, The British Academy, 10–11 Carlton House Terrace, London SW1Y 5AH

You must not circulate this book in any other form and you must impose this same condition on any acquirer

British Library Cataloguing in Publication Data
Data available

Library of Congress Cataloging in Publication Data
Data available

Typeset by Newgen Publishing UK
Printed in Great Britain by TJ Books Ltd, Padstow, Cornwall

ISBN 978-0-19-726710-3
ISSN 0068-1202

For my parents, Riva and Eli,
and for Nil, the hero of the family.
A.A.S.

For my dear wife Meltem,
and kids Selen and Alp Efe.
E.E.K.

For my sister Tuğçe, the strongest
tie to the best years of my life.
T.B.

Contents

List of Figures	x
Colour Plates	xiii
List of Tables	xxi
Notes on Contributors	xxii
Preface	xxxii

Part I: Introduction — 1

1 New Data Sources and Computational Approaches to Migration and Human Mobility — 3
ALBERT ALI SALAH, TUBA BIRCAN, AND EMRE EREN KORKMAZ

2 Ethical and Legal Concerns on Data Science for Large-Scale Human Mobility — 24
ALBERT ALI SALAH, CANSU CANCA, AND BARIŞ ERMAN

Part II: Data Sources — 49

3 CESSDA Data Catalogue: Opportunities and Challenges to Explore Mobility and Migration — 51
DIMITRA KONDYLI, RON DEKKER, AND IVANA ILIJASIC VERSIC

4 Leveraging Mobile Phone Data for Migration Flows — 71
MASSIMILIANO LUCA, GIANNI BARLACCHI, NURIA OLIVER, AND BRUNO LEPRI

5 Analysing Refugees' Secondary Mobility Using Mobile Phone Call Detail Records — 94
HARALD STERLY AND LARS WIRKUS

6 Remote Sensing Data for Migration Research — 115
TUBA BIRCAN

7 Using Facebook and LinkedIn Data to Study International Mobility — 141
CAROLINA COIMBRA VIEIRA, MASOOMALI FATEHKIA, KIRAN GARIMELLA, INGMAR WEBER AND EMILIO ZAGHENI

8	Twitter Data for Migration Studies JISU KIM, LAURA POLLACCI, GIULIO ROSSETTI, ALINA SÎRBU, FOSCA GIANNOTTI, AND DINO PEDRESCHI	159
9	Indicators and Survey Data to Understand Migration and Integration Policy Frameworks and Trends in the EU GIACOMO SOLANO	183
10	Financial Datasets: Leveraging Transactional Big Data in Mobility and Migration Studies MERT GÜRKAN, BURÇIN BOZKAYA, AND SELIM BALCISOY	211

Part III: Visualisation — 239

11	Visual Exploration of Large Multidimensional Trajectory Data ALEXANDRU TELEA AND MICHAEL BEHRISCH	241
12	Voyage Viewer: A Multivariate Visualisation Tool for Migration Analysis ISABELLA LOAIZA, GERMÁN SÁNCHEZ, SERENA CHAN, FELIPE MONTES JIMÉNEZ, MOHSEN BAHRAMI, AND ALEX PENTLAND	267

Part IV: Case Studies and Applications — 289

13	Combining Mobile Call Data and Satellite Imaging for Human Mobility TUĞBA BOZCAGA AND ASLI CANSUNAR	291
14	Using Machine Learning and Synthetic Populations to Predict Support for Refugees and Asylum Seekers in European Regions CARLOS ARCILA-CALDERÓN, JAVIER J. AMORES, AND MIKOLAJ STANEK	310
15	Issues about Analysing Multilingual Communication in Immigrant Contexts A. SEZA DOĞRUÖZ	336
16	Applying Computational Linguistic and Text Analysis to Media Content about Migration WILLIAM L. ALLEN	352
17	Exploring Digital Connectivities in Forced Migration Contexts: 'Digital Making-Do' Practices AMANDA ALENCAR AND MARIE GODIN	366

18	Conflict and Forced Migration: Social Media as Event Data H. AKIN UNVER AND AHMET KURNAZ	383

Part V: A Final Word — **403**

19	Eight Theses on Migration Studies and Big Data EMRE EREN KORKMAZ	405
	Glossary	419
	Index	423

List of Figures

1.1	Stakeholders and collaborators in data science for migration and mobility.	12
2.1	*The Box* tool for visualising the strengths and weaknesses of a technology from an ethical perspective.	37
3.1	The CESSDA Data Catalogue in a nutshell.	55
3.2	How the CESSDA Data Catalogue looks.	55
3.3	Metadata record of a dataset in the CESSDA Data Catalogue.	56
3.4	Searching and locating migration datasets via the CESSDA Data Catalogue portal.	60
3.5	Migration topics related to the migration studies in the CDC.	61
3.6	The EthmigSurveyDataHub registry.	65
3.7	Overview of the Data Management Expert Guide.	68
4.1	Example of area covered by different antennas in a cellular network.	73
5.1	Number of unique users who are recorded in Dataset 3 as calling or texting on a given day, for all 365 days of 2017, by refugee status.	102
5.2	'Mobile' and 'less mobile' callers in the dataset.	104
5.3	Net migration of refugees between Turkish provinces in 2017.	106
5.4	Mobility of refugees between districts in 2017; all movements over 100 km between districts shown.	106
5.5	Mobility per day, expressed as the ratio of mobile by total refugee/non-refugee callers on that day.	109
5.6	Mobility per week into and out of the northern hazelnut provinces, expressed as the ratio of mobile callers to total refugee/non-refugee callers in these provinces in this week.	109
6.1	Remote sensing sensor systems.	118
6.2	Schematic depiction of the remote sensing process.	124
7.1	Facebook's advertising platform for an advertisement targeting women living in Colombia who used to live in Venezuela.	144
7.2	Facebook and American Community Survey (ACS) profiles of stocks of migrants by age and sex for Mexicans in California and in Texas.	145
7.3	Example for LinkedIn's advertising platform.	149
7.4	A circular plot showing estimates for the number of people who studied in one European country, but are currently living in another.	150
7.5	Estimates of the number of college-educated people from Syria living in the European Union (EU).	151
7.6	The approach used to combine data from the Facebook advertising platform and data from the ACS.	156
8.1	Twitter user terms of service over time.	169

List of Figures

8.2	The top 20 countries in terms of number of Twitter users (in millions) as of January 2021.	175
9.1	Example of indicators from IMPIC.	185
9.2	Example of aggregation structure from CITRIX.	186
9.3	Topics covered by existing indices.	188
9.4	Countries covered by existing indices (world).	191
9.5	Countries covered by existing indices (Europe).	192
9.6	Years covered by existing indices.	193
9.7	Policy areas included in MIPEX, and indicators for each area.	194
9.8	Example of MIPEX indicators.	195
9.9	MIPEX interactive tool.	195
9.10	Eurostat database.	198
9.11	Eurostat database explorer example.	199
10.1	The numbers of transactions per spending category in the transactions dataset.	219
10.2	The top 20 cities in terms of the number of transactions in the dataset.	220
10.3	The top 20 cities with respect to the number of unique customers in the dataset.	221
10.4	Heatmap of transactions with a sample size of 25,000.	222
10.5	Distributions of gender and marital status in the dataset.	222
10.6	Distributions of education status, gender, and income in the dataset.	223
10.7	Origin and destination cities of customers.	225
10.8	Spending categories of customers in origin and destination cities.	227
10.9	Spending categories of customers in origin and destination cities.	228
10.10	Diversity metrics of customers.	229
10.11	Choropleth maps of the findings of Scenario 0.	230
10.12	Choropleth maps of the findings of Scenario 2.	231
11.1	Refugee movements between origin and destination (asylum) countries in 2000 visualised with four methods.	244
11.2	(a) Schema for storing migration data. (b) Relation of path-sets, graphs, and graph drawings.	246
11.3	Examples of straight-line path data (a) and trail data (b,c).	248
11.4	Aggregate visualisations of geographical movement data.	250
11.5	Visualisation of US migration dataset by several methods.	251
11.6	Visualisation of dynamic motion data using (a) small multiples and (b) animation.	253
11.7	Other visualisation types for migration data: (a) matrix metaphor; (b) MatLink; (c) MapTrix; (d) OD Maps; (e) SpaceCuts.	255
11.8	Visual analytics workflow for exploring commuter flow in the greater São Paulo area.	260
12.1	Heat map comparing different visualisations for migration.	271
12.2	Examples of visualisations for migration.	272
12.3	Voyage Viewer inputs and resources, outputs and outcomes.	275

12.4	Voyage Viewer MERN (MongoDB, Express, React, Node) application architecture.	277
12.5	World map visualisation in Voyage Viewer.	278
12.6	Layers of Voyage Viewer's World Map.	279
12.7	Some of the visualisations that are created by the People Like Me feature.	282
12.8	People Like Me: Employment and Income.	283
12.9	Policy actors use case.	285
13.1	Internal migration patterns of four refugees by number of movements.	298
13.2	CORINE land cover, Turkey, 2018.	299
14.1	Random forest features.	323
14.2	Jupyter notebook to create synthetic populations.	324
14.3	Jupyter notebook to estimate the probability of acceptance of refugees for each region.	324
14.4	Comparative visualisation of the estimates on refugee support with the six predictive models in all regions of Europe.	326
14.5	Summarised visualisation with the average probability of acceptance for the six models and all the analysed periods (2015–2017).	327
14.6	Average level of support for refugees by country and total descriptive statistics.	328
14.7	Estimated refugee support in regions of Spain, Italy, and Greece.	328
14.8	Longitudinal estimates of support for refugees in Europe by period.	330
18.1	A sample workflow for automated violent event data extraction and processing.	391
18.2	Region-level violent event data comparison in geographic relationship to the nearest refugee camps.	395
18.3	Town-level (Afrin) violent event data comparison.	396
18.4	Time-series graph showing ACLED, Twitter, and UCDP data frequencies corresponding to major violent events.	397

Colour Plates

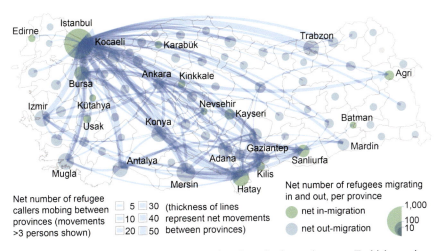

Plate 1 Colour version of Figure 5.3. Net migration of refugees between Turkish provinces in 2017; only movements between first and last residence over 100 km are shown. (Source: Sterly *et al*. (2019), modified)

xiv   *Colour Plates*

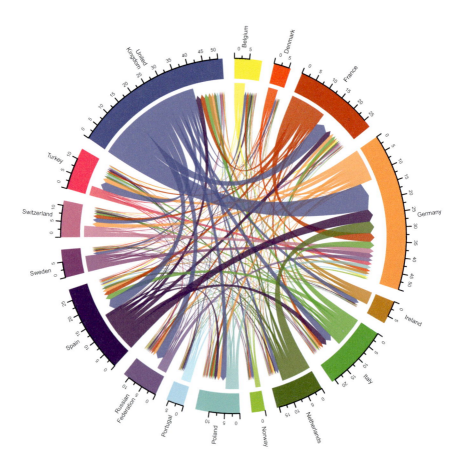

Plate 2 Colour version of Figure 7.4. A circular plot showing estimates for the number of people who studied in one European country, but are currently living in another. The numbers are in hundred thousands (100,000s). The estimates were obtained through LinkedIn's advertising platform, and corrected for LinkedIn penetration rates in the host country. Assuming migrants are overrepresented on LinkedIn compared to non-migrants, the estimates would be upper bounds for the true numbers.

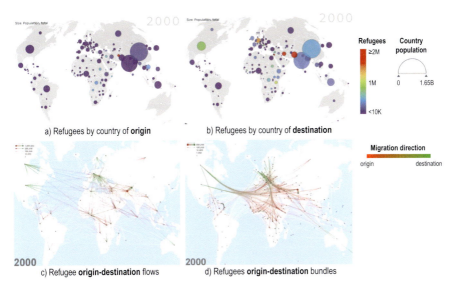

Plate 3 Colour version of Figure 11.1. Refugee movements between origin and destination (asylum) countries in 2000 visualised with four methods. (a,b) Refugee counts per origin, respectively destination, countries shown in GapMinder (Gapminder, 2020). (c) Refugee flows depicted as straight lines (red = origin, green = destination) in JFlowMap (Boyandin, 2010). (d) The same image as (c) but simplified by trail bundling.

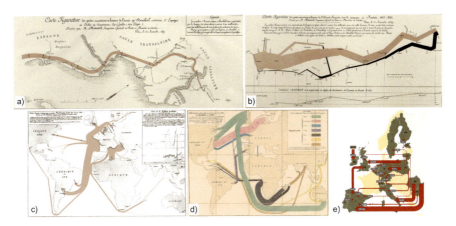

Plate 4 Colour version of Figure 11.4. Aggregate visualisations of geographical movement data. Flow maps of (a) the campaign of Hannibal (Minard, 1869); (b) the campaign of Napoleon in Russia (Minard, 1869); (c) French wine exports (Minard, 1864); (d) word migration map (Minard, 1862); (e) intra-European migrations in 2006 (Hossmann et al., 2008).

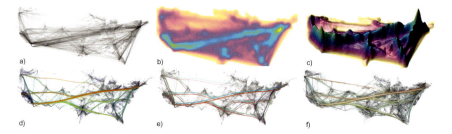

Plate 5 Colour version of Figure 11.5. Visualisation of US migration dataset by several methods. From simple to involved: (a) blending of straight-line trails; (b) colour-coded density map; (c) height- and colour-coded density map; (d) bundled trails using path-length colouring; (e) directional bundling; (f) pseudo-shading of bundles. Figures generated with the open-source CUBu software (van der Zwan et al., 2016).

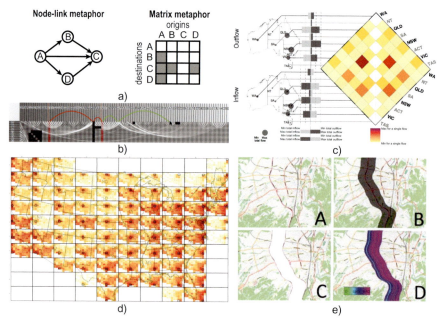

Plate 6 Colour version of Figure 11.7. Other visualisation types for migration data: (a) matrix metaphor; (b) MatLink (Yang et al., 2017); (c) MapTrix (Yang et al., 2017); (d) OD Maps (Wood et al., 2010); (e) SpaceCuts (Buchmüller et al., 2016).

Colour Plates xvii

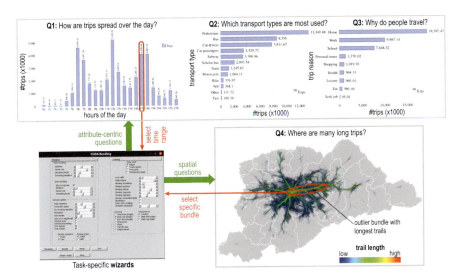

Plate 7 Colour version of Figure 11.8. Visual analytics workflow for exploring commuter flow in the greater São Paulo area (Martins *et al.*, 2020), constructed using the CUBu open-source tool (van der Zwan *et al.*, 2016).

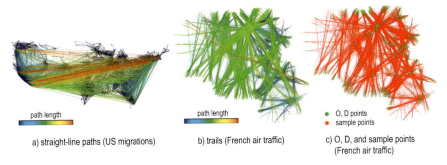

Plate 8 Colour version of Figure 12.2. Examples of straight-line path data (a) and trail data (b,c). Figures generated with the open-source CUBu software (van der Zwan *et al.*, 2016).

xviii   Colour Plates

Plate 9 Colour version of Figure 11.3. Examples of visualisations for migration. This figure shows screenshots of selected visualisations about migration. A The interface to the Refugee Project. B The interface of the World in Numbers. C The visualisation prepared for UNICEF with the data from the Uprooted report of 2016.

Colour Plates xix

Plate 10 Colour version of Figure 12.9. Policy actors use case. A Intercity flows for five origin cities exporting the highest number of migrants to Adana city in the sample dataset, and a bar plot to show the aggregated number of migrants by month. When hovering on paths detailed information is shown. B Sankey diagram of refugees migrating to Adana. C Choropleth for refugee social integration index at city level.

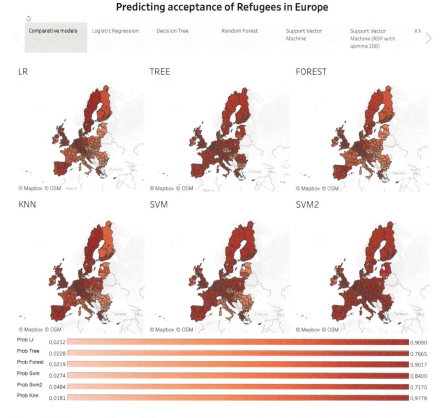

Plate 11 Colour version of Figure 14.4. Comparative visualisation of the estimates on refugee support with the six predictive models in all regions of Europe.

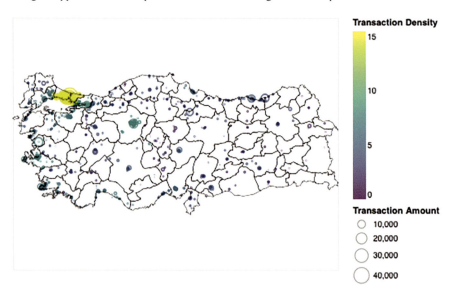

Plate 12 Colour version of Figure 10.4. Heatmap of transactions with a sample size of 25,000. Lighter colours denote areas with higher transaction density. Transaction amount information is encoded with circle sizes drawn on the heatmap.

List of Tables

1.1	Organising empirical modelling along two dimensions proposed by Hofman *et al.* (2021), simplified from the original	7
4.1	Example CDR for user u_1 for a specific date	74
5.1	Example data rows for Dataset 3	102
6.1	Overview of major remote sensing data sources	119
6.2	Overview of major remote sensing derived land products	126
9.1	Characteristics of indices on migration policy	187
9.2	Characteristics of data on migration and integration trends	197
9.3	Gaps in data	204
10.1	Statistical properties of the transactions dataset	218
10.2	Details of the transactions dataset with the introduced filtering options	224
10.3	Number of unique customers with minimum transactions per city	224
10.4	Number of customers categorised as settled to a new city	226
10.5	Findings from scenarios and estimated migration numbers	232
10.6	Correlation coefficients between case study findings and estimates published by the Turkey Statistical Institute	233
11.1	Software for processing and visualising (multivariate) motion data	261
13.1	CORINE land types by group	300
13.2	Characteristics of receiving districts by measurement strategy	303
14.1	Variables from Eurobarometer to model the level of support for refugees in Europe	321
14.2	Evaluation metrics and parameters of the general models	322
14.3	Logistic regression coefficients	322
18.1	A sample meta-keyword list containing macro-level violent event types	394
18.2	Actor-specific entity recognition list for Kurdish groups in, or relevant to, northern Syria	394

Notes on Contributors

Amanda Paz Alencar is a digital migration scholar specialising in the study of media and social media in Europe and Latin America, with a focus on how communication technologies are shaping (forced) migration processes. She is an associate professor in the Department of Media & Communication at Erasmus University Rotterdam, and Chair of the Intercultural Communication Division within International Communication Association. Amanda has guest-edited two special issues in the peer-reviewed journals *International Communication Gazette* and *Media and Communication* on media, communication, and forced migration. Alongside her academic work, she coordinates a digital training programme at EUR for students with a refugee background.

William Allen is a British Academy postdoctoral fellow at the Department of Politics and International Relations (DPIR), University of Oxford. His research agenda uses migration as a lens onto the dynamics, causes, and consequences of citizen engagement with political and economic information, particularly via digital media. This work has been recognised with awards from the UK Political Studies Association and the American Political Science Association. He also has interests in developing new approaches that connect computational, experimental, and causal inferential methods to address applied social scientific questions. He currently serves as associate editor for *Journal of Refugee Studies* and *Evidence & Policy*.

Javier J. Amores is a communication researcher and member of the Observatory of Audiovisual Contents (OCA). A graduate in audiovisual communication and master in audiovisual communication research with an Extraordinary Award from the University of Salamanca, he is currently developing his PhD dissertation at the same university, with the financial support of the Castilla y León Regional Government and the European Social Fund. His lines of research are focused on the analysis of news media and social networks, social communication, hate speech, and computational methods applied in social sciences.

Carlos Arcila-Calderón is an associate professor at the University of Salamanca (Spain) and a member of the OCA. He holds a PhD in communication from Universidad Complutense de Madrid, a master's in data science and a master's in journalism. He is the principal investigator of the European project Preventing Hate Against Refugees and Migrants (PHARM; funded by the REC programme of the European Commission) and the national project Data Science in Spain: Knowledge and Public Perception of Big Data and Artificial Intelligence (funded by

FECYT), as well as local principal investigator of enhanced migration measures from a multidimensional perspective (HumMingBird; funded by H2020).

Mohsen Bahrami is a postdoctoral researcher at the Connection Science group at the MIT Institute for Data, Systems, and Society. His research field is computational social science and he has been working on data-driven behavioural analytics to analyse, describe, and predict individual and group behaviour using large-scale datasets from various industries. He has conducted academic research and completed industry projects under the supervision of Professor Pentland. He is currently conducting research concerning how human mobility, social interactions, and peer influence can affect health and economic outcomes in urban areas.

Selim Balcisoy is professor at Sabancı University, Faculty of Engineering and Natural Sciences. He previously held positions at Nokia Research Center, Dallas, USA and EPFL Computer Graphics Lab, Lausanne, Switzerland, and co-founded VisioThink and Health Mobile Software.

Gianni Barlacchi is a machine learning scientist at Amazon Alexa, working on deep learning for natural language processing. He obtained his PhD in computer science from the University of Trento (Italy), with a thesis on machine learning models for urban computing, focusing in particular on human mobility and land use classification through semantic data. During his PhD he was a visiting researcher at Telefonica Research, IBM Research, and Amazon, and he is one of the authors and core developers of scikit-mobility, a Python library for human mobility analysis.

Michael Behrisch is an assistant professor for visual analytics in the Visualization and Graphics Group at the Utrecht University, Department of Information and Computing Sciences. His research seeks to develop interactive data analysis methods for non-expert users, with respect to visualisation and data mining, that enable understanding and reasoning in bigger and more complex datasets. He focuses on the effective combination of techniques from visualisation, human–computer interaction, statistics, machine learning, and data mining. In these so-called visual analytics systems the enormous processing power of computers and the problem-solving creativity of humans coalesce through visual interactive interfaces.

Tuba Bircan is an assistant professor at the Department of Sociology and the research coordinator of the Interface Demography research group, at Vrije Universiteit Brussel (VUB), Belgium, and a senior research associate at HIVA (KU Leuven). She has held visiting fellowships at Utrecht University and the University of Cambridge. As an interdisciplinary researcher, her scholarly interests cover a wide range from migration, refugees, inequalities, equal opportunities, and social and public policies to new methodologies and use of big data and artificial intelligence (AI) for studying societal challenges.

Tugba Bozcaga is an assistant professor in politics and political methodology at King's College, London, and a fellow at Harvard University's Middle East Initiative. Previously she was a postdoctoral fellow at the Middle East Initiative at Harvard University's Kennedy School. She completed her PhD at MIT. Her work has been awarded the Mancur Olson Best Dissertation Prize (Honorable Mention) from the APSA Political Economy Section, the Weber Best Conference Paper Award from the APSA Religion and Politics Section, the Best Comparative Policy Paper Award from the APSA Public Policy Section, and Best Paper awards from the APSA MENA Politics Section. She is also a faculty fellow at the Association for Analytic Learning about Islam and Muslim Societies (AALIMS) and the Program on Governance and Local Development (GLD).

Burcin Bozkaya is director of data science and professor of data science at New College of Florida. He holds a PhD in management science from the University of Alberta, Canada. Dr. Bozkaya has been a professor of business analytics at Sabanci University's Sabanci School of Management in Istanbul, Turkey, and a visiting professor at the Media Lab at MIT, analysing high-dimensional datasets.

Cansu Canca is a moral and political philosopher, with a PhD specialising in applied ethics. She is the founder and director of the AI Ethics Lab. She is also the ethics lead and research associate professor at the Institute for Experiential AI at Northeastern University, and serves as an AI ethics and governance expert consultant at the United Nations. she was formerly in the faculty at the University of Hong Kong, and an ethics researcher at Harvard Law School, Harvard School of Public Health, Harvard Medical School, National University of Singapore, Osaka University, and the World Health Organization. Canca started the AI Ethics Lab in late 2016 (based in Cambridge, MA) focusing on integrating ethics into the innovation process. In 2018, she was listed among the '30 Influential Women Advancing AI in Boston', and in 2019 among the '100 Brilliant Women in AI Ethics'. She is a founding editor for *AI and Ethics* journal.

Asli Cansunar is an assistant professor of Political Science at the University of Washington. She holds a PhD in political science (2018) and an MA in economics (2014) from Duke University. Her research lies at the intersection of comparative political economy, comparative politics, and economic history, focusing on the political consequences of economic inequality. She teaches courses on economic inequality, political methodology, politics of the Middle East, and geospatial analysis.

Serena Chan is a first-generation, second-year undergraduate student at Wellesley College majoring in political science and cinema & media studies. She has assisted in researching visualisations for depicting international migration for Voyage Viewer.

Notes on Contributors

Carolina Coimbra Vieira is currently a PhD student at Max Planck Institute for Demographic Research (MPIDR). She holds her master's degree in computer science from the Federal University of Minas Gerais in Brazil. She has been exploring the use of social media data to assess the bidirectional relation between migration and cultural diffusion.

Ron Dekker is the owner of Open Science Apex (www.osapex.eu) and associated consultant at Technopolis Group Belgium where he coordinates the Open Science Team. Until 2021, he was the director of CESSDA ERIC, the Consortium of Social Science Data Archives, with its main office in Bergen, Norway. CESSDA is a European Infrastructure with 23 members (countries) and combines the work and expertise of these countries' social science data service providers, see www.cessda.eu. Ron studied econometrics and worked for ten years in labour market research at Dutch universities. He was at the national research council for almost twenty years – running a data agency and program committees, and in general management (institutes, infrastructure, and open science). This included secondment to the Dutch government for project leadership on open science for the Dutch EU Presidency in 2016, and as national expert at the European Commission in Brussels in 2017.

A. Seza Doğruöz is a tenured faculty at Ghent University. Dr. Doğruöz investigates the link between multilingual language use and society through spoken and online datasets combining qualitative and computational methods of analysis.

Barış Erman has a law degree from Istanbul University, Faculty of Law, and has held positions at Istanbul University and Istanbul Bilgi University. He is currently an assistant professor at Yeditepe University, and lectures on comparative and international penal law.

Masoomali Fatehkia is a research assistant at the Social Computing group of the Qatar Computing Research Institute (QCRI). He works on data for social good research projects, in particular studying the use of social media advertising data for monitoring development goals such as mapping poverty and monitoring digital gender inequalities.

Kiran Garimella is the Michael Hammer postdoc at the Institute for Data, Systems, and Society at MIT. Before joining MIT he was a postdoc at EPFL, Switzerland. His research focuses on using digital data for social good, including areas like polarisation, misinformation, and human migration. His work on studying and mitigating polarisation on social media won the best student paper awards at top computer science conferences. Kiran received his PhD in computer science at Aalto University, Finland, and master's and bachelor's from IIIT Hyderabad, India. Prior to his PhD he worked as a research engineer at Yahoo Research, Barcelona, and QCRI, Doha.

Fosca Giannotti is a director of research in computer science at the Information Science and Technology Institute 'A. Faedo' of the National Research Council, Pisa, Italy. She is a pioneering scientist in mobility data mining, social network analysis, and privacy-preserving data mining. Fosca leads the Pisa Knowledge Discovery and Data Mining (KDD) Laboratory, a joint research initiative of the University of Pisa and ISTI-CNR. She has coordinated tens of European projects and industrial collaborations. She was recently the recipient of a prestigious ERC Advanced Grant entitled XAI – Science and technology for the explanation of AI decision-making.

Marie Godin is a British Academy postdoctoral fellow at the Refugee Studies Centre (University of Oxford). She holds an MSc in forced migration from the same institution, and a PhD in social sciences from the University of East London. Her research project looks at the nexus between forced migration, social protection, and digital technologies, with a particular focus on international migration from sub-Saharan Africa to Europe. Her broader research interests lie in the area of migration and development, with a focus on diaspora engagement, and gender and political activism. Marie has published extensively on the Congolese diaspora and the politics of 'home' and belongings in different contexts.

Mert Gürkan is a researcher at the Behavioral Analytics and Visualization Lab, and recently finished his master's degree in computer science and engineering at Sabancı University, Turkey. He has assisted in research projects on computational social science, behavioural analysis, and the application of data-driven methods in medical domains. His recent research has covered the integration of innovative data sources for studying migration movements.

Ivana Ilijasic Versic holds a postgraduate degree in economic sciences and a PhD in psychology. For more than 15 years she has also been involved in the project management and coordination of around 20 European Union funded projects and has participated in the development of around 100 project proposals. Ivana has been Chief Operations Officer of CESSDA ERIC since 2017, and is responsible for the overall coordination and supervision of external and internal developments at CESSDA, as well as strategic direction and planning as part of the management board. She is also coordinating the work of CESSDA Working Groups.

Jisu Kim obtained her PhD in data science at Scuola Normale Superiore in Italy and is a research scientist at Max Planck Institute for Demographic Research (MPIDR). She holds a master's degree in applied economics from University of Paris 1 Panthéon-Sorbonne. She has been working on exploring and developing novel methods to improve relevant statistics of international migration using social media data.

Dimitra Kondyli is a research director at the Institute of Social Research, National Centre for Social Research (EKKE), and is one of this with scientific responsibility for the EKKE Repository. She has studied sociology, political sciences, and anthropology in France. Her main research interests include social research methodological issues pertaining to the development of research infrastructure and migration from a gender perspective. She has coordinated European as well as national research projects and has been part of the core research team in more than 40 research projects. She has published in Greek and English.

Emre Eren Korkmaz is a departmental lecturer in migration and development at the University of Oxford's Department of International Development, where he teaches on the MSc course in migration studies. From October 2016 to September 2018 he was a British Academy Newton International Fellow at ODID. He was also a junior research fellow at St Edmund Hall (2017–20) and a research associate at the Centre for Technology and Global Affairs of the Department of Politics and International Relations (2018–20). In recent years he has been driven by a passion for examining the social and political impact of new digital and frontier technologies on migration.

Ahmet Kurnaz is a computer engineer and political scientist. He holds a PhD in political science from Çanakkale Onsekiz Mart University, Turkey. His research focuses on computational social science methods, online polarisation and digital political communication. He was a visiting researcher at the Oxford Internet Institute in 2017 and 2018, and at the University of Maryland, College Park in 2015.

Bruno Lepri leads the Mobile and Social Computing Lab (MobS) at the Bruno Kessler Foundation (FBK; Trento, Italy); he is a research affiliate at the MIT Connection Science initiative, and a senior research affiliate of Data-Pop Alliance. In 2010 he won a Marie Curie Cofund postdoc fellowship and he has held postdoc positions at FBK and at the MIT Media Lab. He holds a PhD in computer science from the University of Trento.

Isabella Loaiza is a PhD student and research assistant in the Human Dynamics lab at the MIT Media Lab. Her research focuses on understanding social learning and building tools that help communities to accumulate data about themselves to empower them to make better decisions. She is also interested in improving the representation of underserved communities in the data used to build data dashboards and to train machine learning algorithms.

Massimiliano Luca is a PhD student in the Faculty of Computer Science at the Free University of Bolzano and in the Mobile and Social Computing Lab at Fondazione Bruno Kessler. He is broadly interested in computational sustainability and machine learning methods to predict, generate, and explain human mobility using alternative data sources.

Felipe Montes Jimenez is an associate professor and director of the master's in analytics of the Department of Industrial Engineering and fellow of the Fogarty

Institute of the National Institutes of Health (USA). His main interest is the study of complex social and organisational systems, mainly by using methodologies that integrate organisational strategy with social network analysis, agent-based models, system dynamics, and statistics. He has particularly developed projects in the sectors of health, higher education, and technology.

Nuria Oliver is a computer scientist. She is Chief Scientific Adviser at the Vodafone Institute, Chief Data Scientist at DataPop Alliance, an independent director on the board of directors of Bankia, and Commissioner of the Presidency of Valencia for AI and COVID-19. Previously, she was Director of Data Science Research at Vodafone, Scientific Director at Telefónica, and a researcher at Microsoft Research. She holds a PhD from the Media Lab at MIT, and is an IEEE Fellow, ACM Fellow, a member of the board of ELLIS, and elected permanent member of the Royal Academy of Engineering of Spain. She is one of the most cited female computer scientists in Spain, with her research having been cited by more than 19,000 publications. She is well known for her work in computational models of human behaviour, human–computer interaction, mobile computing, and big data for social good.

Dino Pedreschi is professor of computer science at the University of Pisa, and a pioneering scientist in mobility data mining, social network mining, and privacy-preserving data mining. He leads the Pisa KDD Lab, a joint initiative with the CNR. Dino has been visiting scientist at the Centre for Complex Network Research of Northeastern University, Boston (2009–2010), at the University of Texas at Austin (1989–90), at CWI Amsterdam (1993), and at UCLA (1995). Dino is the author of many influential publications and has been a principal investigator of numerous EU projects in the KDD Lab.

Alex Pentland directs the MIT Connection Science and Media Lab Human Dynamics labs, was previously co-creator of the MIT Media Lab, the Media Lab Asia in India, and the Center for Future Health at Strong Hospital. He has served on advisory boards for the UN Secretary General, the American Bar Association, Google, and AT&T. A member of the US National Academies and discussion leader at the World Economic Forum, he was central in the discussions that led to GDPR and metrics for the UN Sustainable Development Goals. He is one of the most-cited computational scientists in the world, and a serial entrepreneur whose spin-off companies serve the health and security needs of hundreds of millions of people.

Laura Pollacci is a postdoctoral researcher at the Department of Computer Science of the University of Pisa. In 2015 and 2014 she graduated *cum laude* in digital humanities (MSc and BSc) at the University of Pisa. Both theses were developed in the computational linguistics area at the Computational Linguistic Laboratory. She received a PhD in computer science from the same institution with a thesis on the conjunct usage of big data and sentiment analysis for the study of human migration. She is currently a member of the Knowledge Discovery and Data Mining Laboratory.

Giulio Rossetti is a permanent researcher at the Institute of Information Science and Technology 'A. Faedo' of the Italian National Research Council (CNR-ISTI). Since 2011 he has been performing research in complex network analysis and data science as a member of the Knowledge Discovery and Data Mining Laboratory. His recent work focuses on the modelling and studying of dynamics of networks and on feature-rich networks.

Albert Ali Salah is Professor of Affective and Social Computing at Utrecht University, Department of Information and Computing Sciences, and Adjunct Professor at Boğaziçi University, Department of Computer Engineering. He has previously held research positions at Centrum Wiskunde & Informatica (CWI), University of Amsterdam, and Nagoya University. His work focuses on computer analysis of human behaviour. He was the scientific coordinator of the Data for Refugees Challenge, and leads a work package in the HumMingBird EU project. He is a senior member of IEEE and ACM, and a research affiliate of the Datapop Alliance.

German Sanchez is a PhD student and research assistant at the Biomicrosystems group and the Social and Health Complexity Center (SHCC) at Los Andes University, Colombia. He holds a bachelor's in electrical and electronics engineering from Universidad de Los Andes in Bogotá, Colombia. His research focuses on wearables to autodiagnose health care systems and data analysis to better understand how society behaves using networks and visualisation tools. He is collaborating with the MIT Human Dynamics group to generate migration data analysis and a voyage viewer for migrants.

Alina Sîrbu is assistant professor of computer science at the University of Pisa. She holds a PhD in computer science (2011) from Dublin City University in Ireland. After her PhD, she was a postdoctoral researcher at the Institute for Scientific Interchange in Turin, Italy, and at the University of Bologna, Italy. She was a visiting assistant professor at NYU Shanghai (2014) and NYU Abu Dhabi (2017). Her research is in complex systems modelling, machine learning, and data science, with applications in a wide variety of fields. She has been involved in several interdisciplinary EU projects.

Giacomo Solano is Head of Research at the Migration Policy Group (MPG). His research interests include the comparative analysis of migration and integration statistics and policies (in particular, in the EU) and labour market integration of migrants (e.g., migrant entrepreneurship). He holds a PhD joint degree in sociology from the University of Amsterdam and University of Milan-Bicocca.

Mikolaj Stanek is associate professor at the Sociology and Communication Department, University of Salamanca. He holds a doctoral degree in sociology from the

Complutense University of Madrid. His research interests include demographic dynamics of immigrant populations and immigrants' labour market integration. He is a principal investigator of the project 'Convergences and divergences of demographic patterns of natives and migrants' funded by the Spanish Ministry of Science and Innovation.

Harald Sterly is a senior scientist at the Department of Geography and Regional Research at the University of Vienna. He has an MSc in geography from the University of Cologne and a completed a postgraduate course in international development cooperation with the SLE at the Humboldt-University Berlin. His PhD thesis focused on mobile communication and translocal social relations of rural-to-urban migrants in Bangladesh. In the past, he has coordinated the TransRe research group at the University of Bonn, which focuses on the linkages between migration, translocal connections, and social resilience in Thailand.

Alexandru Telea is Professor of Visual Data Mining at Utrecht University, Department of Information and Computing Sciences. His research interests include information visualisation, high-dimensional data visualisation, visual analytics, and multiscale shape and image processing. He previously held positions at the Eindhoven University of Technology and the University of Groningen.

Hamid Akın Unver is an associate professor at the Department of International Relations at Özyeğin University, Istanbul, and a fellow at the Centre for Technology and Global Affairs at Oxford University. He has taught at Kadir Has, Sabancı, Princeton, Essex, and Michigan Universities, and held visiting research positions at the Oxford Internet Institute and the Alan Turing Institute, London. He is a member of the executive committee of the International Studies Association, and the National Academy of Sciences of Turkey.

Ingmar Weber is the Research Director for Social Computing at the Qatar Computing Research Institute (QCRI). His interdisciplinary research looks at what online user-generated data can tell us about the offline world and society at large. Working closely with sociologists and demographers he has pioneered the use of online advertising data for complementing official statistics on international migration, digital gender gaps, and poverty. His work is regularly featured in UN reports, and analyses performed by his team have been used to improve operations by UN agencies and NGOs ranging from Colombia to the Philippines.

Lars Wirkus is Head of Research Infrastructure and Data at the Bonn International Centre for Conflict Studies (BICC). He coordinates and is responsible for research data management and information and communication technology (ICT). From 2007 to early 2011, Lars worked on a part-time basis as a senior researcher with BICC and as a research associate with the United Nations University–Institute for Environment and Human Security. Between 2011 and 2020 Lars held the position of Head of Data and Geomatics.

Emilio Zagheni studied economics, statistics, and social sciences at Bocconi University in Milan. In 2006 and 2008 he received MA degrees in demography and statistics from the University of California, Berkeley, where he was also awarded a PhD in demography in 2010. From 2010 to 2012 he worked as a research scientist at the MPI for Demographic Research in Rostock. Since 2014 he has been employed as a professor of sociology at the University of Washington in Seattle, first as an assistant professor, and, since 2016, as an associate professor. He is the Director and Scientific Member at the Max Planck Institute for Demographic Research as of 2018.

Preface

LARGE AND COMPLEX datasets collecting digital breadcrumbs of human behaviour have become non-negligible sources for social science researchers, students, and practitioners. 'Big data' has made a place for itself as a commodity in academic, commercial, and non-commercial settings. There have been numerous new descriptions for defining social scientists with quantitative expertise: empirical social scientist, computational social scientist, quantitative social scientists, social data scientist, etc. Nonetheless, a social scientist with solid big data skills is not yet a common profile in academia and research institutions. Neither is a computer scientist with broad interdisciplinary skills in social sciences. As the amount of published material increases exponentially in many disciplines, specialisation seems to be a reasonable response to keep up with the state of the art, and to produce technically and conceptually solid research. Interdisciplinary teams are vital in providing the critical synthesis from these separate specialisations, and this book is put together to help bridge the language gap between the different specialisations needed for migration analysis from big data sources.

In this volume we spend little time on explaining actual data scientific methods (we provide information boxes in the chapters for some basic terminology), and focus on the use of data science for migration and mobility. Consequently, the book deals with an intrinsically multifaceted research domain combining sociology, policy, computational social science, statistics, and behavioural sciences. In it, the reader will find different voices, different disciplinary concerns, and the widely differing scientific languages of these disciplines, but also examples of excellent collaborations between these disciplines. We see it as a step to help scholars of this burgeoning research area to learn more about the rich canvas of tools, methodologies, and conceptualisations, and as a call for more interdisciplinary dialogue to address the thorny issues in this domain.

Despite the vast amount of quantitative research in migration and mobility, big data and the use of advanced data science techniques have not been very prevalent amongst migration and mobility researchers, and there is a gap we need to address. Social scientists stand to benefit from the analysis of the new data sources, but may lack the computational tools; data scientists have the theoretical and practical knowledge in dealing with these data sources but may have no familiarity with the relevant questions of migration research. We argue that it is possible to bridge this gap and to guide migration scholars in the proper use of new data sources usable for migration research, while familiarising data scientists with the concerns and questions of migration scholars.

The goal of the book is to provide the reader with useful definitions of new data sources and relevant case studies to demonstrate potential applications. We have separated the book into different logical sections, and invited experts to address issues in each of the sections. In the preparation of the book, experts were contacted individually to solicit the chapters, which were reviewed extensively (between three and eight reviews per chapter) by the editors, authors of other chapters, and external reviewers, including graduate students. The revised chapters were then edited for consistency and coherence.

Part I contains two chapters. The opening chapter of the book, written by the editors, is an overarching look at the domain, and sets the stage. It also serves to address some of the important issues that are not covered in depth by other chapters in the book, such as new developments in privacy-aware data processing. It is followed by Chapter 2 on conceptual tools of ethical data processing in migration and mobility, as this is one of the most important concerns. Chapter 2 also deals with the legal issues related to data processing, algorithm creation, and deployment.

Part II provides extensive information on the new data sources and their potential for studying migration and human mobility related questions. The first chapter in this section (Chapter 3) is about the Consortium of European Social Science Data Archives (CESSDA) catalogue, which provides information about more than 30,000 datasets, and seeks to realise the vision of FAIR (findable, accessible, interoperable, and reusable) data. Chapters 4 and 5 cover a major data source that can provide very detailed information on mobility patterns of migrants, but is difficult to obtain, namely, mobile call detail records (CDR). Chapter 4 provides examples from data challenges such as Telecom Italia and Data for Refugees, and showcases uses of CDR for applications on refugees, climate-based migration, and labour migration. Chapter 5 focuses on the refugee case, and interleaves technical discussions about data preparation and spatiotemporal analysis with issues on bias, ethics, and consent. Chapter 6 covers remote sensing, which is particularly important for climate-induced migration, starting from major data sources and major applications such as land cover maps and night lights, with two detailed examples from Uganda and Mexico, and further examples from migration and humanitarian aid. The next important data source is social media. Chapter 7 describes work on Facebook and LinkedIn, and Chapter 8 on Twitter, both chapters providing links to code and resources to work with these platforms, as well as highlighting challenges and limitations. Analysis on Twitter often relies on natural language processing, which is an informative dimension for studying immigrants. Chapter 9 is on the main sources and datasets for analysing migration policy, trends, and integration, including surveys like DEMIG, IMPIC, and MIPEX. The final chapter of this section, Chapter 10, is about another difficult-to-obtain data source, namely, financial datasets. The locations, types, and amounts of financial transactions provide some insights into the economic activities of migrants, but the available data volumes are typically limited, which makes it very challenging to obtain reliable estimates.

Part III is about visualisation, a tool that is used at all stages of data analysis. Chapter 11 is a tour de force of visualisation approaches particularly suitable for studying human mobility. Chapter 12 is an in-depth description of Voyage Viewer, an open online tool for visualising and investigating migration-related datasets.

Part IV is a special section exploring the possibilities that arise when big data and migration research come together. It provides examples of new data sources in action, including a look at the applications for specific mobility-related research questions. Chapter 13 combines mobile CDR with land cover maps for investigating how employment opportunities influence refugee mobility. Chapter 14 is a case study on the acceptance and integration of refugees and asylum seekers, delving into survey data with the help of big data analysis and simulation techniques. Chapter 15 discusses the challenges and opportunities in analysing multilingual language use within immigrant communities. Chapter 16 is about an unusual data source from media, namely a large corpus of British newspaper texts about migration, asylum seekers, and refugees. Chapter 17 is an empirical study using a socio-anthropological approach and investigates refugee inclusion in the digital solutions developed for them. Using the migration of Venezuelans in Brazil and migrants cross the French–UK border, the chapter highlights many issues for vulnerable groups and precarious experiences in forced migration. The last chapter of this section, Chapter 18, looks at event datasets and evaluates the potential of social media vs off-the-shelf datasets in this area.

The last section of the book contains an opinion piece on some of the policy aspects of artificial intelligence and data science technologies described in the book, as well as a projection about the future of this area. Similar to the chapter that precedes it, it defends the view that refugees and migrants should be at the centre of the big data analysis solutions developed in this area. While the potential of technology is great in creating timely solutions, or in providing decision-makers with actionable data, the risks are not to be taken lightly. In that sense, this chapter also complements Chapter 2 on the ethical and privacy aspects, as well as addressing some of the issues raised in the first chapter of the book.

Our work is supported by European Union's Horizon 2020 Research and Innovation Programme under grant agreement 870661. We would like to take the opportunity to thank all the authors of the book, Portia Taylor from the British Academy for her support, as well as our colleagues who reviewed the material and provided extensive feedback: A.A. Akdag Salah, C. Arcila, B. Aydoğdu, S. Balcısoy, T. Bozcağa, A. Cansunar, D. Kondyli, A.S. Doğruöz, I. Gorantis, L. Schrijver, A. Sîrbu, G. Solano, B. van Enk, and the anonymous reviewers contacted by the publisher. We hope that this book will serve as a solid entry point into the inspiring world of data science for migration research.

Additional author resources are available at: https://www.thebritishacademy.ac.uk/publishing/proceedings-british-academy/data-science-for-migration-and-mobility/

Part I

Introduction

1

New Data Sources and Computational Approaches to Migration and Human Mobility

ALBERT ALI SALAH, TUBA BIRCAN, AND EMRE EREN KORKMAZ

Introduction

SCHOLARS FROM DIFFERENT disciplines have been seeking to understand the societal dynamics in migration[1] and mobility, which concerns itself with long-term human movements within and between countries, as well as ways to estimate and predict such movements.

While qualitative research methods have been instrumental in gaining insights into the factors influencing human movements, quantitative approaches were essential for tasks like prediction and estimation. The digital era ushered in by extremely widespread use of digital tools, such as mobile phones and social media, brought new possibilities for quantitative analysis. Especially with the onset of the Covid-19 pandemic, the potential value of new data sources such as mobile phones was recognised in capturing the statics and dynamics of large-scale human movements (Oliver et al., 2020).

In this work we provide an overview of the potential benefits and risks, as well as the challenges, of using big data analysis for migration and mobility. Our aim is to illustrate, with examples, how approaches based on large-scale data analysis can be used to gain insights into the multilayered and complex issues surrounding this area. Our take-away lesson is that such methods are not wholesale solutions providing definitive answers, but have different strengths and weaknesses compared to traditional methods and, as such, can be complementary to them.

---

[1] A full-blown glossary of technical terms in migration and mobility is beyond the scope of this chapter, but we provide definitions of some key terms in a glossary at the end of the book. The International Organization for Migration (IOM) maintains an up-to-date glossary on migration at https://publications.iom.int/system/files/pdf/iml_34_glossary.pdf

This chapter is organised as follows. The first section is devoted to the conceptual groundwork. In 'Why new data sources for migration?', we discuss the potential benefits of new data sources, and give examples from the literature. 'Data sharing practices' is about the stakeholders, and how data can be shared among them. We do not discuss ethical, legal, or privacy-related risks associated with the collection and use of big data solutions here, but we provide a case study to illustrate one of the risks in more depth in 'A case study on risks: Digital identity, big data, and the power of corporations'. We end with some conclusions.

Conceptual groundwork

Migration and mobility

Although the migration process refers to relocating across an (inter)national boundary for a period of time, the precise operationalisation of this concept in practice varies amongst countries, institutes, and disciplines. We are all 'mobile individuals' living in a world that has been structured by mobility, and people move for various purposes and lengths of time. The forms of mobility and migration are diversifying globally (see, e.g., Favell 2011; Skeldon 2017; Vertovec 2007). Hence, when focusing on different aspects of migration, it is important to distinguish different forms of movement and migration. Migratory movements can be: within or across borders; voluntary (for work, study, or family reasons) or forced (as a result of conflict or natural disasters); regular (with documentation) or irregular (without documentation); and temporary, seasonal or longer term / permanent. Definitions can change during the process. For instance, if a non-native student (a voluntary, regular migrant) overstays her/his allowance for the academic year for which s/he was registered, s/he may become an undocumented migrant. This will also lead to a gap in keeping the records and following up the migratory movements and status changes.

As a first step in studying migratory movements with new methodologies, the terminology of migration and mobility needs to be set clearly, especially for the scholars working on these topics and not having a social sciences background. In order to avoid any confusion between mobility and migration, we can start by distinguishing the two terms. Every migratory movement is 'mobility' but the other direction is not true: every mobility movement cannot be counted as 'migration'. Therefore, for traditional migration statistics, the term 'mobility' is not commonly used.

The data perspective

Computational social science is defined as 'the development and application of computational methods to complex, typically large-scale, human (sometimes simulated) behavioural data' (Lazer et al., 2009). It is a research area that fosters (or rather, demands) collaborations between data and computer scientists and statistical physicists, and with many disciplines whose inquiries extend into issues touching on human behaviour, such as epidemiology, economics, policy, governance, public health, and, naturally, migration. The most important aspect of these collaborations is the sharing (and subsequent analysis) of large-scale human behavioural data, which are gathered by diverse stakeholders for diverse purposes, but can be repurposed for addressing specific research questions (Lazer *et al.*, 2020).

In the context of migration and mobility, what we call 'new data sources' are those that are not widely adopted for studying questions in this area. To give a specific example, satellite remote sensing systems have frequently been used to study bird migrations, which are more regular and 'visible' than migrating humans, but such data are extremely useful in sensing environmental conditions that can be used to gain insights into economic factors, population estimates, environmental conditions, and proxy indicators of wealth (Bircan, 2022). Similarly, mobile phone and social media usage leaves digital traces that can be very informative on different aspects of migration (Coimbra Vieira *et al.*, 2022; Kim *et al.*, 2022; Luca *et al.*, 2022; Sterly and Wirkus, 2022).

The interest from computational social scientists, computer scientists, and data scientists in the utilisation of alternative data sources for varied societal challenges led to an increase in studies addressing human migration and mobility. This is also related to the newly burgeoning field of 'data science and artificial intelligence for social good', which typically adapts United Nations' Sustainable Development Goals (SDGs) as a framework for addressing problems with socially beneficial outcomes (Tomašev *et al.*, 2020; Cowls *et al.*, 2021). From the data science and methodological perspectives, these studies consider 'migration' more of an application case, rather than contributing to the existing theoretical frameworks. Acknowledging the benefits of these innovative techniques, there are still numerous challenges to be tackled to pave analytical and sustainable paths to nurture interdisciplinary studies and to strengthen the new computational approaches to long-lasting questions about migration.

Data science is a very broad term and encompasses all methods used to turn data into knowledge and insights. Machine learning, on the other hand, is about creating models that optimise certain functions over such data. Some of these models are concerned with prediction, in which case the data that are consumed by these models are treated as input, and the predictions as the output. For example, the number of immigrants and emigrants for a specific country can be predicted based on past data (Robinson and Dilkina, 2018). However, this problem is very challenging, as there are many factors that play a role in migration, and their interaction is complex. Other machine learning approaches are concerned with finding patterns in data (such as clusters and groups that exhibit differences), or with modelling spatiotemporal dynamics. A type of machine learning algorithm called 'deep learning' has received enormous interest in recent years, but these are typically mathematical models with millions of free parameters, and their success depends on using very large datasets for training them, i.e., setting their parameters (Alpaydin, 2016). What make machine learning and data science very interesting for migration and mobility is the availability of the new data sources we have mentioned, as they allow the development of complex mathematical models.

Big data refers to extremely large datasets that may be analysed computationally to reveal patterns, trends, and associations, especially relating to human behaviour and interactions. As Hilbert (2013) states, big data differs from data based on traditional household surveys as it does not refer to a random sample of individuals but to the totality of the population using, for instance, mobile phones or internet-based platforms, and these data are accessible in near real time. Big data is not only 'big' because of its volume; the speed ('velocity') at which it is generated and the complexity ('variety') of the information are also considered as distinguishing features of this kind of data (Hilbert, 2013). In relation to migration research, the term 'big data' refers to anonymised data generated by users of mobile phones, internet-based platforms (i.e., social media) and applications, or by digital sensors and meters such as satellite imagery. Big data analysis requires specific technical and analytical methods to extract meaningful insights from the big data and transform these data into 'value' (De Mauro *et al.*, 2016).

Approaches to empirical modelling

At this point, it is useful to stress some important distinctions in the way computational and social sciences approach their empirical problems. Since computer modelling is more limited in handling semantic information than structured and numeric information, it is not a surprise that it supports quantitative approaches better than qualitative approaches. But what is more important is that in computational sciences there is a heavier emphasis on predictive models as opposed to explanation-based models in social sciences (Hofman *et al.*, 2021). One of the promises of computational social science is the possibility of creating models with both predictive and explanatory powers.

If we apply the conceptual model proposed by Hofman *et al.* (2021) to empirical modelling in migration and mobility, we get two main distinctions along which to look at research. The focus of the study can be on specific features and effects, to explain the factors that caused a certain phenomenon under study, or conversely, it can be about predicting outcomes, to try to see what would happen if some of these factors are changed, for example through policy decisions. The second dimension proposed by Hofman *et al.* (2021) is whether there are any interventions or distributional changes for the described situation. Table 1.1 summarises the four possibilities under this conceptual model. To exemplify the possibilities of new data sources and computational approaches in migration and mobility, we provide different examples that fall into these four quadrants.

Descriptive modelling is about describing the features or effects for a certain situation. Consider the question of integration and assimilation of migrants, which is typically studied via surveys. This limits the number of people from which data are obtained, but allows detailed insights for some of the factors. For example, the

EUCROSS Survey[2] that investigated the Europeanisation of immigrants included telephone interviews with 1000 subjects from different nationalities (Pötzschke, 2015). Contrast this with the study of Marquez *et al.* (2019), where mobile phone data traces of over one million users (including over 200,000 Syrians in Turkey) were used together with 65,000 tweets collected from Twitter to measure integration and sentiments against refugees in Turkey. The use of such large data sources allowed the researchers to analyse integration and segregation in great spatiotemporal detail, even though factors such as demographics were not visible due to the anonymisation of the data.

Explanatory modelling is for estimating the effects of changing some of the factors that affect a situation. This goes beyond descriptive modelling, in that there is an effort to explain the causes of changes in the observed variables. Many mathematical models in empirical sociology and economics fall under this quadrant, including the gravity and radiation models in migration analysis (Zipf, 1946; Simini *et al.*, 2012). As an example of using new data sources, we can consider the application of computational linguistic and text analysis to media content about migration (Allen, 2022; Koch *et al.*, 2020). Koch *et al.* (2020) studied the empirical relationship between public debates in the media and asylum acceptance rates in Europe from 2002–2016 by using a large news repository called GDELT,[3] which contains about 2.5 terabytes of media material per year (see also Unver and Kurnaz, Chapter 18, this volume). The advantages of using GDELT over traditional data sources are the large coverage and the possibility of having a rich representation for public debate as a factor.

Predictive modelling, the third quadrant in Table 1.1, is about predicting the outcomes, without paying much attention to the specific factors that play a role in those outcomes. This is a very typical setting for machine learning scenarios, where a complex model is trained for achieving supervised classification (i.e., the model learns to predict output labels from a set of input features, based on a training set of pre-labelled data points). The model can achieve excellent accuracy, which is the main criterion of success, but it may not give any usable insights about the input

Table 1.1 Organising empirical modelling along two dimensions proposed by Hofman *et al.* (2021), simplified from the original

	No intervention or distributional changes	Under interventions or distributional changes
Focus on specific features or effects	Descriptive modelling	Explanatory modelling
Focus on predicting outcomes	Predictive modelling	Integrative modelling

---

[2] The Europeanisation of Everyday Life: Cross-Border Practices and Transnational Identities among EU and Third-Country Citizens, https://cordis.europa.eu/project/id/266767
[3] The GDELT Project, https://www.gdeltproject.org/

factors, especially if there are many such factors and each contributes a little to the outcome, as well as having complex relationships with other factors. Bircan (2022) discussed the use of remote sensing data for migration and mobility research. In (Dietler *et al.*, 2020), researchers developed a machine learning based prediction model for quantifying settlement growth in rural communities in Burkina Faso, using such remote sensing data. Since other data sources were lacking, a multi-annual training dataset was created using historic Google Earth imagery and good prediction results were obtained.

The main problem with such predictive modelling approaches is that the machine learning model only learns the variation in its training set, and has limited generalisation capabilities. When there is an unexpected change of conditions and dynamics, the models cannot handle these automatically. Instead, the experts need to intervene, and retrain the models by taking relevant factors into account. To illustrate the difficulty of fully automatic incorporation of the relevant factors in machine learning models, consider the example given by Earney and Jimenez (2019) about the UNHCR's Jetson project in Somalia, where the predictive models for drought-related migration failed, until the researchers, based on interviews they had conducted, factored in the local goat prices. Because goats did not survive the journey to the border, they had to be sold before moving out.

The fourth quadrant, integrative modelling, seeks to predict outcomes in terms of interpretable factors and causal relationships between them. An example study was conducted by Bosetti *et al.* (2019), where mobile phone data was used to create realistic models of refugee mobility and integration, to assess scenarios of a measles epidemic starting in different cities of Turkey. The vaccinated local population and largely unvaccinated refugee population had different mixing opportunities in different cities, derived from the mobile data, and the influence of this integration indicator in the spreading of the epidemic was assessed via agent-based modelling.

Why new data sources for migration?

Limitations of traditional data sources

Migration, influenced by multiple and interlinked factors, is growing globally in scope, complexity, and diversity. Despite a large amount of official statistics and administrative data on migration, only part of the complexity of migration phenomena can be captured through traditional migration data. Notable amounts of data on migration have been collected by several countries; however, the mechanisms to centralise, disaggregate, and cross reference all data collected from various branches of the government are lacking. Additional important data sources are provided by international organisations, such as the UN International Organization for Migration (IOM), the Organisation for Economic Co-operation and Development (OECD), and the United Nations, and these also need to be integrated for wider insights.

The main purpose of much of these data is to answer local/national situations. Data collection methodology is therefore often tailored to local circumstances, which restricts data comparability across countries. Major gaps across the migration data landscape are summarised in four categories (Santamaria and Vespe, 2018):

- problems with existing data;
- issues with the way the data are presented or disseminated;
- data that are not widely collected or are not easily accessible;
- potentially useful data that are currently inaccessible.

The global-level migration indicators are relatively underdeveloped and the problems with existing data include drawbacks and inconsistencies in definitions and typologies, drivers of migration, representation of gender and hidden populations, geographical coverage, and timeliness (Ahmad-Yar and Bircan, 2021; Bircan *et al.*, 2020). To elaborate further, traditional data collection is mostly limited to certain periods. Country-wide survey studies are expensive and performed once every few years. Field work involves in-depth, concentrated data collection, but it does not have the spatiotemporal coverage of new data sources. Continuous collection of real-time data by various corporations such as mobile phone operators, financial institutions, and technology platform companies serving people on the move can provide much more detail on some aspects. Such data seem to be largely untapped for global-level migration indicators at the moment.

These challenges can be addressed by improving the existing datasets by promoting different data sources, specifically big data for estimations of migration, and by proposing validated best practices for data collection and sharing.

Challenges for new data sources

There are commercial and/or privacy issues to solve concerning access to new data sources, and substantial research and analysis are required. The challenges with the use of big data for migration are: (1) institutional interests of political actors shape the decisions about the data collection; (2) methodological heterogeneity due to the different definitions, methods, and data sources; (3) nation-state policies on quantifying migration (Scheel and Ustek-Spilda, 2018). Moreover, researchers in the field have, increasingly more often, faced the paradoxical problem of data abundance. The questions about this new data upsurge are threefold. First, sifting through is a much bigger task than it was in the past, and warrants larger resources. Second, there are limited and emerging regulations concerning data use and release. Third is the challenge of working with partial, incomplete, and imperfect data.

These challenges with new data sources for migration studies give rise to a thorough exploration of innovation and cooperation regarding simulations, triangulation, and big data analytics. In the meantime, the scholarly field of migration studies remains vulnerable and prone to the damage of pseudoscience or excitement of experiments with data.

Big data and migration research in practice

Global Migration Group and others (2017) group main big data sources that have so far been used in migration-related studies under three broad categories:

- mobile phone based, e.g. call records;
- internet based, e.g. social media;
- sensor based, e.g. Earth observation data (satellite imagery).

In addition, there are other alternative data sources in use, such as financial datasets (Gürkan *et al.*, 2022) and media archives (Koch *et al.*, 2020). Increasing numbers of studies and initiatives are working on the insights on migration phenomena that can be provided through analysis of big data. In this section we provide a few illustrative examples of the use of data in practice.

Our first two examples are about the use of mobile call detail records (CDR). The great spatiotemporal granularity of mobile CDR allows detailed investigation of mobility within a country, but also serves to derive proxy indicators of socioeconomic factors. In a landmark study, Blumenstock *et al.* (2015) used mobile CDR metadata from Rwanda to infer proxy indicators for wealth. In order to do that, they complemented the CDR with a comparatively small (i.e., less than 1000 subjects) sample of follow-up phone surveys, which provided them with wealth ground truth. This in turn served as labels for a supervised model that was able to predict wealth across the country, at a fraction of the cost of a national household survey, and in a much faster way. This study is also a very good example of the integrative modelling discussed earlier, as the analysis revealed mobile data factors about wealth prediction. The authors noted that 'features related to an individual's patterns of mobility are generally predictive of motorcycle ownership, whereas factors related to an individual's position within his or her social network are more useful in predicting poverty and wealth' (Blumenstock *et al.*, 2015).

A second interesting study is by Bakker *et al.* (2019), where mobile CDR was used for measuring social integration of refugees. Using the Data for Refugees Challenge data (Salah *et al.*, 2018), the researchers developed a number of proxy indicators for measuring social integration for each city, such as the amount of space where Syrian refugees and Turkish locals come together, and the ratio of calls made from refugees to locals, as opposed to other refugees. Using 2017 data, they illustrated that some of the cities in Turkey had very low integration scores, and indeed, violent events in 2018 confirmed these insights. An obviously interesting aspect of such analysis is that it can be performed continuously, and used to monitor changes over time, as well as to assess the effect of policy decisions, or changing social factors.

Two important problems in migration research, for which big data approaches based on social media may be useful, are estimating and predicting migrant stocks in a country, and the migration flow from one country to another (Sîrbu *et al.*, 2021).

In nowcasting migrant stocks, typical data sources are official statistics and administrative data, but different countries differ in the amount and quality of such data, and it is difficult to combine multiple sources. Some of the data will be outdated or not properly updated. Zagheni *et al.* (2014) investigated the use of Twitter to nowcast migrant stocks. Using either geolocated tweets or migrant language (when it is different from the host country's language), it is possible to find migrants in a country. However, Twitter users have a particular demographic distribution, and only a fraction of the population under study will be using it. Subsequently, such biases must be carefully taken into account. Combining social media and survey studies may result in even better estimates (Alexander *et al.*, 2020).

For predicting migration flows, one problem of traditional models like the gravity model is predicting variations over time for a single migration corridor, as these models depend on variables that do not change over time, such as distance between the countries, or colonial past history. Böhme *et al.* (2020) illustrated that Google trends data, which collects the frequency of words used in search queries in a country, can be used to predict migration intentions, provide faster estimates compared to official data releases, and improve conventional model estimates. However, as the 'parable of Google Flu' (see Lazer *et al.*, 2014) illustrated before, algorithmic changes in Google's search recommendation system, possibilities of external manipulations, and drift in the system may eventually invalidate such a system for prediction. Since Google trends data are not designed for the express purpose of migration flow estimation, such changes may damage its validity and reliability over time. Controlling for dependencies among data, paying attention to measurement and construct validity (Lazer *et al.*, 2014), and creating explanations for more transparent processing of the data will enable researchers to use this data source for a longer time. For more specific migration flows, other social media channels or data repositories can be used. For instance, LinkedIn data can be used to investigate migration of professionals (State *et al.*, 2014), or Scopus can be used for migration of researchers (Miranda-González *et al.*, 2020).

Satellite imaging, the third major data source on our list, can be used to gain insight into dynamic settlement of refugee encampments. Quinn *et al.* (2018) proposed the use of deep learning algorithms on satellite images to estimate refugee occupancy rates in 13 such settlements in Sudan, Nigeria, and Iraq, by detecting structures automatically. While it is possible to use the satellite images for manual estimation, this would take a significant amount of time, as there are thousands of structures in each of the settlements investigated.

Data sharing practices

Migration research adopting new technological developments and methodologies can only improve and attain its goals when strong cooperation between the collaborators who provide and/or require the new data sources is established. There are commercial and/or privacy issues to solve to get access to such data, and substantial research and analysis are required before it can meet ethical requirements from both research and societal perspectives.

Stakeholders and collaborators

Figure 1.1 illustrates the stakeholders and collaborators network in data science for migration and mobility, which includes migrants (who are often the true data owners), researchers, data collectors, data providers, policy-makers, and decision-makers. We briefly discuss the main concerns and issues from a stakeholder perspective.

Researchers

New data sources offer new analysis tools to researchers, but also create new methodological challenges, particularly in assessing the representativeness of such datasets. Analytical techniques from computer science are increasingly being used to solve social science problems, including migration and mobility related challenges, but these are mainly implemented by information and communication technology (ICT) experts and data scientists, and require interdisciplinary collaborations.

Collaboration between data scientists and social scientists requires negotiating the interdisciplinary language gap, paying attention to both data-driven and theory-driven aspects of the problem, and applying rigorous methodologies that satisfy both disciplines. A focus on predictive modelling, common in computational

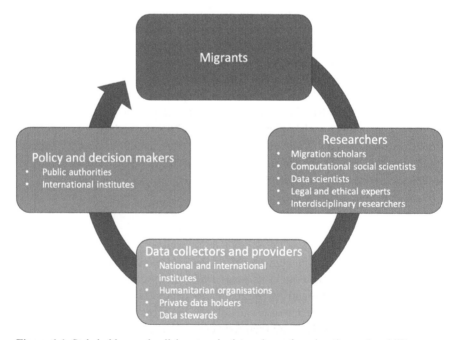

Figure 1.1 Stakeholders and collaborators in data science for migration and mobility.

sciences, requires careful controls on model complexity and generalisation. A focus on explanation-based modelling, on the other hand, demands caution about underlying assumptions, valid research design, and spurious relationships between factors.

Social scientists should be able to understand the assumptions that drive algorithms when assessing their societal implications. Algorithmic approaches affect society in different ways. They may be used to generate analysis results that are taken up by policy-makers and thus influence choices in the public sphere. They can also be incorporated into decision-making systems, and directly influence the decisions on a day-to-day basis. For researchers, it may be alluring to use new modelling tools, such as those based on machine learning or agent-based simulations, to build more powerful and insightful models and, as we argued in the previous section, to integrate explanation-based models with predictive models. These approaches can enhance social scientific inquiry in novel ways, address data gaps, save time and other resources, allow more granular and continuous analysis, and provide greater coverage.

Data collectors and providers

Both public and private data collectors have a stake in this area. For private companies, the purpose of sharing data can be the realisation of humanitarian goals, and social good (Letouzé and Oliver, 2019). In order to do that, the legal and ethical problems of data sharing must be solved (Salah *et al.*, 2022), and the financial aspects must be considered. In particular, for sustainable and long-term social good projects, financing the data collection and sharing is essential.

Policy- and decision-makers

These groups, including international institutes and non-governmental and intergovernmental institutions, have a very clear stake. They need knowledge to operate efficiently and effectively, and data may be the key to obtaining this knowledge. However, policy-makers are centres of authority and having them access large amounts of data is not without its risks.

Migrants

The final, and arguably most important, stakeholders are the migrants and refugees themselves, as data owners, as well as the group most influenced by the policy decisions and decision-making systems that consume the data. Alencar and Godin (2022) argued that initiatives developed for migrants and refugees under social good initiatives may fail to improve the realities of refugees, or even create technological dependencies that are harmful in the long run. Grassroots movements by migrants and refugees, as well as reappropriation of data and technologies, are essential in expanding the discussions in this area. It is also important to adopt an international human rights perspective to look at technology use in migration and 'migration management', with all the debates that come with the term (Geiger and Pécoud, 2010; Molnar, 2019).

Found data and private data

Found data describes data collected for a purpose different than its present use.[4] For example, mobile call detail records are originally collected by telecommunications companies for marketing insights and customer relationship management, but as they contain very detailed information about human movements in a country they can be repurposed for analysing mobility (Salah et al., 2019). Some of the found data repositories are publicly available, but the telecommunications data are typically not. These are both sensitive and valuable assets for these companies. Accessing such privately owned data sources is difficult. Researchers' access to privately owned data is a significant step for enabling further computational applications to address diverse questions about migration. However, critical privacy questions arise about the legal requirements, confidentiality, and rules of engagement. Any approach to securing personal data and protecting residents from being predicted, manipulated, or outright controlled via their personal data requires strong encryption and cybersecurity, without back doors.

Industry can generate data and data products that could be potentially accessible to scientists, practitioners, and the public. However, the integration at global level of public data curated and owned by industry is not always feasible or practical. The reasons can be summarised as the lack of shared open access policies and the potential conflict between the regional/national interests of industry and the international dimension and perspective of data sharing. Nevertheless, new industrial collaborations of this kind do occur. While broad strategies and regional mechanisms are being explored, a sharper focus on accountability and monitoring mechanisms are needed. The growing role of the private sector in the governance of AI and data science applications, also for migration studies, highlights the movement away from state responsibility. We discuss some of the risks this may entail in the section entitled 'A case study on risks: Digital identity, big data, and the power of corporations'.

Before we go into the potential benefits and risks of new data sources, we briefly discuss in Box 1.1 various models of accessing large-scale private data. Based on an earlier taxonomy proposed by De Montjoye et al. (2018), Letouzé and Oliver (2019) discussed five major data sharing models, which we summarise here. These models have different advantages and disadvantages.

---

[4] In social sciences, such data are generally called 'secondary data'.

Box 1.1 Data sharing models

Limited data sharing is when a data holder signs a non-disclosure agreement (NDA) with a selected group and shares data with them. Some of the data challenges in the social good domain have used this model, including the Data for Refugees Challenge (Salah *et al.*, 2018, 2019). The NDA has some legal guarantees about what is done with the shared data, but not really the practical means to enforce them. This model is also less usable in a continuous analysis scenario, where data insights are regularly provided to policy-makers.

Remote access also requires an NDA, but allows access to some form of data remotely. Typically, the data are internally sanitised, and privacy-sensitive information is removed by anonymisation and data aggregation. This sharing model can be somewhat more flexible than the limited data sharing model, but the essential difference is in logistics of data.

Application programming interfaces (APIs) and open algorithms are more systematic ways of approaching the remote access scenario, where an interface is designed to allow data access by queries. The principle is that the entity sending the queries will not access the actual data, but only the outcome of the queries, which are designed to satisfy privacy concerns (Letouzé, 2019). This approach, also called 'Question and Answer' (De Montjoye *et al.*, 2018), provides transparency and mutual trust, but the development of the necessary APIs is costly.

Precomputed indicators and synthetic data, as the name implies, shares only transformed data. Precomputed indicators are variables that are computed from the raw data, such as wealth proxies based on mobility patterns (Blumenstock *et al.*, 2015). Synthetic data are typically produced by simulations, based on feature distributions of the original data. While producing such transformed data can be easily done in a way to protect individual privacy, group privacy still needs to be considered.

Data collaboratives are 'public–private partnerships that allow for collaboration and information sharing across sectors and actors' (Verhulst and Young, 2019). This is a general approach in which 'data stewards' within private companies curate and facilitate data sharing for public good. Issues of consent and legal permissions are regulated by the private partner.

Differential privacy seeks to develop data access mechanisms that permit gaining insights about the population without learning anything specific about individuals (Dwork *et al.*, 2014). The core idea here, particularly relevant for the migration domain, is that the anonymisation and aggregation of data, while facilitating data sharing, means a loss of precious information, such as demographics. Differential privacy allows creation of models without developers accessing the raw data. For example, in *federated learning*, a model is sent to many data centres holding some sensitive data, and each time a slightly updated model is passed onwards (Li *et al.*, 2020). This way, the data are not aggregated in a single centre, and the developers of the model do not have actual access to the sensitive details.

A case study on risks: Digital identity, big data, and the power of corporations

So far we have discussed what data science offers for studies in migration and mobility, and the significance of accessible data. In this section we consider the practice of implementing technological solutions, and analyse a concrete case study on irregular migration for discussing risks. Biased and unfair algorithms, data gaps, non-transparent algorithmic decisions, function creep for collected data, and loss of privacy and control are all issues raised as significant risks in this domain (Salah *et al.*, 2022). But there are also issues related to conflicting interests of the stakeholders, which we illustrate with an example.

Consider the role of corporations and their relations with the UN agencies and humanitarian organisations in collecting, storing, and processing data in the name of financial integration of refugees at digital identification projects. This is a hot topic in the humanitarian context, and we aim here to demonstrate how the collection, processing, and storage of refugee data could create risks by ignoring the fundamental rights of refugees and serve the corporate interests. This debate also illustrates that large-scale data analysis is not only a methodological and technical issue but is part of a highly political power struggle.

The identification problem

As the number of refugees and forcibly displaced people worldwide has reached 79.5 million,[5] the issue of what to do for their financial and social integration in the countries in which they take refuge comes to the fore.[6] The push to find solutions is all the more urgent considering that conflicts, civil wars, and other factors that cause immigration will continue, and those who leave their homes and countries cannot return for years, maybe even for generations. Likewise, more than one billion people around the world cannot currently benefit from basic rights and services, nor can they participate in financial life due to their lack of identity. Insufficient state capacity or exclusionary political decisions may explain why these people lack formal identification. The United Nations' Sustainable Development Goals scheme aims to overcome the identification question, and granting digital identity is one of these solutions (UN, 2015), which is mainly promoted by financial and technological corporations and mobile phone operators (Coppi and Fast, 2019).

A calculation of the lives potentially transformed by solving the identification question goes from 26 million refugees to 80 million when displaced people are included, and even upwards of one billion people when those currently lacking a legal identity are considered. This is first and foremost a data collection and management problem. Regardless of their status, each of these individuals faces obstacles to

---
[5] The UN Refugee Agency: Figures at a Glance, https://www.unhcr.org/figures-at-a-glance.html
[6] GSMA: Using Mobile Technology to provide Functional Identities, https://www.gsma.com/mobilefordevelopment/blog-2/using-mobile-technology-provide-functional-identities/

enjoying their fundamental rights and services, and are relegated to remain outside of financial services and markets.

There are two main reasons for solving the identification question. It is a critical problem that people without a legal identity cannot access essential public services such as education and health, because they are not officially registered. This is particularly true for refugees, asylum seekers, and undocumented immigrants. The other issue is to fulfil the 'know your customer' (KYC) requirement that financial institutions and mobile operators must comply with when they provide services and acting from this, paving the way for refugees to receive cash transfers as part of the humanitarian assistance. In this way, it will also be possible for refugees and anyone who does not have an identity card to open a bank account or buy SIM cards for their mobile phones, and become a customer of these corporations.

Stakeholders and suppliers

The global companies entering the field of refugees and humanitarian aid with innovative solutions became prominent upon the call by the United Nations on the private sector to reach the Sustainable Development Goals by 2030 (UN, 2015). The 'UN Guiding Principles on Business and Human Rights' explain how companies can play a progressive role in solving social problems. To integrate refugees into social life, global companies are requested to support the development of refugee-hosting countries through investments and creating employment. In this way they are encouraged to position refugees as employees or suppliers in the global supply chain, and refugees as employees or entrepreneurs are expected to contribute economically to the host country.[7]

Here, companies are given a progressive, transformative role. In the 1960s and 70s, global companies were accused of being the reason for underdevelopment and the exploitation of the labour force with underground and aboveground resources. However, with these calls, they are attributed a positive role of bringing the corrupt administrators of undeveloped countries to their knees, introducing international standards in these countries, and developing the domestic workforce in terms of technical skills and qualification.

Understanding this approach is important in terms of seeing how global companies mobilise and use other institutions as intermediaries. With the desire to expand the market and access new data, both as a supplier of these institutions and as a strong 'stakeholder' in this field, together with states, UN organisations, and humanitarian aid organisations. One of the first steps in this context is to give identity to refugees, the forcibly displaced, and those who do not have official registration. It is preferable that this identity is not a paper or plastic one, because it is not possible to fill it with all the information, it can be lost and forged, and, more importantly, it

---

[7] Business & Human Rights Resource Centre: UN Guiding Principles, https://www.business-humanrights.org/en/big-issues/un-guiding-principles-on-business-human-rights/

remains with the holder, hence preventing a technology or financial company from accessing these data. However, if the identity is digital, it may be possible to store a wide variety of data items, including name, birthplace, and date, as well as vaccine shots, diplomas, and aids received. In addition, security issues such as a person's relationship with criminal organisations can be checked. This way, states, UN agencies, and corporations can access very important information about the background of a person besides their name and place and date of birth.

The question is, who will collect this information and transfer it to digital media? The United Nations and humanitarian organisations are taking on this hard work. These institutions, which set up camps where people took refuge, distribute aid, determine their refugee status, and perform other difficult and risky tasks, also query the identity of applicants for aid and transfer the data they obtain to the digital environment. These technological solutions are expensive, and require serious investment. They require not only a technical infrastructure, but also expert teams. Since UN agencies or humanitarian organisations that need to produce quick solutions to emergencies in short-term projects do not have the money and capacity to make this investment, these organisations have to work with mobile phone operators, banks, and technology companies, to which they have to give a significant part of the funds they receive. Of course, donor countries can also fund some organisations to develop their own technological infrastructure, but this is not preferred.

This is where the risk of data exploitation enters the picture. As global supplier companies provide technical infrastructure, they are able to access the data of millions of people and control the shaping of the market, thanks to the work of these institutions. In this way, banks organise cash transfers in the field of humanitarian aid, mobile operators distribute SIM cards and offer communication and mobile banking services, while technology companies offer and develop a range of technological products from blockchain to big data analysis and machine learning. The technological literacy required to understand how systems like blockchain operate is very high, and it would be naive to expect the refugees to fully understand the implications. The controversy surrounding the UN's collection of biometric information from ethnic Rohingya refugees (discussed by Salah et al., Chapter 2, this volume) illustrated that the refugees often did not fully understand the forms used in data collection, or were afraid of negative consequences in case they did not share data.

As a summary, although digital solutions enable the financial integration of refugees, the forcibly displaced, undocumented immigrants, and those without an official identity, as well as their participation in the capitalist economy as customers and employees, this process remains at the initiative of companies, and within the limits set by them. The issue of the rights and freedoms of these communities remains incomplete. Having many stakeholders creates additional risks for the vulnerable, because while data are shared, the conditions under which this is achieved and the influence of different parties in determining what is stored and processed is not fully transparent.

Conclusions

Migration is a complex and dynamic phenomenon that requires multifaceted expansion of the quantitative approaches through a multidimensional lens. We have illustrated in this work that data science and the analysis of secondary data sources can provide valuable insights with high spatiotemporal granularity. One can argue that, so far, scattered efforts have been made with regards to attempts to enhance the knowledge base on migration- and mobility-related challenges in quantitative terms via new data sources, but coordinated and significant systems have not yet been established.

The use of big data and machine learning allows the creation of complex models, with which simple measurements and behaviours, accumulated and integrated over time, can turn into reliable estimators. However, issues of generalisation and model validity, as well as societal and ethical issues, stand as challenges before these approaches turn into mainstream solutions. Traditional approaches using well-controlled and in-depth measurements cannot be replaced by analysis of secondary data, but only be complemented.

When these new tools are added to the toolbox of the researcher, they offer enhanced flexibility in dealing with practical issues. Each country is different in its conditions, resources, and needs. Official statistics and national surveys provide excellent data in some countries, which can afford to dedicate plenty of resources for high-quality data. In other countries, secondary data sources may address much needed data gaps. The data scientific tools developed naturally serve primary data sources as well and, in time, cause better theoretical models to be developed.

The use of secondary data sources to observe human movements is not without its societal risks. Unchecked, it may bestow undesired surveillance capabilities on governments and corporations. The analysis outcomes, or systems built on such data, may end up acquiring biases, or providing outcomes that are not sufficiently transparent or accountable. Clearly, these risks need to be openly discussed and solved before these technologies become usable. We believe the efforts will be worthwhile.

Acknowledgements

This study is supported by the European Union's Horizon 2020 Research and Innovation Programme under grant agreement No. 870661.

References

Ahmad-Yar, A. W. and Bircan, T. (2021), 'Anatomy of a misfit: International migration statistics', *Sustainability* 13(7), 4032.

Alencar, A. and Godin, M. (2022), 'Exploring digital connectivities in forced migration contexts: Digital "making do" practises', *in* A. A. Salah, E. E. Korkmaz, and T. Bircan, eds, *Data Science for Migration and Mobility*, Proceedings of the British Academy, British Academy / Oxford University Press, London, UK.

Alexander, M., Polimis, K., and Zagheni, E. (2020), 'Combining social media and survey data to nowcast migrant stocks in the United States', *Population Research and Policy Review* 41, 1–28.

Allen, W. (2022), 'Applying computational linguistic and text analysis to media content about migration: Opportunities and challenges for social scientific domains', *in* A. A. Salah, E. E. Korkmaz, and T. Bircan, eds, *Data Science for Migration and Mobility*, Proceedings of the British Academy, British Academy / Oxford University Press, London, UK.

Alpaydin, E. (2016), *Machine Learning: The New AI*, MIT Press, Cambridge, MA.

Bakker, M. A., Piracha, D. A., Lu, P. J., Bejgo, K., Bahrami, M., Leng, Y., Balsa-Barreiro, J., Ricard, J., Morales, A. J., Singh, V. K., Bozkaya, B., Balcisoy, S., and Pentland, A. (2019), 'Measuring fine-grained multidimensional integration using mobile phone metadata: The case of Syrian refugees in Turkey', *in Guide to Mobile Data Analytics in Refugee Scenarios: The 'Data for Refugees Challenge' Study*, Springer Nature, New York, 123–40.

Bircan, T. (2022), 'Remote sensing data for migration research', *in* A. A. Salah, E. E. Korkmaz, and T. Bircan, eds, *Data Science for Migration and Mobility*, Proceedings of the British Academy, British Academy / Oxford University Press, London, UK.

Bircan, T., Purkayastha, D., Ahmad-yar, A. W., Lotter, K., Iakono, C. D., Göler, D., Stanek, M., Yilmaz, S., Solano, G., and Ünver, Ö. (2020), 'Gaps in migration research: Review of migration theories and the quality and compatibility of migration data on the national and international level', HumMingBird project report.

Blumenstock, J., Cadamuro, G., and On, R. (2015), 'Predicting poverty and wealth from mobile phone metadata', *Science* 350(6264), 1073–6.

Böhme, M. H., Gröger, A., and Stöhr, T. (2020), 'Searching for a better life: Predicting international migration with online search keywords', *Journal of Development Economics* 142, 102347.

Bosetti, P., Poletti, P., Stella, M., Lepri, B., Merler, S., and Domenico, M. D. (2019), Reducing measles risk in Turkey through social integration of Syrian refugees, *in* 'Data for Refugees Challenge Workshop'.

Coimbra Vieira, C., Fatehkia, M., Garimella, K., Weber, I. and Zagheni, E. (2022), 'Using Facebook and LinkedIn data to study international mobility', *in* A. A. Salah, E. E. Korkmaz, and T. Bircan, eds, *Data Science for Migration and Mobility*, Proceedings of the British Academy, British Academy / Oxford University Press, London, UK.

Coppi, G. and Fast, L. (2019), 'Blockchain and distributed ledger technologies in the humanitarian sector', HPG commissioned technical report.

Cowls, J., Tsamados, A., Taddeo, M., and Floridi, L. (2021), 'A definition, benchmark and database of AI for social good initiatives', *Nature Machine Intelligence* 3(2), 111–15.

De Mauro, A., Greco, M., and Grimaldi, M. (2016), 'A formal definition of big data based on its essential features', *Library Review* 65(3), 122–35.

De Montjoye, Y.-A. *et al.* (2018), 'On the privacy-conscientious use of mobile phone data', *Scientific Data* 5(1), 1–6.

Dietler, D., Farnham, A., de Hoogh, K., and Winkler, M. S. (2020), 'Quantification of annual settlement growth in rural mining areas using machine learning', *Remote Sensing* 12(2), 235.

Dwork, C., et al. (2014), 'The algorithmic foundations of differential privacy', *Foundation Trends in Theoretical Computer Science* 9(3–4), 211–407.

Earney, C. and Jimenez, R. M. (2019), 'Pioneering predictive analytics for decision-making in forced displacement contexts', in A. A. Salah, A. Pentland, B. Lepri, and E. Letouzé, eds, *Guide to Mobile Data Analytics in Refugee Scenarios*, Springer, New York, 101–19.

Favell, A. (2011), *Eurostars and Eurocities: Free movement and mobility in an integrating Europe*, IJURR Studies in Urban and Social Change vol. 56, John Wiley & Sons, Chichester.

Geiger, M. and Pécoud, A. (2010), 'The politics of international migration management', in M. Geiger and A. Pécoud, eds, *The Politics of International Migration Management*, Springer, New York, 1–20.

Global Migration Group and others (2017), *Handbook for Improving the Production and Use of Migration Data for Development*, Global Knowledge Partnership for Migration and Development (KNOMAD).

Gürkan, M., Bozkaya, B., and Balcisoy, S. (2022), 'Financial datasets: Leveraging transactional big data in mobility and migration studies,, in A. A. Salah, E. E. Korkmaz, and T. Bircan, eds, *Data Science for Migration and Mobility*, Proceedings of the British Academy, British Academy / Oxford University Press, London, UK.

Hilbert, M. (2013), 'Big data for development: From information-to knowledge societies', *SSRN Electronic Journal*, 2205145.

Hofman, J. M., et al. (2021), 'Integrating explanation and prediction in computational social science', *Nature* 595, 181–8.

Kim, J., Pollacci, L., Rossetti, G., Sîrbu, A., Giannotti, F., and Pedreschi, D. (2022), 'Twitter data for migration studies', in A. A. Salah, E. E. Korkmaz, and T. Bircan, eds, *Data Science for Migration and Mobility*, Proceedings of the British Academy, British Academy / Oxford University Press, London, UK.

Koch, C. M., Moise, I., Helbing, D., and Donnay, K. (2020), 'Public debate in the media matters: Evidence from the European refugee crisis', *EPJ Data Science* 9(1), 1–27.

Lazer, D., Kennedy, R., King, G., and Vespignani, A. (2014), 'The parable of Google Flu: Traps in big data analysis', *Science* 343(6176), 1203–5.

Lazer, D. M., et al. (2020), 'Computational social science: Obstacles and opportunities', *Science* 369(6507), 1060–62.

Lazer, D., et al. (2009), 'Life in the network: The coming age of computational social science', *Science* 323(5915), 721–3.

Letouzé, E. (2019), 'Leveraging open algorithms (opal) for the safe, ethical, and scalable use of private sector data in crisis contexts', in A. A. Salah, A. Pentland, B. Lepri, and E. Letouzé, eds, *Guide to Mobile Data Analytics in Refugee Scenarios*, Springer, New York, 453–64.

Letouzé, E. and Oliver, N. (2019), *Sharing is Caring: Four Key Requirements for Sustainable Private Data Sharing and Use for Public Good*, Data-pop Alliance and Vodafone Institute for Society and Communications, London.

Li, T., Sahu, A. K., Talwalkar, A., and Smith, V. (2020), 'Federated learning: Challenges, methods, and future directions', *IEEE Signal Processing Magazine* 37(3), 50–60.

Luca, M., Barlacchi, G., Oliver, N., and Lepri, B. (2022), 'Leveraging mobile phone data for migration flows', in A. A. Salah, E. E. Korkmaz, and T. Bircan, eds, *Data Science for Migration and Mobility*, Proceedings of the British Academy, British Academy / Oxford University Press, London, UK.

Marquez, N., Garimella, K., Toomet, O., Weber, I. G., and Zagheni, E. (2019), 'Segregation and sentiment: Estimating refugee segregation and its effects using digital trace data', *in* A. A. Salah, A. Pentland, B. Lepri, and E. Letouzé, eds, *Guide to Mobile Data Analytics in Refugee Scenarios*, Springer, New York, 265–82.

Miranda-González, A., Aref, S., Theile, T., and Zagheni, E. (2020), 'Scholarly migration within Mexico: Analyzing internal migration among researchers using Scopus longitudinal bibliometric data', *EPJ Data Science* 9(1), 34.

Molnar, P. (2019), 'Technology on the margins: AI and global migration management from a human rights perspective', *Cambridge International Law Journal* 8(2), 305–30.

Oliver, N., *et al.* (2020), 'Mobile phone data for informing public health actions across the COVID-19 pandemic life cycle', *Science Advances* 6(23), 764.

Pötzschke, S. (2015), 'Migrant mobilities in Europe: Comparing Turkish to Romanian migrants', *Migration Letters* 12(3), 315–26.

Quinn, J. A., Nyhan, M. M., Navarro, C., Coluccia, D., Bromley, L., and Luengo-Oroz, M. (2018), 'Humanitarian applications of machine learning with remote-sensing data: Review and case study in refugee settlement mapping', *Philosophical Transactions of the Royal Society A: Mathematical, Physical and Engineering Sciences* 376(2128), 20170363.

Robinson, C. and Dilkina, B. (2018), 'A machine learning approach to modeling human migration', *in Proceedings of the 1st ACM SIGCAS Conference on Computing and Sustainable Societies*, pp. 1–8.

Salah, A. A., Canca, C., and Erman, B. (2022), 'Ethical and legal concerns on data science for large-scale human mobility', *in* A. A. Salah, E. E. Korkmaz, and T. Bircan, eds, *Data Science for Migration and Mobility*, Proceedings of the British Academy, British Academy / Oxford University Press, London, UK.

Salah, A. A., Pentland, A., Lepri, B., and Letouzé, E. (2019), *Guide to Mobile Data Analytics in Refugee Scenarios*, Springer, New York.

Salah, A. A., Pentland, A., Lepri, B., Letouzé, E., Vinck, P., de Montjoye, Y.-A., Dong, X., and Dağdelen, Ö. (2018), 'Data for refugees: The D4R challenge on mobility of Syrian refugees in Turkey', arXiv:1807.00523.

Santamaria, C. and Vespe, M. (2018), 'Towards an EU policy on migration data: Improvements to the EU migration data landscape', Publications Office of the European Union, Luxembourg, available at http://dx.doi.org/10.2760/645367

Scheel, S. and Ustek-Spilda, F. (2018), 'Big data, big promises: Revisiting migration statistics in context of the datafication of everything', Border Criminologies, available at https://www.law.ox.ac.uk/research-subject-groups/centre-criminology/centreborder-criminologies/blog/2018/06/big-data-big

Simini, F., González, M. C., Maritan, A., and Barabási, A.-L. (2012), 'A universal model for mobility and migration patterns', *Nature* 484(7392), 96–100.

Sîrbu, A., *et al.* (2021), 'Human migration: The big data perspective', *International Journal of Data Science and Analytics* 11(4), 341–60.

Skeldon, R. (2017), 'International migration, internal migration, mobility and urbanization: Towards more integrated approaches', Population Division, Department of Economic and Social Affairs, United Nations.

State, B., Rodriguez, M., Helbing, D., and Zagheni, E. (2014), 'Migration of professionals to the US', *in* L. M. Aiello and D. McFarland, eds, *Social Informatics*, Springer, New York, 531–43.

Sterly, H. and Wirkus, L. (2022), 'Analysing refugees' secondary mobility using mobile phone call detail records', *in* A. A. Salah, E. E. Korkmaz, and T. Bircan, eds, *Data Science for Migration and Mobility*, Proceedings of the British Academy, British Academy / Oxford University Press, London, UK.

Tomašev, N., *et al.* (2020), 'AI for social good: Unlocking the opportunity for positive impact', *Nature Communications* 11(1), 1–6.

UN (2015), *Transforming Our World: The 2030 Agenda for Sustainable Development*, A/RES/70/1.

Unver, H. A. and Kurnaz, A. (2022), 'Conflict and forced migration: Social media as event data', *in* A. A. Salah, E. E. Korkmaz, and T. Bircan, eds, *Data Science for Migration and Mobility*, Proceedings of the British Academy, British Academy / Oxford University Press, London, UK.

Verhulst, S. G. and Young, A. (2019), 'The potential and practice of data collaboratives for migration', *in* A. A. Salah, A. Pentland, B. Lepri, and E. Letouzé, eds, *Guide to Mobile Data Analytics in Refugee Scenarios*, Springer, New York, 465–76.

Vertovec, S. (2007), 'Introduction: New directions in the anthropology of migration and multiculturalism', *Ethnic and Racial Studies* 30(6), 961–978.

Zagheni, E., Garimella, V. R. K., Weber, I., and State, B. (2014), 'Inferring international and internal migration patterns from Twitter data', *in WWW'14 Companion: Proceedings of the 23rd International Conference on World Wide Web*, 439–44.

Zipf, G. K. (1946), 'The $P_1 P_2 / D$ hypothesis: On the intercity movement of persons', *American Sociological Review* 11(6), 677–86.

2

Ethical and Legal Concerns on Data Science for Large-Scale Human Mobility

ALBERT ALI SALAH, CANSU CANCA, AND BARIŞ ERMAN

Introduction

BIG DATA BASED analysis of human mobility relies on various data sources and combines these to address a range of 'wicked' social problems, i.e., complex problems without a clear analytical solution and with many dimensions that need to be optimised simultaneously. These problems may not have clear-cut causal relationships but, as in most complex systems, they are driven by feedback loops, circular causality, and parameters that involve many stakeholders. A purely data-driven approach could be dangerous, simply because it fails to address this complexity properly and thereby generates various side issues while only solving the problem in focus.

This chapter introduces the ethical and legal aspects of data science, with the aim of providing the reader with a basic understanding of the ethical risks, legal issues, and tools to mitigate them. These risks may ensue from the use of a particular approach or methodology, or they may have deep-seated causes such as problems in key definitions, issues related to specific data sources, and issues in policy recommendations.

The 'Applying ethics and ethics principles' section introduces applied ethics and ethics principles in the context of data science. 'Ethical issues in data science for migration and mobility' details some common ethical issues in data science and technologies that build on data science, describing how these issues may manifest in the migration and mobility domains. 'Data ethics tools' provides a list of ethics tools for projects and initiatives, while 'Legal risks for data science in migration and mobility' briefly addresses legal concepts and concerns, which are more closely related to policy-makers and end users but still relevant to researchers. Further reading is provided at the end of the chapter.

Applying ethics and ethics principles

What is applied ethics?

When we discuss the ethics of a particular technology, our goal is to determine how we can ethically develop and use that technology in various domains. This requires an understanding of the ethical risks already entailed in the proposed technology and existent in the domain within which it is meant to be utilised. Through an ethics analysis that explicates how these risks may manifest as the technology enters into use in a given domain, we can determine the best course of action to mitigate ethical risks. In this chapter we focus on the ethical questions and concerns related to data science technologies as they apply to the domain of migration and mobility.

Ethics, more specifically *applied ethics*, aims to guide actions. Applied ethics is a normative subdiscipline of philosophy, where the core question is, what is the *right* thing to do in a given situation? Here, 'right' is understood in terms of *good* and *just*. This might be, for example, about a developer choosing which dataset or algorithm to use in order to minimise harm, or a policy-maker deciding which safeguards to set up in order to reduce algorithmic discrimination. In order to guide such decisions, an ethics analysis would employ theories from moral and political philosophy, engage with morally relevant concepts, and use analogies and thought experiments to test the argument. Since the questions at hand are real-world questions, such an analysis would also require information provided by other disciplines. For example, if the question is whether it is ethical to mandate stricter border controls during a pandemic, we need information regarding the transmission mode and rate of the virus, the mortality and morbidity rate of the disease, the expected social and economic impact of the policy on various groups, the feasibility and cost of this policy, and details of the other available options, just to name a few. Once this information is provided by health sciences and social sciences, we can analyse the ethical justifications and implications of the question in terms of harm and benefit, individual freedom and autonomy, and distribution of benefits and burdens within the society to determine whether the policy is ethically permissible, necessary, or ethically prohibited.

Ethics in data science

When it comes to data science for migration and mobility, ethical questions arise from the domain of migration itself, from the types of technologies that can be utilised or developed in relation to migration, and from the intersection of these two. These questions are present from the conception of a project to the presentation of the results, including ethically loaded decisions in formulating the problem and choosing the methods and tools for researching it.

Concerns in data ethics can be distinguished as those related to data, algorithms, and practices (Floridi and Taddeo, 2016). Ethics of data pertain to the collection, storage, and usage of large-scale data, re-identification and privacy issues, consent of data owners, the biases inherent in the dataset itself, and risks and benefits arising from the analysis of the data. Ethics of algorithms focus on the complexities of algorithms, designers' and developers' responsibilities for ethical design, and auditing and transparency. Finally, ethics of practice relate to the practise of data science: the results of data analysis and actual deployment of algorithms, and their effects on real-world decisions, focusing on power, authority, policy, and user rights. These areas are necessarily intertwined, and the boundaries are not clearly distinguishable.

For example, a big data project investigating migrants' access to schools and educational facilities should take into account potential issues in the formulation of the project and the use of different data sources. This may, for instance, include considerations like data coverage in rural areas, to ensure there are no data gaps, and the consent of data owners. Mamei et al. (2019) provided an example in this area that used mobile call detail records (CDR) to compute refugees' physical access to educational institutions. The algorithms used to estimate access should take specific biases into account (e.g., assumptions about modes of transport or considering gender-related issues in transportation). Once such an analysis is completed, the policy recommendations could take a broad range of possible consequences and complex factors into account, as the changing use of educational facilities may have different impacts on different populations. Clearly, considering all three levels of ethical concerns (i.e., data, algorithm, and practice) is necessary to fully assess and address the ethical risks and benefits. An example is the closing down of the temporary language centres in Turkey in order to integrate Syrian children into Turkish primary schools, rather than teach them at the language centres. This was done to improve their social integration, and indeed served this aim. However, this policy had a strong negative effect on the older female refugee population, who were able to attend the centres but not able to attend the primary schools to learn the local language (Haznedar et al., 2018; Salah et al., 2019). Having a small set of objectives to improve can easily result in neglecting other dimensions of the issue and cause other problems while fixing the initial problem.

The questions related to the use of data science tools can also be placed in the broader context of migration ethics and political theory, where the responsibilities of the stakeholders, practical conditions, and normative positions in the discourse are questioned (Carens, 2013; Owen, 2020). For the purposes of this chapter we address a narrower set of concerns related to the use of specific technologies, but we acknowledge that the issues discussed here have a wide range of implications and the conceptual framing of these problems must be carefully considered. The last few years of increased technology use have taught us that some consequences of the wide-ranging adoption of technologies are very difficult to predict. An example can be found in social media, where content filtering algorithms designed to improve user experience end up widening the gaps within the society and polarising it. Such risks are exacerbated when the computer scientists who design the algorithms are unaware of the nuances and debates around the topic and in related domains, and treat questionable assumptions as solid foundations. For this reason, a basic understanding of data ethics is crucial for the ethical practise of data science.

Ethics principles

In recent discussions in ethics of technology, data, and artificial intelligence (AI), ethics principles have been dominant. Since 2015, over 100 sets of ethics principles have been published around the world just for AI practices.[1] This number is higher when we include data ethics principles and, more broadly, technology ethics principles. Each one of these sets covers a wide range of ethics principles such as transparency, privacy, diversity, and sustainability. While these sets of principles differ slightly from each other by emphasising different principles, their basic structure is in line with the *principlism* approach developed in 1979 for research ethics with three *core principles*: respect for persons, beneficence, and justice.[2]

These core principles are loosely derived from theories in moral and political philosophy. Autonomy, minimisation of harm, and justice are argued to be intrinsically valuable within these theories.[3] They are valued for themselves and not as a means to achieve other goals; they are the goals of ethics. In comparison, *instrumental principles* such as privacy or transparency are valuable as a means to achieve these ends. For example, privacy allows us to exercise our autonomy without interference from others and protects us from harm; transparency allows us to acquire the necessary understanding and information so that we can make rational and informed choices and thereby exercise our autonomy, and it helps uphold justice by uncovering unfair and unequal treatments. Such instrumental principles are not goals of ethics, i.e., we do not value privacy or transparency simply for their own sake (Canca, 2020).

---

[1] AI Ethics Lab, *Toolbox: Dynamics of AI Principles*, February 2020; see https://aiethicslab.com/big-picture/

[2] The Belmont Report (The National Commission for the Protection of Human Subjects of Biomedical and Behavioral Research, 1979) lays out the foundation of *principlism*, which is further developed in the seminal book *Principles of Biomedical Ethics* (Beauchamp and Childress, 2013). While the Belmont Report lists three 'basic ethical principles', principlism often lists four, dividing the principle of beneficence into beneficence and non-maleficence principles.

[3] In humanitarian aid and forced migration literature, the 'do no harm' principle makes up a core concept derived from medical ethics. However, strictly speaking, 'do no harm' is an ethically problematic principle. A good example is life-saving surgery: surgery necessarily involves harm (that is, cutting open the patient and risking their life), although it is justified by another risk of harm already present (that is, the patient's medical condition which poses harm to the patient in the absence of surgery) and the potential of benefits which would outweigh the harm of surgery (that is, the cure). A strict 'do no harm' principle would not allow life-saving surgery, because while doing surgery involves doing harm, allowing the patient to die from their existing medical condition is not an active *doing* of harm. Clearly, this reasoning poses serious ethical problems. Therefore, 'do no harm' functions as a loose title for a more nuanced ethical approach, i.e., recognising and minimising the risk of harm due to (humanitarian or medical) intervention, and minimising the risk of overall harm while maximising overall benefits to ensure that the benefits outweigh the harm. The exact procedures to achieve this end and the threshold of risk for justifiable interventions are further discussed in the relevant literature.

Why does this distinction of core and instrumental principles matter? Because in order to apply and utilise these principles, we need to understand which of them are interchangeable and which are fundamental. (We will return to this distinction in 'Data ethics tools' with *The Box* tool.) Let's take the example of using aggregate anonymous mobile phone data to study migration patterns in order to predict the spread of an infectious disease (Wesolowski *et al.*, 2012). The goal here is to control the spread of the disease and thus minimise the harm. However, the data are not collected through individual consent, because collecting individual consent, even if possible, would slow down the process to such a degree that the project would fail. Is this an ethical violation? The answer depends on the purpose of consent and the other related ethical concerns. Consent, as an instrumental principle, serves to protect and promote individual autonomy by ensuring that individuals can make decisions regarding their life, their space, and their body. If the data are aggregated and anonymised properly, it cannot be re-identified or connected back to the individuals and therefore its use will not directly affect the individual's life. In other words, through another instrumental principle, privacy, the ethical need for consent to protect individual autonomy can be satisfied. One could still argue that if the project results in decisions that would negatively affect the individual's group (for example, travel bans for seasonal workers), the individual might have refused to allow their anonymised data to be used, if they were given the chance to do so beforehand.

At this point we are pitting core principles against each other. Will a certain action result in unfair discrimination of a group? Is the harm done to this group outweighed by the benefit this group and/or others might receive? Would protecting individual autonomy in this broad manner result in violation of the autonomy of others? In order to ensure that the project is ethically justifiable, these questions must be answered by a thorough ethics analysis that takes into account the empirical evidence and, if need be, appeals to the theories behind these principles to flesh out their specific demands. Once this analysis lays out the extent of the ethical risks, we can determine the best course of action to mitigate these risks through project and algorithm design and safeguards for the use of the results.

Ethical issues in data science for migration and mobility

Here, we take a brief look at some of the most common ethical issues in data science and AI technologies. These include issues related to (1) consent; (2) de-identification, anonymisation, and re-identification; (3) black box, transparency, and explainability; (4) algorithmic bias; (5) dual use of technologies; and (6) complexity and risk assessment. As we sketch out the main ethical concerns with respect to each of these points, we also provide examples from the migration and mobility domain to illustrate the issues within the proper context of this book.

Consent

Consent is a practice to ensure individual autonomy is protected and promoted. Proper consent has three conditions: the individual consenting must be informed and rational, and the consent must be voluntary. The ethical and sometimes legal need for consent arises in various stages of data science and AI technologies. In research, consent plays a crucial role in the individual's participation and the sharing of identifiable personal data.

In emerging technologies, a major problem with consent arises from a lack of understanding around the technology and its potential for harm and benefits. As we will discuss in detail in the next sections, difficulties in the risk assessment of technologies, the lack of transparency in models, risks for re-identification of data, and dual use of technologies make it particularly difficult for individuals to engage in meaningful consent procedures. This is also due to the fact that even researchers are often unclear about these risks and benefits. Furthermore, power relations between authorities and vulnerable populations, as well as ownership of surveillance and data collection technologies, affect practices of consent. For example, it is difficult for a refugee living in a camp to decline consent for an iris scan, if it is the only way to get food and fundamental help.[4]

Data collected and research conducted using online platforms through reliance on the terms and conditions of those platforms also raise a problem about consent. Since it has been shown that individuals cannot practically or reasonably read and understand all of the terms and conditions of all the platforms they use, these agreements cannot constitute proper consent (McDonald and Cranor, 2008).[5] From a regulatory perspective, these agreements are superseded by communication laws of the countries where these platforms reside, which may explicitly permit aggregated and anonymised processing of such data for humanitarian or research purposes.

Failure to properly obtain consent from refugees and asylum seekers may result not only in a violation of the right to privacy and self-determination, but also the right to liberty and security, and even the right to life. A striking example of this is the controversy about the United Nations Refugee Agency (UNHCR) collecting and sharing of Rohingya refugees' personal data with Bangladesh, which then shared it with the Myanmar authorities. Allegedly, the UNHCR collected the Rohingya refugees' personal data by having them sign a document, where a checkbox indicated that their data might be shared for repatriation purposes. However, this checkbox was in English only, and many refugees thought that they had to agree to the terms in order to get their identity cards. According to Human Rights Watch

---

[4] #UN4RefugeeMigrants: Iris scan helps Syrian refugees in Jordan receive UN supplies in 'blink of eye', https://refugeesmigrants.un.org/ar/node/100042481
[5] PC Mag: It Would Take 17 Hours to Read the Terms & Conditions of the 13 Most Popular Apps, https://www.pcmag.com/news/it-would-take-17-hours-to-read-the-terms-conditions-of-the-13-most-popular

(HRW), this constitutes a breach of the policies of the UNHCR, who subsequently released a statement to respond to the allegations.[6]

De-identification, anonymisation, and re-identification

Consent is often not needed if an individual's personal data can be successfully de-identified or anonymised, meaning that the data can no longer be associated with an individual. However, this is easier said than done. As algorithms become more powerful and more datasets become available, it is increasingly difficult to completely anonymise the data and prevent re-identification (Sweeney, 2002; Waldo, 2016). Re-identification poses a problem to privacy and thereby to individual autonomy.

Anonymisation removes personal identifiers such as names, addresses, identifying numbers, and keys from a database, but the remaining patterns may still be sufficient to identify a person uniquely. For example, behaviour can also be used as a biometric (De Montjoye *et al.*, 2013). In some cases, researchers have ensured anonymity under certain assumptions, but later research developed methods invalidating these assumptions and made identification possible. One should be cautious of sharing an anonymous dataset with a party who might possess additional information that can be used to remove the anonymity from (some of) the records. This does not mean that privacy is impossible. Aggregation of data is an additional step that can be taken to ensure privacy is secured. Appropriately anonymised and aggregated mobile phone data has been successfully used to estimate population distributions, where other data sources are scarce, outdated, or unreliable (Deville *et al.*, 2014). For example, the Data for Development (D4D) Challenge opened a large set of mobile CDR to the research community with the aim of providing insights to policymakers about development (Blondel *et al.*, 2012). The initial challenge contained communication graphs, which illustrated some of the properties of the social networks of the users. Later, Sharad and Danezis (2013) managed to de-anonymise part of these communication graphs by using graph-theoretic analyses. Subsequently, the following Data for Refugees (D4R) Challenge, which also made a large mobile CDR dataset from Turkey available to help create insights about Syrian refugees in Turkey (Salah *et al.*, 2018), abstained from making the communication graph data available.

Black box, transparency, and explainability

The increasing use of complex machine learning models results in systems that are often referred to as 'black boxes', where it is not clear how the system reaches its outcome. These systems lack transparency regarding how the model engages with

---

[6] Human Rights Watch: UN Shared Rohingya Data Without Informed Consent, https://www.hrw.org/news/2021/06/15/un-shared-rohingya-data-without-informed-consent; The UN Refugee Agency: News comment: Statement on refugee registration and data collection in Bangladesh, https://www.unhcr.org/uk/news/press/2021/6/60c85a7b4/news-comment-statement-refugee-registration-data-collection-bangladesh.html

the data to produce the outcome. In contrast to 'black box' AI, *explainable* AI models are those whose outcome can be understood by humans. There are at least two different aspects to explainability that need considering. One is explainability for the designer, who benefits from an improved understanding of how the model is reaching its decisions. The designer can then use these insights to identify potential issues. Such insights would allow the designer to reduce various risks of harm, including those related to safety, security, and unjustified discrimination. The second aspect of explainability is related to the user, who thereby achieves a better understanding of the decisions of the system and can factor it in to further deliberations. Enabling the user to engage with the system in this way promotes user autonomy.

Consider a (hypothetical) satellite imaging based AI system that predicts whether an area will experience climate-related forced migration within the next 10 years. The input of the AI system is a satellite image, and the output is a binary decision about the target variable. Such a system may be created via supervised learning, where past data are used to predict future cases. A system that is more explainable for the designer could use the concept of attention and highlight those areas of the satellite image that were most important for its decision. The designer can then notice, for example, that the system invariably pays more attention to the centre of the image (which can be a bias in training image selection) and the designer can take measures to rectify this bias, for example by selecting randomly cropped images. On the other hand, a system that is more explainable for the user may point to the lack of forested areas and distance to water sources, which affected the outcome. This can prompt the user to examine potential solutions and policies in dealing with the issue. In the first case, explainability is used to improve the AI system and protects it from incorrect and biased design and training, whereas the second case is about making the system more useful as a tool in decision-making.

Algorithmic bias

Algorithmic bias occurs when the AI model systematically and unfairly discriminates against certain groups. This is different from the statistical concept of bias in machine learning, although related to it. To clarify this point, let us first explain the latter. Suppose we have a sample and we are estimating a parameter θ based on this sample. In machine learning terminology, the bias of our estimator is the difference between θ that we are trying to estimate and the expected value of the estimator (Alpaydin, 2020). For example, for a properly collected sample, the sample average is an unbiased estimator for the population mean, as the expected difference between them is zero. We want this kind of bias to be as small as possible. If we are estimating a population parameter by means of a sample, a large bias can be created by incorrect sampling from the population. For example, if you would like to estimate the education level of a migrant group in a country, but sample only migrants from a small university town, you will create a bias; the expected average education level of your sample will be higher than the expected average education level of the population.

Algorithmic bias, on the other hand, is about systematic and unfair outcomes of an AI system. This might be intentional or (more often) unintentional. The bias can enter the model through various routes: unrepresentative datasets, datasets that reflect existing social biases, discriminatory labelling of data, variables and proxies used within the models, and framing of the problem for the model. Some of these biases are straightforward to fix (such as unrepresentative datasets), and some of them are nearly impossible to eliminate (such as social biases within datasets). Algorithmic bias constitutes a serious problem for social justice because systems and technologies can amplify existing biases while hiding them behind a facade of mathematical objectivity. Algorithmic bias (and bias more generally) is necessarily related to the concepts of *justice* and *fairness*. Theories of justice in political philosophy offer us various definitions of justice and how to apply them. To achieve useful results, research on algorithmic bias and fairness in machine learning has to engage with this literature.

When investigating biases, a useful concept is a *protected attribute*; these are data attributes that need to be tested for potential biases, such as ethnicity, gender, and age. Discrimination based on a protected attribute can happen in different ways. Mehrabi *et al.* (2019) described five major categories, of which the most important are *direct discrimination*, which happens when a protected attribute directly leads to a biased outcome, and *indirect discrimination*, which happens when the system is not taking any protected attributes into account, but seemingly neutral attributes are acting as proxies for directed attributes. An example of the latter is the usage of postal codes, which may contain information about the ethnicity of subjects if ethnic groups are more densely populated in certain areas of a city. Indirect discrimination requires extra attention, especially if the outcomes of data analysis are used for policy decisions.

Dealing with issues of bias requires looking at the data collection and analysis process critically and holistically. Who collects the data (e.g., a private vs public entity) and whether this entity has a specific agenda, how the data are sampled (whether there are any structural issues and whether representativeness is ensured), and how the data are annotated are all issues that can introduce bias even before the analysis is initiated.

Biases may also arise inadvertently from incorrect analysis. In data science, the collection of large-scale data from a heterogeneous sample may lead to a phenomenon called *Simpson's paradox* (Blyth, 1972). Put simply, this issue happens when one has subgroups that exhibit biases that cancel each other out when the data are aggregated. Clemens (2020) provided an example of this for the emigration–income relationship, which shows very different patterns for the aggregate population compared to subgroups with different income levels. Another example related to demographics is given in Escalante *et al.* (2022), where a model was initially examined for gender bias and found to have none, but further investigation into different age groups revealed a strong preference for younger women and older men in the system, which cancelled each other out in the age-aggregated analysis. Simpson's paradox can also happen with trend analysis, where aggregation can make trends appear or disappear (Alipourfard et al., 2018). Shuffling and randomisation-based tests can be used to determine whether Simpson's paradox has any effect on the outcomes of a study (Lerman, 2018).

Dual use of technologies

Most technologies have a dual use: They can be utilised to benefit individuals and society, but they can also be used against them. This issue of dual use of technology becomes bigger as it gets easier to modify the developed systems for ethically problematic purposes and have them adopted by actors with different political agendas. Dual use of technology is not a novel problem, but it is amplified due to the adaptability and the scale of deployment of emerging technologies.

Some of the most important ethical issues in the context of mobility arise from the dual use of technology. A population-level mobility tracking application could be the key to controlling a pandemic, but also a dangerous surveillance tool in the hands of an autocratic government that can use it to suppress and punish any actions against its authority (Oliver et al., 2020). Similarly, a remote-sensing application designed to support and save refugee boats in the Mediterranean Sea can also be used to stop them before reaching European shores.[7]

It is worth noting that inadequate use of ethical instruments may end up masking the problems instead of helping to solve them. An ethical assessment committee that is available but not consulted, data management plans that are written in detail but not followed, and stakeholder consultations where function creep and dual use are hidden can function as ethics-washing, where ethics is used more as lip service than as a tool. To avoid circumventing ethical safeguards, 'data protection by design and default' is a good practice to follow, where protection is incorporated in the design stage to prevent misuse. For example, in the Data for Refugees Challenge, which created a mobile CDR database from one million customers, including Syrian refugees and natives, this practice was followed to anonymise the data as a one-way transformation during data collection (Salah et al., 2018; Vinck et al., 2019). Since the original data, as well as the mapping, were removed before the database was shared, the anonymity of individuals would have been preserved even if a data breach were to compromise the dataset.

Complexity and risk assessment

A major source of difficulty in ethical design, development, and use of technologies comes from the complexity of human social dynamics and the difficulty of

---

[7] See, for example, the discussions around humanitarian rescue operations in the Mediterranean reported by Médecins sans Frontières; e.g., MSF and Sea Watch ship becomes the fifth search and rescue vessel to be detained in five months - condemning people to die at sea, http://prez.ly/Yg0b

estimating technologies' effects on these dynamics. Many factors influence human behaviour, such as human mobility across the globe, and while it is possible to design experiments that control a large number of variables to study the effects of a few factors, the mutual interactions of these factors are difficult to model. The hallmark of complex systems is that a linear relationship between a set of causes and a set of effects is inadequate for modelling the system dynamics. Rather, these systems can be better conceptualised by stable and unstable attractors, equilibria, limit cycles, and bifurcations (Strogatz, 2018). When a technology is designed and put into use, it interacts with the society that uses it and changes it in unexpected ways. A good example is again social media, which ended up occupying a role in the society that no one could have predicted, as it slowly transformed practices of communication and commerce.

Complexity has three implications for ethical design in the domain of migration and mobility. The first is that the models and systems relying on big data analysis should be seen as potential agents of change. A technology that is initially designed to help in classifying asylum cases may create a benchmark that changes the behaviour of asylum-seeking individuals. The second implication is that, like most complex systems, a control framework is required to properly monitor the system, where measurements should be obtained and continuously checked for drift. Finally, and most importantly, the conceptual tools of complex systems should be used effectively, instead of simpler but inadequately linear cause-and-effect explanations (Lauer, 2021).

In addition to the complexity problem, the problems of re-identification, black box, algorithmic bias, and dual use contribute to the difficulty of weighing the potential risks and benefits of systems and technologies. Difficulties in risk assessment pose a direct problem for minimisation of harm, and they feed into other ethical issues such as consent and protection of vulnerable groups. When the risks are not well understood and well calibrated even by the researchers and developers, it becomes increasingly difficult for them to minimise the risk of harm to individuals, to vulnerable groups, and to the society, as well as to explain these risks to individuals for their informed consent when sharing personal data or participating in research.

To give an example, the processing of mobile CDR in the Data for Refugees project clearly showed refugees working in areas for which no work permits were issued to them (e.g., a large airport construction project). Publishing this result (as a purely scientific finding) at the time might have caused people to lose their jobs. Risk assessment must take into account the reality of vulnerable groups and not be restricted to an idealised situation. In doing so, it is also worth understanding what constitutes a vulnerable group. Traditionally, what constitutes a group in this context involves national, ethnic, religious, or racial ties. However, groups can be formed by internal or external perceptions of commonalities and identities (Verkuyten, 2018). Furthermore, as Kammourieh *et al.* (2017) pointed out, big data processing can create groups by matching people via commonalities. Subsequently, group privacy also needs to be considered as a risk factor. Vulnerability can be legally defined (e.g., asylum seekers), but in many occasions it can also be contextual and it needs to be considered in relation to power and authority. Political systems and agendas may sustain, create, or fail to alleviate vulnerabilities. Migrants and refugees may be disadvantaged in a certain context; they may have limited access to rights and services, even fundamental and human rights like the right for asylum. Big data and technology based projects need to be assessed from this perspective as well.

The complexity of the technology–society interaction and the various facets of risk assessment also inform how we should understand and position ethics and ethics analysis with respect to technology development and use. Ethics analysis must take the gaps and uncertainties in risk assessment into account and evaluate technologies for their multiple impacts on individuals, groups, and the society. As technology transforms society and society transforms the technology, ethics analysis must function as a tool to detect and mitigate arising risks. To do that, ethics analysis must remain as a continuous and integral part of technology development and use.

Data ethics tools

This section serves as an entry point for useful tools and resources for evaluating a data science project from an ethics perspective. We strongly recommend working with ethics experts for any major initiative, as paying lip service to a few ethics guidelines will not be sufficient to thoroughly analyse and vet a project. Ethics expertise is necessary to engage with the ethics literature that would constitute the backbone of any ethics analysis and help utilise ethics tools fully.

In several major initiatives on mobility analysis, dedicated ethics committees were formed and operated at each stage of the project. For example in the Data for Development challenge project (Blondel *et al.*, 2012), an ethics panel (DEEP, Data for Development external ethics panel) was created, which evaluated project proposals submitted to obtain a large mobile phone dataset, as well as the reports of the groups who did obtain the data, and finally wrote a report on the problematic issues and recommendations for such data (DEEP, 2015). This report, for example, acknowledged that 'Big Data can enable understanding and modelling large scale human behaviour with a temporal and spatial granularity never achieved before', and pointed to several challenges:

- Local knowledge is necessary to interpret how people are using the technology in question. Forming local collaborations is an important aspect of the work.
- In low- and middle-income countries (LMIC) there is less awareness of the risks of making personal data public, which does not mean that this is an opportunity to make more data public from LMIC, but that there is a need to take extra precautions and protect these people against risks they may not be aware of.
- Anonymisation should ensure a minimum security and trade-off granularity of detail in a risk-based approach.

- While most legislation is aimed at individual privacy, group privacy needs to be taken into account.
- Local legislation may be missing or insufficiently developed for digital data protection. International standards should be observed nonetheless.
- The statistical biases in proprietary data can be difficult to understand and quantify. Having reputable institutions analyse the data, and providing access to many scrutinising eyes, can address this only partially.
- The publication of research results may touch on culturally sensitive subjects, or through some correct or incorrect inferences may be harmful to the groups under study. The risk assessment should also consider publication and public dissemination as potential risk elements.

As this report shows, having a dedicated ethics committee can help bring ethical problems and concerns to the surface that would not necessarily have been acknowledged otherwise.

Data ethics tools and guidelines can bring order into the process of assessing ethical issues by emphasising various key concerns, and questioning the involvement and (potentially conflicting) aims of all stakeholders. Some such tools are *The Data Ethics Canvas* of the Open Data Institute (ODI), *The Box* by the AI Ethics Lab, and *Data Ethics Decision Aid* from Utrecht University.

The Data Ethics Canvas from the ODI[8] is a tool that groups a number of ethics-related questions under 15 headings, and prompts the researcher to answer each question in turn. For example, one of the headings is 'Negative effects on people', and under that heading the following questions are asked:

- Who could be negatively affected by this project?
- Could the way that data are collected, used, or shared cause harm or expose individuals to risk of being re-identified? Could it be used to target, profile, or prejudice people, or unfairly restrict access (e.g., exclusive arrangements)?
- How are limitations and risks communicated to people? Consider: people who the data are about, people impacted by its use, and organisations using the data.

The Box by the AI Ethics Lab[9] is a tool for operationalising ethics principles (Figure 2.1). It aims to help researchers, developers, and designers think through the ethical implications of the technologies they are building. *The Box* is a simplified tool that lists important ethical concerns by putting 18 instrumental ethics principles in relation to three core principles: respect for autonomy, minimisation of harm and maximisation of benefits, and securing justice. For example, instrumental principles of human control, transparency, explainability, information, agency, consent, and privacy mainly help promote the core principle of respecting individual autonomy. Once we correctly distinguish between core and instrumental principles we can turn many vague AI principles into an operational checklist to guide practice, because

---

[8] ODI: What is the Data Ethics Canvas?, https://theodi.org/article/data-ethics-canvas/
[9] AI Ethics Lab: TOOL: The Box, https://aiethicslab.com/the-box/

Figure 2.1 *The Box* is a tool for visualising the strengths and weaknesses of a technology from an ethical perspective.

the core principles reveal the underlying values practitioners should aim to achieve, while the instrumental principles offer various paths for achieving them. The categorisation of the instrumental principles in relation to specific core principles helps researchers and practitioners focus on different aspects of each core principle, and offers a way to determine how to best satisfy the core principles by substituting or supporting one instrumental principle with another (Canca, 2020). In *The Box*, each of these instrumental principles is further detailed through prompt questions. Once the researcher engages with all of these questions, the tool also helps them visualise the ethical strengths and weaknesses of the technologies that they are evaluating and enables visual comparison of these technologies.

Another example is the *Data Ethics Decision Aid* (DEDA), developed at Utrecht University for reviewing public projects with social impact using large-scale citizen data (Franzke *et al.*, 2021). Especially for municipalities and local governance, data-driven management is an important tool, because near-real-time monitoring helps with rapidly responding to the needs of the city. The authors point out that legal frameworks and regulations are inadequate to deal with all the issues related to such data usage, and that there are legal usage instances which are ethically problematic. The main difference of DEDA is that it defines a number of roles (such as project lead and policy officer) within the organisation, and associates specific actions with these roles. DEDA also structures its activities around asking a predetermined set of questions, which are organised into the headings of data-related considerations (collection algorithms, source, data use, including anonymisation and visualisation, data storage, including access, sharing, reusing and repurposing) and general considerations (responsibility, communication, transparency, privacy, and bias).

Legal risks for data science in migration and mobility

Ethical guidelines are necessary, because legal frameworks do not cover everything related to the development and use of technological solutions. Legal frameworks, even the human rights framework, leave many questions open in real-life practice (Canca, 2019). There are many cases where data collection and processing practices might be legal but not ethical, such as using excessive but legally permitted surveillance measures to observe the behaviour of employees (Franzke *et al.*, 2021). It is therefore important to separate the ethical and the legal issues. We discuss the latter in this section.

Legally, researchers and developers only make themselves liable if they fail to comply with the national and international standards and regulations they are subject to. While in some cases they must deal with issues of dual loyalty (e.g., involvement with multiple jurisdictions), they may expect to be exempt from any individual legal responsibility for the possible damages their products cause if they are operated diligently. However, if such damages and human rights violations are the result of governmental operations of the systems the developers created, they can still result in state responsibility under international human rights law, or administrative liability under the relevant national jurisdiction.

We discuss the legal aspects in three stages: a collection, algorithm development, and actual deployment and policy. For data collection, the most important concepts are 'consent', 'data protection', and 'identity'. For algorithm development we will discuss 'fairness', 'transparency', and 'bias', and for deployment, 'accountability' and 'power'. We do not attempt an exhaustive treatment of these complex issues here; we merely point to some of the important concepts and considerations.

Data collection, processing, and sharing

The central issue in big data, from a legal perspective, is 'consent', without which data collection (and processing) may be illegal. In Europe and the US, the legal traditions lead to different paths when it comes to consent (Boehm, 2015). The European Union (EU) and the Council of Europe (CoE) regulations on the issue, such as the General Data Protection Regulation (GDPR),[10] and the Data Protection Convention, emphasise substantive law guarantees, including fairness, lawfulness, adequacy, and purpose limitation. The latter implies that collected data should not be further processed in a way incompatible with the purpose for which it was collected. The US regulations, however, lack such guarantees. In addition, the US and Canadian regulations treat foreigners outside of their territory differently by not applying the legal standards applicable in their countries (Hayes, 2017). As a result, what is considered as a legal consent in a given context may differ greatly according to jurisdiction.

---

[10] General Data Protection Regulation (GDPR): Article 4: Definitions, https://gdpr.eu/article-4-definitions/

The second important issue is 'data protection', which pertains to the security of the collected and stored data. The GDPR asserts that *data protection* means keeping data safe from unauthorised access and *data privacy* means empowering users to make their own decisions about who can process their data and for what purpose. The right to privacy is subsequently also connected to the user's understanding of how their private data are shared with other parties, and to consent to any such sharing of data.

Especially in cases where data from vulnerable populations are collected, data protection has serious legal implications. Refugees, human trafficking victims, and political asylum seekers are examples of these cases. If a data leak may jeopardise or endanger the data owners, regulations like GDPR require that the data are kept encrypted and secure, and prevent data being shared with third parties that do not meet the required standards. Failure to comply with these standards may result in legal responsibilities for states or individuals. Protection extends beyond the lifetime of a project, and while designing the project one should regulate whether data will be archived or destroyed at the end of it. In many cases there are legal mandates for the maximum storage duration of particular types of data.

The third issue is 'identity', which, from a legal perspective, is connected to the processing of personal data, as the latter is defined as any information that relates to an identified or identifiable living individual. From an EU perspective, Regulation (EU) 2016/679 of the European Parliament and of the Council of 27 April 2016 (GDPR) define a set of human rights related principles and rules regarding the processing of personal data. As regulated under Article 5 of the GDPR, these principles include lawfulness, fairness and transparency, purpose limitation, data minimisation, accuracy, storage limitation, integrity, confidentiality, and accountability. Additionally, any processing of personal data must be based on the data subject's consent (in cases of special categories data, this consent must, as a rule, be specific), and be subject to the principle of proportionality. While GDPR is an EU regulation, these principles have worldwide ramifications, particularly because personal data can only be transferred from the EU to third countries in compliance with the conditions and standards set out in the GDPR.

On 14 May 2019 the EU adopted Regulations 2019/817[11] and 2019/818,[12] establishing a framework for the interoperability between EU information systems in the area of freedom, security, and justice. These regulations aim to establish an interoperability regime between various existing EU databases by creating four new components that will be accessible to border control and law enforcement authorities of EU member states, and to Europol and Interpol. Blasi Casagran (2021) notes that these components actually constitute new databases since they will be processing and storing data in a structured manner, and incorporate new objectives. As such, they may constitute a separate interference with human rights, particularly the right to privacy of the subjects.

---

[11] EUR-Lex: Document 32019R0817, https://eur-lex.europa.eu/eli/reg/2019/817/oj
[12] EUR-Lex: Document 32019R0817, https://eur-lex.europa.eu/eli/reg/2019/818/oj

The interoperability regulations also raise concerns regarding the right to non-discrimination of third-country nationals that travel or migrate to EU countries. The merger of data affected by the components created through these regulations only concerns third-country nationals, and might constitute, in and of itself, a discriminatory attitude toward them by subjecting them to other standards than EU citizens, and by regarding them as potential criminals (Blasi Casagran, 2021).

Algorithm development

Personal data regarding migrants, refugees, and asylum seekers may be subject to automated decision-making processes, some of which may be using AI algorithms. Algorithms intended to be used in migration, asylum, or border-control management may have an adverse impact on the fundamental rights of the subject. We have already discussed algorithmic fairness and transparency earlier in this chapter. Here, we briefly mention some additional points.

A proposal for an EU Regulation laying down harmonised rules on AI addresses such algorithms as 'high-risk' AI systems and aims to establish requirements and standards for the development, commercialisation, and use of those AI systems 'that pose significant risks to the health and safety or fundamental rights of persons'.[13] The proposal stresses the importance of accuracy, transparency, and the non-discriminatory nature of these systems when intended to be used as polygraphs and similar tools or to detect the emotional state of a person, for risk assessment of persons entering the territory of an EU member state or applying for visa or asylum, for verifying the authenticity of their documents, or for determining the eligibility of their applications. If put into force, developers and users of such high-risk AI systems will have to meet certain requirements, such as establishing a risk management system, and guaranteeing high-quality data, transparency, human oversight, accuracy, robustness, and cybersecurity.

Developers of high-risk AI systems should be particularly aware that AI systems may be inadequate in dealing with non-standard situations. In such cases, the lack of effective human oversight may lead to an infringement of fundamental rights. In order to reduce or eliminate legal risks arising from conformity requirements for high-risk systems, the system should incorporate appropriate human–machine interface tools to allow effective human oversight. The human overseer must be able to correctly interpret and override the output of the system and to refrain from overly relying on it. To this end, developers and producers should provide necessary information, tools, and education for users.

Deployment and policy

Legal problems related to the deployment of big data systems are mainly associated with powerful users, which may be government agencies or private corporations.

---

[13] European Commission: Proposal for a Regulation laying down harmonised rules on artificial intelligence, https://digital-strategy.ec.europa.eu/en/library/proposal-regulation-laying-down-harmonised-rules-artificial-intelligence-artificial-intelligence

Algorithmic approaches, based on big data and AI technologies, are used to inform policies of governments and intergovernmental organisations. In the area of migration and mobility, an example is IOM's Displacement Tracking Matrix (DTM), which relies on several big data sources like mobile phone data and social media analysis to monitor movements of people across the globe. According to its website, DTM 'gathers and analyses data to disseminate critical multi-layered information on the mobility, vulnerabilities, and needs of displaced and mobile populations that enables decision-makers and responders to provide these populations with better context specific assistance'.[14]

Two important considerations here are accountability and relations of power between data collectors and data owners. In this context, accountability (and oversight) are about the existence of regulatory mechanisms to protect people against unfair decisions taken by automated systems. When formulated as a supervised learning problem, an automated decision-making system may be designed, for example, to make a recommendation about the admittance of a person through a border. The mathematical formulation of the system and the preparation of its parameters (i.e., training) requires a cost function, where each error the system makes has a certain cost. Admitting someone incorrectly may not have the same cost as denying someone entry incorrectly. One could argue that the cost of an error is a human cost, and it is perhaps impossible to reduce that to a numeric value. Accountability is about holding the organisations operating such systems accountable for the errors.

While the processing of personal data may be used to better allocate migration management services and to protect potential victims of human trafficking (Beduschi, 2017), it may also cause human rights infractions. Particularly in the case of processing methods utilising AI, automated decisions may impact migrants, refugees, and asylum seekers disproportionately. It should be considered that such individuals may be disadvantaged regarding their ability to recognise that they are dealing with an AI, to be informed about their rights to submit the decision to a human supervisor, and to use such rights in an effective way.

The already asymmetrical power structure between the public authorities and the migrants can be furthered through the use of advanced technologies. Countries receiving large numbers of migrants use migration management approaches that are increasingly reliant on technology (Geiger and Pécoud, 2010). Molnar (2019b) argued that such technologies do not prioritise human rights and that states deliberately keep international regulation to a minimum. Risk assessment techniques utilising big data for immigration and border control may result in criminalising migration and putting vulnerable groups in jeopardy (Beduschi, 2017). Additionally, accountability gaps are created when states outsource part of their responsibilities in this area to private companies. Large-scale surveillance data are being collected via satellites and drones for border control (e.g., Frontex and the European Border Surveillance System in the EU), leading to (further) militarisation

---

[14] Global DTM, https://www.globaldtm.info

of border control agencies and to the entrenchment of the image of migrants as a threat to be averted (Csernatoni, 2018).

The use of technology for the detection and pushback of migrants, refugees, and asylum seekers has ramifications regarding the extraterritorial jurisdiction of the state utilising such methods. It is possible for states to employ humanitarian technology to detect and track asylum seekers, and ultimately to implement pushback strategies. In *Hirsi Jamaa and others v. Italy*, the European Court of Human Rights decided that migrants intercepted by Italian forces in open sea and then deported to Libya fell under the jurisdiction of Italy, although they never entered Italian territorial waters. Furthermore, the Court decided that the deportation to Libya constituted a violation of Article 3 of the European Convention of Human Rights due to the risk of suffering ill-treatment in that country.[15] Marin and Krajčíková (2016) argued that this judgment had an effect on European countries increasingly seeking the cooperation of North African countries. Nonetheless, the use of data processing technologies to pushback vulnerable migrants, particularly refugees and asylum seekers, may result in a breach of the *non-refoulement* principle if the people in question would be subject to torture, ill-treatment, political persecution, or death penalty in the country they would be deported to. Additionally, such actions could violate positive obligations of states to protect the life and liberty of persons arising from international law and human rights law (Molnar, 2019b).

One of the risks associated with the processing of big data is that connected databases create a number of cross-references, which, when used out of context, may result in discriminatory or restrictive decisions by law enforcement or border management authorities. The EU interoperability regulations mentioned above constitute a good example. Any official accessing one of the components would be pinged with a match if the data in question is included in any of the databases, without needing to access the contents of that database. In such cases, even a faulty or legally insignificant match (i.e., cases of double identity without any illegal reason), may result in a denial of entry to a country if the decision-making official pursues a risk-averse attitude. Researchers should bear in mind that legal standards should serve to protect the individual from abuse or misuse of power by the authorities, and allow for safeguards to prevent such consequences.

Data ethics and the Global Compact for Safe, Orderly, and Regular Migration

The relevance of data ethics in the context of migration and refugees is also emphasised in the Global Compact for Safe, Orderly and Regular Migration (GCM), as policies at the United Nations (UN) level have the potential to affect the legal system of many countries. On 19 December 2018, the UN General Assembly

---

[15] European Court of Human Rights: Case of Hirsi Jamaa and Others v. Italy, http://hudoc.echr.coe.int/spa?i=001-109231

adopted a GCM.[16] The GCM comprises 23 objectives and commitments based on the 2016 New York Declaration for Refugees and Migrants. Objective 1 of the GCM addresses the need to collect and utilise accurate and disaggregated data as a basis for evidence-based policies. Commitments following this objective call for a 'comprehensive strategy for improving migration data at the local, national, regional and global levels' through 'harmonising data collection methodologies' and 'strengthening analysis and dissemination of migration-related data and indicators'. The same objective also supports 'further development of and collaboration between existing global and regional databases and depositories'.

Additionally, the GCM addresses the needs for an integrated, secure, and coordinated border management policy (Objective 11) and for strengthening 'certainty and predictability in migration procedures for appropriate screening, assessment and referral' (Objective 12), among others.

While these objectives and commitments allow and encourage the collection, processing, and sharing of migration data to prevent illegal migration, the GCM also emphasises the need to protect the human rights and the principles of non-discrimination and non-regression for all migrants. In particular, Objective 17 includes a commitment to 'establish mechanisms to prevent, detect and respond to racial, ethnic and religious profiling of migrants by public authorities, as well as systematic instances of intolerance, xenophobia, racism, and all other multiple and intersecting forms of discrimination, in partnership with national human rights institutions, including by tracking and publishing trend analyses, and ensuring access to effective complaint and redress mechanisms'.

As a legally non-binding instrument, the GCM cannot set legal obligations on states or individuals, but may be considered as a benchmark for future policies of states willing to implement it. Already, a majority of UN Member States have made it a priority to eliminate discriminatory procedures against migrants and to introduce a concept of responsibility for states that follow this commitment (Guild, 2018).

Conclusion

Data science in migration and human mobility involves dealing with a number of ethical questions and concerns at every stage of a project. These ethical questions cannot be separated from the development and design of the project, since they arise in defining the goal of the project; in data collection, labelling, and storage; in interactions with research subjects; and in the application of the results in real life. For that reason, ethics must be considered an integral part of data science projects from the very start as something that requires not only care but also problem-solving skills using ethics tools.

Ethical and legal concerns regarding human mobility and migration are deeply intertwined since new legal regulations arise from developing emerging practices,

---

[16] IOM: Global Compact for Migration, https://www.iom.int/global-compact-migration

which in turn take existing ethical standards into consideration. Discussions to determine which regulations to put in place must first necessarily engage in ethical debate on what would be the 'right' and 'fair' practices in development and use of technologies. Regardless of how detailed the legal framework becomes, there are and will always be questions that fall into grey areas and require ethical decision-making during the technology development and deployment process. National and international legal instruments do not always and immediately result in a binding law, but in many cases involve ethical self-assessment procedures or general policy guidelines. As such, it is imperative for researchers and developers to be aware of the ethical risks associated with their analyses and products, particularly if the systems are expected to interfere with human rights.

Document repositories and further reading

There are several documents that are relevant and useful when it comes to addressing legal and ethical aspects of big data projects. User licence agreements are necessary for datasets collected or shared by private companies. GovLab maintains a repository of agreements to form a starting point for any new project, which can lighten the load of the legal team tremendously.[17] The DARIAH project collects a repository of consent forms for users.[18] During the course of a project it is important that data access is clearly regulated, which is typically achieved with a data management plan (DMP). Many universities and funding agencies have their own standards or templates for these documents, and Stanford University Library has a useful repository of DMPs.[19]

Applied ethics must take into account the context within which the ethical questions arise. We have mentioned several ethics frameworks for reviewing projects. In order to use these tools properly we need to engage with the demands and details of the context. A large amount of resources are available on the websites of Ethics in Context,[20] the Oxford Institute of Internet,[21] and Stanford Institute for Human-Centered AI.[22]

The concept of privacy, in its multiple forms, is extensively discussed in Solove (2006), and neatly summarised in Kitchin (2016). Gambs *et al.* (2014) is a good starting point for understanding the risks of sharing geolocated data, and how these can be deanonymised.

---

[17] The GOVLAB: Contracts for Data Collaboration, https://www.thegovlab.org/project/project-contracts-for-data-collaboration
[18] DARIAH-EU: DARIAH ELDAH Consent Form Wizard, https://www.dariah.eu/2020/09/17/dariah-eldah-consent-form-wizard/
[19] Stanford Libraries: Data management plans, https://library.stanford.edu/research/data-management-services/data-management-plans
[20] Ethics in Context, https://c4ejournal.net/
[21] Oxford Internet Institute, https://www.oii.ox.ac.uk/
[22] Stanford University: Human-Centred Artificial Intelligence, https://hai.stanford.edu/

The domain-specific terminology and knowledge are very important; for data scientists not familiar with the area of migration and mobility, UNHCR and IOM provide white papers and reports that can serve as a starting point. A key document in assessing proportionality and power usage for issues with regard to vulnerable populations is 'Principles and Guidelines, supported by practical guidance, on the human rights protection of migrants in vulnerable situations' prepared by the United Nations Human Rights Office of the High Commissioner.[23] The 1951 Geneva Convention and its 1967 Protocol are the most important legal documents to clarify definitions and rights for refugees, and to determine the obligations of the states which signed the protocol.[24] However, there are special cases to consider. For example, while Turkey is party to the 1951 Geneva Refugee Convention, it only acknowledged 'refugee' status for people originating from Europe. Consequently, the Syrian refugees in Turkey were officially considered 'temporarily protected foreign individuals'.

Several researchers published seminal work on the role of AI and big data technologies in migration management. Ana Beduschi's work discusses both the role of technology (Beduschi, 2017, 2021) and the concept of digital identity (Beduschi, 2019). Molnar and Gill (2018) wrote an influential report on automated decision-making employed in Canada's immigration and refugee system, and Akhmetova (2020) extended this discussion with the concept of an 'invisible border wall'. Other work by Molnar contributes important ideas from a human rights perspective (Molnar, 2019a,b).

On the data science side, proper statistical or machine learning based experiment design is a key issue. Mehrabi *et al*. (2019) provided a comprehensive survey of bias and fairness in machine learning and algorithmic decision-making, and Lepri *et al*. (2018) provided an overview of technical solutions to enhance fairness, accountability, and transparency in such settings.

Acknowledgements

This study is supported by the European Union's Horizon 2020 Research and Innovation Programme under grant agreement No. 870661.

References

Akhmetova, R. (2020), 'Efficient discrimination: On how governments use artificial intelligence in the immigration sphere to create and fortify "invisible border walls"', Centre on Migration, Policy and Society Working Paper 149.

---

[23] UN Human Rights Office: Principles and Guidelines, https://www.ohchr.org/Documents/Issues/Migration/PrinciplesAndGuidelines.pdf

[24] The UN Refugee Agency: The 1951 Refugee Convention, https://www.unhcr.org/1951-refugee-convention.html

Alipourfard, N., Fennell, P. G., and Lerman, K. (2018), 'Can you trust the trend? Discovering Simpson's paradoxes in social data', *in Proceedings of the 11th ACM International Conference on Web Search and Data Mining*, 19–27.

Alpaydin, E. (2020), *Introduction to Machine Learning*, 4th edn, MIT Press, Cambridge, MA.

Beauchamp, T. L. and Childress, J. F. (2013), *Principles of Biomedical Ethics*, 7th edn, Oxford University Press, Oxford.

Beduschi, A. (2017), 'The big data of international migration: Opportunities and challenges for states under international human rights law', *Georgetown Journal of International Law* 49, 981–1018.

Beduschi, A. (2019), 'Digital identity: Contemporary challenges for data protection, privacy and non-discrimination rights', *Big Data & Society* 6(2), 2053951719855091.

Beduschi, A. (2021), 'International migration management in the age of artificial intelligence', *Migration Studies* 9(3), 576–96.

Blasi Casagran, C. (2021), 'Fundamental rights implications of interconnecting migration and policing databases in the EU', *Human Rights Law Review* 21(2), 433–57.

Blondel, V. D., Esch, M., Chan, C., Clérot, F., Deville, P., Huens, E., Morlot, F., Smoreda, Z., and Ziemlicki, C. (2012), 'Data for development: The D4D challenge on mobile phone data', arXiv:1210.0137.

Blyth, C. R. (1972), 'On Simpson's paradox and the sure-thing principle', *Journal of the American Statistical Association* 67(338), 364–6.

Boehm, F. (2015), 'A comparison between US and EU data protection legislation for law enforcement purposes', European Parliament, Study for the LIBE Committee.

Canca, C. (2019), 'Human rights and AI ethics – why ethics cannot be replaced by the UDHR', United Nations University, Centre for Policy Research.

Canca, C. (2020), 'Operationalizing AI ethics principles', *Communications of the ACM* 63(12), 18–21.

Carens, J. (2013), *The Ethics of Immigration*, Oxford University Press, Oxford.

Clemens, M. A. (2020), 'Migration from developing countries: Selection, income elasticity and Simpson's paradox', Centro Studi Luca d'Agliano Development Studies Working Paper 465.

Csernatoni, R. (2018), 'Constructing the EU's high-tech borders: FRONTEX and dual-use drones for border management', *European Security* 27(2), 175–200.

De Montjoye, Y.-A., Hidalgo, C. A., Verleysen, M., and Blondel, V. D. (2013), 'Unique in the crowd: The privacy bounds of human mobility', *Scientific Reports* 3(1), 1–5.

DEEP (2015), 'Data for development Senegal: Report of the external review panel', Technical report, Institute of Business Ethics.

Deville, P., Linard, C., Martin, S., Gilbert, M., Stevens, F. R., Gaughan, A. E., Blondel, V. D., and Tatem, A. J. (2014), 'Dynamic population mapping using mobile phone data', *Proceedings of the National Academy of Sciences* 111(45), 15888–93.

Escalante, H. J., *et al.* (2022), 'Modeling, recognizing, and explaining apparent personality from videos', *IEEE Transactions on Affective Computing* 13(2), 894–911.

Floridi, L. and Taddeo, M. (2016), 'What is data ethics?', *Philosophical Transactions of the Royal Society Series A* 374, 20160360.

Franzke, A. S., Muis, I., and Schäfer, M. T. (2021), 'Data ethics decision aid (DEDA): A dialogical framework for ethical inquiry of AI and data projects in the Netherlands', *Ethics and Information Technology* 23, 551–67.

Gambs, S., Killijian, M.-O., and del Prado Cortez, M. N. (2014), 'De-anonymization attack on geolocated data', *Journal of Computer and System Sciences* 80(8), 1597–614.

Geiger, M. and Pécoud, A. (2010), 'The politics of international migration management', *in* M. Geiger and A. Pécoud, eds, *The Politics of International Migration Management*, Springer, New York, 1–20.

Guild, E. (2018), 'The UN global compact for safe, orderly and regular migration: What place for human rights?', *International Journal of Refugee Law* 30(4), 661–3.

Hayes, B. (2017), 'Migration and data protection: Doing no harm in an age of mass displacement, mass surveillance and "big data"', *International Review of the Red Cross* 99(904), 179–209.

Haznedar, B., Peyton, J. K., and Young-Scholten, M. (2018), 'Teaching adult migrants', *Critical Multilingualism Studies* 6(1), 155–83.

Kammourieh, L., Baar, T., Berens, J., Letouzé, E., Manske, J., Palmer, J., Sangokoya, D., and Vinck, P. (2017), 'Group privacy in the age of big data', *in* L. Taylor, L. Floridi, and B. van der Sloot, eds, *Group Privacy*, Springer, New York, 37–66.

Kitchin, R. (2016), 'The ethics of smart cities and urban science', *Philosophical Transactions of the Royal Society A: Mathematical, Physical and Engineering Sciences* 374(2083), 20160115.

Lauer, D. (2021), 'You cannot have AI ethics without ethics', *AI and Ethics* 1(1), 21–5.

Lepri, B., Oliver, N., Letouzé, E., Pentland, A., and Vinck, P. (2018), 'Fair, transparent, and accountable algorithmic decision-making processes', *Philosophy & Technology* 31(4), 611–27.

Lerman, K. (2018), 'Computational social scientist beware: Simpson's paradox in behavioral data', *Journal of Computational Social Science* 1(1), 49–58.

Mamei, M., Cilasun, S. M., Lippi, M., Pancotto, F., and Tümen, S. (2019), 'Improve education opportunities for better integration of Syrian refugees in Turkey', *in* A. A. Salah, A. Pentland, B. Lepri, and E. Letouzé, eds, *Guide to Mobile Data Analytics in Refugee Scenarios*, Springer, New York, 381–402.

Marin, L. and Krajčíková, K. (2016), 'Deploying drones in policing southern European borders: Constraints and challenges for data protection and human rights, *in* A. Završnik, ed, *Drones and Unmanned Aerial Systems*, Springer, New York, 101–27.

McDonald, A. M. and Cranor, L. F. (2008), 'The cost of reading privacy policies', *A Journal of Law and Policy for the Information Society* 4(3), 543–68.

Mehrabi, N., Morstatter, F., Saxena, N., Lerman, K., and Galstyan, A. (2019), 'A survey on bias and fairness in machine learning', arXiv:1908.09635.

Molnar, P. (2019a), 'New technologies in migration: Human rights impacts', *Forced Migration Review* 61, 7–9.

Molnar, P. (2019b), 'Technology on the margins: AI and global migration management from a human rights perspective', *Cambridge International Law Journal* 8(2), 305–30.

Molnar, P. and Gill, L. (2018), 'Bots at the gate: A human rights analysis of automated decision-making in Canada's immigration and refugee system', Citizen Lab and International Human Rights Program.

Oliver, N., *et al.* (2020), 'Mobile phone data for informing public health actions across the COVID-19 pandemic life cycle', *Science Advances* 6(23), 764.

Owen, D. (2020), *What Do We Owe to Refugees?*, Polity, Cambridge.

Salah, A. A., *et al.* (2019), 'Policy implications of the D4R challenge', *in* A. A. Salah, A. Pentland, B. Lepri, and E. Letouzé, eds, *Guide to Mobile Data Analytics in Refugee Scenarios*, Springer, New York, 477–95.

Salah, A. A., Pentland, A., Lepri, B., Letouzé, E., Vinck, P., de Montjoye, Y.-A., Dong, X., and Dağdelen, Ö. (2018), 'Data for refugees: The D4R challenge on mobility of Syrian refugees in Turkey', arXiv:1807.00523.

Sharad, K. and Danezis, G. (2013), De-anonymizing D4D datasets, *in Workshop on Hot Topics in Privacy Enhancing Technologies*.

Solove, D. (2006), 'A taxonomy of privacy', *University of Pennsylvania Law Review* 154(3), 477–564.

Strogatz, S. H. (2018), *Nonlinear Dynamics and Chaos with Student Solutions Manual*, CRC Press, Boca Raton, FL.

Sweeney, L. (2002), 'Achieving k-anonymity privacy protection using generalization and suppression', *International Journal of Uncertainty, Fuzziness and Knowledge-Based Systems* 10(05), 571–88.

The National Commission for the Protection of Human Subjects of Biomedical and Behavioral Research (1979), *The Belmont Report: Ethical Principles and Guidelines for the Protection of Human Subjects of Research*.

Verkuyten, M. (2018), *The Social Psychology of Ethnic Identity*, Routledge, Abingdon.

Vinck, P., Pham, P. N., and Salah, A. A. (2019), ' "Do No Harm" in the age of big data: Data, ethics, and the refugees', *in* A. A. Salah, A. Pentland, B. Lepri, and E. Letouzé, eds, *Guide to Mobile Data Analytics in Refugee Scenarios*, Springer, New York, 87–99.

Waldo, J. (2016), 'Big data and the social sciences: Can accuracy and privacy co-exist?', *in Proceedings, Data for Policy 2016: Frontiers of Data Science for Government: Ideas, Practices and Projections*, University of Cambridge.

Wesolowski, A., Eagle, N., Tatem, A. J., Smith, D. L., Noor, A. M., Snow, R. W., and Buckee, C. O. (2012), 'Quantifying the impact of human mobility on malaria', *Science* 338(6104), 267–70.

Part II

Data Sources

3

CESSDA Data Catalogue: Opportunities and Challenges to Explore Mobility and Migration

DIMITRA KONDYLI, RON DEKKER, AND IVANA ILIJASIC VERSIC

Introduction

THIS CHAPTER SEEKS to contribute to the overall aims of the book by promoting tools and services that are a product of transnational collaboration at the crossroads of various scientific disciplines and multicultural/multilingual research.

We will describe multilingual tools that the Consortium of European Social Science Data Archives (CESSDA) developed within its members' community of service providers to provide data and services that support worldwide data-driven research communities to discover, use, and adequately produce high-quality research. CESSDA has developed core tools to provide seamless access to data across Europe. These tools are an ambitious ongoing effort to make data and metadata available to research communities worldwide, supporting and promoting FAIR and responsible research in compliance with EU excellence science pillars. One of them is the CESSDA Data Catalogue,[1] a multilingual catalogue that provides information (metadata) on more than 36,000 datasets, making it the largest social science data catalogue in the world. These datasets cover a wide range of social science research topics that investigate phenomena and aspects of contemporary societies at national, European, and international level.

Among these datasets, aspects of 'social mobility' research are being studied via approximately 3000 datasets that are available today. Focusing on the CESSDA Data Catalogue, social mobility research data will be examined and highlighted as a use case for migration research worldwide.

---

[1] CESSDA Data Catalogue, https://datacatalogue.cessda.eu/.

Consortium of European Social Science Data Archives

CESSDA[2] has existed since 1976 as an umbrella organisation for social science data archives across Europe. In early 2000 it was decided to establish CESSDA as a formal research infrastructure, with European countries as its members. CESSDA has been on the European Strategic Forum for Research Infrastructures (ESFRI) Roadmap since 2006, became an ESFRI Landmark in 2016, and in 2017 it was assigned European legal status as an ERIC: European Research Infrastructure Consortium.

One of the major tasks of ERICs is to create pan-European infrastructure systems needed by science to produce high-quality research, as well as to utilise the vast amount of data and information that already exist or should be generated in Europe (European Strategy Forum on Research Infrastructures, 2006). Via the establishment of the CESSDA ERIC and other domains' research infrastructures, EU efforts have been put to promoting world-class social science research infrastructures. This is operationalised by responding to the fragmentation of data, information, and adequate knowledge scattered in different geographical locations, divided by language, cultural, economic, legal, and institutional barriers (European Strategy Forum on Research Infrastructures, 2006).

The purpose of CESSDA is to provide a distributed and sustainable research infrastructure that enables the research community to conduct high-quality research in the social sciences, to facilitate teaching and learning by sharing expertise and training, and to contribute to responses to major societal challenges.

CESSDA funds core services that are developed by its national social data archives that are in the core of the organisation and act as service providers to researchers and other users. CESSDA's service providers develop, participate in, use, enable, and provide core services such as:

- data ingestion and curation;
- distribution of research data;
- training activities;
- tools, software, and middleware;
- use of the European Language Social Science Thesaurus (ELSST) as well as maintenance of national languages within this multilingual thesaurus;
- common single-sign-on user authentication systems recommended by CESSDA ERIC,
- the harvesting of their resource discovery metadata and relevant additional metadata for inclusion in the CESSDA Data Catalogue, to render FAIR (findable, accessible, interoperable, and reusable; see Box 3.1) data to potential user communities worldwide.

---

[2] CESSDA: The CESSDA Consortium, https://www.cessda.eu/About/Consortium

> **Box 3.1** FAIR principles for data sharing
>
> FAIR is an acronym for findability, accessibility, interoperability, and reuse, and was introduced by Wilkinson *et al.* (2016) as a set of guiding principles for improving data sharing and stewarding practices. This box summarises these principles, as described at https://www.go-fair.org/fair-principles/.
>
> F1   (Meta)data are assigned a globally unique and persistent identifier.
> F2   Data are described with rich metadata (defined by R1 below).
> F3   Metadata clearly and explicitly include the identifier of the data they describe.
> F4   (Meta)data are registered or indexed in a searchable resource.
>
> A1   (Meta)data are retrievable by their identifier using a standardised communications protocol.
>   A1.1   The protocol is open, free, and universally implementable.
>   A1.2   The protocol allows for an authentication and authorisation procedure, where necessary.
> A2   Metadata are accessible, even when the data are no longer available.
>
> I1   (Meta)data use a formal, accessible, shared, and broadly applicable language for knowledge representation.
> I2   (Meta)data use vocabularies that follow FAIR principles.
> I3   (Meta)data include qualified references to other (meta)data.
>
> R1   (Meta)data are richly described with a plurality of accurate and relevant attributes.
>   R1.1   (Meta)data are released with a clear and accessible data usage licence.
>   R1.2   (Meta)data are associated with detailed provenance.
>   R1.3   (Meta)data meet domain-relevant community standards.

Catalogues as a vehicle of collaborative research: Migration studies use cases

Migration studies have been conducted by many disciplines such as anthropology, sociology, political science, economics, demography, law, and history, which all used different analytical tools and brought to light different aspects and types of migration as well as explanations (Boyd and Grieco, 2014). In recent years, new data types and disciplines have gradually become involved in the migration 'research landscape' given the increasing numbers of displaced populations and people moving from one country to another or moving towards other continents. Thus, migration research became quite eclectic in terms of the disciplines involved. Data produced in such research spans from census data to various registries and surveys collected by different authorities (national statistical offices, government agencies, or academics) in many EU countries, including many of CESSDA member countries, and are archived in designated archives by CESSDA service providers.[3]

---

[3] CESSDA: The CESSDA Consortium, https://www.cessda.eu/About/Consortium

The CESSDA Data Catalogue can serve as a starting point for both thematic data regarding migration studies and additional services to researchers. This is described below in more detail.

The Data Catalogue explained

The CESSDA Data Catalogue (CDC) can be a starting point for many research topics and collaborative research. There are some prerequisites allowing a smooth search through one single catalogue, such as a metadata model, to be followed when preparing data for deposit or concerning data being FAIR.

On the latter, FAIR principles address salient value added to data: they give data greater value and strengthen their exploitation by users and by technological applications. FAIR principles are inclusive in the sense that they include both open data as well as data provided under submissions. Nevertheless, in the context of open science and in the current conjuncture of the European Open Science Cloud (EOSC), all stakeholders of the data landscape, including CESSDA ERIC, apply the principle of data 'as open as possible and as closed as necessary', at least for data provided by publicly funded research (Collins et al., 2018).

Both the metadata model and the FAIR requirements ease secondary use of data, for example the comparison of different datasets or even combining original datasets into a new dataset.

Catalogue development

The CESSDA Data Catalogue harvests the metadata from its national service providers. This gives users a one-stop-shop to search for data in (currently) 22 European social data archives (see Figure 3.1).[4] The user interface provides filters and free text search for the discovery of data (see Figure 3.2).

Before the catalogue could be deployed, several technical issues needed to be resolved. Different service providers used different (national) systems for their metadata, and CESSDA had to develop harvesters that connect to all these systems. In addition, the common CESSDA metadata profile needed to be agreed, in particular which subset of the global Data Documentation Initiative (DDI)[5] would be used, and some of the metadata items require controlled vocabularies to ensure consistency. Another important aspect was that the CESSDA metadata profile was compatible with other pre-existing profiles such as OpenAIRE and Google schema.[6]

---

[4] CESSDA Data Catalogue, https://datacatalogue.cessda.eu/
[5] The Data Documentation Initiative (DDI) is an international standard for describing data produced by surveys and other observational methods in the social, behavioural, economic, and health sciences. It supports the documentation of the entire research life cycle (i.e., conceptualisation, collection, processing, distribution, discovery, archiving).
[6] Google schema is a semantic vocabulary of tags that you can add to your HTML pages to improve the way search engines read and process your page.

CESSDA DATA CATALOGUE

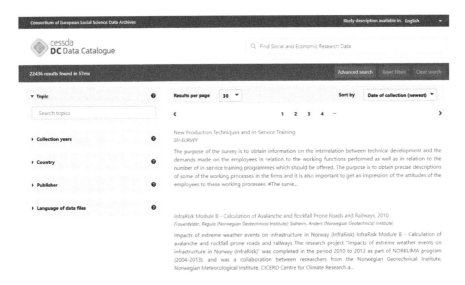

Figure 3.1 The CESSDA Data Catalogue in a nutshell.

Figure 3.2 How the CESSDA Data Catalogue looks. Captured from https://datacatalogue.cessda.eu.

In this process, some service providers had to clean up existing metadata profiles or add relevant metadata.

CESSDA decided to develop its own catalogue user interface as there were no suitable existing tools in 2015. In addition to free search, filters to reduce the number of selected data files and features dealing with multilingual metadata were needed.

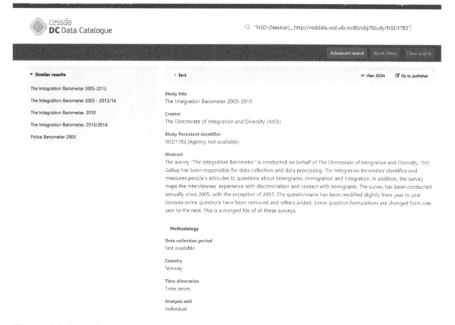

Figure 3.3 Metadata record of a dataset in the CESSDA Data Catalogue.

CESSDA currently provides sets of metadata by language and, to connect the different languages, the ELSST is used. To be useful, the catalogue needs to be up to date (CDC is refreshed each night), fast in searching, and easy to use (no training or instruction manual required).

The CESSDA Data Catalogue does not contain any data – it only has metadata (see Figure 3.3). If a user wants to go to the data, the system forwards the user to the national database of the service provider. This approach is efficient as the data are not duplicated and it prevents ownership discussions. It is also a safe solution as the datasets remain where they are being archived, taking into consideration that a substantial part of the data contains sensitive information and access will require additional checks.

Catalogues and multilinguality

Building on extensive experience in international data transfer, CESSDA has systematically worked towards networked solutions that ideally allow interested researchers to remotely access the data holdings of its members from any geographical location.

During the last 20 years many content-oriented initiatives and projects have been developed, aimed at producing high-quality multilingual metadata and tools to render Data Catalogue holdings as high in quality and as FAIR as possible. EU data projects such as MADIERA[7] (FP5 – Human Potential, 2002–2006) and Preparatory Phase Project for a Major Upgrade of the CESSDA Research Infrastructure (FP7 – Infrastructures, 2008–2010)[8] have contributed to the creation of a CESSDA data portal, providing seamless access to data holdings maintained and provided by its members since the late 1990s.

Another initiative to enable users to discover, search, and use multilingual data is the multilingual thesaurus that CESSDA ERIC maintains. This thesaurus contains translations of terms used between different human languages in social sciences research. It is referred to as the ELSST and has been coordinated until recently by the UK Data Service, a service provider for CESSDA. From 2020, coordination and maintenance has been transferred to CESSDA ERIC, ensuring continuity. ELSST is currently available in 14 languages: Czech, Danish, Dutch, English, Finnish, French, German, Greek, Lithuanian, Norwegian, Romanian, Slovenian, Spanish, and Swedish. The thesaurus is updated annually, and this is coordinated by a multi-national ELSST Thesaurus Management Team responsible for content changes and management. In the years to come, search in the CESSDA Catalogue will integrate the multilingual thesaurus and replace the CESSDA topic classification system, which is a sub-lexical category of ELSST.

Searching the catalogue: The case of migration datasets

The CDC contains descriptions (metadata) of more than 36,000 data collections in 10 languages held by CESSDA service providers, currently representing 22 European countries. A free text search in CDC on 'migration' gives 1355 hits and 'mobility' gives 3414 hits in the English language. Filters and advanced search (using logical operators) can reduce and fine-tune the search for relevant data. The number of datasets that appear are linked to different service providers. Metadata is in the English language, while the datasets can be either in the local language or in English. The visitor can very easily have metadata information which allows further refinement of the search. Once the user locates the 1355 hits classified under the keyword 'migration', the discovery of the datasets themselves is launched.

The CDC provides basic search, filtered search, and advanced search. Filters (such as by topic) can be used to refine the results provided by the basic (free text) search, or vice versa. Some of the constructs in advanced search can be quite complex and are meant for advanced users (e.g., fuzziness and sloppiness). Theoretically, the topic filter should contain only ELSST terms, but in current practice it uses the values found in the 'topics' field of the metadata record. CESSDA is continuously working on improving the quality of this content.

Free text search can be restricted to certain fields (typically the study title, abstract, and creator), or one can search all fields. However, 'boosting' can be used

---

[7] CORDIS: Multilingual access to data infrastructures in the European research area, https://cordis.europa.eu/project/id/HPSE-CT-2002-00139
[8] CESSDA PPP: Rationale for the CESSDA PPP project, https://ppp.cessda.eu/rationale.html

to give preference to a word or phrase found in the study title, abstract, and creator fields over matches found elsewhere. CESSDA currently uses this approach, with the study title receiving a bigger boost than abstract or creator. The practice of 'boosting' one or more fields when running a search query is generally preferred to increasing the time needed to create the search indices.

Approximately 10 service providers are providing datasets that respond to the search on 'migration'. These datasets, usually surveys conducted at national or European and international level, have as a main objective the investigation of migration or studying migration in a specific module or set of questions. An analysis of the available datasets at the level of metadata has shown that a variety of aspects and components related to migration are available. Additionally, the time perspective offers an interesting insight for further use, as migration research varies across time and this variation is reflected in the datasets and years of collection. Thus, the changing aspects of migration phenomena studied are findable via datasets produced by comparative analysis, including studies between countries, groups, and historical periods, as well as qualitative, quantitative, and mixed methods studies at the international, European, or national level.

Topics include migratory movements of the local population (meaning internal migration, e.g., the datasets from the beginning of the century available at CESSDA service providers such as the Norwegian Centre for Research Data (NSD)[9] or the Netherlands Data Archiving and Networked Services (DANS)[10]) and international migration statistics, investigating aspects of international migration covering a period from 1816 to 1924 and beyond. There are datasets from major organisations such as the Organisation for Economic Co-operation and Development (OECD) and its international migration database, showcasing flows and stocks of the total immigrant population and immigrant labour force together with data on the acquisition of nationality dating from 1980, as well as general-purpose multi-country survey projects collecting data on push-and-pull factors of international migration in selected origin and destination countries (datasets that are further available via the UK Data Archive (UKDA)[11]).

Migrant integration seems to occupy a central role regarding datasets dating mainly from the 1980s, reflecting the evolution of migration research and studied concepts. There are also studies investigating immigration and immigrants, asylum seekers, and national identity studied through the attitudes and opinions of the general public or migrants within concrete societies in relation to integration, with subtopics like educational attainment and employment or unemployment of migrant populations compared to the native populations.

Under the term 'social stratification', and in particular clash and ethnicity, studies regarding specific communities of migrant workers conducted mainly in the UKDA can be found. From the late 2010s many mixed studies provide valuable

---

[9] NSD - Norwegian Centre for Research Data, https://www.nsd.no/en/
[10] DANS - Data Archiving and Networked Services, https://dans.knaw.nl/en/
[11] UK Data Archive, https://www.data-archive.ac.uk/

insights concerning aspects of humanitarian services, assistance, condition of asylum seekers, and the broader data landscape with regards to displaced populations arriving in Europe recently. Rich material including in-depth interviews and biographical research depicting migrants' narratives as well as survey questionnaires providing information, documentation, and the data themselves to research communities. Phenomena related to migration studies, such as the brain drain of the 21st century, can also be found in the UKDA via surveys conducted in 1950–1960, allowing potential comparative analysis with recent surveys archived by CESSDA service providers.

Recent trends affecting migration studies like climate change and population mobility are being archived as well. One of the core comparative surveys harvested by the CDC is the European Social Survey (ESS), documented by the NSD, a service provider of CESSDA ERIC. The module focusing on immigration and asylum issues was first fielded in 2002 during the first round of ESS. Some items like immigration attitudes or perceptions of social realities were repeated in the ESS seventh round (2014) alongside some new items focusing on contact with migrants and minorities, attitudes towards different types of migrants, and biological and cultural racism to strengthen the measurement of symbolic threats.

The second example of comparative research is the Eurobarometer, the public opinion survey conducted within the European Union since 1973. This survey has been archived and managed by the Leibniz Institute for Social Science (GESIS), another CESSDA service provider (i.e., Eurobarometer 4 (1975), 8 (1977), 30 (1988), 70.1 (2008)) findable mainly under the topics of migration, mass political behaviour, attitudes, and opinions. Another comparative survey to be found via the CDC includes the International Social Survey Programmes (1995–2003, 2013) as well as panel surveys at national level classified under the topics of national and cultural identity, social exclusion, or social mobility.

The above-mentioned surveys can be further located and accessed under the following terms of access depending on the sensitive character of the data, prior agreements with data depositors, or the additional specific legal framework of each CESSDA service provider. The terms of data access usually encompass data open to all, data available upon registration, or restricted data access, and more rarely data under an embargo period. Commercial use is in principle not permitted, while the use of these data for research and teaching purposes is widely acknowledged by all CESSDA service providers.

The infographic in Figure 3.3 attempts to classify the number of service providers archiving data related to migration and social mobility, method of data collection, number of data, as well as type of data harvested by CDC as of May 2021.

An analysis of 200 datasets out of 1400 hits in the CESSDA Data Catalogue has been carried out based on the available topics for every above-mentioned study (or dataset), and may be presented under a word cloud visualisation, shown in Figure 3.5.

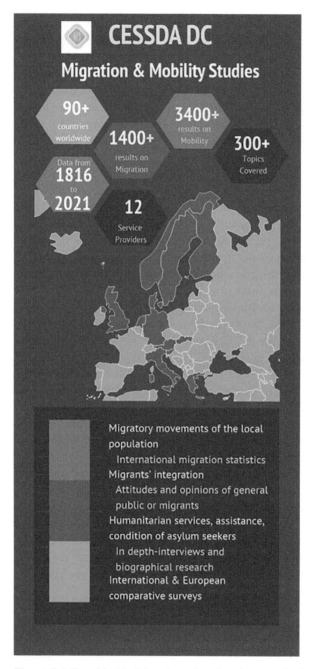

Figure 3.4 Searching and locating migration datasets via the CESSDA Data Catalogue portal.

Figure 3.5 Migration topics related to the migration studies in the CDC.

FAIR in practice

With a thematic catalogue or thematic archive based on this catalogue, the findability and accessibility requirements of FAIR are met; it is known which data are available, where they are, and how they can be accessed. Still, with over 1000 hits on migration, investigating the datasets themselves could be a time-consuming task.

Another time-consuming task is to combine data, e.g., to combine original datasets into a new research dataset. For example, CESSDA service provider GESIS contains over 500 studies on immigration per country and time (GESIS Historical Statistics Database[12]). Combining these data over countries and over time is a demanding process including investment in skilled permanent personnel, considering, and constantly updating changes in definitions, reclassification or harmonisation with the new terms in the CESSDA controlled vocabularies or topics related to the ELSST maintained by CESSDA. In the EC-funded SSHOC project[13]

---

[12] GESIS Historical Statistics Database, https://histat.gesis.org/histat/en/index
[13] This project has received funding from the European Union's Horizon 2020 Research and Innovation Programme under grant agreement No. 823782. Available at: https://www.sshopencloud.eu

(Social Sciences and Humanities Open Cloud), an SSH Market Place[14] has been created (currently in a beta version) where researchers can share the tools that were used to prepare, combine, enrich, etc. datasets.

Besides this data-driven and rather technical approach, another way would be to organise research communities around datasets or to provide existing research communities with data services, e.g., a common platform for sharing data and tools, or application programming interfaces (APIs) that curate these data. This approach connects to the EOSC that wants to develop, deploy, and evolve 'a trusted environment ... to share, curate, discover, access, process and reuse research outputs of all kinds across borders and scientific disciplines' (European Open Science Cloud, 2021, p. 8).

Use cases on migration

Even though migration is a permanent phenomenon within societies, the late 20th as well as the 21st centuries have been marked by intense migration movements involving international partnership and innovative methods of collecting related data, as well as policy implications at the local, regional, European, and international levels. Hence, migration is a topic that remains high on the EC agenda and stretches over multiple framework programmes (see Box 3.2).

The Mobility and Migration Research Platform,[15] founded by the European Commission in 2020, gathers all activities done in the framework of H2020 funding related to migration. Dominating domains in this research are social sciences and humanities, aiming at overarching and substantial understanding of migration phenomena by in-depth exploration of socioeconomic research on migration and contributing directly to the data-based evidence for migration policies and their development. Since 1994, around 80 projects on migration have been funded within the social sciences and humanities under research and innovation funding programmes.

In Horizon 2020, migration-related research has been granted over 200 million EUR in the period from 2018 to 2020 (European Union, 2017). Out of this amount, 120 million EUR was planned to be spent on research tackling types of migration, effects on host countries, or barriers for social integration, and, as the final goal, modelling and managing migration flows.

The EC encouraged proposed projects to focus on the drivers of migration, but also to explore deeper roots of migration challenges such as unstable political situations, trends in demographics, poverty, or globalisation of transport and communications, etc., all resulting in increased numbers of international migrants. According to the European Union (2020), these projects covered different aspects

---

[14] SSH Open Marketplace, https://marketplace.sshopencloud.eu
[15] European Commission: Why the EU supports social sciences and humanities (SSH) research, https://ec.europa.eu/info/research-and-innovation/research-area/social-sciences-and-humanities/migration-and-mobility_en

> **Box 3.2** European Union Framework Programmes
>
> The European Union Framework Programmes (FPs) have constituted the main instrument for research funding in the EU since 1984. They were proposed by the European Commission and adopted by the Council and the European Parliament following a co-decision procedure. FPs used to cover a period of five years, with the last year of one FP and the first year of the following FP overlapping. FPs were contributed as a financial instrument to help make the European Research Area (ERA) a reality. A historical overview is provided in Reillon (2017).
>
> ERA is the internal market for science and technology aimed at fostering scientific excellence, competitiveness, and innovation through the promotion of better cooperation and coordination between relevant actors at all levels. The sixth FP (FP6) 2002–2006 had a catalytic role in the creation of transnational projects and cooperation, introducing a European along with an international dimension. Funding for specific research infrastructures was added to the FP6 pillars to better structure the ERA. Some major projects building CESSDA were implemented in that period.
>
> From FP7 (2007–2014) the programme and funding periods were extended to seven years. Horizon 2020 (FP8) was operational from 1 January 2015 to 31 December 2020, to be followed by Horizon Europe. Horizon 2020 projects have led to the creation of ERICs in general, and CESSDA in particular, in order to promote the enhancement of scientific excellence and efficacy in European research in the social sciences, but also to facilitate access to data and metadata beyond physical borders. Hence, CESSDA involvement in EU funding has been significant in H2020, with several milestone projects strengthening cooperation and expertise among CESSDA members.

of the migration phenomenon, including, but not limited to, immigrant integration, temporary/circular migration, transnationalism, migration and gender relations, migration and development, migration flows, migration data and statistical modelling, diversity, economic impact of immigration, and transnational families.

Two migration-related projects funded over recent years through different EC programmes are described below as an example of synergies between CESSDA and migration-related projects: the CESSDA Data Catalogue stores research datasets that are being conducted within the framework of the HumMingBird[16] project, and the International Survey Data Network has collaborated with CESSDA within the framework of the SSHOC cluster project.

The HumMingBird Project

HumMingBird is a Horizon 2020 project with 16 partners across Europe aimed at improving understanding of dynamics of migration flows and their drivers

---

[16] HumMingBird project (2019–2024). This project has received funding from the European Union's Horizon 2020 Research and Innovation Programme under grant agreement No. 870661. Available at:https://hummingbird-h2020.eu

by analysing patterns, motivations, geographical route changes, etc., ultimately forecasting emerging and future trends.

To provide a holistic view of migration and migration processes and to highlight some of the major global developments around migration in the future, mixed data techniques, new data types and sources (satellite data, big data), as well as more traditional quantitative and qualitative data sources (international comparative surveys, statistical offices' data, small-scale qualitative surveys conducted during the project, etc.) have been used.

In the HumMingBird project, CESSDA's role is to ensure that collected data feeds into the CESSDA Data Catalogue, ensuring it is FAIR and enriching it with valuable input that will be made accessible to a large variety of stakeholders. HumMingBird survey outcomes can further be linked with thematic datasets of the CESSDA catalogue to provide designated research communities, potential interested policy makers, and the wider public with post-project exploitation of data and indicators.

International Survey Data Network

The International Ethnic and Immigrant Minorities' Survey Data Network[17] (ETHMIGSURVEYDATA)[18] covers 35 countries and has more than 200 members. The network was funded for four years (2017–2021) in the framework of the COST action (an EU funding instrument) and gathered researchers from different sectors (academic, think tanks, government, civil society organisations, private companies) to work on and increase access to and usability and dissemination of survey data on the economic, social, and political integration of ethnic and migrant minorities (EMMs).

One of the main outputs of the network was setting up the 'EthmigSurveyDataHub';[19] a data hub to facilitate knowledge sharing and transfer, as well as opportunities for depositing and access to EMM survey data across Europe. This data hub includes the following components: survey registry, survey question bank, post-harmonised survey data bank, and survey data playground.

The Ethnic and Migrant Minorities (EMM) Survey Registry has started operating in a beta version. The EMM registry is a free online tool available to designated communities of users to locate existing quantitative surveys in order to enhance knowledge and facilitate research work on ethnic/migrant minority populations through the compiled survey-level metadata. The content of the current EMM Survey Registry results from the contribution of a national delegation of 35 participating countries in the COST action to an initial collection of all surveys targeting

---

[17] Ethmig Survey Data, https://ethmigsurveydatahub.eu/
[18] COST ACTION 16111 – International Ethnic and Immigrant Minorities' survey data Network (2017–2021). Available at: https://www.sciencespo.fr/centre-etudes-europeennes/fr/node/17084
[19] Ethmig Survey Data: About, https://ethmigsurveydatahub.eu/the-action/

Figure 3.6 The EthmigSurveyDataHub registry. See https://ethmigsurveydatahub.eu/emmregistry/.

ethic and migrant minority populations from 2000 to 2018 in their respective countries. In Figure 3.6 the fields used for the metadata representing a specific survey are shown.

This project also collaborates with the CESSDA-led EOSC interoperability project SSHOC as a data community pilot, thus bringing forward interdisciplinary challenges related to different SSH data communities, and serving as a use case for the use of tools and services, including APIs (see Box 3.3), provided by SSH research infrastructures in the project.

Challenges and prospects for collaborative research

Despite the huge amounts of data produced by various sources, numerous challenges persist in our era that are connected to the collection, deposit, search, use, analysis, and reuse of data. These challenges depend widely upon methods and techniques that allow primary or secondary use of data as well as the data-sharing culture of research communities producing these data. Regarding data findability, for instance, the large international datasets are findable and accessible. However, data collected and curated by individual researchers or for the purpose of a specific research question might not be easily findable or accessible for secondary use. The reasons can be either that the data are not archived in a trusted repository, or the metadata do not meet standards and are of limited use.

As to the data-sharing culture, many researchers agree that data should be accessible and reusable, but at the same time they are reluctant to share their own data. A study by Stieglitz et al. (2020) revealed that researchers connect sharing data with considerable effort to make data shareable and an increased risk of losing publication opportunities, while the benefits (increasing one's network, higher efficiency, academic credit, and recognition) remain uncertain.

> **Box 3.3** Application programming interfaces
>
> **What are APIs?**
>
> An API is a set of definitions and protocols for building and integrating application software. The precise specification of the API helps with conceptual simplification: the user of the API does not need to know the implementation details of the individual services provided by the API, and only deals with its function and proper syntax. The actual implementation can be improved over time without changing the interface, which helps maintain a continued service that can be updated.
>
> Three different release policies are used for APIs. Public APIs are available to everyone and, since they can be adopted by many users, bring better interoperability and legibility in software design. Private APIs are used internally within companies, and allow control and a competitive edge. Partner APIs are shared with specific partners.
>
> See more at https://www.redhat.com/en/topics/api/what-are-application-programming-interfaces.
>
> **Example of an API for social policy**
>
> In WP4 'Innovations in Data Production' of the SSHOC project a social policy API has been developed. It can be embedded in social surveys to efficiently collect accurate policy-relevant micro-level information across different fields. Based on the OECD Family Database (The Family Support Calculator,[a] 2016), the API allows users to calculate net income or social benefits. It relies on the integration of a policy imputation algorithm into social surveys. Existing algorithms (e.g., EUROMOD (2020) on tax benefit systems, the Generations & Gender Programme (GGP) on family policies, or Wage Indicator on employment conditions) could be easily integrated into a social survey through an API. The initial design of the API covered around 20 indicators for 28 member states covering family policy, employment, labour markets, and pensions. The API is usable by all European survey infrastructures and the wider research community.
>
> ---
> [a] https://www.oecd.org/els/soc/

To overcome these barriers, researchers should be provided with tools to describe their data and get a persistent identifier (e.g., DOI or handle) automatically if metadata and data are archived via trusted repositories. Next, the research community, including the universities and funding organisations, should give credit for sharing data and providing tools to enrich data. One way to do this is to standardise data references in publications, especially journal articles, and to provide metrics on data views and data downloads (e.g., from the Zenodo platform).

Another challenge is related to metadata standards or metadata profiles (subsets of these standards). There is a clear need for interdisciplinary cooperation, such as already exists between EOSC cluster projects[20] (e.g., social data with environmental or health data). Regarding interoperability: connecting and combining data takes

---
[20] H2020 INFRAEOSC-2018-04 call funded projects covering different scientific domains: ENVRI-FAIR, EOSC-Life, ESCAPE, PANOSC, SSHOC.

huge effort and may induce data quality issues. Trusted repositories, provenance of data, or sustainability of tools and services, a need for disciplinary expertise, or building communities are only some of the additional challenges to be addressed in more detail.

As an essential component to meet the challenges, the EU has put in place open access policy principles, meaning that open science is the new model of research practice, with tools and collaboration for the production and distribution of scientific work and research outcomes going beyond scientific impact by addressing economic and social impact as well.

Turning FAIR data into reality (Collins *et al.*, 2018) relies heavily on a data-sharing culture in which data research infrastructures like CESSDA and peer European infrastructures have a major role to play. The use and reuse of data and metadata respond to the transparency and accountability principles the research communities and organisations should engender when producing publicly funded research (Kondyli and Klironomos, 2022). CESSDA service providers have for many years been offering their high-quality expertise, tools, and services to designated researchers. Besides the Data Catalogue, CESSDA also provides training services for data management plans.

A data management plan (DMP) should be produced early in the research workflow, often as a prerequisite of research funding institutions. It is a 'live' and formal document that reflects the whole research data management life cycle aimed at the reproducibility of research results. A DMP meets time and resources constraints and can be updated throughout the life cycle of a research project. CESSDA has created the Data Management Expert Guide (CESSDA Training Team, 2020) to assist social scientists in making their research data findable, interoperable, sustainable, accessible, and reusable (FAIR). This guide contributes to professionalism in data management and increases the value of research data. The seven chapters of the guide (see Figure 3.7) respond to the various phases of the whole research data life cycle from planning, organising, documenting, processing, storing, and protecting data to sharing and publishing them.

The first chapter is connected to the initial phase of the data research life cycle, data planning, while the second one concentrates on the organisation and documentation phase by providing information on appropriate data file and folder structures. The chapter on process introduces data management topics such as data entry and coding, integrity of data, and learning about version and edition management. The chapter on storage teaches how to plan a storage and backup strategy, as well as the advantages and disadvantages of different storage and backup solutions. Also, measures to protect data from unauthorised access are explained. The chapter on protection highlights the legal and ethical obligations and shows how a combination of gaining consent, anonymising data, gaining clarity over who owns the copyright to data, and controlling access can enable the ethical and legal sharing of data, while the chapter on archiving and publishing provides valuable knowledge for researchers to inform their decisions on where to archive and publish their data in a way that others can properly access, understand, use, and cite them. The final

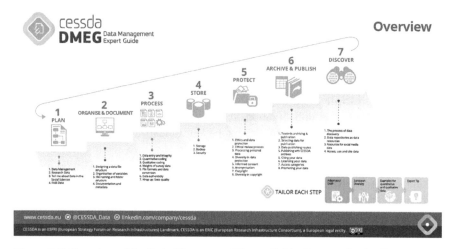

Figure 3.7 Overview of the Data Management Expert Guide. See text for details.

chapter explains techniques for discovering and reusing existing or previously collected datasets, as well as the different types of social science data sources in Europe and around the world.

CESSDA put the extension, enrichment, and technical improvement of its Data Catalogue as a high priority in its strategic plan for the period 2021–2024. New datasets are linked to the Data Catalogue provided either by its members or as results of implemented projects like the following example. The Open Archives Initiative Protocol for Metadata Harvesting (OAI-PMH)[21] tool was developed by the Finnish Data Service (Jääskeläinen, 2020) to allow harvesting data from the Data Catalogue to other data catalogues (e.g., in the European Open Science Cloud) and has since been implemented in several EC-funded projects.

Conclusion

Migration will constantly be in the political and social agendas for years to come, rendering responsible research necessary to investigate the multiple aspects of meeting the societal needs of people on the move. One of the challenges is to facilitate research worldwide by providing FAIR data via trusted repositories. Beyond the constant enrichment of migration studies and related metadata in the CESSDA Data Catalogue, datasets can be enriched by adding the original questionnaires, connecting questions and variables, and studying the original concepts and questions by the successful implementation of the European Question Bank, a project implemented

---

[21] OAI-PMH is a protocol developed for harvesting metadata descriptions of records in an archive so that services can be built using metadata from many archives.

by CESSDA ERIC. The European Question Bank considers the multiple language and translation issues and can facilitate the reuse of existing datasets, as well as serving as an input for new surveys or linking to controlled vocabularies[22] in order to promote the multilingual datasets provided by CESSDA archives.

The linkage to various digital objects and data via various tools developed by CESSDA service providers will also provide fertile ground for secondary data use and research. In other words, mapping and identifying relationships among all digital research objects (publications, data, software) is key to the successful maintenance and further development of the CESSDA Data Catalogue. Another sustainable idea to further enhance migration research is the establishment of thematic archives. By adding new information (e.g., tagging 'migration' in one of the filters), thematic archives can be set up with a focus on specific topics. This requires that all depositors add relevant keywords to their metadata. Currently, CESSDA is running several pilot cases and collaborating with different research communities, including migration, to further elaborate the concept of thematic archives.

Several CESSDA service providers offer safe data centres to access sensitive data available under specific terms of use for researchers. CESSDA could also capitalise on the experience of other infrastructures like the National Institute of Health (NIH), which developed and deployed a Data Commons,[23] a secure infrastructure for sharing data. Similarly, ELIXIR[24] developed the Core Data Resources, and in other disciplines virtual research environments (VRE) are being developed. Within such VREs, data producers (including researchers) can manage access to the data. They can also store common and heavily used data (instead of downloading these data repeatedly, which is inefficient but also increases the chance of security breaches).

The European Commission is considering data spaces on relevant societal topics such as mobility, health, and financial data (European Union, 2020). In addition to these common data spaces, there are ideas to develop personal data spaces in which researchers could store and control access to their data.

To conclude, the CESSDA Data Catalogue offers to the social science domain and researchers a reliable and rich overview of datasets collected in Europe and worldwide concerning migration research topics. It provides a unique opportunity to gain time and effort by getting descriptive information on the data before downloading it, and functions as a sustainable and reliable platform for the development of new services. In addition, social researchers can also deposit their own data in their native languages to any CESSDA service provider, thus rendering their data accessible, sustainable, and findable for the benefit of both science and society.

---

[22] Controlled vocabularies definition available at https://www.getty.edu/research/publications/electronic_publications/intro_controlled_vocab/what.pdf.

[23] National Institutes of Health: New Models of Data Stewardship - Data Commons Pilot, https://commonfund.nih.gov/commons

[24] ELIXIR: ELIXIR Core Data Resources, https://elixir-europe.org/platforms/data/core-data-resources

References

Boyd, M. and Grieco, E. (2014), 'Women and migration: Incorporating gender into international migration theory', Migration Information Source, Washington DC, available at http://www.migrationinformation.org/Feature/print.cfm?ID=106

CESSDA Training Team (2020), *CESSDA Data Management Expert Guide*, CESSDA ERIC, Bergen, Norway.

Collins, S., Genova, F., Harrower, N., Hodson, S., Jones, S., Laaksonen, L., Mietchen, D., Petrauskaitė, R., and Wittenburg, P. (2018), *Turning FAIR into Reality: Final Report and Action Plan from the European Commission Expert Group on FAIR Data*, European Commission Publications Office, Luxembourg.

European Open Science Cloud (2021), 'Strategic research and innovation agenda of the European Open Science Cloud, version 1.0', available at https://www.eosc.eu/sites/default/files/EOSC-SRIA-V1.0_15Feb2021.pdf

European Strategy Forum on Research Infrastructures (2006), *European Roadmap for Research Infrastructures: Report 2006*, Office for Official Publications of the European Communities, Luxembourg.

European Union (2017), *H2020 Migration Factsheet*, HORIZON 2020 Work Programme for Research & Innovation 2018–2020, available at https://ec.europa.eu/programmes/horizon2020/sites/horizon2020/files/migration_fact_sheet_2018-2020.pdf

European Union (2020), 'Communication from the Commission to the European Parliament, the Council, the European Economic and Social Committee and the Committee of the Regions: A European strategy for data', COM(2020) 66 final, EURLex, Brussels.

Jääskeläinen, T. (2020), 'CESSDA Data Catalogue: UI changes and metadata requirements'. Unpublished presentation slides for the CESSDA webinar on 20/11/2020.

Kondyli, D. and Klironomos, N. (2022), 'The impact of "FAIR" and open science on the research infrastructures', *in Documentation and Management of Empirical Research: Research Infrastructures for Social Science*, Alexandria.

Reillon, V. (2017), 'EU framework programmes for research and innovation: Evolution and key data from FP1 to Horizon 2020 in view of FP9', European Parliamentary Research Service, available at https://www.europarl.europa.eu/RegData/etudes/IDAN/2017/608697/EPRS_IDA%282017%29608697_EN.pdf

Stieglitz, S., Wilms, K., Mirbabaie, M., Hofeditz, L., Brenger, B., López, A., and Rehwald, S. (2020), 'When are researchers willing to share their data? Impacts of values and uncertainty on open data in academia', *PLOS One* 15(7), e0234172.

Wilkinson, M. D., *et al.* (2016), 'The FAIR guiding principles for scientific data management and stewardship', *Scientific Data* 3(1), 1–9.

4

Leveraging Mobile Phone Data for Migration Flows

MASSIMILIANO LUCA, GIANNI BARLACCHI, NURIA OLIVER, AND BRUNO LEPRI

Introduction

AS REPORTED BY the United Nations, the number of migrants worldwide is constantly growing, with an estimation of 280 million migrants in 2020.[1] Climate change, wars, and economic distress are some of the reasons behind these increasing migratory flows. Indeed, according to the International Organization for Migration (IOM),[2] migration is recognised as one of the critical issues of the 21st century, posing fundamental challenges to governments in many regions of the world. For instance, policies are needed to guarantee access to health care, education, jobs and public services, social integration, and many other aspects related to migration, such as infrastructure and urban planning, resource allocation, border security, etc. To implement such policies, having up-to-date data about migratory movements is of paramount importance. However, traditional data sources, e.g., official statistics, cannot offer this type of information due to intrinsic limitations such as low sampling frequency, given that migrations may change rapidly (Crawley *et al.*, 2016; Pradhan, 2004). Moreover, official statistics are usually published after significant time gaps of several years (or even decades) due to the complexity of the data collection and data preparation processes and high costs. Thus, alternative data sources are urgently needed.

In this context, mobile phones have become ubiquitous in both developed and developing economies. As reported by the International Telecommunication Union (ITU) and the GSMA (International Telecommunication Union, 2020; GSMA Intelligence, 2020), in 2019 there were more than 5.2 billion unique subscribers (67% of

---

[1] Migration Data Portal, https://migrationdataportal.org
[2] IOM, https://www.iom.int/

the world population) with eight billion active SIM cards, therefore accounting for a penetration rate with respect to the population of 103%. While penetration rates are larger in developed economies, small island developing states, least-developed countries, and landlocked developing countries are also experiencing rapid growth in mobile phone adoption (International Telecommunication Union, 2020).

In recent years, passively collected, anonymised/pseudonymised, aggregated mobile network data has been leveraged to study different types of migration (e.g., refugees (Salah *et al.*, 2019a), climate migration (Pastor-Escuredo *et al.*, 2014), labour migration (Bruckschen *et al.*, 2019), and others (Deville *et al.*, 2014)) and to understand daily habits, levels of integration (e.g., Bakker *et al.*, 2019; Boy *et al.*, 2019; Alfeo *et al.*, 2019), access to education (e.g., Mamei *et al.*, 2019) and to health services (e.g., Altuncu *et al.*, 2019), and other aspects of the everyday life of migrants (e.g., Salah *et al.*, 2019a).

Mobile phone data also have some limitations to be considered, including biases in the data (e.g., certain social groups might be underrepresented, such as women, children, and the elderly), ethical challenges, and privacy and regulatory problems. These issues should be carefully taken into account when dealing with mobile phone data. We introduce some of these limitations later in this chapter, while ethical and legal challenges were discussed in detail in Chapter 2 (Salah *et al.*, 2022).

This chapter discusses the importance of leveraging passively collected mobile network data as an alternative data source to gather precious and previously unavailable insights on migration flows. First, the 'Mobile phone data: Call detail records' section describes what call data records are. In 'Application of mobile phone data for migration' we show how to use this data source to monitor different aspects and types of migration such as refugees, climate migrants, and labour migrants. In 'Mobile phone data for migration: Challenges and limitations' we discuss a few key limitations that may play a crucial role in capturing indicators about migration and migrants (e.g., technical challenges, biases, ethical issues, regulatory and financial issues, and others). Finally, we derive some conclusions.

Mobile phone data: Call detail records

This section describes the most commonly used type of passively collected mobile network data: call detail records (CDRs). CDRs are collected by telecommunication companies for billing purposes and contain information about customers' interactions with the mobile network.

CDRs are generated in the base transmission stations (also referred to as antennas or cell towers) every time a phone makes or receives a phone call or sends/receives a short message (SMS). While CDRs contain many fields, the most commonly used fields for research purposes are the pseudonymised phone numbers of the caller/callee, the timestamp of when the phone call/SMS took place, the duration of the phone call, and the unique identifiers (IDs) of the cell towers to which the mobile phones of the caller/callee were connected. Note that if the caller (or the

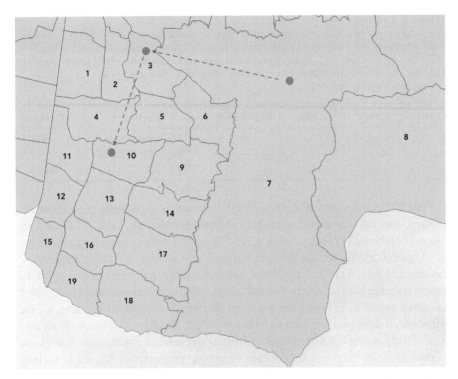

Figure 4.1 Example of area covered by different antennas in a cellular network. Note how the size of the area of coverage changes between urban areas (e.g., area 10) and rural areas (e.g., area 7).

callee) is a customer of a different mobile operator, then the cell tower ID where it was connected is unknown. Moreover, no content is registered in the CDRs, but only information about the events is recorded. Thus, CDRs are often referred to as *metadata*.

In mathematical notation for this chapter, a CDR is a tuple $\langle u_i, u_j, t, a_o, a_d, d \rangle$ where $u_i, u_j \in U$ (U is the set of users' identifiers) and represent the encrypted identifiers of the caller and the callee; t is the timestamp of when the call took place, or the SMS was sent/received; $a_o, a_d \in A$ are the identifiers of the antennas pinged at time of the event. The former (a_o) is the cell phone tower handling the outgoing communication. The latter (a_d) is the receiving tower, and d is the duration of the communication which only applies to phone calls. The two antennas are known only if both caller/callee are customers of the same mobile operator. Otherwise, only one of the antennas is known. By knowing the location of the antennas and their respective areas of coverage, one can roughly estimate the positions of u_i and u_j at an antenna level. In rural areas, the location estimation is typically within an area of a few kilometres. In urban areas, where there is a larger density of cell towers, the location estimation is within an area of around 100 m by 100 m. An example of such differences is shown in Figure 4.1.

Table 4.1 Example CDR for user u_1 for a specific date.
For instance, the first line of the table shows that u_1 called u_{3652} at 11:50:32 on 1 January 2020. Moreover, we know that u_1 was connected to the antenna with identifier 7 when they made the call. Similarly, u_{3652} was connected to antenna 8. Note how the last record does not have information for the antenna to which the callee was connected as u_{3131} is a customer from another mobile network.

Caller	Callee	Origin	Destination	Timestamp	Duration
u_1	u_{3652}	7	8	01-01-2020 11:50:32	48 s
u_1	u_{1713}	3	7	01-01-2020 14:07:24	93 s
u_1	u_{3131}	10	?	01-01-2020 18:11:37	189 s

The CDRs are stripped of all personal information to preserve the customers' privacy, and the customers' identifiers are pseudonymised. Table 4.1 shows an example of three CDRs of customer u_1, and Figure 4.1 shows their inferred mobility.

Although mobile phone data are not typically publicly available for privacy reasons (de Montjoye et al., 2018), the community has made some effort to enable research with such data. For instance, several telecommunication companies launched data sharing initiatives, e.g., data challenges, to release large-scale CDRs for research upon request, such as Telecom Italia's Big Data Challenge (Barlacchi et al., 2015). Along a similar line, the EU-funded research infrastructure SoBigData (Grossi et al., 2018) opens regular calls for project proposals on datasets of various types, including mobility data (Andrienko et al., 2020). Currently, the SoBigData catalogue includes CDRs from Tuscany, Italy, and Rome, Italy.

Although there are some access limitations, the ubiquity of mobile devices has enabled the analysis of CDRs to quantify and model large-scale human mobility: 97% of the world's population lives in an area covered by mobile cellular signal (International Telecommunication Union, 2020), and 90% of people have access to a mobile phone (Poushter et al., 2016). Thus, researchers and policy-makers have an unprecedented opportunity to investigate both *individual* and *aggregated* mobility patterns (Gonzalez et al., 2008; Schneider et al., 2013; Blondel et al., 2015; Luca et al., 2020). See Box 4.1 for details of how geographical data is used for processing CDRs.

Application of mobile phone data for migration

Mobile phone data represent a unique opportunity to investigate migration. Researchers may, for example, use such data to support policy-makers, organisations, and authorities in taking data-driven decisions related to migration (Hughes et al., 2016). In the past, mobile network data have been used to solve a variety of societal challenges (Blondel et al., 2015), including modelling migration, assessing migrants' well-being (e.g., Sîrbu et al., 2021; International Organization for Migration – UN Migration Agency 2018; UNHCR 2016; Salah et al., 2019b; Lai et al., 2019) and estimating population displacements (e.g., Deville et al., 2014;

Box 4.1 Record linkage and tools for geographical mobility data

Geographical data processing involves modelling, visualisation, and processing of spatial data. Multiple open-source Python libraries may help to process mobile phone data and, more generally, mobility data. For example, GeoPandas (https://geopandas.org) is a generic library useful for dealing with geospatial data in pandas format. It allows loading different data sources (e.g., shapefile, GeoJSON, and others) into a pandas-like data structure and enables geographical operations such as spatial joins. Shapefile is a digital vector storage format for storing geographic location and associated attribute information. It is possible to encode many shapes (such as points, polygons, and multipatches) with this format (see http://www.esri.com/library/whitepapers/pdfs/shapefile.pdf for the complete specification). While shapefile stores binary information, GeoJSON is text based, and follows the popular JSON format (see https://en.wikipedia.org/wiki/GeoJSON). The pandas library uses a two-dimensional, potentially heterogeneous tabular data format called a DataFrame. This data structure enables labelled rows and columns, and permits SQL-like inner join operations via a merge operation, where two DataFrames are combined by using the columns of either one as primary keys (see https://pandas.pydata.org/docs/reference/api/pandas.DataFrame.merge.html for examples).

Classical join operations rely on feature values, used as keys. Spatial join operations, on the other hand, can join columns based on location or proximity, as defined by the location information contained in the data. It then becomes possible to select records physically close to a specific point of interest.

Some libraries are more specific to human mobility. Examples of such libraries are MovingPandas (Graser, 2019) and scikit-mobility (Pappalardo *et al.*, 2019).

In scikit-mobility, a set of trajectories is described by a data structure called a TrajDataFrame, which is an extension of the pandas DataFrame that has specific column names and data types. With a TrajDataFrame, each row represents a point of a trajectory, described by a latitude, longitude, and a date-time variable, and can be extended by an object identifier. This data structure is suitable for storing GPS trajectories of many objects (e.g., humans or vehicles). Apart from extracting mobility metrics and patterns from existing data at individual and collective level (e.g., length of displacements, characteristic distances, origin–destination matrices, etc.), scikit-mobility can also generate synthetic individual trajectories using standard mathematical models (random walk models, exploration and preferential return model, etc.) and synthetic mobility flows using standard migration models like the gravity model and the radiation model (see https://github.com/scikit-mobility/scikit-mobility).

Tatem, 2017; Pastor-Escuredo *et al.*, 2019; Koebe, 2020). This section describes how mobile phone data have been used to monitor different types of migration.

Refugees

According to the United Nations High Commissioner for Refugees (UNHCR), 'refugees are people who have fled war, violence, conflict, or persecution and have crossed an international border to find safety in another country' (UNHCR,

2020). In recent years, the mobility and behaviours of refugees have been studied via the analysis of CDRs. The more prominent series of research studies related to refugees and mobile phone data was introduced with the Data for Refugees (D4R) Challenge (Salah *et al.*, 2019b). For D4R, Türk Telekom shared a one-year CDR dataset to allow researchers, practitioners, and activists to tackle urgent social problems that emerged in Turkey after a drastic increase in Syrian refugees since the 2011 civil war. The data have been analysed to estimate the refugees' well-being and gained insights on the refugees' living conditions (e.g., health, education, and segregation). Differently from standard CDRs, in D4R, users are flagged as refugees when one of the following conditions holds: (1) having ID numbers given to refugees and foreigners in Turkey; (2) being registered with Syrian passports; and/or (3) using special tariffs reserved for refugees. It is not guaranteed to include only and exclusively refugees in the categories mentioned above, which serves as a layer of protection (Salah *et al.*, 2018). Multiple studies based on the analysis of this dataset have suggested ways to measure the social and economic integration of refugees (e.g., Bakker *et al.*, 2019; Boy *et al.*, 2019; Andris *et al.*, 2019; Bertoli *et al.*, 2019). In particular, Bakker *et al.* (2019) defined three metrics to measure social, spatial, and economic integration. To succeed, the authors integrated CDRs with the arriving and departing visitors by district provided by the Ministry of Culture and Tourism and with the votes per polling station during the 2015 and 2018 general elections from the Ballot Result Sharing System of the Turkish Supreme Electoral Council. Social integration was measured with individual CDRs, and it was defined as the ratio of calls from a minority group to a majority group and the total number of calls from minority groups (regardless of the group of the callee).

Regarding the spatial integration, Bakker *et al.* suggested using CDRs to estimate the number of people of a given group in a specific area and used the Gini coefficient to measure the presence of different groups. In this case, higher values represent more diversity, and therefore more integration. Individual CDRs were also used to compute the probability that a minority group shares an area with a person of a majority group. Finally, the authors suggested measuring economic integration by calculating mobility similarity matrices for some key timestamps (e.g., weekends, evening, working hours) and used the Frobenius norm[3] to measure the employment score.

According to the authors, refugees in Istanbul were more spatially integrated than those living in Southeastern Anatolia. However, there was a higher and positive correlation of spatial, social, and economic integration in Southeastern Anatolia. Finally, the authors showed that the presence and integration of refugees had an impact on political outcomes. For instance, their study showed that social integration was correlated with an increase of votes for pro-refugee parties. Economic integration was instead correlated with the opposite.

---

[3] The Frobenius norm is the square root of the sum of all squared elements of a matrix, and results in a larger value if there are elements that are large in absolute value.

Boy et al. (2019) measured the segregation (i.e., an imposed restriction on the interaction between people that are considered to be different (Freeman, 1978)), isolation (i.e., to which extent different groups share residential areas (Massey and Denton, 1988)), and homophily (i.e., the tendency of people to associate with groups they share similar traits with (Currarini et al., 2016)), and they used such metrics as a proxy for the social integration of refugees. The authors used individual CDRs and aggregated mobility matrices (e.g., origin–destination matrices derived from CDRs) to look at the evolution of mobility and communication patterns of refugees.

Another study aiming to investigate the integration of refugees is described in Alfeo et al. (2019). They computed the similarity between locals and refugees using their mobility and communication patterns as a proxy for social integration. More precisely, they defined four metrics to measure social integration: (1) district attractiveness, (2) residential inclusion by district, (3) refugees' interaction level, and (4) refugees' mobility similarity. The authors found that mobility similarity is positively correlated with the refugees' interaction level, showing that sharing urban spaces among locals and refugees can improve social integration. To perform their analyses, the authors had to infer the home location of the individuals involved in the study. To do so, they used individual CDRs and some heuristics like the ones introduced in Pappalardo et al. (2020). A similar study by Andris et al. (2019) showed that the presence of certain types of amenities such as community centres, social centres, schools, and places of worship plays a crucial role in the integration of refugees. In this study, CDRs analysed at an individual level were integrated with points of interest (POIs) derived from the Humanitarian Open Street Map.[4] Moreover, to measure the distances between POIs and the refugee camps, the authors used Turkish refugee campsites sourced from the UNHCR and the Regional Information Management Working Group, Europe.

Other works integrated alternative data sources to measure the refugees' social integration. This is the case with Bertoli et al. (2019), where the authors relied on CDRs, the Global Dataset of Events, Language, and Tone (GDELT), and housing data. Hu et al. (2019) used both CDRs and POIs, while Bozcaga et al. (2019) combined mobile phone data with official statistics from different sources (e.g., Ministry of Interior, Turkish Census, and other government statistics). Marquez et al. (2019) also used data from Twitter, and Kılıç et al. (2019) employed multiple official statistics to explore several factors of the Syrian refugee crisis (e.g., home and work location of the refugees, meaningful places for the refugees, and others).

More recently, mobile phone data have been used as a source for a gravity model to better understand the factors governing the refugees' mobility (e.g., changes of income, propensity to leave camps, transit through Turkey and agricultural business cycles, and others; Beine et al., 2021). In this study, CDRs were used to understand whether mobility can be modelled with a gravity model (Barbosa et al., 2018). Mobile phone data were integrated with the gross domestic product (GDP) provided

---

[4] Humanitarian Open Street Map, https://www.hotosm.org/

by the Turkish Statistical Institute to measure income levels, and with data from the Directorate General of Migration Management in Turkey for information about the propensity to leave camps.

Mobile phone data, integrated with additional data sources, are also employed to measure the access of refugees to health care services (Salman *et al.*, 2021; Altuncu *et al.*, 2019) and education (Mamei *et al.*, 2019), and, more generally, to investigate the effect of displacement on the mobility and communication patterns (Beine *et al.*, 2019; Frydenlund *et al.*, 2019).

Human flows can also be used to estimate the spread of infectious diseases. Bosetti *et al.* (2020) used mobile phone data to quantify the risk of measles outbreaks. The authors found that heterogeneity in immunity, population distribution, and human-mobility flows are critical factors that augment the possibility of having an outbreak. Conversely, social integration and vaccine campaigns were found to be winning formulas to reduce such risks.

Finally, Mancini *et al.* (2019) discussed opportunities and risks of using mobile phone data to monitor the refugees' daily experiences. The authors investigated the role of mobile phones in the refugees' day-to-day life, their journeys (based on mobile phone and other data sources, such as surveys and interviews), their social relations, self-empowerment, education, and health. Most of the studies investigated in the review focused on Syrian refugees and multiple countries were involved, such as Germany (Borkert *et al.*, 2018; Wall *et al.*, 2017) and others (e.g., Smets 2018; Charmarkeh 2013).

Loaiza *et al.* (2020) combined surveys with mobile phone data to measure refugees' integration. The authors used a modified version of the gravity model to contrast the mobility patterns and economic integration of people that left Venezuela to move to Colombia and of Colombians who used to live in Venezuela and went back to Colombia in the context of the recent migration crisis across South America. Using aggregated mobile phone data, combined with the monthly household survey of National Administrative Department of Statistics of Colombia (DANE), the authors showed that the drivers behind the mobility patterns and destination choices are different.

Several observations emerge from the literature on the analysis of mobile data related to international refugees. First, mobile phone data are primarily used to investigate the refugees' socioeconomic and living conditions in the host country. Second, the use of GPS information from the refugees' smartphones may pose severe security and privacy issues (Beduschi, 2017). Finally, mobile phone data are usually integrated with statistical data and surveys (both official and not) to get a more complete picture of the context.

Climate-based migration

Climate change is a long-term change in the average weather patterns affecting the Earth's local, regional, and global climates. Such weather patterns are exemplified by changes in the frequency and intensity of severe phenomena such as floods, storms, and droughts. These extreme natural phenomena have a significant impact on migration flows and mobility patterns. Examples are the rainfalls in Burkina Faso (Henry *et al.*, 2004) and the drought in Ethiopia (Meze-Hausken, 2000). Environmental migration is defined by the International Organization for Migration (IOM) as characterised by 'people who, predominantly for reasons of sudden or progressive changes in the environment that adversely affect their lives or living conditions, are obliged to leave their habitual homes or choose to do so, either temporarily or permanently, and who move within their country or abroad' (IOM-MECC, 2019).

Two examples of leveraging location data to model climate-based migration are found in Sakaki *et al.* (2010) and Wang and Taylor (2014), where the authors analysed geolocated tweets to model mobility changes after an earthquake in Japan and after Hurricane Sandy, respectively. Regarding studies that rely on mobile phone data, Isaacman *et al.* (2018) analysed CDRs to investigate environmental migration in La Guajira, Colombia. In 2014, the area was affected by a prolonged drought period that pushed the population, mainly those living in rural zones, to move to other places. In this case, mobile phone data at an individual level were used to detect the home location of the users before and after the period under analysis, and therefore to estimate the number of migrants.

The authors investigated mobility on a national level. They found that 90% of the people on the move stayed in the region of La Guajira but moved to a different municipality. In contrast, the other 10% moved to other districts in Colombia. The findings confirmed a general theory indicating that only short-distance moves appeared to be affected by climatic factors (Henry *et al.*, 2004). To model people on the move, the authors proposed a home detection algorithm and they modelled migrants using the gravity model (Zipf, 1946) and the radiation model (Simini *et al.*, 2012). Finally, since weather data play a pivotal role in mobility patterns, the authors proposed a modified version of the radiation model to deal with meteorological data.

An analysis aiming to estimate evacuation, displacement, and migration based on mobile phone data was conducted by Lu *et al.* (2016) in the context of the tropical cyclone Mahasen in Bangladesh. The authors showed that mobility patterns allowed the estimation of the effectiveness of early warning strategies based on early and mid-storm population movements. In Chittagong, the early warning accomplished the aim of motivating evacuation during appropriate times. The authors analysed individual CDRs of millions of users covering a period between one month before and one month after. Moreover, to reduce potential noise and bias, the authors considered only SIMs already registered with the telecommunication company before the natural disaster. To detect the effectiveness of interventions, they investigated anomalies in the cell phone tower activities. At the same time, to estimate mobility patterns they derived mobility matrices at a tower level by aggregating the CDRs. Similarly, Moumni *et al.* (2013) highlighted that during the Oaxaca earthquake, they faced a moderate increase of mobility with respect to the baseline, showing anomalies in mobility patterns. Also, in this study, the role of CDRs at an individual level was to detect anomalies in the activities. The studies mentioned above showed that mobility networks could eventually be used to estimate people's displacement before, during, and after a natural disaster. Along this line, Pastor-Escuredo et al. (2014) used aggregated CDRs combined with additional information such as rainfall data and remote sensing imagery to characterise the activity patterns after the floods in Tabasco, Mexico. The authors found abnormal communication patterns and stated that such insights could locate damaged areas and optimise the resource allocation in the first hours after a natural disaster. The authors also highlighted that communication activity could also be used to measure the awareness of the at-risk population.

An additional study by Lu et al. (2016a) aimed at quantifying the incidence and duration of migrations in Bangladesh and long-term mobility patterns in areas stressed from a climate perspective. In this study, the authors also highlighted the importance of integrating mobile phone data with other targeted phone-based and household-based panel surveys to characterise vulnerable, underrepresented groups in the mobile data (e.g., women, children, and the poorest). CDRs were preprocessed as in Lu et al. (2016): only users that were already active before the cyclone were considered. Note that users who activated a SIM less than 10 days before the cyclone were not considered.

Bengtsson et al. (2011) showed that mobile phone data could be used to estimate the displacement of the population after the Haiti earthquake of 2010. The authors demonstrated the validity of their findings by comparing the obtained results with the data collected in an extensive retrospective population-based survey carried out by the United Nations. Similarly to other studies, the authors used individual CDRs to follow users for 42 days before and 158 days after the natural disaster to detect changes in outgoing and incoming mobility patterns.

Based on the case studies conducted on Haiti's disasters (2010, 2016) and in Nepal (2015), the International Migration Organization, in cooperation with other partners, released FlowKit by Flowminder.[5] FlowKit is a software tool that facilitates mobile phone data analysis and ensures data privacy to leverage partnerships with mobile phone operators (Power et al., 2020). In particular, FlowKit allows near real-time assessment of population displacement after natural disasters in various contexts.

Timely analysis of the data is of paramount importance, especially when dealing with environmental migration and refugees. Most, if not all, the work carried out so far has not been performed in real time but after the fact. Having tools to enable fast partnerships with the custodians of the data to ease the data sharing and analysis process is thus of critical importance.

Mobile phone data are also widely used to investigate changes in the communication patterns in areas affected by natural disasters (Moumni et al., 2013; Lu et al., 2016). In general, mobile phone data have been shown to play a crucial role

---

[5] Flowminder, https://www.flowminder.org

in understanding the displacement of people before, during, and after natural disasters, assessing the effects of early warnings for evacuation orders, and investigating long-term mobility impacts caused by climate change. They are particularly valuable when complemented by and integrated with traditional data sources, such as household surveys.

A recently published dataset that may be useful for future investigations of climate-based migrations is the Geocoded Disasters (GDIS) dataset (Rosvold and Buhaug, 2021). The dataset contains geographic information about almost 40,000 locations connected to nearly 10,000 natural disasters. Each disaster is mapped to a class (e.g., drought, extreme temperature, storm, and others). Finally, it contains an identifier that allows researchers to easily integrate information from the popular EM-DAT dataset[6] that records natural disasters.

Labour migration

The International Labor Organization (ILO)[7] defines migrant workers as 'all international migrants currently employed or unemployed seeking employment in their current country of residence'. Obtaining timely information about labour migration is an open challenge at all stages of the migration journey (International Labour Organization, 2019). Alternative data sources may help to obtain up-to-date statistics and measure social aspects of the migrants' lives (e.g., safety, access to communication technologies, social integration, and others). As an example, Neubauer et al. (2015) used Twitter geotagged posts to estimate work migration patterns.

Recently, a study on women migrant workers in the Association of South-East Asian Nations (ASEAN) countries used mobile phones as proxies for access to the internet and new technologies (International Labour Organization, 2019). In particular, they proposed using mobile phones as a tool for measuring access to information on their rights, support services, and response to violence. Alışık et al. (2019) used mobile phone data to investigate mobility patterns of Syrian refugees in Turkey that might be related to seasonal jobs in fields such as seasonal agriculture and seasonal tourism. The authors found that, in general, for Syrians, labour is a vital mobility driver. Antalya and Mugla are considered to be the two regions with the highest incoming mobility related to the seasonal work opportunities in the field of tourism, and Rize, Ordu, Giresun, Nigde, and Malatya for agriculture. As already mentioned, vulnerable groups such as refugees can be difficult to track with mobile phones. Vulnerable groups may also be exploited for cheap, or even free, labour in high-risk scenarios.

Bruckschen et al. (2019) proposed a framework to detect fine-grained socioeconomic occurrences with a limited training dataset. The authors used CDRs to spot

---

[6] EM-DAT - The International Disaster Database, https://www.emdat.be/
[7] International Labour Organisation, https://www.ilo.org/global/lang--en/index.htm

potentially undeclared employment of refugees in Turkey by analysing seasonal migration patterns in two scenarios: the hazelnut harvest in Ordu and the construction of Istanbul's third airport. In their study, work-related commuting patterns suggesting potential undeclared employment emerged.

Olivieri *et al.* (2020) analysed mobile phone data, used in combination with household survey data, to measure the impact of the Venezuelan migrants in Ecuador on the labour market. In this case, CDRs were used to associate mobile phones held by Venezuelans with a census tract that most likely contains their home location. The authors found that regions with higher inflows of Venezuelans do not affect the labour market or employment. In contrast, low-educated Ecuadorian workers in these regions had a reduction in employment quality and earning.

In Nigeria, mobile phones were leveraged to measure the impact of technology accessibility for labour migrants (Aker *et al.*, 2011). This study showed that having access to information and communications technology increases the probability of rural to urban migrations. Such patterns are primarily due to increased communication with social networks (e.g., information on the labour market and work opportunities).

Conversely, Ciacci *et al.* (2020) showed that having access to mobile phone signals reduces the probability of migration by members of a household. This is due to the positive effects of mobile phones on the labour market and access to well-being. In this paper, however, mobile phone signal access was not measured with mobile phone data, but with a survey.

Other uses of mobile phone data

While the works mentioned above target a specific definition or aspect of migration, other relevant papers use mobile phone data to tackle additional migration-related phenomena, such as internal migration and mobile phones as an alternative data source to official statistics. In this section we summarise the most relevant among such papers.

Deville *et al.* (2014) analysed mobile phone data to estimate the population density at a national and seasonal scale in Portugal and France. This paper contains important insights on how to map a population by time and, therefore, to highlight temporal shifts that may be related to some types of internal migration. Similarly, Furletti *et al.* (2014) used mobile phone data to observe inter-city mobility patterns. Other studies used mobile phone data as a potential alternative to national statistics in developing economies, such as Namibia (Lai *et al.*, 2019) and Rwanda (Blumenstock, 2012).

The WorldPop project (Tatem, 2017) integrated mobile phone data with censuses, surveys, and other data sources to estimate the population density worldwide with a spatial granularity of 100 m × 100 m cells. Finally, Chi *et al.* (2020) provided a general framework to detect migration events. The authors empirically validated their approach using Twitter data for the United States and mobile phone data in Rwanda.

Mobile phone data for migration: Challenges and limitations

While CDRs have the potential to enable us to overcome many of the intrinsic limitations of traditional methods (e.g., surveys), such as infrequent sampling and high costs, they present specific challenges that need to be addressed before this type of data can be used effectively to measure and model human migration. In this section we highlight the main limitations of leveraging mobile network data in the context of human migrations. These limitations are different, including technical, regulatory, financial, and ethical dimensions. Our goal is to highlight that such limitations should be carefully considered when using this type of data for migration-related purposes.

Technical challenges

There are numerous technical challenges posed by analysing mobile network data for migration; the following is a summary of the most prominent ones. A more detailed discussion on some of these limitations is presented in Chapter 2 (Salah et al., 2022).

Geographic and temporal resolution

While CDRs might be available for a large portion of the population, their spatial granularity depends on the geographic density of antennas, which, in turn, is proportional to the density of the population served by those antennas. Thus, the coverage of an antenna might range from a few kilometres in rural areas to 100 metres in urban areas. Figure 4.1 shows an example of regions covered by antennas in a city. As illustrated in this figure, the difference in coverage area between antenna 7 and antenna 2 stands out.

In terms of temporal resolution, CDRs are event based, which means that the data are only generated when the phone is used (making/receiving a phone call or sending/receiving an SMS). There are no data related to the customers' behaviours when they do not interact with their devices. Thus, the temporal granularity of the CDRs depends on the intensity of usage of the mobile phones by the customers, leading to demographic and socioeconomic differences which affect the representativeness of the data, as explained below. This limitation is partially solved by the so-called extended detail records (XDRs). XDRs measure the number of bytes downloaded/uploaded at each antenna. Thus, they are dramatically less sparse temporally than CDR data but have rarely been analysed for migration purposes.

Representativeness of the data

Understanding the representativeness of the data is of paramount importance when modelling migrations. Mobile phone data are known to be biased: users are unevenly distributed by demography, geography, and socioeconomic groups (Arai *et al.*, 2016; Wesolowski *et al.*, 2012, 2013). For example, Sekara *et al.* (2019) highlighted that in Turkey in 2018 the mobile phone subscriber penetration was 65%, showing that 35% of Turks do not have a SIM registered to their name. In other words, we have individuals with multiple SIMs and others with no SIM. Other studies highlight that tracking particular portions of the population may pose significant challenges. For example, in their study concerning the spread of malaria, Marshall *et al.* (2016) highlighted the potential biases of tracking people using mobile phones in regions of sub-Saharan Africa. There, men are more likely to be mobile phone owners, phone sharing is common among rural women, and many individuals use multiple SIM cards due to non-overlapping provider coverage. Similar biases have shown to be a key challenge in tracking children in Turkey (Sekara *et al.*, 2019). Other issues related to the representativeness of mobile phone data have been investigated by Arai *et al.* (2016).

Data integration

Combining data from different sources and/or countries/regions is especially relevant when dealing with migration. Whenever people cross a border, their mobile phones switch to roaming on the infrastructures of different operators. Hence, modelling the behaviour of international migrants requires significant economic effort for researchers who would need to buy the data or establish partnerships with multiple companies. Moreover, substantial technical effort is necessary to integrate CDRs from different sources, with potentially different biases and temporal and spatial resolutions. For instance, while mobile phone records in Kenya are an excellent proxy for mobility, regardless of socioeconomic factors (Wesolowski *et al.*, 2013), mobile phone data in Rwanda are a good proxy only for the mobility of wealthy and educated men (Blumenstock and Eagle, 2012). In general, integrating data with very different levels of representativeness poses significant challenges.

Timeliness of the data

When dealing with migration, an essential goal of researchers and organisations is to provide timely insights on the situation of migrants. However, real-time access to CDRs has proven to be very difficult and remains an open challenge. Having such an access model would require institutional partnerships with telecommunications (telco) operators and significant investments in infrastructures and mechanisms to guarantee security and privacy (Pastor-Escuredo *et al.*, 2019). Founded by the MIT

Media Lab, Imperial College, London, Orange, the World Economic Forum, Telefonica, and the Data-Pop Alliance, OPAL aims to provide open-source tools to unlock the potential of private sector data (to date, mainly mobile phone data, as in the case of the OPAL for telco program developed by the Flowminder Foundation since late 2021) for public good purposes by 'sending the code to the data' in a safe, participatory, and sustainable manner (Oehmichen et al., 2019; Lepri et al., 2018).

Ethical, regulatory, and financial challenges

In this section we touch upon the ethical, regulatory, and financial challenges that were discussed in detail in Chapter 2 (Salah et al., 2022), with a focus on mobile phone data.

Ethical challenges

The broad adoption of mobile phones has opened new regulatory and ethical challenges. As an example, with 67% of the world population having a subscription with a mobile phone operator, it would be possible to implement massive surveillance projects by tracking such devices. Ethical challenges may have a tremendous impact particularly on communities or groups that are already vulnerable, as in the case of migrants. For instance, mobile phone data may be of critical importance to help policy-makers or international organisations take actions to support migrants. However, the same data can also be used for non-social-good purposes such as discrimination, to stand in the way of migrants, and many others. For this reason, guaranteeing the ethical usage of data is a significant challenge. Competitions such as D4R, as an example of data access policies, have implemented a scientific committee and a project evaluation committee aiming to also evaluate the ethical aspects of the submitted research proposals (Salah et al., 2019b). Data were made available only after the approval of such committees. Another discussion on ethical challenges using mobile phone data especially for analysing vulnerable communities is presented in Taylor (2016) using the Data for Development challenge based in Côte d'Ivoire as a case study. A perspective on ethical challenges focusing on migration can be found in Vinck et al. (2019); Salah et al. (2022).

Privacy and regulatory challenges

Privacy represents a fundamental right in modern society. Even if the data shared by the operators are aggregated and de-identified, there might be ways to re-identify a user depending on aggregation and anonymisation tools and the procedures used to prepare the dataset (de Montjoye et al., 2013).

In general, to avoid privacy issues the data are collected and shared without including names, phone numbers, or identifying information. In some cases, some sociodemographic characteristics of users may be associated with CDRs. Moreover, in theory the users involved in the studies must agree to sharing their data for each specific usage. In practice, for example in the case of refugees, people may not have full control over how their data are collected and stored by authorities or organisations (Vinck *et al.*, 2019).

To guarantee people's privacy, authorities started to design frameworks such as the GDPR in Europe, CCPA in California, and many others to ensure privacy for everyone.

Companies also use such frameworks for sharing data. However, there are cases in which countries do not have frameworks to govern the release of data. This is the case of the D4D Challenge in Côte d'Ivore (de Montjoye *et al.*, 2014). Unlike the other states in West Africa that were using the same data protection regularities used in France at the time of the competition, Côte d'Ivoire did not have a data protection regulation. In that case, data have been released using a non-disclosure agreement between the researchers and the telco company. The agreement, in this case, was also the only commitment to privacy and data protection (Taylor, 2016).

Difficulty of access and lack of financially sustainable models

CDRs are privately held by telecommunication companies. While several mobile phone datasets have been shared with researchers and practitioners in the context of data challenges (Salah *et al.*, 2019b; Blondel *et al.*, 2012), they are generally not publicly available. Even if the data are fully anonymized, aggregated, and only meant to be used for public interest purposes, access to this type of data has proven difficult. Recognising the value that different types of privately held data could have for social good, in 2018 the European Commission created a high-level expert group on business-to-government data sharing.[8] In February 2020 this group published their report (High-Level Expert Group on Business-to-Government Data Sharing, 2020), which put forward several recommendations to foster an environment where privately held data could be leveraged by the public sector for public interest purposes. Similarly to other privately held datasets (e.g., financial data and data from social platforms and digital products), the difficulties related to accessing mobile data result in (1) high costs to scientists and practitioners who need to pay to access the data, and (2) lack of reproducibility of the works based on the analysis of such proprietary datasets. In addition to the barriers mentioned before, there is also a lack of financially sustainable business models to support companies in data sharing efforts for the public interest.

---

[8] European Commission: Commission appoints Expert Group on Business-to-Government Data Sharing, https://digital-strategy.ec.europa.eu/en/news/commission-appoints-expert-group-business-government-data-sharing

Conclusion

Nowadays, more people than ever before are on the move. Policy-makers face tremendous issues in developing evidence-driven policies to address the challenges associated with migrations. In this context, mobile phones are the most widely adopted piece of technology today, with more than 5.2 billion subscribers and a penetration rate of the 103%. Hence, pseudonymised, aggregated, and passively collected mobile data have the potential to help shed light on the living conditions of migrants, providing relevant insights to policy-makers, international organisations, and humanitarian actors. In this chapter we have described the most commonly used types of mobile data, together with their peculiarities and limitations. Next, we provided an overview of how these types of data have been used to monitor the mobility of migrants and other aspects of their life, including their integration, access to services, and working conditions. We are excited about the opportunities that mobile phone data bring to enable us to better understand this complex problem. While mobile phone data are not exempt from limitations, it is a valuable tool to complement existing data sources and contribute to achieving our vision of evidence-driven policy-making. As mobile phone penetration increases, we are hopeful for a future where everybody counts and is counted.

References

Aker, J. C., *et al.* (2011), 'Mobiles and mobility: The effect of mobile phones on migration in Niger', *in Proceedings of the German Development Economics Conference, Berlin 2011*, number 2, Verein für Socialpolitik, Research Committee Development Economics.

Alfeo, A. L., Cimino, M. G., Lepri, B., and Vaglini, G. (2019), 'Using call data and stigmergic similarity to assess the integration of Syrian refugees in Turkey', *in* A. A. Salah, A. Pentland, B. Lepri, and E. Letouzé, eds, *Guide to Mobile Data Analytics in Refugee Scenarios*, Springer, New York, 165–78.

Alışık, S. T., Aksel, D. B., Yantaç, A. E., Kayi, İ., Salman, S., İçduygu, A., Çay, D., Baruh, L., and Bensason, I. (2019), 'Seasonal labor migration among Syrian refugees and urban deep map for integration in Turkey', *in* A. A. Salah, A. Pentland, B. Lepri, and E. Letouzé, eds, *Guide to Mobile Data Analytics in Refugee Scenarios*, Springer, New York, 305–28.

Altuncu, M. T., Kaptaner, A. S., and Sevencan, N. (2019), 'Optimizing the access to healthcare services in dense refugee hosting urban areas: A case for Istanbul', *in* A. A. Salah, A. Pentland, B. Lepri, and E. Letouzé, eds, *Guide to Mobile Data Analytics in Refugee Scenarios*, Springer, New York, 403–16.

Andrienko, G., *et al.* (2020), '(So) Big Data and the transformation of the city', *International Journal of Data Science and Analytics* 11, 311–40.

Andris, C., Godfrey, B., Maitland, C., and McGee, M. (2019), 'The built environment and Syrian refugee integration in Turkey: An analysis of mobile phone data', *in Proceedings of the 3rd ACM SIGSPATIAL International Workshop on Geospatial Humanities*, 1–7.

Arai, A., Fan, Z., Matekenya, D., and Shibasaki, R. (2016), 'Comparative perspective of human behavior patterns to uncover ownership bias among mobile phone users', *ISPRS International Journal of Geo-Information* 5(6), 85.

Bakker, M. A., et al. (2019), 'Measuring fine-grained multidimensional integration using mobile phone metadata: The case of Syrian refugees in Turkey', in A. A. Salah, A. Pentland, B. Lepri, and E. Letouzé, eds, *Guide to Mobile Data Analytics in Refugee Scenarios*, Springer, New York, 123–40.

Barbosa, H., Barthelemy, M., Ghoshal, G., James, C. R., Lenormand, M., Louail, T., Menezes, R., Ramasco, J. J., Simini, F., and Tomasini, M. (2018), 'Human mobility: Models and applications', *Physics Reports* 734, 1–74.

Barlacchi, G., De Nadai, M., Larcher, R., Casella, A., Chitic, C., Torrisi, G., Antonelli, F., Vespignani, A., Pentland, A., and Lepri, B. (2015), 'A multi-source dataset of urban life in the city of Milan and the Province of Trentino', *Scientific Data* 2(1), 1–15.

Beduschi, A. (2017), 'The big data of international migration: Opportunities and challenges for states under international human rights law', *Georgetown Journal of International Law* 49, 981.

Beine, M., Bertinelli, L., Cömertpay, R., Litina, A., and Maystadt, J.-F. (2021), 'A gravity analysis of refugee mobility using mobile phone data', *Journal of Development Economics* 150, 102618.

Beine, M., Bertinelli, L., Cömertpay, R., Litina, A., Maystadt, J.-F., and Zou, B. (2019), 'Refugee mobility: Evidence from phone data in Turkey', in A. A. Salah, A. Pentland, B. Lepri, and E. Letouzé, eds, *Guide to Mobile Data Analytics in Refugee Scenarios*, Springer, New York, 433–49.

Bengtsson, L., Lu, X., Thorson, A., Garfield, R., and Von Schreeb, J. (2011), 'Improved response to disasters and outbreaks by tracking population movements with mobile phone network data: A post-earthquake geospatial study in Haiti', *PLOS Med* 8(8), e1001083.

Bertoli, S., Cintia, P., Giannotti, F., Madinier, E., Ozden, C., Packard, M., Pedreschi, D., Rapoport, H., Sîrbu, A., and Speciale, B. (2019), 'Integration of Syrian refugees: Insights from D4R, media events and housing market data', in A. A. Salah, A. Pentland, B. Lepri, and E. Letouzé, eds, *Guide to Mobile Data Analytics in Refugee Scenarios*, Springer, New York, 179–99.

Blondel, V. D., Decuyper, A., and Krings, G. (2015), 'A survey of results on mobile phone datasets analysis', *EPJ Data Science* 4(1), 10.

Blondel, V. D., Esch, M., Chan, C., Clerot, F., Deville, P., Huens, E., Morlot, F., Smoreda, Z., and Ziemlicki, C. (2012), 'Data for development: The D4D challenge on mobile phone data', arXiv:1210.0137.

Blumenstock, J. E. (2012), 'Inferring patterns of internal migration from mobile phone call records: Evidence from Rwanda', *Information Technology for Development* 18(2), 107–25.

Blumenstock, J. E. and Eagle, N. (2012), 'Divided we call: Disparities in access and use of mobile phones in Rwanda', *Information Technologies & International Development* 8(2), 1–16.

Borkert, M., Fisher, K. E., and Yafi, E. (2018), 'The best, the worst, and the hardest to find: How people, mobiles, and social media connect migrants in (to) Europe', *Social Media+ Society* 4(1), 2056305118764428.

Bosetti, P., Poletti, P., Stella, M., Lepri, B., Merler, S., and De Domenico, M. (2020), 'Heterogeneity in social and epidemiological factors determines the risk of measles outbreaks', *Proceedings of the National Academy of Sciences* 117(48), 30118–25.

Boy, J., Pastor-Escuredo, D., Macguire, D., Jimenez, R. M., and Luengo-Oroz, M. (2019), 'Towards an understanding of refugee segregation, isolation, homophily and ultimately integration in Turkey using call detail records', *in* A. A. Salah, A. Pentland, B. Lepri, and E. Letouzé, eds, *Guide to Mobile Data Analytics in Refugee Scenarios*, Springer, New York, 141–64.

Bozcaga, T., Christia, F., Harwood, E., Daskalakis, C., and Papademetriou, C. (2019), 'Syrian refugee integration in Turkey: Evidence from call detail records', *in* A. A. Salah, A. Pentland, B. Lepri, and E. Letouzé, eds, *Guide to Mobile Data Analytics in Refugee Scenarios*, Springer, New York, 223–49.

Bruckschen, F., Koebe, T., Ludolph, M., Marino, M. F., and Schmid, T. (2019), 'Refugees in undeclared employment: A case study in Turkey, *in* A. A. Salah, A. Pentland, B. Lepri, and E. Letouzé, eds, *Guide to Mobile Data Analytics in Refugee Scenarios*, Springer, New York, 329–46.

Charmarkeh, H. (2013), 'Social media usage, tahriib (migration), and settlement among Somali refugees in France', *Refuge: Canada's Journal on Refugees* 29(1), 43–52.

Chi, G., Lin, F., Chi, G., and Blumenstock, J. (2020), 'A general approach to detecting migration events in digital trace data', *PLOS One* 15(10), e0239408.

Ciacci, R., García-Hombrados, J., and Zainudeen, A. (2020), 'Mobile phone network and migration: Evidence from Myanmar', Technical report, Max Planck Institute for Demographic Research, Rostock, Germany.

Crawley, H., Jones, K., McMahon, S., Duvell, F., and Sigona, N. (2016), 'Unpacking a rapidly changing scenario: Migration flows, routes and trajectories across the Mediterranean', Technical report, Unravelling the Mediterranean Migration Crisis (MEDMIG) Research Brief No. 1.

Currarini, S., Matheson, J., and Vega-Redondo, F. (2016), 'A simple model of homophily in social networks', *European Economic Review* 90, 18–39.

de Montjoye, Y.-A., *et al.* (2018), 'On the privacy-conscientious use of mobile phone data', *Scientific Data* 5(1), 1–6.

de Montjoye, Y.-A., Hidalgo, C. A., Verleysen, M., and Blondel, V. D. (2013), 'Unique in the crowd: The privacy bounds of human mobility', *Scientific Reports* 3(1), 1–5.

de Montjoye, Y.-A., Smoreda, Z., Trinquart, R., Ziemlicki, C., and Blondel, V. D. (2014), 'D4D-Senegal: The second mobile phone data for development challenge', arXiv:1407.4885.

Deville, P., Linard, C., Martin, S., Gilbert, M., Stevens, F. R., Gaughan, A. E., Blondel, V. D., and Tatem, A. J. (2014), 'Dynamic population mapping using mobile phone data', *Proceedings of the National Academy of Sciences* 111(45), 15888–93.

Freeman, L. C. (1978), 'Segregation in social networks', *Sociological Methods & Research* 6(4), 411–29.

Frydenlund, E., Şener, M. Y., Gore, R., Boshuijzen-van Burken, C., Bozdag, E., and de Kock, C. (2019), 'Characterizing the mobile phone use patterns of refugee-hosting provinces in Turkey', *in* A. A. Salah, A. Pentland, B. Lepri, and E. Letouzé, eds, *Guide to Mobile Data Analytics in Refugee Scenarios*, Springer, New York, 417–31.

Furletti, B., Gabrielli, L., Giannotti, F., Milli, L., Nanni, M., Pedreschi, D., Vivio, R., and Garofalo, G. (2014), 'Use of mobile phone data to estimate mobility flows. Measuring urban population and inter-city mobility using big data in an integrated approach', *in Proceedings of the 47th Meeting of the Italian Statistical Society*.

Gonzalez, M. C., Hidalgo, C. A., and Barabasi, A.-L. (2008), 'Understanding individual human mobility patterns', *Nature* 453(7196), 779–82.

Graser, A. (2019), 'Movingpandas: Efficient structures for movement data in Python', *GIForum* 1, 54–68.

Grossi, V., Rapisarda, B., Giannotti, F., and Pedreschi, D. (2018), 'Data science at SoBigData: The European research infrastructure for social mining and big data analytics', *International Journal of Data Science and Analytics* 6(3), 205–16.

GSMA Intelligence (2020), 'The mobile economy', Technical report, GSMA Intelligence.

Henry, S., Schoumaker, B., and Beauchemin, C. (2004), 'The impact of rainfall on the first out-migration: A multi-level event-history analysis in Burkina Faso', *Population and Environment* 25(5), 423–60.

High-Level Expert Group on Business-to-Government Data Sharing (2020), 'Towards a European strategy on business-to-government data sharing for the public interest', Technical report, European Commission.

Hu, W., He, R., Cao, J., Zhang, L., Uznalioglu, H., Akyamac, A., and Phadke, C. (2019), 'Quantified understanding of Syrian refugee integration in Turkey', in A. A. Salah, A. Pentland, B. Lepri, and E. Letouzé, eds, *Guide to Mobile Data Analytics in Refugee Scenarios*, Springer, New York, 201–21.

Hughes, C., Zagheni, E., Abel, G. J., Sorichetta, A., Wi'sniowski, A., Weber, I., and Tatem, A. J. (2016), 'Inferring migrations: Traditional methods and new approaches based on mobile phone, social media, and other big data: Feasibility study on inferring (labour) mobility and migration in the European Union from big data and social media data', Technical report, European Commission project #VT/2014/093.

International Labour Organization (2019), 'Mobile women and mobile phones: Women migrant workers' use of information and communication technologies in ASEAN', Technical report, International Labour Organization.

International Organization for Migration – UN Migration Agency (2018), 'Big data and migration. How data innovation can serve migration policymaking.', Technical report, International Organization for Migration – UN Migration Agency.

International Telecommunication Union (2020), 'Measuring digital development 2020', Technical report, International Telecommunication Union.

IOM-MECC (2019), 'MECLEP: Migration, environment and climate change: Evidence for policy', Technical report, IOM Migration, Environment and Climate Change (MECC) Division.

Isaacman, S., Frias-Martinez, V., and Frias-Martinez, E. (2018), 'Modeling human migration patterns during drought conditions in La Guajira, Colombia', *in Proceedings of the 1st ACM SIGCAS Conference on Computing and Sustainable Societies*, 1–9.

Kılıç, Ö. O., Akyol, M. A., Işık, O., Kılıç, B. G., Aydınoğlu, A. U., Surer, E., Düzgün, H. Ş., Kalaycıoğlu, S., and Taşkaya-Temizel, T. (2019), 'The use of big mobile data to gain multilayered insights for Syrian refugee crisis', in A. A. Salah, A. Pentland, B. Lepri, and E. Letouzé, eds, *Guide to Mobile Data Analytics in Refugee Scenarios*, Springer, New York, 347–79.

Koebe, T. (2020), 'Better coverage, better outcomes? Mapping mobile network data to official statistics using satellite imagery and radio propagation modelling', *PLOS One* 15(11), e0241981.

Lai, S., zu Erbach-Schoenberg, E., Pezzulo, C., Ruktanonchai, N. W., Sorichetta, A., Steele, J., Li, T., Dooley, C. A., and Tatem, A. J. (2019), 'Exploring the use of mobile phone data for national migration statistics', *Palgrave Communications* 5(1), 1–10.

Lepri, B., Oliver, N., Letouzé, E., Pentland, A., and Vinck, P. (2018), 'Fair, transparent, and accountable algorithmic decision-making processes', *Philosophy & Technology* 31(4), 611–27.

Loaiza, I, Novak, M., Morales, A. J., and Pentland, A. (2020), 'Looking for a better future: Modeling migrant mobility', *Applied Network Science* 5(1), 1–19.

Lu, X., *et al.* (2016a), 'Unveiling hidden migration and mobility patterns in climate stressed regions: A longitudinal study of six million anonymous mobile phone users in Bangladesh', *Global Environmental Change* 38, 1–7.

Lu, X., *et al.* (2016b), 'Detecting climate adaptation with mobile network data in Bangladesh: Anomalies in communication, mobility and consumption patterns during cyclone Mahasen', *Climatic Change* 138(3), 505–19.

Luca, M., Barlacchi, G., Lepri, B., and Pappalardo, L. (2020), 'Deep learning for human mobility: A survey on data and models', arXiv:2012.02825.

Mamei, M., Cilasun, S. M., Lippi, M., Pancotto, F., and Tümen, S. (2019), 'Improve education opportunities for better integration of Syrian refugees in Turkey', *in* A. A. Salah, A. Pentland, B. Lepri, and E. Letouzé, eds, *Guide to Mobile Data Analytics in Refugee Scenarios*, Springer, New York, 381–402.

Mancini, T., Sibilla, F., Argiropoulos, D., Rossi, M., and Everri, M. (2019), 'The opportunities and risks of mobile phones for refugees' experience: A scoping review', *PLOS One* 14(12), e0225684.

Marquez, N., Garimella, K., Toomet, O., Weber, I. G., and Zagheni, E. (2019), 'Segregation and sentiment: Estimating refugee segregation and its effects using digital trace data', *in* A. A. Salah, A. Pentland, B. Lepri, and E. Letouzé, eds, *Guide to Mobile Data Analytics in Refugee Scenarios*, Springer, New York, 265–82.

Marshall, J. M., *et al.* (2016), 'Key traveller groups of relevance to spatial malaria transmission: A survey of movement patterns in four sub-Saharan African countries', *Malaria Journal* 15(1), 1–12.

Massey, D. S. and Denton, N. A. (1988), 'The dimensions of residential segregation', *Social Forces* 67(2), 281–315.

Meze-Hausken, E. (2000), 'Migration caused by climate change: How vulnerable are people in dryland areas?', *Mitigation and Adaptation Strategies for Global Change* 5(4), 379–406.

Moumni, B., Frias-Martinez, V., and Frias-Martinez, E. (2013), 'Characterizing social response to urban earthquakes using cell-phone network data: The 2012 oaxaca earthquake', *in Proceedings of the 2013 ACM Conference on Pervasive and Ubiquitous Computing Adjunct Publication*, Association for Computing Machinery, New York, NY, 1199–208.

Neubauer, G., Huber, H., Vogl, A., Jager, B., Preinerstorfer, A., Schirnhofer, S., Schimak, G., and Havlik, D. (2015), 'On the volume of geo-referenced tweets and their relationship to events relevant for migration tracking', *in* R. Denzer, R. M. Argent, G. Schimak, and J. Hřebíček, eds, *Environmental Software Systems: Infrastructures, Services and Applications*, Springer, New York, pp. 520–30.

Oehmichen, A., Jain, S., Gadotti, A., and de Montjoye, Y.-A. (2019), 'OPAL: High performance platform for large-scale privacy-preserving location data analytics', *in Proceedings of 2019 IEEE International Conference on Big Data*, 1332–42.

Olivieri, S., Ortega, F., Carranza, E., and Rivadeneira, A. (2020), *The Labor Market Effects of Venezuelan Migration in Ecuador*, The World Bank.

Pappalardo, L., Ferres, L., Sacasa, M., Cattuto, C., and Bravo, L. (2020), 'An individual-level ground truth dataset for home location detection', arXiv:2010.08814.

Pappalardo, L., Simini, F., Barlacchi, G., and Pellungrini, R. (2019), 'scikit-mobility: A Python library for the analysis, generation and risk assessment of mobility data', arXiv:1907.07062.

Pastor-Escuredo, D., Imai, A., Luengo-Oroz, M., and Macguire, D. (2019), 'Call detail records to obtain estimates of forcibly displaced populations', in A. A. Salah, A. Pentland, B. Lepri, and E. Letouzé, eds, *Guide to Mobile Data Analytics in Refugee Scenarios*, Springer, New York, 29–52.

Pastor-Escuredo, D., *et al.* (2014), 'Flooding through the lens of mobile phone activity', *IEEE Global Humanitarian Technology Conference (GHTC 2014)*, 279–86.

Poushter, J., *et al.* (2016), 'Smartphone ownership and internet usage continues to climb in emerging economies', *Pew Research Center* 22, 1–44.

Power, D., Thom, M., Gray, J., Albert, M., Delaporte, S., Li, T., Harrison, J., Greenhalgh, J., Thorne, N., and Bengtsson, L. (2020), 'Flowkit: Unlocking the power of mobile data for humanitarian and development purposes', Technical report, Flowminder; Digital Impact Alliance; WorldPop.

Pradhan, P. K. (2004), 'Population growth, migration and urbanisation. Environmental consequences in Kathmandu Valley, Nepal', in J. D. Unruh, M. Krol, and N. Kliot, eds, *Environmental Change and its Implications for Population Migration*, Springer, New York, 177–99.

Rosvold, E. L. and Buhaug, H. (2021), 'GDIS, a global dataset of geocoded disaster locations', *Scientific Data* 8(1), 1–7.

Sakaki, T., Okazaki, M., and Matsuo, Y. (2010), 'Earthquake shakes twitter users: Real-time event detection by social sensors', in *Proceedings of the 19th International Conference on World Wide Web*, 851–60.

Salah, A. A., Canca, C., and Erman, B. (2022), 'Ethical and legal concerns on data science for large scale human mobility', in A. A. Salah, E. E. Korkmaz, and T. Bircan, eds, *Data Science for Migration and Mobility*, Proceedings of the British Academy, British Academy / Oxford University Press, London, UK.

Salah, A. A., Pentland, A., Lepri, B., and Letouzé, E. (2019a), *Guide to Mobile Data Analytics in Refugee Scenarios*, Springer, New York.

Salah, A. A., Pentland, A., Lepri, B., Letouzé, E., de Montjoye, Y.-A., Dong, X., Dağdelen, Ö., and Vinck, P. (2019b), 'Introduction to the data for refugees challenge on mobility of Syrian refugees in Turkey', in A. A. Salah, A. Pentland, B. Lepri, and E. Letouzé, eds, *Guide to Mobile Data Analytics in Refugee Scenarios*, Springer, New York, 3–27.

Salah, A. A., Pentland, A., Lepri, B., Letouzé, E., Vinck, P., de Montjoye, Y.-A., Dong, X., and Dagdelen, O. (2018), 'Data for refugees: The D4R challenge on mobility of Syrian refugees in Turkey', arXiv:1807.00523.

Salman, F. S., Yücel, E., Kayı, İ., Turper-Alışık, S., and Coşkun, A. (2021), 'Modeling mobile health service delivery to Syrian migrant farm workers using call record data', *Socio-Economic Planning Sciences* 77(1), 101005.

Schneider, C. M., Belik, V., Couronné, T., Smoreda, Z., and González, M. C. (2013), 'Unravelling daily human mobility motifs', *Journal of The Royal Society Interface* 10(84), 20130246.

Sekara, V., Omodei, E., Healy, L., Beise, J., Hansen, C., You, D., Blume, S., and Garcia-Herranz, M. (2019), 'Mobile phone data for children on the move: Challenges and opportunities', in A. A. Salah, A. Pentland, B. Lepri, and E. Letouzé, eds, *Guide to Mobile Data Analytics in Refugee Scenarios*, Springer, New York, 53–66.

Simini, F., González, M. C., Maritan, A., and Barabási, A.-L. (2012), 'A universal model for mobility and migration patterns', *Nature* 484(7392), 96–100.

Sîrbu, A., *et al.* (2021), 'Human migration: The big data perspective', *International Journal of Data Science and Analytics* 11(4), 341–60.

Smets, K. (2018), 'The way Syrian refugees in Turkey use media: Understanding "connected refugees" through a non-media-centric and local approach', *Communications* 43(1), 113–23.

Tatem, A. J. (2017), 'WorldPop, open data for spatial demography', *Scientific Data* 4(1), 1–4.

Taylor, L. (2016), 'No place to hide? The ethics and analytics of tracking mobility using mobile phone data', *Environment and Planning D: Society and Space* 34(2), 319–36.

UNHCR (2016), 'Connecting refugees: How internet and mobile connectivity can improve refugee well-being and transform humanitarian action', Technical report, UNHCR.

UNHCR (2020), 'What is a refugee?', available at https://www.unhcr.org/what-is-a-refugee.html

Vinck, P., Pham, P. N., and Salah, A. A. (2019), ' "Do no harm" in the age of big data: Data, ethics, and the refugees', *in* A. A. Salah, A. Pentland, B. Lepri, and E. Letouzé, eds, *Guide to Mobile Data Analytics in Refugee Scenarios*, Springer, New York, 87–99.

Wall, M., Otis Campbell, M., and Janbek, D. (2017), 'Syrian refugees and information precarity', *New Media & Society* 19(2), 240–54.

Wang, Q. and Taylor, J. E. (2014), 'Quantifying human mobility perturbation and resilience in Hurricane Sandy', *PLOS One* 9(11), e112608.

Wesolowski, A., Eagle, N., Noor, A. M., Snow, R. W., and Buckee, C. O. (2012), 'Heterogeneous mobile phone ownership and usage patterns in Kenya', *PLOS One* 7(4), e35319.

Wesolowski, A., Eagle, N., Noor, A. M., Snow, R. W., and Buckee, C. O. (2013), 'The impact of biases in mobile phone ownership on estimates of human mobility', *Journal of the Royal Society Interface* 10(81), 20120986.

Zipf, G. K. (1946), 'The $P_1 P_2/D$ hypothesis: On the intercity movement of persons', *American Sociological Review* 11(6), 677–86.

5

Analysing Refugees' Secondary Mobility Using Mobile Phone Call Detail Records

HARALD STERLY AND LARS WIRKUS

Introduction

IN THIS CHAPTER we provide insights into the process of human mobility analysis using call detail records (CDRs). It is written from the perspective of migration and mobility researchers with a more qualitative research background, and the data science part should be quite accessible. We therefore believe that the chapter can be particularly helpful for those who come from a similar background, which is the case for many migration researchers. In this introduction we start with a brief background of CDR analysis for mobility and migration research, then give some information on the context of Syrian refugees in Turkey, and provide an overview of data and research ethics, as we believe this is important in this case. Readers familiar with Luca *et al.* (Chapter 4 in this volume) can skip the first part of this section. In the main part we juxtapose our steps in data analysis with ethical considerations that we have incorporated during the process: we give a short 'portrait' of the data and its preparation, and show how we derived general, spatial, and temporal information from the CDR data. We finally reflect on the ethical aspects of voluntariness and informed consent, do no harm, and bias and representation. Code (in R) and simulated data can be retrieved from the book's accompanying web page.

Mobile phone data and mobility analysis

Mobile phones, and smartphones in particular, are among the most important assets for people on the move, especially for those forcibly displaced, as they are often deprived of access to key information resources. Phones enable and guarantee access to necessary or even vital information on destinations, routes, and security issues before moving, help to cope with the numerous challenges that arise during the journeys, and facilitate digital connectivity and mutual support within refugee communities (Dekker *et al.*, 2018; Frouws *et al.*, 2016; Kozlowska, 2015). The importance of information and communication technology (ICT), and of smartphones in particular, is symbolised not least by the term 'smartphone refugee' (Jungbluth, 2017, p. 76). On the downside, digital traces constantly produced by mobile phones can also pose a major risk for people on the run, as these traces could be used to impose control and sanctions on migrants and refugees. Thus, such traces have huge implications for research ethics in the academic mobility studies community and beyond (Taylor *et al.*, 2017).

Whenever a mobile phone is used for calling, texting, or accessing data services, a CDR, or an extended data record (XDR) in the case of data usage, is generated that stores the time and day, duration, type of communication, and the ID of the cellular base transmission station (tower) handling the call request. These data are used for billing purposes by the mobile phone providers. However, these CDRs are also seen as one of the most important new data sources for human mobility research that have emerged in the past decade (Barbosa *et al.*, 2018). CDRs have been applied widely to study mobility in a variety of contexts, such as assessing disaster displacement (e.g., Lu *et al.*, 2016), improving mobility-related data for epidemiological models (see, e.g., Engebretsen *et al.* (2020) for influenza, Finger *et al.* (2016) for cholera), or for monitoring population mobility after restrictions during the Covid-19 pandemic (Oliver *et al.*, 2020). They have served as a basis for improving demographic data in otherwise data-scarce environments (e.g., Lai *et al.*, 2019) and for urban transportation planning (see, for example, Steenbruggen *et al.* (2013) for a systematic review). Blondel *et al.* (2015) and Luca *et al.* (Chapter 4, this volume) provide systematic overviews of the use of CDRs in a variety of different areas.

A range of approaches and metrics have been developed to derive mobility data from CDRs, from 'flat' conceptions of mobility (treating all forms of mobility similarly) to more advanced approaches such as spatiotemporal thresholds (Lai *et al.*, 2019) or matrices of individual trajectories (Zufiria *et al.*, 2018). The Flowminder Foundation provides an extensive list of mobility metrics that can be derived from CDR data, for example home and work locations that are assigned as subscribers' residence and work places, respectively; locations of interest such as main travel routes or hotspots that are visited by many subscribers; subscriber presence as the frequency and regularity of subscribers' visits to a given location; intra-regional and inter-regional travel, as the quantity of subscribers moving within a given region or across regions; and also indicators on data quality such as changes in the number of calls or callers.[1]

However, access for researchers to CDR data remains a major challenge: mobile phone providers are often hesitant to provide CDR data (including derived or aggregated and anonymised data) for scientific purposes for several reasons. First, data

---

[1] See Flowminder COVID-19 Resources: Mobility indicators (https://covid19.flowminder.org/mobility-indicators) for more indicators and more detailed explanations.

protection regulations in many countries (rightly) restrict the storage, usage, and transfer of such data; in addition, even where legally possible, telephone providers might prefer to avoid getting a reputation for giving customer data to third parties. Second, providers increasingly see such data as an economic resource and exploit it for their own sake or through subsidiaries. Third, technical and organisational issues also play a role, as not all providers have the necessary prerequisites to store, process, and make available such data (Oliver et al., 2020).

Institutional and social networks can play an important role here. In recent years, clusters have formed in some countries and locations that do a lot of research on CDR data; in Estonia, for example, where access to digital data is often easier, government institutions have cooperated with mobile operators to improve statistics on tourism and travel. Institutions with a high professional reputation, proven experience, and existing working relationships with mobile service providers are in a better position than others in gaining access to CDR data.

Background: Syrian refugees in Turkey, and the Data for Refugees (D4R) Challenge

Since the onset of the armed conflict in Syria in 2011/2012, many millions of Syrian civilians have fled across the borders; by 2020, Turkey accommodated about 3.5 million of these refugees,[2] making the country the largest host of refugees worldwide. In the early stages of the Syrian conflict and the refugee movement to Turkey, most Syrian refugees were accommodated in camps that the Turkish government had set up close to the Syrian border; many of the refugees later moved onwards to seek employment and better living conditions in other places. At present, the majority of Syrian refugees in Turkey live in towns and cities throughout the country, and in larger urban centres like Istanbul or Ankara (UNHCR, 2019). Although refugees under the status of temporary protection do receive humanitarian assistance and services, their situation remains a matter of concern, including issues of housing, health, education, employment, social integration, and discrimination, among others (Saraçoğlu and Bélanger, 2019; Woods, 2016).

Against this background, Türk Telekom, the Turkish Academic and Research Council (TÜBITAK), and Boğaziçi University, together with other national and international organisations, organised the Data for Refugees (D4R) Challenge,[3] with the aim of exploring the possibilities of phone data for improving the living situation of the refugees. Carefully anonymised CDR data was provided to selected research projects to enable them to conduct research in the five fields of health, education, unemployment, safety, and social integration (Salah et al., 2019b). Data availability and use was restricted to the duration and scope of the respective projects through legally binding usage contracts.

---

[2] The UN Refugee Agency: Registered Syrian Refugees https://data2.unhcr.org/en/situations/syria/location/113
[3] Originally hosted at http://d4r.turktelekom.com.tr/, now accessible at https://web.archive.org/web/20200502180141/http://d4r.turktelekom.com.tr/

As part of the D4R Challenge, the authors of this chapter were involved in a project that explored the extent and spatiotemporal patterns of *secondary mobility* of refugees (see Sterly et al., 2019). Secondary mobility here is understood as the onward movement of refugees from the place of (first) registration to other places. It often poses challenges for humanitarian aid, as it can make it difficult to effectively and efficiently organise and provide services such as shelter, health care, or education, which are usually tied to stationary infrastructures. There is very little research and data about the quantitative extent, destinations, and routes for secondary mobility of refugees; the few existing studies are mainly qualitative in nature (e.g., Skov, 2016; Kvittingen et al., 2019; Tuzi et al., 2019).

In the following sections we introduce the type of data and how it was prepared, present some analytical steps to derive information on spatiotemporal mobility from this data, and some ethical reflections. The research presented here has a certain 'proof-of-concept' quality to it, for several reasons. As we attempt to gain insights into general patterns and trends, it is an exploratory study from the viewpoint of migration and environmental researchers. We did not apply rigorous data science testing methods to control for spurious patterns; instead, we relied on the existing expertise of the research group in these areas. Furthermore, the representativity of the CDR data can be challenged, as the noise sources are difficult to characterise exactly (see also Luca et al., Chapter 4, this volume).

Research and data ethics: Protection of research participants

Data ethics involves the study and evaluation of moral problems related to data, algorithms, and corresponding practices, in order to formulate and enable morally good solutions (Floridi and Taddeo, 2016). Against this definition, key issues posed by the collection and analysis of CDRs as one type of large dataset concern possible re-identification of individuals through data mining, linking, and merging, and reuse of datasets. In addition to the general ethical questions that are raised when using large-scale data, including mobile phone data, for studying social phenomena (see also Salah et al., Chapter 2, this volume), the special research context of the project and the high vulnerability of refugees call for additional reflections and awareness of research and data ethics. The ways in which digital (meta-)data are produced, shared, and used raise new issues of research and data-related ethics that go beyond 'classic' aspects of protecting research subjects (Letouzé et al., 2015). We list some of the main concerns here:

- The concept of *voluntary and informed consent* partially loses its substance, because the use for (specific) research purposes is not foreseeable when the data are created. Although the producers or collectors of the data often obtain the legal right (e.g., in contracts for mobile phone use or for smartphone apps) for the use or transfer of the 'obtained' data, it is difficult to speak of 'informed consent' here (see also Kitchin, 2014). This is a general problem of any secondary use of data, but it is exacerbated by the often widespread transfer of large digital datasets, especially in commercial contexts. In the case of the D4R challenge, it has to be noted that the research use of aggregated and anonymous data was permitted by the communication law of Turkey, as privacy was ensured.

- *Non-identification:* What makes CDRs so valuable is the predictability and uniqueness of individual human behaviour, but that also comes with the risk of 're-identification'. There have been a number of cases where anonymised data could be de-anonymised either through errors in the anonymisation procedures or through combination with other data; a prominent example is the data of 173 million New York taxi rides that were published anonymously in 2013, but could then be quickly attributed to individual drivers and customers (Metcalf and Crawford, 2016).
- *Data security:* Large digital data stocks with a high potential to violate personal rights or be misused, but also with a potentially high commercial value, require particularly careful and thorough protection against unauthorised access or disclosure.
- *Do no harm:* Apart from the potential benefits of big-data analyses (e.g., epidemiology, traffic planning, etc.), such data can also be used by government and commercial actors to monitor and discipline population (groups) (Zook et al., 2017). Scientists must ensure that their work does not result in discrimination or harm, especially for already disadvantaged groups. Results of analyses, but also the generation of new analysis methods and tools, can, for example, contribute to the exclusion of groups from credit, insurance, or health services through profiling or social sorting. If methods and data are unintentionally transferred from their original context, this is also referred to as 'control creep' (Kitchin, 2014).
- *Bias/representation:* The representativity (or lack thereof) of data is also of particular importance in big data. In cases of secondary use of data (for example, when analysing CDRs) it is often unclear to what extent they represent the population in focus. CDRs and their subsequent analytics reflect the market share of the company whose CDRs are being analysed, unless information from different operators can be obtained. This is a (scientific) problem of the external validity of data, but it also concerns ethical aspects, namely the (non-) representation of groups, regions, or structures, rendering them 'invisible' in the otherwise publishable and impactful results (Kitchin, 2014).
- *Group privacy* becomes relevant when the analysis of large-scale digital data affects groups, either already existing groups or algorithmically, ad hoc formed groups, as happens, for example, through profiling (Mittelstadt, 2017). This can put such groups at risk, for example by revealing features that could lead to discrimination, even if the privacy of each individual member is protected. Thus, group privacy is an emergent property and relevant ethical category on its own, between individual privacy and collective interests. Individuals belonging to such a group have a legitimate interest in how and what data on them is collected and what information is produced (Taylor et al., 2017).

- *Delimitation of private/public data:* As a large number of extensive digital datasets are publicly available (e.g., Twitter data, Facebook entries, product reviews, etc.), it is often argued that rules or principles of data protection should not apply to them. This is problematic because the combination of several publicly accessible datasets may allow conclusions to be drawn about otherwise sensitive and private areas of an individual's life (e.g., health status, sexual orientation, political views, etc.) (Kosinski *et al.*, 2013).

In the course of this chapter we will return to three of these aspects (voluntariness/informed consent, do no harm, and bias/representation) and discuss them with regard to their implications for our data analysis and the decisions taken.

Data preparation and analysis, and ethical reflections

A short 'portrait' of the data, and data preparation

For the data challenge project, we were granted access to CDR data of the Turkish mobile operator Türk Telekom for more than 70,000 refugee and non-refugee phone users for the time interval from 1 January 2017 to 31 December 2017. This data was a subsample from a database of about 1.2 million refugee and non-refugee phone users that had been produced from the entire customer base of Türk Telekom in a longer process. This database was established on the one hand to safeguard the privacy and non-traceability of individuals, and on the other to improve representativity; the non-refugee Turkish customers in given administrative areas, for example, were sampled proportionally to the number of refugee callers who were registered in these areas, to allow for comparison. The special feature of the data was a refugee 'flag' that had been assigned to customers who either had an ID number given to refugees or foreigners in Turkey, were registered as customers with a Syrian passport, or had made use of special tariffs reserved for refugees (Salah *et al.*, 2019b). This meant some degree of uncertainty concerning the refugee/non-refugee identity of callers, as there were also Syrian non-refugees among the users with the refugee flag, as well as non-Syrian refugees and migrants.

A total of three datasets were provided in the challenge. *Dataset 1* contained the 'antenna traffic' (i.e., all calls and text messages) between the locations of Türk Telekom's mobile phone base transmission stations; *Dataset 2* was a collection of 26 'real' CDR datasets each containing the anonymised metadata of about 65,000 Türk Telekom users' calls and text messages for two-week periods. In this dataset, users had been resampled every 14 days and the ID numbers were newly reassigned to prevent re-identification through the fine-grained mobility patterns. *Dataset 3* consisted of the calling data for a sample of approximately 55,000 users over the entire 12-month period. In order to prevent re-identification, the spatial resolution of base transmission stations was aggregated to the level of the administrative districts of Turkey (Salah *et al.*, 2019b). About two thirds of the users in Dataset 3 had the status 'refugee'. In addition, two datasets with the geo-coordinates of the approximately 100,000 mobile phone base transmission stations of Türk Telekom and the 973 districts of Turkey were provided. In the following we describe the approach with Dataset 3, because it provided the most comprehensive information for our project, namely on mobility over a longer period of time and over greater distances.

Data preparation

We report the particular steps of data preparation in detail, because they illustrate the kinds of issues large-scale data collection efforts may exhibit. We also want to show that attention needs to be paid to making sure that there are no data issues that will invalidate the results obtained through subsequent analysis. All analysis steps were performed with the open-source software R on a standard desktop computer. Box 5.1 provides a short overview of the data preparation steps commonly used in data science.

First, the data of Dataset 3 were reviewed for consistency as well as for temporal coverage, and some data problems were corrected. For the months of January, February, March, and April, some data was missing (e.g., in February and March, data for incoming calls only included four and eight days, respectively). In some months there was duplicate data that needed to be removed, and the file for the month of September included almost all of the data for August in addition to the September data. The file containing geolocation and other information for the 973 administrative districts could not be assigned to the CDR datasets at first, because reference IDs were missing; these had to be created first. To minimise the gaps in temporal coverage, the separately stored data records for incoming and outgoing telephone calls and text messages were merged. After consolidation, Dataset 3 contained about 56 million entries of the following form:

- CALLER_ID: the randomly assigned identification number of the user; the first digit marks the status (1 = refugee, 2 = non-refugee)
- TIMESTAMP: date and time of calling/texting activities in the format dd-mm-yyyy hh:mm
- DIST_ID: ID number of the district
- PROV_ID: ID number of the province.

Table 5.1 shows an example of the data from Dataset 3. Figure 5.1 shows the number of unique users who called or texted on a given day, for all 365 days of 2017. Some things are worth noting here. First, the numbers of callers flagged as refugees rise between January and September, and then they drop again until the end of the year, while the numbers of non-refugee callers remain more or less stable. Second, the extent of the missing data becomes apparent, with the larger gaps in February and March, as well as in April. Third, some systematic and non-systematic fluctuations in the calling activity or data availability shows up: there seems to be a weekly pattern with weekend drops in calling in both refugee and non-refugee groups; and in June, July, and October there are some larger fluctuations. These fluctuations

Box 5.1 Data preparation

In data science, it is important to work with data collected and processed for a specific purpose, but sometimes it is necessary to work with *secondary data*, such as mobile CDRs, which may initially be prepared for a different purpose. Data preparation is a necessary step to deal with issues of data quality, and requires some insight into the data collection and subsequent modelling. Furthermore, modelling may also impose (or suggest) certain data preprocessing steps, and these can be included in the data preparation.

Missing data To deal with missing data, one needs to know whether missing values are occurring due to a systematic issue, or randomly. Small amounts of missing data may be ignored, but, depending on the model choice, it may be necessary to provide values. These can be selected randomly in the data range, filled with mean or median values of the existing data items, filled with the most frequent value (i.e., the mode, which works well with categorical values but can introduce a bias), filled with the value of the nearest neighbour (which can be sensitive to outliers), or imputed with a regression model. The latter includes sophisticated estimators, such as deep learning, provided that there are enough data points to train them. When doing *data imputation*, it is important to preserve variable relationships (i.e., the correlation structure). If, for example, a variable has a different set of values for males and females in the population, ignoring this during the imputation will create inconsistent results. It is also important to use an *unbiased estimator* for imputation, where the expected value of the estimator is equal to the true value of the estimated parameter. For example, if the age of a subject is a missing value to be imputed, it can be filled by a process that on the average produces the mean sample age.

Data normalisation Especially when combining heterogeneous data sources, normalisation can improve the model stability of numerical methods. Two frequently used methods are *min–max normalisation*, where the data are shifted to the [0, 1] range by subtracting the minimum value and dividing by the difference between the maximum and minimum values, and *z-normalisation*, where the mean is subtracted and the values divided by the standard deviation. In the evaluation of predictive models, it is important to use the training set values for normalising the validation and test sets, otherwise the test set is no longer independent. For explanation-based models, the normalisation may be adapted.

Data augmentation Most machine learning methods are hurt by redundant and highly correlated variables in the analysis, as well as constant variables (i.e., zero variance). Removing these variables may improve modelling. It is also possible to augment the data with variables or samples derived from existing data. This is either performed to improve the generalisation ability of the model (for instance, by adding noisy samples to enhance noise resilience) or to simplify the task of the model (for instance, by adding composite variables at a higher semantic level).

Dealing with outliers Algorithms have different levels of sensitivity to outliers. Pruning or trimming extreme variables can be helpful with generalisation, but this should be done carefully, and with an accompanying analysis of what is being removed and why.

Table 5.1 Example data rows for Dataset 3

CALLER_ID	TIMESTAMP	DIST_ID	PROV_ID
1100016958	13-06-2017 23:33	445	27
2424850506	09-06-2017 23:40	513	34
2768064772	29-06-2017 21:42	108	63
1464108283	18-06-2017 09:00	68	6
⋮	⋮	⋮	⋮

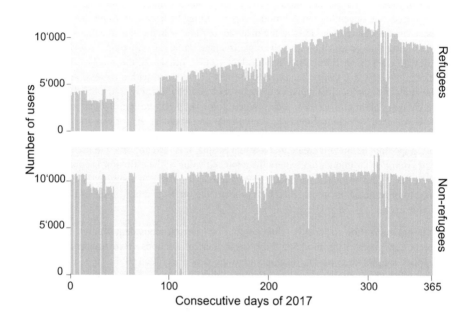

Figure 5.1 Number of unique users who are recorded in Dataset 3 as calling or texting on a given day, for all 365 days of 2017, by refugee status. (Source: Sterly et al. 2019, modified)

need to be taken into account; for example, when calculating the number of people starting migration moves on a certain day, this would need to be expressed as the ratio of moving persons to the number of persons covered on this day.

Ethics: Bias and representation

As outlined above, external validity is often unclear for the secondary use of data, i.e., data that are analysed outside the context where they were created. CDR data are subject to a whole range of systematic errors or biases that must be taken into account when analysing and interpreting the results correctly. On the one hand, this is a matter of scientific methodology; on the other, these errors can also lead to social groups being misrepresented or not represented at all. In the CDR data (not only) of the Challenge, for example, the following biases play a role when conclusions about the population are to be drawn from the analysis results: sociodemographic biases (whether people own a cell phone at all varies by age, gender, or socioeconomic status); the market share of Türk Telekom varies (provider or market-share bias); phones are sometimes used by several people, or one user owns several phones; the marker for 'refugees' in the datasets included all persons with temporary protection status (asylum seekers, recognised refugees).

As we saw the project as an exploration of the possibilities of CDR analysis for mobility analyses, and due to resource constraints, we did not strive to control the data for these biases and to achieve greater representativity. This would have included, for example, the consideration of sampling biases through harmonisation with other existing data on the distribution of refugees in Turkey, or of provider biases (the potential for socio-spatially and temporally unequal distribution of penetration by Türk Telekom), or of gender and social biases in phone ownership and usage (see also Luca et al., Chapter 4, this volume, on the issue of representativity of CDR data). When interpreting the results of the analysis, this must be acknowledged as a clear limitation; we thus see our findings from the analysis as *indicating trends, overall structures, and key dynamics* rather than as figures and values that are exact representations of reality.

CDR analysis: Some key insights

The analysis of the CDR data followed two basic tracks: the first was geared towards identifying major *spatial* patterns of mobility, and the second aimed at identifying major *temporal* patterns of mobility.

In a first step, common for both tracks, we determined the home locations of users. This is particularly important for higher-resolution CDR data (e.g., Dataset 2 of the D4R challenge) in order to correctly understand everyday mobility. In the postprocessed version of Dataset 3, data were provided already spatially aggregated at district level, which means that a large proportion of small-scale everyday mobility no longer appeared in the data. However, as fine-grained everyday mobility can also involve the frequent crossing of district boundaries, it is useful to specify the home location. In order to determine the home location, often the base transmission station where users spend the night hours are used; we chose a similarly pragmatic approach by defining the home location as the district where a user places the last call on a day.

To get an understanding of the spatial and temporal patterns of mobility, we manually explored a small sample of users. Based on this, we then made two choices for proxies to distinguish permanent migration from temporary movements. The first proxy for migration was the first and the last place of residence of users in the dataset. We selected the two places for any given user where she first and last appeared in the dataset and determined the distance between the two places

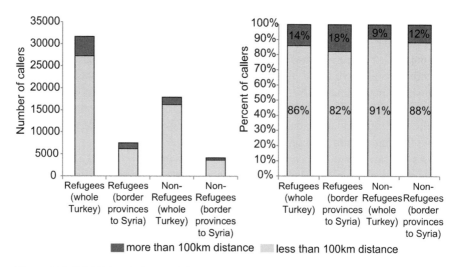

Figure 5.2 'Mobile' and 'less mobile' callers in the dataset (mobile = more than 100 km between first and last district, less mobile = less than 100 km). Left: Absolute figures. Right: Per cent. Border provinces: Hatay, Gaziantep, Şanlıurfa, Kilis, and Mardin. (Source: Sterly et al., 2019, modified)

(i.e., between the district centroids). Short-term commuting movements and circular migration, where the data include both outward and return movement, are thus removed. The second proxy for migration was a threshold of movement of more than 100 km, since movements of less than 100 km in many cases seemed to represent rather small-scale and short-term commuting movements whose (outward or) return movements were, for example, 'cut off' by the one-year time limit of the dataset. We then aggregated the dataset by users and the first and last places where they appeared in the dataset, obtaining a 'user-by-places table'.

Figure 5.2 shows the number of 'mobile' and 'less mobile' users according to these two proxies. If we take this as an indication of migration or secondary mobility, about 14% of users flagged as refugees and 9% of users flagged as non-refugees shifted their place of residence within Turkey during the course of the year 2017. The proportion is slightly higher when considering movement away from the provinces bordering Syria (about 18% for refugees and 12% for non-refugees).

It is notable here that, even if we take these figures as rough approximations, *a very clear majority of refugee users do not move more than 100 km on a permanent basis*, even if the border provinces to Syria are considered separately. This is consistent with previous research that many Syrian refugees either stay close to the border (to be able to return easily if possible) or stay in places where they have social networks and can find accommodation and work. While, up to 2015, Syrian refugees were free to move to and settle at their place of choice in Turkey (Erdoğan, 2019), since 2015 their access to social services is tied to the location of their registration, which can take several months to change. Baban et al. (2017) reported that since

2016 Syrian refugees wishing to relocate to other places and cities require a change of registration. However, for occupations in seasonal agriculture Syrian refugees do not need a work permit, which allows them to take up such work without changing their registration (Akar and Erdoğdu, 2019).

Ethics: Voluntariness and informed consent

The example of CDR data in the context of forced migration highlights the problem of voluntariness and informed consent in big data. Although all Türk Telekom users have legally agreed to the use of data for research purposes when signing a contract, typical procedural limitations come into play: (1) most users do not read (long and complicated) privacy policies of such contracts; (2) if they do read them, they do not understand them; (3) if they do read and understand them, they often lack the expertise to make an informed decision; and (4) even if none of these apply, the decision is often not free, for example if users urgently need the services in question and there are no other providers (Kitchin, 2014). It should be noted here that in humanitarian emergencies, people are often particularly vulnerable and find themselves in multiple dependency relationships with state and non-state actors (authorities, NGOs, companies, etc.). Due to additional linguistic and cultural barriers, it is therefore questionable whether one can even speak of voluntariness and informed consent here.

As a project team we discussed these aspects before the submission of a project proposal for the D4R challenge. After an internal debate and with the involvement of local stakeholders, including weighing up the expected gain in knowledge and the possible risks and negative aspects, we decided to submit a project application. The decisive factors were the multilevel anonymisation of the data, i.e., that it was not possible to trace back individuals according to the current state of knowledge, and the fact that the projects of the D4R Challenge were supervised and guided by an external ethics committee. This committee consisted of representatives from universities, NGOs, and government bodies, and evaluated and reviewed all project proposals for the Challenge, as well as the reports and publications that were produced. Regarding the privacy risks associated with such data analysis projects, guidance by an existing or the setting up of an independent ethical review panel seems indispensable. During the runtime of our project and the process of the data analysis we continued to discuss interim results and adapted our project in such a way that no negative effects on refugees were to be expected.

CDR analysis: Spatial patterns

To gain a perspective on the spatial patterns of refugee mobility, we constructed a mobility matrix of the 973 Turkish districts and the numbers of refugees and non-refugees moving between them, according to the proxies for migratory movements (more than 100 km between first and last appearance in the dataset). This was done

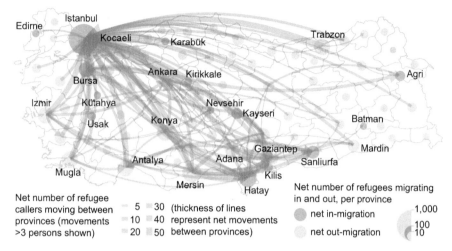

Figure 5.3 Net migration of refugees between Turkish provinces in 2017; only movements between first and last residence over 100 km are shown. (Source: Sterly et al. (2019), modified). Colour version printed as Plate 1.

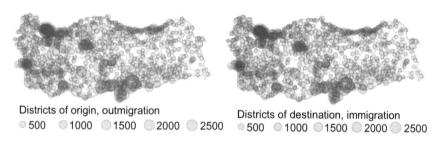

Figure 5.4 Mobility of refugees between districts in 2017; all movements over 100 km between districts shown. (Source: Sterly et al. (2019), modified)

by aggregating the user-by-places table (see 'CDR analysis: Some key insights') by first and last place and summing the number of users departing from and arriving at these places. Between almost all districts there were movements in both directions, so we determined the net migration between districts. For more clarity of representation, we then aggregated these data at the level of the 81 provinces. Figure 5.3 shows the net migration aggregated at province level. For comparison, Figure 5.4 shows the districts of origin and destination for all movements.

The data confirm large-scale migration patterns or systems that are already known, for which, however, quantitative basis on this granularity was largely lacking: (1) larger urban centres as destinations (especially Istanbul, Bursa, Ankara, and others); (2) general migration routes from south to north and from east to west; and (3) movements within the Western Turkish–Syrian border region, including migration to cities and provinces bordering with Syria (Hatay, Kilis, Şanlıurfa), suggesting some return migration. Apart from permanent relocation, there is also bidirectional mobility to and from more rural places in central and northern Turkey, which indicates labour migration into local agricultural labour markets. Although visible to some extent, this seasonal mobility seems to be less pronounced in the data than we had originally expected, in terms of agricultural labour demand in central Turkey.

Ethics: Do no harm

Especially in the refugee context, which deals with disadvantaged and often extremely vulnerable groups, the avoidance of harm and disadvantages for research participants is extremely important. In the context of the D4R Challenge, we discussed this in the project team before and during the project and identified the following areas as particularly sensitive that may contribute to disadvantages for refugees:

- the use of analysis results by security authorities and/or private companies to the disadvantage of refugees ('results creep');
- the use of analysis methods developed in the project to the disadvantage of refugees ('methods creep');
- media representation of the project or its results that may lead to negative or hostile reactions towards refugees.

To address these problematic aspects, we designed the project in terms of content and methodology. It also has to be mentioned that the D4R Challenge took place in a 'secured' framework (in a kind of sandbox, so to speak): all project proposals were checked with regard to research ethics aspects before the projects were approved and data were handed out; the user agreement limited the use of data in terms of content and time to exactly the project context; results had to be submitted to the committee prior to publication.

In order to avoid generating results that could be misused, we kept the analyses relatively general and descriptive in nature, and, in the course of the project, also decided not to consider aspects that could potentially make refugees the object of hostility or that were already controversial in the media (for example, competition for agricultural jobs). Here, the concept of group privacy also becomes relevant, as through the analysis, properties of the group of refugees could be identified, or sub-groups could be constructed that could then lead to discrimination. Methodologically, we did not aim for the development of analysis methods or algorithms that could potentially contribute to surveillance or control mechanisms. The content and scope of the final report was discussed within the project team, and we included only content that we deemed non-harmful. The discussions of ethical aspects were important at all stages of the project, including the decision of whether to participate in the D4R Challenge or not, the initial proposal design, the implementation, and the publication and dissemination of results. These would not have been possible without the broad expertise within our team, which included one expert on data ethics, two topical experts on refugees, and one local expert from an NGO working with Syrian refugees in Turkey. Based on these experiences, we would highly recommend conducting projects of this nature with a team consisting of topical and local experts and or/stakeholders, and in collaboration with ethical experts, not only for the sake of ethical soundness, but also to be able to successfully interpret the analysis results.

CDR analysis: Temporal patterns

For the analysis of mobility over time, the idea was to determine the number of users that move or migrate on each day. In a first run, we tried this for permanent migration moves (with the two proxies of first and last appearance in the dataset and $distance > 100\,km$) and did not get very informative results. We then decided to widen the scope of mobility definitions by using a proxy for movement of more than 100 km within 24 hours. This excluded small-scale and short-term, everyday commuting mobilities, but still included weekly and also more episodic circular (back and forth) movements, in addition to permanent movement. We then identified, for every user, the dates at which they moved more than 100 km between their daily home locations (i.e., the districts where they made the last call or text message on a day). These data were then aggregated by date, with the number of users summarised. Because of the high temporal variability of callers covered in the dataset (see Figure 5.1), we calculated the ratio of the number of mobile callers to the total number of callers on each particular day, in order to ensure comparability over time.

The results (movement over time, Figure 5.5) show that there was a clear increase in mobility before the two Eid festivals (Eid al-Fitr from 21 to 25 June and Eid al-Adha from 1 to 4 September 2017), and then a gradual decline. The non-refugee population was much more mobile around Eid al-Fitr than the refugee population, probably due to their better economic situation, allowing for leisure travel and family visits. However, it also becomes clear that the refugee population was also much more mobile during the Eid festivals than at other times of the year. The strong contrast in weekend mobility is notable, which is much stronger among the non-refugee group and probably related to commuting, while it is very weak in the refugee group.

Although visible, seasonal mobility seems to be less pronounced on a national level than we had expected, given the importance of the seasonal labour market in agricultural production. To contextualise this, also with regard to the findings on seasonal agricultural labour mobility of Alışık et al. (2019), we checked for movements into and out of the northern provinces with hazelnut production (Ordu, Samsun, Giresun, Sakarya, Düzce, Trabzon, Zonguldak; cf. İslam (2018)). Figure 5.6 shows the weekly movements of refugees and non-refugees into (dashed) and out of (solid) these northern provinces. For the analysis we only included those callers who had neither their first nor their last 'appearance' in the data in these

ANALYSING REFUGEES' SECONDARY MOBILITY 109

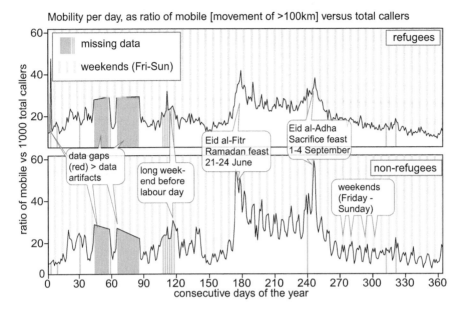

Figure 5.5 Mobility per day, expressed as the ratio of mobile callers (moving more than 100 km on that particular day) by total refugee/non-refugee callers on that day. (Source: Sterly et al. (2019), modified)

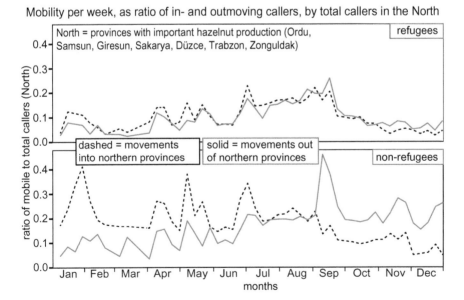

Figure 5.6 Mobility per week into and out of the northern hazelnut provinces (Ordu, Samsun, Giresun, Sakarya, Düzce, Trabzon, and Zonguldak), expressed as the ratio of mobile callers to total refugee/non-refugee callers in these provinces in this week.

northern provinces, in order to exclude temporary movements out and in, permanent movements into, and residents of these provinces. The results clearly show seasonal movements of both refugees and non-refugees. The overall movement pattern of non-refugees is more pronounced, with a higher ratio of callers moving in general, and a more distinct dominance of mobility towards the north from January to June, and out of the north from September to December. For refugees, the temporal difference in mobility into and out of the northern provinces was less distinct, but there was a certain amount of in- and outward mobility that strongly increased during the main months of the hazelnut harvest (late July to September). For both refugee and non-refugee callers, there were mobility peaks around the time of the two Eid festivals.

Conclusion

In this chapter we have shown with a simple example how spatiotemporal mobility patterns can be derived from CDR data. The following issues seem important to us to conclude.

First, regarding the method and data, the analysis of CDRs has made it possible to reveal mobility and migration patterns at an unprecedented level of detail, both spatially and temporally, which is difficult to obtain through 'traditional' means (e.g., surveys, registers, or census data). Even the very simple approach we followed can already reveal a range of interesting findings. However, the complexity of human mobility requires a more intricate and in-depth analysis of mobility patterns than we followed here that was beyond the scope of our project and capacities. Exciting avenues in this direction include, for example, multilevel analyses of spatiotemporal patterns (cf., for example, Alessandretti et al., 2020).

Second, regarding the findings, general patterns of refugee secondary movement in Turkey (south to north, east to west, to urban centres and the coast, to and from agricultural areas) are clearly reflected in the data. Cultural motivations for migration (e.g., Eid) are more important than originally expected, and are overlayed with seasonal movements due to the need for agricultural labour. But the CDR analysis also suggests that migration flows are more complex, and that the boundaries between commuting, visiting, temporary, seasonal, and permanent migration may be more fluid than definitions in migration studies often suggest.

Third, the analysis of CDR data touches on a whole range of ethical aspects or even problems that require systematic consideration; such data should only be used if ethical criteria can be met. The organisers of the D4R Challenge paid particular attention to these issues, including the anonymisation of datasets, the validation process to protect the interests of refugees, and the establishment of clear contractual agreements for the research teams using the data. Similar standards are needed for the analysis of these data in other contexts. The prevention of potential negative consequences, particularly for vulnerable groups such as refugees, also needs special attention from all the researchers and stakeholders involved.

Fourth, CDR data also impose certain limitations. There are research questions that are not easy or possible to address with CDR data, for example when a high spatial granularity of less than hundreds of meters (depending on location) is required, or when a consistent temporal resolution for all users is necessary. The frequency of CDRs from active events varies greatly, depending on the intensity of use of a device; for some users there are several records per hour, while for others there are only a few per month. Controlling for the biases inherent in CDR data (for example, phone ownership or provider bias) requires knowledge, for example, of the socioeconomic characteristics of users and market shares, that providers might be unwilling to share. And CDR data are relatively 'content scarce' and, in anonymised form (which should be the standard when dealing with CDRs from a data protection point of view), hardly or only indirectly allow conclusions to be drawn about demographic characteristics (e.g., gender, age), socioeconomic status, or reasons and goals for actions. This becomes especially apparent in the case of mobility and migration analyses, as most migration decisions are multilayered and multicausal.

Finally, regarding practical aspects, as social scientists often lack the necessary technical skills, and data analysts may lack the necessary thematic and contextual knowledge to fully realise the potential of such data, one consequence of this could be to foster the formation of interdisciplinary teams to successfully analyse CDR and similar data. Such teams should also include, or at least involve, ethics experts, as ethical challenges arise during all stages of research. Access of researchers to CDR data remains an issue, as phone providers are often hesitant to provide CDR data (including aggregates or derivatives) for scientific purposes, for legal, economic, and organisational reasons. However, working with CDRs and similar data, while respecting ethics and privacy concerns, would certainly benefit both the academic community and general society.

Further reading

On technical-methodological aspects of the analysis of CDRs and mobile data:

- The Flowminder Foundation has put together a very detailed collection of metrics for analysing CDRs.[4]
- The organisers of the D4R Challenge have edited a book containing a large number of excellent examples of how CDR data can be combined with other data and used to construct advanced metrics to study mobility, inequality, integration, and other issues (Salah *et al.*, 2019a).
- UNSTATS has issued a very informative internet document.[5]

---

[4] Flowminder COVID-19 Resources: Mobility indicators: Descriptions, https://covid19.flowminder.org/mobility-indicators/mobility-indicators-descriptions

[5] UNSTATS: Handbook on the Use of Mobile Phone Data for Official Statistics, https://unstats.un.org/bigdata/task-teams/mobile-phone/MPD%20Handbook%2020191004.pdf

On ethical issues of big data and research:

- Taylor (2016) very concisely discusses the ethical and methodological dilemmas of mobile phone data analysis (it has to be noted that the paper predates Covid-19, and in the fields of non-pharmaceutical interventions it severely underplays the potential of mobile data analysis for tracking and controlling epidemics).
- Zook *et al.* (2017) very compactly lay out a comprehensive list of principles for research with big data.

References

Akar, S. and Erdoğdu, M. M. (2019), 'Syrian refugees in Turkey and integration problem ahead', *Journal of International Migration and Integration* 20(3), 925–40.

Alessandretti, L., Aslak, U., and Lehmann, S. (2020), 'The scales of human mobility', *Nature* 587(7834), 402–7.

Alışık, S. T., Aksel, D. B., Yantaç, A. E., Kayi, I., Salman, S., Içduygu, A., Çay, D., Baruh, L., and Bensason, I. (2019), 'Seasonal labor migration among Syrian refugees and urban deep map for integration in Turkey', *in* A. A. Salah, A. Pentland, B. Lepri, and E. Letouzé, eds, *Guide to Mobile Data Analytics in Refugee Scenarios*, Springer, New York, 305–28.

Baban, F., Ilcan, S., and Rygiel, K. (2017), 'Playing border politics with urban Syrian refugees', *Movements* 3(2), 81–102.

Barbosa, H., Barthelemy, M., Ghoshal, G., James, C. R., Lenormand, M., Louail, T., Menezes, R., Ramasco, J. J., Simini, F., and Tomasini, M. (2018), 'Human mobility: Models and applications', *Physics Reports* 734, 1–74.

Blondel, V. D., Decuyper, A., and Krings, G. (2015), 'A survey of results on mobile phone datasets analysis', *EPJ Data Science* 4(1), 10.

Dekker, R., Engbersen, G., Klaver, J., and Vonk, H. (2018), 'Smart refugees: How Syrian asylum migrants use social media information in migration decision-making', *Social Media+ Society* 4(1), 2056305118764439.

Engebretsen, S., Engø-Monsen, K., Aleem, M. A., Gurley, E. S., Frigessi, A., and de Blasio, B. F. (2020), 'Time-aggregated mobile phone mobility data are sufficient for modelling influenza spread: The case of Bangladesh', *Journal of the Royal Society Interface* 17(167), 20190809.

Erdoğan, M. (2019), 'Syrian refugees in Turkey', Technical report, Konrad–Adenauer-Stiftung Report, available at https://www.kas.de/en/web/tuerkei/veranstaltungsberichte/detail/-/content/syrian-refugees-in-turkey

Finger, F., Genolet, T., Mari, L., de Magny, G. C., Manga, N. M., Rinaldo, A., and Bertuzzo, E. (2016), 'Mobile phone data highlights the role of mass gatherings in the spreading of cholera outbreaks', *Proceedings of the National Academy of Sciences* 113(23), 6421–6.

Floridi, L. and Taddeo, M. (2016), 'Introduction. what is data ethics?', *Philosophical Transactions of the Royal Society A: Mathematical, Physical and Engineering Sciences* 374, 20160360.

Frouws, B., Phillips, M., Hassan, A., and Twigt, M. (2016), 'Getting to Europe the WhatsApp way: The use of ICT in contemporary mixed migration flows to Europe', Regional Mixed Migration Secretariat Briefing Paper.

İslam, A. (2018), 'Hazelnut culture in Turkey', *Akademik Ziraat Dergisi* 7(2), 259–66.

Jungbluth, S. (2017), '"Smartphone refugees": Mobility, power regimes, and the impact of digital technologies', Master's thesis, Faculty of Social Sciences, Tampere University.

Kitchin, R. (2014), *The Data Revolution: Big Data, Open Data, Data Infrastructures and their Consequences*, Sage, New York.

Kosinski, M., Stillwell, D., and Graepel, T. (2013), 'Private traits and attributes are predictable from digital records of human behavior', *Proceedings of the National Academy of Sciences* 110(15), 5802–5.

Kozlowska, H. (2015), 'The most crucial item that migrants and refugees carry is a smartphone', *Quartz*, available at http://qz.com/500062/the-most-crucial-item-that-migrants-and-refugees-carry-is-a-smartphone

Kvittingen, A., Valenta, M., Tabbara, H., Baslan, D., and Berg, B. (2019), 'The conditions and migratory aspirations of Syrian and Iraqi refugees in Jordan', *Journal of Refugee Studies* 32(1), 106–24.

Lai, S., zu Erbach-Schoenberg, E., Pezzulo, C., Ruktanonchai, N. W., Sorichetta, A., Steele, J., Li, T., Dooley, C. A., and Tatem, A. J. (2019), 'Exploring the use of mobile phone data for national migration statistics', *Palgrave Communications* 5(1), 1–10.

Letouzé, E., Vinck, P., and Kammourieh, L. (2015), 'The law, politics and ethics of cell phone data analytics', Data-Pop Alliance.

Lu, X., *et al.* (2016), 'Unveiling hidden migration and mobility patterns in climate stressed regions: A longitudinal study of six million anonymous mobile phone users in Bangladesh', *Global Environmental Change* 38, 1–7.

Luca, M., Barlacchi, G., Oliver, N., and Lepri, B. (2022), 'Leveraging mobile phone data for migration flows', *in* A. A. Salah, E. E. Korkmaz, and T. Bircan, eds, *Data Science for Migration and Mobility*, Proceedings of the British Academy, British Academy / Oxford University Press, London, UK.

Metcalf, J. and Crawford, K. (2016), 'Where are human subjects in big data research? The emerging ethics divide', *Big Data & Society* 3(1), 2053951716650211.

Mittelstadt, B. (2017), 'From individual to group privacy in big data analytics', *Philosophy & Technology* 30(4), 475–94.

Oliver, N., *et al.* (2020), 'Mobile phone data for informing public health actions across the COVID-19 pandemic life cycle', *Science Advances* 6(23), eabc0764.

Salah, A. A., Canca, C., and Erman, B. (2022), 'Ethical and legal concerns on data science for large-scale human mobility', *in* A. A. Salah, E. E. Korkmaz, and T. Bircan, eds, *Data Science for Migration and Mobility*, Proceedings of the British Academy, British Academy / Oxford University Press, London, UK.

Salah, A. A., Pentland, A., Lepri, B., and Letouzé, E. (2019a), *Guide to Mobile Data Analytics in Refugee Scenarios*, Springer, New York.

Salah, A. A., Pentland, A., Lepri, B., Letouzé, E., de Montjoye, Y.-A., Dong, X., Dağdelen, Ö., and Vinck, P. (2019b), 'Introduction to the data for refugees challenge on mobility of Syrian refugees in Turkey', *in* A. A. Salah, A. Pentland, B. Lepri, and E. Letouzé, eds, *Guide to Mobile Data Analytics in Refugee Scenarios*, Springer, New York, 3–27.

Saraçoğlu, C. and Bélanger, D. (2019), 'The Syrian refugees and temporary protection regime in Turkey: A spatial fix for Turkish capital', in I. D. Karatepe, T. Toren, and G. Yilmaz, eds, *Integration through Exploitation: Syrians in Turkey*, Rainer Hampp, Munich, 96.

Skov, G. (2016), 'Transfer back to Malta: Refugees' secondary movement within the European Union', *Journal of Immigrant & Refugee Studies* 14(1), 66–82.

Steenbruggen, J., Borzacchiello, M. T., Nijkamp, P., and Scholten, H. (2013), 'Mobile phone data from GSM networks for traffic parameter and urban spatial pattern assessment: A review of applications and opportunities', *GeoJournal* 78(2), 223–43.

Sterly, H., Etzold, B., Wirkus, L., Sakdapolrak, P., Schewe, J., Schleussner, C.-F., and Hennig, B. (2019), 'Assessing refugees' onward mobility with mobile phone data: A case study of (Syrian) refugees in Turkey', *in* A. A. Salah, A. Pentland, B. Lepri, and E. Letouzé, eds, *Guide to Mobile Data Analytics in Refugee Scenarios*, Springer, New York, 251–63.

Taylor, L. (2016), 'No place to hide? The ethics and analytics of tracking mobility using mobile phone data', *Environment and Planning D: Society and Space* 34(2), 319–36.

Taylor, L., Floridi, L., and Van der Sloot, B. (2017), *Group Privacy: New Challenges of Data Technologies*, Springer, New York.

Tuzi, I. *et al.* (2019), 'From insecurity to secondary migration: "Bounded mobilities" of Syrian and Eritrean refugees in Europe', *Migration Letters* 16(4), 551–61.

UNHCR (2019), *Turkey*, Fact sheet (July).

Woods, A. (2016), 'Urban refugees: The experiences of Syrians in Istanbul', Istanbul Policy Center, Sabanci University.

Zook, M., *et al.* (2017), 'Ten simple rules for responsible big data research', *PLOS Computational Biology* 13(3), e1005399.

Zufiria, P. J., *et al.* (2018), 'Identifying seasonal mobility profiles from anonymized and aggregated mobile phone data. Application in food security', *PLOS One* 13(4), e0195714.

6

Remote Sensing Data for Migration Research

TUBA BIRCAN

Introduction

IN RECENT DECADES, remote sensing, the science of obtaining information about objects or areas from a distance, typically from aircraft or satellites, has become a valuable data source for performing large-area measurements of the physical conditions of the Earth's surface. Recent technological and methodological developments in satellite remote sensing have proven to provide highly detailed information on environmental conditions. Remote sensing technologies include conventional radar, laser altimeters, altimeters, acoustic ultrasound, aerial photographs, hyperspectral imaging, and multispectral platforms.

As remote sensing is available over time even in parts of the world that would otherwise be lacking in the availability of census and other types of data (Elvidge *et al.*, 2009; Henderson *et al.*, 2012), remote sensing is an important resource in the spatial examination of economic, environmental, and migration phenomena. Data from a variety of different sensors are available for large areas and free of cost, hence allowing researchers and decision-makers to gather information, to answer questions about environmental conditions, and to monitor global change.

Several international institutions built early-warning systems (EWS) using satellite data. An EWS is a tool for disaster prediction information, in particular for extreme events as a result of natural hazards, sociopolitical factors, etc. Some examples are the GIEWS (Global Information and Early Warning System, by the Food and Agriculture Organisation of the United Nations), the ASAP (Anomaly Hotspots of Agricultural Production, by the European Union Directorate General, Joint Research Centre), which uses remote sensing to detect food security alerts, and Vietnam's advanced water forecasting system as an early warning for floods (by the Vietnam National Center for Water Resources Planning and Investigation). Although the role of satellite remote sensing is commonly acknowledged for the observation of natural landcover (Melesse *et al.*, 2007; Xie *et al.*, 2008), scientific studies which demonstrate the potential of remote sensing in a social and humanitarian context are relatively scarce.

Regarding human migration, the use of remote sensing data for migration-related topics is of rising importance as detailed data can be acquired rapidly. Different platforms are applicable for gathering remote sensing data, such as satellites, aircraft, and drones. Given the strength of the remote sensing data to monitor the environment, both human migration induced by environmental factors or armed conflicts and the humanitarian aid planning for internally displaced persons[1] upon extreme weather events can be investigated through computational methods. To be more specific, the information derived from Earth observation (EO) images could include the number and size of dwellings, dwelling type classification, and derived population estimations (Spröhnle *et al.*, 2014); or the number and dynamics of the displaced population in camps (Lang *et al.*, 2010). Applications of remote sensing have provided humanitarian operations with several benefits, such as assisting in decisions concerning the positioning of refugee camps and monitoring their size and state (e.g., Lang *et al.* 2017; Kemper and Heinzel 2014); identifying the best roads on which to dispatch aid relief (e.g., bridge destroyed, flooded area), and tracking, the movement of displaced people (e.g., Voigt *et al.* 2016; Lang *et al.* 2018); and identifying some crucial characteristics of the environment (e.g., Hein *et al.* 2018). However, there are also some concerns in the development of this technology and its use. When social and humanitarian application areas for remote sensing are considered, the vulnerability of the corresponding populations and governmental involvement in the initiatives contribute to raising ethical concerns, including violation of human and fundamental rights, along with the misuse of potential early warning systems to detect the direction and timing of future migratory trends.

The ultimate goal of this chapter is to examine different remote sensing data sources to describe the specific advantages and limitations of different remote sensing platforms in the context of migration and humanitarian aid. The chapter will first identify the basic concepts of remote sensing, then elaborate on the sensors and satellite systems with specific details regarding the data content and access. After explaining the most widely used and publicly available remote sensing data products, how these indices have been used for environment-induced human migration and humanitarian aid studies will be discussed in detail through two case studies. Finally, we will comb through the ethical aspects of the use of remote sensing for studies and applications concerning migration and migrants.

---

[1] The UN defines internally displaced individuals as 'persons who have been forced to flee their homes suddenly or unexpectedly in large numbers, as a result of armed conflict, internal strife, systematic violations of human rights or natural or man-made disasters, and who are within the territory of their own country'.

An overview of remote sensing

The commonality in the definitions of remote sensing lies in data collection 'at a distance'. To be able to capture information about objects or areas, various platforms such as aircraft, spacecraft, near-space vehicles, and satellites are equipped with EO sensors. The information collected by these sensors is the electromagnetic (EM) radiation emitted from objects on the Earth's surface. The EM spectrum describes the range of all possible frequencies/wavelengths of radiation; only a portion of the EM spectrum is visible/detectable by the human eye (i.e., the visible portion). Other portions of the spectrum include infrared, microwave, and radio waves, none of which are detectable by the human eye. To gather information, EO sensors are designed to make measurements in specific portions/divisions of the EM spectrum.

Most common EO platforms are remote sensing satellites, and several of these collect and provide imagery by observing the entire globe or a specific part of it within a defined time period (Guo et al., 2016). After an elaborate review of the scientific definitions, Campbell and Wynne (2011, p. 6) concludes that 'Remote sensing is the practice of deriving information about the Earth's land and water surface using images acquired from an overhead perspective, using EM radiation in one or more regions of the electromagnetic spectrum, reflected or emitted from the Earth's surface.'

The spatial and temporal coverage of a satellite relies on its orbit. The orbit of a satellite is one of several predefined curved paths around the Earth. Depending on the proportion of the gravitational pull of the Earth and the velocity of the satellite, satellites move in a particular orbit considering their height above the Earth's surface, orientation, and rotation with respect to the Earth. The selection of the best orbit for a satellite depends on the ultimate goal of the satellite and the sensor(s) it carries. The time required for completing one revolution of the orbit is called the *orbital period*, but a satellite in a geostationary orbit remains static to observers on Earth.

Remote sensing sensors

Earth observation is the process of acquiring observations of the Earth's surface and atmosphere through detecting, measuring, and recording changes in the spectral-radiometric and spatial characteristics of energy radiated by Earth-surface components via remote sensing instruments from different platforms such as aerial platforms, drones (remotely piloted aircraft systems, RPAS), and satellites.

As illustrated in Figure 6.1, remote sensing sensors are of two primary types, active and passive (Schowengerdt, 2007; Liu and Mason, 2013). Active sensors are the devices that emit their own energy (radiation) in the direction of the target to be examined under most atmospheric conditions. The sensor then records the radiation reflected back to the satellite. Examples of active systems are radar (microwave remote sensing) and light detection and ranging (LiDAR).

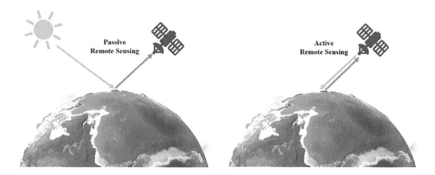

Figure 6.1 Remote sensing sensor systems.

Passive sensors focus on detecting natural energy (electromagnetic radiation) generated by the Sun that is emitted or reflected by the object being observed or the Earth's surface. Passive remote sensing systems mostly work in the visible, infrared, thermal infrared, and microwave portions of the EM spectrum.

The most common and accessible remote sensing data comes from satellites, equipped with various sensors depending on their missions. While some satellites have optical (passive) sensors, others carry high-resolution synthetic-aperture radar (SAR) systems (active). SAR is employed for building two-dimensional images or three-dimensional features (such as landscapes) since it works in various weather conditions (Kirscht and Rinke, 1998) and offers the opportunity to cover large areas of interest.

Remote sensing satellite systems

A variety of remote sensing satellite systems exist from which satellite imagery of Earth is acquired through different satellite operators, manufacturers, and data providers. In line with the objective of this chapter, those that are commonly used for migration and/or humanitarian applications will be discussed. The selection of a data product depends highly on the research questions; therefore, a remote sensing satellite data user should be aware of the different data sources available, the data products provided by those sources, and applications of those processed data and derived indices. The most common remote sensing data sources are summarised in Table 6.1, where free access data sources are elaborated in detail.

Commercial remote sensing satellites

DigitalGlobe is an American commercial vendor of space imagery and geospatial content. As part of Maxar Technologies, DigitalGlobe operates a civilian remote sensing spacecraft. Its active satellite constellation includes GeoEye-1,

Table 6.1 Overview of major remote sensing data sources

Satellite code	Provider	Content coverage	Raw data access and restrictions
QuickBird, Ikonos	DigitalGlobe	Mapping, change detection, planning (engineering, natural resources, urban, infrastructure), land use, environmental impact assessment, tourism, military, crop management, environmental monitoring	Paid; purchased from Digital Globe (https://www.satimagingcorp.com/satellite-sensors/ikonos/)
SPOT	EADS Astrium	Mapping, change detection, planning (engineering, natural resources, urban, infrastructure), land use, environmental impact assessment, tourism, military, crop management, environmental monitoring	Paid. Purchased from EADS Astrium (https://www.intelligence-airbusds.com/imagery/constellation/spot/)
ASTER	NASA, Government of Japan	Vegetation, ecosystem dynamics, hazard and disaster monitoring, change detection, Earth science	Paid. Purchased from NASA; free access possibility for research and education purposes upon permission from NASA (https://asterweb.jpl.nasa.gov/data.asp)
Landsat-5 TM and Landsat-7 ETM+	NASA / US Geological Survey (USGS)	Oceanography, aerosols, bathymetry, vegetation types, peak vegetation, biomass content analysis, moisture analysis, thermal mapping, mineral deposit identification	Free access (https://www.usgs.gov/core-science-systems/nli/landsat-data-access)
Landsat-8	NASA/USGS	Oceanography, aerosols, bathymetry, vegetation types, peak vegetation, biomass content analysis, moisture analysis, cloud cover analysis, thermal mapping, soil moisture estimation	Free access (https://www.usgs.gov/core-science-systems/nli/landsat-data-access)

(continued)

Table 6.1 (*continued*)

Satellite code	Provider	Content coverage	Raw data access and restrictions
Terra (EOS AM) and Aqua (EOS PM)	NASA (MODIS)	Vegetation health using time-series analyses with vegetation indices, long-term land cover changes, global snow cover trends, water inundation from pluvial, riverine, or sea-level rise, flooding in coastal areas, change of water levels, detection and mapping of wildland fires.	Free access (https://modis.gsfc.nasa.gov/data/)
Suomi National Polar Partnership Satellite	NASA (NOAA)	Visible Infrared Imaging Radiometer Suite (VIIRS): products from night-time data including nightfire (VNF), day/night band low imaging data (NTL), and VIIRS Boat Detection (VBD)	Free access upon registration (https://earthdata.nasa.gov/earth-observation-data/near-real-time/download-nrt-data/viirs-nrt)
19 DMSP satellites	Air Force Space Command (AFSC) /NOAA	Night-time observation of light and combustion sources worldwide, 1992–2013.	Free access upon registration (https://www.wmo-sat.info/oscar/satellites/view/dmsp_f19)
Sentinel-1	ESA/Copernicus	Continuous all-weather, day and night radar imaging for land and ocean services	Free access (https://scihub.copernicus.eu/)
Sentinel-2	ESA/Copernicus	High-resolution optical imaging for land services (e.g., imagery of vegetation, soil, and water cover, inland waterways, and coastal areas)	Free access. VHR data purchased from ESA. Free access possibility for EU-funded research upon permission of ESA. (https://scihub.copernicus.eu/)

WorldView-1, WorldView-2, and WorldView-3. Archive satellite data are also available from IKONOS for 1999–2015 and QuickBird for 2001–2015.

LANDSAT programme

The Earth Resources Satellite Program involves a series of Earth observation satellites jointly managed by NASA and the United States Geological Survey (USGS) since 1972. The first satellite, Landsat 1, was followed by others; more recently, Landsat 7 and Landsat 8, were launched in 1999 and 2013 respectively, and they are currently in orbit and collecting data. Landsat 7 data has eight spectral bands with spatial resolutions ranging from 15 m to 60 m (49 ft to 197 ft) with a temporal resolution of 16 days. Landsat 8 collects approximately 740 scenes a day. Landsat 9, which replicates the technologically advanced instruments on Landsat 8, launched in 2021 and allows the collection of continuous high-quality data required for advancing Earth applications, including our ability to map surface temperature and surface water quality. Landsat has been the 'world's longest continuously acquired collection of space-based moderate-resolution land remote sensing data' (Emery and Camps, 2017, p. 26). As discussed by Roy *et al.* (2014), the optimal ground resolutions and spectral bands of the Landsat satellites enable efficient tracking of land use and land change due to natural changes (i.e., climate change, drought, wildfire, etc.) or human-caused changes (i.e., urbanisation, biomass changes, etc.). Most of the Landsat images are divided into scenes to allow easy downloading. Millions of satellite images and derived products are archived and publicly available for research purposes through EarthExplorer,[2] GloVis,[3] and the LandsatLook (formerly LandLook Viewer).[4]

Defence Meteorological Satellite Programme

The Defence Meteorological Satellite Program (DMSP), initiated by the United States Air Force in 1962, launched a series of satellites to monitor meteorological, oceanographic, and environmental data for clouds, bodies of water, snow, fire, and pollution in the visual and infrared spectra (Nichols, 1975). The combination of data from four satellites (day and night, dawn, and dusk satellites) collects global information every six hours. Such information is acquired by scanning radiometers to identify cloud type and height, land and surface water temperatures, water currents, ocean surface features, ice, and snow. The data are publicly available at the Earth Observation Group (EOG)[5] within the National Center for Environmental Information (NCEI) Solar Terrestrial Physics (STP) Division.

[2] USGS EarthExplorer, https://earthexplorer.usgs.gov/
[3] USGS GloVis, https://glovis.usgs.gov/
[4] USGS LandsatLook, https://landsatlook.usgs.gov/
[5] Earth Observation Group, https://payneinstitute.mines.edu/eog/

Moderate-Resolution Imaging Spectroradiometer

Moderate-Resolution Imaging Spectroradiometer (MODIS) is a sensor on board the Terra (EOS AM) and Aqua (EOS PM) satellites, which were launched by NASA in 1999 and 2002. This key instrument, which covers the highest number of spectral bands of any global-coverage moderate-resolution imager and has 250 m and 500 m spatial resolutions, provides a valuable compromise between high temporal frequency and high spatial resolution to map the land surface. Based on images of the entire Earth every one to two days, Terra and Aqua provide global measurements such as changes in Earth's cloud cover, radiation budget, and the processes occurring in the oceans, on land, and in the lower atmosphere. Main MODIS land indicators include the Enhanced Vegetation Index (EVI), Leaf Area Index, FAPAR, and Net Primary Production (Justice *et al.*, 2002), and the data can be downloaded from the USGS website.[6]

Suomi National Polar-orbiting Partnership

MODIS has been succeeded by the Visible Infrared Imaging Radiometer Suite instrument on board the Suomi National Polar-orbiting Partnership (Suomi NPP) satellite launched in 2011 by the United States National Oceanic and Atmospheric Administration (NOAA). Suomi NPP is a weather satellite that was previously known as the National Polar-Orbiting Operational Environmental Satellite System Preparatory Project (NPP) and NPP-Bridge. NPP is designed as a pathfinder to bridge the gap between the old Earth Observing System (EOS) of NASA and the United States' next generation of operational environmental satellites (Joint Polar Satellite System) by flying new instruments providing climate measurements that continue the prior observations by the EOS on a new satellite bus and using a new ground data network (Murphy, 2006). The primary imager on Suomi NPP is the Visible Infrared Imaging Radiometer Suite (VIIRS) (Elvidge *et al.*, 2013, 2017). A variety of VIIRS data can be freely accessed globally from EOG's website.[7] These products include Nightfire (VNF) data, which provides locations and times of hot pixel detections along with estimates of temperatures and source sizes, and is available in 24 hour increments; day/night band: low-light imaging data (NTL), which covers lighting from cities, towns, villages, combustion sources, and lit fishing boats for monthly or annual cloud-free composites; and VIIRS Boat Detection (VBD) data, which detects bright sea vessels at night using the VIIRS day/night band (DNB) and is provided in CSV and KMZ format.

---

[6] USGSL LP DAAC, https://lpdaac.usgs.gov/
[7] Earth Observation Group: VIIRS, https://payneinstitute.mines.edu/eog-2/viirs/

Copernicus programme

The Copernicus programme, formerly Global Monitoring for Environment and Security (GMES), was launched by the European Union in 2003 and is designed to improve the management of the environment, our understanding of it, and to help us mitigate the effects of climate change and ensure civil security.[8] Copernicus' services can be summarised in six categories: land management, the marine environment, atmosphere, emergency response, security, and climate change. Its aim is real-time dynamic monitoring of the environment by providing accurate, timely, and easily accessible observation data from existing and future European and non-European satellites. The European Commission manages the programme. It is implemented in partnership with the Member States, the European Space Agency (ESA), the European Organisation for the Exploitation of Meteorological Satellites (EUMETSAT), the European Centre for Medium-Range Weather Forecasts (ECMWF), EU agencies and Mercator Océan. One of the major assets of the Copernicus programme is that the data and information services provided within its framework are free and openly accessible to users[9] through the Copernicus Open Access Hub (previously named the Sentinels Scientific Hub).

Within the Copernicus programme, the European Commission acts on behalf of the European Union and is in charge of the overall initiative, setting requirements, and managing the services. ESA is responsible for the development of a new family of satellites, called Sentinels. Currently, three complete two-satellite constellations (Sentinel-1A, -1B; Sentinel-2A, -2B; and Sentinel-3A, -3B) are in orbit along with an additional single satellite, Sentinel-5P. Sentinel-1A and -1B, which were launched respectively in 2014 and 2016, collects a unique set of observations comprising all-weather, day and night radar images. Sentinel-2A was launched in 2015 and Sentinel-2B in 2017, with the aim of producing high-resolution optical images for land services. These two satellites are significant data sources since Sentinel-1 gathers radar imaging data for land and ocean services (Sayedain *et al.*, 2020), while Sentinel-2 provides a robust dataset for multispectral high-resolution imaging for monitoring land, inland waters, and coastal areas (Phiri *et al.*, 2020). In addition, the two Sentinel-3 satellites, launched in 2016 and 2018, collect data for services relevant to the ocean and land (Yang *et al.*, 2020). Sentinel-5P, launched in 2017, is the first Copernicus mission in orbit dedicated to monitoring the atmosphere.

In addition to the satellite data, the Copernicus programme includes licensed in situ data, which are defined as observation data from ground, sea, or airborne sensors, reference, and ancillary data. These data are used to validate and calibrate Copernicus products.

---

[8] The European Space Agency: Europe's Copernicus programme, http://www.esa.int/Applications/Observing_the_Earth/Copernicus/Overview3

[9] 'Regulation (EU) No 377/2014 of the European Parliament and of the Council of 3 April 2014 establishing the Copernicus Programme and repealing Regulation (EU) No 911/2010'. European Union, 3 April 2020. Retrieved 23 July 2020.

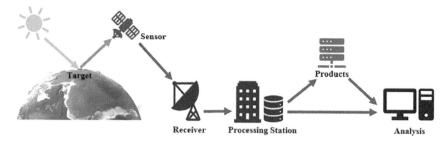

Figure 6.2 Schematic depiction of the remote sensing process.

The remote sensing process and data products

As in any other social science study, the starting point in remote sensing is the identification of a problem. Remote sensing applications are multidisciplinary in nature, and hence both inductive and deductive approaches can be applied. Remote sensing analysis results can be the final output for a research question or can be used as part of a mixed methods approach for a more elaborate utilisation. Consequently, the selected methodology depends on the origin of a specific research question and the overall methodology of the research.

The remote sensing process (see Figure 6.2) starts with the recording of the information (radiation) by the sensors on the platforms (i.e., satellite). Recorded data sent to the receivers on Earth are transferred to the processing station. Collected data are saved as raw data (satellite images) at full instrument resolution (level 0 products) and then they are processed (converted to products) by the satellite owner/institute or data providers to derive numerous products such as parameters, variables, indicators, maps, etc. As described above, most of the satellite systems allow free access to the collected data. Researchers might request raw data to process themselves, which requires advanced technical and computing skills and high-capacity computing devices, or they might get derived products to use in their analysis.

As discussed, the selection of satellite data products needs great caution. Following the definition of the problem, the data requirements should be determined to select the most appropriate data type and data source. The most common data measurements are:

- in situ data (Global Positioning System (GPS) receivers);
- resolution (radiometric, spatial, spectral, and temporal);
- electromagnetic spectrum (EM bands/segments).

These measurements are employed to develop remote sensing products. Remote sensing data can be analysed with analogue (visual) or digital image processing methods (Jensen, 1996). Digital image processing aims to operate on a digital image through a multi-step process to extract information that cannot be inferred from the original form. Three general steps in digital image processing (Jensen, 1996) are:

- preprocessing (radiometric corrections, geometric corrections);
- information enhancement (point operations, local operations);
- information extraction (expert systems, neural networks).

Concerning the methodology, the state of the art in machine learning on satellite data demonstrates that machine learning is the most appropriate and most successful approach to image recognition (LeCun *et al.*, 2015; Zhang *et al.*, 2016; Cao *et al.*, 2017; Cheng *et al.*, 2017; Zhu *et al.*, 2017). In this chapter, rather than illustrating how to develop indicators through digital image processing, we will focus on processed remote-sensing indicators as available data products that can be employed for studying human migration and humanitarian aid.

Numerous standard remote sensing data products have been developed and made available for further analysis by the programmes elaborated above. This section provides some detail (without explaining the scientific calculations behind them) for two themes which are most common in the study of human migration: (1) land cover and land use, and (2) night-lights. Additional information regarding the variables, data availability, and access can be found in Table 6.2, including the indices provided by different programmes.

Land cover and land use

Land cover and land use data are mostly based on time-series remote sensing images and made available as categorical maps inferred through semiautomated methods (Diogo and Koomen, 2016). Many global land models use vegetation-type data derived from annual satellite imagery (Friedl *et al.*, 2010). All relevant indices are related, but have small differences in terms of methodology or data source (satellites and sensors).

Normalised Difference Vegetation Index (NDVI)   Distinguishes actively growing vegetation from background features and can be used to estimate the density of green on an area of land. This is the most widely used vegetation index in remote sensing studies (Hansen *et al.*, 2000; Song *et al.*, 2018).

Soil Adjusted Vegetation Index (SAVI)   Developed to correct NDVI for the effect of varying conditions like different soil colour and different soil moisture in the areas where vegetative cover is low (Gilabert *et al.*, 2002).

Modified Soil Adjusted Vegetation Index (MSAVI)   Minimises the effect of bare soil on SAVI (Qi *et al.*, 1994). SAVI and MSAVI are commonly used to measure cover.

Enhanced Vegetation Index (EVI)   Mainly used for detecting stress related to drought over different landscapes, to monitor the development of droughts affecting agriculture (Karnieli *et al.*, 2013).

Transformed Soil Adjusted Vegetation Index (TSAVI)   A vegetation index that intends to minimise soil brightness effects by modelling the soil line with a random slope and intercept (Ren and Zhou, 2014).

Table 6.2 Overview of major remote sensing derived land products

Provider	Resolution	Indices
MODIS[a]	250 m–1 km	Surface Reflectance, Land Surface Temperature and Emissivity (MOD11), Land Surface Temperature and Emissivity (MOD21), Land Cover Products, Vegetation Index Products (NDVI and EVI), Thermal Anomalies – Active Fires, Fraction of Photosynthetically Active Radiation (FPAR) / Leaf Area Index (LAI), Evapotranspiration, Gross Primary Productivity (GPP) / Net Primary Productivity (NPP), Bidirectional Reflectance Distribution Function (BRDF) / Albedo Parameter, Vegetation Continuous Fields, Water Mask, Burnt Area Product
Copernicus[b]	250 m–500 m[c]	Land Cover Products[d], fraction of photosynthetically active radiation absorbed by the vegetation, fraction of green vegetation cover, LAI, Normalized Difference Vegetation Index, Vegetation Condition Index, Vegetation Productivity Index, Dry Matter Productivity, Burnt Area Product, Soil Water Index (SOI), Surface Soil Moisture, Land Surface Temperature, Top of Canopy Reflectance, Surface Albedo
CORINE[e]	100 m	Land cover products for the European Economic Area, changes in land cover in 44 classes with a minimum mapping unit (MMU) of 5 ha in 1990, 2000, 2006, 2012, and 2018
NOAA[f]	1 km–16 km	LAI, FAPAR, Vegetation Index, Global Vegetation Index, Normalized Difference Vegetation Index, Fractional Vegetation Index, Precipitable Water Index, Vegetation Health Fraction Product, Surface Reflectance[g], annual, monthly, and daily global night-time lights, VIIRS Boat Detection

[a]https://modis.gsfc.nasa.gov/data/dataprod/
[b]https://land.copernicus.eu/global/access
[c]Near real time to be resampled from 300 m.
[d]Spatial resolution for the land cover products of the Copernicus programme is 50 m–100 m.
[e]Coordination of Information on the Environment; https://land.copernicus.eu/pan-european/corine-land-cover
[f]Land cover: https://www.ospo.noaa.gov/Products/land/vegetation.html; night lights: https://payneinstitute.mines.edu/eog/
[g]Spatial resolution for the Surface Reflectance product of the NOAA programme is 375 m–750 m.

Soil Water Index (SWI) Quantifies the moisture condition at various depths in the soil, and is mainly driven by precipitation via the process of infiltration (Albergel *et al.*, 2008), since the soil moisture is a very heterogeneous variable and varies on small scales with soil properties and drainage patterns.

Vegetation Continuous Fields (VCF) Includes estimates of areal proportions of life form, leaf type, and leaf longevity. VCF provides global sub-pixel estimates of three land cover components (per cent tree cover, per cent non-tree vegetation, and per cent non-vegetated) at 250 m spatial resolution; a global water mask (MOD44W) is also included as an embedded ancillary layer (Pickens *et al.*, 2020).

Leaf Area Index (LAI) A dimensionless quantity that characterises plant canopies, it is defined as the one-sided green leaf area per unit ground surface area (LAI = leaf area (m^2) / ground area (m^2)) in broadleaf canopies (Zheng and Moskal, 2009). LAI is used to predict photosynthetic primary production and evapotranspiration, and as a reference tool for crop growth.

Night-time lights

Night-time lights data are a beneficial by-product of a meteorological satellite programme. The most common data sources for night-time lights are DMSP and the VIIRS Day/Night Band (DNB) data covering both day- and night-time (low-light) conditions. Although the main application area for night-time lights focuses on estimating total population or population density (Lo, 2001; Sutton *et al.*, 2003), DNB data have been used for a wide range of applications such as ship tracking and fishing activity (Straka *et al.*, 2015); estimating access to electricity and electrification, as well as community resilience and power outage, industrial output, and economic activities (Bennett and Smith, 2017; Yeh *et al.*, 2020); total population or population density (Lo, 2001; Sutton *et al.*, 2003); economic growth at both national and subnational levels (Bruederle and Hodler, 2018); understanding armed conflicts (Li *et al.*, 2015, 2020); the extent and characteristics of urbanisation processes (Pandey *et al.*, 2013); and estimating migration and mobility patterns (Chen, 2020) and migration distances (Niedomysl *et al.*, 2017).

Satellite data utilisation for studying climate-induced migration

The notion of accelerating environmental change and a deteriorating ecosystem leading to growing human migration has been burgeoning since the 1970s (Black, 2001). Since then, climate change and environmental factors have been hot topics among scholars and policy communities in Europe and globally. In the last decade in particular there has been a rapid increase in empirical studies where environmental factors are included in modelling human migration. Nevertheless, the statistics and a wide range of methodological approaches fail to support any evidence on environmental factors as marginal migration drivers. For the assessment of environment–migration relationships, many discussions are based on a Malthusian assumption of climate refugees, that climate change would lead to large-scale human displacements (IPCC, 1992; Myers, 2002; Gray and Wise, 2016).

The interlinkage between sociodemographic, political, and security-related factors and the aftermath of climate and environmental factors for migration have recently been investigated in depth. A large body of literature has tested climate- or environment-induced migration hypotheses, also considering the confounding factors, by linking environmental and climate data to geolocated data on human migration, rarely from official statistics but mostly household surveys (Bohra-Mishra *et al.*, 2014; Gray and Mueller, 2012a,b; Mueller *et al.*, 2014). The results of such studies are striking as although they confirm the positive relationship between accelerating extreme climate events and increasing human migration, they also reveal the significance of the intersectional relationship of environmental factors with non-environmental factors, which does not fit the prevailing 'environmental refugee/migrant' narrative (Deressa *et al.*, 2009; Hunter *et al.*, 2014; Gray and Wise, 2016). To be more specific, the drivers of migration are functioning through confounding factors of environment, social, political, economic, and demographic determinants, and distress migration following climate shocks can be just one of many possible adaptations to environmental change (McLeman and Smit, 2006; Jäger *et al.*, 2009; McLeman and Hunter, 2010; Black *et al.*, 2011; McLeman, 2014; Parrish *et al.*, 2020).

In light of these examples, three case studies will be elaborated in order to illustrate how indicators developed through satellite data are used to understand the relationship between human migration and climate- and environment-related aspects.

Case study 1: Impact of ethnic migration on a protected area landscape in western Uganda

Hartter *et al.* (2015) were interested in the relationship between ethnic migration and the landscape surrounding Kibale National Park in western Uganda. For the analyses, they combined historical narratives with interviews, census, and satellite data. Satellite data for land cover were analysed for the period between 2000 and 2010 for the areas dominated by two specific ethnic groups (Bakiga and Batoro). Derived data products of forested area change (per cent tree cover in 2000 and 2010 and per cent tree cover change from 2000 to 2010) were extracted from MODIS data. Annual estimates of per cent tree cover in 2000 and 2010 were extracted from the VCF at 250 m resolution from the pixels inside each polygon. A lower proportion of forest coverage in an area was taken as a proxy for cultivated/farmed areas. To compare three areas, they tested mean differences by ANOVA and Tukey–Kramer honest significant difference (HSD) tests for multiple comparisons of cover in 2000 and 2010, as well as the change in per cent cover 2000–2010. Moreover, they compared initial land cover maps (for 2001 and 2009) with the survey data on the types

Box 6.1 Triangulation and mixed method approaches

Triangulation can be defined as employing several approaches to study the same research question. For the purposes of this book, this includes the use of qualitative and quantitative approaches jointly, but also, within each main approach, it is possible to use triangulation to improve any analysis. The main difficulty of triangulation is in combining methods that rest on different assumptions, load different meanings to similar concepts, or bring different perspectives to the study. This is also one of the main issues of *mixed methods* research, where qualitative and quantitative methods are brought together pragmatically in a research project.

Data triangulation, one of the four triangulation types defined by Denzin (1970), is the use of a variety of data sources, including time, space, and persons, in a study to improve the richness of the data and compensate for its weaknesses by complementary strengths of other data (Flick, 2007). Data triangulation increases the validity and reliability of the results by providing alternatives to validation and hence by diminishing the risk of false interpretations (Flick, 2002, 2007).

Theory triangulation is the assessment of alternative (even competing) theories to explain a phenomenon, whereas *method triangulation* is, as its name implies, the use of multiple methods, including at the design and data collection stages. Finally, Denzin (1970) defined *investigator triangulation* as two or more skilled (and independent) researchers examining the same data. This is particularly challenging for domains where large, private datasets (such as mobile CDRs) are analysed, as data sharing may be difficult.

To study migration and human mobility, the integration of new data sources calls for a mixed methods approach and for multiple types of triangulation (Fielding, 2012), which 'provides a rationale for hypotheses/theories/guiding assumptions to compete and provide alternatives' (Niaz, 2008, p. 64).

Taking remote sensing as an example, while these approaches are considered primarily quantitative, they can be combined with qualitative methods (for a broad review of these studies, see Jiang 2003). Considering that the interaction of environmental factors with non-environmental factors may account for the drivers of migration (Parnell and Walawege, 2011), information on physical processes and spatial relations will not be sufficient to inform us of the dynamics of the society–landscape relationship. Satellite images can provide an in-depth view of the geographical landscape in either rural or urban settings, yet while studying human actions and their cultural landscape, further information and insights are indispensable to provide a clearer picture of the overall situation.

of crops grown by Batoro and Bakiga households, as a check on agricultural differences and practices between the three regions. Their results show that in the last half of the twentieth century, the area around Kibale National Park transformed into a densely settled agricultural landscape from a barely populated woodland. More interestingly, the drivers of migration to this region were not primarily based on economic factors, and social and cultural determinants together with environmental change need to be investigated to understand human migration.

Case study 2: Non-linearities and thresholds for the relationship between climate shocks and rural–urban migration in Mexico

To investigate the odds of migration between rural and urban areas in Mexico, Nawrotzki *et al.* (2017) gathered Mexican census data for 2000 and 2010 with high-resolution climate data from Terra Populus that are linked to census data at the municipality level. Moreover, to address the significant non-linearities, the climate shocks are measured as monthly deviations from a 30 year (1961–1990) long-term climate normal period. In terms of measures for climate extremes, they used monthly average precipitation and maximum temperature (a 50 year time series, 1961–2010) and the number of drought and heat months. In addition to the climate shocks, they used satellite data to measure the urban extents in order to examine four internal migration patterns (rural–urban, rural–rural, urban–urban, and urban–rural) based on sending and receiving municipality categories. To do this, the municipality classifications of the urban area were built on MODIS urban extents for the year 2000. To address the clustered structure (individuals nested in municipalities), multilevel models were employed. The findings pointed out different linear and non-linear relationships between heat months and migration to urban destinations, whereas migration to rural destinations was only weakly associated with climate factors.

Case study 3: Dynamics of armed conflict, forced migration, and urbanisation in Colombia

Camargo *et al.* (2020) investigated the anthropogenic and demographic processes in Colombia by the spatial relationship between forced migration, armed conflicts, and socioeconomic factors. They combined municipal-level spatial data on forced displacements for both expulsed and received populations with satellite data of night-time lights, including all available images in Google Earth Engine, to measure anthropogenic change and urbanisation. The night-lights data were measured for three politically relevant time intervals (1991–1998, 1999–2006, and 2006–2013) and were used to develop three indicators of land use and land cover change, based on night-time changes: night-lights intensity (average anthropogenic change), the proportion by which high light intensity areas had expanded (anthropogenic print spatial expansion), and the proportion of an area that stops emitting light during each period (anthropogenic print spatial contraction). Accordingly, they managed to examine the land use/cover changes across space and time for different geographic scales (national, regional, or metropolitan levels) while controlling for different sociodemographic variables. The results showed that forced migration affected smaller populations significantly, and smaller urban areas experienced larger distress from internal displacement processes compared to large urban centres.

Satellite data applications for migration and humanitarian aid

From a technical perspective, remote sensing and satellite data provide measurements and spatial patterns for a more comprehensive look at the Earth's surface. During the past five decades, the purpose of Earth observation has moved from surface monitoring towards contributing to the development of human society (Guo, 2014). Liverman et al. (2000) termed this 'socialising the pixel' to emphasise the potential of the use of remote sensing imagery in addressing 'social' concerns. Rindfuss and Stern (1998) made an important point in the same book and emphasised the fusion of different scientific traditions in addition to the fusion of different data sources. Remote sensing data are widely acknowledged, and the most prevalent applications of remote sensing techniques are seen in the natural sciences, yet utilisation of remote sensing data for disaster management and humanitarian aid is more common than for migration research, which is concerned with why, how, and when people migrate and what happens before, during, and after migration.

Considering humanitarian crises, the potential role of remote sensing data as a tool in addressing displacement has already been highlighted (IDMC, 2019). Satellite imagery can be tapped to identify vulnerable areas for enabling humanitarian help, building resilience, and developing intervention strategies before or during a crisis. As described above in detail, remote sensing data include, but are not limited to, climate and land cover, such as vegetation and drought, night lights, and urbanisation extents. This information can help to assess the regions at risk due to environmental extremes with direct impact on residential areas, croplands, and access to water, and epidemics and/or armed conflicts, which might induce internal or international displacement of populations. There have been numerous cases where satellite images have been employed for humanitarian aid following climate extremes and large-scale displacement (Heslin and Thalheimer, 2020). For instance, an improved agricultural drought indicator (for Ethiopia) was developed in direct collaboration with a humanitarian aid organisation, namely Doctors without Borders (Médecins sans Frontières), to provide drought and food security monitoring as well as early drought warnings (Enenkel et al., 2016). Likewise, the use of satellite imagery of flood extent, destroyed structures, or burned areas has been demonstrated for emergency mapping applications for governments and humanitarian aid organisations to support crises by estimating the land area and the number of affected people (Boccardo and Tonolo, 2015). On the other hand, some practitioners like the Red Cross Climate Centre (RCCC) have been testing forecast-based financing, which is based on scientific models of remote sensing data to develop early-warning systems and providing information for short-term humanitarian assistance (Coughlan de Perez et al., 2015).

Besides natural disasters, the size of already displaced populations has been examined through remote sensing data by mapping refugee settlements and detecting and counting tents and buildings in and around the camps (Bjorgo, 2000; Kemper and Heinzel, 2014; Quinn et al., 2018), as well as by estimating population density mapping for humanitarian health aid (Greenough and Nelson, 2019). Better predictions for the people in need and hence better estimations for requirements and necessities mean that local and national authorities and humanitarian help organisations can improve their aid allocations. Also, the opportunities of remote sensing data for night lights have been seized for conflicting activities (Witmer and O'Loughlin, 2011; Witmer, 2015; Pech and Lakes, 2017), for estimating the number of people in a given location (Bennett and Smith, 2017; Lang et al., 2018, 2020), or the humanitarian emergency settings for enduring conflicts and crises, such as in the cases of Syria and Yemen (Corbane et al., 2016; Jiang et al., 2017; Garber et al., 2020).

Accordingly, the applications of migration and humanitarian aid present a grand potential for future research, but also bring aspects such as ethical concerns into focus. We will discuss the limitations in the last section and provide a broad picture of remote sensing applications for monitoring climate change, extreme weather events, and disasters, determining environmental factors and mapping, indirect measures for internal displacement, human mobility, and the potential use for humanitarian purposes.

Discussion: Opportunities and limitations

While satellite or remote sensing data provide an outsider view from a distance, the content will not be comprehensive enough to overtake the significance of micro data (such as surveys) and macro data (such as official statistics and register data) based on specific information of the area or population and qualitative information based on field and personal experiences such as ethnographic field work and in-depth interviews. However, given the notable gaps in the international migration statistics, in particular irregular migration (Bircan et al., 2020; Ahmad-Yar and Bircan, 2021), satellite data can serve as a complementary information source for triangulation and improved estimations. Nevertheless, researchers should be aware of the existing limitations of remote sensing data and applications. The major shortcomings of satellite data for studying migration can be summarised as spatial resolution, complexity, data processing challenges, lack of evidence for use in practical examples, and ethical aspects.

Remote sensing data have a complex structure and advanced data processing is needed to develop products such as indicators and maps. Thanks to rich sources due to the numerous (both public and commercial) satellites orbiting the Earth, data availability and richness in content (in terms of resolution and coverage) are improving steadily. Publicly available data are usually at a lower resolution and with less precision, while very high resolution (VHR) satellite imagery can be purchased at different costs. In the case of Europe, ESA allows VHR remote sensing data to be used free of charge for large-scale scientific projects supported by EU institutions. However, publicly available raw data in its unprocessed form requires high-performance computing systems and proficient data scientists. Fortunately, many organisations (such as NASA, ESA, etc.) make derived products and indices publicly available. Yet, gathering, analysing, and interpreting satellite data require expertise. In short, the data compatibility of these indices (most of which are in geospatial formats) with traditional and new data sources is not straightforward for non-expert users.

Having said that, satellite data have been actively used by geographers and data scientists for environmental and ecology-related questions. The studies also covered specific cases linked to human migration and humanitarian aid, as discussed in the previous sections. However, because of the technical complexity and the focus on modelling and methods, as opposed to societal aspects, possible future applications are not ready in terms of validity, reliability, and insightful inferences when viewed from a social science perspective. Nevertheless, the complex nature of the migration phenomenon and the humanitarian responses to environmental crisis and conflict areas have drawn attention to the intricate relations between varied factors and provided scholars from all disciplines with insights on the need for more comprehensive perspectives and horizons.

There are also ethical issues to consider in processing such data. High-resolution data can help to improve indicator development and models; however, increasing the accuracy from dozens of meters to centimetres poses a significant threat of misuse and human tracking. Even low-resolution visual remote sensing data capture enables the observation of private property and collecting of sensitive personal information, which will pose as a violation of individual privacy and potentially be placing people in harm's way (Gilman, 2014; Berman *et al.*, 2018). When the overall application areas of satellite data such as forced migration and vulnerable populations are reckoned with, it is crucial that all stakeholders (i.e., governments, international organisations, and civil society organisations) are informed and endorse the data collection, processing, and, above all, how the results will be exploited within ethical considerations. Power relations of data access, control, and ownership are of great importance when satellite imagery and digital technologies are employed mostly by developed countries for developing or under-developed countries, which are vulnerable due to environmental crises or armed conflict, and are consequently the main migrant-sending countries. To elaborate the data ownership and the ethical considerations a bit more, satellite companies with commercial interests and their products, which could be purchased with minimum legal boundaries, do not differentiate between purposes of use. For instance, a non-profit organisation called Sea-Eye[10] developed an artificial intelligence system trained on satellite images that can detect and assist migrant boats on the Mediterranean. When the developers and the users of this system are humanitarian organisations, it can serve to help the vulnerable migrants and refugees travelling on boats to Europe, or in providing evidence for human rights violations, such as failure to render assistance in emergencies by civilian or military vessels. On the other hand, considering

---

[10] Sea-Eye, https://sea-eye.org/en/

that irregular migration is mostly an 'unwanted' notion in Europe, there is no reason to assume that such a system has not been used for preventive migration management by public authorities or military services to detect the approaching migrant boats and prevent them landing on the European coasts.

To conclude, we have demonstrated that remote sensing data from satellites can provide important opportunities to improve population estimates for at-risk communities, displaced people, and refugee groups, and predict forced migration flows, notably in the context of natural disasters, climate extremes, and conflict zones. Satellite imagery can also be deployed to provide relevant and beneficial information to address first-concern needs and to design adaptation measures in emergency cases where data are mostly not available in real time or in the short run due to geographical, political, or other reasons. As discussed, with the help of remote sensing data, mapping a crisis, identifying the location, frequency, and intensity of affected areas, and determining at-risk and vulnerable populations will facilitate assistance and support for pre- and during-crisis/disaster resilience-building interventions. The availability of and open access to satellite data does not directly allow the stakeholders to utilise it for further analysis and interpret the information available. Consequently, capacity building amongst and collaborations between social scientists and practitioners is a priority in order to benefit from the opportunities that remote sensing provides, and to address the challenges and developing human rights compliant applications.

Acknowledgements

This study was supported by the European Union's Horizon 2020 Research and Innovation Programme under grant agreement no. 870661.

References

Ahmad-Yar, A. W. and Bircan, T. (2021), 'Anatomy of a misfit: International migration statistics', *Sustainability* 13(7), 4032.

Albergel, C., Rüdiger, C., Pellarin, T., Calvet, J.-C., Fritz, N., Froissard, F., Suquia, D., Petitpa, A., Piguet, B., and Martin, E. (2008), 'From near-surface to root-zone soil moisture using an exponential filter: An assessment of the method based on in-situ observations and model simulations', *Hydrology and Earth System Sciences* 12(6), 1323–37.

Bennett, M. M. and Smith, L. C. (2017), 'Advances in using multitemporal night-time lights satellite imagery to detect, estimate, and monitor socioeconomic dynamics', *Remote Sensing of Environment* 192, 176–97.

Berman, G., de la Rosa, S., and Accone, T. (2018), 'Ethical considerations when using geospatial technologies for evidence generation', Technical report, UNICEF Office of Research – Innocenti.

Bircan, T., Purkayastha, D., Ahmad-yar, A. W., Lotter, K., Iakono, C. D., Göler, D., Stanek, M., Yilmaz, S., Solano, G., and Ünver, Ö. (2020), 'Gaps in migration research:

Review of migration theories and the quality and compatibility of migration data on the national and international level', Technical Report (Deliverable 2.1), HumMingBird Project.

Bjorgo, E. (2000), 'Using very high spatial resolution multispectral satellite sensor imagery to monitor refugee camps', *International Journal of Remote Sensing* 21(3), 611–16.

Black, R. (2001), 'Environmental refugees: Myth or reality?', Technical report, United Nations High Commissioner for Refugees.

Black, R., Adger, W. N., Arnell, N. W., Dercon, S., Geddes, A., and Thomas, D. (2011), 'The effect of environmental change on human migration', *Global Environmental Change* 21, S3–S11.

Boccardo, P. and Tonolo, F. G. (2015), 'Remote sensing role in emergency mapping for disaster response', *in* G. Lollino, A. Manconi, F. Guzzetti, M. Culshaw, P. T. Bobrowsky, and F. Luino, eds, *Engineering Geology for Society and Territory*, Vol. 5, Springer, New York, 17–24.

Bohra-Mishra, P., Oppenheimer, M., and Hsiang, S. M. (2014), 'Nonlinear permanent migration response to climatic variations but minimal response to disasters', *Proceedings of the National Academy of Sciences* 111(27), 9780–5.

Bruederle, A. and Hodler, R. (2018), 'Nighttime lights as a proxy for human development at the local level', *PLOS One* 13(9), e0202231.

Camargo, G., Sampayo, A. M., Peña Galindo, A., Escobedo, F. J., Carriazo, F., and Feged-Rivadeneira, A. (2020), 'Exploring the dynamics of migration, armed conflict, urbanization, and anthropogenic change in colombia', *PLOS One* 15(11), e0242266.

Campbell, J. B. and Wynne, R. H. (2011), *Introduction to Remote Sensing*, Guilford Press, New York.

Cao, G., Wang, B., Xavier, H.-C., Yang, D., and Southworth, J. (2017), 'A new difference image creation method based on deep neural networks for change detection in remote-sensing images', *International Journal of Remote Sensing* 38(23), 7161–75.

Chen, X. (2020), 'Nighttime lights and population migration: Revisiting classic demographic perspectives with an analysis of recent European data', *Remote Sensing* 12(1), 169.

Cheng, G., Han, J., and Lu, X. (2017), 'Remote sensing image scene classification: Benchmark and state of the art', *Proceedings of the IEEE* 105(10), 1865–83.

Corbane, C., Kemper, T., Freire, S., Louvrier, C., and Pesaresi, M. (2016), 'Monitoring the Syrian humanitarian crisis with the JRC's global human settlement layer and night-time satellite data', Publications Office of the European Union, Luxembourg.

Coughlan de Perez, E., van den Hurk, B., Van Aalst, M., Jongman, B., Klose, T., and Suarez, P. (2015), 'Forecast-based financing: An approach for catalyzing humanitarian action based on extreme weather and climate forecasts', *Natural Hazards and Earth System Sciences* 15(4), 895–904.

Denzin, N. K. (1970), *The Research Act*, Aldine, Chicago, IL.

Deressa, T. T., Hassan, R. M., Ringler, C., Alemu, T., and Yesuf, M. (2009), 'Determinants of farmers' choice of adaptation methods to climate change in the Nile Basin of Ethiopia', *Global Environmental Change* 19(2), 248–55.

Diogo, V. and Koomen, E. (2016), 'Land cover and land use indicators: Review of available data', Technical report, OECD.

Elvidge, C. D., Baugh, K., Zhizhin, M., and Hsu, F. C. (2013), 'Why VIIRS data are superior to DMSP for mapping nighttime lights', *Proceedings of the Asia-Pacific Advanced Network* 35(0), 62.

Elvidge, C. D., Baugh, K., Zhizhin, M., Hsu, F. C., and Ghosh, T. (2017), 'VIIRS night-time lights', *International Journal of Remote Sensing* 38(21), 5860–79.

Elvidge, C. D., Sutton, P. C., Ghosh, T., Tuttle, B. T., Baugh, K. E., Bhaduri, B., and Bright, E. (2009), 'A global poverty map derived from satellite data', *Computers & Geosciences* 35(8), 1652–60.

Emery, B. and Camps, A. (2017), *Introduction to Satellite Remote Sensing: Atmosphere, Ocean, Land and Cryosphere Applications*, Elsevier, Amsterdam.

Enenkel, M., Steiner, C., Mistelbauer, T., Dorigo, W., Wagner, W., See, L., Atzberger, C., Schneider, S., and Rogenhofer, E. (2016), 'A combined satellite-derived drought indicator to support humanitarian aid organizations', *Remote Sensing* 8(4), 340.

Fielding, N. G. (2012), 'Triangulation and mixed methods designs: Data integration with new research technologies', *Journal of Mixed Methods Research* 6(2), 124–36.

Flick, U. (2002), 'Qualitative research: State of the art', *Social Science Information* 41(1), 5–24.

Flick, U. (2007), *Managing Quality in Qualitative Research*, Sage, Thousand Oaks, CA, 38–54.

Friedl, M. A., Sulla-Menashe, D., Tan, B., Schneider, A., Ramankutty, N., Sibley, A., and Huang, X. (2010), 'MODIS collection 5 global land cover: Algorithm refinements and characterization of new datasets', *Remote Sensing of Environment* 114(1), 168–82.

Garber, K., Fox, C., Abdalla, M., Tatem, A., Qirbi, N., Lloyd-Braff, L., Al-Shabi, K., Ongwae, K., Dyson, M., and Hassen, K. (2020), 'Estimating access to health care in Yemen, a complex humanitarian emergency setting: A descriptive applied geospatial analysis', *The Lancet Global Health* 8(11), e1435–43.

Gilabert, M., González-Piqueras, J., García-Haro, F., and Meliá, J. (2002), 'A generalized soil-adjusted vegetation index', *Remote Sensing of Environment* 82(2-3), 303–10.

Gilman, D. (2014), *Unmanned Aerial Vehicles in Humanitarian Response*, United Nations Office for the Coordination of Humanitarian Affairs, New York.

Gray, C. L. and Mueller, V. (2012a), 'Natural disasters and population mobility in Bangladesh', *Proceedings of the National Academy of Sciences* 109(16), 6000–5.

Gray, C. L. and Mueller, V. (2012b), 'Drought and population mobility in rural Ethiopia', *World Development* 40(1), 134–45.

Gray, C. and Wise, E. (2016), 'Country-specific effects of climate variability on human migration', *Climatic Change* 135(3–4), 555–68.

Greenough, P. G. and Nelson, E. L. (2019), 'Beyond mapping: A case for geospatial analytics in humanitarian health', *Conflict and Health* 13(1), 1–14.

Guo, H. (2014), 'Special section guest editorial: Earth observation for global environmental change', *Journal of Applied Remote Sensing* 8(1), 084501.

Guo, H., Dou, C., Zhang, X., Han, C., and Yue, X. (2016), 'Earth observation from the manned low Earth orbit platforms', *ISPRS Journal of Photogrammetry and Remote Sensing* 115, 103–18.

Hansen, M. C., DeFries, R. S., Townshend, J. R., and Sohlberg, R. (2000), 'Global land cover classification at 1 km spatial resolution using a classification tree approach', *International Journal of Remote Sensing* 21(6–7), 1331–64.

Hartter, J., Ryan, S. J., MacKenzie, C. A., Goldman, A., Dowhaniuk, N., Palace, M., Diem, J. E., and Chapman, C. A. (2015), 'Now there is no land: A story of ethnic migration in a protected area landscape in Western Uganda', *Population and Environment* 36(4), 452–79.

Hein, C., Hünemohr, H., and Lasch, R. (2018), 'Remote sensing in humanitarian logistics: An integrative approach', *in The Road to a Digitalized Supply Chain Management: Smart and Digital Solutions for Supply Chain Management*, Proceedings of the Hamburg International Conference of Logistics (HICL), Vol. 25, epubli GmbH Berlin, 271–90.

Henderson, J. V., Storeygard, A., and Weil, D. N. (2012), 'Measuring economic growth from outer space', *American Economic Review* 102(2), 994–1028.

Heslin, A. and Thalheimer, L. (2020), 'The picture from above: Using satellite imagery to overcome methodological challenges in studying environmental displacement', *Oxford Monitor of Forced Migration* 8(2), 75–87.

Hunter, L. M., Nawrotzki, R., Leyk, S., Maclaurin, G. J., Twine, W., Collinson, M., and Erasmus, B. (2014), 'Rural outmigration, natural capital, and livelihoods in South Africa', *Population, Space and Place* 20(5), 402–20.

IDMC (2019), 'Global report on internal displacement 2019', Technical report, NRC.

IPCC (1992), 'Climate change 1992: The supplementary report to the IPCC scientific assessment', Technical report, Intergovernmental Panel on Climate Change.

Jäger, J., Frühmann, J., Grünberger, S., and Vag, A. (2009), 'Environmental change and forced migration scenarios, synthesis report', ATLAS Innoglobe Ltd., Hungary.

Jensen, J. (1996), *Introductory Digital Image Processing: A Remote Sensing Perspective*, Pearson, London, 197–256.

Jiang, H. (2003), 'Stories remote sensing images can tell: Integrating remote sensing analysis with ethnographic research in the study of cultural landscapes', *Human Ecology* 31(2), 215–32.

Jiang, W., He, G., Long, T., and Liu, H. (2017), 'Ongoing conflict makes Yemen dark: From the perspective of nighttime light', *Remote Sensing* 9(8), 798.

Justice, C., Townshend, J., Vermote, E., Masuoka, E., Wolfe, R., Saleous, N., Roy, D., and Morisette, J. (2002), 'An overview of MODIS land data processing and product status', *Remote Sensing of Environment* 83(1–2), 3–15.

Karnieli, A., Bayarjargal, Y., Bayasgalan, M., Mandakh, B., Dugarjav, C., Burgheimer, J., Khudulmur, S., Bazha, S., and Gunin, P. (2013), 'Do vegetation indices provide a reliable indication of vegetation degradation? A case study in the Mongolian pastures', *International Journal of Remote Sensing* 34(17), 6243–62.

Kemper, T. and Heinzel, J. (2014), 'Mapping and monitoring of refugees and internally displaced people using EO data', *in* Q. Weng, ed, *Global Urban Monitoring And Assessment Through Earth Observation*, CRC Press, Boca Raton, FL, 195.

Kirscht, M. and Rinke, C. (1998), '3D reconstruction of buildings and vegetation from synthetic aperture radar (SAR) images', *in Proceedings of the IAPR Workshop on Machine Vision Applications*, 228–31.

Lang, S., et al. (2020), 'Earth observation tools and services to increase the effectiveness of humanitarian assistance', *European Journal of Remote Sensing* 53(sup2), 67–85.

Lang, S., Füreder, P., and Rogenhofer, E. (2018), 'Earth observation for humanitarian operations', *in* C. Al-Ekabi and S. Ferretti, eds, *Yearbook on Space Policy 2016*, Springer, New York, 217–29.

Lang, S., Schoepfer, E., Zeil, P., and Riedler, B. (2017), 'Earth observation for humanitarian assistance', *in Proceedings of the GI Forum*, Vol. 1, 157–65.

Lang, S., Tiede, D., Hölbling, D., Füreder, P., and Zeil, P. (2010), 'Earth observation (EO)-based ex post assessment of internally displaced person (IDP) camp evolution and population dynamics in Zam Zam, Darfur', *International Journal of Remote Sensing* 31(21), 5709–31.

LeCun, Y., Bengio, Y., and Hinton, G. (2015), 'Deep learning', *Nature* 521(7553), 436–44.

Li, X., Zhang, R., Huang, C., and Li, D. (2015), 'Detecting 2014 Northern Iraq Insurgency using night-time light imagery', *International Journal of Remote Sensing* 36(13), 3446–58.

Li, X., Zhou, Y., Zhao, M., and Zhao, X. (2020), 'A harmonized global nighttime light dataset 1992–2018', *Scientific Data* 7(1), 1–9.

Liu, J. G. and Mason, P. J. (2013), *Essential Image Processing and GIS for Remote Sensing*, John Wiley & Sons, Chichester.

Liverman, D., Moran, E. F., Rindfuss, R., and Stern, P. C. (2000), 'People and pixels: Linking remote sensing and social science (book review)', *The Geographical Bulletin* 42(1), 61.

Lo, C. (2001), 'Modeling the population of China using DMSP operational linescan system nighttime data', *Photogrammetric Engineering and Remote Sensing* 67(9), 1037–47.

McLeman, R. A. (2014), *Climate and Human Migration: Past Experiences, Future Challenges*, Cambridge University Press, Cambridge.

McLeman, R. A. and Hunter, L. M. (2010), 'Migration in the context of vulnerability and adaptation to climate change: Insights from analogues', *Wiley Interdisciplinary Reviews: Climate Change* 1(3), 450–61.

McLeman, R. and Smit, B. (2006), 'Migration as an adaptation to climate change', *Climatic Change* 76(1), 31–53.

Melesse, A. M., Weng, Q., Thenkabail, P. S., and Senay, G. B. (2007), 'Remote sensing sensors and applications in environmental resources mapping and modelling', *Sensors* 7(12), 3209–41.

Mueller, V., Gray, C., and Kosec, K. (2014), 'Heat stress increases long-term human migration in rural Pakistan', *Nature Climate Change* 4(3), 182–5.

Murphy, R. E. (2006), 'The NPOESS preparatory project', *in* J. J. Qu, W. Gao, M. Kafatos, R. E. Murphy, and V. V. Salomonson, eds, *Earth Science Satellite Remote Sensing*, Springer, New York, 182–98.

Myers, N. (2002), 'Environmental refugees: A growing phenomenon of the 21st century', *Philosophical Transactions of the Royal Society of London. Series B: Biological Sciences* 357(1420), 609–13.

Nawrotzki, R. J., DeWaard, J., Bakhtsiyarava, M., and Ha, J. T. (2017), 'Climate shocks and rural-urban migration in Mexico: Exploring nonlinearities and thresholds', *Climatic Change* 140(2), 243–58.

Niaz, M. (2008), 'A rationale for mixed methods (integrative) research programmes in education', *Journal of Philosophy of Education* 42(2), 287–305.

Nichols, D. A. (1975), 'The defense meteorological satellite program', *Optical Engineering* 14(4), 144273.

Niedomysl, T., Hall, O., Archila Bustos, M. F., and Ernstson, U. (2017), 'Using satellite data on nighttime lights intensity to estimate contemporary human migration distances', *Annals of the American Association of Geographers* 107(3), 591–605.

Pandey, B., Joshi, P., and Seto, K. C. (2013), 'Monitoring urbanization dynamics in India using DMSP/OLS night time lights and SPOT-VGT data', *International Journal of Applied Earth Observation and Geoinformation* 23, 49–61.

Parnell, S. and Walawege, R. (2011), 'Sub-Saharan African urbanisation and global environmental change', *Global Environmental Change* 21, S12–S20.

Parrish, R., Colbourn, T., Lauriola, P., Leonardi, G., Hajat, S., and Zeka, A. (2020), 'A critical analysis of the drivers of human migration patterns in the presence of climate change: A new conceptual model', *International Journal of Environmental Research and Public Health* 17(17), 6036.

Pech, L. and Lakes, T. (2017), 'The impact of armed conflict and forced migration on urban expansion in Goma: Introduction to a simple method of satellite-imagery analysis as a complement to field research', *Applied Geography* 88, 161–73.

Phiri, D., Simwanda, M., Salekin, S., Nyirenda, V. R., Murayama, Y., and Ranagalage, M. (2020), 'Sentinel-2 data for land cover/use mapping: A review', *Remote Sensing* 12(14), 2291.

Pickens, A. H., Hansen, M. C., Hancher, M., Stehman, S. V., Tyukavina, A., Potapov, P., Marroquin, B., and Sherani, Z. (2020), 'Mapping and sampling to characterize global inland water dynamics from 1999 to 2018 with full Landsat time-series', *Remote Sensing of Environment* 243, 111792.

Qi, J., Chehebouni, A., Huete, A., Kerr, Y., and Sorooshian, S. (1994), 'Modified soil adjusted vegetation index (MSAVI)', *Remote Sensing of Environment* 48, 119–26.

Quinn, J. A., Nyhan, M. M., Navarro, C., Coluccia, D., Bromley, L., and Luengo-Oroz, M. (2018), 'Humanitarian applications of machine learning with remote-sensing data: Review and case study in refugee settlement mapping', *Philosophical Transactions of the Royal Society A: Mathematical, Physical and Engineering Sciences* 376(2128), 20170363.

Ren, H. and Zhou, G. (2014), 'Determination of green aboveground biomass in desert steppe using litter-soil-adjusted vegetation index', *European Journal of Remote Sensing* 47(1), 611–25.

Rindfuss, R. R. and Stern, P. C. (1998), 'Linking remote sensing and social science: The need and the challenges', *in* National Research Council, *People and Pixels: Linking Remote Sensing and Social Science*, National Academies Press, Washington DC, 1–27.

Roy, D. P., *et al.* (2014), 'Landsat-8: Science and product vision for terrestrial global change research', *Remote Sensing of Environment* 145, 154–72.

Sayedain, S. A., Maghsoudi, Y., and Eini-Zinab, S. (2020), 'Assessing the use of cross-orbit Sentinel-1 images in land cover classification', *International Journal of Remote Sensing* 41(20), 7801–19.

Schowengerdt, R. (2007), *Remote Sensing, Models and Methods for Image Processing*, Elsevier, Amsterdam.

Song, X.-P., Hansen, M. C., Stehman, S. V., Potapov, P. V., Tyukavina, A., Vermote, E. F., and Townshend, J. R. (2018), 'Global land change from 1982 to 2016', *Nature* 560(7720), 639–43.

Spröhnle, K., Tiede, D., Schoepfer, E., Füreder, P., Svanberg, A., and Rost, T. (2014), 'Earth observation-based dwelling detection approaches in a highly complex refugee camp environment: A comparative study', *Remote Sensing* 6(10), 9277–97.

Straka, W. C., Seaman, C. J., Baugh, K., Cole, K., Stevens, E., and Miller, S. D. (2015), 'Utilization of the Suomi national polar-orbiting partnership (NPP) visible infrared imaging radiometer suite (VIIRS) day/night band for arctic ship tracking and fisheries management', *Remote Sensing* 7(1), 971–89.

Sutton, P. C., Elvidge, C., and Obremski, T. (2003), 'Building and evaluating models to estimate ambient population density', *Photogrammetric Engineering & Remote Sensing* 69(5), 545–53.

Voigt, S., *et al.* (2016), 'Global trends in satellite-based emergency mapping', *Science* 353(6296), 247–52.

Witmer, F. D. (2015), 'Remote sensing of violent conflict: Eyes from above', *International Journal of Remote Sensing* 36(9), 2326–52.

Witmer, F. D. and O'Loughlin, J. (2011), 'Detecting the effects of wars in the Caucasus regions of Russia and Georgia using radiometrically normalized DMSP-OLS nighttime lights imagery', *GIScience & Remote Sensing* 48(4), 478–500.

Xie, Y., Sha, Z., and Yu, M. (2008), 'Remote sensing imagery in vegetation mapping: A review', *Journal of Plant Ecology* 1(1), 9–23.

Yang, J., Zhou, J., Göttsche, F.-M., Long, Z., Ma, J., and Luo, R. (2020), 'Investigation and validation of algorithms for estimating land surface temperature from Sentinel-3 SLSTR data', *International Journal of Applied Earth Observation and Geoinformation* 91, 102136.

Yeh, C., Perez, A., Driscoll, A., Azzari, G., Tang, Z., Lobell, D., Ermon, S., and Burke, M. (2020), 'Using publicly available satellite imagery and deep learning to understand economic well-being in Africa', *Nature Communications* 11(1), 1–11.

Zhang, L., Zhang, L., and Du, B. (2016), 'Deep learning for remote sensing data: A technical tutorial on the state of the art', *IEEE Geoscience and Remote Sensing Magazine* 4(2), 22–40.

Zheng, G. and Moskal, L. M. (2009), 'Retrieving leaf area index (LAI) using remote sensing: Theories, methods and sensors', *Sensors* 9(4), 2719–45.

Zhu, X. X., Tuia, D., Mou, L., Xia, G.-S., Zhang, L., Xu, F., and Fraundorfer, F. (2017), 'Deep learning in remote sensing: A comprehensive review and list of resources', *IEEE Geoscience and Remote Sensing Magazine* 5(4), 8–36.

7

Using Facebook and LinkedIn Data to Study International Mobility

CAROLINA COIMBRA VIEIRA, MASOOMALI FATEHKIA,
KIRAN GARIMELLA, INGMAR WEBER AND
EMILIO ZAGHENI

Introduction to advertising data

ONLINE SOCIAL NETWORKS are well known for promoting social interaction between people by connecting them even when they are physically separated, whether by a few miles or across continents. To deliver their free service to their users, most online social networks rely on targeted advertisements as their business model. Facebook, for example, hosts over a quarter of the world's population, and the Facebook Advertising Platform (Facebook Ads) alone is responsible for more than 98% of the company's total revenues. Similarly, Twitter, Instagram, and TikTok are social networks whose business models are based on advertising. Even social networks that are based on a freemium model such as LinkedIn, where many features are available for free, but some require a paid membership, rely on targeted advertisements via the LinkedIn Advertising Platform (LinkedIn Ads) for additional revenues.

The key appeal to advertisers who are considering using these platforms to promote their products lies in the targeting capabilities offered by the social networks. Highly targeted advertisements can, potentially, deliver the right message to the right consumer, and thus offer a good return on investment. Social networks are able to offer these targeting capabilities due to the rich user data they collect, which include detailed demographic information, such as information on the user's age, gender, home location, income level, and education level, but also on their topical interests and certain behaviours. Some of these attributes are explicitly self-declared by the users, such as their age and gender, while others are derived from meta-information on how they access the social network, such as their likely home location or their device type; and some are inferred through machine learning models, using their likes, social interactions, or status updates as input.[1]

In other words, we can see social network advertising as the process of matching social network users by their profile data available on the social network to target groups specified by the advertiser to deliver advertisements. Thanks to the personalised targeting and scalability of online advertising, advertisers benefit from huge increases in their conversions and sales at a lower cost of acquisition. According to the non-profit Interactive Advertising Bureau, social network advertising has thus become a popular form of advertising, with a projected $43 billion spent on it in 2020.[2]

The richness of the aggregated data provided by online social network advertising platforms has also been explored by the academic community using the same tools the platforms provide to advertisers. These tools allow advertisers to obtain audience estimates referring to the estimated number of users on a social network that matches the given input criteria based on demographic attributes before the advertisement is launched. Using these tools, researchers can obtain data for studying demographic characteristics across several research areas, including mobility and migrant assimilation (Dubois *et al.*, 2018). Facebook and LinkedIn host two of the main advertising platforms researchers use to study migration, in part because these platforms have features that make it easy to target migrants.[3]

Facebook is the most popular online social network, and its purpose is very generic, as its users can utilise the platform for different purposes in their daily lives, such as contacting friends, sharing emotions, or reading the news. Similarly, users on LinkedIn can use the social network to connect and build a professional network. By using Facebook's advertising manager[4] it is possible, for example, to target users by their current location as well as by their home town, which allows us to identify potential migrants. Similarly, LinkedIn provides information on each user's previous and current place of work or study, which can be used to study migration. The information the network users provide about their native language and the languages they speak can also be used as a proxy for their nationality or home country, and to study migration.

When performing research involving Facebook Ads, it is possible to study, for example, the process of migration at a high level, and to examine the assimilation levels of migrants based on the interests they express online. For instance, in the 'Facebook examples' section we show how Facebook Ads can be used to collect anonymous and aggregate audience estimates for women aged 18+ living in Colombia who used to live in Venezuela and who primarily use a 4G connection to access

---

[1] Facebook: About detailed targeting, https://www.facebook.com/business/help/182371508761821?id=176276233019487
[2] IAB, https://www.iab.com/
[3] While Twitter has similar features, to the best of our knowledge there has so far been no research conducted using Twitter advertising data (at the time of writing, April 2021).
[4] Facebook Ads Manager, https://www.facebook.com/business/tools/ads-manager

the social network site. Since it is possible to collect information about users' educational institutions or employers through LinkedIn data, LinkedIn Ads can be used to study professional migration. LinkedIn Ads may also be used to harvest information about where migrants have studied, where they live and work, and their professional connections. As an example, in 'LinkedIn examples' we show how LinkedIn Ads can be used to estimate the number of female LinkedIn members who hold a PhD, studied at the University of Cambridge, and are now living in Germany.

These data are publicly accessible (Facebook/LinkedIn account needed) for every user, and there are no special access requirements. The advertising platform web page allows for the most intuitive and user-friendly interactions. On this web page, the advertiser can select the desired demographic attributes, while the platform provides the audience estimates. However, this approach is relatively slow, and does not scale. To automate the data collection process we can use dedicated application programming interfaces (APIs) provided by the platforms. This approach requires certain levels of programming and web-scraping skills. These APIs, which are used for serving data to the website's front end, are not publicly advertised. They can, however, be easily identified using network monitoring in any modern web browser.

Thus, a key advantage of these data is that they are available for free. Another highly attractive feature of both platforms is that they allow researchers to segment the advertising and to target specific audiences (without actually placing an advertisement). When compared to the work involved in collecting data using other data sources, such as surveys and census data, the data collection process through online social network platforms requires less time, effort, and cost to deliver the desired data. The amount of data available, the scalability, and the speed of updates are among the other advantages of using these low-cost, real-time platforms. In particular, these platforms are interesting to researchers because they offer access to large numbers of users who provide their information on social networks, and because they offer APIs. Although there are a lot of advantages to using these platforms as data sources, doing so also raises ethical issues. In addition, the platforms are structured as a black box, which imposes limits on the use of such data for research. We discuss these limits in 'General limitations/challenges', after discussing examples from two major social networks that provide free advertising data: Facebook and LinkedIn.

Facebook examples

As is the case for most social networks, Facebook's main revenue stream is from targeted online advertising. Facebook offers advertisers a rich set of targeting options to reach the desired audience. In addition to providing advertisers with the ability to target users based on age, gender, device type, or topical interests, Facebook Ads allows advertisers to target users based on their previous country of residence ('users who used to live in country X'). For a specified set of targeting criteria, the platform then provides an estimate of the audience size called the Monthly Active

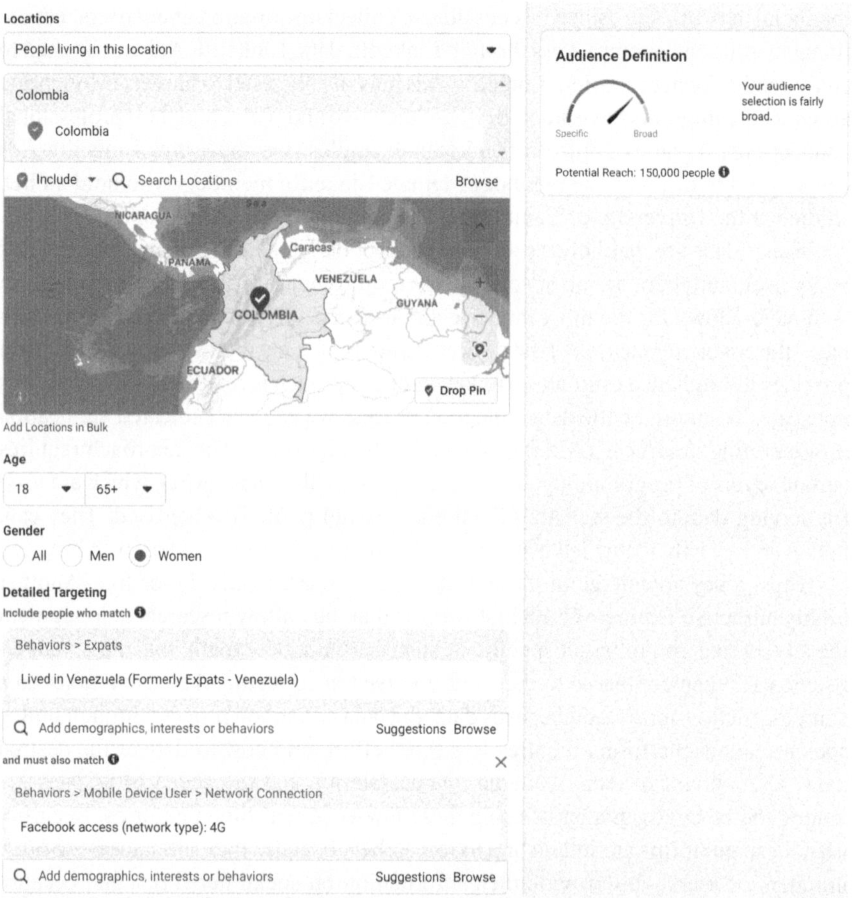

Figure 7.1 Screenshot of Facebook's advertising platform for an advertisement targeting women aged 18+ living in Colombia who used to live in Venezuela and who primarily use a 4G connection to access the social network site. The advertising platform displays an estimated audience of 150,000 users matching these targeting criteria.

Users (MAU). For example, Figure 7.1 shows the specifications for an advertisement targeting women aged 18+ living in Colombia who used to live in Venezuela and who primarily use a 4G connection to access the social network. For this target group, the advertising platform displays an estimated 150,000 users matching these criteria.[5] While the example here is at the country level, these estimates can be requested at various subnational spatial resolutions, including for regions, for

---

[5] Accessed on 10 November 2020. Note that the marketing API returns rounded estimates, whereby values in the thousands are rounded to the nearest hundred, values in the tens of thousands are rounded to the nearest thousand, and so on.

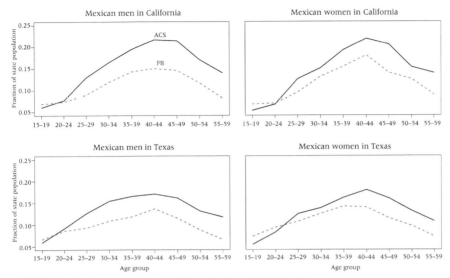

Figure 7.2 Facebook and American Community Survey (ACS) profiles of stocks of migrants by age and sex for Mexicans in California and in Texas. Source: Zagheni *et al.* (2017).

cities, and, at the lowest spatial granularity, for a specified radius around a given latitude/longitude coordinate. However, at more fine-grained spatial resolutions, data sparsity can become an issue, as the number of available Facebook users decreases, especially in countries with lower Facebook penetration. These estimates can be collected programmatically through an API[6] for various combinations of targeting options providing aggregated and anonymized data[7] on the distribution of Facebook users in a given location. Such data can provide opportunities for social science research, including for studies on migration. This section reviews some studies that have used these data for migration research, and the methods they have employed to analyse the data and to address bias.

Zagheni *et al.* (2017) and Spyratos *et al.* (2019) studied how migration researchers can complement migration statistics by using Facebook's audience estimates of users with different countries of previous residence to estimate the sizes of migrant populations. Zagheni *et al.* (2017) observed strong correlations between the fractions of Facebook users with various countries of previous residence across US states, the sizes of foreign-born populations estimated by the American Community Survey (ACS), and the country-level estimates of the sizes of migrant stocks in the World Bank data. When the authors compared the ACS data to Facebook's audience estimates, they observed patterns of bias across the information on age and country

---

[6] Meta for Developers: Marketing API, https://developers.facebook.com/docs/marketing-apis/
[7] The Python library https://github.com/maraujo/pySocialWatcher can be used to collect advertising data from the Facebook Marketing API.

of previous residence (Figure 7.2), which they corrected for by including country and age fixed effects in a regression model that predicted the survey data from the Facebook audience estimates. They observed improved model accuracy in estimating the sizes of migrant populations when this bias correction was done. Spyratos *et al.* (2019) used these data to compute estimates of migrant populations by country of origin globally in different destination countries. They addressed the selection biases in the sample of Facebook users by dividing the audience estimates for each migrant group by the Facebook penetration rate. This approach enabled them to correct for differences in Facebook usage across different countries of origin and destination, as well as across different age and gender groups. The Facebook penetration rates for each demographic group in each country were estimated by dividing the number of monthly active users on Facebook from the API by the respective population's size from the survey data. They then developed a model to compute the Facebook penetration level for each migrant group as a weighted average of the Facebook penetration rates in the countries of current and previous residence. These weight parameters were then estimated to give the best predictive fit between the corrected Facebook estimates and survey data.

Alexander *et al.* (2019) studied the utility of such data for estimating short-term population movements, such as in the aftermath of natural disasters, while focusing on the case of the outmigration of Puerto Ricans to the continental US after Hurricane Maria. They estimated the percentage change in the population of Puerto Ricans by comparing the number of Facebook users in the United States who previously lived in Puerto Rico in the periods before and after Hurricane Maria. In order to account for changes not due to the hurricane, such as changes related to an update to Facebook's estimation algorithm that may have affected audience estimates, they adopted a difference-in-differences approach whereby the observed change in the audience estimates for other migrant groups was deducted from the observed change in the audience estimates for Puerto Ricans. Given that changes in Facebook's audience estimates for other migrant groups generally moved in lock-step with those for Puerto Ricans in the periods prior to the hurricane, this approach was used to isolate changes in the population of Puerto Ricans that resulted from the hurricane. The authors then estimated the number of Puerto Ricans who moved to the continental US by multiplying the estimated percentage increase in the population of Puerto Rican Facebook users by the number of Puerto Ricans in the United States prior to the hurricane based on the survey data. The authors observed an increase in the number of Puerto Ricans living in the US, including a marked increase in the number of younger, working-age Puerto Ricans.

Palotti *et al.* (2020) studied how the estimates of Facebook users from Venezuela could be used to estimate the sizes of the Venezuelan refugee populations at the national and subnational levels for various countries in Latin America. To estimate the number of Venezuelan refugees, they corrected Facebook's audience estimates of users who previously lived in Venezuela by the overall Facebook penetration rate in the destination country. For example, if the total number of Facebook's monthly active users in the destination country, as per the advertising API, was estimated as equal to 60% of the destination country's population, then the raw estimates would be scaled up by a factor of 100/60. The authors found a strong correlation between these estimates and the available survey data at national and subnational geographic resolutions. In addition to estimating the sizes of the refugee populations, the authors explored the insights that could be gained from these estimates about the educational and economic situations of these populations. They developed regression models to estimate the users' income levels based on the device types they used on the social network, and drew on the self-declared information on the users' educational levels to learn more about the educational qualifications of the Venezuelan refugees across countries, and across regions in a country.

Beyond these quantitative estimates of the sizes of migrant populations, Dubois *et al.* (2018) and Stewart *et al.* (2019) studied qualitative aspects of cultural assimilation by using the interest-based targeting options of the platform. Dubois *et al.* (2018) collected the audience estimates of Facebook users for a list of interests in both the destination country and the home country of the target migrant group under study. They compared the numbers of users with these different interests in the home country and in the destination country in order to filter the interests to those that were more popular in the destination countries. Using the filtered list of interests, they then computed an assimilation score that compared the relative popularity of these interests in the destination country and among the targeted migrant groups in the destination country. Dubois *et al.* (2018) applied their approach to studying migrant assimilation among Arabic-speaking migrants in Germany across different demographic groups. Stewart *et al.* (2019) used the methodology of Dubois *et al.* (2018) to study the assimilation of Mexican migrants to the Anglo and African-American populations in the United States. For their study, Stewart *et al.* (2019) focused on the Mexican migrants' interests in musical genres in order to study their assimilation levels, while taking into account demographic dimensions such as age, gender, educational level, and language.

The wide range of targeting criteria provided on Facebook Ads makes it possible to study other aspects of migration and mobility as well. Spyratos *et al.* (2020) used data on estimates of users by travel frequency (using the option to target users who are 'frequent travelers' or 'frequent international travelers') to study the travelling behaviour of migrant groups by country of previous and current residence. As a validation step, the authors observed strong correlations between the estimates of Facebook users by country of previous residence who were frequent travellers or frequent international travellers, and the per capita number of international travellers by nationality in the United Kingdom, and the per capita income by nationality in the United States, respectively. To model the travelling behaviour of the migrants in this sample of Facebook users the authors fitted various regression models to explain the fraction of users who were frequent (international) travellers as a function of other variables, such as the users' demographics, and the characteristics of the country of previous or current residence, such as the country's income and gender inequality levels or its Facebook penetration rates.

As the studies reviewed here have shown,[8] the audience estimates from Facebook Ads represent a useful data source for studies of migration and mobility. Among the potential applications of these data are estimating the sizes of migrant populations; complementing traditional migrant statistics; estimating short-term migration movements in response to natural disasters, or in the context of a refugee crisis in which official data may be lacking or appearing with a time lag; and gaining further insights into other aspects of migration, such as education, socioeconomics, cultural assimilation, and travelling behaviour. However, these audience estimates also have limitations. 'General limitations/challenges' discusses the limitations of using social network advertising platforms for studies of migration.

LinkedIn examples

Unlike Facebook, LinkedIn's advertising platform does not provide a mechanism to explicitly target users based on countries they have lived in before. However, LinkedIn supports targeting users by 'Member Schools' to 'reach members who completed a course at a specific school, college, university or other learning institution'. This targeting is available for schools that have a dedicated page on LinkedIn, such as https://www.linkedin.com/school/university-of-cambridge/ for the University of Cambridge. Using the appropriate search API endpoint, one can look up the corresponding ID, in this case *urn:li:school:12691*. This ID is needed for API calls to obtain audience estimates through the corresponding endpoint.[9]

Figure 7.3 shows an example of the specifications for an advertisement targeting women living in Germany who studied at the University of Cambridge, and who hold a PhD. For this target group, the advertising platform displays an estimated audience of 530 users matching these criteria.[10]

To approximate the criterion of 'having lived in country X', we compiled a list of higher education institutions in country X, so that we could construct a query for LinkedIn users who 'studied at a higher education institution in country X'. Concretely, for each European country, including territories such as the Isle of Man, we (1) obtained a list of universities from uniRank[11] to search for, (2) searched for academic institutions for each city, region, or country targetable by LinkedIn, and (3) later filtered the returned results to remove kindergartens and high schools, as well as false positives, such as universities with ambiguous names from non-European countries (since we were only interested in European countries).

Figure 7.4 shows a circular plot of the estimate of LinkedIn users who (1) studied in country X (origin of the arrow), and (2) who now[12] live in country Y (target

---

[8] Interested readers are invited to contact the study authors for access to the data used in their study.
[9] LinkedIn API Documentation, https://learn.microsoft.com/en-us/linkedin/
[10] Accessed on 20 April 2022.
[11] uniRank, https://www.4icu.org/
[12] As of the time of data collection, i.e., October 2018.

USING FACEBOOK AND LINKEDIN DATA   149

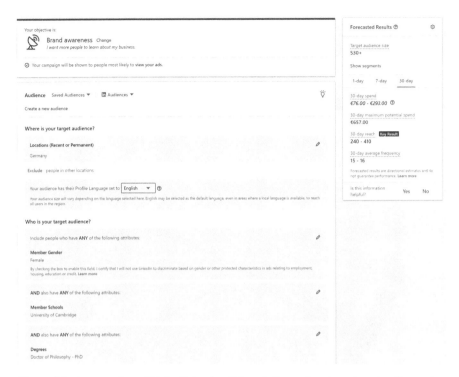

Figure 7.3 A screenshot of LinkedIn's advertising platform, showing a target audience size of 530 members for the selection of female LinkedIn users who studied at the University of Cambridge, hold a PhD, and are living in Germany.

of the arrow), rather than in country X. The audience estimates are in hundred thousands, and small countries are not shown to avoid clutter. Furthermore, the audience estimates are rescaled to correct for LinkedIn penetration in the target country: for a host country with a population of P and a total number of resident LinkedIn users L, all audience estimates are scaled upward by P/L. Assuming that migrants are more likely than non-migrants to be on LinkedIn, these rescaled audience estimates would be upper bounds for the true numbers.[13]

Whereas the fairly large country-to-country mobility shown in Figure 7.4 might not be surprising given the European context and programmess such as Erasmus,[14] the same methodology can be applied to shine a light on otherwise overlooked highly skilled migrants. Figure 7.5 shows similarly obtained estimates for LinkedIn users who (1) studied at a university in Syria, but (2) are currently[15] living in a

---

[13] Zagheni et al. (2017) observed that generally Facebook overestimates the (migrant)/(non-migrant) ratio compared to ground truth data from the World Bank. This overestimation was most pronounced in poorer, African countries. This suggests that migrants, compared to non-migrants, are more likely to be on Facebook and that this gap is biggest in poorer countries. In other words, if you migrate to a poor country, you are more likely to be on Facebook than the host population. But the same does not hold in countries such as the US or countries with high Facebook penetration.
[14] European Commission: Erasmus+, https://ec.europa.eu/programmes/erasmus-plus/node_en
[15] As of 2018.

150 Coimbra Vieira et al.

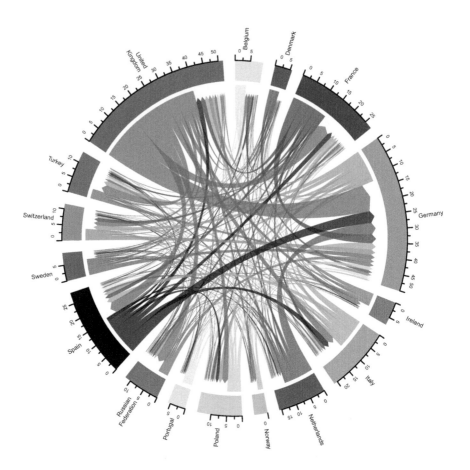

Figure 7.4 A circular plot showing estimates for the number of people who studied in one European country, but are currently living in another. The numbers are in hundred thousands (100,000s). The estimates were obtained through LinkedIn's advertising platform, and corrected for LinkedIn penetration rates in the host country. Assuming migrants are overrepresented on LinkedIn compared to non-migrants, the estimates would be upper bounds for the true numbers. Colour version printed as Plate 2.

European country. These audience estimates, which were generated by Michele Vespe and Spyridon Spyratos at the European Commission, were obtained by scaling up the raw audience estimates by the LinkedIn penetration among college graduates. Concretely, for each host country separately, they computed the ratio of 'LinkedIn users with a self-declared BA, MA, or PhD' and 'population with a university degree according to Eurostat[16]'. Assuming the LinkedIn penetration among university-educated Syrians is similar to the LinkedIn penetration among the host population, this correction factor appropriately corrects for the undersampling. This case study and the corresponding figure were shared by Vespe and Spyratos (2019), and are being used with permission.

[16] Eurostat, https://ec.europa.eu/eurostat

Figure 7.5 Estimates of the number of college-educated people from Syria living in the European Union (EU). The estimates were derived from LinkedIn Ads with an attempt to correct for selection bias (see text). A similar method was proposed by Vespe and Spyratos (2019).

Note that one challenge researchers face in this type of data collection is that LinkedIn users who studied in *several* countries are counted multiple times. Thus, a LinkedIn user who studied in both Germany and the United Kingdom, and who currently lives in Spain, would be counted both as having moved to Spain from the United Kingdom, and as having moved to Spain from Germany. This double count could conceptually be addressed by iterating over pairs or triples of origin countries. Concretely, a researcher could obtain a separate estimate for the number of people who have lived in two countries, such as Germany and the United Kingdom, and then subtract these estimates from the bigger count based on single countries of origin. While theoretically possible, this would increase the number of queries that would need to be issued to the appropriate API by roughly a factor of $n = 28$, which was the number of European Union member countries in 2018.

Another practical challenge researchers face in using these data is that, unlike Facebook, LinkedIn does not offer documentation for their existing free-of-charge APIs, which are somewhat hidden. The documentation offered online by LinkedIn instead refers to a premium API that is aimed at bigger advertisers. Therefore, we advise researchers who want to automate data collection from LinkedIn to study the hidden API using the network monitoring tools that are built into the browser.[17] These network monitoring tools log the requests sent to the LinkedIn server by the web browser. These requests are being made, usually unnoticed by the user, while the LinkedIn Campaign Manager is being used normally. Using these tools it is easy to understand which API call is being used to search for a school of a particular name, or which API call provides the actual audience estimates. Using the appropriate structure of API calls, together with the required cookies obtained after signing in, it is relatively easy to automate data collection using the APIs. In 'General limitations/challenges' we discuss the limitations and challenges that typically arise when working with advertising platforms.

General limitations/challenges

While there are many advantages to using these novel methods to obtain data for demographic research, it is important to be aware of their limitations and their risks.

Self-selection bias

The first limitation is integral to all social network research: namely, that the data are subject to self-selection bias. As most social network users self-select to be on the social network, they do not constitute a representative sample of the society. Certain features offered by the social networks also make them amenable to certain types of user sets. For instance, highly educated users are overrepresented on LinkedIn, and urban users are overrepresented on Twitter (Perrin and Anderson, 2019).

Self-reporting bias

Even if we correct for such biases, there are issues with using observational data that are subject to self-reporting bias. Users might not always provide the right information. For instance, in many cases we rely on self-reported data such as information about educational level on Facebook or about schools attended on LinkedIn. While it is generally assumed when using such datasets that the information users provide can be taken at face value, this may not always be the case.

Algorithmic bias

A more serious issue that is particular to advertising data is that these data were not devised to be used for the purposes we have illustrated in this chapter. First,

---

[17] See https://developer.mozilla.org/en-US/docs/Tools/Network_Monitor for Firefox, or https://developers.google.com/web/tools/chrome-devtools/network for Chrome.

these datasets were generated for advertising purposes, and not to study migration. Hence, the designers of these datasets might have different objectives. Second, the data are generated by black-box algorithms, which are, in most cases, company secrets that will not be revealed. Thus, any biases that were programmed into these black-box algorithms will be replicated in the data, and, eventually, in our analysis. Moreover, any errors in the inference processes of these algorithms will also be replicated in our analysis. Third, given the proprietary nature of the data and the processes through which they are generated, the data might undergo regular updates that are not apparent to the researchers, who mistakenly assume that the data collection process is consistent. For instance, Facebook has been changing its definition of 'users who lived in country X' every year. As a result, even though we see the ease of obtaining new data from these sources as positive (e.g., data for measuring how trends changed after an event, such as a natural disaster), we cannot be sure whether the changes in the data we observe are due to changes in Facebook's algorithms or to the new users who came onto the social network.

Brittleness of the APIs

From a practical perspective, the APIs researchers can use to obtain the data may change frequently or disappear altogether, which can make it difficult to replicate research. For instance, in our own experience, the LinkedIn advertising API changed from HTTP GET to HTTP POST unannounced, which forced us to rewrite all of our code.

Privacy concerns

The next big concern that arises when using such data is the privacy risks they pose. The datasets we proposed using in this chapter are aggregated anonymized data. They only provide counts of users who satisfy certain criteria. However, previous studies have demonstrated how such aggregated data and other tools that Facebook provides could be misused (Speicher *et al.*, 2018). Although these risks have now been fixed, there is no guarantee that the aggregated data will always be anonymized. To preserve individual anonymity, these advertising APIs do not return any user counts below a certain minimum threshold (1000 users on Facebook and 300 users on LinkedIn in November 2020). A practical side effect of the aggregation in research studies is that this aggregation could lead to biases. For example, accurate counts of small populations may not be possible. One technique for reducing these biases was recently proposed by Rama *et al.* (2020). It is even more important to bear in mind that having anonymized, aggregated data does not necessarily mitigate all privacy concerns. Privacy is not just of concern to individuals. Group-level harms can occur, even with aggregated data, that could be misused by bad actors. For instance, authoritarian governments could use such data to obtain aggregate statistics of regions in a country with high immigrant populations, or with people of a certain faith.

Ethical and legal concerns

Finally, there are ethical and legal challenges when using such data that remain unresolved. It is important to keep in mind that some of the data, particularly the data used to infer the interests of users, are collected by the platforms without the consent of the users. The use of data brokers (Venkatadri *et al.*, 2019) might lead to data being collected without the consent of the users, or without the users being given the opportunity to opt out. There are some interesting ongoing legal arguments about whether the computation and targeting of such interests complies with General Data Protection Regulation (GDPR).[18]

Summary

In summary, although advertising data might appear to be a viable source of data for demographic research, these data have specific caveats and limitations that we should be aware of when using such datasets in our research. This is especially important given that the output of such research could be used to inform policy. In these cases it is important to acknowledge biases, which may change the interpretation of results, but also to actively engage in bias mitigation. Box 7.1 summarises selected approaches for dealing with biases.

The next frontier: Combining data and fully leveraging the infrastructure of the digital age

In this last section of the chapter we discuss research developments in this area that may occur in the future. More specifically, we focus on the new opportunities offered by the ability to combine different types of data sources with those provided by the advertising platforms for Facebook and LinkedIn. The first main way of combining probabilistic samples and passively collected data involves developing statistical models, often using Bayesian approaches. The second main way of combining sources and tools involves using advertising platforms to recruit participants for surveys.

An emerging line of literature that we expect to develop further in the years to come focuses on combining different types of data sources using Bayesian statistical methods. The underlying idea is that different types of data have different types of

---

[18] Techcrunch: Facebook faces fresh criticism over ad targeting of sensitive interests, https://techcrunch.com/2018/05/16/facebook-faces-fresh-criticism-over-ad-targeting-of-sensitive-interests/

Box 7.1 Dealing with bias

There are different approaches that could be used to address different types of bias.

Settling for relative trends: Usually, relative trends, i.e., trends over time or differences across space, are somewhat robust against biases. For example, if globally only an unknown percentage x% of migrants are using Facebook, but if this percentage is stable across time and/or space, then an increase of 20% in the biased measure still corresponds to an increase of 20% in the true count. This general line of thought underlies the work of Palotti et al. (2020).

Machine learning and regression: Another approach is applicable if there is good ground truth to calibrate against and the aim is to extrapolate out to other locations or time points. Then the biased data can be used as features and the machine learning model takes care of the 'calibration' or 'de-biasing'. This approach assumes that the bias is a function that can be learned as any other function, as long as the machine learning model is suitable and there are enough training samples. This approach underlies the work of Spyratos et al. (2019).

Parametric approaches: If there are reasonable assumptions about how the bias behaves, it is possible to use parametric approaches. A structural form is derived from the related variables, and used to correct for the bias. For example, Zagheni and Weber (2012) analysed mobility patterns of email users in order to estimate population-level age and gender-specific migration rates, assuming a certain relationship between internet penetration and mobility to deal with selection biases. The profiles by age and gender were first rescaled to match official statistics, and then the estimated number of migrants, by age group and gender, was multiplied by a correction factor to adjust for overrepresentation of more educated and mobile people in groups for which the internet penetration was projected to be low.

Non-parametric difference-in-differences (DiD) approach: Without any type of data to calibrate against, this approach is a more formal version of trend analysis. But if there is some data to 'anchor' against then it becomes a kind of hybrid between machine learning and trend analysis. DiD involves comparing the difference in the size of a group of interest before and after an event to the difference in the size of a 'control' group before and after the same event. For example, Alexander et al. (2019) used it to model Puerto Rican migrant movements in the continental US before and after Hurricane Maria. Provided that the biases affect all groups equally, their effects are reduced.

Bayesian approaches: Bayesian formulation offers a coherent and probabilistic formalism to integrate various sources of uncertainty in the modelling, including the prior information and biases in the form of inflated or deflated values. The important parameters are modelled with statistical distributions, bias is adjusted over these parametrically, and prior distributions can be taken into account based on expert opinions or through (more) reliable data sources. Good examples are Raymer et al. (2013); Hsiao et al. (2020); Alexander et al. (2020) and, more recently, Rampazzo et al. (2021).

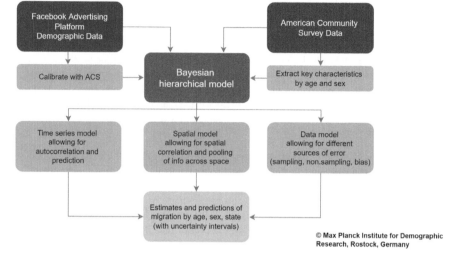

Figure 7.6 Schematic illustration of the approach used to combine data from the Facebook advertising platform and data from the ACS to produce more accurate short-term forecasts of migrant stocks in the United States. Source: Alexander *et al.* (2020).

biases and imperfections. These issues, which can affect data quality, can be explicitly modelled by incorporating additional information. This can be done in a formal and reproducible way using Bayesian methods. More specifically, researchers can incorporate beliefs, either via the use of so-called priors, or by structuring models so that certain types of information are pooled across space and time.

In a recent example centred around nowcasting stocks of migrants in the United States, Alexander *et al.* (2020) showed that a Bayesian hierarchical model that combined data from Facebook Ads and data from the ACS produced more accurate short-term forecasts than either a model that relied only on Facebook data or a model that relied only on time series from the ACS.

Figure 7.6 shows a schematic illustration of the approach used to combine data from Facebook Ads and data from the ACS to produce more accurate short-term forecasts of migrant stocks in the United States. While the figure refers to the paper by Alexander *et al.* (2020), the approach is quite general, and a number of studies are testing Bayesian models for combining social network and survey data to estimate stocks or flows of migrants (e.g., Hsiao *et al.*, 2020; Rampazzo *et al.*, 2021).

The second main area of development is the use of the advertising infrastructure to collect data via surveys. Migrants are a hard-to-reach population. Targeted advertisements may provide the tools necessary to reach these populations and to invite them to participate in a survey. Initial approaches have demonstrated that this is a cost-effective way of collecting data (Pötzschke and Braun, 2017). A rapidly expanding related literature in public health has also shown that when appropriate post-stratification weights are used, surveys run via advertising platforms can generate estimates that are close approximations of those obtained from probabilistic samples (Grow *et al.*, 2020).

In summary, we expect that the next frontier will involve blending approaches from classic data collections, survey methods, and Bayesian statistics with the infrastructure of the digital age, which offers not just access to digital trace data, but new opportunities for data collection and survey experiments.

Acknowledgements

We thank Carlos Callejo Peñalba, who was a master's degree student at Aalto University in Finland in 2018–2019. As part of his course project, Carlos collected and visualised LinkedIn data on the number of users who studied in one European country, but who now live in another European country.

We also thank Michele Vespe and Spyros Spyratos at the Joint Research Center of the European Commission in Ispra, Italy. Michele and Spyros let us use their analysis of the number of LinkedIn users who studied in Syria but who now live in a European country.

References

Alexander, M., Polimis, K. and Zagheni, E. (2019), 'The impact of Hurricane Maria on out-migration from Puerto Rico: Evidence from Facebook data', *Population and Development Review* 45(3), 617–30.

Alexander, M., Polimis, K., and Zagheni, E. (2020), 'Combining social media and survey data to nowcast migrant stocks in the United States', *Population Research and Policy Review* 41, 1–28.

Dubois, A., Zagheni, E., Garimella, K., and Weber, I. (2018), 'Studying migrant assimilation through Facebook interests', *in* S. Staab, O. Koltsova, and D. I. Ignatov, eds, *Social Informatics*, Vol. 2, Springer, New York, 51–60.

Grow, A., Perrotta, D., Del Fava, E., Cimentada, J., Rampazzo, F., Gil-Clavel, S., and Zagheni, E. (2020), 'Addressing public health emergencies via Facebook surveys: Advantages, challenges, and practical considerations', *Journal of Medical Internet Research* 22(12), e20653.

Hsiao, Y., *et al.* (2020), 'Modeling the bias of digital data: An approach to combining digital and survey data to estimate and predict migration trends', Technical report, Max Planck Institute for Demographic Research, Rostock, Germany.

Palotti, J., Adler, N., Morales-Guzman, A., Villaveces, J., Sekara, V., Herranz, M. G., Al-Asad, M., and Weber, I. (2020), 'Monitoring of the Venezuelan exodus through Facebook's advertising platform', *PLOS One* 15(2), e0229175.

Perrin, A. and Anderson, M. (2019), 'Share of US adults using social media, including Facebook, is mostly unchanged since 2018', Pew Research Center.

Pötzschke, S. and Braun, M. (2017), 'Migrant sampling using Facebook advertisements: A case study of Polish migrants in four European countries', *Social Science Computer Review* 35(5), 633–53.

Rama, D., Mejova, Y., Tizzoni, M., Kalimeri, K., and Weber, I. (2020), 'Facebook Ads as a demographic tool to measure the urban–rural divide', *in Proceedings of The Web Conference 2020*, 327–38.

Rampazzo, F., Bijak, J., Vitali, A., Weber, I., and Zagheni, E. (2021), 'A framework for estimating migrant stocks using digital traces and survey data: An application in the United Kingdom', *Demography* 58(6), 2193–218.

Raymer, J., Wiśniowski, A., Forster, J. J., Smith, P. W., and Bijak, J. (2013), 'Integrated modeling of European migration', *Journal of the American Statistical Association* 108(503), 801–19.

Speicher, T., Ali, M., Venkatadri, G., Ribeiro, F. N., Arvanitakis, G., Benevenuto, F., Gummadi, K. P., Loiseau, P., and Mislove, A. (2018), 'Potential for discrimination in online targeted advertising', *Proceedings of Machine Learning Research* 81, 5–19.

Spyratos, S., Vespe, M., Natale, F., Iacus, S. M., and Santamaria, C. (2020), 'Explaining the travelling behaviour of migrants using Facebook audience estimates', *PLOS One* 15(9), e0238947.

Spyratos, S., Vespe, M., Natale, F., Weber, I., Zagheni, E., and Rango, M. (2019), 'Quantifying international human mobility patterns using Facebook Network data', *PLOS One* 14(10), e0224134.

Stewart, I., Flores, R. D., Riffe, T., Weber, I., and Zagheni, E. (2019), 'Rock, rap, or reggaeton? Assessing Mexican immigrants' cultural assimilation using Facebook data', *in* L. Liu and R. White, eds, *WWW'19: The World Wide Web Conference*, Association for Computing Machinery, New York, 3258–64.

Venkatadri, G., Sapiezynski, P., Redmiles, E. M., Mislove, A., Goga, O., Mazurek, M., and Gummadi, K. P. (2019), 'Auditing offline data brokers via Facebook's advertising platform', *in* L. Liu and R. White, eds, *WWW'19: The World Wide Web Conference*, Association for Computing Machinery, New York, 1920–30.

Vespe, M. and Spyratos, S. (2019), 'A changing migration data landscape?', Global Working Group on Big Data for Official Statistics, International Meeting on Measuring Human Mobility.

Zagheni, E. and Weber, I. (2012), 'You are where you e-mail: Using e-mail data to estimate international migration rates', *in Proceedings of the Fourth Annual ACM Web Science Conference*, 348–51.

Zagheni, E., Weber, I., and Gummadi, K. (2017), 'Leveraging Facebook's advertising platform to monitor stocks of migrants', *Population and Development Review* 43(4), 721–34.

8

Twitter Data for Migration Studies

JISU KIM, LAURA POLLACCI, GIULIO ROSSETTI,
ALINA SÎRBU, FOSCA GIANNOTTI, AND DINO PEDRESCHI

Introduction

MIGRATION RESEARCH COVERS a wide area of disciplines and is typically performed using various data types such as census data, registries, and surveys collected by governmental institutions and national statistics offices. Social big data have been proposed to fill some of the gaps and complement traditional data types (Sîrbu *et al.*, 2021). Among the various types of social big data, user-generated content from Twitter can be a valuable resource in migration studies. This has been proven by recent works using Twitter data to study various migration-related problems. These include estimating migration stocks and flows from Twitter data (Zagheni *et al.*, 2014; Kim *et al.*, 2020; Mazzoli *et al.*, 2020; Lenormand *et al.*, 2015; Valle *et al.*, 2017), introducing and studying new migrant integration indices (Kim *et al.*, 2021b), evaluating cultural diversity (Pollacci, 2019), language mobility (Moise *et al.*, 2016), and social network activity (Kim *et al.*, 2021a). However, data collection, preprocessing, and analysis is far from straightforward and can result in biased data that might influence the final results. Furthermore, ethical and privacy issues need to be considered carefully, as biased results and publication of sensitive information might harm migrants.

In this chapter we provide an overview of the various stages required to conduct a study on Twitter. We start with a series of recent works that employ Twitter data for migration studies in the 'Migration case studies' section. We then continue with a more technical description of the Twitter APIs and of the format of the resulting data ('Downloading: API and libraries' and 'Data format'). We perform an in-depth review of the terms of service, especially in relation to the protection of personal information included in these data, including ethics considerations

('Terms of service'). We continue with a description of example processing pipelines for natural language processing and geolocation ('Processing Twitter data'). A thorough discussion of gaps and biases in these data is also provided, linking with existing analyses on selection bias and representativity ('Gaps and biases'). To conclude the chapter, we underline the challenges and open issues with these data in 'Discussion and conclusions'.

Migration case studies

Among big data, Twitter is one of the most used resources for the study of human migration. Despite the number of gaps and biases discussed above, numerous studies have used tweets in different ways, sometimes even in combination with other data sources, both conventional and unconventional.

Works that use official data to validate migration stocks and flows obtained via Twitter include, among others, Kim *et al.* (2020), Pollacci (2019), and Hawelka *et al.* (2014). In the first (Kim *et al.*, 2020), a generic methodology is developed to identify migrants within the Twitter population. This describes a migrant as a person who has their current residence different from their nationality. Residence is defined as the location where a user spends most of his/her time in a year. Nationality is 'inferred from linguistic and social connections to a migrant's country of origin'. The authors validate the results with an internal gold standard dataset and with two official statistics, and they show strong performance scores and correlation coefficients. Pollacci (2019) introduced the *superdiversity index* based on the changes in the emotional content of words used by a multicultural community compared to the standard language. The index is validated by comparing it with official immigration statistics available from the European Commission's Joint Research Center through the D4I data challenge. In most cases, the superdiversity index correlates well with immigration rates at various geographical resolutions for most countries. Hawelka *et al.* (2014) analyse global mobility patterns and compare countries' mobility characteristics. The investigation aims to discover spatial patterns and clusters of regional mobility. The authors assign users to a residence country, dividing residents and foreigners, and compare countries' mobility and temporal profiles to understand inflow and outflow dynamics. Finally, using country-to-country networks of travels, global regions of mobility are identified. The results obtained are validated with both worldwide tourism statistics and previously used models of human mobility.

A different aspect studied using Twitter data are travel patterns, investigated at local (Azmandian *et al.*, 2012), national (Krumm *et al.*, 2013; Valle *et al.*, 2017), and global (Lenormand *et al.*, 2015) scales. Azmandian *et al.* (2012) study travel patterns of Twitter users in three big cities and characterise groups across space and time. At the national scale, Krumm *et al.* (2013) aim to understand when individuals move between different regions according to the distances between the regions themselves and the demographic and spatial features of both. Furthermore,

Valle et al. (2017) present a method to group individual Twitter users with similar movement patterns. The method has also been applied to the movements of people in Florida. In this case, the approach allows for determining the origin of visitors (tourists) in the state, identifying patterns according to the different origins. At the global scale, Lenormand et al. (2015) quantify city influence to characterise human mobility. The method focuses on the ratio of locals to non-local visitors, and the authors concentrate only on urban residents' mobility flows to build city-to-city networks. They analyse centrality measures at different scales according to the built networks.

Mazzoli et al. (2020) present one of the most recent works to detect migration flows worldwide using geolocated Twitter data. The approach focuses on the migration crisis in Venezuela, and it is compared with official statistics. The proposed method can be used to understand preferred routes, mobility across countries, as well as settlement areas and spatial integration in cities. The flows of migrants are also analysed in (Zagheni et al., 2014), where the authors use geolocated Twitter data of about 500,000 users in OECD countries. The work aims to analyse geographic movements within and between countries to infer migration patterns. The authors propose a difference-in-differences approach aimed at reducing selection bias for out-migration rates. In the literature, this work has been a crucial testimony of how geolocated tweets can improve the study of the relationship between internal and international migration. Moreover, the proposed method can be used to infer turning points in migration trends, which is crucial for migration forecasting.

Nguyen and Garimella (2017) describe trends in global human migration by exploiting a novel tool, tensor decomposition. In this work, human migration is modelled as a three-mode tensor composed of origin country, destination country, and migration time. In Moise et al. (2016), the authors exclusively relate to geolocalised data obtained through a preprocessing phase to extract coupled information on location and language at the tweet level. The authors propose a two-step quantitative analysis. The first step focuses on the temporal dimension by exploring the temporal evolution of languages and multilinguistic landscapes (e.g., Switzerland). The second step shifts the perspective from the dimensional to the spatial, and finally combines them. The authors perform a study on both temporal and spatial dimensions by investigating how language mobility over time is reflected in Twitter data after illustrating the languages' diffusion.

Finally, Twitter data can help understand spatial events (Andrienko et al., 2015), infer users' nationalities (Mahmud et al., 2014), build classification models based on features such as language, hashtags, and the geographical location of social ties (Huang et al., 2014), and study the impact of language, boundaries, geographic distance, and air travel frequency in the shaping of social ties on Twitter (Takhteyev et al., 2012). In the most recent works, Twitter data was further exploited to measure cultural integration levels of international migrants using hashtags (Kim et al., 2021b) and to explore the structure of the social networks between migrants and natives (Kim et al., 2021a). In the same direction of studying integration, the sentiment of tweets can provide useful observations on the (non-)

acceptance of topics, social trends, or ideological currents (Sánchez-Holgado and Arcila-Calderón, 2018). Thus, an important usage of Twitter data is monitoring, assessing, and studying sentiments against migrants and refugees using Sentiment Analysis[1] techniques. With this assumption, many studies have focused on specific events (Arcila-Calderón *et al.*, 2021; Abdul-Mageed *et al.*, 2013), highly sensitive communities such as refugees (Öztürk and Ayvaz, 2018; Lucić *et al.*, 2020; Coletto *et al.*, 2016), and on the general (im)migration discourse (de Rosa *et al.*, 2021; Harlow and Johnson, 2011; Flores, 2017).

Acquiring data

The data collection phase can follow several strategies. On one hand, it is possible to use the tools made available by the platform itself, through the various APIs (application programming interfaces) available. On the other hand, numerous methods have been developed over time in different programming languages and are available for free online. An exhaustive list of both official and community libraries can be found on the 'Twitter Libraries' page of the platform site.[2]

Downloading: API and libraries

As discussed, Twitter data can be accessed and collected through public APIs, a well-defined set of endpoints that make accessible, in a structured format, several pieces of information related to the platform users and their activities.

Indeed, the API endpoints are not frozen once and for all: since their first release to the developer community they have been updated, extended, and revised to better comply with both community requests and company choices for the exposed data. At the time of writing, early access to a novel version of the API (v2) has been released, a release that became publicly available in 2021. This includes a special product for researchers, the so-called 'Academic Research Track', that is available upon request. All researchers can apply with their project to perform non-commercial research.

To avoid being tied to a specific API version, here we discuss only the macro categories of Twitter data that the API enables us to collect, focusing on the ones that are relevant for migration studies. We will therefore not discuss individual endpoints, but only the typologies of the accessible information.

We can identify three broad families of data to be collected: user profiles, user tweets, and user social contact data.

---

[1] Sentiment analysis uses natural language processing techniques to identify and quantify affective states and subjective information automatically.
[2] Twitter Developer Platform: Libraries, https://developer.twitter.com/en/docs/developer-utilities/twitter-libraries

User profiles: Similar to other online social platforms, Twitter allows its users to specify a few pieces of information on their profile (e.g., username, home location, description, etc.) and associates with it several indicators (e.g., account registration date, number of tweets, number of followers/friends, etc.). All such information can be downloaded from Twitter and used to study, at a high level of abstraction, the aggregate degree of activity of users. However, user-provided data are often partial/wrong/misleading (e.g., fake home locations).

User tweets: Tweets are the core of Twitter data. Tweets are composed not only of the text written by the users, but they also carry with them several items of metadata and annotations (ranging from hashtags, that can be used to identify topics, to geolocation information). Tweet collection can be approached following two different macro strategies: (1) accessing the online *stream*, and (2) focusing on the historical activity of individual users. Both approaches have their own advantages and drawbacks. Approach (1) allows us to obtain a real-time view of the discussion happening on the platform: APIs allow us to focus on tweets originating from a specific location (by specifying a geographic bounding box) and/or containing a given set of keywords/hashtags. The downside of such flexibility lies in the quantity of data accessible: Twitter allows access to only a small random sample of the stream (a limit that can be increased through premium/paid API access or through the Academic Research Track). Strategy (2), on the other hand, allows for looking into the past, collecting historical data from individual profiles, and thus enabling a more detailed analysis of user behaviour. Here, the limitation lies in the fixed number of tweets collectable for each account that, given the variable activity level of Twitter users, does not guarantee a common temporal collection window. The academic access to the API allows access to the entire Twitter history for the search API.

User social contacts: Finally, APIs allow access to the list of users that follow (the so-called 'followers'), and are followed by (the so-called 'friends'), a given account, thus allowing us to build the 'social' neighbourhood of each user. Indeed, such a directed graph describes the potential interactions involving the observed user. However, to get a more dynamic view it is also possible to observe interactions through the mentions appearing in the user's tweets.

As anticipated, several tools and libraries have been developed to ease the access to API endpoints, Tweepy[3] and Twarc[4] being the most used for their simplicity and easy setup. Such libraries are developed to simplify some of the most common operations needed to access Twitter data: application authentication, data request, response pagination, limit on the number of API calls. In particular, authentication and rate limits are among the most important components to be familiar with. Twitter APIs require the existence and authentication of a developer account

---

[3] Tweepy Documentation, http://docs.tweepy.org/en/latest/
[4] GitHub: DocNow/twarc, https://github.com/DocNow/twarc

having active credentials (API keys). Developer accounts can have different levels of access to the endpoints due to their status ('basic' or 'premium', and the recently introduced 'research'). The authentication is performed through the standard OAuth2 protocol.[5] Moreover, different types of accounts are characterised by different rate limits[6] (e.g., the number of calls in a given unit of time for each specific endpoint). The Academic Research Track has increased limits compared to the basic user, allowing, for instance, access to the complete Twitter history.

Finally, it is worth mentioning that an alternative strategy to access Twitter data is via the so-called *hydrating* Twitter ID datasets (see, for instance, Hydrator[7]). Hydrating means downloading the complete Twitter content corresponding to a certain tweet ID. Hydrating tweets allows the reconstruction of existing datasets without sharing sensitive data such as tweet contents (see also 'Terms of service' for a discussion on how to share Twitter data). During the last few years, several repositories have started to collect Twitter ID datasets to allow for research replicability (see, for instance, the DocNow catalogue[8]).

Data format

The Twitter developer platform provides several tools and endpoints grouped in APIs. For our purposes, we concentrate only on fields relevant to migration.[9] Twitter APIs provide data encoded using JavaScript Object Notation (JSON), a lightweight data-interchange format.[10]

Tweet object

Tweets are the core of the Twitter platform. Each Tweet object has several root-level attributes, some of which are returned by default, such as `id` and `text`, while others must be explicitly requested or expanded at query time. Given the platform's structure and functionality, Tweet objects are also 'parent' objects of several child objects: user, place, media, and poll (see below). Moreover, tweets generate `entities` objects: lists of Twitter-specific contents parsed out of the tweet text, such as #hashtags, @mentions, URLs, and $cashtags. Given the high number of attributes, we report only the most relevant for migration studies.

`created_at`   Contains the creation time of the tweet.
`lang`   Provides the language of the tweet, if detected by Twitter.

---

[5] Twitter Developer Platform: Authentication, https://developer.twitter.com/en/docs/authentication/overview
[6] Twitter Developer Platform: Rate limits, https://developer.twitter.com/en/docs/rate-limits
[7] GitHub: DocNow/hydrator, https://github.com/DocNow/hydrator
[8] DocNow Catalog, https://catalog.docnow.io/
[9] For a complete list of the endpoints available on the platform see the API reference index, https://developer.twitter.com/en/docs/api-reference-index.
[10] Introducing JSON, https://www.json.org/json-en.html

user   In addition to the identifier of the user who posts the tweet, the API can return a User object if the author_id expansion parameter is included in the request. The User object contains the Twitter user account metadata. It is returned in the User Lookup endpoint but can also be found as a Tweet child object. As a Tweet, a User has several root-level attributes and, in turn, is 'parent' of other child objects, including entities. In addition to generic features, such as name, username, and created_at (the UTC datetime that the user account was created on Twitter), the endpoint can include the location field if the user has provided one. It may not be an actual location, and most of the time it is not machine parseable as this is a free-form value. Furthermore, as stated in the Twitter documentation, the pinned_tweet_id field may help to infer the user's language since it refers to a tweet pinned to the top of the user's profile. Regarding ethics and privacy concerns, the protected field indicates if the user protects their tweets, i.e., if the user's tweets are private, while withheld contains withholding details when applicable, e.g., countries where the user is not available.[11]

geo   The object contains information about the location tagged by the user in a tweet, if they specified one. These include the coordinates of the location tagged in the tweet, the precise location of the user (latitude, longitude),[12] and the place identifier if referring to a point of interest tagged in the tweet.

place   The Place object can only be found in the Tweet object since it is not a primary object on any endpoint. The root-level attributes include some default information, such as full_name and the place's identifier if it is a point of interest tagged in the tweet. Additional fields can include the short name, country, country_code, i.e., the country this place belongs to, and the place type (such as a city name or a point of interest). Finally, the geo object contains place details in GeoJSON format.

Finally, the following fields are relevant to the study of migration as they relate to ethical or privacy aspects:

possibly_sensitive   This field is displayed if a tweet contains a link. It indicates that the URL may hold sensitive contents.

withheld   When present, the object contains details for withheld contents, such as the countries where the content is not available, the copyright infringement, and type of withheld content (tweet or user).

Terms of service

While, in traditional research, data are typically collected specifically for the research purpose, Twitter data counts as secondary usage of existing data, as its

---

[11] Depending on the country and related laws, following specific requests, it may be necessary to withhold access to users and contents.
[12] This value could be null unless the user explicitly shares their exact location.

collection is intermediated by Twitter. This facilitates access to larger amounts of data, but at the same time creates other issues in terms of data usage. The use of Twitter data are subject to a series of terms and conditions. These include the user terms of service[13] that each individual user agrees to when creating an account, and the developer terms,[14] including the developer agreement[15] that typically the researcher agrees to when creating a new application to download data. Here we will describe the parts of these terms of service that we deem important for the migration researcher.

User terms of service

The public Twitter API gives access to Twitter data that was made public by the Twitter users themselves. When connecting to Twitter, users accept the terms and conditions of use, and in particular users agree to the following statements:

> You understand that through your use of the Services you consent to the collection and use (as set forth in the Privacy Policy) of this information, including the transfer of this information to the United States, Ireland, and/or other countries for storage, processing and use by Twitter and its affiliates.
>
> You should only provide Content that you are comfortable sharing with others.
>
> By submitting, posting or displaying Content on or through the Services, you grant us a worldwide, non-exclusive, royalty-free license (with the right to sublicense) to use, copy, reproduce, process, adapt, modify, publish, transmit, display and distribute such Content in any and all media or distribution methods now known or later developed (for clarity, these rights include, for example, curating, transforming, and translating). This license authorizes us to make your Content available to the rest of the world and to let others do the same.
>
> By publicly posting content when you Tweet, you are directing us to disclose that information as broadly as possible, including through our APIs, and directing those accessing the information through our APIs to do the same.

Thus, when downloading data from the public Twitter API, one obtains data that the users allowed Twitter to distribute. However, studies show (Williams *et al.*, 2017b; Obar and Oeldorf-Hirsch, 2020) that very few users are aware of the extent of this redistribution, and that many users do not even read the terms of service. As such, using Twitter data for research requires evaluation of the privacy and ethics issues involved, to ensure that individuals are not harmed. This is because Twitter data includes possibly sensitive personal data such as real names, geolocation, opinions, that the user has made public, but not specifically for the purpose of research. This is particularly important for the protection of possibly sensitive groups in migration research.

---

[13] Twitter: Terms of Service, https://twitter.com/en/tos
[14] Twitter Developer Platform: Policies and agreements, https://developer.twitter.com/en/more/developer-terms
[15] Twitter Developer Platform: Developer Agreement, https://developer.twitter.com/en/developer-terms/agreement

Developer terms of service and links to privacy and ethics in migration research

The developer terms of service define what can be done with Twitter data. Even if in theory these data are public, they cannot be used in uncontrolled contexts. Indeed, the terms allow developers to 'use the Twitter API to integrate Twitter Content into your Services or conduct analysis of such Twitter Content, as explicitly approved by Twitter'. Some limitations apply and we will review the most relevant from the viewpoint of migration research.

General terms relate to downloading, storing, and sharing data. Researchers need to comply with rate limits when downloading data, and not attempt to circumvent these. The API keys need to be kept safe and not shared with others. Any Twitter content downloaded through the API needs to be kept 'confidential and secure from unauthorised access by using industry-standard organisational and technical safeguards for such data'. If the need arises to share data, whether with collaborators or to ensure reproducibility of research, only tweet ids or user ids can be shared. The other party can then 'rehydrate' the content directly through the APIs. Even so, only a small number of ids can be shared in a limited amount of time. The limits on the number of IDs shared do not apply if data sharing is done for research purposes.[16]

An important clause in the developer terms of service is that related to user protection. This prohibits a series of use cases, some of which can be relevant for migration research. The first such use case is 'conducting or providing surveillance or gathering intelligence, including but not limited to investigating or tracking Twitter users or Twitter Content'. Migration researchers have to ensure that the methods they develop do not permit tracking of individuals in space and time, as this could harm individuals.

Another clause forbids 'monitoring sensitive events (including but not limited to protests, rallies, or community organising meetings)'. This is very related to the previous point: methods should not track individuals, but also sensitive events or communities. Researchers need to be very careful when studying migrant groups and events, and ensure no harm can come to those communities.

A third important clause mentions:

> targeting, segmenting, or profiling individuals based on sensitive personal information, including their health (e.g., pregnancy), negative financial status or condition, political affiliation or beliefs, racial or ethnic origin, religious or philosophical affiliation or beliefs, sex life or sexual orientation, trade union membership, Twitter Content relating to any alleged or actual commission of a crime, or any other sensitive categories of personal information prohibited by law.

Migration research is, by definition, concerned with migrants, who are distinguished based on their country of origin and for which many demographic or cultural characteristics that are typically studied are also listed in the clause above. Therefore,

---

[16] Twitter Developer Platform: More about restricted uses of the Twitter APIs, https://developer.twitter.com/en/developer-terms/more-on-restricted-use-cases

using Twitter data for migration studies needs to be extremely carefully done, so that individuals or groups cannot be targeted based on the research. This could be the start of a very long discussion on ethics; however, that is not the purpose of this section, and we direct the user to Chapter 2 (Salah et al., 2022). However, it is important to mention one aspect: Twitter data are not anonymous. With traditional data, the practice is to either anonymise the data or to obtain informed consent from participants. Informed consent on Twitter, where data comes potentially from millions of users, is quite impossible to obtain. At the same time, anonymisation and pseudonymisation are not straightforward, and are currently an area of research in itself. This is because of the possibility of re-identification (Henriksen-Bulmer and Jeary, 2016), facilitated by the fact that the original data, and possibly other types of data related to the same persons, are public so also available to an attacker. For instance, simply by citing a full tweet, one can possibly enable the uncovering of the identity of the person who posted it (Ogawa et al., 2015), even if the identifying information such as name, screen name, etc. was removed. Similarly, showing the exact locations of a user on a map could cause a security issue, since with enough timestamped geolocations, individuals can be re-identified (Yoshiura, 2019; Cecaj et al., 2016; Monreale et al., 2010). This brings us back to the necessity to keep data very safe, and only publish information that does not permit identification of users or groups, and is aggregated at a high enough level.

A different clause related to user protection is that of off-site matching of users. This applies to situations when data needs to be integrated, and accounts or content on Twitter matched with corresponding off-Twitter data. An example usage could be combining survey data with Twitter data, by matching the users with the survey participants (see Sloan et al., 2020 for a discussion of privacy and ethics in this context). From the viewpoint of the Twitter terms of service, this can be performed either with the informed consent of the participants (e.g., ask for consent during the survey itself) or by using only public information (public biographies, tweets, screen name, etc.).

Some Twitter users decide to publish the location of their tweets together with the message that they share. This information is very relevant for migration research, since this allows a glimpse at international mobility flows. However, again, using location data is not allowed in certain contexts. We have already seen that tracking of users is forbidden. Furthermore, the terms state that 'any use of location data or geographic information on a standalone basis is prohibited'. Geolocation information needs to be saved with the original tweet, and it is forbidden to extract locations to show where individuals have been over time. However, the terms specify that showing aggregated geo activity is permitted: 'Heat maps and related tools that show aggregated geo activity (e.g., the number of people in a city using a hashtag) are permitted.' Therefore, again, migration researchers should never show individual geolocation data, since this can be used to track individuals, and as already discussed, possibly re-identify them.

TWITTER DATA FOR MIGRATION STUDIES 169

Figure 8.1 User terms of service over time. Updated December 2021 from https://twitter.com/en/tos/previous

To conclude this section, while Twitter appears to be an 'easy' source of data for migration research, extreme care needs to be taken to respect the terms and conditions and comply with privacy and ethics regulations so as not to harm individuals or groups. Given the complexity of the issue, and the use of public but potentially sensitive personal data, all research employing personal information from Twitter data should go through a process of ethics approval by a qualified body before being published.

Changes in the terms of service

The above-mentioned points of the Twitter terms of service relate to the version available at the moment of writing of this chapter (last updated December 2021). However, an important point to keep in mind when designing a new study based on Twitter data are that the terms of service change rather often. Figure 8.1 shows the timing of the various versions of the user terms of service, which changed 16 times in 16 years. If we compare version 1[17] with version 16, we observe that the terms have become more and more inclusive of increasingly complex issues. While in version 1 users were simply asked to comply with simple rules of conduct, publish suitable content, and not tamper with the Twitter software, nowadays the terms explain carefully to users issues such as privacy, data usage, rights, etc. Also, it is important to note that the terms of service change slightly from one country to another.

The developer API, which enables researchers to download Twitter data, has also undergone changes over time. Three main versions have been published: V1 in 2006, V1.1 in 2012, and V2 in 2020. Intermediate releases with small changes have also been made. In 2021 Twitter introduced the academic research product track,[18] which requires developers to apply for access. This allows for enhanced features and higher rate limits compared to the public or enterprise APIs.

---

[17] Twitter: Previous Terms of Service, https://twitter.com/en/tos/previous/version_1
[18] Twitter Developer Platform: Academic Research access, https://developer.twitter.com/en/solutions/academic-research/products-for-researchers

Processing Twitter data

Twitter data includes structured data, in JSON format, that describes various attributes of users and tweets, and also unstructured data in the form of natural text produced by the users (the tweet itself) plus all the other media included (images, videos). Analysing Twitter data thus requires a preprocessing stage to clean the data and extract the relevant information. Clearly, the cleaning phase depends on the purpose of the analysis and therefore the information to be extracted. It is therefore not possible to define a complete preprocessing phase, but rather to indicate a few steps that are typically necessary. While the structured format makes it straightforward to extract information, several issues need to be handled during the cleaning phase. We concentrate here on two different aspects: processing of natural language and of geolocations. The general pipeline for natural language processing (NLP) is described in Box 8.1.

Natural language processing

This preprocessing phase can be performed following three strategies:

- predefined: by using existing libraries for Twitter data, e.g., Preprocessor;[19]
- custom: by coding bespoke functions and methods to process data;
- mixed: combine existing approaches with custom-defined functions.

While libraries may be more suitable for non-experts since they simplify several operations, the results may not always be accurate or customisable. On the other hand, coding a full preprocessing pipeline involves managing several issues in favour of more customisation and data accuracy. The preprocessing strategies strongly depend on tasks to be performed, and typically involve removing some content and information, while adding some extra knowledge. However, while some items that are removed can be ignored (remove strategy), others, such as entities, can be removed from the text but saved in separate fields as additional content (remove and save strategy). For instance, entities can be extracted using named entity recognition methods, and then used to identify sub-datasets. When preprocessing the text of tweets, one needs to take into account some potential issues and provide strategies to manage them. Common issues that one may find, together with possible approaches, are:

- Emoticons and emojis may include a lot of information using a small number of characters, so their correct interpretation is important:
    - old-school emoticons: use dictionaries of emoticons to recognise them;
    - emojis: group content into emoticons, symbols and pictographs, transport, map symbols, and flags.

---

[19] Preprocessor is a preprocessing library for tweet data written in Python: https://pypi.org/project/tweet-preprocessor/

> **Box 8.1** Natural language processing
>
> Natural language processing (NLP) refers to computer-based processing of natural (human) language data. For this purpose, large text databases (*text corpora*) are used to train symbolic and machine learning based algorithms.
>
> There are a number of standard tasks in NLP, and most of these require tools to be developed for each specific language. Morphological analysis includes tasks related to word structures, syntactic analysis relates to grammatical structure, and semantic analysis pertains to the actual meaning or affect associated with the text. The latter includes *sentiment analysis*, which is important in the area of migration, to gauge social media sentiments against migrants, refugees, and policies related to them.
>
> When dealing with social media text, a *cleaning* step is essential, as there will be many extra symbols, repeated letters, ungrammatical fragments, and links. After cleaning, the text goes through a phase of word analysis to process the text to extract the necessary information according to the task to be performed. Typically, the first level is *tokenisation*, i.e., the identification of linguistically meaningful units from the text, e.g., words, punctuation marks, numeric digits. *Part-of-speech tagging* is the task of determining the part of speech for each word, such as noun, verb, or adjective.
>
> There are some special words that may require attention. *Stopwords* are language-specific words that are used to simplify the NLP task by identifying some natural boundaries, where the analysis can be broken down. *Named entities*, on the other hand, are names of people, places, events, monetary values, quantities, etc. *Named entity recognition* tasks typically aim to identify and classify named entities in unstructured text into predefined entity categories.
>
> The identified words undergo *lemmatisation*, where a lemma is the base dictionary form of a word. In languages where a word can take many different forms this is a very important step. For example, Turkish is an *agglutinative language* with case markers, and a single word can have thousands of forms. A *stemming* phase may be necessary, depending on the task, which aims to reduce words to their root form (e.g., computer, compute, computing).
>
> The grammar of a language describes the syntax of well-formed sentences. A *formal grammar* is a formalism that includes an alphabet and a set of production rules that allow the generation of syntactically well-formed sentences. Formal grammars are described in classes of increasing power, which translates to the intricacy of permitted derivations. *Regular expressions* are simple character strings that are used for text matching tasks, and are at the simple end of this spectrum. Natural languages are quite complex, and can hardly be described by small sets of grammatical production rules. Syntactic analysis can be performed by dividing a sentence into its fragments via its formal grammar, which is also called *parsing*.

- Users tend to employ general and Twitter-specific stopwords ('RT', 'lol'): one can use precompiled and manually created stopword lists to recognise these.
- Fuzzy terms and repeated letters: a typical strategy is to remove three or more consecutive repeated characters (e.g., transform 'haaaapppyy' into 'happy').

This type of spelling error can be fixed using existing tools and dictionaries (e.g., Hunspell,[20] PAISA (Lyding *et al.*, 2014) for Italian language, etc.).
- URLs, hashtags, user mentions, and links: These are typically identified automatically by the Twitter API, hence present in the resulting JSON, or can be extracted using libraries or manually using regular expressions.

The processes of cleaning, lemmatisation, and tokenisation are rather complex, but fortunately there are libraries that perform them automatically. There are approximately 7000 spoken languages across the world. Despite this variety, and in particular on social platforms, the majority of the population uses only a small fraction of these languages, such as English, Mandarin Chinese, Spanish, Arabic, and Hindi. After a long period of English language exclusivity, several NLP tools now focus on major languages and standardised varieties, although some resources are still available only for the English language, e.g., NLTK[21] and TextBlob.[22] However, there are also freely available resources able to manage other languages, such as TreeTagger,[23] Stanza (a native Python NLP library that uses the Java CoreNLP library; Qi *et al.*, 2020), Polyglot,[24] and Spacy.[25] This is particularly important in the context of migration studies since migrants typically speak more languages, and being able to study the content they produce can become challenging.

Although there has been considerable evolution and diffusion of tools and resources in multiple languages, the linguistic question still poses considerable challenges today. When dealing with multilingual models with low resource languages, one can also evaluate transfer learning. This refers to the set of machine learning methods that aim to transfer the knowledge acquired in one context to another context, where the context can be either another task or another language. A basic approach may employ automatic machine translation via browser and libraries, e.g., Google Translate. Despite the naïveté of this approach, it should be underlined that in the last few years the performance has significantly improved thanks to recent advances in deep learning and the availability of resources. Besides basic approaches, the literature is rich in techniques applicable to particular domains, available resources, and the tasks to perform. These include: *cross-lingual transfer learning*, which aims to transfer resources from resource-rich sources to poor target languages (Das and Hasegawa-Johnson, 2015); *zero-shot learning*, that trains a one-domain model and assumes it generalises the low resources domains (Wang *et al.*, 2019, 2020); and *one-shot learning*, that foresees training a one-domain model and adapting it by using a few examples from the target low resource domain (Wang *et al.*, 2020). However, these topics need separate discussion and are not the focus of this chapter, since they introduce specific issues, especially on social

---

[20] Hunspell: About, http://hunspell.github.io/
[21] NLTK, https://www.nltk.org/
[22] TextBlob: Simplified Text Processing, https://textblob.readthedocs.io/en/dev/index.html
[23] TreeTagger, https://www.cis.uni-muenchen.de/~schmid/tools/TreeTagger/
[24] The number of languages supported varies depending on the task, i.e., tokenisation 165 languages, part of speech tagging 16 languages. https://polyglot.readthedocs.io/
[25] SpaCy, https://spacy.io/

platforms, such as translation reliability and 'slang' interpretation. In contrast to the transfer models, multilingual models jointly train models on resource-rich and resource-poor data, as the name suggests.

Besides preprocessing tweets, NLP (sub)tasks are widely employed to study human migration from various perspectives. Information extraction tasks such as named entity recognition could be used to identify the geolocation of social media users and specific community-related terms. For instance, Han *et al.* (2014) observed that some topics like 'Piccadilly and tube' are more often used in tweets by people located in London than in another city. Moreover, Adnan and Longley (2013) performed an investigation on Twitter activities in European capitals by comparing names, possible ethnicities, and genders of Twitter users in these cities.

Geolocation pipeline

The geolocation of tweets is a very important task for migration studies. Twitter data has two classes of geographical metadata: the tweet location, available when users share the location at the time of tweeting, and the account location, a free-form character field providing a hint on the region and country where the user is located. Twitter introduced geotagging support in 2009. However, in June 2019 the platform removed support for precise geotagging. This means that tweets no longer include the exact geographical coordinates. To perform analyses considering geographical information, one can follow an *a priori* or a post-collection strategy.

In the post-collection strategy, the tweets of interest are selected *a posteriori* from the dataset, based on the geographic information included with the tweet. This is mostly used when working with preexisting datasets from which one intends to select only a subset of interest. Two possible analyses can be done: geocoding, the process of converting addresses into geographic coordinates, and reverse geocoding, the process of converting geographic coordinates into a human-readable address, or mapping to standardised geographical nomenclatures such as the NUTS system.[26]

The *a priori* strategy assumes that the initial collection of tweets takes place on a geographical basis, i.e., collect all the tweets posted in a specific country or region. This is possible by limiting the stream or search API to a bounding box of interest. Tweet-specific location information can be represented as specific latitude/longitude Point coordinates or within the Place object. The tweets that fall into the first category were generated by GPS-enabled devices and therefore included the exact GPS location of the tweet. However, be aware that tweets with Point coordinates do not provide any further information about the GPS location, such as country or city. Conversely, tweets with a Place object contain four longitude–latitude coordinates that define a polygon, thus the general area, within which the given tweets were posted (geo.bbox field).

---

[26] Eurostat - NUTS: Background, https://ec.europa.eu/eurostat/web/nuts/background

As stated in 'Data format', the Place is not the primary object of any endpoint. Still, it falls under the so-called *expansions*, i.e., further requests to obtain additional data objects related to returned tweets. The Place-related fields enable specifying which Place fields will be included with returned tweets; these may include name, type (e.g., city, neighbourhood, country) and the country code corresponding to the country where the Place is located, among other fields.

To date, numerous libraries and methods have been created to extract and obtain geographic information from tweets. One of the most used libraries, in particular for the Python language, is CARMEN (Dredze *et al.*, 2013), a geolocation system that can determine structured location information from tweets. The framework uses geocoding tools and a combination of automatic and manual resolution methods to infer location from GPS positions. UnicodeCNN (Izbicki *et al.*, 2019) is a method that allows the prediction of GPS locations of tweets written in any language by using a mixture of von Mises–Fisher distributions. The Google Maps Geocoding API[27] is a Google API which allows for both geocoding and reverse geocoding. Using the Google Maps Geocoding API it is possible to standardise tweets' geolocation information. It should be noted that there is a limit of 2500 coordinates per day for standard Google Map API users. Finally, Geopy[28] is a Python client for several popular geocoding web services that allows the location of the coordinates of addresses, cities, and countries.

For geolocalised tweets, it is also possible to combine different libraries, maximising the result. Pollacci (2019) needed to match tweet locations with NUTS regions from an immigration-related dataset (the Data for Integration (D4I) dataset[29]). For this, the author checked whether the information included in the metadata matched places in the D4I data. To geo-allocate remaining tweets, the author combined several Python libraries to build a specific pipeline. First, the algorithm exploited the MediaWiki API[30] using the tweets' locations. If the API did not allow for extracting the tweet's origin city, the location was used as a Google Search API[31] parameter to extract URLs from the first five pages. URLs pointing to Wikipedia were used to extract the city referred to by the location from the information box. Finally, remaining locations were passed as parameters to the Google Maps API and in Geopy. As stated in Pollacci (2019), the latter two libraries are generally more accurate but suffer from rate and call limits.

Gaps and biases

Various types of biases and gaps exist when using Twitter data to study migration. One of the most notable challenges is that the Twitter population does not represent

---

[27] Google Maps Platform: Use API Keys with Geocoding API, https://developers.google.com/maps/documentation/geocoding/get-api-key
[28] geopy, https://pypi.org/project/geopy/
[29] European Commission: Data for Integration (D4I), https://ec.europa.eu/knowledge4policy/migration-demography/data-integration-d4i_en
[30] MediaWiki: API, https://www.mediawiki.org/wiki/API:Main_page
[31] Google: Programmable Search Engine, https://developers.google.com/custom-search/

TWITTER DATA FOR MIGRATION STUDIES

Figure 8.2 The top 20 countries in terms of number of Twitter users (in millions) as of January 2021. Source: https://www.statista.com/statistics/242606/number-of-active-twitter-users-in-selected-countries/

the offline population (Weber, 2015; Yildiz et al., 2017), i.e., there is a so-called 'selection bias'. First, because different internet penetration rates across countries cause over-/underrepresentation of certain populations. Second, Twitter lacks population coverage compared to other social media platforms such as Facebook and Instagram.[32]

The popularity of Twitter is also variable across countries. Most Twitter users are from the United States, Japan, India, the United Kingdom, and Brazil,[33] as shown in Figure 8.2. The popularity of Twitter varies from 69.3 million users in the United States down to 5.2 million in South Korea based on the number of Twitter users as of July 2021.[33]

A different but related gap is the fact that sociodemographic information is missing from Twitter data. This makes research more difficult, and even the evaluation of selection bias is hindered. Existing studies have employed various methods to estimate sociodemographic information such as age, sex, and education level. For instance, studies on migration gathered profile photos and used face-recognition software to estimate the gender and age of the users (Zagheni et al., 2014; Huang et al., 2014). Otherwise, according to a survey conducted by Pew Research, the Twitter population has characteristics that are different from other social media platforms (Wojcik and Hughes, 2019). In the United States, Twitter users tend to have more education and higher income than the general public. As for the genders, they are equally represented on Twitter. When it comes to ethnicity, white ethnicity is prominently present on Twitter. Although there are studies on the demographics of general Twitter users using Twitter data (Mislove et al., 2011; Longley et al., 2015), studies that focus on migrants are missing in the literature. Therefore, it is difficult to understand socioeconomic demographic components of migrants. We can, however, understand from these works that young people, age 15 and above,

---

[32] Facebook has over 2.7 billion monthly active users as of the second quarter of 2020, and Twitter has on average 330 million monthly active users as of the first quarter of 2019. Instagram has more than one billion monthly active users (see https://www.facebook.com/business/marketing/instagram).

[33] Statista: Leading countries based on number of Twitter users as of January 2022, https://www.statista.com/statistics/242606/number-of-active-twitter-users-in-selected-countries/

and white ethnicity are over-represented on Twitter in the United States and in London.

Along with selection bias in the user population, bias also exists in the process of collecting and cleaning data. There are two main methods collecting data from Twitter: using the Streaming API or the Firehose. Twitter's Streaming API has a 1% sample limit extraction where the methodology of how the 1% sample is extracted is unknown. Firehose has the advantage of collecting more than 1% of a sample, but it is costly. Often, researchers choose to use the Streaming API. With the newly opened Academic Research track, this should change in the future, and researchers should be able to access more data. However, in the study of migration, one additional challenge is the fact that the geolocation information is often missing, further restricting the available data. The proportion of geotagged tweets ranges from 3.17% from the Streaming API to 1.45% from Firehose (Morstatter and Liu, 2017). Not all users enable geolocation, and it is not clear how the demographics of those who do are different from the rest of the population. Furthermore, during the data cleaning process researchers often encounter several issues. There is frequently a lot of noise, including typos, incomplete tweets, false information on profiles, and so on. Removing and cleaning unrelated information reduces the data size significantly, and it is not clear if this affects the Twitter population uniformly or whether some users are more prone to having their tweets removed.

Other types of gaps originate from third-party entities. Creating bots on Twitter is one of the ways to manipulate information (Kollanyi *et al.*, 2016; Ferrara, 2017). These may artificially increase the number of followers and friends, or post large numbers of tweets to increase audiences' attention. Another example would be manipulating the trendy topics. For instance, during election periods the trendy topics have been used to influence voting behaviours (Howard and Kollanyi, 2016).

Discontinuity of the service may become an issue as well. For instance, after the modification of Twitter's conditions, the profile language is no longer available. The discontinuity of service makes replication of preexisting methods difficult for further improvements of migration statistics. In addition, changes in rate limits also occur, slowing the speed of the data collection process.

As also explained in 'Terms of service', researchers are required to respect the terms of service and data protection regulations. This limits free sharing of data as Twitter contains a lot of personal information. It is obligatory for researchers to ensure confidentiality, security, and ethical concerns when using sophisticated data.

Overall, the gaps and biases that exist in Twitter data make it difficult for researchers to generalise their findings to the general population. Extra efforts are required to handle the bias. For instance, Zagheni *et al.* (2014) employ a difference-in-difference approach to control for different Twitter user compositional changes across different countries under the assumption that the changes are constant in the short term. By doing so, they were able to successfully monitor general trends of out-migration in real time for OECD countries (see also Box 7.1, this volume).

Discussion and conclusions

This chapter has provided a summary of the steps involved in using Twitter data for migration research. This included downloading data, typical processing pipelines, and complying with the terms of service. Gaps and biases were identified, and a short literature review described various exciting applications of these data for migration studies, demonstrating that they can be applied in a variety of areas of research, from estimating stocks and flows to studying diversity and integration, or understanding the effects of specific natural or political events.

The discussion identified a series of issues, challenges, and open questions regarding these types of novel data sources. First of all, it is clear that the data collection step is not straightforward. While efforts are being made to develop tools that can facilitate the use of the API by researchers with little programming expertise, frequent changes in the API and the sheer amount of data to be downloaded mean that this remains a challenge. Storing and processing the large amounts of data, while being careful not to breach the terms of service, still requires specific computer science expertise.

Furthermore, in the context of studying migration flows or stocks, or migrant behaviour, even if we are in the field of big data, the relevant data resulting from the collection step could still be reduced by filtering out irrelevant data in consecutive processing stages. For instance, if we only think of the restrictions of the public Streaming API, allowing for only 1% of data to be downloaded, coupled with the filtering of non-geolocalised tweets (about 98.5%), that leaves us with 0.015% of data alone, referring to the entire user population. If we want to restrict this to migrants, the data risks becoming very limited. This could particularly happen if migrants are less represented in the data compared to the general population. We have seen that Twitter users tend to be better remunerated, have higher education levels, and are white, therefore some migrant groups could be less represented. A different consideration could be that some migrant groups could be less prone to disclose their geolocation, which means their data will disappear when filtering out non-geolocalised tweets. Some of these issues could be reduced by accessing the newly introduced Academic Research API. At the same time, these issues are less substantial in studies that analyse migration by considering the entire population, not only migrants. Examples are the study of sentiment towards migration, or evaluation of cultural diversity.

A different aspect where there are a lot of open issues is that of privacy and ethics. The terms and conditions of the public APIs can, at times, be vague, and may not cover all the ethics issues involved. There have been some attempts to produce ethics and privacy guidelines for using social media data in research (Townsend and Wallace, 2016; Williams *et al.*, 2017a); however, they are general and do not consider the special case of migration research. In this field we are facing a very difficult problem. On one hand, sensitive personal information such as ethnicity, geolocation, and demographics are key to developing suitable analyses and advancing the state of the art. On the other hand, we are studying possibly very sensitive groups, hence these pieces of personal information should be protected, for the sake of both individual and group privacy. In these conditions special guidelines are necessary, including on privacy, ethics, and legality.

Currently, most migration research using Twitter data does not publish the data it is based on, thus impeding replicability, which is one of the pillars of good-quality research. At the same time, privacy regulations make it very difficult to publish the original data (Bishop and Gray, 2017), while anonymisation studies, especially for Twitter, are still in their infancy. Some works exist describing de-anonymising and re-identification for social graphs (Narayanan and Shmatikov, 2009), social network content (Henriksen-Bulmer and Jeary, 2016; Ogawa *et al.*, 2015), and geolocation (Yoshiura, 2019; Cecaj *et al.*, 2016; Monreale *et al.*, 2010); however, widely accepted guidelines and solutions to publishing such data do not exist. Privacy risk assessment is an ongoing topic (Pellungrini *et al.*, 2017), and further results, especially related to migration, are needed.

Acknowledgements

This work was supported by the European Commission through the Horizon2020 European projects 'SoBigData++: European Integrated Infrastructure for Social Mining and Big Data Analytics' (grant agreement no. 871042) and 'HumMingBird – Enhanced migration measures from a multidimensional perspective' (Research and Innovation Action, grant agreement no. 870661).

References

Abdul-Mageed, M., Brown, C., and Abu-Elhij'a, D. (2013), 'Twitter in the context of the Arab Spring', *AoIR Selected Papers of Internet Research*, 3, available at https://spir.aoir.org/ojs/index.php/spir/article/view/9084

Adnan, M. and Longley, P. (2013), 'Analysis of Twitter usage in London, Paris, and New York City', *in Proceedings of the 16th AGILE Conference on Geographic Information Science*, 1–7.

Andrienko, N., Andrienko, G., Fuchs, G., Rinzivillo, S., and Betz, H.-D. (2015), 'Detection, tracking, and visualization of spatial event clusters for real time monitoring', *in Proceedings of the 2015 IEEE International Conference on Data Science and Advanced Analytics (DSAA)*, 1–10.

Arcila-Calderón, C., Blanco-Herrero, D., Frías-Vázquez, M., and Seoane, F. (2021), 'Refugees welcome? Online hate speech and sentiments in Twitter in Spain during the reception of the boat Aquarius', *Sustainability* 13(5), 2728.

Azmandian, M., Singh, K., Gelsey, B., Chang, Y.-H., and Maheswaran, R. (2012), 'Following human mobility using tweets', *in* L. Cao, Y. Zeng, A. L. Symeonidis, V. I. Gorodetsky, P. S. Yu, and M. P. Singh, eds, *Agents and Data Mining Interaction*, Springer, New York, 139–49.

Bishop, L. and Gray, D. (2017), 'Ethical challenges of publishing and sharing social media research data', *in* K. Woodfield, ed, *The Ethics of Online Research*, Emerald Publishing Limited, Bingley.

Cecaj, A., Mamei, M., and Zambonelli, F. (2016), 'Re-identification and information fusion between anonymized CDR and social network data', *Journal of Ambient Intelligence and Humanized Computing* 7(1), 83–96.

Coimbra Vieira, C., Fatehkia, M., Garimella, K., Weber, I., and Zagheni, E. (2022), 'Using Facebook and LinkedIn data to study international mobility', *in* A. A. Salah, E. E. Korkmaz, and T. Bircan, eds, *Data Science for Migration and Mobility*, Proceedings of the British Academy, British Academy / Oxford University Press, London.

Coletto, M., Esuli, A., Lucchese, C., Muntean, C. I., Nardini, F. M., Perego, R., and Renso, C. (2016), 'Sentiment-enhanced multidimensional analysis of online social networks: Perception of the Mediterranean refugees crisis', *in Proceedings of the 2016 IEEE/ACM International Conference on Advances in Social Networks Analysis and Mining (ASONAM)*, 1270–77.

Das, A. and Hasegawa-Johnson, M. (2015), 'Cross-lingual transfer learning during supervised training in low resource scenarios', *in Proceedings of the Sixteenth Annual Conference of the International Speech Communication Association*.

de Rosa, A. S., Bocci, E., Bonito, M., and Salvati, M. (2021), 'Twitter as social media arena for polarised social representations about the (im)migration: The controversial discourse in the Italian and international political frame', *Migration Studies* 9(3), 1167–94.

Dredze, M., Paul, M. J., Bergsma, S., and Tran, H. (2013), Carmen: 'A Twitter geolocation system with applications to public health', *in Proceedings of the Workshops at the Twenty-Seventh AAAI Conference on Artificial Intelligence*.

Ferrara, E. (2017), 'Disinformation and social bot operations in the run up to the 2017 French presidential election', arXiv:1707.00086.

Flores, R. D. (2017), 'Do anti-immigrant laws shape public sentiment? A study of Arizona's SB 1070 using Twitter data', *American Journal of Sociology* 123(2), 333–84.

Han, B., Cook, P., and Baldwin, T. (2014), 'Text-based Twitter user geolocation prediction', *Journal of Artificial Intelligence Research* 49, 451–500.

Harlow, S. and Johnson, T. J. (2011), 'The Arab spring: Overthrowing the protest paradigm? How the New York Times, global voices and Twitter covered the Egyptian revolution', *International Journal of Communication* 5, 16.

Hawelka, B., Sitko, I., Beinat, E., Sobolevsky, S., Kazakopoulos, P., and Ratti, C. (2014), 'Geo-located Twitter as proxy for global mobility patterns', *Cartography and Geographic Information Science* 41(3), 260–71.

Henriksen-Bulmer, J. and Jeary, S. (2016), 'Re-identification attacks: A systematic literature review', *International Journal of Information Management* 36(6), 1184–92.

Howard, P. N. and Kollanyi, B. (2016), 'Bots,#Strongerin, and #Brexit: Computational propaganda during the UK-EU referendum', available at https://ssrn.com/abstract=2798311

Huang, W., Weber, I. and Vieweg, S. (2014), 'Inferring nationalities of Twitter users and studying inter-national linking', *in Proceedings of the 25th ACM Conference on Hypertext and Social Media*, 237–42.

Izbicki, M., Papalexakis, V., and Tsotras, V. (2019), 'Geolocating tweets in any language at any location', *in Proceedings of the 28th ACM International Conference on Information and Knowledge Management*, 89–98.

Kim, J., Sîrbu, A., Giannotti, F., and Gabrielli, L. (2020), 'Digital footprints of international migration on Twitter', *in* M. R. Berthold, A. Feelders, and G. Krempl, eds, *Advances in Intelligent Data Analysis XVIII*, Springer, New York, 274–86.

Kim, J., Sîrbu, A., Rossetti, G., and Giannotti, F. (2021a), 'Characterising different communities of Twitter users: Migrants and natives', *in* R. M. Benito, C. Cherifi, H. Cherifi, E. Moro, L. M. Rocha, and M. Sales-Pardo, eds, *Complex Networks and Their Applications X*, Springer, New York, 130–41.

Kim, J., Sîrbu, A., Rossetti, G., Giannotti, F., and Rapoport, H. (2021b), 'Home and destination attachment: Study of cultural integration on Twitter', arXiv:2102.11398.

Kollanyi, B., Howard, P. N., and Woolley, S. C. (2016), 'Bots and automation over Twitter during the first US presidential debate', Data Memo 2016.3, Project on Computational Propaganda, Oxford.

Krumm, J., Caruana, R., and Counts, S. (2013), 'Learning likely locations', *in* S. Carberry, S, Weibelzahl, A. Micarelli, and G. Semeraro, eds, *User Modeling, Adaptation, and Personalization*, Springer, New York, 64–76.

Lenormand, M., Gonçalves, B., Tugores, A., and Ramasco, J. J. (2015), 'Human diffusion and city influence', *Journal of The Royal Society Interface* 12(109), 20150473.

Longley, P. A., Adnan, M., and Lansley, G. (2015), 'The geotemporal demographics of Twitter usage', *Environment and Planning A* 47(2), 465–84.

Lucić, D., Katalinić, J., and Dokman, T. (2020), 'Sentiment analysis of the Syrian conflict on Twitter', *Medijske Studije* 11(22), 46–61.

Lyding, V., Stemle, E., Borghetti, C., Brunello, M., Castagnoli, S., Dell'Orletta, F., Dittmann, H., Lenci, A., and Pirrelli, V. (2014), 'The PAISA corpus of Italian web texts', *in Proceedings of the Ninth Web as Corpus Workshop (WaC-9) @ EACL 2014*, 36–43.

Mahmud, J., Nichols, J., and Drews, C. (2014), 'Home location identification of Twitter users', *ACM Transactions on Intelligent Systems and Technology (TIST)* 5(3), 1–21.

Mazzoli, M., Diechtiareff, B., Tugores, A., Wives, W., Adler, N., Colet, P., and Ramasco, J. J. (2020), 'Migrant mobility flows characterized with digital data', *PLOS One* 15(3), e0230264.

Mislove, A., Lehmann, S., Ahn, Y.-Y., Onnela, J.-P., and Rosenquist, J. (2011), 'Understanding the demographics of Twitter users', *in Proceedings of the International AAAI Conference on Web and Social Media*, Vol. 5.

Moise, I., Gaere, E., Merz, R., Koch, S., and Pournaras, E. (2016), 'Tracking language mobility in the Twitter landscape', *in Proceedings of the 16th IEEE International Conference on Data Mining Workshops (ICDMW)*, 663–70.

Monreale, A., Andrienko, G. L., Andrienko, N. V., Giannotti, F., Pedreschi, D., Rinzivillo, S., and Wrobel, S. (2010), 'Movement data anonymity through generalization', *Transactions on Data Privacy* 3(2), 91–121.

Morstatter, F. and Liu, H. (2017), 'Discovering, assessing, and mitigating data bias in social media', *Online Social Networks and Media* 1, 1–13.

Narayanan, A. and Shmatikov, V. (2009), 'De-anonymizing social networks', *in Proceedings of the 30th IEEE Symposium on Security and Privacy*, 173–87.

Nguyen, H. and Garimella, K. (2017), 'Understanding international migration using tensor factorization', *in Proceedings of the 26th International Conference on World Wide Web Companion*, 829–30.

Obar, J. A. and Oeldorf-Hirsch, A. (2020), 'The biggest lie on the internet: Ignoring the privacy policies and terms of service policies of social networking services', *Information, Communication & Society* 23(1), 128–47.

Ogawa, Y., Hashimoto, E., Ichino, M., Echizen, I., and Yoshiura, H. (2015), 'Deanonymising social network posts by linking with résumé', *in* W. Abramowicz, ed., *Business Information Systems Workshops*, Springer, Cham, 248–60.

Öztürk, N. and Ayvaz, S. (2018), 'Sentiment analysis on Twitter: A text mining approach to the Syrian refugee crisis', *Telematics and Informatics* 35(1), 136–47.

Pellungrini, R., Pappalardo, L., Pratesi, F., and Monreale, A. (2017), 'A data mining approach to assess privacy risk in human mobility data', *ACM Transactions on Intelligent Systems and Technology (TIST)* 9(3), 1–27.

Pollacci, L. (2019), 'Superdiversity: (Big) Data analytics at the crossroads of geography, language and emotions', PhD thesis, University of Pisa.

Qi, P., Zhang, Y., Zhang, Y., Bolton, J., and Manning, C. D. (2020), 'Stanza: A Python natural language processing toolkit for many human languages', arXiv:2003.07082.

Salah, A. A., Canca, C., and Erman, B. (2022), 'Ethical and legal concerns on data science for large-scale human mobility', *in* A. A. Salah, E. E. Korkmaz, and T. Bircan, eds, *Data Science for Migration and Mobility*, Proceedings of the British Academy, British Academy / Oxford University Press, London, UK.

Sánchez-Holgado, P. and Arcila-Calderón, C. (2018), 'Towards the study of sentiment in the public opinion of science in Spanish', *in Proceedings of the Sixth International Conference on Technological Ecosystems for Enhancing Multiculturality*, 963–70.

Sîrbu, A., *et al.* (2021), 'Human migration: The big data perspective', *International Journal of Data Science and Analytics* 11(4), 341–60.

Sloan, L., Jessop, C., Al Baghal, T., and Williams, M. (2020), 'Linking survey and Twitter data: Informed consent, disclosure, security, and archiving', *Journal of Empirical Research on Human Research Ethics* 15(1–2), 63–76.

Takhteyev, Y., Gruzd, A., and Wellman, B. (2012), 'Geography of Twitter networks', *Social Networks* 34(1), 73–81.

Townsend, L. and Wallace, C. (2016), 'Social media research: A guide to ethics', University of Aberdeen Technical Report, available at https://www.gla.ac.uk/media/Media_487729_smxx.pdf

Valle, D., Cvetojevic, S., Robertson, E. P., Reichert, B. E., Hochmair, H. H., and Fletcher, R. J. (2017), 'Individual movement strategies revealed through novel clustering of emergent movement patterns', *Scientific Reports* 7(1), 1–12.

Wang, W., Zheng, V. W., Yu, H., and Miao, C. (2019), 'A survey of zero-shot learning: Settings, methods, and applications', *ACM Transactions on Intelligent Systems and Technology* 10(2), 1–37.

Wang, Y., Yao, Q., Kwok, J. T., and Ni, L. M. (2020), 'Generalizing from a few examples: A survey on few-shot learning', *ACM Computing Surveys* 53(3), 1–34.

Weber, I. (2015), 'Demographic research with non-representative internet data', *International Journal of Manpower* 36(1), 13–25.

Williams, M. L., Burnap, P., and Sloan, L. (2017a), 'Towards an ethical framework for publishing Twitter data in social research: Taking into account users' views, online context and algorithmic estimation', *Sociology* 51(6), 1149–68.

Williams, M. L., Burnap, P., Sloan, L., Jessop, C., and Lepps, H. (2017b), 'Users' views of ethics in social media research: Informed consent, anonymity, and harm', *in* K. Woodfield, ed, *The Ethics of Online Research*, Emerald Publishing Limited, Bingley.

Wojcik, S. and Hughes, A. (2019), 'Sizing up Twitter users', Pew Research Center, Washington DC.

Yildiz, D., Munson, J., Vitali, A., Tinati, R., and Holland, J. A. (2017), 'Using Twitter data for demographic research', *Demographic Research* 37, 1477–514.

Yoshiura, H. (2019), 'Re-identifying people from anonymous histories of their activities', *in Proceedings of the 10th IEEE International Conference on Awareness Science and Technology*, 1–5.

Zagheni, E., Garimella, V. R. K., Weber, I., and State, B. (2014), 'Inferring international and internal migration patterns from Twitter data', *in Proceedings of the 23rd International Conference on the World Wide Web*, 439–44.

9

Indicators and Survey Data to Understand Migration and Integration Policy Frameworks and Trends in the EU

GIACOMO SOLANO

Introduction

MANY FACTORS CONTRIBUTE to the initiation and perpetuation of migration to destination countries over time, and influence the integration of migrants. Migration trends emerge as an interaction between structural factors (e.g., economic context and policies), formal and informal institutions, and individual agency (e.g., human capital and social capital). Among these factors, the migration policies of the destination country play a role. The openness or closedness of migration policies influence migration dynamics and integration outcomes. Migration policies, in particular admission policies, can provide (or constrain) specific migration infrastructures and shape migration flows and stocks, e.g., they may influence the number and the characteristics of migrants entering a country and staying there (Czaika and De Haas, 2013; Helbling and Leblang, 2019). Similarly, the policies implemented by policy-makers to support migrants' integration shape their integration outcomes (Solano and Huddleston, 2020).

This chapter aims at presenting the main sources and datasets on migration policy, and migration trends and integration outcomes. Since the early 2000s, an increasing number of data sources have emerged (Kraler and Reichel, 2022; Solano and Huddleston, 2021). This chapter introduces these sources of quantitative data.

Key in the analysis of migration policy is the distinction between outputs and outcomes (Gest *et al.*, 2014). Policy outputs refer to the formulation of laws and policies, while outcomes are, at least in part, the result of the implementation of those laws and policies. Policy outputs are policy measures, such as the adoption of a law/policy by government entities on topics related to migration. Policy outcomes refer to the impact that a policy might have (e.g., immigration stock and flows). For example, concerning integration of refugees in the labour market, a possible policy output is a law granting refugees immediate access to self-employment, and the number of self-employed refugees represents the policy outcome.

Quantitative data on migration policy outputs and outcomes are particularly useful in conducting cross-country comparative analysis and in understanding trends over time. Furthermore, data allow for the addressing of the role that policies play in influencing migration trends and migrants' integration outcomes. This chapter first addresses the data availability, gaps, and possible future developments by analysing the field of migration policy indicators. After that, I carry out the same analysis for the outcomes, namely migration trends and integration outcomes. For each topic, I first address the issue of data accessibility and then illustrate the topics and groups of migrants addressed, as well as the data's geographical and temporal scope. The chapter concludes with some reflections on the remaining gaps and on the possible use of the presented data sources and data. The conclusions address possible links between the presented data sources, data science, and big data.

Output: Migration policy indicators

Since the early 2000s, many undertakings have provided a comparative analysis of migration and integration policies in EU countries (Solano and Huddleston, 2021). To this end, researchers have developed indicators and indices to analyse trends and differences in migration policy, including admission, citizenship acquisition, and integration policies. Gest *et al.* (2014, p. 274) underline that indices 'are understood as highly aggregated, composite measures of immigration policy, while indicators are understood as more specific, disaggregated elements that are individually coded'. An indicator is an observable entity that captures a specific concept and provides a measure of that concept. Indicators can be aggregated into an index. Figure 9.1 displays an example of an indicator (from IMPIC, on admission policies). Figure 9.2 shows the aggregation structure of another index (CITRIX on naturalisation policies).

These sets of indicators are designed to analyse the differences and trends in migration policy and are then used by the research community to assess the determinants and effects of policies. Policy outputs refer to the formulation of laws and policies, and are different from implementation, which refers to the concrete application of the on-paper policy outputs. 'Implementation' indicators measure whether these laws and policies are properly interpreted and delivered as practices. As it is usually difficult to measure the implementation of policies, existing indices and sets of indicators on migration policy have mainly focused on policy outputs.

Existing research has analysed the nature of policy by using two main methodological approaches. The majority of previous projects carried out an overall assessment of migration policies in one or more areas (e.g., integration policies, admission policies), while others addressed the changes that occurred in the policy framework over time and assessed the nature of each change (e.g., introduction of a

A6.1 & A6.2 Language skills

Question: For the years 1980 - 2010, were minimum language skills required from the sponsored spouses?

[R_a06_1] Minimum language skills required?

Values	Label
-2	No
-1	Yes

Question: If minimum language skills were required: Were language skills tested?

Values	Label
0	No
0.5	Yes, required but not specified
0.6	Yes, required but not tested
0.7	Yes, required and tested after arrival
0.8	Yes, required and tested before arrival
0.9	Yes, required and tested before and after arrival
1	No family reunification policy

Figure 9.1 Example of indicators from IMPIC. Source: (Bjerre et al., 2016, pp. 57–58)

new law). IMPIC (Immigration Policies in Comparison, Helbling et al., 2017) and MIPEX (Solano and Huddleston, 2020; Huddleston et al., 2015) are examples of the former, while DEMIG (Determinants of International Migration, De Haas et al., 2015) is a case in point for the latter. In what follows, I examine existing indices by looking at data accessibility, topics and groups covered, and geographical and temporal coverage (see Table 9.1).

Data accessibility

One of the main issues when it comes to data availability on migration policy indices is their accessibility. Data are often not publicly available. Some aggregated data (index scores) are available through the International Organization for

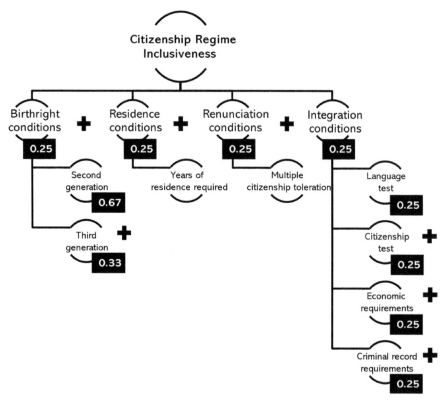

Figure 9.2 Example of aggregation structure from CITRIX. Source: Schmid (2021, p. 345)

Migration (IOM) Data Portal.[1] The portal includes many migration policy related topics from different indices: migration governance (migration governance index from the IOM); emigration, immigration and return policy (from UN); migration policy changes (from DEMIG); migration control and labour migration policy (from IMPIC); asylum/refugee policy (IMPIC); family reunification policy (IMPIC); and integration policy (MIPEX). Other aggregated data can be derived from publications using these indices as part of quantitative analysis. However, the scores and the information on the indicators composing the index are often not publicly available. There are, of course, some exceptions, though, and there is increasing pressure on researchers in the field to make index data publicly available. For example, among others, datasets from DEMIG (on migration policy changes), IMPIC (on immigration policy), and MIPEX (on integration policy) are fully accessible. They can be used by other researchers to conduct additional analysis, or can be independently updated or used as a reference by others.

Due to the limitations in data accessibility, indices often remain the product of one-off projects (Scipioni and Urso, 2018): they normally cover the years of the

---

[1] Migration Data Portal, https://migrationdataportal.org/

Table 9.1 Characteristics of indices on migration policy

Data accessibility	Indices remain often the product of one-off projects.
	Data are often not publicly available. Among others, some exceptions are DEMIG,[a] IMPIC,[b] and MIPEX.[c]
Topics	Many topics have been addressed. However, most existing indices focus on admission and citizenship policies.
	When it comes to the study of integration policies, the focus is mainly on labour market integration.
	Other areas of research, e.g., irregular migration, return and diaspora policies, are covered by a small number of policy indicators.
Groups	Many indices focus on migrants in general.
	Specific categories of migrants are also well covered by more sectoral indices, e.g., high-skilled labour migrants, and asylum seekers and beneficiaries of international protection.
	A gender perspective is largely absent.
Geographical coverage	Existing indices vary widely in the number of countries covered, ranging from 3 to 200+.
	Most indices analyse EU15 or Western countries (e.g., Australia, Canada, and USA).
	The majority of indices focus on the national level, while only a minority address the sub-national level (regional or local level).
Temporal coverage	Most indices are longitudinal in nature.
	However, the temporal coverage of existing indices is limited, as most focus on a small number of years.
	The timeframe that is covered most often is the period between 2000 and 2010, while more recent years are covered to a lesser extent.
	The large majority of indices focus on the contemporary age, while a historic perspective is missing.

[a] https://www.migrationinstitute.org/data/demig-data/demig-policy-1
[b] http://www.impic-project.eu/
[c] https://www.mipex.eu/

project and, sometimes, some years before (through back-scoring). Given that data are not freely available, other researchers do not normally update existing indices, but rather create a new set of indicators (almost) from scratch. This imposes limitations on the monitoring purpose of these indices and on the analysis of the evolution of the nature of migration policy frameworks.

Topics and groups covered

Topics

Migration policy indicators and indices have addressed many topics (Bjerre *et al.*, 2015). However, according to a recent analysis conducted by Solano and Huddleston (2021), sets of indicators and indices are disproportionately concentrated in

Areas	Frequency
Admission	36
Integration	29
Residence/Citizenship	49
Expulsion and return	13
Sub-areas	
Economic/labour migration (admission)	27
Education purpose/student migration (admission)	8
Family reunification	28
Asylum and humanitarian protection	17
Education (integration)	15
Labour market integration	23
Social Inclusion (in general)	17
Political participation	18
Health	16
Antidiscrimination	13
Citizenship	39
Residence permits	27
Return	7
Irregular migration/Expulsion	15

Figure 9.3 Topics covered by existing indices. Source: (Solano and Huddleston, 2021, p. 331)

a few areas of migration policy research (see Figure 9.3). The majority of policy indicators relate to admission and citizenship policies. For example, IMPALA (International Migration Policy and Law Analysis, Beine *et al.*, 2016) compares immigration policy in nine countries over ten years. It covers policies on admission and access to nationality. The index includes several categories of migration: economic migration, family reunification, asylum and humanitarian migration, and student migration.

Integration policies are underrepresented compared to the high number of articles on integration in migration studies (Pisarevskaya *et al.*, 2020; Solano and Huddleston, 2022). Furthermore, when it comes to the study of integration, the focus is mainly on labour market integration. By contrast, other relevant areas of integration (education, health, political participation, etc.) are overlooked (Solano and Huddleston, 2021). An exception is MIPEX (Solano and Huddleston, 2020), which measures policies to integrate migrants in 52 countries including EU28 and OECD countries. It encompasses eight areas of integration: labour market mobility, family reunification, education, political participation, permanent residence, access to nationality, anti-discrimination, and health.

Other areas of research, e.g., irregular migration, return and diaspora policies, are covered by a small number of policy indicators (Solano and Huddleston, 2021). The IMISEM (Every Immigrant Is an Emigrant)[2] dataset represents an exception to this tendency, as it addresses emigrant, emigration, immigration, immigrant, and citizenship policies.

Groups

While many indices focus on migrants in general, others look at specific categories of migrants, or distinguish between them. Comprehensive indices, which often focus on admission policies, address labour migrants, migrant residents on family reunification permits, asylum seekers/refugees, and international students. All four are included in DEMIG (De Haas *et al.*, 2015), IMPALA (Beine *et al.*, 2016), and IMPIC (Helbling *et al.*, 2017).

Specific categories of migrants are also well covered by more sectoral indices, e.g., high-skilled labour migrants, asylum seekers, and beneficiaries of international protection. Several indices focus on high-skilled labour migrants. For example, Cerna (2014) created an index to assess changes over time on policies to attract and support high-skilled migrants in the labour market. Similarly, IMMEX (Immigration for Employment Index, Migration Policy Group, 2012) analyses admission schemes for migrant workers, looking at both general-worker schemes and schemes for high-skilled migrants (e.g., EU Blue Card). Other indices focusing on this topic are the high-skilled migration policy indicators (Czaika and Parsons, 2017) and Lowell's index for policies on high-skilled workers (Lowell, 2005).

The topic of beneficiaries of international protection has been widely analysed by existing indices, although mainly with regard to admission policies. For example, the Asylum Policy Index (Hatton, 2009) addresses the change in the nature (restrictiveness) of policies for asylum seekers for three different aspects: admission policies, procedures to acquire refugee status, and welfare policies for asylum seekers and refugees. This index covers 19 OECD countries between 1999 and 2006. IMPIC (Helbling *et al.*, 2017) focuses on admission policies for migrants by focusing on four different kinds of migration: (1) labour migration, (2) family reunification, (3) refugees and asylum, and (4) co-ethnics. Within the refugees and asylum category, IMPIC covers eligibility and conditions of access to the status, as

---

[2] GIGA: Every Immigrant Is an Emigrant: How Migration Policies Shape the Paths to Integration (IMISEM), https://www.giga-hamburg.de/en/research-and-transfer/projects/immigrant-emigrant-migration-policies-shape-paths-integration-imisem

well as the security of this status and the associated rights. NIEM (National Integration Evaluation Mechanism, Wolffhardt et al., 2019a), represents an interesting case as it considers integration policies for these categories in 15 European countries, rather than only admission policies.

Finally, a gender perspective is largely absent (Scipioni and Urso, 2018). There is no index that systematically compares differences in policies for migrant men and women. On the one hand, this makes sense as policies address migrants in general and are often gender neutral. On the other hand, the gender dimension is relevant on some specific topics. For example, the literature shows that gender matters when it comes to integration patterns, and that women migrants face additional challenges in comparison with those faced by men (EWSI, 2018). Nearly all migration and integration indices only look at policy differences by status, some of which are more relevant for women (e.g., family reunification, domestic work, victims of trafficking). Other than that, a gender focus in policy is lacking. Some indices on integration do indeed include questions on gender, but such focus is always very marginal. For example, MIPEX addresses targeted policies to support the inclusion of migrant women in the labour market. MIPEX also covers anti-discrimination policies, but the focus is on ethnic/religious/nationality discrimination and not on gender. The Multicultural Policy Index (Banting and Kymlicka, 2013) also analyses affirmative actions for disadvantaged migrant groups, including women.

Geographical and temporal coverage

The geographical coverage of indices varies widely from case to case. Existing indices vary widely in the number of countries covered, from 3 to 200+ (Solano and Huddleston, 2022). The UN Inquiry among Governments on Population and Development has the widest geographical coverage, as it covers 206 countries, both developed and developing. Focusing on a more limited topic, the MACIMIDE Global Expatriate Dual Citizenship Database (Vink et al., 2015) covers dual citizenship for migrants in 200 countries.

The majority of indices focus on the national level, while only a minority address the sub-national level (regional or local level). Sub-national indices have been created mainly in federal states (e.g., India, Switzerland, USA). For example, Manatschal (2011) analysed sub-national variation in integration policies by addressing Swiss cantons. At city level, the most notorious effort is represented by the Intercultural Cities Index (ICC)[3] created by the Council of Europe. The ICC focuses on policies to support intercultural integration in European and non-European cities.

A recent meta-analysis of existing indices (Solano and Huddleston, 2021) shows that many indices analyse European countries (often, EU Member States) or, at best, OECD/developed countries (e.g., Australia, Canada, and USA); see also Figure 9.4). The focus on Western/developed countries still holds within Europe,

---

[3] Council of Europe: About the Intercultural Cities Index, https://www.coe.int/en/web/interculturalcities/about-the-index

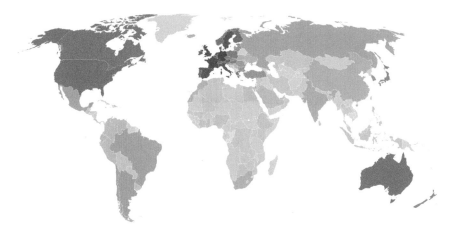

Figure 9.4 Countries covered by existing indices (world). Note: The darker the shade, the higher the number of indices covering the country. Source: Elaboration based on data from (Solano and Huddleston, 2021)

as there is a strong tendency to focus on EU15 countries (see Figure 9.5). Countries such as Germany, Italy, Spain, the Netherlands, Sweden, and the United Kingdom are among those almost always included in the analysis. This seems to reflect immigration trends, as these are among the oldest European countries of immigration and the largest new destination countries (although additional new countries are currently subject to sizeable immigration flows, e.g., Greece).

Most of the indices are longitudinal in nature. They can be considered as panel data, as they cover the same countries over a given period of years. However, the temporal coverage of existing indices is limited, as most of them focus on a small number of years. The timeframe covered most often is the period between 2000 and 2010 (see Figure 9.6), while more recent years are covered to a lesser extent (Solano and Huddleston, 2021).

There are indices that encompass a greater number of years. This is done by assessing policies for either a number of continuous years or every n years. IMPIC, which covers four decades (1980–2018), and MIPEX, which spans 12 years (2007–2019), are examples of the former, while the Multiculturalism Policy Index (Banting and Kymlicka, 2013) is an example of the latter, as it covers 1980, 2000, and 2010.

Furthermore, as indices have been developed by sociologists and political scientists, a large majority focus on the contemporary age, while a historic perspective is missing. One of the noteworthy exceptions to this trend is the set of indicators developed by Timmer and Williams (1998), who analysed the development of migration policies for the period 1860–1930 in five countries that were relevant immigration countries at the time (Australia, Argentina, Brazil, Canada, and the United States). Another exception is Peters' set of indicators (Peters, 2015), which covers immigration policies in 19 European and non-European countries from the late 18th century through to the early 21st century.

Figure 9.5 Countries covered by existing indices (Europe). Note: The darker the shade, the higher the number of indices covering the country. Source: (Solano and Huddleston, 2021, p. 333)

An example index: The Migrant Integration Policy Index

MIPEX is a tool that measures policies to integrate migrants in countries across six continents, including all EU and OECD Member States. MIPEX has been regularly updated and expanded since 2007 (the pilot edition was implemented in 2004).

The MIPEX score is based on a set of 58 indicators covering eight policy areas and has been designed to benchmark current laws and policies against the highest standards, through consultations with top scholars and institutions using and conducting comparative research in their area of expertise. The policy areas of integration covered by MIPEX are the following: labour market mobility, family reunification, education, political participation, permanent residence, access to nationality, anti-discrimination, and health (see Figure 9.7).

A policy indicator is a question relating to a specific policy component of one of the eight policy areas. For each indicator, there is a set of options with associated values (from 0 to 100, *e.g.*, 0-50-100), see Figure 9.8. The maximum of 100 is awarded when policies meet the highest standards for equal treatment. Within each of the eight policy areas, the indicator scores are averaged together to give the policy area score for each of the eight policy areas per country, which, averaged together one more time, lead to the overall scores for each country.

INDICATORS AND SURVEY DATA

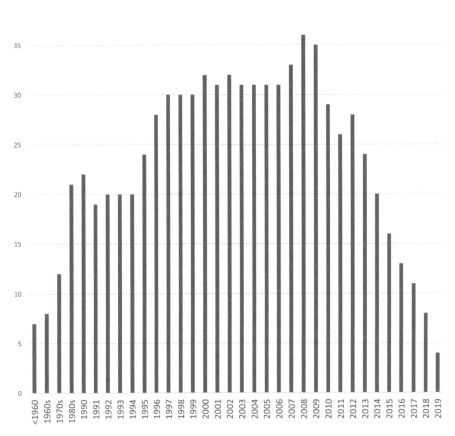

Figure 9.6 Years covered by existing indices. Source: (Solano and Huddleston, 2021, p. 335)

The MIPEX questionnaires are completed by national experts (at least one per country). The health strand was completed by a separate set of migrant health policy experts, and only for 2014 and 2019. The Migration Policy Group (MPG) central research staff check the experts' responses to guarantee full comprehension of and consistent responses to the questions across countries. When concerns arise, MPG's research staff request additional information from country experts. In addition, the MPG research team conducts a final question-by-question consistency check, and a check of changes over time, to ensure that similar situations and changes have received the same score/change across all countries.

The finalised data for each country are input and analysed centrally by the MPG research team. The team conducts quantitative analysis to understand the state of integration policies in the MIPEX countries, and overall trends and changes over time. Results are then presented and displayed in an interactive, easy-to-use, online tool (Figure 9.9).

1. LABOUR MARKET MOBILITY

1.1. Immediate access to labour market;
1.2. Access to public sector;
1.3. Access to self employment;
1.4. Public employment services;
1.5. Education, vocational training and study grants;
1.6. Recognition of academic qualifications;
1.7. Economic integration measures of TCNs;
1.8. Economic integration measures of youth and women;
1.9. Access to social security;

3. EDUCATION

3.1. Access to compulsory and non-compulsory education;
3.2. Access to higher education;
3.3. Educational guidance at all levels;
3.4. Provision of support to learn language of instruction;
3.5. Measures to address educational situation of migrant groups;
3.6. Teacher training to reflect migrants' learning needs;
3.7. School curriculum to reflect diversity;
3.7. Measures to bring migrants into the teacher workforce;
3.8. Teacher training to reflect diversity

5. PERMANENT RESIDENCE

5.1. Residence period;
5.2. LTR Language requirement;
5.3. Economic resources;
5.4. Duration of validity of permit;
5.5. Renewable permit;
5.6. Periods of absence allowed;
5.7. Access to social security and assistance;

7. ANTI-DISCRIMINATION

7.1. Law covers direct/indirect discrimination, harassment, instruction;
7.2. Employment & vocational training;
7.3. Education;
7.4. Social protection;
7.5. Access to and supply of public goods and services, including housing;
7.6. Enforcement mechanisms;
7.7. Mandate of specialized equality body - grounds;
7.8. Mandate of specialized equality body - powers;
7.9. Law covers positive action measures

2. FAMILY REUNION FOR FOREIGN CITIZENS

2.1. Residence period;
2.2. Eligibility for dependent parents/grandparents and dependent adult children;
2.3. Pre-entry integration requirement;
2.4. Post-entry integration requirement;
2.5 Economic resources;
2.6. Accommodation;
2.7. Duration of validity of permit;
2.8. Grounds for rejection, withdrawal, refusal;
2.9. Personal circumstances considered;
2.10. Right to autonomous residence permit for partners and children;

4. POLITICAL PARTICIPATION

4.1. Right to vote and stand in national and local elections;
4.2. Membership in political parties;
4.3. Strength of national consultative body;
4.3. Active information policy;
4.4. Public funding/support for national immigrant bodies;

6. ACCESS TO NATIONALITY

6.1. Residence period;
6.2. Citizenship for immigrant children (birthright and socialisation);
6.3. Naturalisation language requirement;
6.4. Naturalisation integration requirement;
6.5. Economic resources;
6.6. Criminal record;
6.7 Dual nationality for first generation;

8. HEALTH

8.1 ENTITLEMENT TO HEALTH SERVICES

8.1. Health entitlements for legal migrants;
8.2. Health entitlements for asylum-seekers;
8.3. Health entitlements for undocumented migrants;
8.4. Administrative discretion and documentation for legal migrants;
8.5. Administrative discretion and documentation for asylum-seekers;
8.6. Administrative discretion and documentation for undocumented migrants;
8.7. Information for migrants concerning entitlements and use of health services;
8.8. Information for migrants concerning health education and promotion;
8.9. Availability of qualified interpretation services;
8.10. Involvement of migrants in information provision, service design and delivery;
8.11. Support for research on migrant health;
8.12. Whole organisation approach;

Figure 9.7 Policy areas included in MIPEX (and indicators for each area). Source: (Solano and Huddleston, 2020)

Indicator	Description	Option 1 (100)	Option 2 (50)	Option 3 (0)
Access to self employment	Are foreign residents able to take up self-employed activity under equal conditions as nationals?	Yes. There are no additional restrictions than those based on type of permit	Other limiting conditions that apply to foreign residents, e.g. linguistic testing (please specify)	Certain sectors and activities solely for nationals (please specify)

Figure 9.8 Example of MIPEX indicators. Source: https://www.mipex.eu

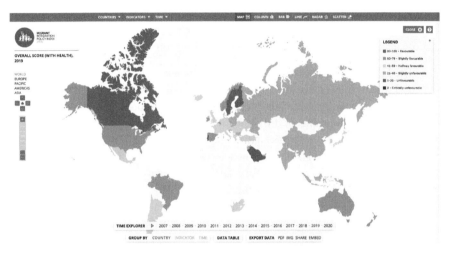

Figure 9.9 MIPEX interactive tool. Source: https://www.mipex.eu/play/

Outcomes: Migration and integration trends

As a result of different developments and initiatives involving national data providers and international actors at both the EU and national levels, data availability and accessibility have expanded enormously in recent decades, allowing data users to tap vast and expanding sources of information on migration trends and integration outcomes (Kraler and Reichel, 2022; Wolffhardt et al., 2019b). This is due to effort by the EU, in particular with the adoption of Regulation (EC) No. 862/2007 and Regulation (EU) 2020/851 (amending Regulation (EC) No. 862/2007), which made it compulsory for EU Member States to regularly provide Eurostat with data on migration issues.

The main data source is Eurostat, which is the statistical office of the European Union. Eurostat provides data on both national and sub-national scales in a wide range of migration- and integration-related areas. Data are gathered through national statistical offices and EU surveys. Many EU-level surveys complement aggregate data with individual-level information. These surveys, commissioned by EU institutions or coordinated at the European level, contribute to a better understanding of migration- and integration-related issues.

This section focuses on the data displayed on the Eurostat website and illustrates the key EU-wide surveys. This chapter considers the following surveys: the EU Labour Force Survey (EU-LFS), the EU Statistics on Income and Living Conditions Survey (EU-SILC), the European Social Survey (ESS), Eurobarometer, the European Values Study (EVS), and the EU Minorities and Discrimination Survey (EU-MIDIS).

There are indeed other EU-wide surveys that have been carried out by European projects or university consortia, such as LOCALMULTIDEM,[4] the Integration of the European Second generation (TIES),[5] and the Immigrant Citizens Survey (ICS),[6] but these surveys are not included in this chapter. For a more comprehensive list of surveys, I suggest referring to the following sources:

- The GESIS Leibniz Institute for the Social Sciences is a European data archive and research infrastructure provider. The GESIS data catalogue provides data and documentation materials, including reports, codebooks/questionnaires, and datasets, on thousands of different social surveys.[7]
- The COST Action 'International Ethnic and Immigrant Minorities Survey Data Network', the main aim of which is to facilitate the coordination of past, present, and future research efforts that produce and analyse data on migrants.[8]
- The Migration research Hub,[9] managed by IMISCOE[10] and produced in the frame of the EU-funded Horizon2020 CrossMigration project,[11] gathers information on research papers and datasets on migration.

As in the section on migration policy, the topic of data on migration trends and integration outcomes is addressed by looking at data accessibility, the topics and groups covered, and the geographical and temporal scope (see Table 9.2).

Data accessibility

Figures produced by Eurostat are available at the country or sub-country aggregate level in the Eurostat database (see Figure 9.10).[12] Figures are freely accessible and

---

[4] Localmultidem: Description of Project, https://www.um.es/localmultidem/description.html
[5] European Commission: The integration of the Second Generation, https://cordis.europa.eu/project/id/36077
[6] Migration Policy Group: Immigrant Citizens Survey, https://www.migpolgroup.com/_old/diversity-integration/immigrant-citizens-survey/
[7] GESIS Search, https://search.gesis.org
[8] COST: CA16111 - International Ethnic and Immigrant Minorities' Survey Data Network (ETHMIGSURVEYDATA), https://www.cost.eu/actions/CA16111/; Ethmig Survey Data, http://www.ethmigsurveydatahub.eu/
[9] Migration Research Hub, https://migrationresearch.com/
[10] IMISCOE (International Migration, Integration and Social Cohesion in Europe) is Europe's largest network of scholars in the area of migration and integration. See https://www.imiscoe.org/
[11] European Commission: Current European and Cross-National Comparative Research and Research Actions on Migration, https://cordis.europa.eu/project/id/770121
[12] Eurostat: Database, https://ec.europa.eu/eurostat/data/database

Table 9.2 Characteristics of data on migration and integration trends

Data accessibility	Eurostat figures are freely accessible, and can be downloaded from the website.
	Complete datasets with individual-level data from EU-wide surveys (e.g., Eurobarometer, EU-LFS, and EU-SILC) are not publicly available but often accessible upon request.
Topics	The Eurostat database focuses on four main thematic areas related to migration: demography and migration, asylum and managed migration, migrant integration, children in migration.
Groups	The Eurostat website generally covers both foreign-born population groups and third-country nationals.
	Eurostat provides breakdowns of statistics according to various characteristics, usually age and sex.
	EU-wide surveys focus on the entire population (migrants and natives) and address a wide range of areas that are only broadly linked to migration and migrant integration.
	Key EU-wide surveys are the following: EU Labour Force Survey (EU-LFS), EU Statistics on Income and Living Conditions Survey (EU-SILC), European Social Survey (ESS), Eurobarometer, European Values Study (EVS), the EU Minorities and Discrimination Survey (EU-MIDIS).
Geographical coverage	Eurostat limits its geographical scope of analysis to European countries. Most of the time, figures cover the EU28 countries (including the UK), and EFTA countries (Iceland, Liechtenstein, Switzerland, and Norway).
	Figures are mostly available at the country level. In some cases, statistics are also available at the sub-national level, for example on migration stock (number of migrants), employment and education of migrants.
	Eurostat also provides figures based on the degree of urbanisation (e.g., on migrant population, or employment and education), distinguishing between cities, towns and suburbs, and rural areas.
	EU-wide surveys generally cover the EU28 Member States and sometimes the EFTA countries.
Temporal coverage	Eurostat provides annual statistics, as of the 1990s. However, coverage is discontinuous until 2009, both in terms of countries and years. Since 2009, statistics have generally been updated annually for nearly all the EU-28/EFTA countries.
	EU-wide surveys produce longitudinal data, as they cover several years, but not panel data, as different individuals are interviewed in each wave. Surveys started in the late 1980s (EU-LFS and EVS), the 1990s (Eurobarometer), or 2000s (EU-SILC, ESS and EU-MIDIS).

can be downloaded from the website through the data explorer (see Figure 9.11). Eurostat also provides aggregate data based on the EU-wide surveys (e.g., EU-LFS and EU-SILC). Complete datasets with individual-level data (called microdata) are not publicly available but often accessible upon request.

198   Solano

Figure 9.10 Eurostat database. Source: https://ec.europa.eu/eurostat/data/database

Most microdata from the surveys considered are accessible upon request in the GESIS repository: Eurobarometer surveys,[13] EVS,[14] and EU-MIDIS.[15] Datasets

---

[13] GESIS: Eurobarometer Data Service, https://www.gesis.org/en/eurobarometer-data-service/home
[14] COST: CA16111 - International Ethnic and Immigrant Minorities' Survey Data Network (ETH-MIGSURVEYDATA), https://www.cost.eu/actions/CA16111/
[15] GESIS: Second European Union Minorities and Discrimination Survey (EU-MIDIS II), 2016, https://dbk.gesis.org/dbksearch/sdesc2.asp?no=6703&db=e&doi=10.4232/1.13514

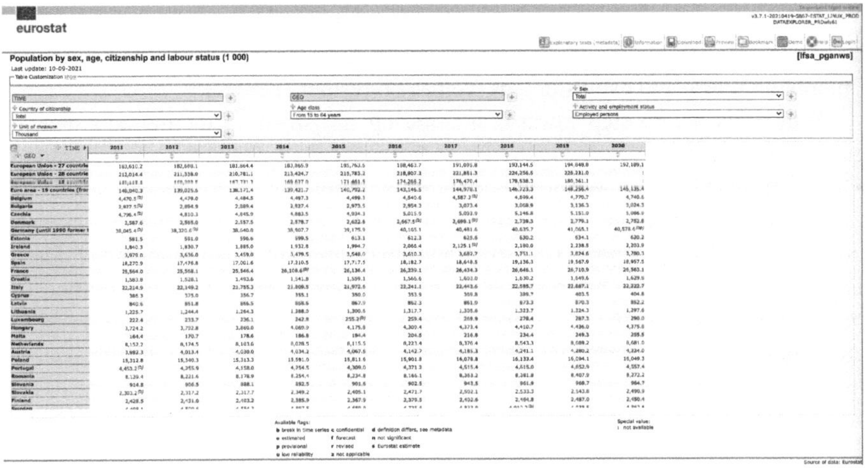

Figure 9.11 Eurostat database explorer (example). Source: https://ec.europa.eu/eurostat/data/database

from the waves of the ESS can be downloaded, after registration, directly from the ESS website.[16]

The procedure for accessing data from EU-LFS and EU-SILC is slightly more difficult, as Eurostat grants access to data for scientific purposes only. If not yet recognised as a research organisation, researchers should first apply to have their organisation recognised as a research entity. As soon as the organisation is recognised as such, the researcher can apply for access by submitting a research proposal.

Topics and groups covered

Topics

Data in the Eurostat database focus on five main thematic areas related to migration trends and integration outcomes: international migration and citizenship, asylum, managed migration, migrant integration, and children in migration.

First, Eurostat addresses 'International migration and citizenship' (available under 'Population and social conditions/Migration') by providing figures on immigration and emigration flows, as well as acquisition and loss of citizenship.

Second, the 'Asylum' section (available under 'Population and social conditions/Migration') includes statistics on asylum applicants, decisions on asylum applications, resettlement, and information related to the Dublin regulation (Regulation No. 604/2013).

---

[16] European Social Survey: Data and Documentation, https://www.europeansocialsurvey.org/data/

Third, the 'Managed migration' section (available under 'Population and social conditions/Migration') includes statistics on enforcement of immigration legislation (mainly on return and expulsion), as well as on resident permits.

Fourth, as a first step towards monitoring the situation of migrants and to enhance comparability between the EU Member States, in the Zaragoza declaration (2010)[17] Member States established a set of common indicators, the so-called EU Zaragoza integration indicators (Huddleston *et al.*, 2013). The section on migrant integration (available under 'Cross cutting topics/migrant integration and children in migration') provides information on the following areas of the integration of migrants in their country of destination: city statistics (population by citizenship and country of birth), social inclusion (poverty and living conditions), health, education (country- and regional-level series), employment (country- and regional-level series), active citizenship.

Lastly, the 'Children in migration' section (available under 'Cross cutting topics/migrant integration and children in migration') addresses migrant minors. It includes asylum statistics, residence permit statistics, and figures on the enforcement of immigrant legislation on migrant minors.

Groups

Information in the Eurostat website is generally available on both (1) people that were born in a country different from the country in which they reside (foreign-born population), and (2) people that have the citizenship of a country other than the one in which they reside (so-called third-country nationals). Furthermore, Eurostat provides breakdowns of these statistics according to various characteristics, usually age and sex. For many topics (e.g., on 'Demography and migration' and 'Migrant integration'), Eurostat also allows for comparison with non-migrants. Data on minors are also presented, especially relating to asylum and managed migration.

The key EU-wide surveys focus on the entire population (migrants and natives) and address a wide range of areas only broadly linked to migration and migrant integration:

- EU-LFS is the main data source for labour market statistics in the EU. The labour situation of migrants and their descendants has been the subject of the LFS 2008 and 2014 ad-hoc modules. The collection of data on reasons for migration allows for the distinguishing of labour migrants from refugees, family migrants, students, and others.
- EU-SILC is the main data source for comparative statistics on income and living conditions, including poverty and social exclusion. It collects data on

---

[17] European Commission: Declaration of the European Ministerial Conference on Integration (Zaragoza, 15 & 16 April 2010), https://ec.europa.eu/migrant-integration/library-document/declaration-european-ministerial-conference-integration-zaragoza-15-16-april-2010_en

income, poverty, social exclusion, housing, labour, education, and health. EU-SILC targets the whole resident population. However, migrant-related questions (information about country of birth, nationality, and year of immigration) are collected. This allows for comparison between natives and migrants.
- ESS is an individual-level, cross–national survey. The ESS measures social integration and attitudes, beliefs, and behaviours. ESS1 (2002) and ESS7 (2014) contained a set of questions exploring differing aspects of migration (e.g., attitudes on migration and perceptions of social realities, opinions on public policy, and knowledge about immigration).[18]
- Eurobarometer surveys monitor the evolution of public opinion in Europe. The Standard Eurobarometer survey consists of approximately 1000 face-to-face interviews per country. The survey is conducted twice yearly. Special Eurobarometer reports are based on in-depth thematic studies. A Special Eurobarometer report on the integration of migrants in the European Union was released in 2018. In October 2017, a survey was carried out in 28 EU Member States to measure the attitudes of Europeans towards migration and the integration of non-EU migrants.
- EVS provides insights into the ideas, beliefs, preferences, attitudes, values, and opinions of citizens all over Europe. Indicators allow the identification of first- and second-generation migrants, and comparison with natives. Data from the EVS is often employed to understand majority-group individuals' perceived level of threat from migrants. The section of EVS on politics and society contains several items referring to attitudes towards migrants.

The surveys that focus on a whole resident population allow for comparison between natives and migrants. However, as the above-mentioned surveys were designed to target the whole resident population rather than specific sub-populations, there are some limitations when considering the coverage of migrant populations. If a random probability sampling strategy is applied, a representative sub-sample of migrants should be available, but the size of this sub-sample may not allow for statistical inference, especially in countries where the number of migrants is particularly low (e.g., in Eastern European countries).

Furthermore, the adaptation of general population surveys to include migrants and non-EU nationals is not merely a matter of sampling size (or design). For example, the EU-LFS ad hoc modules deal not only with an increase in sample size, but also with the incorporation of a set of questions that facilitated identification of different types of migrants and descendants of migrants.

Other surveys provide an additional contribution by addressing (specific groups of) migrants (specific countries of origin, second generation migrants, etc.). The one considered here, EU-MIDIS, covers EU-wide information on ethnic minorities and migrants' experiences of discrimination in different areas of life (labour

---

[18] For students and other users, the ESS EduNet platform is available. It is a training resource mainly developed for use in higher education: https://essedunet.nsd.no/cms/

market, education, housing, health and other services, criminal victimisation, social inclusion, and societal participation). The population surveyed is broadly termed 'migrants' or 'descendants of migrants'. The EU-MIDIS sample is representative of the selected population groups that were surveyed in each country.

Geographical and temporal coverage

Eurostat limits its geographical scope of analysis to European countries. Most of the time, figures cover the EU28 countries (including the UK), EFTA countries (Iceland, Liechtenstein, Switzerland, and Norway), and, on integration outcomes only, Montenegro, North Macedonia, Turkey, and Serbia. There are sometimes gaps due to a lack of data from a country's statistical office.

Eurostat provides data at different geographical levels (using the European Union's Nomenclature of Territorial Units for Statistics, NUTS):

- country level;
- NUTS-1, which refers to the macro-regional level;
- NUTS-2, which refers to the macro-regional, regional/sub-regional (provinces) level (depending on the country);
- NUTS-3, which refers to the sub-regional level (provinces or metropolitan areas, depending on the country).

Figures are mostly available at the country level. This allows for comparative analysis of trends in different European countries. In some cases, statistics are also available at NUTS-1 and NUTS-2 levels, for example on migration stock (number of migrants), and employment and education of migrants. On migration stock, statistics on cities and greater cities (lower than NUTS-3) are also available. Eurostat also provides figures based on the degree of urbanisation (e.g., on migrant population, and employment and education), distinguishing between cities, towns and suburbs, and rural areas. This is particularly useful for understanding intra-country differences on migration trends and integration outcomes.

Concerning temporal coverage, available statistics have a longitudinal nature, as they cover the same countries over a given period of years. Eurostat provides annual statistics, as of the 1990s. However, coverage is discontinuous until 2009, both in terms of countries and years. Since 2009, statistics have generally been updated every year and for nearly all the EU-28/EFTA countries. This allows analysis of trends and changes over time.

Overall, EU-wide surveys produce longitudinal data, as they cover several years, but not panel data as different individuals are interviewed in each wave. An exception is EU-SILC, which also produces data on individual-level changes over time, observed over a four-year period. Surveys generally cover the EU28 Member States and sometimes the EFTA countries:

- EU-LFS has been conducted since 1983 in the 28 Member States of the European Union, two candidate countries, and three EFTA countries.

- EU-SILC has been conducted since 2004 in all EU28 countries, Iceland, Norway, and Switzerland.
- ESS consists of six waves (2002–2018, every two years). The number of countries varies from wave to wave. In the most recent edition, the survey covered 31 European countries.
- Standard Eurobarometer has been conducted in the EU28, candidate countries, and occasionally EFTA countries since 1995. The Special Eurobarometer on the integration of migrants was carried out in the 28 EU Member States.
- EVS covers a period spanning from 1981 to 2017–2020 (every nine years). Not all European countries have been represented from the beginning, but the fifth wave of EVS (2017) included 35 European countries.
- EU-MIDIS consists of two waves (2008 and 2016). It covers the EU28 countries.

Many EU-wide surveys produce data at the national level, or do not allow for statistical inference at the sub-national level, due to the sampling strategy at a national level. However, there are some promising factors and exceptions. EU-LFS microdata including the NUTS-2 level codes are provided by all participating countries with a good degree of geographical comparability. Activity, employment, and unemployment rates are now available to be disaggregated by country of birth and country of citizenship at regional level (NUTS-2), and by degree of urbanisation. In the ESS, almost every country addressed provides the possibility of analysing data at NUTS-2 level (at least). In almost two-thirds of the countries the data allow for statistical inference. Similarly, the EVS allows for sub-national analysis, such as the analysis of the perceived threat of immigration at the national, regional, and local levels. Unfortunately, migrant sample sizes do not allow for sub-national analysis.

Data quality, gaps, and limitations

The previous sections illustrated the multiple and growing sources of data on both migration policy and migration trends and integration outcomes in the EU. Despite this increase, some gaps and limitations persist in the available data on both migration policy and migration trends and integration outcomes (see Table 9.3).

In the field of migration policy, at least four main gaps should be the subject of future development. First, some migration policy areas are underrepresented (e.g., emigration, governance, and return/expulsion), while there is strong overlap and redundancy of information on some topics (e.g., admission and citizenship). This means that we are less able to draw conclusions on trends and changes in some areas of migration policy-making. Second, a large majority of existing indices focus on EU15 and Western countries, while other European countries have been less frequently analysed. Other countries should be studied to also address migration trends outside the EU15. Third, the field also lacks a gender perspective. While indicators account for different types of migrants by status or skills, e.g.,

Table 9.3 Gaps in data

	Integration policy (outputs)	**Migration and integration trends (outcomes)**
Data accessibility	Data on many indices are not publicly accessible.	—
Topics	Some migration policy areas are understudied (e.g., emigration, governance, and return and expulsion).	EU-wide surveys do not produce a statistically representative sample of migrants for each country.
		Missing key migrant-related questions and information, because EU-wide surveys address the general population.
Groups	A focus on gender-related aspects is missing.	—
Geographical coverage	Non-EU15/non-Western countries have been less frequently analysed.	Many EU-wide surveys produce data that do not allow for statistical inference at the sub-national level, due to country-level sampling strategies.
Temporal coverage	Lack of up-to-date data (especially after 2015).	—

distinguishing between labour migrants and refugees or between high-skilled and low-skilled migrants, a gender perspective has rarely been introduced. Fourth, most data from the produced indices are not accessible. To enhance cooperation with other researchers and to sustain indices over time, researchers should publish their index data with open access. Lastly, while there is redundancy of information for the period 2000–2010, there is also a lack of more up-to-date data. Existing indices should be updated, accounting for changes in policies over the last 10 years (especially after 2015).

There is a wealth of data at both the aggregate and the individual level on migration trends and integration outcomes. Datasets are often published with open access, allowing researchers to analyse the data produced. However, due to sampling strategies and focus on the entire population, some issues arise when it comes to attempting a migrants-only focus and a sub-national focus (Wolffhardt et al., 2019b). First, EU-wide surveys are representative of the entire population and a representative sub-sample of migrants is often not available, especially in countries where the number of migrants is particularly low. Second, given that most EU-wide surveys address the general population, they miss a certain number of key migrant-related questions and information. The adaptation of general-population surveys to include migrants is indeed not merely a matter of sampling size (or design). For example, the EU-LFS ad hoc modules entailed not only an increase in sample size, but also the incorporation of a set of questions that facilitated the identification of different types of migrants and descendants of migrants. Third, many EU-wide surveys produce data that do not allow for statistical inference at the sub-national level, due to country-level sampling strategies. There appears to be a lack of infrastructure for monitoring integration processes at the local level in a reliable and consistent way.

Beside these gaps, there is also the issue of data quality. Data on migration and migrant integration policies are often collected by means of national experts (e.g., in the case of MIPEX or IMPIC) who fill in a standardised questionnaire. Experts translate qualitative information (from laws and policy documents) into something quantitative. Therefore, there is a certain degree of subjectivity in the interpretation of the laws and policy documents. However, data producers normally conduct a set of checks to ensure consistency and accuracy of analysis, as well as comparability of results. For example, the research coordinators of MIPEX first check all the experts' responses to guarantee that they properly understood the questions and answered them in a manner consistent with other countries. They also double-check questions based on publicly available data and legal texts (e.g., GLOBALCIT, the European Equality Law Network, the European Migration Network). In addition, the research team conducts a final question-by-question consistency check to ensure that similar situations receive the same score across all countries (Solano and Huddleston, 2020). Therefore, despite the challenges posed by the comparative analysis of countries with different legislative frameworks and specific situations, data have proved to be, by and large, rather accurate and reliable (Helbling, 2013; Koopmans et al., 2012; Koopmans, 2013; Scipioni and Urso, 2018).

Concerning data on migration and integration trends (outcomes), Eurostat always conducts reliability and other data quality checks on the collected data, in close connection with the national statistical authorities. Quality assurance work is carried out centrally by Eurostat through regular quality reviews of the statistical production processes. In addition, the statisticians have integrated various quality assurance measures into their day-to-day business. This can take the form of guidelines, production and data validation procedures, and standards, amongst others (European Commission, 2020). Eurostat data are the most reliable comparative data that are available on migration and migrant integration trends in Europe.

The link between policies and migration trends and integration outcomes

The use of quantitative data is particularly effective when it comes to understating the effect that these policies have (Czaika and De Haas, 2013; Helbling et al., 2020; Solano and Huddleston, 2020). To understand the effect of migration policy on migration dynamics, integration outcomes and, more generally, on society as a whole, researchers should link indicators on migration policy with existing datasets on migration/integration.

The increased availability of data on migration in Europe has led to new opportunities for research. Researchers have analysed the link between policies and migration trends and integration outcomes by means of multivariate analysis techniques (e.g., regression models). However, the full potential of the available data is still to be exhausted. Although an increasing number of papers have analysed this link, a consensus about the influence of migration polices is far from being reached (Czaika and De Haas, 2013). On the one hand, many scholars have argued that efforts by states to regulate and restrict immigration often fail (e.g., Bhagwati, 2003; Cornelius et al., 2004; Düvell, 2006). The argument is that international migration is mainly driven by structural factors such as labour market imbalances, inequalities in wealth, and political conflicts in origin countries, factors on which migration policies have little or no influence. On the other hand, others disagree with this sceptical view, and have demonstrated that migration policies have been increasingly effective in influencing the magnitude and composition of migration flows (Beverelli, 2021; Hatton, 2005; Helbling et al., 2020; Mayda, 2010; Ortega and Peri, 2013).

Several articles have analysed the effect of integration policies (Solano and Huddleston, 2020). These studies show that major differences in integration outcomes and attitudes around the world reflect the major disparities in integration policies around the world. Integration policies also shape how immigrants and the public respond to these inequalities. Inclusive policies contribute to closing gaps in key integration outcomes. They also create a 'virtuous circle' of integration that promotes openness and interaction.

Conclusions

This chapter has presented the main sources of quantitative data on both migration policy and migration trends and integration outcomes in the EU. Since the early 2000s, an increasing number of data sources has emerged in Europe and at the international level (Kraler and Reichel, 2022).

Indicators and indices have been used over recent decades to measure the nature of migration policy frameworks and to compare them across different countries and periods of time. Many indices have been produced on different aspects of migration policy (e.g., admission and citizenship policies). These indices cover many years; mainly the period 2000–2010, but also before and after. Data on migration trends and integration outcomes are available at both aggregate and individual levels on a wide range of topics, such as migration and asylum trends, and migrant integration. New venues for the use of these datasets are emerging, thanks to the new opportunities created by new data science techniques. Machine learning approaches are particularly beneficial due to their predictive capacity. If models are provided with quality data, they can make estimates with a high level of precision and reliability. For example, Arcila-Calderón *et al.* (2022) estimated the level of support for refugees based on sociodemographic data and data from European surveys. To assess the reliability of the estimate, they compared their results with the Eurobarometer survey, and the results corresponded.

New opportunities also arise through the availability of big data (e.g., social media or mobile phone data; see Luca *et al.*, 2022; Kim *et al.*, 2022). These new data sources can be combined with traditional data sources (Eurostat) and data on policies to produce meaningful analysis of the new trends. For example, satellite and social media data can be used to complement and back up official statistics, which are often released with some delay (e.g., approximately one year in the case of Eurostat).

In conclusion, although data gaps persist, the available data allow researchers and policy-makers to understand migration policies and their effects.

Recommended reading

There are several key references when it comes to indicators and survey data to understand migration and integration policy frameworks and trends in the EU. The chapter from Kraler and Reichel (2022) and the DG Home[19] publication (Huddleston *et al.*, 2013) represent two excellent introductions to EU statistics on migration and migrant integration. There are also several articles that provide overviews of the existing literature on indices on migration and migrant integration policies, such as Bjerre *et al.* (2015) and Scipioni and Urso (2018). The most recent and comprehensive review is currently the one from Solano and Huddleston (2021). Finally, to know more about the link between migration and migrant integration policies and trends/outcomes, the publications from Czaika and De Haas (2013), Helbling *et al.* (2020), and Solano and Huddleston (2020) represent three relevant references.

References

Arcila-Calderón, C., Jiménez Amores, J., and Stanek, M. (2022), 'Using machine learning and synthetic populations to predict support for refugees and asylum seekers in European regions', *in* A. A. Salah, E. E. Korkmaz, and T. Bircan, eds, *Data Science for Migration and Mobility*, Proceedings of the British Academy, British Academy/Oxford University Press, London.

Banting, K. and Kymlicka, W. (2013), 'Is there really a retreat from multiculturalism policies? New evidence from the multiculturalism policy index', *Comparative European Politics* 11(5), 577–98.

Beine, M., Boucher, A., Burgoon, B., Crock, M., Gest, J., Hiscox, M., McGovern, P., Rapoport, H., Schaper, J., and Thielemann, E. (2016), 'Comparing immigration policies: An overview from the IMPALA database', *International Migration Review* 50(4), 827–63.

---

[19] DG Home stands for Directorate-General for Home Affairs.

Beverelli, C. (2021), 'Pull factors for migration: The impact of migrant integration policies', *Economics & Politics* 34(1), 171–91.
Bhagwati, J. (2003), 'Borders beyond control', *Foreign Affairs* 82, 98.
Bjerre, L., Helbling, M., Römer, F., and Zobel, M. (2015), 'Conceptualizing and measuring immigration policies: A comparative perspective', *International Migration Review* 49(3), 555–600.
Bjerre, L., Helbling, M., Römer, F., and Zobel, M. (2016), 'The Immigration Policies In Comparison (IMPIC) dataset', WZB Berlin Social Science Center Discussion Paper, 2016–201.
Cerna, L. (2014), 'Attracting high-skilled immigrants: Policies in comparative perspective', *International Migration* 52(3), 69–84.
Cornelius, W. A., Martin, P. L., and Hollifield, J. F. (2004), *Controlling Immigration: A Global Perspective*, Stanford University Press, Stanford, CA.
Czaika, M. and De Haas, H. (2013), 'The effectiveness of immigration policies', *Population and Development Review* 39(3), 487–508.
Czaika, M. and Parsons, C. R. (2017), 'The gravity of high-skilled migration policies', *Demography* 54(2), 603–30.
De Haas, H., Natter, K., and Vezzoli, S. (2015), 'Conceptualizing and measuring migration policy change', *Comparative Migration Studies* 3(1), 1–21.
Düvell, F. (2006), 'The irregular migration dilemma: Keeping control, out of control or regaining control?', in F. Düvell, ed, *Illegal Immigration in Europe*, Palgrave Macmillan, London, 3–13.
European Commission (2020), 'European statistical system handbook for quality and metadata reports', Technical report, Publications Office of the European Union, Luxembourg.
EWSI (2018), 'Integration of migrant women: A key challenge with limited policy resources', available at https://ec.europa.eu/migrant-integration/special-feature/integration-migrant-women_en
Gest, J., Boucher, A., Challen, S., Burgoon, B., Thielemann, E., Beine, M., McGovern, P., Crock, M., Rapoport, H., and Hiscox, M. (2014), 'Measuring and comparing immigration, asylum and naturalization policies across countries: Challenges and solutions', *Global Policy* 5(3), 261–74.
Hatton, T. J. (2005), 'Explaining trends in UK immigration', *Journal of Population Economics* 18(4), 719–40.
Hatton, T. J. (2009), 'The rise and fall of asylum: What happened and why?', *The Economic Journal* 119(535), F183–F213.
Helbling, M. (2013), 'Validating integration and citizenship policy indices', *Comparative European Politics* 11(5), 555–76.
Helbling, M., Bjerre, L., Römer, F., and Zobel, M. (2017), 'Measuring immigration policies: The IMPIC database', *European Political Science* 16, 79–98.
Helbling, M. and Leblang, D. (2019), 'Controlling immigration? How regulations affect migration flows', *European Journal of Political Research* 58(1), 248–69.
Helbling, M., Simon, S., and Schmid, S. D. (2020), 'Restricting immigration to foster migrant integration? A comparative study across 22 European countries', *Journal of Ethnic and Migration Studies* 46(13), 2603–24.
Huddleston, T., Bilgili, Ö., Joki, A.-L., and Vankova, Z. (2015), *Migrant Integration Policy Index 2015*, CIDOB and MPG, Barcelona/Brussels.
Huddleston, T., Niessen, J., and Tjaden, J. D. (2013), *Using EU Indicators of Immigrant Integration*, Final Report for Directorate-General for Home Affairs, EUR-OP, Brussels.

Kim, J., Pollacci, L., Rossetti, G., Sîrbu, A., Giannotti, F., and Pedreschi, D. (2022), 'Twitter data for migration studies', *in* A. A. Salah, E. E. Korkmaz, and T. Bircan, eds, *Data Science for Migration and Mobility*, Proceedings of the British Academy, British Academy/Oxford University Press, London.

Koopmans, R. (2013), 'Indices of immigrant rights: What have we learned, where should we go?', *Comparative European Politics* 11(5), 696–703.

Koopmans, R., Michalowski, I., and Waibel, S. (2012), 'Citizenship rights for immigrants: National political processes and cross-national convergence in Western Europe, 1980–2008', *American Journal of Sociology* 117(4), 1202–45.

Kraler, A. and Reichel, D. (2022), 'Migration statistics', *in* P. Scholten, ed, *Migration Studies*, Springer, Cham, pp 439–62.

Lowell, B. L. (2005), 'Policies and regulations for managing skilled international migration for work', United Nations, Mortality and Migration Section of the Population Division/DESA.

Luca, M., Barlacchi, G., Oliver, N., and Lepri, B. (2022), 'Leveraging mobile phone data for migration flows', *in* A. A. Salah, E. E. Korkmaz, and T. Bircan, eds, *Data Science for Migration and Mobility*, Proceedings of the British Academy, British Academy/Oxford University Press, London.

Manatschal, A. (2011), 'Taking cantonal variations of integration policy seriously — or how to validate international concepts at the subnational comparative level', *Swiss Political Science Review* 17(3), 336–57.

Mayda, A. M. (2010), 'International migration: A panel data analysis of the determinants of bilateral flows', *Journal of Population Economics* 23(4), 1249–74.

Migration Policy Group (2012), 'IMMEX: Immigration for Employment Index: A research project on European immigration policies', Technical report, MPG, Brussels.

Ortega, F. and Peri, G. (2013), 'The effect of income and immigration policies on international migration', *Migration Studies* 1(1), 47–74.

Peters, M. E. (2015), 'Open trade, closed borders: Immigration in the era of globalization', *World Politics* 67(1), 114–54.

Pisarevskaya, A., Levy, N., Scholten, P., and Jansen, J. (2020), 'Mapping migration studies: An empirical analysis of the coming of age of a research field', *Migration Studies* 8(3), 455–81.

Schmid, S. D. (2021), 'Stagnated liberalization, long-term convergence, and index methodology: Three lessons from the CITRIX citizenship policy dataset', *Global Policy* 12(3), 338–49.

Scipioni, M. and Urso, G. (2018), *Migration Policy Indexes*, no. JRC109400, ISPRA: Joint Research Centre (European Commission).

Solano, G. and Huddleston, T. (2020), *Migrant Integration Policy Index 2020*, CIDOB and MPG, Barcelona/Brussels.

Solano, G. and Huddleston, T. (2021), 'Beyond immigration: Moving from Western to global indexes of migration policy', *Global Policy* 12(3), 327–37.

Solano, G. and Huddleston, T. (2022), 'Migration policy indicators', *in* P. Scholten, ed, *Migration Studies*, Springer, Cham, pp 439–62.

Timmer, A. S. and Williams, J. G. (1998), 'Immigration policy prior to the 1930s: Labor markets, policy interactions, and globalization backlash', *Population and Development Review* 24(4), 739–71.

Vink, M. P., De Groot, G.-R., and Luk, N. C. (2015), 'MACIMIDE global expatriate dual citizenship dataset', *Harvard Dataverse* 5.

Wolffhardt, A., Conte, C., and Huddleston, T. (2019a), 'The European benchmark for refugee integration: A comparative analysis of the national integration evaluation mechanism in 14 EU countries', Fundacja Instytut Spraw Publicznych, Warsaw.

Wolffhardt, A., Joki, A.-L., and Solano, G. (2019b), 'Facilitating evidence-based integration policies in cities', Options report of the Stakeholder Working Group.

10

Financial Datasets: Leveraging Transactional Big Data in Mobility and Migration Studies

MERT GÜRKAN, BURÇIN BOZKAYA, AND SELIM BALCISOY

Introduction

IN THE GLOBALISED world of the 21st century, all types of human migration are widely encountered phenomena. Unfortunately, the most recent decade has witnessed many tragic cases of human migration, such as the Syrian refugees fleeing from the civil war in Syria to neighbouring countries including Turkey, Lebanon, and Jordan, and Venezuelan citizens seeking refuge in Colombia and other countries. However, not all cases of migration necessarily carry a negative sentiment. Choice of migration for better work opportunities (e.g., the case of Turkish migrants to Germany in the post World War II era) or educational opportunities (e.g., many international students migrating to and staying in the USA) can lead to happiness and positive impacts on the lives of individuals. As these examples may hint, migration has many effects on individuals, as well as societies, in areas such as education, healthcare, employment and income, and economic and social integration with the receiving country or society. Hence, policy-makers are charged with a great responsibility to facilitate the socioeconomic well-being of both migrant and migrant-receiving communities.

The United Nations Migration Agency defines a migrant as

> any person who is moving or has moved across an international border or within a State away from his/her habitual place of residence, regardless of (1) the person's legal status; (2) whether the movement is voluntary or involuntary; (3) what the causes for the movement are; or (4) what the length of the stay is.[1]

---

[1] Migration of United Nations (2020), https://www.un.org/en/sections/issues-depth/migration/index.html

To effectively manage massive relocations of families and individuals, it is critical to understand and account for all of the dimensions included in this definition as well as others, which, thankfully, can be mostly identified and/or measured in this era of big data availability. Many studies, such as Palotti *et al*. (2020) and Blumenstock *et al*. (2019), have aimed to provide a better understanding of international migration patterns by analysing the data collected from various sources. Salah *et al*. (2019) provides extensive coverage of how mobile call detail record (CDR) data can be used in many diverse ways to understand major difficulties and problems faced by Syrian refugees in Turkey and to make recommendations to alleviate these problems. Similar methods are also employed in studies for internal migration patterns. Fudolig *et al*. (2021) utilised CDR data to explain the mobile communication behaviours of internal migrants. Miranda-González *et al*. (2020) made use of bibliometric network data of academicians to infer the internal migration of scholars within Mexico. In addition to these, a variety of other datasets and data sources can be used for a better understanding of both internal and international migration movements.

The goal of this chapter is to shed light on how transactional datasets from the finance industry, a rather less known and scarcely used source of data to describe migration, can be used in identifying and understanding the internal migration patterns of a country. These datasets, widely used in mobility analysis by Singh *et al*. (2015), Li *et al*. (2018), and Bounie *et al*. (2020) in various other contexts, can include signs of when and where individuals move and change their places of residence or work, through credit card purchases, ATM withdrawals, and money transfers. In our work, we first describe the attributes of the dataset we work with, then we present a case study where such transactional records can be used to identify the movement of individuals from their former places of residence/work to new places. In many cases, individuals may not officially declare such moves, nor will they update their records promptly with the financial institution or other government offices. Yet, as suggested by El Mahrsi *et al*. (2017) and more studies in the literature that analyse spatiotemporal characteristics of big data to determine homes or workplaces of individuals, it is possible to detect new after-migration residence locations by analysing certain categories of transactions such as supermarket and gasoline purchases. We utilise such approaches to detect migration between cities and provinces within a country.

While financial datasets may be used for the purposes described above, there are also limitations involved with this approach. It is clear that the entire population of individuals who are of interest for migration purposes will not all have accounts with financial institutions. This 'unbanked population' will not be represented in financial datasets and hence it would not be possible to consider them in migration analysis. Even for the population represented in these datasets, there will be bias towards individuals, such as working professionals (as opposed to unemployed population or youth of school age), who are more likely to be affiliated with financial institutions by having accounts with them.

An additional selection bias can also be present, as the case study depicted in this chapter is structured on a sample transactional dataset of a commercial and private bank. Due to possible differences in the demographic and socioeconomic profiles of the customers, the results discussed here may not be applicable for a dataset from a different financial organisation. Hence, this may limit the reproducibility of the results of this study with customer bases from organisations with a different specific focus. Nevertheless, we show that even with the available limited data, it is possible to carry out analysis to detect migration. Furthermore, as we demonstrate in our work, analysis of the demography of which individuals are moving between which locations may provide clues on the possible causes or reasons for migration.

The chapter is organised as follows. In the 'Literature review' section we provide a literature review on the use of financial and other datasets in human mobility studies, and we point out the gap in the literature regarding migration analysis. In 'Datasets' we describe a transactional dataset that we have been using in many mobility studies, which is donated to us by a major bank in Turkey. In 'Case study' we present a case study where we propose a methodology to analyse our financial dataset for detecting traces of human migration within the country boundaries. Finally, in 'Discussion and conclusion' we present our concluding remarks, including the limitations of our research and possibilities for future work.

Literature review

As the world experienced a pandemic, research groups from a variety of backgrounds had the chance to perceive the importance of human mobility. Studies on human mobility datasets publicly shared by companies like Apple[2] and Google[3] made it possible to associate the course of the epidemic with the aggregated mobility of individuals. Although it brings the pandemic to our minds when it is mentioned now, mobility studies are integral parts of understanding social phenomena that involve human behaviours and actions. Among these social phenomena, migration necessitates the adaptation of the mobility study approach as it implies a displacement. As the estimated number of migrants corresponds to 3.5% of the total population of the world, social realities such as integration, inequality, and policies that emerge from this human movement should be recognised.[4] Since human migration and human mobility are concepts deeply linked together, studies that aim to uncover migration patterns with a data-driven approach can also reveal valuable insights about these social realities.

Inequalities in the social, economic, and demographic sense, the lack of education and employment opportunities, violation of human rights, and scarcity of

---

[2] Mobility Trend Reports of Apple (2020), https://covid19.apple.com/mobility
[3] Google Community Mobility Report of Google (2020), https://www.google.com/covid19/mobility
[4] International Migrant Stock 2019 of United Nations (2019), https://www.un.org/en/development/desa/population/migration/data/estimates2/estimates19.asp

resources to live can create the roots of migration mobility patterns.[5] Globalisation and the ease of international transportation are some of the factors that contribute to this increase in mobility and displacement. As argued by Batsaikhan *et al.* (2018), the underlying reasons and their results reflecting on the mobility along with the policy implications of these patterns are topics which are frequently investigated with data-driven studies. It is stated that it is crucial to understand migration mobility patterns for countries and organisations to be able to create efficient migration policies.[6] Additionally, grasping these patterns could allow countries and policy-makers to foresee the necessary policy adaptations to achieve more inclusive social, economic, and political policies. With this set of objectives, insights from data-driven migration mobility studies can be essential for uncovering migration patterns.

To facilitate data-driven studies on human migration and the mobility that emerges with it, the available datasets are often divided into three categories. The first category are statistical data sources consisting of population demographics, and household surveys are the primary sources to consider. These datasets provide worldwide migrant stock information. In addition to statistical sources, administrative sources are also frequently utilised. As these types of data sources are produced with various countries' data collection mechanisms, they are taken into account to help convey migrant stock and migrant flow. The rapid development of technology also allows private organisations to produce human migration or human mobility related to datasets. These datasets generated by people's digital footprints, such as data from a mobile phone, social media, credit cards, payments, GPS, etc., are considered innovative data sources.[7]

Although statistical and administrative data sources provide reliable migration data, the first form of shortcomings of these data sources comes with the coverage and the timeliness of the data. As such datasets are usually published annually after complex data collection processes, they do not help address current flows and trends. In addition to this, Spyratos *et al.* (2019) pointed out that these datasets also lack detail about migrant populations apart from the demographic insights. The inadequacy of statistical and administrative data sources on complex migration topics such as migrant integration, irregular migration, and impact of migration policies have been stated.[8] Integration of innovative data sources can be beneficial for resolving these shortcomings. Unstructured big data, usually gathered from various social media sources, that reflect the digital footprints of individuals can support statistical and administrative datasets published by international organisations such as the UN and OECD.

---

[5] Migration and Human Mobility of International Organization for Migration (2012), https://www.un.org/millenniumgoals/pdf/Think%20Pieces/13_migration.pdf
[6] Migration and Mobility of Eurofound (2020), https://www.eurofound.europa.eu/topic/migration-and-mobility
[7] Migration Data Portal of International Organisation for Migration (2017), https://migrationdataportal.org
[8] Migration Data Sources of International Organization for Migration (2017), https://migrationdataportal.org/themes/migration-data-sources

How big data can help to understand the phenomenon of migration is a question asked by many researchers. One of the common approaches is the usage of traditional data sources like census and surveys with alternative data sources like retail data and geolocated Twitter data to find migration flows and stocks. Sîrbu *et al.* (2021), which focused on migration and distinguished the three stages thereof as the journey, stay, and return, claimed that big data have a positive impact on studying the journey, and various datasets including Twitter and retail help to reveal the integration of migrants in society. A combination of statistical and administrative data with big data sources can also contribute to the validation of these innovative sources. Likewise, big data sources can close the data gaps of traditional sources thanks to their continuous availability. Box 10.1 describes approaches to inference from quantitative data sources.

In addition to the shortcomings of traditional datasets described above, Fatehkia *et al.* (2020a) stated that these datasets can be hard to collect for some countries or for different time intervals. In such cases, as demonstrated in Spyratos *et al.* (2018) and Gendronneau *et al.* (2019), the usage of non-traditional big data sources such as Facebook and Twitter may allow studies to proceed. In addition to these, Giannotti *et al.* (2011), Gonzalez *et al.* (2008), Lulli *et al.* (2017), and Pappalardo *et al.* (2015) provide significant examples of studies that have also been done by taking advantage of mobile CDRs. While Fatehkia *et al.* (2020b) stated that the data obtained from Facebook can provide more detailed insights about the demographic and socioeconomic structures of migrants, Blumenstock *et al.*, 2019 stated that Twitter and CDR datasets can be used for creating social networks from communication patterns of migrant communities. Kikas *et al.* (2015) made use of online communication services like Skype for similar migrant network analysis.

The main advantage of using financial data in migration studies compared to other forms of big data is the introduction of economic indicators. With these data, in addition to insights on demographic and socioeconomic structures, economic and financial behaviour patterns of migrant communities can be analysed as well. Massey (1989) described the significance of economic and financial indicators for studies aiming to uncover the driving factors of migration patterns. Gravity models presented by Ramos and Suriñach (2016) and Karemera *et al.* (2000) can be exemplified for such studies, where migration flows are aimed to be modelled with existing demographic, socioeconomic, and also financial indicators of countries. The gravity model presented in the International Migration Drivers study (Migali *et al.*, 2018) put forward the GDP per capita as one of the most significant factors for emigration movements from countries.

The utilisation of financial data for migration studies is not limited to aggregated indicators such as GDP or GDP per capita. Some studies use more direct financial behaviour of migrant communities. Studies that use remittance data of migrant communities can analyse their financial transfers in destination regions. Although remittances are usually conceptualised as monetary transfers made by migrants from destination regions to origin regions, income earned by temporary migrant workers

Box 10.1 Approaches to inference

Inference about a phenomenon that cannot be observed directly or fully can be tricky. Often, the researcher needs to rely on other, (more) observable, variables that are known to correlate with the phenomenon of interest. These observable variables act as *proxy indicators*, and the target variable is inferred by a combination of such variables. The more diverse the proxies, the more complementary they will be in telling the researcher about the target variable. Variables which are included in the analysis but do not contain relevant information can act as *confounding variables*, and their random variations can be picked up as spurious patterns if powerful analysis methods are used.

One way of integrating proxy indicators is by *Bayesian inference*, which is a method of statistical inference in which Bayes' theorem is used to update the probability for a hypothesis as more evidence or information becomes available. In this approach, the prior probability of the hypothesis is denoted with $p(H)$, and the conditional probability of the hypothesis, given evidence E, is written as

$$p(H \mid E) = \frac{p(E \mid H)p(H)}{p(E)},$$

where $p(E)$ is typically approximated by a marginalisation over all possible hypotheses, or cancelled out in comparative analysis, as it does not contain model elements and thus remains constant for all models or hypotheses.

When the data have a temporal nature, the Bayesian inference can be extended with variables that are indexed with a time indicator, such as E_t, denoting evidence at time t. There are models, such as the *Kalman filter*, which permit modelling temporal dependencies, and thereby enable *trend analysis* and *seasonality*.

Most approaches in the literature rely on the analysis of correlations, and tell us little about *causality*, which is itself a fickle notion. Halpern (2015) used a definition of actual causality where 'A is a cause of B if, had A not happened, B would not have happened'. We can think of examples like a civil war causing forced migration. However, each of these events can involve many factors themselves. In recent years, *Granger causality* has also been used as a statistical hypothesis test for determining whether one time series is useful in forecasting another (Granger, 1969). While this is not strictly a measure of causality, the idea is that if A 'Granger-causes' B, the predictions of the value of B based on its own past values and on the past values of A are better than predictions of B based only on B's own past values. These formulations also allow modern prediction approaches, such as machine learning models, to be used in inferences.

Halpern and Pearl (2005) proposed using *structural equations*, where variables are split into two groups: 'the *exogenous variables*, whose values are determined by factors outside the model, and the *endogenous variables*, whose values are ultimately determined by the exogenous variables' (Halpern, 2015). A causal model simply describes the relationship between these variables mathematically (and probabilistically). Pearl (2009) is an excellent text that discusses causality and its mathematical modelling, and argues that the grammar of probability calculus alone is insufficient to model causal knowledge.

in the hosting regions also falls under the definition of remittances.[9] Hence, studies with remittance data can also produce valuable insight into the economic relations of different regions or countries.

Levitt (1998) pointed out the potential social value of studies with remittance data, as these datasets can reveal clues about behaviours and identities towards the origin country of migrants in the destination country. Although studies with these data do not reveal the mobility patterns of migrants, they indicate how they communicate with their country of origin. However, studies with available remittance data are criticised by Alvarez *et al.* (2015) for being misleading, as the data fail to represent accurate estimations. Brown *et al.* (2014) stated that the main source of criticism for such data stems from the sensitivity issues that emerge from face-to-face interviews conducted during the data collection periods.

Concerning migration studies, one can see that a major use of financial datasets has been through indicators and data obtained from official organisations. In Beaton *et al.* (2017) and Lim and Basnet (2017), remittances are considered to be money transfers from migrants to their families or relatives in the origin country. These studies often handle these monetary transfers as media for investigating the volume of present international migration and developmental differences between the origin and destination countries. Another major use of financial data is in the form of economic indicators in gravity or similar predictive models. In addition to these, financial indicators can also be derived from other existing data sources. Bakker *et al.* (2019) is an example of this type of financial data utilisation where an economic integration measure is defined based on the employment activity of migrant communities.

It can be noticed that in the study of human mobility and human migration there is limited use of financial data. Many studies often refer to economic and financial indicators published by international organisations such as the World Bank and the IMF. The difficulty of obtaining data from other financial organisations is usually due to privacy regulations and sensitivity issues on sharing such data. When available, the use of financial datasets to study human mobility reveals significant insights into the relationship between human mobility and socioeconomic indicators. However, the focus seems not to be on human migration. As Sobolevsky *et al.* (2014) argued, it is rather on the operational and topological solutions for human interactions. With datasets, as described in the 'Datasets' section, which contain both mobility patterns of individuals as well as their socioeconomic indicators, migration and related phenomena can be analysed by mobility patterns with a financial data perspective. In addition to this, although there are studies that approach the internal migration patterns of Turkey with financial indicators, such as Gökhan (2008) and Gezici and Keskin (2005), these studies do not make use of big data sources. Therefore, we aim to bridge the gap by using financial datasets from one of the largest private Turkish banks to study internal human migration.

---

[9] IOM and Remittances of International Organization for Migration (2009), https://publications.iom.int/system/files/pdf/iom_and_remittances.pdf

Datasets

Being able to combine transactional and demographic data of customers enables analysis of sophisticated questions. Transactional data of customers can be employed to better understand the spending behaviours of individuals, to create a network of customers and networks, or to uncover economic and well-being indicators of a region or the country. If the data at hand also have coordinates available for transactions, these datasets can also be utilised for mobility studies. In this way, the spending behaviours of individuals during and after their movements can be investigated. Additionally, combining customer spending with demographic data can allow the study of the similarities and differences of the spending behaviour of the various demographic and socioeconomic groups in the data. Our study utilises a combination of transactional and demographic data to analyse internal migration patterns of Turkey. In this section, the datasets are covered in more detail.

Our research work relies on a comprehensive set of credit card transactions recorded and shared by a private bank in Turkey between July 2014 and June 2015. Transactions in the dataset are derived from a larger sample that was collected from all provinces of Turkey from Turkish residents who hold a credit or debit card issued by the bank. As also reported in Table 10.1, the sample transaction dataset utilised in this study contains more than nine million transactions. Among these available transactions, almost 40%, more than 3.7 million transactions, have their location information available as latitude and longitude coordinates. While the dataset contains the transactions of 102,893 unique customers, there are only 98,834 customers whose transaction coordinates are available. As the dataset also contains information on points of interest (POIs) with masked identifiers for each transaction, unique POI locations can also be traced with the dataset. As such, the dataset contains location information from 94,803 unique POIs with latitude and longitude pairs. In addition to the transactions dataset, the study described here also utilises an additional dataset consisting of demographic information about customers included in the sample dataset.

Table 10.1 Statistical properties of the transactions dataset

Statistical Property	Numerical Value
Number of transactions	9,334,625
Number of transactions with coordinates available	3,729,193
Number of unique customers	102,893
Number of unique customers with transaction coordinates available	98,834
Number of unique POI locations	94,811
Number of unique POI locations with transaction coordinates available	94,803

FINANCIAL DATASETS 219

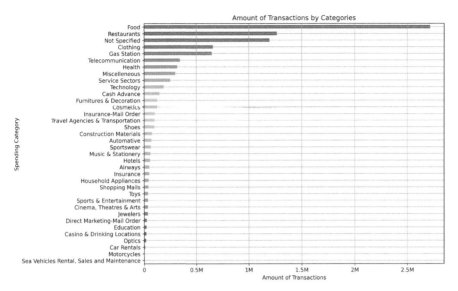

Figure 10.1 The numbers of transactions per spending category in the transactions dataset. The majority of the transactions are in the 'Food' and 'Restaurants' categories, followed by a large number of transactions without categories. 'Clothing' and 'Gas Station' are also categories with large numbers of transactions.

The numbers of transactions per spending category in the transactions dataset can be observed from Figure 10.1. As can be seen, the majority of the transactions are spent in the 'Food', 'Restaurants', 'Clothing', and 'Gas Station' categories. The third-largest group of transaction are transactions with missing category values, marked as 'Not Specified'.

Location frequencies for transactions can be observed in Figure 10.2. One can see that the majority of the transactions originated in Istanbul. It should also be noted that the values denoting the number of transactions in Figure 10.2 are log-transformed, showing that the exact number of transactions originating in Istanbul is larger than the bar chart displays. To convey the exact statistics, while there are more than 3.4 million transactions originating from Istanbul, there are only 40,478 transaction instances available for Kocaeli, although it has the second-highest number of transactions. This suggests that for possible case study practices, Istanbul will be a key location for studying migration patterns, as the data are more reliable for the city because of the available volume.

Similar to the distribution of transactions in the dataset, the distribution of the number of unique customers also favours studies for Istanbul. Among the 102,893 unique customers available in the dataset, 95,910 of them have their bank branch recorded to be in Istanbul. Again, Kocaeli follows Istanbul in our sample, with only 1,402 unique customers. These statistics are shared in Figure 10.3.

To analyse the distribution of transactions and customers within Turkey, Figure 10.4 displays a heatmap of a sample of the transactions in the dataset. The

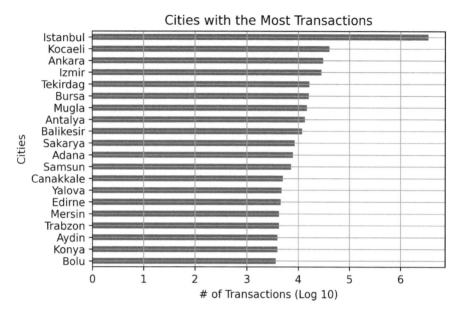

Figure 10.2 The top 20 cities in terms of the number of transactions in the dataset. To be able to fit the chart, a base-10 log transform of the number of transactions was taken.

heatmap also suggests that the majority of transactions, and the transactions with the highest amounts, originate in the area around Istanbul. Ankara, Kocaeli, Izmir, and Bursa are the other cities with a high density of transactions.

Demographic information about the customers can be seen from Figures 10.5 and 10.6. Figure 10.5 suggests that the majority of the dataset consists of male customers. Additionally, more than half of the customers in the selected sample are married individuals. When Figure 10.6 is analysed, it can be seen that the majority of customers are high school graduates. This group is followed by university graduates. The mean income levels of individuals in the dataset with respect to their education status can also be observed from the figure.

Case study

'Human migration' is defined as the movement of people from one place to another with the intention of settling, permanently or temporarily, at the new geographic location. As one of the forms of the broader migration phenomena, internal migration (or domestic migration) is defined as human migration within one geopolitical entity, usually a nation-state. As the datasets used in this study consist of customers and their transactions originating from Turkey, we target internal migration patterns of Turkey in this work.

As also described in earlier sections, the datasets utilised in this research were presented as transactions of customers of a major private bank in Turkey for

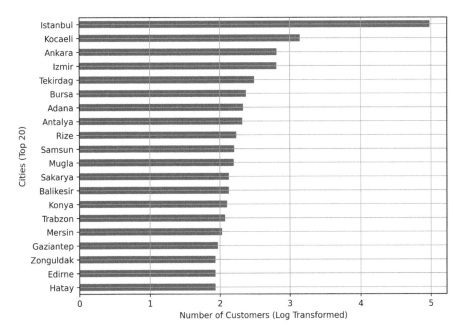

Figure 10.3 The top 20 cities with respect to the number of unique customers in the dataset. To be able to fit the chart, a base-10 log transform of the number of transactions was taken.

2014–2015. To provide more context for the scenario, according to the World Bank Global Index,[10] in Turkey 33% of the adult population owns a credit card. Among the population of credit card users, this bank has a market share of roughly 10%–11% for the period of available transactions.[11] Therefore, the bank had approximately a 3%–3.3% share of the adults who uses credit cards in Turkey. Also, arguably, those adults who are using credit cards are more financially literate than their other peers; Lusardi and Mitchell (2011) suggested that Turkey has 29% of adults who are financially literate and only half of them understand compound interest.

It should also be taken into account that for decades the Turkish population dynamics have been impacted by internal migration. The 2000 population census revealed that almost 30% of the population were born in a province different from where they now reside. Filiztekin and Gökhan (2008) claimed that this ratio rises to

---

[10] Global Findex Database of The World Bank, https://globalfindex.worldbank.org/sites/globalfindex/files/2018-05/Global%20Findex%20Database.xlsx

[11] Committed to Sustainable Leadership of Akbank, https://www.akbank.com/doc/Akbank_Investor_Presentation.pdf; Executional Excellence in 2016 and Beyond of Akbank, https://www.akbank.com/en-us/investor-relations/Documents/InvestorPres2Q16.pdf

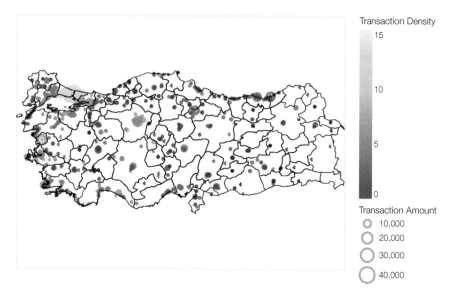

Figure 10.4 Heatmap of transactions with a sample size of 25,000. Lighter colours denote areas with higher transaction density. Transaction amount information is encoded with circle sizes drawn on the heatmap. Colour version printed as Plate 12.

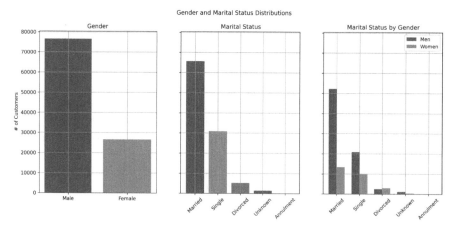

Figure 10.5 Distributions of gender and marital status in the dataset.

62% for Istanbul. Therefore, Istanbul can be considered as the main province that attracts migrants from other cities of Turkey.

The main goal of this study is to infer the internal migration patterns of the country with the help of transactional data. As a secondary goal, we also aim to study the spending behaviour of individuals before and after moving to a new city. To this end, the methodology adopted is based on investigating the transaction periods of customers from origin and destination cities. Similar period-based methods were adopted in Chi *et al.* (2020) and Fiorio *et al.* (2017) to infer migration patterns from innovative data sources. In our work, the methodology described incorporates an iterative constraint structure. Each set of constraints is applied to transactions of customers and aims to reflect an internal migration case. We consider three sets of constraints, and the scenarios resulting from their respective applications are called Scenario 0, Scenario 1, and Scenario 2.

To detect the internal migration patterns of Turkey, the constraints discussed above are in the form of various threshold values for customer transactions and some assumptions about their spending behaviours. With these restrictions on transactions and customer behaviour, various patterns of individual spending during migration scenarios are intended to be covered. In the following discussion of detecting migration patterns, these threshold values and assumptions, along with the different scenarios they create, will be discussed.

In addition to the operations described above, some data filtering operations are also performed on the transaction dataset. By filtering the customers in the dataset by transactions originating from multiple cities, only customers with an inter-city displacement are selected. In addition to this, a filtering option on the number of available transactions per customer is also introduced. To this end, only customers who had more than 10 transactions are kept in the dataset. With this option, we aim to gather individuals with more reliable data. These processes reduced the number of transactions available in the dataset from 3,729,193 (the original number of transactions with coordinates available) to 2,583,101. Also, through these processes, the number of unique customers is reduced to 42,139. These values are also presented in Table 10.2.

In addition to the threshold for the minimum number of transactions per customer, we introduce different threshold values for the minimum number transactions required per customer from each different city. As threshold values, 5, 10, 20, and 30 were used. Again, we aim to have more reliable data through higher

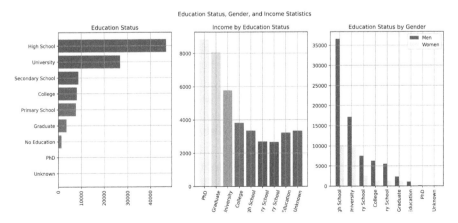

Figure 10.6 Distributions of education status, gender, and income in the dataset.

Table 10.2 Details of the transactions dataset with the introduced filtering options

Statistical Property	Numerical Value
Transactions with coordinates available	3,729,193
Transactions with coordinates with each customer > 10 transactions	2,583,101
Unique customers with coordinates available	98,834
Unique customers with > 10 transactions and coordinates available	42,139

Table 10.3 Number of unique customers with minimum transactions per city

Applied Threshold	Number of Customers
Number of customers with 5 different transactions for each city	2153
Number of customers with 10 different transactions for each city	649
Number of customers with 20 different transactions for each city	155
Number of customers with 30 different transactions for each city	53

values for the applied threshold. Also, these threshold values allow analyses on the distributions of the number of customers who performed spending in different cities. The resulting number of unique customers can be observed from Table 10.3.

For the first scenario of detecting individuals from the dataset as patterns, labelled Scenario 0, a homogeneous flux of transactions is considered. This homogeneous flux assumes that transactions for a migrant in our dataset start and end in the original city before beginning to occur in the destination city. As the dataset utilised in the research also included the timestamp of transactions, reflecting this assumption in the analysis was straightforward. To perform analyses for this scenario, only the customers whose time intervals of transactions from different cities do not overlap were considered as individuals with inter-city displacement. This scenario is then combined with the minimum transaction thresholds defined above. Unfortunately, with the minimum transactions per city as 30, no customers could be categorised as settled into a new city. With the minimum transactions per city set as 20, 10, and 5, respectively 6, 25, and 150 individuals fit the requirements above. When the threshold is applied as 10, the distributions of origin and destination cities of displacements are presented in Figure 10.7. It can be observed that, as the majority of the transactions in the dataset are from Istanbul, the majority of displacement patterns also revolve around Istanbul.

Re-evaluating the assumption described above, one can argue that the transactions of a customer who is about to relocate to another city may not be completely homogeneous, since an assumption of homogeneous transaction flux also presumes that the individual moves from the origin city to the destination city once and only once. However, this presumption is probably too rigid, as moving to another city usually requires multiple visits to the destination city to prepare the new living conditions. Considering this, the assumption of a direct change in transactions is relaxed

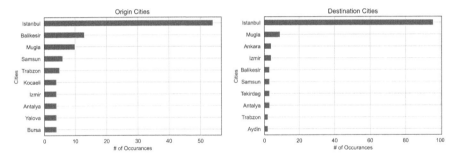

Figure 10.7 Origin and destination cities of customers. Obtained after applying a minimum transactions per city threshold of 5 with the assumption of homogeneous flux of transactions from cities per customer.

in an additional scenario, named Scenario 1, to offer individuals a period for moving to another city. To achieve this, the recorded timestamps of individuals can be utilised by letting transactions from the origin and destination cities overlap for a certain amount of time. In this way, a certain period can be allocated for individuals to move to another city.

Here, in addition to the analyses reported earlier, the period of allowing transactions from different cities is set to two months, and the other parameters for transactions of individuals are kept as before. This change in the constraints is reflected by filtering the individuals who have at least two months between the last transaction from the origin city and the first transaction from the destination city. With the minimum transactions per city as 30, 3 customers were categorised as settled into a new city compared to no customers with the more restrictive scenario employed above. Also, with minimum transactions per city set to 20, 10, and 5, respectively 12, 70, and 368 customers were categorised as displaced to a city different from their origin.

As the current inferences may also include people on vacation, a further restriction on transactions of customers needed to be introduced to discard individuals whose transaction sequences resemble a vacation or moving to a summer house rather than settling in another city. To establish this distinction, a requirement was introduced to create a new scenario, Scenario 2, where it is ensured that the transactions from the destination city cover more than two months. After this restriction, 205, 54, 9, and 3 customers were categorised as settling in a different city with the minimum transactions per city selected as 20, 10, and 5, respectively. In Table 10.4 these results and the resulting number of customers categorised as settled in a new city for the different scenarios can be observed.

Figures 10.8 and 10.9 display the numbers of transactions per category recorded for individuals categorised as settled into a new city. As can also be observed from these figures, for most of the categories the numbers of transactions do not change drastically. However, it should also be noted that the numbers of transactions in both scenarios increase in the destination city, as can be observed from the x-axis

Table 10.4 Number of customers categorised as settled to a new city.
Scenario 0 denotes numbers categorised with the homogeneous flux of transactions assumptions. Scenario 1 denotes numbers categorised with a two month tolerance for overlapping transactions. Scenario 2 denotes numbers categorised by introducing the minimum time period needed for transactions from a city restriction as two months.

Minimum Transactions per City	Scenario 0	Scenario 1	Scenario 2
30	—	3	3
20	6	12	9
10	25	70	54
5	150	368	205

limits of these figures. The most noticeable change seems to be the increase in the rankings of restaurant spending in both scenarios. The fact that the number of restaurant transactions increases for customers who settled in a new city may suggest an adjustment period of these customers, where they opt for more practical solutions.

Because of the datasets utilised in this study, transactions of customers can also be analysed without aggregating them. To this end, as also performed in the earlier study of Singh et al. (2015) with similar datasets, different metrics can be produced from the existing attributes. As this sample contains category, amount, and POI information for each transaction, how these attributes vary with the customer behaviour in both origin and destination cities can be analysed. For this subject, three new metrics are derived and calculated for each customer. Then, these metrics are studied with two samples of customers that were also used in earlier results. The metrics employed here are categorical diversity, POI diversity, and transaction amount diversity; they are described below, and the results are shown in Figure 10.10.

Categorical diversity This is defined as the number of unique category occurrences over the number of transactions per customer who is considered as settled to another city. The formula for categorical diversity is:

$$D_{i_{cat}} = \frac{uniq(cat)_i}{t_i}, \quad (10.1)$$

where $D_{i_{cat}}$ is the categorical diversity value for customer i, $uniq(cat)_i$ is the number of unique categories for the given transactions, and t_i is the number of available transactions for customer i. The resulting categorical diversity values of customers are in the range $(0, 1]$, as the number of unique categories can at most be equal to the number of transactions.

For both samples of customers described above, the average categorical diversity seems to be decreasing after settling to a new city. For the first sample, customers with at least five transactions for each city, the mean value of this

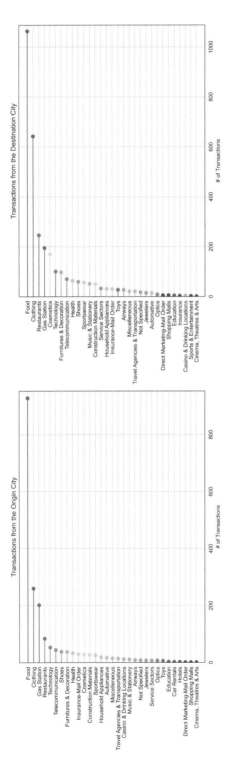

Figure 10.8 Spending categories of customers in origin and destination cities. The figures were obtained with the initial scenario where the only requirement on customers was having at least five transactions in both the origin and destination city.

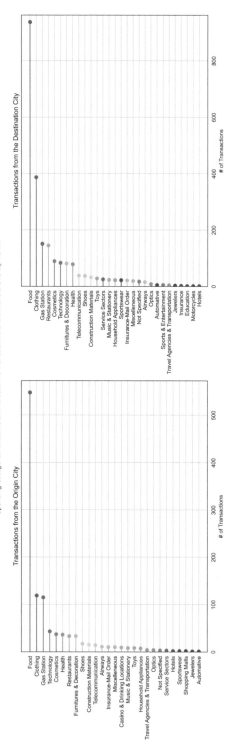

Figure 10.9 Spending categories of customers in origin and destination cities. The figures were obtained with at least 10 transactions for both origin and destination city and a two-month time period allowance for overlaps from transactions in origin and destination cities.

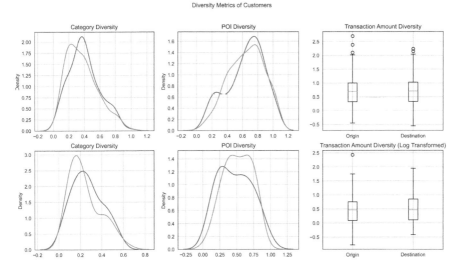

Figure 10.10 Diversity metrics of customers. The figures on the upper row are obtained from customers with at least five transactions for each city. The figures at the bottom are obtained from customers with at least 10 transactions for each city and two months of overlap period. Similar trends for category and POI diversity can be observed in both origin and destination cities. While the average categorical diversity decreases slightly after settling in a new city, POI diversity slightly increases.

diversity metric decreased from 0.402 to 0.372 in the origin city. For the second sample, customers with at least 10 transactions and a two-month overlap period, categorical diversity decreased from 0.265 to 0.242. These results show that customers tend to narrow their spending in terms of categories when they first settle in another city. The categorical diversity of customers in the second sample being lower also suggests this finding, as the increase in the number of transactions does not increase the variety of categories.

POI diversity This is defined as the number of unique POI occurrences over the number of transactions per customer who is considered as settled to another city. The formula for POI diversity is:

$$D_{i_{POI}} = \frac{uniq(POI)_i}{t_i}, \qquad (10.2)$$

where $D_{i_{POI}}$ is the POI Diversity value for customer i, $uniq(POI)_i$ is the number of unique POI occurrences for given transactions, and t_i is the number of available transactions for customer i. Again, the resulting POI diversity values of customers are in the range $(0, 1]$, as the number of unique POI occurrences can at most be equal to the number of transactions.

Unlike the categorical diversity, the average POI diversity increases for both samples in the destination city. For the first sample, POI diversity increases from 0.641 to 0.650. For the second sample, this metric increases from 0.475 to 0.514.

The findings here show that customers tend to visit more POIs after they settle in a new city. It can also indicate that these customers are more open to exploration in their spending behaviour in the destination city.

Transaction amount diversity This is defined as the standard deviation of transaction amounts over the number of transactions per customer who considered as settled to another city. The formula for the transaction amount diversity is:

$$D_{i_{TRX}} = \frac{\sigma_{t_i}}{t_i}, \qquad (10.3)$$

where $D_{i_{TRX}}$ is the POI diversity value for customer i, σ_{t_i} is the standard deviation of the given transaction amounts, and t_i is the number of available transactions for customer i. Unlike the previous metrics, transaction amount diversity is not bound in the range between 0 and 1.

Similar to categorical diversity, transaction amount diversity also decreases for both samples in the destination city. The average value of transaction amount diversity decreases from 15.69 to 13.60 for the first sample. For the second sample, this metric decreases from 11.8 in the origin city to 8.32 in the destination city. The decrease in this metric can be interpreted as a smaller number of transactions with higher amounts in the destination city. The findings suggest that customers who settle in a new city behave more cautiously in terms of their amounts of spending.

Choropleth maps, in which cities are categorised according to the frequency of moving patterns, can be observed in Figures 10.11 and 10.12. These maps display the results of Scenarios 0 and 2, respectively. The frequencies of origin and destination cities are displayed in separate maps for a better understanding of the underlying patterns. When the results are compared, one can see that Scenario 0

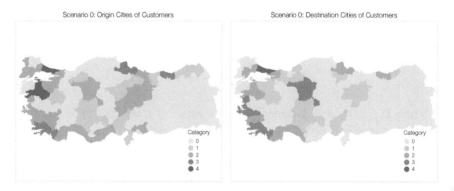

Figure 10.11 Choropleth maps of the findings of Scenario 0. The figure on the left displays the frequency of origin cities, while the figure on the right displays the frequency of the destination cities.

Figure 10.12 Choropleth maps of the findings of Scenario 2. The figure on the left displays the frequency of origin cities, while the figure on the right displays the frequency of the destination cities.

reveals more patterns in both origin and destination cities, as the transaction requirement makes the scenario more flexible. In the results of both scenarios, Istanbul is the city with the maximum frequency for both origin and destination city. The remaining large cities of the country and the Aegean cities are other candidates for creating origin–destination city pairs with Istanbul.

The findings from the scenarios covered in this section are compared with the official migration statistics shared by Turkish Statistical Institute (TURKSTAT). The dataset published by TURKSTAT reports annual origin–destination city pairs for migration estimates in Turkey. As the transactions in our dataset start in July 2014 and end in June 2015, it would be most accurate to check the official estimates for both 2014 and 2015. In Table 10.5, the most frequent origin–destination city pairs from the different scenarios and the official migration estimates of Turkey for the years 2014 and 2015 are listed. Although the absolute numbers in the findings and the official statistics differ severely, it can be argued that the methods employed are accurate in identifying migration trends. The results of the scenarios covered are successful in terms of reporting that the majority of origin–destination city pairs involve Istanbul.

The findings in both Scenario 0 and Scenario 2 also overlap with the official statistics in terms of the regions in which internal migration generally takes place. As can be observed from Table 10.5, the majority of migration to Istanbul takes place from provinces close to Istanbul or the other largest cities of the country. Even though a numeric comparison between the findings of the methods here and the official estimations cannot be performed, one can see that many of the origin–destination city pairs in the findings overlap with the official statistics. The results of the scenarios also seem to capture the migration patterns revolving around Istanbul.

Table 10.5 Findings from scenarios and estimated migration numbers

Comparison between official statistics of migration estimates of Turkey published by the Turkish Statistical Institute and the findings of the scenarios discussed in this section. For all four statistics, a maximum of 20 values are displayed.

Scenario 0 (total of 150 city pairs)		Scenario 2 (total of 54 city pairs)		2014 Estimates		2015 Estimates	
City Pair	Est. Value	City Pair	Est. Value	City Pair	Est. Value	City Pair	Est. Value
Balıkesir–Istanbul	13	Izmir–Istanbul	6	Kocaeli–Istanbul	28,272	Kocaeli–Istanbul	29,475
Muğla–Istanbul	10	Balıkesir–Istanbul	6	Tekirdağ–Istanbul	23,170	Tekirdağ–Istanbul	25,422
Istanbul–Muğla	9	Yalova–Istanbul	3	Istanbul–Tokat	19,388	Ordu–Istanbul	21,420
Samsun–Istanbul	6	Bursa–Istanbul	3	Istanbul–Ankara	19,021	Ankara–Istanbul	18,907
Trabzon–Istanbul	5	Istanbul–Antalya	3	Ankara–Istanbul	18,775	Istanbul–Ankara	18,066
Antalya–Istanbul	4	Istanbul–Kocaeli	3	Izmir–Istanbul	16,129	Giresun–Istanbul	17,935
Yalova–Istanbul	4	Ankara–Istanbul	3	Istanbul–Izmir	15,559	Izmir–Istanbul	17,124
Istanbul–Izmir	4	Samsun–Istanbul	3	Tokat–Istanbul	15,395	Tokat–Istanbul	17,035
Bursa–Istanbul	4	Muğla–Istanbul	2	Istanbul–Kocaeli	14,952	Bursa–Istanbul	14,215
Izmir–Istanbul	4	Kocaeli–Istanbul	1	Istanbul–Van	13,155	Istanbul–Kocaeli	13,939
Istanbul–Ankara	4	Kırıkkale–Istanbul	1	Ordu–Istanbul	12,934	Istanbul–Tokat	13,844
Kocaeli–Istanbul	4	Antalya–Istanbul	1	Bursa–Istanbul	12,901	Istanbul–Izmir	13,237
Kayseri–Istanbul	3	Aydın–Istanbul	1	Istanbul–Balıkesir	12,494	Istanbul–Van	12,908
Istanbul–Tekirdağ	3	Tekirdağ–Istanbul	1	Istanbul–Ordu	12,437	Sakarya–Istanbul	12,047
Istanbul–Samsun	3	Konya–Istanbul	1	Sakarya–Istanbul	11,888	Samsun–Istanbul	10,924
Istanbul–Antalya	3	Diyarbakır–Istanbul	1	Istanbul–Giresun	11,814	Antalya–Istanbul	10,141
Kocaeli–Balıkesir	3	Erzurum–Istanbul	1	Istanbul–Bursa	11,132	Istanbul–Bursa	10,128
Gaziantep–Istanbul	2	Sakarya–Istanbul	1	Istanbul–Tekirdağ	11,101	Istanbul–Tekirdağ	10,104
Çanakkale–Istanbul	2	Istanbul–Istanbul	1	Antalya–Istanbul	10,887	Manisa–Izmir	9,479
Istanbul–Kocaeli	2	Istanbul–Çankırı	1	Istanbul–Sivas	10,403	Balıkesir–Istanbul	9,479

Discussion and conclusion

We have attempted to capture patterns of individuals who settled in a different city in the period of the sample. In this process, the scenarios followed a restrictive trend in transactions of customers to eliminate mobility patterns that are very unlikely to be instances of domestic migration. The first scenario, Scenario 0, includes all of the customers that have transactions originating from a different city than their initial location after a certain time. Scenario 1 introduces a tolerance period for customers. With this, we aimed to include additional customers in the analyses by creating a settlement process. With Scenario 1, the assumption of homogeneous transactions that ensures the transactions of a customer start with the origin city and pass to the destination city is removed. The effect of removing the assumption can be observed from Table 10.4 with an increase in the number of individuals categorised as settled to another city compared to Scenario 0. By the addition of a further time constraint on transaction periods from different cities in Scenario 2, we attempted to rule out individuals who travel to different cities with no intention of migrating, rather with a higher probability of having a vacation, visiting relatives, or moving to a summer house for a shorter period of time. By utilising multiple scenarios, we have aimed to cover various behaviour patterns and make the requirements on customer transactions resemble the process of settling in a new city gradually.

Although the numbers estimated for internal migration patterns are different from the official statistics in terms of magnitude, it can be seen that the patterns discovered in different scenarios do match with the migration patterns from the official migration estimates. Although the magnitude of the estimates inferred with both scenarios is not large enough to validate through TURKSTAT statistics, we applied Pearson correlation tests on the findings and the official statistics to base the study on statistical results. We tested the findings of both Scenarios 0 and 2 against the official statistics from 2014 and 2015. The resulting correlation scores can be seen in Table 10.6. Obtaining correlation scores in the range of 0.225 and 0.246 indicates a weak positive correlation for each pair of tested sets. Hence, it can be claimed that there is some parallel between our findings and migration estimates from official sources.

The main reason why few customers are categorised as settled to another city in the scenarios was because of the limited number of transactions available for each customer. Most of the customers did not have an adequate number of transactions

Table 10.6 Correlation coefficients between case study findings and estimates published by the Turkey Statistical Institute

Compared Set 1	Compared Set 2	Correlation Coefficient
Scenario 0	2014 estimations	0.266
Scenario 0	2015 estimations	0.225
Scenario 2	2014 estimations	0.223
Scenario 2	2015 estimations	0.246

from multiple cities to be considered as transactions of individuals who possibly migrated to another city. This can also be observed in the case study. When the number of transactions required from both origin and destination city is increased to 30, no transactions were eligible to be analysed in Scenario 0.

As mentioned earlier, having a very small sample size may result in difficulties replicating the findings discussed in this study. As we worked only with a sample of customers of a private bank, one can claim that two types of bias exist in the study. The first is due to the bank customers not representing the demographics of the whole population. Our work was only able to analyse the behaviour of individuals who were customers of a particular bank. An additional bias is also present due to our sample of customers being from only a single financial organisation among many available in the country. Though the private bank that provided this dataset did not have a particular focus for its customers, our study is still affected by the underlying demographic and socioeconomic structure of customers of the specific bank. To address these coverage issues, a more comprehensive study can be performed with data from multiple organisations. Comparing results from different financial organisations can provide more concrete estimates about internal migration and better understanding of the behaviour of individuals after their movement. However, the biggest challenge for such a study is obtaining the data since there are many obstacles that prevent financial organisations sharing their transactional data.

On the other hand, apart from having a few individuals who fit the requirements introduced, the presence of the high granularity in the dataset paves the way for new research that cannot be performed with only internal migration estimates. The diversity studies presented in the 'Case study' section can be exemplified as such research. The results of analyses made about the diversity metrics of individuals show that customers who settle in a new city visit more different POIs, while they tend to narrow their spending in terms of category and amount. These can be interpreted as customers behaving more conservatively with their spending behaviour. Moreover, at the same time, their spending habits are not well established and they do not have the usual go-to places for various needs.

One of the limitations in the study presented was the fact that the majority of transactions of the dataset consisted of customers and transactions from Istanbul. It may have led to the absence of discoveries of migration patterns that do not involve Istanbul as an origin or destination city. However, migration estimates published by TURKSTAT also demonstrate the presence of Istanbul either as the origin or the destination city in the most frequent migration patterns. It can be argued that the processes presented in this document were successful in reflecting the main migration patterns of the country. Further scenarios that include higher numbers of individuals could be created with a dataset containing a larger number of transactions. The patterns discussed in the study can be processed in a more detailed and reliable way if they can be linked with other possible data sources. It should be noted that the patterns revealed in this study are not directly presented as migration estimates, as it was difficult to rule out the variety of possible reasons that may have caused individuals to move to a different city. Additionally, it should also be stated that the dataset used in the study covered transactions of customers for one year. The methods employed could be validated with a dataset containing transactions from a longer period.

Acknowledgements

The authors are grateful to the officials of the bank who made this study possible by making the transaction dataset available.

References

Alvarez, S. P., Briod, P., Ferrari, O., and Rieder, U. (2015), 'Remittances: How reliable are the data?', *Migration Policy Practice* 5(2), 42–6.

Bakker, M. A., Piracha, D. A., Lu, P. J., Bejgo, K., Bahrami, M., Leng, Y., Balsa-Barreiro, J., Ricard, J., Morales, A., Singh, V. K., Bozkaya, B., Balcisoy, S., and Pentland, A. (2019), 'Measuring fine-grained multidimensional integration using mobile phone metadata: The case of Syrian refugees in Turkey, *in* A. A. Salah, A. Pentland, B. Lepri, and E. Letouzé, eds, *Guide to Mobile Data Analytics in Refugee Scenarios*, Springer, New York.

Batsaikhan, U., Darvas, Z., and Raposo, I. G. (2018), 'People on the move: Migration and mobility in the European Union', Bruegel Blueprint Series 28.

Beaton, K., Cerovic, S., Galdamez, M., Hadzi-Vaskov, M., Loyola, F., Koczan, Z., Lissovolik, B., Martijn, J., and Ustyugova, Y. (2017), *Migration and Remittances in Latin America and the Caribbean: Engines of Growth and Macroeconomic Stabilizers?*, International Monetary Fund.

Blumenstock, J., *et al.* (2019), 'Migration and the value of social networks', Technical report, CEPR Discussion Papers (13611).

Bounie, D., Camara, Y., and Galbraith, J. W. (2020), 'Consumers' mobility, expenditure and online–offline substitution response to COVID-19: Evidence from French transaction data', available at https://ssrn.com/abstract=3588373

Brown, R., Carling, J., Fransen, S., and Siegel, M. (2014), 'Measuring remittances through surveys: Methodological and conceptual issues for survey designers and data analysts', *Demographic Research* 31(41), 1243–74.

Chi, G., Lin, F., Chi, G., and Blumenstock, J. (2020), 'A general approach to detecting migration events in digital trace data', *PLOS One* 15(10), 1–17.

El Mahrsi, M. K., Côme, E., Oukhellou, L., and Verleysen, M. (2017), 'Clustering smart card data for urban mobility analysis', *IEEE Transactions on Intelligent Transportation Systems* 18(3), 712–28.

Fatehkia, M., Coles, B., Ofli, F., and Weber, I. (2020a), 'The relative value of Facebook advertising data for poverty mapping', *in Proceedings of the International AAAI Conference on Web and Social Media*, Vol. 14, 934–8.

Fatehkia, M., Tingzon, I., Orden, A., Sy, S., Sekara, V., Garcia-Herranz, M., and Weber, I. (2020b), 'Mapping socioeconomic indicators using social media advertising data', *EPJ Data Science* 9(1), 22.

Filiztekin, A. and Gökhan, A. (2008), 'The determinants of internal migration in Turkey', *Proceedings of the International Conference on Policy Modelling, EcoMod 2008*.

Fiorio, L., Abel, G., Cai, J., Zagheni, E., Weber, I., and Vinué, G. (2017), 'Using Twitter data to estimate the relationship between short-term mobility and long-term migration', *in Proceedings of the 2017 ACM Conference on Web Science*, 103–10.

Fudolig, M. I. D., Monsivais, D., Kunal, B., Hang-Hyun, J., and Kimmo, K. (2021), 'Internal migration and mobile communication patterns among pairs with strong ties', *EPJ Data Science* 10, 16.

Gendronneau, C., Yıldız, D., Hsiao, Y., Stepanek, M., Abel, G., Hoorens, S., Wiśniowski, A., Zagheni, E., Fiorio, L., and Weber, I. (2019), 'Measuring labour mobility and migration using big data: Exploring the potential of social-media data for measuring EU mobility flows and stocks of EU movers', European Commission Publications Office, Luxembourg.

Gezici, F. and Keskin, B. (2005), 'Interaction between regional inequalities and internal migration in Turkey', ERSA Conference Papers, ersa05p132.

Giannotti, F., Nanni, M., Pedreschi, D., Pinelli, F., Renso, C., Rinzivillo, S. and Trasarti, R. (2011), 'Unveiling the complexity of human mobility by querying and mining massive trajectory data', *The VLDB Journal* 20, 695–719.

Gökhan, A. (2008), 'The determinants of internal migration in Turkey', PhD thesis, Sabancı University.

Gonzalez, M. C., Hidalgo, C.. and Barabasi, A.-L. (2008), 'Understanding individual human mobility patterns', *Nature* 453, 779–82.

Granger, C. W. (1969), 'Investigating causal relations by econometric models and cross-spectral methods', *Econometrica: Journal of the Econometric Society* 37(3), 424–38.

Halpern, J. (2015), 'A modification of the Halpern–Pearl definition of causality', *in Proceedings of the Twenty-Fourth International Joint Conference on Artificial Intelligence*.

Halpern, J. Y. and Pearl, J. (2005), 'Causes and explanations: A structural-model approach. Part I: Causes', *British Journal for the Philosophy of Science* 56(4), 843–87.

Karemera, D., Oguledo, V. I., and Davis, B. (2000), 'A gravity model analysis of international migration to North America', *Applied Economics* 32(13), 1745–55.

Kikas, R., Dumas, M., and Saabas, A. (2015), 'Explaining international migration in the Skype network: The role of social network features', *in SIdEWayS '15: Proceedings of the First ACM Workshop on Social Media World Sensors*, Association of Computing Machinery, New York.

Levitt, P. (1998), 'Social remittances: Migration driven local-level forms of cultural diffusion', *The International Migration Review* 32(4), 926–48.

Li, J., Xu, L., Tang, L., Wang, S., and Li, L. (2018), 'Big data in tourism research: A literature review', *Tourism Management* 68, 301–23.

Lim, S. and Basnet, H. C. (2017), 'International migration, workers' remittances and permanent income hypothesis', *World Development* 96, 438–50.

Lulli, A., Gabrielli, L., Dazzi, P., Dell'Amico, M., Nanni, M., and Ricci, L. (2017), 'Scalable and flexible clustering solutions for mobile phone-based population indicators', *International Journal of Data Science and Analytics* 4(4), 285–99.

Lusardi, A. and Mitchell, O. S. (2011), 'Financial literacy around the world: An overview', *Journal of Pension Economics and Finance* 10(4), 497–508.

Massey, D. S. (1989), 'Economic development and international migration in comparative perspective', *Population and Development Review* 14(3), 383–413.

Migali, S., *et al.* (2018), 'International migration drivers', Joint Research Centre, Ispra, Italy.

Miranda-González, A., Aref, S., Theile, T., and Zagheni, E. (2020), 'Scholarly migration within Mexico: Analyzing internal migration among researchers using Scopus longitudinal bibliometric data', *EPJ Data Science* 9(1), 34.

Palotti, J., Adler, N., Morales-Guzman, A., Villaveces, J., Sekara, V., Garcia Herranz, M., Al-Asad, M., and Weber, I. (2020), 'Monitoring of the Venezuelan exodus through Facebook's advertising platform', *PLOS One* 15(2), 1–15.

Pappalardo, L., Pedreschi, D., Smoreda, Z., and Giannotti, F. (2015), 'Using big data to study the link between human mobility and socio-economic development', *in Proceedings of the 2015 IEEE International Conference on Big Data*, 871–8.

Pearl, J. (2009), *Causality*, Cambridge University Press, Cambridge.

Ramos, R. and Suriñach, J. (2016), 'A gravity model of migration between the ENC and the EU', *Tijdschrift voor economische en sociale geografie* 108(1), 21–35.

Salah, A. A., Pentland, A., Lepri, B., and Letouzé, E. (2019), *Guide to Mobile Data Analytics in Refugee Scenarios*, Springer, New York.

Singh, V. K., Bozkaya, B., and Pentland, A. (2015), 'Money walks: Implicit mobility behavior and financial well-being', *PLOS One* 10(8), 1–17.

Sobolevsky, S., Sitko, I., Combes, R. T. D., Hawelka, B., Arias, J. M., and Ratti, C. (2014), 'Money on the move: Big data of bank card transactions as the new proxy for human mobility patterns and regional delineation. The case of residents and foreign visitors in Spain, *in Proceedings of the 2014 IEEE International Congress on Big Data*, 136–43.

Spyratos, S., Vespe, M., Natale, F., Weber, I., Zagheni, E., and Rango, M. (2018), *Migration Data using Social Media: A European Perspective*, Publications Office of the European Union, Luxembourg.

Spyratos, S., Vespe, M., Natale, F., Weber, I., Zagheni, E., and Rango, M. (2019), 'Quantifying international human mobility patterns using Facebook Network data', *PLOS One* 14(10), e0224134.

Sîrbu, A., Andrienko, G., Andrienko, N., Boldrini, C., Conti, M., Giannotti, F., Guidotti, R., Bertoli, S., Kim, J., Muntean, C., Pappalardo, L., Passarella, A., Pedreschi, D., Pollacci, L., Pratesi, F., and Sharma, R. (2021), 'Human migration: The big data perspective', *International Journal of Data Science and Analytics* 11(4), 341–60.

Part III

Visualisation

11

Visual Exploration of Large Multidimensional Trajectory Data

ALEXANDRU TELEA AND MICHAEL BEHRISCH

Introduction

THE LAST DECADE has witnessed the rapid increase of data sources concerning many societal aspects, including migration. Such data sources, e.g., Refugee Processing Center (RPC) admissions and arrivals (Refugee Processing Center, 2020) or the Migration Data Portal (MDP, 2020) provide increasingly rich and diverse data concerning the origins, categories, amounts, and paths followed by migrating individuals and groups. As such portals collect and aggregate data from a variety of sources and types, they provide an alternative, and important, source for migration researchers, policy-makers, and the grand public for studying and understanding migration-related phenomena (Bilsborow, 2016).

However, data availability is only one of the necessary ingredients to support insight forming and decision-making. The other key ingredient is the availability of *tools* allowing stakeholders to clean, analyse, and present data in ways that support answering their questions and completing their tasks. Such tools include statistical analysis, data mining, and, last but not least, data *visualisation*.

Visualisation tools applicable to migration data cover a variety of approaches. As geographical attributes, such as the origin and destination of migration flows and the paths taken in between, are key to migration data, many visualisation approaches use map-based presentation to encode spatial information, and overlay this with additional attributes on demand, such as types, sizes, and time of migratory flows (Gapminder, 2020). However, efficiently and effectively visualising large amounts of migration data in this spatial metaphor is challenging. One of the key issues here is the *relational* nature of such data, which relates origins to destinations by paths. Displaying large datasets containing thousands of such paths or more, each one potentially annotated with multiple attributes, can easily create a high amount of clutter, which makes analysis hard or even impossible.

This chapter provides a practical overview of visualisation methods, techniques, and workflows for the exploration of large trajectory datasets such as present in migration data. The main aim is to provide data scientists and, at a wider level, researchers interested in studying migration data who do not have a visualisation background, with guidelines on how to choose and use existing visualisation tools and techniques to study their trajectory-centric data. When the practitioner involved with migration data has a better understanding of the process of preparing and creating visualisations, he or she will be in a better position to understand the shortcomings, biases, and ways of deceiving the viewer by these visualisations, and thereby be able to avoid such issues.

This chapter is structured as follows. The 'Background' section introduces a generic model to store and manipulate migration-related, or, more generally, trajectory-based, data. Next, the same section introduces several classes of visualisation methods for such data, outlining their advantages and limitations for specific tasks. After having discussed data and tools, 'Creating visualisations' details the typical workflow that the data scientist follows from the moment when a new data source, or dataset, is made available up to and including the iterative and interactive exploration of created visualisations to answer actual questions on the data. 'Discussion and conclusion' unifies the discussion on data modelling, tools, and visual exploration, outlining key open challenges related to the study of trajectory-based data, and also sketching directions for further reading and research.

Background

Designing and validating visualisations typically follows a so-called nested model (Munzner, 2009) consisting of four steps: (1) The *domain* problem is characterised by eliciting the terms and high-level tasks that are commonly used by specialists in the respective field (migration study, in our case). (2) The data that describe these tasks and terms are abstracted into a so-called *data model*. (3) The data and tasks elicited during the previous steps are mapped to *visual encodings*, i.e., mapping *data* to visual shapes that are to be rendered on the screen, and interaction design, i.e., mapping *tasks* to interactive operations that one can execute on the visual shapes. (4) The visual and interaction designs proposed in the previous step are subsequently implemented in concrete software *tools*.

Constructing visualisations ideally follows all the steps (1)–(4), which are executed iteratively several times to refine the understanding of the users' needs and thereby the creation of visualisations that optimally address these needs. Doing this, however, requires considerable amounts of effort and specialised knowledge, both in the problem domain and in visualisation, computer graphics, and interaction programming. Moreover, such paths require a *concrete*, specific problem with particular users and their needs. Detailing the design of such specific visualisations is possible, but less interesting for the wider public.

In this chapter we aim to provide actionable knowledge to *non-specialist* users interested in understanding the *types* of visualisations that can help the study of migration data in general, as opposed to the design of *custom* visualisations for a specific problem. Moreover, we focus here on migration data that involves spatiotemporal *trails*. These data are the least supported by generic visualisation tools known to a wider public, and thus where our discussion of more advanced visualisation tools is of greatest added value. As such, we next only cover a subset of the entire four-step nested model, as follows. 'Problem domain' outlines the problem domain, listing generic questions and tasks that users of trail-centric migration data want to address. 'Data model' proposes a simple but generic model for representing trail-centric migration data that covers most use cases from the problem domain. 'Visualisation techniques' presents several types of visualisation techniques that can handle the aforementioned data model, focusing mainly on techniques that are well proven and battle-tested within the visualisation community, and which are supported by open-source implementations.

Problem domain

Characterising a problem domain for visualisation design starts by identifying the entities that are to be analysed (Munzner, 2009). For migration data, these include origins and destination locations, e.g., countries, migration time moments, gross migration amounts, and migrant population characteristics, e.g., profession, age group, or refugee status. Consequently, the tasks imply answering questions revolving around these entities.

As outlined in 'Introduction', one of the particularly challenging aspects of migration data is that they are *spatial* and *relational* in nature; that is, they inherently consist of multiple spatial locations being *linked* by multi-attribute migratory flows. As such, we next focus only on tasks that take into account this relational nature. Other tasks, e.g., that consider the migration data as a set of tables listing the values of entities to be analysed, are far simpler to address by using established charting tools for tabular data, e.g., Tableau (Tableau Inc., 2020) or Google Charts (Google Inc., 2020), and are thus not discussed in this chapter. Specific questions that visualisation addresses related to migration data are outlined below:

Q1 Where (between which origins and destinations) are the strongest migration flows?
    Q1a Which attributes, e.g., trail characteristics, contribute to the success of a migration trail? And, how can migration flows be steered?

Q2 Are there similar migration patterns over different space and/or time intervals?
    Q2a Can we extrapolate root causes that lead to these migration flows at a specific point in time?

Q3 Are there migration patterns having a specific structure, e.g., migration from a country to a large set of neighbour countries?

Q4 Is there a reversal of migration over specific geographical regions and, if so, during which time periods?

Q5 Which reasons exist for emigrating from a specific origin? Which reasons exist for immigrating to a specific destination?

Figure 11.1 illustrates the above challenge of visualising trail-based data. We consider here a simple dataset that records the number of refugees by *origin* (leaving a country) and by *destination* (entering a country), for all countries, for the year 2000. Figure 11.1(a) and (b) show these numbers, visualised using GapMinder (Gapminder, 2020), colour-coded on a blue-to-red colour map. For reference, the country populations are encoded by the disk sizes. The overall technique is known as a bubble chart. These images allow us to see some patterns, e.g., that Europe and North America receive a significant share of refugees (warm colours, image (b)); Afghanistan has the highest refugees leaving it (small red dot in the centre of image (a)); and Iran and Pakistan are the highest receivers of refugees (small red dots in the centre of image (b)). However, we cannot, for instance, see where the Afghan refugees are going to, or where those arriving in Iran and Pakistan come from. On a higher level, we cannot see any *displacement* patterns indicating actual flows of refugees between different parts of the world. Figure 11.1(c) shows actual

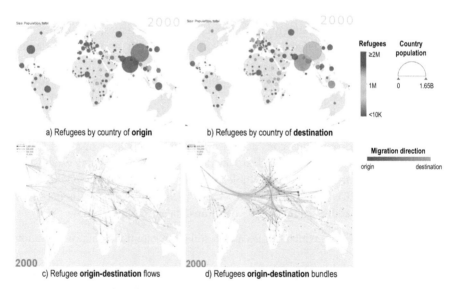

Figure 11.1 Refugee movements between origin and destination (asylum) countries in 2000 visualised with four methods. (a,b) Refugee counts per origin, respectively destination, countries shown in GapMinder (Gapminder, 2020). (c) Refugee flows depicted as straight lines (red = origin, green = destination) in JFlowMap (Boyandin, 2010). (d) The same image as (c) but simplified by trail bundling. Colour version printed as Plate 3.

refugee flows: origin–destination (OD) flows above a certain person count (selected by the user so as to diminish visual clutter) are drawn as straight lines linking the respective countries' centres, and coloured using a red (origin) to green (destination) gradient (Boyandin et al., 2010). Some additional patterns become immediately visible, such as the net influx of refugees in Europe and North America (green lines ending there). We also see that these lines originate mainly from Central and South America, respectively Africa, the Middle East, and Central Asia. Figure 11.1(d) further simplifies the visualisation by reducing visual clutter by 'bundling' spatially close trails. This creates a more schematic view of the migration flows which shows more clearly the two main refugee streams arriving in North America and Canada, and also that the majority of refugees that leave Africa arrive in Northwest Europe. While kept simple on purpose, Figure 11.1 already illustrates both the difficulty, but also the added value, of visualising migration trails as opposed to simple per-country aggregates.

From the above simple example, we see a few specific aspects of the questions that visualisation aims to address. First and foremost, these are less of a quantitative nature, but more of a qualitative nature. Indeed, questions that relate *strictly* to attribute values, e.g., finding the range or average of a migration flow, or the point in time where a migration flow has peaked, can be accomplished using standard database tools, and benefit (far) less from visualisation. Simple visual depictions such as plain-text tables or bar charts can already support answering such questions. Conversely, questions which involve *multiple* data aspects (attributes), some of which are of spatiotemporal nature, and questions whose answers are not single values, but rather spatiotemporal *patterns*, are naturally better served by visualisation. For example, the easiest way to convey what a distribution looks like is actually to *draw* it, especially in the case that its nature cannot be easily captured by a simple mathematical model. The qualitative aspect of the above questions, as opposed to quantitative aspects, is outlined by the presence of keywords such as 'where' (requires the description of potentially multiple locations), 'similar' (requires the description of multiple aspects that make two phenomena alike), 'patterns' (requires the description of multiple data aspects which, when occurring in a certain proportion, cause the appearance of what one calls a pattern), and 'structure' (requires the description of relationships between specific parts of one or several patterns). Other aspects that typically signal the qualitative aspect of questions (which, next, is best approached by visualisation) are the presence of descriptive terms which cannot be measured precisely on a quantitative scale, such as 'strong', 'scattered', 'important', or 'salient'.

A second point common to all the questions listed above is that they all relate to so-called indicators of mobility. Visualisation aims to answer questions concerning such indicators by encoding them into the attributes of the visualisation. For instance, one can colour-code two instances of a country map by unemployment rates, respectively by immigrant numbers, and thereby support answering questions concerning the correlation of the two indicators. We further detail how visualisation relates to questions concerning mobility indicators in the next two sections.

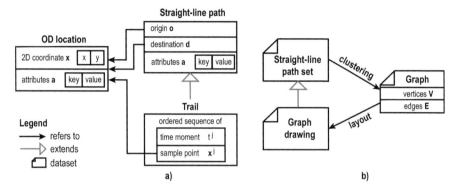

Figure 11.2 (a) Schema for storing migration data. (b) Relation of path-sets, graphs, and graph drawings.

Data model

Preliminaries

Migration scholars use various forms of data representation, such as a wealth of indicators to characterise migration and mobility, e.g. events, economic indicators, sociocultural indicators, and geographic and climate-related data. In visualisation, data are typically represented by means of generic models that aim to capture its structure, typically in as application-independent a way as possible (to foster reusability of the developed visualisation techniques). To ease the learning task of the migration scholar or practitioner interested in (re)using visualisation techniques, we follow next the visualisation terminology of data modelling, thereby introducing and explaining terms and notations that such practitioners will likely encounter, and need to understand, when using visualisation tools. Box 11.1 provides comparative information about graph, network, and trail representations, and their use in visualisation literature.

Figure 11.2a shows a simple schema (using UML-like notation) that allows the storage of migration data. Such a schema can be easily implemented using relational databases (Hoffman, 2003) or even plain-text file formats (Hurter et al., 2012).

Paths vs trails

Straight-line paths and trails typically co-exist in migration data visualisation and serve different purposes. Straight-line paths are necessary when one does not have or use actual location measurements along a trail, but only knows the origin and destination data, or when one wants to perform the analysis at a higher, more abstract, or more aggregated level. In contrast, trails allow finer-grained analyses, and are necessary when the underlying questions target actual motion patterns. Figure 11.3 shows examples of these two data types. Image (a) shows straight-line paths for a

Box 11.1 Graphs, networks, trails

Migration data, and more generally trajectory data, are interchangeably referred to in different sources in the visualisation literature using the terms graphs, networks, and trails (Von Landesberger *et al.*, 2011; Archambault *et al.*, 2013; Lhuillier *et al.*, 2017). Clarifying these terms and how they relate to each other is important, since some visualisation techniques are applicable to only certain data types.

Let $\mathbf{o}_i \in \mathbb{R}^2$ and $\mathbf{d}_i \in \mathbb{R}^2$ be pairs of points denoting the origin (start), respectively destination (end), points of a *journey*. By journey, we mean here the displacement, over a geographical map, of an entity (person, vehicle, or other object carrying information). Let $\mathbf{p}_i \subset \mathbb{R}^2$ denote the *path* being followed by this entity from origin to destination. Such paths are also called *origin–destination (OD) paths*.

We distinguish two path types: *straight-line paths* record only the tuple $(\mathbf{o}_i, \mathbf{d}_i)$, i.e., provide no information on how and where the actual motion occurred, while *trails* record the actual position of the entity over time over its journey as a sequence $\mathbf{x}(t_i^0), \ldots, \mathbf{x}(t_i^N)$ of points $\mathbf{x} \in \mathbb{R}^2$ recorded at consecutive time instants t_i^j. Besides spatial information, OD paths typically also include other data attributes. Per-path attributes $\mathbf{a}(\mathbf{p}_i)$ are values associated to an entire path $\mathbf{p}_i$, e.g., identity of the vehicle, type of vehicle, or cargo weight. Trail-based attributes $\mathbf{a}(\mathbf{x}_i^j)$ are values associated to actual sample points $\mathbf{x}_i^j = \mathbf{x}(t_i^j)$ along a trail, e.g., the speed and flying altitude of an aircraft. Attributes are most conveniently stored as (key, value) pairs, which allows different items (trails, sample points) to have different sets of attributes. Putting it all together, let $OD = \{\mathbf{o}_i, \mathbf{d}_i\}$ be the set of OD pairs under consideration, and let P be the set of straight-line paths or trails. An entire migration dataset is, thus, the tuple $D = (OD, P)$.

Trail data models trajectories, or paths, of entities over (typically) two-dimensional Euclidean space; straight-line OD paths are particular instances of trails containing only two points, the origin (O) and destination (D).

Graph data models abstract relations (also called edges) between node pairs. Formally, a graph is shown as $G = (V, E)$, with V being a vertex set and $E \subset V \times V$ being an edge set. Graphs are visualised by graph *drawings*, which are created by a so-called *graph layout* process. Graph drawings are also called *node–link visualisations*. A graph drawing can use straight lines or curves, which corresponds to straight-line OD path sets, respectively trail sets.

Graphs can be *constructed* from OD sets by clustering spatially close origin, respectively destination, points. Each point cluster c creates a vertex $\mathbf{v} \in V$. Paths linking two clusters c_1 and c_2 create an edge $\mathbf{e} \in E$ linking the clusters' respective vertices $\mathbf{v}_1$ and $\mathbf{v}_2$ from V.

Networks are, in visualisation, typically used as a synonym for the more theoretical term graphs.

dataset of US migrations (Holten and van Wijk, 2009). Every path (9780 in total) shows the migration (relocation) of one person from one city (O) to another city (D) in the US. The paths are colour-coded by their length, to help understand the

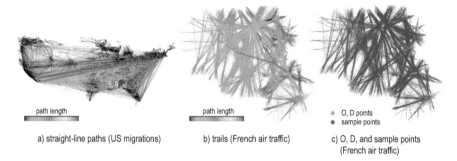

Figure 11.3 Examples of straight-line path data (a) and trail data (b,c). Figures generated with the open-source CUBu software (van der Zwan et al., 2016). Colour version printed as Plate 8.

visualisation. Image (b) shows a trail dataset containing 5255 civil aircraft trajectories recorded by air traffic control over French airspace during one week, also colour-coded by trail length (Hurter et al., 2014). The trails have between 50 and 200 sample points. Image (c) shows the actual O and D points for these trails (green) and their sample points (red).

Modelling time

The data model presented so far can integrate *time* in two different ways. *Sequence* models store consecutive snapshots D_i of the dataset D, recorded at different time instants i. Sequence models are used when one only uses the recording time i of an entire dataset D_i; for example, we have several datasets like the one in Figure 11.3b recorded for several weeks over a year. They only allow comparison of *global* movement patterns between two or more time moments. *Streaming* models store a single dataset D, in which the OD points of each path or trail $\mathbf{p}_i \in P$ have a time attribute. The lifetime of path $\mathbf{p}_i$ is thus the time interval $[t_i^0, t_i^N]$. Streaming models are used when one uses specific recording times for each individual path or trail. When available, they allow finer-grained comparison of motion over different space and/or time ranges. In the following we will cover both time-independent data and streaming and sequence models, outlining visualisation techniques suitable for each of these data types. For a more detailed discussion on visualising temporal multivariate data, we refer to (Archambault et al., 2013).

Visualisation techniques

Arguably the key challenge when visualising geographic movement data is caused by the *size* of the dataset D. When this is too large (roughly, over a few hundred elements) *clutter* occurs due to the many overlapping and/or intersecting paths, as already visible in Figure 11.3a,b. Clutter further impedes accomplishing even basic tasks using the visualisation. As such, visualisation methods aim to reduce such clutter by the various mechanisms described here.

Aggregating methods

These methods do not attempt to directly draw a dataset D. Rather, they simplify D into a dataset D' containing (far) fewer OD pairs and paths. When D' is under a certain size, typically a few tens or hundreds of items, it can be directly drawn with limited clutter, for example using straight-line drawing techniques (discussed next). Note that using straight-line drawing is not mandatory: when D' is small, custom techniques can be used to further reduce clutter, by routing (bending) the drawn paths to minimise overlap and/or intersection. Historically, this has been done by hand-drawing the paths in the simplified path-set P' of D'. Figure 11.4a–d shows four examples of such visualisations created by the French cartographer Minard (2020). This design, where the width of the curved paths is used to encode a path attribute, is also known under the name *flow maps* or *Sankey diagrams*. Image (a) shows a single-trail flow map depicting Hannibal's advance into Gaul and Italy, with path width encoding Hannibal's army size. Image (b) refines this design to show Napoleon's campaign in Russia.[1] As no accurate location data are available, consecutive OD points are now linked by straight-line segments; colour encodes the advance (brown) vs retreat (black) paths. Image (c) generalises this design to show the single-origin, multiple-destination map of French wine exports, with export volume encoded in path width. In contrast to designs (a) and (b), the paths are now curved to minimise overdraw, so the path shapes do not actually encode geographical information, a design we will encounter further on. Finally, image (d) shows a multiple-origin, multiple-destination dataset of people migration in 1858, with path width mapping the number of migrants, and colour encoding the continent of origin. Figure 11.4e shows a recent hand-drawn flow map depicting the intra-European migrations of 2006 (Hossmann *et al.*, 2008). Compared to the earlier Minard maps (Figure 11.4a–d) this design is simpler, as it uses so-called orthogonal (vertical and/or horizontal) path directions only. This follows studies in map visualisation that showed that reading such orthogonal layouts, also called 'metro map layouts', is easier than following layouts using paths drawn at arbitrary angles and/or using variable-angle bends (Wolff, 2007; Nöllenburg, 2014).

Several automatic aggregation methods for a path or trail dataset D exist. The most widespread, and easiest to use, aggregate origin and destination locations based on spatial proximity, thereby replacing clusters of densely located points by single points, typically the cluster centroids. The aggregation radius determines the simplification degree. Alternative techniques use generic clustering methods such

---

[1] While Minard's visualisation is technically impressive, the *insights* it conveys are doubtful. Minard created this visualisation in a period when Napoleon's rule was politically questionable in France, using data sources which highly exaggerated Napoleon's losses in Russia (Tufte, 2002). For a historically more accurate rendition, see (de Caulaincourt, 1933).

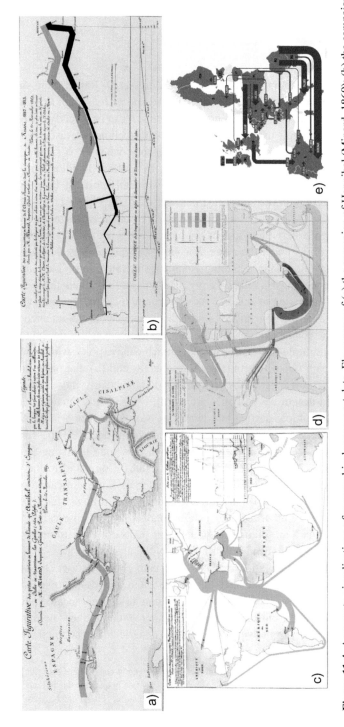

Figure 11.4 Aggregate visualisations of geographical movement data. Flow maps of (a) the campaign of Hannibal (Minard, 1869); (b) the campaign of Napoleon in Russia (Minard, 1869); (c) French wine exports (Minard, 1864); (d) word migration map (Minard, 1862); (e) intra-European migrations in 2006 (Hossmann et al., 2008). Colour version printed as Plate 4.

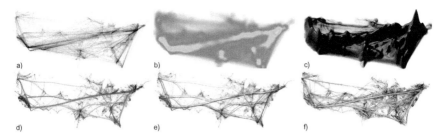

Figure 11.5 Visualisation of US migration dataset by several methods. From simple to involved: (a) blending of straight-line trails; (b) colour-coded density map; (c) height- and colour-coded density map; (d) bundled trails using path-length colouring; (e) directional bundling; (f) pseudo-shading of bundles. Figures generated with the open-source CUBu software (van der Zwan et al., 2016). Colour version printed as Plate 5.

as k-means (Luo et al., 2017). After obtaining the simplified dataset D', this can be depicted using standard graph drawing algorithms, which can carefully optimise the curving of paths to minimise clutter (Tamassia, 2013). Several standard libraries and tools exist that allow non-specialists to create such high-quality graph drawings (Gansner, 2020; Auber, 2004, 2020).

Density maps

These methods, also called heat maps, are motivated by the typical clutter created by directly drawing trails (Figure 11.3a). In contrast to the aggregating methods discussed above, they address this by aggregating the *drawing* of the dataset D rather than the actual *data* (trails). This is done by convolving the drawing of D with a Gaussian or Epanechnikov (parabolic) filter (van Liere and de Leeuw, 2003), a process known in image processing as kernel density estimation (KDE) (Comaniciu and Meer, 2002). The result is a density map that effectively merges trails closer than the width k of the filter, thereby simplifying the visualisation. Figure 11.5 shows this for the US migrations dataset in Figure 11.3a. Image (a) shows a naive computation of trail density, done by drawing the trails half-transparent. While dark regions indicate zones populated by more trails, close (but not exactly in the same position) trails are not grouped together. Image (b) shows the same drawing as in (a), this time convolved (blurred) by a Gaussian filter. We see how close trails get visually merged into high-density zones. This effectively simplifies the visualisation in image space, the simplification level being given by the blurring filter radius. Image (c) shows the same density map as in (b), with density mapped to both colour and height. The dense group of trails that connects the southwest to the northeast of the US now becomes even more salient. Summarising, density maps address Q1 ('Problem domain') well, and also remove small-scale clutter to create a simplified visualisation. For a formal discussion of KDE for trail visualisation, we further refer the reader to (Hurter, 2015).

Bundling methods

These methods share their motivation with the density maps described above, aiming to group similar trails to simplify the visualisation. In contrast to density maps, however, they *deform* the trails to accomplish this. Given a trail set $D = (OD, P)$, bundling (1) finds trails $\mathbf{p}_i \in P$ that are similar to each other, and (2) deforms these so they become even closer spatially. Trail similarity is typically computed using *both* the trail positions $\mathbf{x}_i^j$ and trail attributes $\mathbf{a}(\mathbf{p}_i)$ and/or $\mathbf{a}(\mathbf{x}_i^j)$. Spatial trail similarity, i.e., the term using the positions $\mathbf{x}^j$, is typically computed using Hausdorff distance (Rockafellar and Wetts, 2005; Lhuillier *et al.*, 2017). Attribute similarity is typically computed using the Euclidean distance between the $\mathbf{a}(\mathbf{p}_i)$ values of different trails $\mathbf{p}_i$. The two terms (spatial and attribute) are typically merged by weighting (Telea and Ersoy, 2010).

Formally put, bundling is nothing but applying the mean shift aggregation principle, well known in image analysis (Comaniciu and Meer, 2002), to the drawing of trails. Intuitively put, bundling 'pulls' similar trails in the visualisation towards their local common centre, so that they emerge as compact groups separated by whitespace. This way, one can easily see the main flow patterns present in a trail dataset.

Tens of bundling methods exist in visualisation literature; for a recent survey, we refer to (Lhuillier *et al.*, 2017). From a practical end-user perspective, these differ mainly in terms of ease of use, computational speed, and ease of implementation. As such, we next highlight only those that we consider to be the most interesting for data scientists involved in migration studies (who are not experts in visualisation, and require easy-to-use, scalable, readily available, and predictable methods). From this perspective, two methods stand out. The Kernel Density Estimation Edge Bundling (KDEEB) method (Hurter *et al.*, 2012) pioneered scalable and easy-to-use trail bundling. KDEEB is simple to explain: it computes a KDE density map of the trail set, and then advects (moves) trail sample points $\mathbf{x}^j$ upwards in the density gradient until reaching its maximum, following the mean shift principle (Comaniciu and Meer, 2002). The CUDA Universal Bundling (CUBu) method (van der Zwan *et al.*, 2016) refines and generalises KDEEB to efficiently use graphics hardware (NVIDIA CUDA GPUs) to bundle millions of trails in under one second on modern computers, and also provides different bundling styles in a single implementation.

Figures 11.5d–f show three examples of trail bundling for the US migrations dataset created with CUBu (which subsumes KDEEB and earlier bundling methods). Image (d) colours trails by their length, similar to Figure 11.3a. We see more clearly here than in the unbundled image (Figure 11.3a) where the longest migration trails are located: southwest to northeast, coloured red. Also, spatial migration patterns become clearer than in Figure 11.3a: we see that most migrations happen on the horizontal east–west axis, except for the US coast, where salient north–south patterns exist. Image (b) shows the bundled trails separated by migration *direction*. That is, migration flows between the same origin and destination areas yield distinct,

VISUAL EXPLORATION OF TRAJECTORY DATA   253

parallel, bundles. From this image, we see that migrations in both directions are balanced. Finally, image (f) shows the bundled migration trail-set with pseudo-shading, colour coded again by trail length. Bundles appear here as three-dimensional tubes seen from above, thereby reducing interpretation problems when they cross (see Figure 11.5a). For instance, the southwest–northeast migration bundle appears more saliently in this image than in Figure 11.5a.

Techniques for time-dependent data

For visualising time-dependent migration data (either sequence or streaming, see 'Data model'), two main technique classes exist. First, *small multiples* show separate visualisations of the snapshots D_i recorded at different time instants, side by side, using the same visualisation parameters. This way, users can compare the resulting images to spot (salient) differences and therefore infer (salient) changes. Figure 11.6a shows an example where six snapshots D_i, $1 \leq i \leq 6$, from a time-dependent dataset showing the travel of people using airlines in the US over six days is depicted using KDEEB bundling (Hurter *et al.*, 2013). Comparing the snapshots

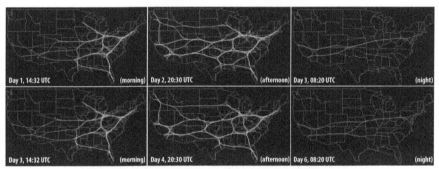

a) Six small-multiple snapshots from a visualization of US flights over a week.

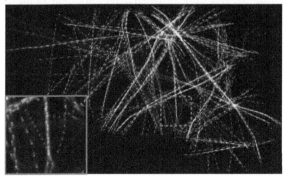

b) Snapshot of a particle visualization of flights over Paris

Figure 11.6 Visualisation of dynamic motion data using (a) small multiples (Hurter *et al.*, 2013) and (b) animation (Hurter *et al.*, 2014). Images generated by open-source software: (a) Hurter *et al.* (2013); (b) van der Zwan *et al.* (2016).

shows how travel patterns change over time; for instance, we see mainly east-coast travel in the morning, travel over the entire map at noon, and mainly long-haul east–west flights during the night. The key problem of small multiples is that it does not scale to more than a few time instants i. The alternative is to use *animation*, i.e., depict how imaginary travellers 'flow' over the paths $\mathbf{p}_i \in P$ over time. This can be done by seeding all $\mathbf{p}_i$ with particles (points) and then animating these over the trajectories of $\mathbf{p}_i$, while at the same time showing only paths whose lifetime $[t_i^0, t_i^N]$ encompasses the current (animation) time. Figure 11.6b shows a snapshot of such a particle visualisation depicting the air traffic over Paris at a given moment in a streaming dataset (Hurter et al., 2014). Animation demands less space than small multiples, but poses a higher burden on the user's memory to remember, and compare, spatial patterns occurring at different times. So far, the visualisation community advocates both small multiples and animation for showing time-dependent data, with no decisive arguments in favour, or against, either technique. More examples of such techniques are given in (Scheepens et al., 2015). Implementations of animation techniques are given in (Hurter, 2020).

Other visual encodings

So far, we have discussed visualisations based on the node–link metaphor. In this metaphor, several visual mappings are predefined: the coordinates of physical locations are mapped to origin and destination points in the screen space $\mathbf{o}_i \in \mathbb{R}^2$, respectively $\mathbf{d}_i \in \mathbb{R}^2$, while the migration flow data attributes are mapped to one or more multiple visual encodings applied to the paths or trails. Typical choices for these edge encodings are colour, thickness, or transparency. Hence, node–link visualisations implicitly emphasise location relationships, making them an effective choice for contextualised displays, e.g., maps.

However, other visualisations for migration data also exist; see Figure 11.7. Historically, these visualisations were designed to address some of the shortcomings of node–link metaphors. Ghoniem et al. (2004), for example, demonstrated that *matrix representations* outperform node–link ones for large or dense relational datasets on several graph analysis tasks. In our context, an (adjacency) matrix of a migration flow graph $G = (V, E)$ is a square matrix M where the cell m_{ij} captures information describing all edges $\mathbf{e}_k \in E$ between vertices $\mathbf{v}_i \in V$ and $\mathbf{v}_j \in V$. Hence, a matrix row or column depicts a node, while a matrix cell depicts edges between two given nodes. At the simplest level, $m_{ij} = 1$ indicates that at least such an edge exist, whereas $m_{ij} = 0$ means that $\mathbf{v}_i$ and $\mathbf{v}_j$ are not directly connected in G. Figure 11.7a shows a simple (directed) graph and its equivalent matrix representation. Note that undirected graphs correspond to symmetric matrices. At a more refined level, m_{ij} can aggregate one, or even multiple, attributes $\mathbf{a}(\mathbf{e}_k)$ defined over all edges $\mathbf{e}_k$. Adjacency matrices shift the emphasis away from the spatial contextualisation of the nodes and paths; that is, one cannot use them to reason about the spatial location or relative position of nodes and edges. In contrast, matrices scale visually very well,

VISUAL EXPLORATION OF TRAJECTORY DATA 255

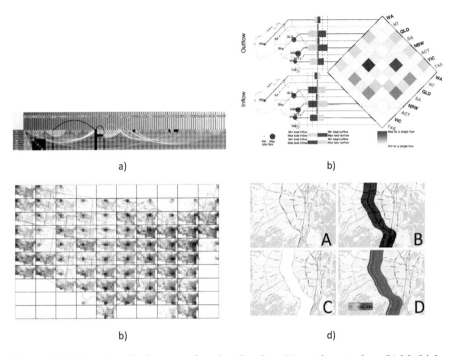

Figure 11.7 Other visualisation types for migration data: (a) matrix metaphor; (b) MatLink (Yang *et al.*, 2017); (c) MapTrix (Yang *et al.*, 2017); (d) OD Maps (Wood *et al.*, 2010); (e) SpaceCuts (Buchmüller *et al.*, 2016). Colour version printed as Plate 6.

as every edge-set $\mathbf{e}_k$ requires, in the limit, a single pixel to be shown. This allows graphs with thousands of nodes and millions of edges to be displayed on a typical computer screen. Also, matrices do not have any of the clutter and overdraw issues of node–link metaphors.

However, for path-related tasks, such as finding how any two vertices are connected (via paths formed by multiple edges), finding shortest routes, and also for contextualising the findings, matrix metaphors are significantly more demanding than node–link ones. Several visual extensions to the basic matrix metaphor aid this. Figure 11.7b shows one of these. Here, apart from showing edges in the matrix cells, these are drawn as curved arcs connecting the respective nodes along both rows and columns (Henry and Fekete, 2007). The user can visually 'follow' a sequence of arcs to find paths that indirectly connect nodes. The MapTrix tool (Yang *et al.*, 2017) re-embeds the geographic (spatial) context of migration flows into matrix displays (Figure 11.7c). This is done by connecting a matrix display (right on the figure) with a classical flow map display (Rae, 2009; left in the figure). The connecting lines (grey in Figure 11.7c) link each row and column (node in the matrix display) with its geographic location on a map, and can also show additional path attributes. OD maps (Wood *et al.*, 2010; Figure 11.7d) show another way to preserve spatial context. In this visualisation, the map is subdivided by a grid. For each grid cell, a heat map shows the density of origins (O) of all flows ending in that cell. This way, users can compare patterns of incoming flows between the grid cells. The heat maps are displayed into their respective cells, thereby conveying information on the destinations (D).

Other methods target depicting additional, potentially time-dependent, attributes of flows. For example, Space-cuts (Buchmüller *et al.*, 2016; Figure 11.7e) distorts the geographic maps by artificially introducing cuts along spatial landmarks, such as streets, rail tracks, or rivers. Flow attributes are shown by rendering them in the space created by the cuts. Contextualised glyph designs (Sun *et al.*, 2017) and interactive lenses (Krüger *et al.*, 2013) are additional solutions to the data scalability problem. However, these solutions are technically more complex to implement and learn to use.

Creating visualisations

Key questions related to the techniques outlined in 'Visualisation techniques' are: How easy is it to create such visualisations for the non-technical user, and how should she proceed to do this? We aim to answer these questions next by detailing the steps of creating an end-to-end visualisation pipeline, from having a data source up to the visual exploration design.

Data collection and curing

The first step, and arguably one of the most laborious, in constructing good visualisations is obtaining good *data*. By this, we mean a dataset D that strictly follows a variant of the schema in Figure 11.2. Obtaining such a D poses several challenges. Some major ones, and possible solutions, are described in this section.

Note that normalisation and value imputation are two important sources of bias in interpreting migration and mobility data. When these operations are used, prior to creating visualisations, they should be reported in the actual visualisation, e.g., by means of suitable legends or captions.

Attributes

The general schema discussed in 'Data model' (Figure 11.2) poses no constraints on path attributes: every path $\mathbf{p}_i$, and even every trail point $\mathbf{x}_i^j$, can have a variable number of attributes $\mathbf{a}(\mathbf{p}_i)$, respectively $\mathbf{a}(\mathbf{x}_i^j)$. To handle such attributes, a *regularisation* pass is needed. First, for all attribute values for the same key, the *types* of all attribute values $\mathbf{a}$ are found, scanning all their values over D, by examining their actual values. Based on their frequency, attributes $\mathbf{a}$ are typically classified as *quantitative* (real-valued numbers), *integral* (integer values), *ordinal* (values that allow ordering but whose absolute values do not capture extra semantics), and *categorical* (values which indicate different classes of objects). These types can be further refined, e.g., categorical values can be split into plain text or URLs. This step is key to the subsequent aggregation and visualisation of attributes. After this step, every value **a** for a path or sample point (Figure 11.2) will have an associated *type*.

Normalisation

Comparing attributes of different types (determined in the previous step), e.g., to compute path or trail similarity further needed for simplification ('Data model') requires normalising them. For numerical attributes, this is typically done by standardisation, i.e., replacing every value **a** by $(\mathbf{a} - \bar{\mathbf{a}})/\sigma(\mathbf{a})$, where $\bar{\mathbf{a}}$ is the attribute's average, and $\sigma(\mathbf{a})$ is the attribute's standard deviation, over all its values in D. Separately, handling trails $\mathbf{p}_i$ typically requires resampling these so that the spatial density of points $\mathbf{x}_i^j$ is roughly uniform over D. This is typically done by linear resampling $\mathbf{p}_i$, which also involves (typically linear) interpolation of the attributes $\mathbf{a}(\mathbf{x}_i^j)$.

Values

Real-world datasets often come with *missing* or *incorrect* values for the attributes **a**. These need sorting out, since virtually all visualisation methods require consistent attribute sets for all their samples $\mathbf{p}_i$ and/or $\mathbf{x}_i^j$. When such values are missing, they are usually replaced, in a process known as value imputation, by *averages* over the entire set of attribute values $\{\mathbf{a}(\mathbf{x}) \mid \mathbf{x} \in D\}$, or by special 'undefined' values if the attribute type of **a** allows this. Incorrect values are treated similarly, i.e., detected based on comparison with the expected range of **a**, and replaced by averages or defaults if non-conforming. (See also Box 5.1, this volume).

Data simplification and filtering

Simplification and filtering are interchangeable terms for two operations: (1) given a dataset D, how to reduce the number of *sample points* **x** (size reduction); and (2) how to reduce the number of *attributes* **a** (attribute reduction). These two simplification directions are orthogonal, and treated as follows.

Size reduction

This *speeds up* the creation and execution of visualisations, since fewer data items need to be drawn. Also, for node–link displays, it reduces clutter. More generally, size reduction allows the user to focus on the main, coarse-scale patterns present in the data. Size reduction can be done by two main mechanisms. *Selection* picks a subset $D' \subset D$ of the data elements to be explored, based, e.g., on specific values of attributes of interest, e.g., migration flows starting from a given country, connecting two given areas, or taking place in a specific time period. Selection works well when one knows *in advance* which are the subsets of interest D' and is extremely easy to implement. Figure 11.6a is an example of selection, as it shows six subsets D' of the entire time-dependent dataset D, selected based on time ranges. *Aggregation*, in contrast, replaces D by a new dataset $\overline{D}$ by replacing elements (paths, origins, destinations) of D that are deemed similar to aggregate versions thereof. The simplest form of aggregation is averaging. For example, the hand-drawn visualisations in Figure 11.4 are obtained this way. Here, the designer has manually grouped all flows between locations of interest. Aggregation can also be done automatically for graph data with tools such as LGC (Fountoulakis *et al.*, 2018) and Tulip (Auber, 2020), and for table-based data with tools such as Tableau (Tableau Inc., 2020). Aggregation does not require the user to select a specific subset of the data. However, it requires selecting a suitable *level of simplification* for the entire dataset.

Attribute reduction

This *simplifies* the visualisation creation, since less data-per-item need to be drawn. As for size reduction, this can be done by selection or aggregation. Selection picks a few attributes **a** from the entire available set, typically based on their keys ('Data model'), and encodes these into different visual channels, such as size, colour, transparency, and position. For example, Figure 11.5d shows the US migration dataset with colour encoding trail length, and position encoding the origin and destination coordinates. Since such visual channels are not independent, typically no more than three to four different attributes **a** can be visualised simultaneously. Aggregation replaces subsets of attributes **a** by a single attribute, again using suitable methods, such as averaging. This is more challenging to do than aggregation for size reduction, since now the attributes to be aggregated can be of different *types*, also having different *ranges*. It is hard to come up with generic guidelines on how to do attribute aggregation. However, a good starting point for practitioners is examining the standardisation and one-hot encoding techniques that have long been used in multidimensional data analysis. A good introductory textbook on this topic is Jolliffe (2002).

Designing the visual exploration

Having suitably cleaned and selected data, the final step is to choose a suitable *set* of visual exploration techniques. By set, we mean here the fact that an effective visualisation never consists of a single, static, image that depicts data. Rather, several techniques are combined, via user interaction, to allow one to *explore* the data and answer specific questions or complete specific tasks. Designing an effective visualisation is a complex process. Nevertheless, several general and well-tested guidelines can be given for this.

Overview, zoom and filter, then details on demand

This concept, also known under the name of 'Shneiderman's visual exploration mantra' (Shneiderman, 1996), is almost invariably used by all visualisation tools. Since users typically do not know *where* to start their exploration, the visualisation starts by presenting a global overview of the entire dataset, computed, e.g., using aggregation techniques ('Data simplification and filtering'). This helps to show interesting spatial patterns, into which the user zooms; alternatively, one can filter out uninteresting data aspects from the overview to simplify its exploration. Next, the user selects the patterns of interest, and examines these in more detail. The process is typically iterated until the questions of interest are answered. Technically, this requires designing visualisations which (1) are tightly coupled with data selection and aggregation mechanisms; and (2) which allow spatial zooming and panning.

Visual analytics loop

At a higher level, Shneiderman's design enables the creation of so-called *visual analytics* (VA) solutions for exploring data. Simply put, these are visualisation and data processing tools whose user interaction options (graphical user interfaces (GUIs), direct manipulation) are designed to best reflect the user's typical *workflow*. That is, rather than offering all options to the user in a 'flat' GUI (which is confusing, since one does not know then which options to use and in which order), options are grouped in wizard-like GUI designs that address specific tasks. The user then selects one such wizard to start the data exploration. The insights obtained allow her to form a *hypothesis* related to the data. Next, other wizards are used to examine the (subsets of the) data in detail to confirm, reject, or refine the hypothesis. The process loops until one arrives at a confirmed hypothesis, or, put more simply, answers one's original questions.

Figure 11.8 shows the workflow of such a VA tool designed to explore an urban mobility data from the greater São Paulo (SP) area in Brazil (Martins *et al.*, 2020). The input dataset D contains over 42 million trips of commuting people in SP over a single day in 2017. Every trip is an OD path annotated with hour of travel, means of transportation (e.g., by foot, bus, train, bike, car, or others), and trip reason (work, school, shopping, seek jobs, and others). Full details of this dataset, collected since 1967 by surveys, are given in Metrô SP (n.d.).

Mobility researchers in SP, including municipalities, want to understand the travel patterns to optimise transport. This implies answering a (wide) set of questions. VA can help here, as follows. The analyst loads the dataset D and first produces a number of aggregated charts showing the distributions or attributes

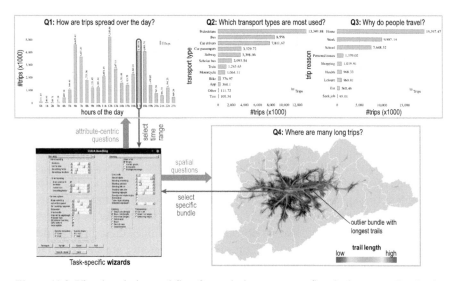

Figure 11.8 Visual analytics workflow for exploring commuter flow in the greater São Paulo area (Martins *et al.*, 2020), constructed using the CUBu open-source tool (van der Zwan *et al.*, 2016). Colour version printed as Plate 7.

a of *D* over the dataset. These simple, attribute-centric, questions can be readily answered by histogram bar charts, like those shown in Figure 11.8(top). There, three basic questions are answered: How are trips spread over the day (Q1)? Which transport types are mostly used (Q2)? Why do people travel? The three respective histograms show that the answers to these questions are, respectively, 'around 6AM, 12AM, and 12AM–6PM' (which would confirm the standard hypothesis related to work start, lunch break, and work end in Brazil); 'people mostly walk, then go by bus, then by car' (which is good to know since public transportation scores second highest, above private cars); and 'people travel most to go home, go to work, and go to school' (which can provide hints as to how one can help improving overall transportation).

Apart from these attribute-centric questions, one can also do spatial questions. A key one is: How are trips spread over the SP area? Figure 11.8(bottom right) shows this by using trail bundling (van der Zwan *et al.*, 2016). Here, trips are coloured by length, and opacity encodes bundled-trip density. We see a red outlier in the middle, signifying *many long trips* that go from west SP to east SP or conversely. Since opacity encodes trip density, the fact that a large part of the SP area is empty (grey) means that there are very few trips spanning peripheral regions. The 'core' of travel is within central SP, and the highest outlier (bottleneck) is the aforementioned west–east trajectory. Hence, if planners want to improve the situation, they should focus on this trajectory.

Given these global insights, users can next select *subsets* of the data, e.g., hours of the day, or particular trails. These are marked in Figure 11.8 in red. After selection, the VA process loops, but now only on the selected data, allowing users to pose more questions to understand *why* these events occur. Questions, and thus the creation of specific visualisations, are done by the GUI *wizards* (Figure 11.8 bottom left). The entire VA lop (queries, marked green, followed by selections, marked red in Figure 11.8, followed by inspecting the newly created visualisations) repeats until one is satisfied with the answers obtained.

This VA example is, obviously, a simple one; space constraints mean we cannot refer to all the existing options (van der Zwan *et al.*, 2016; Martins *et al.*, 2020). Still, it captures the *essence* of designing VA solutions for mobility exploration – visualisations, ranging from simple/aggregated to detailed ones, driven by user selection of data based on visualisation insights: the VA loop.

Putting it all together

A key challenge in implementing (interactive) visualisation systems is the availability of software tools. Visualisation tools are notoriously hard to replicate and/or implement, as underlying technology spans fields as diverse as algorithms and data structures, data mining and querying, computer graphics, image processing, computer vision, interactive techniques, and user interface design (Childs *et al.*, 2013). To assist the reader, Table 11.1 gives a few pointers to established freely available software tools that implement techniques discussed earlier in this chapter, also indicating how the software is available (open source or licence-based model). The

Table 11.1 Software for processing and visualising (multivariate) motion data

Name	Reference	Functionality	Availability	Skills
GraphViz	Gansner (2020)	Small graph layout and rendering	open source	A
Tulip	Auber (2020)	Large graph interactive visualisation	open source	A
KDEEB	Hurter *et al.* (2012)	Bundling spatial trails (basic)	open source	P
CUBu	van der Zwan *et al.* (2016)	Bundling spatial trails (extended)	open source	P
Particles	Hurter *et al.* (2014)	Animating particles along spatial trails	open source	P
Local Graph Clustering	Fountoulakis *et al.* (2018)	Graph simplification	open source	P
Sankey Diagrams	Phineas (2020)	Drawing Sankey diagrams	open source	A
Tableau	Tableau Inc. (2020)	Data cleaning, selection, aggregation	commercial[a]	A

[a] Tableau offers a free academic licence model.

rightmost column indicates the skill-set expected to use the software, i.e., if it targets any (A) users or users with programming (P) skills.

Discussion and conclusion

We have presented a roadmap for selecting and implementing visualisation solutions for exploring multidimensional trail data, such as describing the motion of persons over space and time. We have outlined how to represent such data, which are the main types of visualisation methods, and how to design the assembly of an end-to-end visual exploration pipeline for such data. This provides, we believe, practical guidelines for researchers in different fields (especially those not close to computer science) to select, instantiate, and combine such methods to answer their questions.

Still, it is important to pinpoint several open questions regarding the state of the art, or, more precisely, what current tools can offer, in this respect.

Scalability

How to visually explore large trail sets at interactive rates (millions of trails, hundreds of sample points, tens of attributes)? Bundling and data aggregation methods cover the first two points (number of trails and sample points). Aggregating multiple attributes is still an open question, given the fundamentally different types, and ranges, thereof. Also, given the mentioned hard limit of visualising only a few attributes at a time ('Data simplification and filtering'), this is, we believe, one of the key open issues in the field.

Interpretability

A visualisation conveys, by construction, a *simplified* view of the data D it receives. Hence, it makes needed simplifications. The question is: How do these simplifications affect the *interpretation* of the data, i.e., the conclusions users will draw from it? A case in point is bundling: while reducing occlusion in visualisations, it also *deforms* actual trails, thereby potentially misleading users who expect to see accurate spatial locations. Conveying the fact that (bundled) visualisations are necessary simplifications of the actual data is also an open challenge.

Quality

Given all the inherent limitations of visualisation design discussed in this chapter, it is obvious that one cannot design the 'perfect' visualisation. Hence, ways (metrics) to gauge the quality of a visualisation are needed. For attributed trail data, these are quite scarce. For instance, we still have no theory, let alone metrics, to gauge the quality of a bundling (Lhuillier *et al.*, 2017). Hence, visualisations are most often evaluated by means of controlled studies. However, when deploying them to explore migration data, which is inherently sensitive and open to controversies, ground truth (required by controlled studies) is typically missing.

Replicability

The last, but definitely not the smallest, issue in visualisation is replicability. Using a visualisation proposal presented in academic research (papers) implies being able to *exactly* replicate the setup presented by the authors. This is increasingly hard to do, even for visualisation professionals. The key reason is the increasing complexity of visualisation algorithms and methods, most of which are not available as open-source software. As such, the optimal solution for the interested practitioner is to rely on potentially less cutting-edge methods which are openly available (see, e.g., Table 11.1).

Conclusion

Nevertheless, considering all these challenges, we believe that the current chapter has presented a convincing set of use-cases, with supporting methodology and tooling, that will help migration scientists to explore, experiment with, adopt, and use visualisation methods for trail data, thereby enhancing their understanding and the insights obtained from their respective datasets.

References

Archambault, D., Abello, J., Kennedy, J., Kobourov, S., Ma, K.-L., Miksch, S., Muelder, C., and Telea, A. (2013), 'Temporal multivariate networks', *in* A. Kerren, H. C. Purchase, and M. O. Ward, eds, *Multivariate Network Visualization*, Springer, New York, 151–73.
Auber, D. (2004), 'Tulip: A huge graph visualization framework', *in* M. Junger and P. Mützel, eds, *Graph Drawing Software*, Springer, New York, 105–26.
Auber, D. (2020), 'Tulip graph visualization framework', available at https://tulip.labri.fr
Bilsborow, R. E. (2016), 'The global need for better data on international migration and the special potential of household surveys', *in Proceedings of Improving Data on International Migration: Towards Agenda 2030 and the Global Compact on Migration*, Global Migration Data Analysis Centre, Berlin.
Boyandin, I. (2010), 'JFlowMap flow map visualization tool', available at https://code.google.com/archive/p/jflowmap
Boyandin, I., Bertini, E., and Lalanne, D. (2010), 'Visualizing migration flows and their development in time: Flow maps and beyond', *in Proceedings of the IEEE Symposium on Information Visualization (InfoVis)*.

Buchmüller, J., Jäckle, D., Stoffel, F., and Keim, D. A. (2016), 'SpaceCuts: Making room for visualizations on maps', *in* E. Bertini, N. Elmqvist, and T. Wischgoll, eds, *Proceedings of the Eurographics Conference on Visualization, EuroVis 2016*, Eurographics Association, 67–71.

Childs, H., Geveci, B., Schroeder, W., Meredith, J., Moreland, K., Sewell, C., Kuhlen, T. and Bethel, E. W. (2013), 'Research challenges for visualization software', *Computer* 46(5), 34–42.

Comaniciu, D. and Meer, P. (2002), 'Mean shift: A robust approach toward feature space analysis', *IEEE Transactions on Pattern Analysis and Machine Intelligence* 24(5), 603–19.

de Caulaincourt, A. (1933), *Mémoires*, Editions Plon, Paris.

Fountoulakis, K., Meng, L., Gleich, D. F., and Mahoney, M. W. (2018), 'Local graph clustering software', available at https://github.com/kfoynt/LocalGraphClustering

Gansner, E. (2020), 'GraphViz graph drawing toolkit', available at https://www.graphviz.org

Gapminder (2020), 'Gapminder visualization tool', available at https://www.gapminder.org/tools

Ghoniem, M., Fekete, J., and Castagliola, P. (2004), 'A comparison of the readability of graphs using node–link and matrix-based representations', *in Proceedings of the IEEE Symposium on Information Visualization (InfoVis)*, 17–24.

Google Inc. (2020), 'Google charts API', available at https://developers.google.com/chart

Henry, N. and Fekete, J.-D. (2007), 'MatLink: Enhanced matrix visualization for analyzing social networks', *in* C. Baranauskas, P. Palanque, J. Abascal, and S. Barbosa, *INTERACT'07: Proceedings of the 11th IFIP TC 13 International Conference on Human–Computer Interaction*, Vol. II, Springer, Berlin, 288–302.

Hoffman, D. R. (2003), *Effective Database Design for Geoscience Professionals*, PennWell Corp., Tulsa, OK.

Holten, D. and van Wijk, J. J. (2009), 'Force-directed edge bundling for graph visualization', *Computer Graphics Forum* 28(3), 983–90.

Hossmann, I., Karsch, M., Klingholz, R., Köhncke, Y., Kröhnert, S., Pietschmann, C., and Sütterlin, S. (2008), *Europe's Demographic Future*, Berlin Institute for Population and Development.

Hurter, C. (2015), *Image-Based Visualization: Interactive Multidimensional Data Exploration*, Morgan & Claypool, San Rafael, CA.

Hurter, C. (2020), 'Implementation of particle systems for time-dependent trail visualization'. Open source software, available at http://recherche.enac.fr/~hurter/RealTimeBundling.html

Hurter, C., Ersoy, O., Fabrikant, S. I., Klein, T. R., and Telea, A. C. (2014), 'Bundled visualization of dynamic graph and trail data', *IEEE Transactions on Visualization and Computer Graphics* 20(8), 1141–57.

Hurter, C., Ersoy, O., and Telea, A. (2012), 'Graph bundling by kernel density estimation', *Computer Graphics Forum* 31(3), 865–74. Software available at http://recherche.enac.fr/~hurter/KDEEB.html

Hurter, C., Ersoy, O., and Telea, A. (2013), 'Smooth bundling of large streaming and sequence graphs', *in Proceedings of the IEEE Pacific Visualization Symposium, PacificVis*, 41–48. Software available at http://recherche.enac.fr/~hurter/KDEEB.html

Jolliffe, I. T. (2002), *Principal Component Analysis*, 2nd edn, Springer, New York.

Krüger, R., Thom, D., Wörner, M., Bosch, H., and Ertl, T. (2013), 'TrajectoryLenses: A set-based filtering and exploration technique for long-term trajectory data', *Computer Graphics Forum* 32(3), 451–60.

Lhuillier, A., Hurter, C., and Telea, A. (2017), 'State of the art in edge and trail bundling techniques', *Computer Graphics Forum* 36(3), 619–45.

Luo, D., Cats, O., and van Lint, H. (2017), 'Constructing transit origin–destination matrices with spatial clustering', *Transportation Research Record: Journal of the Transportation Research Board* 2652(1), 39–49.

Martins, T., Lago, N., de Souza, H., Santana, E., Telea, A., and Kon, F. (2020), 'Visualizing the structure of urban mobility with bundling: A case study of the city of São Paulo', *in Proceedings of the SBRC CoUrb Workshop*.

MDP (2020), 'Migration data portal', available at https://migrationdataportal.org

Metrô SP (n.d.), *A mobilidade urbana da região metropolitana de São Paulo em detalhes*, Secretaria Estadual dos Transportes Metropolitanos e Companhia do Metropolitano de São Paulo, São Paulo.

Minard, C.-J. (2020), 'Tableaux graphiques et cartes figuratives'. Bibliothèque numérique patrimoniale des ponts et chaussées, available at https://patrimoine.enpc.fr/document/ENPC01_Fol_10975

Munzner, T. (2009), 'A nested model for visualization design and validation', *IEEE Transactions on Visualization and Computer Graphics* 15(6), 921–8.

Nöllenburg, M. (2014), 'A survey on automated metro map layout methods', *in Proceedings of the Schematic Mapping Workshop*.

Phineas (2020), 'Sankey diagram software', available at http://www.sankey-diagrams.com/sankey-diagram-software

Rae, A. (2009), 'From spatial interaction data to spatial interaction information? Geovisualisation and spatial structures of migration from the 2001 UK census', *Computers, Environment and Urban Systems* 33(3), 161–78.

Refugee Processing Center (2020), 'Refugee data: Admissions and arrivals', available at https://www.wrapsnet.org/admissions-and-arrivals

Rockafellar, R. T. and Wetts, J. R. (2005), *Variational Analysis*, Springer, New York.

Scheepens, R., Hurter, C., van de Wetering, H., and Wijk, J. J. V. (2015), 'Visualization, selection, and analysis of traffic flows', *IEEE Transactions on Visualization and Computer Graphics* 22(1), 379–88.

Shneiderman, B. (1996), 'The eyes have it: A task by data type taxonomy for information visualizations', *in Proceedings of the IEEE Symposium on Visual Languages*, 336–43.

Sterly, H. and Wirkus, L. (2022), 'Analysing refugees' secondary mobility using mobile phone call detail records', *in* A. A. Salah, E. E. Korkmaz, and T. Bircan, eds, *Data Science for Migration and Mobility*, Proceedings of the British Academy, British Academy/Oxford University Press, London, UK.

Sun, G., Liang, R., Qu, H., and Wu, Y. (2017), 'Embedding spatio-temporal information into maps by route-zooming', *IEEE Transactions on Visualization and Computer Graphics* 23(5), 1506–19.

Tableau Inc. (2020), 'Tableau data visualization tool', available at https://www.tableau.com

Tamassia, R. (2013), *Handbook of Graph Drawing and Visualization*, CRC Press, Boca Raton, FL.

Telea, A. and Ersoy, O. (2010), 'Image-based edge bundles: Simplified visualization of large graphs', *Computer Graphics Forum* 29(3), 843–52.

Tufte, E. (2002), 'Minard's sources for the Napoleon campaign visualization', available at https://www.edwardtufte.com/tufte/minard

van der Zwan, M., Codreanu, V., and Telea, A. (2016), 'CUBu: Universal real-time bundling for large graphs', *IEEE Transactions on Visualization and Computer Graphics* 22(12), 2550–63. Software publicly available at http://www.staff.science.uu.nl/~telea001/uploads/Software/CUBu

van Liere, R. and de Leeuw, W. (2003), 'GraphSplatting: Visualizing graphs as continuous fields', *IEEE Transactions on Visualization and Computer Graphics* 2(9), 206–12.

Von Landesberger, T., Kuijper, A., Schreck, T., Kohlhammer, J., van Wijk, J. J., Fekete, J.-D., and Fellner, D. W. (2011), 'Visual analysis of large graphs: State of the art and future research challenges', *Computer Graphics Forum* 30(6), 1719–49.

Wolff, A. (2007), 'Drawing subway maps: A survey', *Informatik Forschung und Entwicklung* 22, 23–44.

Wood, J., Dykes, J., and Slingsby, A. (2010), 'Visualisation of origins, destinations and flows with OD maps', *The Cartographic Journal* 47(2), 117–29.

Yang, Y., Dwyer, T., Goodwin, S., and Marriott, K. (2017), 'Many-to-many geographically-embedded flow visualisation: An evaluation', *IEEE Transactions on Visualization and Computer Graphics* 23(1), 411–20.

12

Voyage Viewer: A Multivariate Visualisation Tool for Migration Analysis

ISABELLA LOAIZA, GERMÁN SÁNCHEZ, SERENA CHAN,
FELIPE MONTES JIMÉNEZ, MOHSEN BAHRAMI, AND
ALEX PENTLAND

Introduction

THE STUDY OF displaced populations is often hampered by missing, scattered, and incomplete data, making it more difficult for researchers, NGOs, policy-makers, and migrants to understand the process of migration and make informed decisions. Some even argue that our knowledge about how to harness data to maximise the benefits and minimise the costs of migration is still at a global shortage (Bilsborrow, 2016). Indeed, some authors declare the need for radical innovation in how we visualise, model, and study human mobility as a multidimensional process that involves space, time, and context (Dodge, 2021).

The shortcomings with migration data are partly due to the traditional survey methods used to collect information about migrants. Surveys are time and resource intensive, they are challenging to scale, and the data collected by different actors is not easy to combine or compare. Recent advances in computational methods, together with the availability of new large-scale datasets, provide governments and NGOs with an effective alternative to analyse, synthesise, and map the mechanics of migrants, refugees, and displaced populations. Smartphone traces and data from social media platforms like Facebook and Twitter are already being used to study migration in cities (Spyratos *et al.*, 2019; Palotti *et al.*, 2020; Hawelka *et al.*, 2014). Despite these efforts, the study of global human mobility remains fragmented across borderlines and limited to snapshots of a migrant's journey, unable to provide a complete picture of the migration process.

An essential step in creating a more cohesive understanding of human migration at a planetary scale is to develop tools that gather the multitude of data available into easily digestible visual representations. This chapter introduces Voyage Viewer, an open, online interactive tool that seeks to advance in this direction. Voyage Viewer harnesses the power of novel datasets and traditional data sources to depict the journeys, the processes, and the challenges that migrants endure on the road and at their destinations. Using data from multiple venues, Voyage Viewer aids in knowledge synthesis, which in turn helps bridge the gap between research and decision-making (Tricco *et al.*, 2011). Thus, by synthesising our disparate information about migration into interactive visualisations that governments, NGOs, citizens, and migrants can use to inform, communicate, and make decisions, Voyage Viewer hopes to revolutionise how we understand and tackle humanitarian crises caused by forced displacement.

Transforming the multi-source data into clear visualisations is another critical aspect in which Voyage Viewer contributes to a better understanding of migration. Visualisations are powerful tools to help the human brain process data more quickly and efficiently than other types of data representations (Morrison and Vogel, 1998; Lazard and Atkinson, 2015). They can illustrate attributes of the data, display associations between variables, and aid in differentiating datasets that may otherwise have identical summary statistics (Avraam *et al.*, 2021).

Visualising migration data can shed light on migration patterns that might be irregular, or occur across large geographical spaces or over long periods. For example, by visualising migrant flows over time, it might be possible to detect seasonal patterns previously thought to be erratic. Similarly, mapping migration can provide insights into where different types of migrants go (Loaiza *et al.*, 2020). Hence, having these visualisations helps local governments more precisely target social programs towards areas where they can have a higher impact on migrant relief.

Web-based applications with interactive and animated charts have enlarged our toolkit to visualise flow data. Interactive visualisations avoid clutter and allow users to focus on the most relevant parts of the information presented. Yet, interactive, web-enabled visualisations about migration or human mobility are still rare (Ho *et al.*, 2011).

This chapter has six sections. The first has introduced Voyage Viewer. The second section summarises related work and compares online visualisations about migrants and migration. The third section describes the design rationale behind Voyage Viewer and details the resources that make up the tool. The fourth section shows how Voyage Viewer may be used in two different use cases. The fifth section discusses Voyage Viewer's current limitations, and the final section provides some conclusions and highlights avenues for future work.

Related work

Creating accurate and clear images with many flows is a challenging task. Displaying thousands or even a few hundred migration routes can quickly produce cluttered and confusing visualisations that hamper comprehension. Some practical ways to tackle this problem in static images are the aggregation, clustering, or bundling of paths (Luo *et al.*, 2017; Lhuillier *et al.*, 2017). These techniques have been widely studied but are outside the scope of this chapter. Instead, in Chapter 11 of this book Telea and Behrisch (2022) provide an in-depth review of such techniques. Other guides and compilations about the best practices on flow representation for non-technical users to produce high-quality visualisations are also available in the literature (Rae, 2009; Chakraborty et al., 2015; Dodge, 2021). This section describes and compares several visualisations about migration and other humanitarian causes, and the second part describes tools meant to visualise migration data.

Visualisations for migration

Interactive, web-based visualisations have been around for almost a decade. Most focus on the flow of goods,[1] economic development[2] (Simoes and Hidalgo, 2011), and city life.[3] However, interactive visualisations for humanitarian crises have a more recent history. Examples of these visualisations include the Humanitarian Needs Overview from United Nations Office for the Coordination of Humanitarian Affairs (OCHA) Centre for Humanitarian Data,[4] the World Health Organisation's Natural Disasters Mortality Dashboard,[5] and the many animated and interactive visualisations created to monitor the evolution of the Covid-19 pandemic[6] and the vaccination efforts that followed it.[7]

To establish what exists in terms of visualisation for migration, we compare 13 different projects from industry, academia, and multilateral organisations. This list is not exhaustive, but it does include essential visualisations made by relevant actors in migration studies. Comparing different visualisations about migration is difficult due to the diverse set of goals, scopes, and datasets used in each project. Therefore, we identified 14 important dimensions to consider when building a visualisation for migration studies or humanitarian crises. Then, we qualified to what extent each of the projects on our list satisfied these dimensions, and summarised our conclusions in the heat map shown in Figure 12.1. Many of the dimensions we consider to remain open areas of research for user interface / user experience (UI/UX) design (see Box 12.1).

The heat map is coloured with a diverging colour map that has blue at one end and pink at the other. The darker the blue, the better that particular visualisation scores in that dimension. When we couldn't find enough information to score a project on any given dimension, that slot on the heat map is coloured red. Thus, the more blue present in one row, the more complete and clear the visualisations. To

---

[1] International trade in goods and services based on UN Comtrade data, https://dit-trade-vis.azurewebsites.net/?reporter=826&type=C&year=2019&flow=2&commodity
[2] The Observatory of Economic Complexity, https://oec.world/
[3] Atlas of Inequality, https://inequality.media.mit.edu
[4] The Centre for Humanitarian Data, https://centre.humdata.org/
[5] WHO: Mortality due to natural disasters, https://apps.who.int/gho/data/node.sdg.13-1-viz?lang=en
[6] New York Times: Tracking coronavirus vaccinations around the world, https://www.nytimes.com/interactive/2021/world/covid-vaccinations-tracker.html; John Hopkins Coronavirus Resource Centre, https://coronavirus.jhu.edu/
[7] Time to Herd, https://timetoherd.com/

Box 12.1 UI/UX dimensions for designing visualisations for big data

We briefly summarise 14 UI/UX dimensions for designing visualisations and their use in Voyage Viewer specifically.

1. *Interactivity:* the extent to which the visualisation lets the user influence or change the content displayed (Kweon et al., 2008; Sundar et al., 2010).
2. *User-friendliness:* the level of difficulty for the user to understand the different elements of the visualisation and how to interact with it.
3. *Mental load:* the amount of 'mental energy' required to process a given amount of information (Feinberg and Murphy, 2000) and the burden put on the user's working memory (previously called short-term memory) (Keller et al., 2019). In general, the higher the mental load, the more difficult it is for the user to understand and remember the information presented.
4. *Map-based representation:* the use of a map, for example to show information about humans on the move.
5. *Non-map-based representation:* whether the project includes other types of visualisations that are not based on maps or geographical representations. Types of visualisations that fall under this category include, but are not limited to, bar charts, bubble charts, scatter plots, line plots, Sankey diagrams, and heat maps.
6. *Flows:* the extent to which the visualisation contains information about the origins, destinations, and paths of humans on the move.
7. *Multiple indicators:* the extent to which the visualisation contains metrics or indicators different from just the number of humans. For migration, these indicators should describe or capture the migrant experience. Examples are demographic indicators, or measures of the level of migrants' economic integration.
8. *Zoom-ability:* the ability to look at the data across different spatial and temporal scales. Can the user see migrant counts at country, state, and county levels? Is it possible for the user to restrict the visualisation output to a few years instead of a decade?
9. *Multiple data sources:* whether the visualisation was built using data from a sole source or several datasets, for example to show migration from various angles.
10. *Multiple types of migrants:* responds to the questions: What kind of migrants does the visualisation show? Does it focus on one type of migrant like 'refugees', or does it encompass different types?
11. *Continuous update:* how often the visualisation is updated to reflect recent data. If there was no information about the regularity of update, we assume the visualisation is not actively maintained.
12. *Geographical scope:* how much of the world the visualisation encompasses – the world, a region, a country.
13. *Transparency:* how easy it is for the user to understand where the data came from, and whether or not the visualisation makes their methodology public.
14. *Call to action:* does the visualisation compel the user to take action to help the migrants either by asking for donations or providing links to relevant literature or tools?

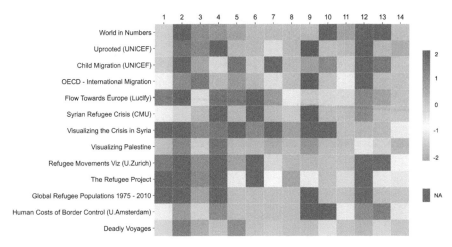

Figure 12.1 Heat map comparing different visualisations for migration. This heat map compares different visualisation projects across 14 dimensions. Rows correspond to individual visualisations and columns to dimensions of analysis. Each column is labelled with a number that corresponds to the same numbered dimension in Box 12.1.

arrive at the final scores in the heat map we averaged the scores given by each of the authors in this chapter.

To begin the comparison, we look at three visualisations made or sponsored by the United Nations. The first, shown in Figure 12.2B, is The World in Numbers[8] from the United Nations High Commissioner for Refugees (UNHCR). It features an interactive map that shows the global stocks of displaced peoples due to conflict, war, persecution, and human rights violations. The interface is straightforward and user-friendly. The information presented is limited to the stocks of migrants per country and does not include data about flows. The emphasis is on the map-based representation, with only one bar chart accompanying it. This project is also limited in its zoomability, since it only shows data at a country level and only uses data recovered by UNHCR. However, in terms of the types of migrants it includes information about, The World in Numbers is one the most encompassing visualisations among those considered here. It includes data about refugees, asylum seekers, internally displaced people, returnees, and stateless people.

The second visualisation in the heat map was created for a UNICEF-sponsored hackathon about child migration using data from the Uprooted report published in 2016 (UNICEF Rapport Uprooted, 2016). A snapshot of this visualisation is shown in Figure 12.2C. Because it was made for the purpose of the hackathon, this project uses only one source of data, it focuses exclusively on one migrant population, migrant children, and it is not constantly updated. Yet, it has a clean, interactive design that does not overload the user's mental capacity. It has two map-based

---

[8] UNHRC Statistics, https://data2.unhcr.org/en/dataviz/6

272   Loaiza et al.

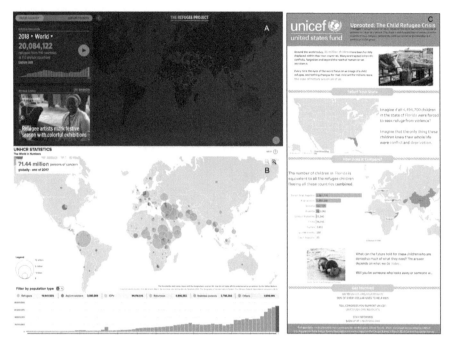

Figure 12.2 Examples of visualisations for migration. This figure shows screenshots of selected visualisations about migration. A The interface to the Refugee Project. B The interface of the World in Numbers. C The visualisation prepared for UNICEF with the data from the Uprooted report of 2016. Colour version printed as Plate 9.

visualisations in addition to a bar chart, a clear call to action, and it has an overall powerful and clear message.

The last project from the UN is the set of visualisations about child migration on UNICEF's website.[9] This visualisation is one of the few in our sample that do not rely heavily on a map-based representation. Instead, UNICEF makes use of other types of charts like bar charts, Sankey diagrams, and chord diagrams. The diversity of diagrams conveys a more holistic picture of child migration around the world.

The fourth visualisation on the list was made by the OECD.[10] It features several bar charts showing the number of migrants per country. This is one of the less complete visualisations in the group, as it has limited interactivity, no map-based visualisation, does not show migrant flows, and is not zoomable. We could not find the source of the data on the website, and thus gave this visualisation a 'Not Applicable' score on the multiple data sources dimension.

The Flow Towards Europe[11] is an example of a visualisation about a humanitarian crisis, created by Lucify (a private company). It is an interactive visualisation

---

[9] UNICEF: Child Migration, https://data.unicef.org/topic/child-migration-and-displacement/migration
[10] OECD: Data visualisation for key OECD data, https://www.oecd.org/statistics/compare-your-country.htm
[11] The flow towards Europe, https://www.lucify.com/the-flow-towards-europe/

that shows the scale of the European refugee crisis based on data from the United Nations. The Flow Towards Europe highlights the scale on which asylum seekers arrived in European countries over time. However, it does not consider other types of migrants. In contrast to other visualisations on the list, this one uses animation to show the flow of migrants. It also uses an aggregation approach by taking each point to represent 25 refugees. While the result is an aesthetically attractive visualisation, it has limitations in how accurately it can depict migration routes and travel times, and it poses a larger mental load on the user. Lucify complements its map-based visualisation by including a Sankey diagram and other visual representations of the number of Syrian refugees seeking asylum in Europe between April 2011 and December 2017. Another instance of a privately created visualisation is Visualising Palestine.[12] While the visualisations available on this site are static images and do not provide any interactivity for users, they clearly show their sources of data and are a good example of how visualisations can be used to show migration crises all over the world.

In a similar vein, the Global Refugee Populations 1975–2010 is a visualisation of the global refugee populations and their evolution over those 35 years.[13] Each country includes a refugee population by year and the number of refugees from the country. It has certain limitations, including estimated data based on refugee arrival through resettlement programs and individual recognition over a 10-year and 5-year period; many industrialised countries do not have a refugee register with reliable data.

Universities and academics have also contributed their visualisations to study migration, with several of them focusing on the Syrian Refugee crisis. At Carnegie Mellon University, a team created a visualisation that shows the monthly progression of refugee movements worldwide to three main locations, Greece, Italy, and Spain, between the years 2014 and 2016.[14] This visualisation across the Mediterranean Sea includes information about destination countries, migrant deaths, and asylum countries, but is limited in the interactivity it provides for users. Other similar efforts are the Syria Visualised Project[15] and the Refugee Movements Visualiser from the University of Zurich.[16]

Other projects created by academia with a broader focus are the University of Amsterdam's The Human Costs of Border Control[17] and the Deadly Voyages visualisation made from Monash University's Australian Border Deaths database.[18] As suggested by their names, both projects gather information about deaths that

[12] Visualizing Palestine: Gaza's untold story, https://visualizingpalestine.org/visuals/gaza-refugee-deaths
[13] Global Refugee Populations 1975–2010, http://c15119308.r8.cf2.rackcdn.com/infographic-global-refugee-populations-1975-2010/index.html
[14] Refugees by Mediterranean Sea, https://explorables.cmucreatelab.org/unreleased/sabbasi/refugees/
[15] Visualizing the Crisis in Syria, https://www.syria-visualized.com/#aboutSection
[16] Refugee Movements, https://refugeemovements.com/main#teambanner
[17] Human Costs of Border Control, http://www.borderdeaths.org/
[18] Monash University: Australian Border Deaths Database, https://www.monash.edu/arts/border-crossing-observatory/research-agenda/australian-border-deaths-database

occurred in the process of migration across different geographies. The Human Costs of Border Control provides a death count for migrants arriving in Southern Europe, and thus its scope is limited at the regional level. When available, it also provides more demographic information about the deceased. The visualisations on its website are simple and easy to understand. A map-based visualisation is included, but it is not clear if they use one or multiple sources of information. The visualisation made using Monash University's data about migrants deaths that occurred in transit to Australia is less interactive and has a smaller scope. The power of these visualisations, however, lies not in their sophistication but in the message they bring forth about the perils of migration.

Finally, The Refugee Project,[19] an interactive online visualisation created by a design studio, is one of the best examples of visualisation applied to migration in our list. It features a map of refugee movements over the last 40 years, while also including historical context to the data in the form of news. The interface, shown in Figure 12.2A, features a map-based representation that shows the stocks of migrants and the flows across countries. With tooltips and charts that update to reflect a country's information when clicked, it is one of the most interactive visualisations on the list. It also cites and links to the sources of data for higher transparency.

Design rationale

Voyage Viewer is a visualisation tool for migration data. It collects public data from conventional sources (governments, multilateral organisations) and anonymised, privacy-preserving digital traces from social media, mobile phone metadata, and mapping applications like OpenStreetMap.[20] By making use of different data sources and combining novel and traditional datasets, Voyage Viewer provides a more complete picture of migration around the world. Additionally, by using data from digital traces, some of the metrics shown in Voyage Viewer capture the process of migration from the viewpoint of migrants themselves (Curry *et al.*, 2019). To explain in detail the different parts of Voyage Viewer, in this section we delve into the inputs and resources needed to build it, the activities and outputs it produces, and outline the outcomes we hope to achieve as charted in Figure 12.3.

Inputs and resources

Traditional data

Voyage Viewer uses traditional data sources collected through the censuses, household surveys, data from government agencies, national statistics offices, and multilateral organisations such as the UNHCR and the International Organisation for

---

[19] The Refugee Project, http://www.therefugeeproject.org/#/1981
[20] OpenStreetMap, https://www.openstreetmap.org/

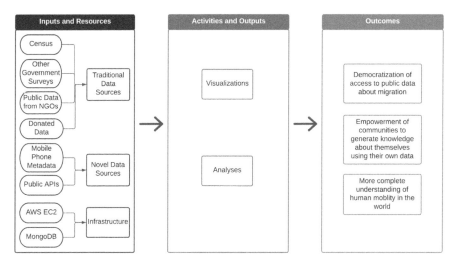

Figure 12.3 Voyage Viewer inputs and resources, outputs and outcomes. This diagram shows the resources that Voyage Viewer is built on, the different outputs it produces, and its expected outcomes.

Migration (IOM). These sources make up the backbone of the data currently available for visualisation with Voyage Viewer. Most countries regularly conduct surveys or censuses that provide public data about their people. Hence, incorporating these kinds of data provides Voyage Viewer with a global-level view of migration around the world. At the time of writing, Voyage Viewer contains information from household surveys for multiple countries in Latin America, Europe, and Australia. Part of these datasets were obtained from the Integrated Public Use Microdata Series Project at the University of Minnesota.[21] Others were obtained directly from the repositories of national statistics bureaus.

These datasets have several constraints regarding their temporal resolution. Due to their cost and limited scalability, most censuses are carried out several years or even decades apart, providing data points that might be too far apart for the effective study of migration. Similarly, the sampling methods used for these surveys are calibrated to produce results that are representative of the local population but are likely to under-sample migrants, especially those who live in poverty, depend on informal jobs, and are without homes.

To supplement these datasets and overcome some of their shortcomings, Voyage Viewer also incorporates other datasets collected with traditional methods, but whose primary purpose is to document migrant populations, their journeys, and characteristics.

To highlight the hardships and challenges that migrants have to overcome in their journeys and the risks that refugees must endure while making their way

---

[21] IPUMS International, https://international.ipums.org/international/

to their destinations, Voyage Viewer includes data about migrant fatalities and disappearances from several external sources. Perhaps most commonly known is the IOM's Missing Migrant Project,[22] which tracks incidents involving migrants, refugees, and asylum seekers who have perished or gone missing in transit around the world. Deaths occurring in transit to the south of Europe are taken from the Human Costs of Border Control Project, and fatalities at the US–Mexico border from the Arizona county medical examiner, which posts data about the deaths of migrants along the US–Mexico border.[23]

Alternative data sources

To date, 95% of the global population has access to at least 2G mobile coverage, and as reported by statista.com, the percentage of individuals who own a smartphone has increased to 44.9% in 2020.[24] This, of course, includes migrants, refugees, and the forcibly displaced. Smartphones and access to the internet have long ceased to be a luxury for migrants. Due to the ubiquity of these technologies, they have become essential tools for the process of migration itself. Refugees, especially those travelling through non-conventional routes, may rely on geolocation, mapping software, and crowd-sourced data like OpenStreetMap (Curry *et al.*, 2019) to find their way to their destination. They also depend on access to the internet to find relevant information about places to stay along the way and where to find resources to support their trip. They also use social networking apps that help them maintain contact with their friends and family back home, communicate their safe arrival, and forge connections with locals and their new communities.

By taking advantage of these technologies, migrants leave digital traces of their online activities. These digital breadcrumbs can be mined and analysed to study the routes, the conditions, and the evolution of migrants' journeys. In opposition to the data traditionally recovered by governments based on costly surveys, these online traces provide a more fine-grained picture of the process of migration from the perspective of migrants themselves. As such, mobile phone and social network data have high potential to transform how we understand, and most importantly, how we can tackle humanitarian crises.

Mobile phone metadata has been used in developed countries like Portugal (Deville *et al.*, 2014; Phithakkitnukoon *et al.*, 2012), France (Deville *et al.*, 2014), and China (Wang *et al.*, 2019) to understand nation-wide migration flows and carry out dynamic population mapping. It has also been used in developing contexts, albeit less regularly, to study internal (Isaacman *et al.*, 2018) and international migration (Phan *et al.*, 2005). Mobile phone metadata has high potential to provide insights on humanitarian crises whenever it is coupled with behavioural science

---

[22] Missing Migrants Project, https://missingmigrants.iom.int/
[23] Arizona OpenGIS Initiative for Deceased Migrants, https://humaneborders.info/
[24] Statista: Global smartphone penetration rate as share of population from 2016 to 2020, https://www.statista.com/statistics/203734/global-smartphone-penetration-per-capita-since-2005/

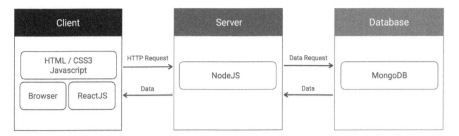

Figure 12.4 Voyage Viewer MERN (MongoDB, Express, React, Node) application architecture. Client: ReactJS web application triggers REST (representational state transfer) application programming interface (API) calls and retrieves server responses mapped to downloadable visualisations. Server: Back-end bridge for the client (APIs) and database. Database: MongoDB non-relational database hosted in a Mongo Atlas cluster.

and machine learning algorithms. It has been used to track epidemics in real time (McGowan *et al.*, 2019), track and prevent disease outbreaks (Tizzoni *et al.*, 2014; Wesolowski *et al.*, 2012, 2016), and uncover and map socioeconomic vulnerabilities (Blumenstock *et al.*, 2015).

In addition to the traditional datasets, Voyage Viewer has aggregated and anonymised data derived from call detail records (CDRs) from different countries to provide more fine-grained data about how migrants move within and across cities.

Infrastructure and system description

Voyage Viewer has a simple structure that is common to most web applications. It has a client or front-end, and a server; both are hosted on Amazon Web Services. The client runs in the user's browser on a computer or mobile device. The server retrieves data and sends it to the client, and it has a database where all the data used to make the visualisations are stored. This simple infrastructure is shown in greater detail in Figure 12.4. A more detailed description of Voyage Viewer's architecture can be found at http://voyageviewer.mit.edu/.

Activities and outputs

Interactive visualisations

Voyage Viewer's interface has five parts: World Map, Country Profiles, People Like Me, and Research. The World Map (Figure 12.5A) is the landing page; thus, it is the first component the user comes into contact with on entering the website. On the World Map, users find information about the number of international migrants globally, the countries that host them, and the direction of migration flows. To begin the exploration, the user has to choose between incoming or outgoing international flows by using the buttons on the upper right corner

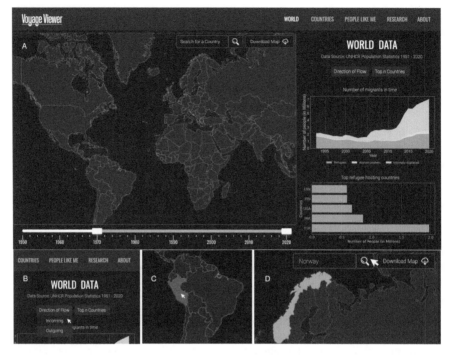

Figure 12.5 World map visualisation in Voyage Viewer. A Voyage Viewer's landing page. B Drop-down menu to select the direction of international migration flows. C Selecting a country by clicking on it directly on the map. D Selecting a country by searching for it on the search bar.

(Figure 12.5B). Then, they must select a country of interest by clicking on the map (Figure 12.5C). If the user is not familiar with the location of the country on the map or is unable to search for it on the screen, they can search for the country by name on the search bar at the top of the map window (Figure 12.5D). To select the time period of interest, users may use the timeline at the bottom of the page.

Once the selection has been made, the visualisations will change to reflect the matching data. The matching data is displayed in five different layers on the map. The first layer (Figure 12.6A) shows the political boundaries that define each country. The second layer (Figure 12.6B) shows a choropleth map highlighting the countries of origin and destination in different colours for clear differentiation. The third layer (Figure 12.6C) draws the paths from the country of origin to the destinations using a colour gradient to further underscore the flow direction. At the time of writing, the paths are not weighted to keep the visualisations clean and less cluttered. However, to access information about the number of migrants by type (refugees, asylum seekers) that have travelled on a particular path, the user can hover over each path. The tooltip will also contain information about the number of deaths that occurred in the passage if the data are

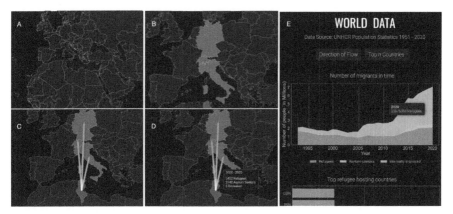

Figure 12.6 Layers of Voyage Viewer's World Map. The World Map is made up of the following layers: A The base map that shows political country boundaries. B A choropleth map on top of the base map that highlights in different colours the origin and destination countries of the user-selected migration flows. C Gradient paths or edges that show the direction of migrant flows. D Tooltips triggered by hovering on a path describe the numbers of refugees, asylum seekers, and other migrants that have travelled that path. In most cases, the tooltip will also show the number of people who have died in the process of traversing that particular path. E Charts that provide additional information about migrants in the user-selected country.

available. These tooltips make up the fourth layer of the World Map visualisation (Figure 12.6D). The last layer is made up of a series of charts that show statistics about the migration patterns in the selected country (Figure 12.6E). The visualisation that results from putting all of these layers together can be downloaded as a static image that is free to use with attribution to Voyage Viewer.

If the user would like to use Voyage Viewer to visualise their own data, this is possible by forking the Voyage Viewer repository from GitHub and running it locally on their machine. Some guidelines are provided to help troubleshoot the process.

The Country Profiles section provides an in-depth look at migration in one specific country selected by the user. Similarly to the World Map, this section also produces choropleth maps and draws network paths connecting places, but only within the selected country. It provides several metrics for a more detailed view of migration, such as the density of migrants per region, or the stocks of migrants disaggregated by gender, age, and education level. Other metrics such as employment and spatial and social integration measures are included only for countries in which these data are available. When they are included, the migrant and local metrics are available for comparison.

On the research page we share links to relevant papers about migration studies and feature some of our own research. In the future, we hope to include research that has been carried out using Voyage Viewer.

People Like Me

The People Like Me feature allows users to learn about the most frequent international and sub-national destinations, economic activities, average income, and other social indicators of migrants who match some of their characteristics. This feature informs users with potentially more relevant information instead of showing general statistics or the average behaviour of a very diverse collective.

At the time of writing, country of origin, state of origin (or equivalent administrative level 1 division), gender, age, highest degree attained, and employment status are used to find matches in the data. While inputs for gender, education, and employment are not mandatory, country, state of origin, and age are required to return results.

While all of the data in our database come from public sources, we use a battery of techniques to ensure that our visualisations are privacy-preserving. The number of inputs required to find matches in the data is limited to only six commonly used variables. Voyage Viewer will also check the number of matches found in the data. If the number of matches is below a certain threshold, Voyage Viewer will not return any information and will prompt the user to change one of the inputs to find more matches.

In addition to finding safety in numbers, Voyage Viewer uses generalisation, the replacement of individual values with broader categories, by binning age into five-year groups and highest degree attained into three broad categories. For example, if the user's age is 27, they would select the bin that indicates ages between 23 and 27, and if their highest degree attained is a PhD, they would select 'Graduate Education'. Voyage Viewer uses spatial aggregation to make sure that the lowest spatial resolution supported is at administrative level 1 (for example, state level in the US) even if the data have a finer spatial resolution. Outliers are removed, and very small or very large values are masked. Finally, displaying data as visualisations helps preserve privacy by reporting only aggregates of data in combination with other anonymisation methods (Chou *et al.*, 2019).

More details about how to use these features and the visualisations they produce are on described later in 'Use cases'.

Outcomes

Voyage Viewer aims to help migrants, researchers, policy experts, and citizens build a more comprehensive and articulate view of human mobility globally. It hopes to do so by helping non-technical users produce clear and beautiful visualisations to inform, communicate, and make decisions around the topic of human mobility and humanitarian crises caused by the massive displacements of people.

It also hopes to promote scientific research about migration processes by lowering the cost to search, find, and retrieve data about human mobility, which is often scattered and difficult to find. By including novel sources of data, Voyage Viewer also opens up the possibility for researchers to ask more and different questions that cannot be answered with only conventional data sources.

Additionally, through its People Like Me feature, Voyage Viewer informs users about the most common destinations for people similar to them, which are the most commonly travelled paths, and provides some outcome measures for migrants in these destinations like the level of unemployment and income distributions. Empowering communities by democratising access to data about themselves is a core value of Voyage Viewer.

Use cases

This section presents a detailed look at the People Like Me section and the Country Profiles. These sections can be used by citizens and policy-makers alike to help advance their distinct goals. We first present a citizen use case for the People Like Me feature, and then describe how a policy-maker might use the Country Profiles.

Citizen use case

On the People Like Me page, users are prompted to fill in a form with their country of origin, state or province of origin, age, gender, highest degree attained, and employment status. Only the first three fields are required, but the more information provided, the more relevant the matches that Voyage Viewer is able to find. With the input provided by the user, Voyage Viewer retrieves data that matches as many variables as possible from its database. The output is then rendered as a set of interactive visualisations in a Migration Outline Report. The different datasets used to make the visualisations are displayed in the lower left corner for transparency (Figure 12.7A).

The Migration Outline (Figure 12.7) begins by showing the number of people in the Voyage Viewer data that match the user's input variables. Then, Voyage Viewer makes two different treemap visualisations containing the most frequent international or sub-national destinations (with respect to the user's country of origin) for data points that match the user in most input variables. When an international destination represents over 40% of individuals among the top destinations, the treemap will contain information about the most common sub-national destinations within that country.

The next part of the Migration Outline contains information about employment and income (Figure 12.8). A heat map shows the percentage of migrants employed, unemployed, or inactive at each of the most frequent sub-national destinations for data points that match the user's input. The heat map is automatically sorted by the number of migrants residing at each of the sub-national destinations, with the destination with the most migrants on top. With help from the the 'Sort by' button, the heat map can be sorted by the percentage of employment, unemployment, or

282   *Loaiza et al.*

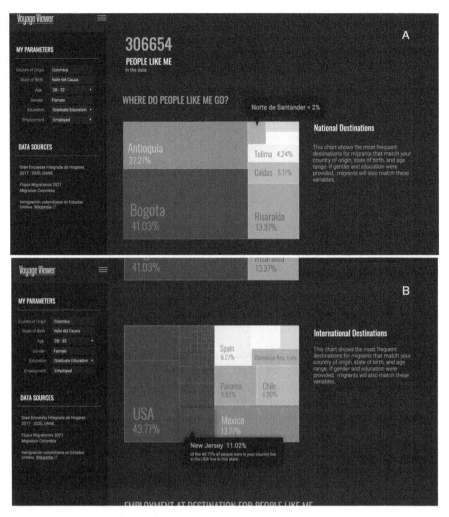

Figure 12.7 People Like Me: Destinations. This figure shows some of the visualisations that are created by the People Like Me feature. A The number of people in the dataset that match the inputs entered by the user. It also shows a treemap with the most common national destinations for people who match the user's input parameters. B A treemap with the most frequent international destinations for people similar to the user. When a destination country represents over 40% of the top destinations, the treemap will also show information about the distribution of migrants within that country.

inactivity. Definitions for employment, unemployment, and inactivity are included to provide clarity on the concepts used in the heat map.

The final part of this feature (see Figure 12.8C) is titled 'Income at destination for people like me'. Here, Voyage Viewer displays a series of distributions that characterise migrants' income at their most frequent destinations. These distributions are contrasted against the distribution of locals' income at these same destinations.

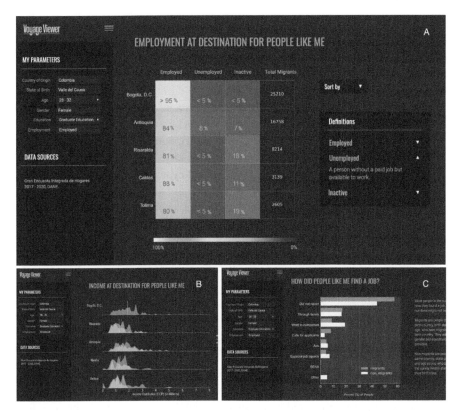

Figure 12.8 People Like Me: Employment and Income. A Distribution of national and international destinations of similar population to the user's profile according to place of birth, gender, age, education level, civil status, and employment status. B Employment rates at the destination country. Migrants at destination are classified as employed, unemployed, and inactive. C Income at different destinations. Distributions on income for locals and migrants.

This comparison provides information about the possible gap between the pay of locals and migrants who are similar to the user. Further development is needed to be able to compare international scenarios. When available, Voyage Viewer will also visualise the means by which migrants and locals found a job (Figure 12.8C).

Policy actors

The use case of data visualisation is illustrated by using a sample of aggregated CDRs and inter-city flows of Syrian refugees in Turkey. The data come from the Turkish telecommunications company Turk Telekom, and was obtained for the 'Data for Refugees' challenge (Salah *et al.*, 2019). The sample we use here was aggregated and used by Bakker *et al.* (2019). The first dataset we upload to Voyage Viewer has the following four columns: Origin, Destination, Flow Count, and Timestamp. For the purposes of this example, the user is visualising the data for the city of Adana. Figure 12.9A shows the bar plot for the number of refugees moving to Adana between January and November 2017. Next, Voyage Viewer visualises the top five origin cities for the sample refugees migrating to Adana. More details are provided as the user hovers over the paths. Figure 12.9B shows the Sankey diagram for the refugees migrating to Adana in our sample during 2017.

For the second use case we use the refugee social integration index (Bakker et al., 2019). Social integration is an index computed from the CDR data. This index measures social integration for a city as the relative number of calls that are made to majority users by minority users while in that city. We visualise this index to compare the social integration across cities in Turkey and see the differences in the distribution. The data uploaded to Voyage Viewer has two columns: City and Social Integration Index. Figure 12.9C shows the resulting choropleth for cities on a map. The difference in the level of Syrian refugees' social integration is visible among different cities.

We have explained two use cases that can shed light on the migration journey and provide insights for policy actors and decision-makers to understanding the integration dynamics and make informed decisions.

Limitations

Voyage Viewer's database is limited to public and accessible datasets. It is likely that these data are not representative of some of the most vulnerable groups of migrants who purposely avoid being surveyed by governments or authorities for fear of persecution or deportation. More effort needs to be put into collecting data about migrants, refugees, and displaced people, especially those living in precarious conditions. Only with better data will important conclusions come to light. Additionally, more work needs to be put into pooling and aggregating techniques so that Voyage Viewer can present a more seamless and integrated picture of migration while avoiding double counting and potential biases from aggregating multiple datasets.

The use of Voyage Viewer to visualise user data from their own computer is also constrained to individuals with sufficient technical skill to fork and run the repository from GitHub locally. Finally, while Voyage Viewer includes several anonymisation and privacy-preserving techniques, more robust controls could be added for data protection.

Conclusions and future work

In this chapter we have introduced Voyage Viewer, an open, online interactive tool that gathers public data about migration and visualises it to help citizens, evidence-based policy-makers, and other stakeholders learn, communicate, and inform about migration issues. We explained the different parts that make up the tool, and

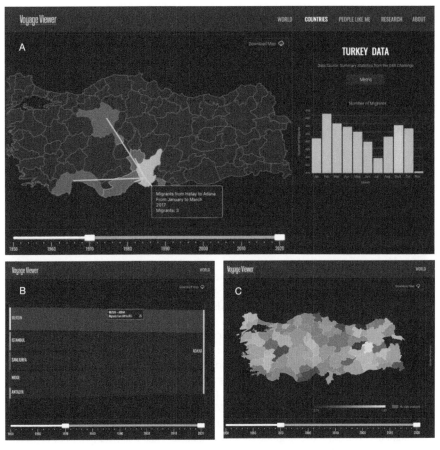

Figure 12.9 Policy actors use case. A Intercity flows for five origin cities exporting the highest number of migrants to Adana city in the sample dataset, and a bar plot to show the aggregated number of migrants by month. When hovering on paths detailed information is shown. B Sankey diagram of refugees migrating to Adana. C Choropleth for refugee social integration index at city level. Colour version printed as Plate 10.

presented two use cases to illustrate how Voyage Viewer might serve different kinds of actors interested in understanding migration patterns.

In the future, we would like to expand Voyage Viewer to contain data about most countries in the world, as well as provide other metrics such as media attention towards refugees and displaced populations at national and sub-national levels, and social integration metrics. Other interesting features we hope to include are forecasts of migration flows, and information about climate change refugees. In terms of privacy, we hope to incorporate more privacy-preserving methods for data platforms such as the ones described in Edge et al. (2020).

We look forward to continuing to improve the tools available for migration studies and engaging with the community via the GitHub repository or the Voyage Viewer website, http://voyageviewer.mit.edu/.

Acknowledgements

The authors would like to thank the team of students and developers who helped build Voyage Viewer. In particular, we would like to thank Vincent Le Put for his expert advice on building large-scale mobility platforms, Julien Hendrickx, Justin Anderson, Jessica Boyd-Doe, and Miguel Casalins for the conversations and comments that helped shape this tool. The authors would also like to thank the reviewers and editors of this book for their insightful feedback.

References

Avraam, D., Wilson, R., Butters, O., Burton, T., Nicolaides, C., Jones, E., Boyd, A., and Burton, P. (2021), 'Privacy preserving data visualizations', *EPJ Data Science* 10(1), 1–34.

Bakker, M. A., *et al.* (2019), 'Measuring fine-grained multidimensional integration using mobile phone metadata: The case of Syrian refugees in Turkey', *in* A. A. Salah, A. Pentland, B. Lepri, and E. Letouzé, eds, *Guide to Mobile Data Analytics in Refugee Scenarios*, Springer, New York, 123–40.

Bilsborrow, R. E. (2016), 'The global need for better data on international migration and the special potential of household surveys', *in Proceedings of the Conference of the International Organisation of Migration's Global Migration Data Analysis Centre (GMDAC) on Improving Data on International Migration: Towards Agenda*.

Blumenstock, J., Cadamuro, G., and On, R. (2015), 'Predicting poverty and wealth from mobile phone metadata', *Science* 350(6264), 1073–6.

Chakraborty, A., Wilson, B., Sarraf, S., and Jana, A. (2015), 'Open data for informal settlements: Toward a user's guide for urban managers and planners', *Journal of Urban Management* 4(2), 74–91.

Chou, J.-K., Wang, Y., and Ma, K.-L. (2019), 'Privacy preserving visualization: A study on event sequence data', *Computer Graphics Forum* 38(1), 340–55.

Curry, T., Croitoru, A., Crooks, A., and Stefanidis, A. (2019), 'Exodus 2.0: Crowdsourcing geographical and social trails of mass migration', *Journal of Geographical Systems* 21(1), 161–87.

Deville, P., Linard, C., Martin, S., Gilbert, M., Stevens, F. R., Gaughan, A. E., Blondel, V. D., and Tatem, A. J. (2014), 'Dynamic population mapping using mobile phone data', *Proceedings of the National Academy of Sciences* 111(45), 15888–93.

Dodge, S. (2021), 'A data science framework for movement', *Geographical Analysis* 53(1), 92–112.

Edge, D., Yang, W., Lytvynets, K., Cook, H., Galez-Davis, C., Darnton, H., and White, C. M. (2020), 'Design of a privacy-preserving data platform for collaboration against human trafficking', arXiv:2005.05688.

Feinberg, S. and Murphy, M. (2000), 'Applying cognitive load theory to the design of web-based instruction', *in Proceedings of the 18th IEEE Annual Conference on Computer Documentation, Technology and Teamwork*, 353–60.

Hawelka, B., Sitko, I., Beinat, E., Sobolevsky, S., Kazakopoulos, P., and Ratti, C. (2014), 'Geo-located Twitter as proxy for global mobility patterns', *Cartography and Geographic Information Science* 41(3), 260–71.

Ho, Q., Nguyen, P. H., Åström, T., and Jern, M. (2011), 'Implementation of a flow map demonstrator for analyzing commuting and migration flow statistics data', *Procedia – Social and Behavioral Sciences* 21, 157–66.

Isaacman, S., Frias-Martinez, V., and Frias-Martinez, E. (2018), 'Modeling human migration patterns during drought conditions in La Guajira, Colombia', *in Proceedings of the First ACM SIGCAS Conference on Computing and Sustainable Societies*, 1–9.

Keller, I., Ahmad, M. I., and Lohan, K. (2019), 'Multi-modal measurements of mental load', arXiv:1906.10557.

Kweon, S. H., Cho, E. J., and Kim, E. M. (2008), 'Interactivity dimension: Media, contents, and user perception', *in Proceedings of the Third International Conference on Digital Interactive Media in Entertainment and Arts*, 265–72.

Lazard, A. and Atkinson, L. (2015), 'Putting environmental infographics center stage: The role of visuals at the elaboration likelihood model's critical point of persuasion', *Science Communication* 37(1), 6–33.

Lhuillier, A., Hurter, C., and Telea, A. (2017), 'State of the art in edge and trail bundling techniques', *Computer Graphics Forum* 36(3), 619–45.

Loaiza, I., Novak, M., Morales, A. J., and Pentland, A. (2020), 'Looking for a better future: Modeling migrant mobility', *Applied Network Science* 5(1), 1–19.

Luo, D., Cats, O., and van Lint, H. (2017), 'Constructing transit origin–destination matrices with spatial clustering', *Transportation Research Record* 2652(1), 39–49.

McGowan, C. J., *et al.* (2019), 'Collaborative efforts to forecast seasonal influenza in the United States, 2015–2016', *Scientific Reports* 9(1), 1–13.

Morrison, J. and Vogel, D. (1998), 'The impacts of presentation visuals on persuasion', *Information & Management* 33(3), 125–35.

Palotti, J., Adler, N., Morales-Guzman, A., Villaveces, J., Sekara, V., Garcia Herranz, M., Al-Asad, M., and Weber, I. (2020), 'Monitoring of the Venezuelan exodus through Facebook's advertising platform', *PLOS One* 15(2), e0229175.

Phan, D., Xiao, L., Yeh, R., Hanrahan, P., and Winograd, T. (2005), 'Flow map layout code', available from http://graphics.stanford.edu/~dphan/code/flowmap.

Phithakkitnukoon, S., Smoreda, Z., and Olivier, P. (2012), 'Socio-geography of human mobility: A study using longitudinal mobile phone data', *PLOS One* 7(6), e39253.

Rae, A. (2009), 'From spatial interaction data to spatial interaction information? Geovisualisation and spatial structures of migration from the 2001 UK census', *Computers, Environment and Urban Systems* 33(3), 161–78.

Salah, A., Pentland, A., Lepri, B., and Letouzé, E. (2019), *Guide to Mobile Data Analytics in Refugee Scenarios*, Springer, New York.

Simoes, A. J. G. and Hidalgo, C. A. (2011), 'The Economic Complexity Observatory: An analytical tool for understanding the dynamics of economic development', *in Proceedings of the Workshops at the 25th AAAI Conference on Artificial Intelligence*.

Spyratos, S., Vespe, M., Natale, F., Weber, I., Zagheni, E., and Rango, M. (2019), 'Quantifying international human mobility patterns using Facebook Network data', *PLOS One* 14(10), e0224134.

Sundar, S. S., Xu, Q., and Bellur, S. (2010), 'Designing interactivity in media interfaces: A communications perspective', *in Proceedings of the SIGCHI Conference on Human Factors in Computing Systems*, 2247–56.

Telea, A. and Behrisch, M. (2022), 'Visual exploration of large multidimensional trajectory data', *in* A. A. Salah, E. E. Korkmaz, and T. Bircan, eds, *Data Science for Migration and Mobility*, Proceedings of the British Academy, British Academy / Oxford University Press, London.

Tizzoni, M., Bajardi, P., Decuyper, A., King, G. K. K., Schneider, C. M., Blondel, V., Smoreda, Z., González, M. C., and Colizza, V. (2014), 'On the use of human mobility proxies for modeling epidemics', *PLOS Computational Biology* 10(7), e1003716.

Tricco, A. C., Tetzlaff, J., and Moher, D. (2011), 'The art and science of knowledge synthesis', *Journal of Clinical Epidemiology* 64(1), 11–20.

UNICEF Rapport Uprooted (2016), 'The growing crisis for refugee and migrant children', UNICEF Nederland, available at https://www.unicef.nl/media/5019459/migratie-rapport-website.pdf

Wang, Y., Dong, L., Liu, Y., Huang, Z., and Liu, Y. (2019), 'Migration patterns in China extracted from mobile positioning data', *Habitat International* 86, 71–80.

Wesolowski, A., Buckee, C. O., Engø-Monsen, K., and Metcalf, C. J. E. (2016), 'Connecting mobility to infectious diseases: The promise and limits of mobile phone data', *The Journal of Infectious Diseases* 214(suppl 4), S414–S420.

Wesolowski, A., Eagle, N., Tatem, A. J., Smith, D. L., Noor, A. M., Snow, R. W., and Buckee, C. O. (2012), 'Quantifying the impact of human mobility on malaria', *Science* 338(6104), 267–70.

Part IV

Case Studies and Applications

13

Combining Mobile Call Data and Satellite Imaging for Human Mobility

TUĞBA BOZCAGA AND ASLI CANSUNAR

Introduction

ACCORDING TO THE Directorate General of Migration Management, Turkey hosted 3.6 million Syrian refugees with temporary protected status as of 2020. Only 59,000 of these refugees lived in settlement camps, while the remainder relocated to various cities. When the refugee influx began in 2011, most of the refugee population initially opted to settle in cities close to the Syrian border. Following the government's decision to gradually close the refugee camps, they then moved to other regions. Syrian refugees are present in almost all Turkish cities, and the variation in settlement patterns is striking. For example, according to official statistics, around 516,510 Syrian refugees chose to reside in Istanbul, Turkey's economic and social centre, and 117,776 individuals moved to a major city in south-central Turkey called Konya. In contrast, only 38 refugees opted to settle in the district in Eastern Anatolia called Tunceli.[1]

The existing literature on the pull factors of migration has two main strands, both based on an analysis of opportunities for easy social and economic integration. First, scholars emphasised the importance of their pre-existing family and home country networks, as well as linguistic and cultural ties, in deciding where to settle in host countries (Åslund, 2005; Damm, 2009a,b). Enclaves can help new refugees find jobs, decrease the cost of acquiring cultural and economic information, and provide a safe social space for newcomers (Crawley and Hagen-Zanker, 2019). Second, the existing research has focused on the prospects of labour market opportunities (Beine *et al.*, 2021; Ostrovsky *et al.*, 2011). The language barrier between

---

[1] Geçici Koruma, https://www.goc.gov.tr/gecici-koruma5638

refugees and employers and the bureaucratic hurdles for formal employment and entrepreneurship have been among the biggest challenges in refugees' social integration. Although successfully finding employment does not guarantee full social integration, it serves as a significant milestone in a refugee's path to becoming an active and self-sufficient member of her new environment. Thus, scholars argued that higher wages and employment prospects were significant determinants of refugees' relocation within their host country.

Yet, the factors that influence where refugees choose to move and settle after arrival remain unclear.[2] Also, the lack of data on the internal migration patterns of refugees within the host countries makes it very hard to track their settlement preferences. Thus, what has been mostly missing from the debate is considering the local industries' impact on attracting refugee populations. To what extent do location choices of refugees respond to the factors of economic attractiveness and employment opportunities? Which types of economic activities are most likely to pull refugees? Given the centrality of employment in refugee integration, in this chapter we focus on the effect of economic and employment opportunities on the relocation decisions of Syrian refugees in Turkey.

Existing studies investigating the impact of economic opportunities on relocation patterns of refugees within their host country encountered four methodological and data-driven problems. First, and most importantly, previous studies investigating the relationship between economic opportunities and refugee settlement patterns assumed that residents gained complete access to all labour market opportunities once they settled within that locality (Beine *et al.*, 2021; Ostrovsky *et al.*, 2011). However, human geography does not always perfectly intersect with politically formulated areas (King, 1997; Soifer and Alvarez, 2017; Lee and Rogers, 2019). If researchers classify places where immigrants settle based just on administrative borders and the characteristics of a given administrative unit, they may miss a crucial piece of information: the labour market demand in the area surrounding an immigrant's home location. A district with few employment opportunities may be close to areas with abundant labour market demand, leading to inaccurate results regarding the underlying motivations of immigrant and refugee mobility in host countries. In this chapter, we assert that the distance to available economic opportunities should be taken into account when examining the determinants of settlement decisions of refugees within their host country. We call the conventional approach, aggregation of residential characteristics by administrative borders, the 'administrative' approach, and our approach, which focuses on the distance to employment opportunities, the 'distance' approach.

Second, the existing literature looks at cross-sectional variations of refugee settlement patterns, which create causal inference problems. In particular, selection bias renders identifying the factors that influence settlement decisions difficult

---

[2] Although Syrian refugees in Turkey should get formal permission to move within the country, these rules are rarely enforced by the government.

because individuals who have settled in a place due only to employment opportunities may have also been from a more disadvantaged background, with fewer pre-existing family or social networks.

Third, while a small number of existing studies highlight employment opportunities as one of the main driving forces of immigrants' and refugees' settlement decisions, their analyses usually use aggregated economic data such as unemployment levels or economic growth rates within large political regions. They do not focus on the effectiveness of particular economic activity in attracting refugee communities (Beine et al., 2021).

Finally, most work focuses on the places of residence formally declared by the refugees or census data (Hatton and Tani, 2005; Maystadt and Duranton, 2019; Mossaad et al., 2020). This strand of literature mainly focuses on the welfare and economic implications of migrant and refugee influx on hosting communities, using formal employment and economic indicators (Docquier et al., 2014; Ottaviano and Peri, 2012; Ceritoglu et al., 2017; Akgündüz et al., 2018). However, census data and formal employment statistics are not very useful in settings like Turkey. It is estimated that in 2017, one million Syrian refugees in Turkey work informally, where 20% of these informal workers are minors (İçduygu and Diker, 2017). Also, informal employment is common within the hosting community: one third of Turkish workers take on informal employment. The prevalence of unregistered Syrian refugees and informal employment means that the relationship between employment opportunities and refugee movements could often not be traced through official data sources (Kadkoy, 2017).

We take on these challenges using an original dataset that brings together mobile call metadata and land cover images. First, rather than using self-reported mobility information or census records, we rely on geolocalised call detail records provided by Salah et al. (2019) within the Data for Refugees challenge. Likewise, rather than relying on formal economic and employment figures disseminated by the government in order to identify labour market and economic opportunities, we use satellite data that describes the type of economic and industrial activity. Combining these two types of data addresses the four limitations mentioned above and allows us to extend existing approaches pertaining to refugee mobility. Second, the over-time structure of mobile call data enables us to control for time-invariant, individual-level, and unobserved variables that confound the relationship between the characteristics of a given district where immigrants settle and settlement decisions. Third, by calculating the distance between employment opportunities (for which we use granular land cover images that classify land zones thematically) and refugee settlement locations, we took into account not only the characteristics of the home location itself but also the areas of the commercial, industrial, construction, and agricultural zones surrounding immigrants' home locations.

To estimate the effect of employment opportunities on refugee mobility patterns in the host countries, we used a longitudinal linear probability model with individual-level fixed effects (see Box 13.1 on linear models), where each observation corresponds to a refugee in a given month for a 12-month period. Specifically, we used mobile call detail records (CDRs) that tracked each user throughout the year 2017 and showed the location of each phone call a user made. While this information is at the district level and does not allow us to observe a user's within-district mobility patterns, we can identify the 'home district' of an individual and detect whether the home district changes over time. We coded all individuals' monthly home locations by identifying variations in cell phone data. If there was a different home district from the previous month's district, we called the current home district a 'receiving district' and the previous home district a 'sending district'.

> **Box 13.1** Fixed effects linear models
>
> When modelling data for which independence assumptions do not hold (for instance in longitudinal data with repeated observations from individuals, or multilevel data with groups of subjects), some factors may be modelled to influence groups of measurements.
>
> *Fixed effects models* assume the levels of independent variables to be fixed (e.g., constant), and that changes in the levels of independent variables lead to changes in the dependent variable. In social sciences, unit fixed-effects regression models are commonly employed for causal inference with longitudinal or panel data, given their rather manageable limitations (Hill *et al.*, 2020) and advantages over cross-sectional models (Angrist and Pischke, 2009; Allison, 2009; Brüderl and Ludwig, 2015; Imai and Kim, 2019).
>
> To use individual-level fixed effects models, the same person/observation should appear multiple times (as in panel data). If individual-specific time-varying covariates are correlated with the time-constant error term, fixed effects linear regression will not work. For modelling correlated data, a model with both fixed effects and random effects, namely a *mixed effects model* (also called a *random effects model*) should be adopted.
>
> A mixed effects model is represented by the sum of fixed and random effects, plus an intercept term. In these models, 'random effects' are allowed to vary over the sample when other effects do not. A well-specified random effects model is considered to be superior to a fixed effects model, as it provides all aspects that fixed effects models provide and goes beyond them (Shor *et al.*, 2007; Bell and Jones, 2015; Bell *et al.*, 2019).
>
> *Panel data*, also called longitudinal data, is data that contain observations about different cross sections across time. In a panel data example, multiple individuals may be measured on multiple occasions, which is different from a simple time series that belongs to a single individual. To be able to model both within- and between-individual effects synchronously in the panel data (i.e., to account for heterogeneity in the effect of individual-level independent variables), a mixed effects linear regression model should include both a fixed part and a random part. The fixed part covers both time-varying and time-invariant independent variables.

This coding allowed us to explore which district characteristics increase the likelihood of being a receiving district. The main independent variables are the distances of a given home location in a given month to the closest areas with potentially high labour demand, as determined by land cover images. We identified industrial-commercial zones, mines, construction areas, agricultural land, forests, salines, urban infrastructure, road-rail network, leisure centres, and water sources by employing the CORINE Land Cover data from 2018, a computerised inventory that categorises land cover into 44 classes relying on satellite images. We measured each district's distance to these economic zones and geographic attributes. We also calculated the percentage of each economic activity zone and geographical attributes within districts.

We found that the distance approach gives substantively and statistically different results compared with the conventional approaches that employ measures aggregated by administrative units. The former results are also more consistent with the findings of the existing literature on internal migration. Adopting the distance approach, we found that individual settlement decisions seem to be affected by *distance* to employment opportunities. Refugees choose to move to districts geographically closer to industrial-commercial, urban zones, and construction sites. On the contrary, refugees are less likely to relocate to districts that are more proximate to mines. The *density* of urban fabric, industrial-commercial zones, and mines, on the other hand, do not significantly affect relocation decisions. In line with our theoretical predictions, distance to economic activity better explains settlement patterns than density measures. These findings emphasise the importance of evaluating refugees' decisions in a spatial framework.

This chapter also makes a methodological contribution to understanding refugee settlement patterns. Recent studies combined satellite imagery with mobile call data to create better wealth and poverty measures, and strong correlations were found between these alternative measures and measures that rely on administrative data. Studies also pointed out that these novel techniques provide an excellent opportunity to create measures for other social science topics that are under studied or studied only with a limited geographical scope due to a lack of data. Examining the motivations underlying refugee mobility by combining mobile call metadata and satellite images, this chapter extends the substantive scope of these contemporary analyses to immigrant and refugee populations. This chapter will also have important implications for research on migration and policy implications for migration receiving countries.

Our chapter is structured as follows: we discuss the data, explain our measurement strategies, and then present an analysis of the mobility of Syrian refugees in Turkey. We conclude by summarising our results and highlighting avenues for further research using big data and a spatial framework to understand refugees' behaviour in host countries.

Data and measurement

Measuring mobility

To investigate the internal migration patterns of refugees, we utilise one of the three datasets made available to the participants of the Data for Refugees (D4R) Challenge; see Salah et al. (2019), and Chapters 4 (Luca et al.) and 5 (Sterly and Wirkus) in this volume. The D4R data are collected from 1,211,839 subscriptions of Turk Telekom, of which 231,142 are tagged as 'refugees', in 2017. A customer was classified as a 'refugee' if she belongs to one of the following categories: (1) has an ID number given to refugees and foreigners in Turkey, (2) is registered with Syrian passports, and (3) uses special tariffs reserved for refugees.[3]

Before discussing the specifics of the dataset we employ, it is worth mentioning several limitations of the D4R data and of mobile call metadata in general. First, mobile call data raise the question of how representative this type of data is of the overall population. Prior research shows that the most vulnerable groups such as women and those on a low income tend to be the least represented in mobile phone usage (Marshall et al., 2016; Wesolowski et al., 2013; Blumenstock and Eagle, 2012). In addition, different operators may have distinct types of customer profiles. The mobile call dataset we employ is collected from 231,142 refugee customers of Turk Telekom, one of the three major telecommunications companies in Turkey. The mobile phone penetration rate in Turkey is high: at the end of March 2017, there were 75,724,413 mobile customers across all operators (excluding the age range of 0–9), corresponding to a mobile penetration rate of approximately 107%. While the overall mobile penetration is high, the market share of Turk Telekom, like most operators across the world, shows fluctuation across provinces and is on average 24.7%. In addition, in the D4R data, only 25% of subscribers are recorded as 'female' (Salah et al., 2019). While this does not mean that women use only 25% of the phone lines, there is admittedly a gender bias in the distribution of phone line owners in our dataset. Given the potential biases in mobile call metadata, studies employing mobile call data should accurately select an empirical design that considers the potential biases in the sample. We believe that, where possible, studies should address at least the internal validity concerns by employing longitudinal observations for the same subject and partial out individual-level fixed effects to isolate the effects of individual-specific characteristics that do not change over time (Angrist and Pischke, 2009, pp. 165–169).

The dataset we employ (D4R's Coarse-Grained Mobility Dataset) consists of timestamped mobile CDRs that contain information on the over 6,600,0731 mobile phone calls of roughly 37,300 randomly sampled individuals from amongst refugee

---

[3] It should be noted that the unique identity number and passport information allow mobile phone operators in Turkey to identify which clients are likely to be refugees. In countries where refugees are registered without such a specific condition, identifying refugees in the data might require additional strategies.

users and show the location of each call at the district level. For each of these call events, we observe a unique identifier for the caller and the date and time of the call. While this dataset does not allow us to identify the cellular phone towers through which the call was routed, it gives us the district where the tower is located. It thus allows us to see whether a user stays mostly within a specific district boundary, which we define as the 'home district', and whether the home district changes across time. Each user is identified by a randomly assigned ID instead of their real phone number. The raw data contain the following fields:

- CALLER_ID: The randomly assigned ID of the user.
- TIMESTAMP: Day and time considered in the format dd-mm-yyyy hh:mm (24 hour format).
- ID: The ID of the district.
- CITY_ID: The ID of the city.

Using the timestamped information on each call's location, we first compute the home district of each individual. Following the approach adopted by existing studies of migration based on CDR data (Blumenstock *et al.*, 2019; Hong *et al.*, 2019), we identify the location at which the individual spends the majority of her evening and night hours (between 6pm and 7am), as calls made during the day may be done from the workplace instead of home. First, for each individual, we compute the most frequently visited district in every hour of the entire dataset, based on the locations of all incoming and outgoing calls. We compute the top modal district for a given day by identifying the district where the user is most commonly found outside of business hours over a day. We then record the frequency with which each district appears as the mode for the user over a given month. The top modal district in a given month is assigned as the home district of the user for that month. In short, refugees who are assigned to a single district throughout a month are assigned to that district, while those who are assigned to more than one district throughout a month are assigned to the district where they had been active for the highest number of days. The end result is a panel of districts by individual/month. Exploiting the longitudinal structure of the data, we determine the home district on a monthly basis for all individual users. If the home district in month t is different from the home district in month $t-1$, we code the home district in month t as a receiving district and the previous home district as a sending district. The dependent variable is a dummy that takes the value one if the refugee moves to a new district and zero otherwise. See Figure 13.1 for several example internal migration patterns.

Measuring the characteristics of origin and destination locations

Which types of economic activities are most likely to pull refugees? What type of economic zones increases the probability of refugee settlement? To investigate the relationship between the prevalence of economic activity and refugee settlement decisions, we identify particular economic activity zones in Turkey using the

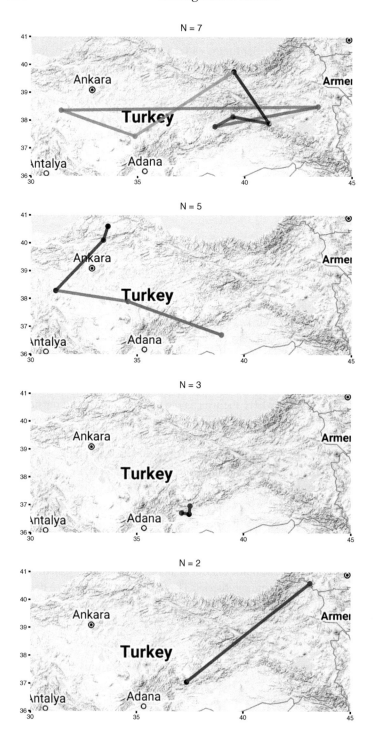

Figure 13.1 Internal migration patterns of four refugees by number of movements.

MOBILE CALL DATA AND SATELLITE IMAGING   299

European Environment Agency (EEA) | Esri, USGS | Esri, HERE, Garmin, FAO, NOAA, USGS | Esri, HERE, Garmin, FAO, NOAA, USGS

Figure 13.2 CORINE land cover, Turkey, 2018.

CORINE land cover inventory (Heymann, 1994). We select the CORINE inventory because it, to our knowledge, provides the most fine-grained information on land use patterns in the region (with a resolution of $100 \times 100\,m^2$ pixels) (see Bircan, Chapter 6, this volume, for information on different sources of remote sensing data). The level of detail is crucial to be able to distinguish small-scale land areas allocated to employment areas such as industrial complexes or construction sites (see Figure 13.2). By making use of 44 different land cover classes, CORINE also allows us to make detailed sectoral classifications and thus accurately identify specific sectors that pull migration. In line with our theoretical approach, the 44 sub-categories are transformed into six main sectoral indicators: industrial-commercial, mines, construction, agricultural land, forests, and salines. One important sector that cannot be detected in land cover images is the service sector. Nevertheless, the areas where service sector employment is available should largely overlap the continuous urban fabric subcategory. In addition, we also control for the following land cover categories to account for other potential factors related to resettlement decisions: urban fabric, road-rail network, leisure, and water sources. Table 13.1 presents the details about the composition of these main categories. We drop the categories that are not theoretically meaningful to explain internal migration patterns: natural grassland; moors and heathland; sclerophyllous vegetation; transitional woodland/shrub; beaches, dunes, and sand plains; bare rock; sparsely vegetated areas; burnt areas; glaciers and perpetual snow; inland marshes; coastal salt marshes; estuaries. Five of these theoretically irrelevant categories are at the same time among the ten least-common land cover types in Turkey (close to zero).

Table 13.1 CORINE land types by group

Category	Original Subcategory	Code
Urban fabric	Continuous urban fabric	111
	Discontinuous urban fabric	112
Industrial-commercial	Industrial or commercial units and public facilities	121
	Port areas	123
	Airports	124
Mines	Mineral extraction sites	131
Construction	Construction sites	133
	Dump sites	132
Road-rail network	Road and rail networks	122
Leisure	Green urban areas	141
	Sport and leisure facilities	142
Agricultural land	Non-irrigated arable land	211
	Permanently irrigated arable land	212
	Rice fields	213
	Vineyards	221
	Fruit tree and berry plantations	222
	Olive groves	223
	Other permanent grasslands under agricultural use	231
	Annual crops associated with permanent crops	241
	Complex cultivation patterns	242
	Land principally occupied by agriculture	243
	Agro-forestry areas	244
Forests	Broad-leaved forest	311
	Coniferous forest	312
	Mixed forest	313
Salines	Salines	422
Water sources	Coastal lagoons	511
	Water bodies	512
	Water sources	521

In the administrative approach, the independent variables are defined as the proportion of the total area of a given land cover type over the total district area. In the spatial approach, the independent variables are defined as the geodesic distance of the home district, specifically its centre, to the nearest zone of a given land cover type. While our results rely on the distances from the centre of districts, which we use as a proxy for refugees' home locations, this is a reasonable assumption given that 99.83% of refugees in Turkey live in urban areas (TCI, 2020, p. 6). To calculate the distances for a given home district, we use the Calculate Distance tool of ArcGIS. To calculate the densities, we use its Point Density tool.

Empirical strategy

Our baseline results assume each individual faces an independent migration decision in each month. She can either stay or migrate to one of the 667 other districts in the sample. We regress the binary migration decision on (lagged) properties of the migrant's current home district, using a linear probability model with a fixed effect for each individual, where each observation corresponds to one refugee. Since the main independent variables are the characteristics of the district where an individual decides to live, due to the use of individual-level effects, individuals staying in the same district throughout 2017 drop from the model. Now, 9262 of 37,300 refugee users in the sample moved to a new home district at least once during 2017. This number corresponds to 24.8% of the whole sample. We use the felm function from the R package lfe to derive our inferences (Gaure, 2013).

One limitation of our approach is that we lack exogenous variation in receiving and sending districts' characteristics. To partially address this concern, we devote considerable attention to causal identification and perform a large number of tests to check the robustness of our results. First, identification is achieved through an extremely restrictive set of fixed effects that limit the potential for individual-level sources of endogeneity. Our preferred specification includes fixed effects for each individual migrant and for each month. The individual fixed effects absorb all time-invariant individual heterogeneity (such as wealth, gender, ethnicity, personality type, family structure, etc.) and address the fact that some people are inherently more likely to migrate than others (and have inherently different preferences for residential location). The month fixed effects account that certain months may face more migration due to political or seasonal conditions. Thus, in our preferred specification, the identifying variation comes from within-individual differences in home district characteristics between destinations and over different months in the 12-month window.

Formally, for a migrant i considering moving from home district h to destination district d in month t, we estimate the effect of land characteristics, $Land_{idt}$, on the migration decision M_{idt}, where M_{idt} is a binary variable equal to 1 if the migrant chooses to move from h to d at t, and 0 otherwise. Using the rich structure of the CORINE land cover data, we can see whether being a receiving district is associated with closeness to (spatial approach) or density of the following land cover types: industrial-commercial, mines, construction, agricultural land, forests, salines, urban fabric, road-rail network, leisure, and water sources. We also add various individual- and district-level control variables in our models. In the equation, X_{it} indicates the individual-level and Z_{idt} the district-level controls. Prior research has argued that immigrants select their residential location based on employment opportunities and welfare benefits and services (Bozcaga et al., 2019; Borjas, 1999; Dodson, 2001).

Other studies highlight that local partisanship is an important determinant as parties and their constituencies differ in their attitudes towards immigrants and refugees (Bloemraad, 2006; Bakker et al., 2019). In this line, we add several district-level control variables to our model: local population; average night-lights density, as a proxy for economic development; literacy rate; and the vote share of the incumbent party AKP. The data on average night-lights density come from an original dataset based on Bozcaga (2020). Since personal factors can also influence relocation choices, we also include individual-level time-varying control variables in our model: the number of calls made, as a proxy for personal income (Blumenstock and Eagle, 2012; Blumenstock et al., 2015), and the number of provinces visited in a given month, as a proxy for the general mobility of the individual. γ_i is the individual-level fixed effects, and ψ_t indicates the month fixed effects. We cluster standard errors by individual.

$$M_{it} = \lambda X_{it} + \beta Z_{idt} + \beta Land_{idt} + \gamma_i + \psi_t + \epsilon_{idt} \tag{13.1}$$

We also implement two robustness checks. First, since refugees' mobility may also depend on temporary job opportunities and seasonal trends (such as harvests and tourism), we repeat the same analysis by excluding the movements in the harvest period (May–September) from our analysis. Second, we attempt to limit the extent to which extreme observations such as fully mobile organisational phone lines used by employees such as truck drivers or cargo carriers influence our analysis by dropping the top 5% of observations with the highest number of across-district movements.

Results

Table 13.2 presents the main results. Across all models, a negative coefficient for the distance variables and a positive coefficient for the density variables indicate a *positive* relationship between the proximity to / density of a given zone in a district and the likelihood to move to that district. We show results for three different samples (original, excluding harvest, trimmed) with two different measurement strategies (distance (log) and density). We only interpret the findings that are robust for at least one of our robustness checks, where we exclude observations during seasonal migration months (Models 3 and 4 in Table 13.2) and with an extreme number of across-district movements (Models 5 and 6 in Table 13.2). The results confirm that the distance to certain economic and labour market opportunities, as well as to urban areas, influences refugees' relocation choices, while the density of economic zones within districts does not significantly predict relocation preferences except for the construction sector.

In analysis with the original and trimmed sample, we find that decreases in the distance to the industrial-commercial zones and urban fabric significantly increase the probability of a refugee relocating into a district. According to Models 1 and 3,

Table 13.2 Characteristics of receiving districts by measurement strategy

	Original		Excluding Harvest		Trimmed	
	Model 1 Distance (log)	Model 2 Density	Model 3 Distance (log)	Model 4 Density	Model 5 Distance (log)	Model 6 Density
Sectoral zones						
Urban fabric	−0.008***	0.009	−0.004	0.021	−0.008**	0.020
	(0.003)	(0.010)	(0.004)	(0.014)	(0.003)	(0.013)
Industrial-commercial	−0.018**	−0.048	0.004	−0.099	−0.026***	−0.036
	(0.008)	(0.039)	(0.013)	(0.061)	(0.009)	(0.049)
Mines	0.012***	0.001	−0.002	0.001	0.013**	−0.003
	(0.004)	(0.005)	(0.007)	(0.007)	(0.005)	(0.006)
Construction	−0.013***	0.363***	−0.017***	0.402**	−0.012***	0.363**
	(0.003)	(0.123)	(0.006)	(0.187)	(0.004)	(0.159)
Agricultural land	0.016	0.002	0.020	0.011*	0.018	0.0003
	(0.010)	(0.004)	(0.017)	(0.006)	(0.012)	(0.005)
Other zones						
Road-rail network	0.004	−0.232	0.012	−1.030**	0.004	−0.451
	(0.007)	(0.308)	(0.012)	(0.489)	(0.008)	(0.381)
Leisure	−0.007**	−0.095	−0.005	−0.052	−0.005	−0.058
	(0.003)	(0.105)	(0.004)	(0.162)	(0.003)	(0.134)
Forests	−0.004	−0.001	−0.002	0.001	−0.005	−0.002
	(0.006)	(0.002)	(0.010)	(0.003)	(0.007)	(0.002)
Salines	0.013	−0.140	−0.002	0.188	0.017	−0.340
	(0.009)	(0.220)	(0.016)	(0.009)	(0.010)	(0.007)
Water sources	−0.004	0.041*	−0.009	−0.002	−0.004	0.052*
	(0.005)	(0.024)	(0.009)	(0.042)	(0.007)	(0.030)

Table 13.2 continued

	Original		Excluding Harvest		Trimmed	
	Model 1 Distance (log)	Model 2 Density	Model 3 Distance (log)	Model 4 Density	Model 5 Distance (log)	Model 6 Density
Controls						
No. calls (log)	−0.026***	−0.026***	−0.021***	−0.020***	−0.023***	−0.023***
	(0.002)	(0.002)	(0.003)	(0.003)	(0.002)	(0.002)
No. provinces (log)	0.066***	0.066***	0.052***	0.052***	0.060***	0.060***
	(0.003)	(0.003)	(0.006)	(0.006)	(0.004)	(0.004)
Population (log)	−0.056***	−0.054***	−0.052***	−0.043***	−0.063***	−0.062***
	(0.007)	(0.006)	(0.012)	(0.011)	(0.008)	(0.008)
Urban population (%)	0.001	0.001*	0.002*	0.002*	0.001**	0.001**
	(0.001)	(0.001)	(0.001)	(0.001)	(0.001)	(0.001)
Incumbent vote share	−0.0003	−0.0004	−0.00001	−0.0003	−0.001	−0.001*
	(0.0004)	(0.0004)	(0.001)	(0.001)	(0.0005)	(0.0005)
Night-lights density	0.0003*	0.001***	0.001**	0.001**	0.0003	0.001*
	(0.0002)	(0.0004)	(0.0003)	(0.001)	(0.0002)	(0.0005)
Literacy rate	−0.005*	−0.007***	−0.008*	−0.011***	−0.005	−0.007***
	(0.003)	(0.002)	(0.004)	(0.004)	(0.003)	(0.003)
Observations	102,367	102,367	46,436	46,436	92,648	92,648
R^2	0.466	0.465	0.569	0.569	0.470	0.469

Note: Standard errors clustered at the individual level. * $p < 0.1$; ** $p < 0.05$; *** $p < 0.01$.

we find that an increase of 18% (one standard deviation) in the distance to industrial-commercial zones decreases the likelihood to move to that district by 0.3 and 0.5 percentage points (i.e., 2% and 3% compared to the sample mean), respectively. Estimates from the same analysis show that an increase of 68% (one standard deviation) in distance to urban areas decreases the likelihood to move to that district by 0.4 percentage points (i.e., 2.4% compared to the sample mean) in Models 1 and 3. We do not observe the same significant relationship when we change the main independent variable's measurement strategy. When we investigate the relationship between the density of industrial-commercial zones and urban fabric within a district and refugee settlement patterns, we fail to find a significant relationship. Furthermore, the coefficient for the density of industrial-commercial zones has a negative sign, suggesting a negative relationship between the density of industrial-commercial zones in a district and the likelihood to move there. Thus, consistent with our expectations, relocating refugees chose to settle in places situated geographically closer to industrial-commercial zones and urban centres.

One of the findings consistent across the two measurement strategies is that geographical proximity to construction zones, as well as their density, increases the likelihood of relocating to a district. Table 13.2 shows that both geographical proximity to construction zones and the density of construction zones positively affect the refugee settlement. Another finding consistent across the two measurement strategies is that neither the distance nor the density of agricultural lands significantly affects refugees' relocation decisions.

Finally, we also fail to reject the hypotheses that the distance to or the density of road-rail networks, leisure facilities, forests, and salines are significant determinants of settlement patterns. Among these geographical attributes, only water sources seem to predict settlement decisions. However, the results here also show variations by the measurement strategy: the density of water sources in a district predicts an increase in the likelihood to move to the district, while the distance of water resources does not seem to predict a statistically significant relationship. However, these results should be approached with caution as they are only significant at a p-value just below 0.1.

The findings above suggest that a potential explanation for the long-term movement of refugees over time, if any, is to a great extent motivated by the geographical proximity of labour prospects in industrial-commercial zones, urban centres, and construction sites. Given the significant effect of the density of water sources, easy access to clean water appears to be a factor as well. When interpreting these results, one should also note that due to the individual-level fixed effects in the model, our sample excludes refugees that did not change their home throughout the year.

Together, these results demonstrate the importance of examining refugee mobility patterns in a spatial framework. We find that the patterns of internal migration of refugees within the host countries are not haphazard and can be predicted by the proximity of economic opportunities. Our results highlight the potential threats for inference based on economic data aggregation, whereby measuring concepts at politically derived units alters empirical results (Amrhein, 1995; Dark and Bram,

2007). By using distance to economic and labour opportunities, instead of employing measures based on the density of economic activity within bureaucratically aggregated large units, we not only show which economic sectors are more likely to pull refugees but also point to the necessity of employing a spatial framework in studying the geographic movement of specific populations through time and space.

One potential concern with using the land cover maps is the possibility of refugees' transformative impact on the geographical and economic characteristics of the settlement district, which might cause endogeneity. However, most features identified through the land cover maps are hard to manipulate through human mobility and activity over a few years, perhaps except for refugee campsites. Thus, we argue that using land cover maps offers an alternative way to measure economic and labour opportunities that might create pull factors for refugees for developing context where quality data on economic activity is not readily available.

Conclusion

In this chapter we focused on the relationship between the internal mobility patterns of Syrian refugees in Turkey and the catchment areas of economic activity. Specifically, we used mobile call detail records and fine-grained land cover data to investigate the extent to which refugees consider the geographic distance from economic activity in deciding where to settle in the host country.

We found consistent evidence that increases in a districts' distance from urban fabric, industrial-commercial zones, and construction sites decrease the probability of attracting Syrian refugees. Conversely, increases in a districts' distance from mines significantly raise the likelihood of being a receiving district. However, when we used the density of these economic activities within a district, rather than the distance from them, the results changed considerably. The density-based measurement strategy suggests that urban fabric, industrial–commercial zones, and mines have no meaningful impact on refugees' relocation decisions.

Throughout the chapter we have emphasised the importance of examining refugee mobility in a spatial framework. We proposed that distance from economic activity is an essential element that shapes refugees' relocation decisions. As geographical distances between communities and economic activity centres vary widely within and across formally defined sub-national units (such as districts, counties, or states), proximity to an economic opportunity should positively affect one's settlement decision. By examining the influence of geographic distance from different types of economic activities and employment opportunities on refugee settlement patterns, our theory builds upon and extends existing research on the push and pull factors of refugees' internal migration patterns in host countries.

References

Akgündüz, Y. E., van den Berg, M., and Hassink, W. (2018), 'The impact of the Syrian refugee crisis on firm entry and performance in Turkey', *The World Bank Economic Review* 32(1), 19–40.

Allison, P. D. (2009), *Fixed Effects Regression Models*, Sage Publications, Thousand Oaks, CA.

Amrhein, C. G. (1995), 'Searching for the elusive aggregation effect: Evidence from statistical simulations', *Environment and Planning A* 27(1), 105–19.

Angrist, J. D. and Pischke, J.-S. (2009), *Mostly Harmless Econometrics*, Princeton University Press, Princeton, NJ.

Åslund, O. (2005), 'Now and forever? Initial and subsequent location choices of immigrants', *Regional Science and Urban Economics* 35(2), 141–65.

Bakker, M. A., et al. (2019), 'Measuring fine-grained multidimensional integration using mobile phone metadata: The case of Syrian refugees in Turkey', *in* A. A. Salah, A. Pentland, B. Lepri, and E. Letouzé, eds, *Guide to Mobile Data Analytics in Refugee Scenarios*, Springer, New York, 123–40.

Beine, M., Bertinelli, L., Cömertpay, R., Litina, A., and Maystadt, J.-F. (2021), 'A gravity analysis of refugee mobility using mobile phone data', *Journal of Development Economics* 150, 102618.

Bell, A., Fairbrother, M., and Jones, K. (2019), 'Fixed and random effects models: Making an informed choice', *Quality & Quantity* 53(2), 1051–74.

Bell, A. and Jones, K. (2015), 'Explaining fixed effects: Random effects modeling of time-series cross-sectional and panel data', *Political Science Research and Methods* 3(1), 133–53.

Bircan, T. (2022), 'Remote sensing data for migration research', *in* A. A. Salah, E. E. Korkmaz, and T. Bircan, eds, *Data Science for Migration and Mobility*, Proceedings of the British Academy, British Academy / Oxford University Press, London.

Bloemraad, I. (2006), *Becoming a Citizen: Incorporating Immigrants and Refugees in the United States and Canada*, University of California Press, Berkeley, CA.

Blumenstock, J., Cadamuro, G., and On, R. (2015), 'Predicting poverty and wealth from mobile phone metadata', *Science* 350(6264), 1073–6.

Blumenstock, J. E., Chi, G., and Tan, X. (2019), 'Migration and the value of social networks', CEPR Discussion Paper No. DP13611.

Blumenstock, J. E. and Eagle, N. (2012), 'Divided we call: Disparities in access and use of mobile phones in Rwanda', *Information Technologies & International Development* 8(2), 1–16.

Borjas, G. J. (1999), 'Immigration and welfare magnets', *Journal of Labor Economics* 17(4), 607–37.

Bozcaga, T. (2020), 'The social bureaucrat: How social proximity among bureaucrats affects local governance', Program on Governance and Local Development Working Paper 35.

Bozcaga, T., Christia, F., Harwood, E., Daskalakis, C., and Papademetriou, C. (2019), 'Syrian refugee integration in Turkey: Evidence from call detail records', *in* A. A. Salah, A. Pentland, B. Lepri, and E. Letouzé, eds, *Guide to Mobile Data Analytics in Refugee Scenarios*, Springer, New York, 223–49.

Brüderl, J. and Ludwig, V. (2015), 'Fixed-effects panel regression', *in* H. Best and C. Wolf, eds, *The Sage Handbook of Regression Analysis and Causal Inference*, Sage, Thousand Oaks, CA, 327–57.

Ceritoglu, E., Yunculer, H. B. G., Torun, H., and Tumen, S. (2017), 'The impact of Syrian refugees on natives' labor market outcomes in Turkey: Evidence from a quasi-experimental design', *IZA Journal of Labor Policy* 6(1), 5.

Crawley, H. and Hagen-Zanker, J. (2019), 'Deciding where to go: Policies, people and perceptions shaping destination preferences', *International Migration* 57(1), 20–35.

Damm, A. P. (2009a), 'Determinants of recent immigrants' location choices: Quasi-experimental evidence', *Journal of Population Economics* 22(1), 145–74.
Damm, A. P. (2009b), 'Ethnic enclaves and immigrant labor market outcomes: Quasi-experimental evidence', *Journal of Labor Economics* 27(2), 281–314.
Dark, S. J. and Bram, D. (2007), 'The modifiable areal unit problem (MAUP) in physical geography', *Progress in Physical Geography* 31(5), 471–9.
Docquier, F., Ozden, Ç., and Peri, G. (2014), 'The labour market effects of immigration and emigration in OECD countries', *The Economic Journal* 124(579), 1106–45.
Dodson, M. E. (2001), 'Welfare generosity and location choices among new United States immigrants', *International Review of Law and Economics* 21(1), 47–67.
Gaure, S. (2013), 'lfe: Linear group fixed effects', *The R Journal* 5(2), 104–17.
Hatton, T. J. and Tani, M. (2005), 'Immigration and inter-regional mobility in the UK, 1982–2000', *The Economic Journal* 115(507), F342–F358.
Heymann, Y. (1994), *CORINE Land Cover: Technical Guide*, Office for Official Publications of the European Communities, Luxembourg.
Hill, T. D., Davis, A. P., Roos, J. M., and French, M. T. (2020), 'Limitations of fixed-effects models for panel data', *Sociological Perspectives* 63(3), 357–69.
Hong, L., Wu, J., Frias-Martinez, E., Villarreal, A., and Frias-Martinez, V. (2019), 'Characterization of internal migrant behavior in the immediate post-migration period using cell phone traces', *in Proceedings of the Tenth International Conference on Information and Communication Technologies and Development*.
İçduygu, A. and Diker, E. (2017), 'Labor market integration of Syrian refugees in Turkey: From refugees to settlers', *The Journal of Migration Studies* 3(1), 12–35.
Imai, K. and Kim, I. S. (2019), 'When should we use unit fixed effects regression models for causal inference with longitudinal data?', *American Journal of Political Science* 63(2), 467–90.
Kadkoy, O. (2017), 'Syrians and labor market integration: Dynamics in Turkey and Germany', available at https://www.gmfus.org/news/syrians-and-labor-market-integration-dynamics-turkey-and-germany
King, G. (1997), *A Solution to the Ecological Inference Problem: Reconstructing Individual Behavior from Aggregate Data*, Princeton University Press, Princeton, NJ.
Lee, D. W. and Rogers, M. (2019), 'Measuring geographic distribution for political research', *Political Analysis* 27(3), 263–80.
Luca, M., Barlacchi, G., Oliver, N., and Lepri, B. (2022), 'Leveraging mobile phone data for migration flows', *in* A. A. Salah, E. E. Korkmaz, and T. Bircan, eds, *Data Science for Migration and Mobility*, Proceedings of the British Academy, British Academy / Oxford University Press, London.
Marshall, J. M., et al. (2016), 'Key traveller groups of relevance to spatial malaria transmission: A survey of movement patterns in four sub-Saharan African countries', *Malaria Journal* 15(1), 1–12.
Maystadt, J.-F. and Duranton, G. (2019), 'The development push of refugees: Evidence from Tanzania', *Journal of Economic Geography* 19(2), 299–334.
Mossaad, N., Ferwerda, J., Lawrence, D., Weinstein, J., and Hainmueller, J. (2020), 'In search of opportunity and community: Internal migration of refugees in the United States', *Science Advances* 6(32), eabb0295.
Ostrovsky, Y., Hou, F., and Picot, G. (2011), 'Do immigrants respond to regional labor demand shocks?', *Growth and Change* 42(1), 23–47.
Ottaviano, G. I. and Peri, G. (2012), 'Rethinking the effect of immigration on wages', *Journal of the European Economic Association* 10(1), 152–97.

Salah, A. A., Pentland, A., Lepri, B., Letouzé, E., de Montjoye, Y.-A., Dong, X., Dağdelen, Ö., and Vinck, P. (2019), 'Introduction to the data for refugees challenge on mobility of Syrian refugees in Turkey', *in* A. A. Salah, A. Pentland, B. Lepri, and E. Letouzé, eds, *Guide to Mobile Data Analytics in Refugee Scenarios*, Springer, New York, 3–27.

Shor, B., Bafumi, J., Keele, L., and Park, D. (2007), 'A Bayesian multilevel modeling approach to time-series cross-sectional data', *Political Analysis* 15(2), 165–81.

Soifer, H. D. and Alvarez, A. M. (2017), 'Choosing units of analysis in subnational research: The modifiable areal unit problem and the study of local violence during civil war', *in Proceedings of the Annual Meeting of the American Political Science Association (APSA)*, San Francisco, CA.

Sterly, H. and Wirkus, L. (2022), 'Analysing refugees' secondary mobility using mobile phone call detail records (CDR)', *in* A. A. Salah, E. E. Korkmaz, and T. Bircan, eds, *Data Science for Migration and Mobility*, Proceedings of the British Academy, British Academy / Oxford University Press, London.

TCI (2020), 'Mülteciler İçin İş birliği', Technical report, T.C. Cumhurbaşkanlığı İletişim Başkanlığı.

Wesolowski, A., Eagle, N., Noor, A. M., Snow, R. W., and Buckee, C. O. (2013), 'The impact of biases in mobile phone ownership on estimates of human mobility', *Journal of the Royal Society Interface* 10(81), 20120986.

14

Using Machine Learning and Synthetic Populations to Predict Support for Refugees and Asylum Seekers in European Regions

CARLOS ARCILA-CALDERÓN, JAVIER J. AMORES, AND MIKOLAJ STANEK

Introduction

THE MASSIVE ARRIVAL of refugees, asylum seekers, returnees, stateless persons and other types of displaced people to Europe[1] is producing relevant social, demographic, economic, and political changes in many member countries. This impact is particularly strong in the countries of first entry (for example, Greece, Italy, and Spain) and in final destinations such as Germany, where the influx of refugees has led to a marked increase in immigration rates since the beginning of the Mediterranean crisis.[2] In the same way, negative and hostile attitudes towards forced migrants seem to have continued to increase. At the same time, policies against immigration, border closures, and incidents of violence based on xenophobic reasons against refugees have also continued to increase, especially focusing on certain countries such as Greece, Germany, or Hungary.

However, this fits in with some research, such as that carried out by the Pew Research Center (Wike *et al.*, 2016). This study indicates that in the wake of the massive arrival of migrants, the feelings of Europeans towards refugees are predominantly negative in most Western countries, mainly because many citizens identify those displaced as an economic or a terrorism-related threat. This becomes a serious problem for the possible integration of refugees, since, from a social perspective, it is extremely important that these newcomers receive help from the host communities. And, in this context, the social integration of newcomers presents an important

---

[1] See UNHCR's Refugee Population Statistics Database, https://www.unhcr.org/refugee-statistics-uat/
[2] Destatis Press Release 246, 14.07.2016. 2015: Höchststände bei Zuwanderung und Wanderungsüberschuss in Deutschland. Available from https://www.destatis.de/DE/PresseService/Presse/Pressemitteilungen/2016/07/PD16_246_12421pdf.pdf

Proceedings of the British Academy, **251**, 310–335, © The British Academy 2022.

challenge for Western states and societies, so it becomes a topic of great academic interest and generates strong public and political debates (Callens and Meuleman, 2017; De Coninck, 2020). Social acceptance is directly related to the perspective of social integration (De Coninck and Matthijs, 2020), that ultimately leads to local integration as a lasting solution, and helps resettlement processes develop properly and without possible conflicts of racist or xenophobic origin.

On the other hand, the (scarce) data available show that the level of acceptance of asylum seekers and, more generally, of immigration, varies greatly not only between countries but also between regions (Drinkwater et al., 2013; Molodikova and Lyalina, 2017). There is also increasing empirical evidence that in several European locations the opposition to allowing asylum seekers to stay is particularly strong (Bansak et al., 2016; Bolin and Lidén, 2015; Zorlu, 2017). In sum, certain works have found that these attitudes towards migration may depend on variables such as nationality, age, education, incomes, or political ideology. This gives great importance to sociodemographic factors to predict refugee acceptance, since they can moderate or influence in some way the degree of acceptance or rejection of refugees (Finney and Peach, 2004; Schweitzer et al., 2005; Cameron et al., 2006; Song, 1992). However, most national and European surveys, such as Eurobarometer or the European Social Survey, which have included questions about the support of refugees or, more generally, migrants, do not have enough geographic data to estimate this support at regional level.

The objective of this work is to estimate and predict on a large scale through big data analysis techniques which European regions are most likely to receive, accept, and support the integration of refugees. For this, we will use data from surveys carried out by Eurobarometer by country, as well as sociodemographic data from each of the basic regions covered by Eurostat, which allow us to extrapolate the results on support for refugees obtained by country to the regional level. This will be achieved through the construction of predictive models based on supervised machine learning algorithms such as logistic regression, decision trees, random forest, support vector machines (SVM) and k-nearest neighbours (KNN; Alpaydin, 2020; Mitchell, 1997; Murphy, 2012), using the available surveys mentioned. Specifically, for the training of the models we will use data about the level of support for refugees presented by European citizens collected from Eurobarometer surveys. Although there are other surveys that could have been used, we chose Eurobarometer because it is one of those that offers non-geolocated data, which helped us to implement and test the proposed method. After estimating the individual probability of accepting refugees, we will use simulation to construct synthetic populations based on Eurostat census data at a regional level, and thus estimate the aggregate probabilities for each region, which will allow us to make final predictions about support for refugees at a regional level. These types of machine learning approaches are useful and beneficial in the field of social sciences due to their predictive capacity. As long as the models are trained with quality data, they can make estimates with a high level of precision and reliability, and in this case the predictions are also representative of each of the regions and generalisable.

The best resulting models will be able to help us draw a map of the geographic areas that are currently most likely to host refugees and which are less likely, and we will also improve our understanding of the possible variables and moderators that affect Europeans' perception of refugees and migrants in general. In addition, this novel predictive approach based on machine learning could help academics, government institutions, NGOs, and other stakeholders to anticipate which populations could present further rejection of future asylum seeker arrivals, and especially which populations could be more likely to accept and contribute to the integration of new refugees or relocated refugees within European borders. The predictive models can also generate a database, as well as interactive visualisation maps, including comparative analyses between models, countries, and regions, and longitudinal analysis of survey periods. In addition, these models can be continually improved and updated with new entries and tagged data (new surveys and even new social media messages), which provide the flexibility needed to adapt to changing contexts.

Understanding that only social support for the reception and integration of refugees in a region is being considered in this case, based on survey data and demographic data, it is worth highlighting that the resulting models are not intended to stigmatise citizens of certain regions with peculiar characteristics (for example, labelling them as 'refugee detractors'). Instead, this predictive analytical approach can help mitigate the risks of exclusion at the aggregate level through the planning of integration policies, including educational strategies, based on existing data. Moreover, the strategy based on machine learning and synthetic populations provided in this chapter can be applied to make estimates considering other dimensions that are not being particularly considered so far, and that may be important in resettlement management taking into account the interests of the refugees themselves, such as employability, schooling opportunities, or housing opportunities. Also, this technology could be applied with multidimensional approaches, which consider different relevant factors to refugee resettlement at the same time, something that is recommended. Ultimately these multidimensional approaches could help European governments and organisations such as UNHCR to establish policies for durable solutions and to implement resettlement programs with new data-driven evidence.

Relocation and resettlement of refugees and asylum seekers in Europe

Migration scholars are aware that the definition of refugee proposed in the 1951 Geneva Convention (art. 1a and 2 of the 1951 Refugee Statute Convention, broadened in the 1967 protocol) is now obsolete, given the complexity of the refugee reality today and the diversity of typologies. Most of these involuntarily displaced people today are part of a massive and anonymous flow of people, generally political, of the mid-20th century, which has little relation with the individual character of the refugee. In addition, the causes of population exoduses that occur today have become diversified and more complex, and should be included in the definition, as suggested by Escalona-Orcao (1995): economic needs (present in any migrant), violations of human rights, but also environmental deterioration, social, political, and/or economic inequalities, or technological gaps. Even UNHCR currently considers that refugee status should not be conditioned by the individual situation, but increasingly by the current situation in the country of origin. Thus, in this new context, sociologists such as Escalona-Orcao offer a classification that considers the different types of forcibly displaced people that exist today, which would include, in addition to asylum seekers themselves, *statutory refugees, refugees for humanitarian reasons, refugees under the UN mandate*, and, finally, *'de facto' refugees*, those who remain in a host country even without having applied for refugee status, or with a denied application.

Even though the nature of the different forcibly displaced persons is complex at present, it is necessary to point out that the International Refugee Law of 1951, still in force, already contemplated that the granting of refugee status should not be permanent or be linked to a specific geographic location. Furthermore, in the 1967 protocol it was agreed that all the actors involved in the migration and settlement processes (governments, international organisations, private companies with social responsibility, etc.) are obliged to make efforts to find lasting solutions to the problems of those forcibly displaced persons. Therefore, applying this premise to the current situation, when migratory pressure increases incessantly, and there are more types of forcibly displaced groups, the European Commission presented in 2015 the 'European Agenda on Migration', which posed a series of immediate measures to be taken in response to the Mediterranean crisis. Among these measures was the so-called Temporary Emergency Relocation Scheme, a programme that allowed the transfer of refugees and asylum seekers from one EU member country to another. From the perspective of the States, this programme aimed to share in a uniform way the responsibility of welcoming, hosting, and integrating refugees, thus complying with their international obligations, and in turn remedying the disproportionate responsibility of those EU countries with external borders that experienced a greater burden of the migratory wave, especially Greece and Italy. Specifically, this relocation was distributed considering the size of the population of the different States, the total GDP, the average number of asylum applications received in the last four years, and the employment rate of the country. Even if the program seemed positive at first, several scholars such as Niemann and Zaun (2018) soon criticised relocation for not being a fair measure of integration of refugees in a third host country, considering only the needs of European countries, and not the real preferences and needs of refugees, since factors such as the probability of integration or the employability opportunities of the relocated people were never included in the relocation criteria. In addition, as Campillo (2017) explains, it was an urgent programme that was born without guarantees of success, due to the lack of a common asylum model in the EU and more convergent migration policies, and due to the lack of participation of some member countries (such as the Czech Republic, Hungary, Romania, or Slovakia).

For this reason, in the same year the European Resettlement Scheme (Commission Recommendation of 8.6.2015) was proposed, from which the European countries agreed to resettle 22,504 refugees in special situations from countries outside the EU to Member States. Resettlement seemed a much more appropriate mechanism to ensure the settlement of refugees in a second home in the long term, since, in theory, this is based on an individualised and detailed analysis of each case. Perhaps that is why this programme, although slower, was more successful than the relocation scheme, as 15,500 displaced people had already been successfully resettled in 21 European countries by April 2017. In fact, the EU-Turkey Declaration of March 2016 was also based on resettlement, since, under this agreement, all irregular migrants arriving in Greece through Turkey from that moment on would be returned to Turkey, on the condition that the EU resettled the same number of Syrian refugees from Turkey. However, this agreement was denounced by academics and activists for somehow legitimising the expulsion of refugees arriving in Greece, and because the EU did not appear to be fulfilling its part of the commitment. Since these agreements, resettlement has become the main mechanism by which current EU programmes commit to providing mobility and protection to refugees in third countries. But, even though more and more causes are considered for why a person may be forced to escape from a certain place and become a refugee, even though the resettlement offers more guarantees to settle these refugees in a durable destination, this does not mean that it takes into account the needs of the displaced persons themselves, or the opportunities they could have to integrate and thrive in the host regions. For this reason, there are still reforms to be carried out that contribute to greater agility in the study of asylum applications, that provide a more durable settlement, and especially that consider the rights, needs, and interests of refugees. And one of the key necessary reforms of these resettlement programs must be precisely the inclusion of scientific and social criteria that allow us to know the relevant factors involved in advance, and thus make decisions based on data. In the case of the Temporary Relocation Scheme, this was an emergency measure to be implemented urgently, and the lack of criteria was understandable, since, as mentioned, it responded more to the needs of some EU countries than to the needs of refugees. But in the case of new resettlement programmes, it is not justifiable that data and empirical knowledge are not yet being used that can help make decisions based on criteria such as employability, schooling opportunities, housing opportunities, and, of course, opportunities for social integration in host regions.

That is why it is understood that it is necessary to develop new strategies that allow us to analyse all the related factors that have not been considered so far in the management of resettlement processes, and thus be able to make predictions that also take into account the needs of the resettled people. With this goal in mind, the present work tries to offer a computational method that helps to predict which are the geographical regions where the social integration of refugees is most likely to be successfully implemented, or which have a lower probability. The developed predictive tool, specifically, will be able to estimate the 'probability of acceptance of refugees' for each of the basic regions of the EU using sociodemographic data from those regions, as well as data related to the support of local citizens to refugees extracted from surveys carried out in member countries. Thus, as aforementioned, the main objective of this chapter is to provide a novel strategy based on machine learning and synthetic populations to predict the future integration of refugees in the different EU regions, knowing that this is just one of many relevant dimensions that must be considered when making decisions that can ensure successful and long-term resettlement processes.

Data-driven migration planning

Although it is true that, especially from 2015, the institutions have been proposing certain relocation and planned resettlement strategies for refugees and asylum seekers based on different factors, as we have seen, most of them are not based on clear criteria or are based only in the needs or requirements of the EU countries themselves. However, at the academic level, nowadays more and more novel migration planning strategies are being proposed that consider empirical evidence based on new factors, information, and data, such as the attributes and preferences of the displaced people, or the characteristics of the receiving societies.

An example of a work exploring the possible types of refugee resettlement is that developed by Colic-Peisker and Tilbury (2003). These authors used conventional data to analyse the resettlement processes of refugees in Australia, proposing a typology of four resettlement styles based on factors such as the social characteristics of the refugees (their human, social, and cultural capital), and the response of the host society to the arrived refugees, in terms of policy and resettlement services. Two types conceived the refugee as an active actor, participant in their own resettlement process, and the two others conceived them passively, as victims and suffering persons not so involved in their resettlement. This work suggests that the most positive models for all parties are the active ones, since they usually have better results in obtaining employment and permanent accommodation for refugees. Nevertheless, these styles are frequently influenced by regional resettlement policies and systems, as well as the refugees' own resources. As aforementioned, the administrations continue making decisions based only on traditional data and urgent needs. Nevertheless, in the last few years the academy has begun to understand the tremendous potential of big data and computational methods to study social processes and movements, including flows of migrants and refugees. In this sense, one piece of research not directly focused on migration processes, but showing the potential of big data available on social networks such as Twitter, is the one developed by Hawelka *et al.* (2014). These authors carried out a mobility study using geographically localised Twitter messages to identify global mobility patterns. The objective was to estimate the number of international travellers based on their place of residence. For this, the authors defined the turning radius and the mobility rate, with the intention of describing migratory movements based on Twitter data. Another work, more focused on the analysis of migratory processes, is the one developed by

Zagheni et al. (2014). In this study, an analysis of 500,000 Twitter users with geographical location was carried out to predict the inflexion points of migration and to gain a better understanding of migratory movements in OECD countries. In this case, the use of a migration rate was introduced considering users who move from one country of origin to another country as a measure to estimate these migratory flows.

On the other hand, Coletto et al. (2016) used a set of Twitter data related to the Mediterranean crisis as a case study to develop an adaptable and scalable multidimensional framework of sentiment analysis in this social medium. In this case, the authors, in addition to collecting tweets with spatial (user and mentioned locations) and temporal information, enriched the data with the sentiment, capable of identifying the polarity of tweets and the users. In contrast to the previous ones, this work was not intended to explore and identify the flows of people through space, but rather to understand the impact on the perception of EU citizens on migrant movements. In the same year, Ahmed et al. (2016) presented a system for the analysis of scenarios and forecasting of mass migration that consisted of multi-scale models to address the need for migration agencies, developed using the Mediterranean crisis as a case study. In this case, the authors used other relevant information available on the internet, such as migrant arrivals' registration data, collected by UNHCR; data on weather conditions and seasonal factors that influence movements, obtained from the Weather Underground service; news data provided by the GDELT Project, with which information about events and political changes was captured; and data aggregated at a country level obtained from other sources (such as the World Bank Group), such as GDP, population, or conflict status. In another line, Lamanna et al. (2018) are the first authors to use big data to make predictions about the integration of migrants and refugees in host regions. They also used data extracted from Twitter, such as language and digital space–time communication patterns of individuals (with which areas of residence are defined), to estimate the power of social integration of the cities around the world. In their study, they carried out an exhaustive analysis on the integration of immigrants in 53 cities of the world by observing the patterns of space–time communication of immigrant and local communities based on the detection of languages on Twitter and on new spatial integration metrics. With the analysis of the spatial distribution from the information extracted from social media, the authors achieved a classification of the cities according to the extent to which they integrate the immigrant communities and people from other cultures.

One of the most relevant studies especially focused on this issue so far is the one developed by Bansak et al. (2018). This work, in addition, has similarities to the strategy proposed in this chapter for its possible application in the management and planning of migration, even though it is focused on employability, a most important factor when considering ensuring refugee integration and a successful resettlement process. In the cited study, the authors developed a model that uses multiple data to assign refugee profiles to resettlement places and thus improve integration results. In this case, information on the basic characteristics of the refugees (country of origin, language skills, gender, age, etc.), the time of arrival, the assigned location, and the average success of employment are used to create a set of supervised machine learning models. The generated tool takes advantage of synergies between refugee attributes and resettlement locations to predict the expected job success of refugees in the different settlement locations based on their background characteristics. The work of Bansak supposed a novel proposal of planned migration based on the estimation of the refugee work success using computational methods and big data.

Although this approach conceived the possible job success of refugees as an influential factor for possible decision-making in terms of resettlement, neither this nor any of the referenced proposals have so far taken into account the extent of the social acceptance of refugees in the reception regions as a variable that should be considered for migration and resettlement management, and especially for a successful integration of the displaced people. For this reason, this chapter aims to offer a new approach, understanding that attitudes towards the migration of host populations are key to the integration of these collectives (Esses *et al.*, 2017). In this sense, we know that, especially from 2015 when the migration pressure in Europe increased, social opposition to allowing asylum seekers to remain in the receiving countries is particularly strong (Bansak *et al.*, 2016; Bolin and Lidén, 2015; Zorlu, 2017). But it is known that this level of acceptance of asylum seekers and, more generally, of immigration, can vary greatly, and not only between countries but also between regions, since it can be influenced by variables such as nationality, age, education, income, or political ideology (Drinkwater *et al.*, 2013; Molodikova and Lyalina, 2017). That is why sociodemographic characteristics are particularly relevant to predicting the acceptance of refugees, since these attributes can moderate or influence the degree of acceptance or rejection (Finney and Peach, 2004; Schweitzer *et al.*, 2005; Cameron *et al.*, 2006; Singer, 1988). However, most national and European surveys which include questions about support for refugees or immigrants, such as the one developed by Gallup's Migrant Acceptance index, do not have enough geographical data to estimate this support at a regional level.

Most of the available data from those surveys are either at the national level or do not allow for statistical inference, due to sampling strategy at a national level. As Wolffhardt *et al.* (2019) mention, there seems to be a lack of infrastructure for monitoring integration processes in a reliable and regular way at the local/urban scale level. It is true that some surveys already allow for infra-national comparisons. The European Social Survey (ESS), for example, allows for regional analysis because it provides available disaggregated data at the NUTS 2 level,[3] but this is not the only one. The European Values Study also allows for sub-national study, such as analysis of the perceived threat of immigration at the national, regional, and local level. Similarly, in the ESS, almost every addressed country provides the possibility of analysing data at NUTS 2, and in almost two thirds of these countries the data

---

[3] See the Glossary for the definition of NUTS. This work has made use of the NUTS 2 division, the level that refers to the basic EU regions.

allow for statistical inference (Wolffhardt *et al.*, 2019). But none of these surveys provide disaggregated data for statistical analysis at the NUTS 3 level.

In the case of Eurobarometer, it does collect geographic location data for the cities chosen in the survey at a NUTS 3 level, but not for all EU regions. In addition, geographically located data are not publicly accessible and can only be retrieved and processed in authorised centres such as GESIS in Germany. For these reasons, the present chapter proposes an innovative strategy with the objective of estimating refugee acceptance using machine learning and the simulation of synthetic populations based on any of the previous public opinion, although in this case data from Eurobarometer have been used. Specifically, we used the first five surveys of Eurobarometer that included the question 'To what extent should "our country" support refugees?'; these were launched between 2015 and 2017, dates that coincided with the worsening of the migration crisis in Europe and the Mediterranean. Thus, after estimating the individual probability of supporting refugees from the collected data, this information is extrapolated using simulation to build synthetic populations based on Eurostat census data throughout Europe, at the NUTS 2 level, only to simplify and test the method, which is perfectly extrapolated and implementable at a NUTS 3 level. By doing this, the most accurate machine learning models are expected to be able to estimate the aggregate acceptance probabilities for each of the basic EU regions. In this way, based on the developed work and the data collected from the resulting predictive models, it is intended to answer the following questions:

RQ1 What machine learning algorithm is suitable for predicting support to help refugees?

RQ2 What descriptive features included in the Eurobarometer surveys are most relevant to predicting support to help refugees?

RQ3 Which regions have greater support for the assistance and reception of refugees and asylum seekers according to the estimate of the synthetic populations generated?

RQ4 Are there temporary differences in the support for the assistance and reception of refugees and asylum seekers between the different moments collected from the survey according to the estimate of the synthetic populations generated?

Method

Predicting individual acceptance

As has been explained, Eurobarometer, like most European surveys, does not offer geolocated data on citizens' attitudes towards refugees at regional and local level.

For this reason, this chapter presents an approach based on machine learning models and synthetic populations, which can be used to make predictions about the support for refugees of European citizens at a regional or local level. To do this, we first used computational methods to mine existing data (Han and Kamber, 2001; Hand, 2007) and to build supervised machine learning models (see Box 14.1) in order to predict which citizens are more likely to receive and support refugees. In this phase, as mentioned above, we used existing sample inputs from survey data regarding opinion and attitudes of Europeans individuals towards refugees. From these surveys, we extracted valuable information about how much European citizens accept refugees (*target feature*) and other relevant variables that might explain this attitude (*descriptive features*). Specifically, we used data from the first five available Eurobarometer surveys that included our target question, 'To what extent should our country support refugees?'[4] (measured on a 1–5 scale), along with other 47 variables. This resulted in a total of 165,089 individuals distributed over five periods: November 2015 ($n = 32,833$), May 2016 ($n = 32,987$), November 2016 ($n = 32,896$), May 2017 ($n = 33,180$), and November 2017 ($n = 33,193$). From the 47 descriptive variables, we only used those related to basic sociodemographic features that can later be identified in a census, such as *country, origin, gender, age, occupation, marital status, education,* and *household composition* (nine in total). To ease the application of the algorithms we converted our *target feature* into a categorical binary variable, recoding the 1–5 scale into just two categories, 'Support helping refugees' or 'No support helping refugees', and nominal descriptive features were transformed into dummy variables (0 and 1). We also rescaled the descriptive variables to use these standardised values when modelling with some algorithms (logistic regression, SVM, and KNN). After dropping missing values, we obtained a final matrix of 112,837 cases × 48 features (Table 14.1).

We run all the models in Jupyter Notebooks in Python 3.4 (available online for reproducibility) using mainly the libraries scikit-learn, pandas, and numpy. Standard machine learning approaches based on *information, similarity, probability* and *error* were used (Kelleher et al., 2015). Specifically, we modelled the social acceptance of refugees using logistic regression (LR), decision tree (DT), random forest (RF), SVM, and KNN over longitudinal data from Eurobarometer and obtained acceptable evaluation metrics in all the surveyed periods and for all the algorithms. For this, we randomly divided the data into a training set (70%) and test set (30%), and we manually tuned the parameters of each algorithm until we found the most optimal configuration. In total we generated 36 models (6×6), corresponding to six algorithms in five different surveys across time (using the data from each period), plus one aggregated summary survey. Table 14.2 shows the parameters and evaluation metrics of the predictive models generated with the data that summarises the five surveys (using k-fold cross-validation).

---

[4] This target question is used for the variable *Support for refugees*, because it is understood as an indicator of this support presented by the European citizen, to the extent that he/she approves that his/her country supports refugees.

Box 14.1 Supervised machine learning models

Machine learning approaches can be classified into several broad categories, depending on the task at hand. A *regression* problem is defined by a mapping from instances to real-valued target variables. Conversely, a *classification* model seeks to learn, from a set of input instances called the *training set*, which class a new instance should belong to. For these types of problems, *discriminative* models will learn boundaries that separate classes, and *generative* models will learn the distribution of instances that belong to a class. The *model selection* problem is about selecting which model should be used to solve the particular problem, and each model comes with a range of assumptions (for example, about the class boundaries), and with different numbers of free parameters that need to be optimised. The data-driven optimisation of these parameters is called the *training* of the model.

Given a set of instances, the training data can be described as $X = \{I_t, r_t\}$, with $t = 1, \ldots, N$, where I_t are instances, r_t are the target labels, and N stands for the total number of training instances. In *supervised learning*, we are provided with the labels during training. The more difficult *unsupervised learning* scenario seeks to find structure in the data without the help of labels, and includes techniques like *clustering* and *density estimation*. For a comprehensive treatment of supervised machine learning, see Alpaydin (2020). We briefly describe the most popular approaches here.

One of the simplest approaches in machine learning is *k-nearest neighbours*, where, given a new instance I, the closest K samples (according to a distance function, which is typically Euclidean distance) are located and their target values are used for estimation (via mean or mode). This model requires keeping the training set in memory, and is therefore slow. When we have two classes that need to be separated, the simplest method is *linear discriminant analysis* (LDA), which fits a linear discriminant function that maximises the variance between the two classes it separates, and minimises the variance within each class. However, classes are not linearly separable for most problems. The *support vector machine* is frequently used for finding a non-linear discriminating boundary between classes. It is an optimisation-based approach that tries to find the optimal hyperplane that separates each class and uses a kernel function to project the points to a higher-dimensional space where they can become linearly separable.

For matrix and tensor data structures (such as images), *neural networks* (NNs) are frequently used. A basic NN (such as a multi-layer perceptron) involves a projection of the data to some intermediate representation, a non-linear transformation and combination of features, followed by a final projection to the desired target function. In a classification problem, typically a *one-hot encoding* is used, where for C classes, a C-dimensional vector is the output, and class membership is indicated by setting the correct class to 1 and the rest to 0. A *deep neural network* is obtained by adding more layers of processing. For image-based data (e.g. satellite images), the *convolution* operation, which is the filtering of a small neighbourhood of the input, provides great translation invariance properties, and *convolutional neural networks* (CNNs) are extremely successful for such problems.

Finally, tree-based classifiers provide their output on progressive filtering of the input based on selected features. *Decision tree* classifiers use information theoretic guidelines to select these features, and *random forest* classifiers bring a large number of randomly constructed decision trees together, to improve generalisation power.

Table 14.1 Variables from Eurobarometer to model the level of support for refugees in Europe

	Variable	Description
0	Support for refugees (target variable)	0 = No support 1 = Support
1	Country	Dummy (0–1): country_BALGARIJA, country_BELGIQUE, country_CESKA REPUBLIKA, country_DANMARK, country_DEUTSCHLAND OST, country_DEUTSCHLAND WEST, country_EESTI, country_ELLADA, country_ESPANA, country_FRANCE, country_GREAT BRITAIN, country_HRVATSKA, country_IRELAND, country_ITALIA, country_KYPROS, country_LATVIA, country_LIETUVA, country_LUXEMBOURG, country_MAGYARORSZAG, country_MALTA, country_NEDERLAND, country_POLSKA, country_PORTUGAL, country_ROMANIA, country_SLOVENIJA, country_SLOVENSKA REPUBLIC, country_SUOMI, country_SVERIGE, country_ÖSTERREICH
2	Origin	0 = Foreigner 1 = Native
3	Marital status	Dummy (0–1): Married, Partnership, Single, Divorced/Separated, Widow
4	Education	0 = No formal education (< 10) 1 = ISCED Level 1. Primary education (10–12) 2 = ISCED Level 2. Lower secondary education (13–15) 3 = ISCED Level 3. Upper secondary education (16–18) 4 = ISCED Level 4. Post-secondary non-tertiary education 5 = ISCED Level 5. First stage of tertiary education
5	Gender	Dummy (0–1): Woman, Man
6	Age	0 = < 15 years 1 = 15–29 years 2 = 30–49 years 3 = 50–64 years 4 = 65–84 years 5 = ≥ 85 years
7	Occupation	Dummy (0–1): Employed, Not active, Unemployed
8	Type of community	Dummy (0–1): Small/middle town, Rural area or village, Large town
9	Household composition	0 = 1 person 1 = 2 persons 2 = 3–5 persons 3 = ≥ 6 persons

Table 14.2 Evaluation metrics and parameters of the general models

Algorithm	Accuracy	F-score	AUC ROC
Logistic regression (LR) ($C = 1000.0, random\_state = 0$)	**0.72**	**0.68**	**0.68**
Decision tree (DT) ($entropy = 3$)	0.67	0.52	0.56
Random forest (RF) ($trees = 10$)	0.68	0.64	0.64
Support vector machines (SVM)	**0.72**	**0.68**	**0.68**
SVM with kernel and gamma (SVM2) ($kernel = rbf, random\_state = 0,$ $gamma = 100, C = 1.0$)	0.69	0.63	0.63
k-nearest neighbours (KNN) ($n = 5$, dist. Euclidean)	0.63	0.41	0.50

Table 14.3 Logistic regression coefficients

Countries
0.41, 0.01, 0.36* (Belgium), −0.15, −0.11, −0.3, 0.15, −0.07, −0.29* (Greece), 0.03, −0.17, −0.01, −0.18, 0.17, −0.07, 0.22, 0.11, −0.19, 0.29* (Luxembourg), −0.15, −0.27, −0.08, 0.06, −0.13, 0.16, 0.11, 0.26, −0.02, −0.28* (Finland), −0.01

Other variables
−0.03, 0.04, −0.01, −0.04, −0.28* (Education), −0.04, 0.04, −0.02, 0.01, −0.03, 0.03, 0.03, −0.03, 0.01, −0.05, 0.08

With these models we could predict the probability (0–1) of support for refugees of any European citizen, with country and education being relevant factors with significant coefficients in logistic regression (Table 14.3) and age and education in random forest (Figure 14.1). For example, using logistic regression for the model of November 2015, we found that a Belgian citizen with 10 years of education has a lower probability (0.62%) of accepting and supporting a refugee than a Greek individual with 30 years of education (0.87%). In this way, predictions were made at an individual level knowing in advance the sociodemographic features of a citizen, something that might be useful for experimental studies or for individual comparisons, but provides little insight into the social acceptance of refugees at a group level.

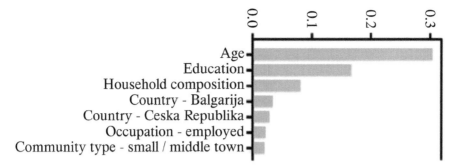

Figure 14.1 Random forest features.

Predicting social acceptance

In order to overcome the limitations of the individual predictions and to extend the predictive models to all European regions, we simulated the sociodemographic features of 2,710,000 European citizens, corresponding to 10,000 in each of the 271 basic regions (NUTS 2). Specifically, we generated *synthetic populations*[5] for each region using *a priori* distributions of the sociodemographic features obtained in the census data from Eurostat. That is, if the *a priori* distribution of gender in a specific region is 45% for men (0) and 55% for women (1), we generated a numeric vector with random assignments of 0 and 1, but with a different probability during the assignments (45% for 0 and 55% for 1). We decided to estimate each variable independently, even when some approaches may prefer to do it conditionally on the other covariates. In the case of the Northern Ireland region (UKN0), for example, with respect to the variable origin, the real population distribution was 23% foreigners and 77% native, and this was translated in a line of code as follows:
```
native = np.array([.23,.77]).cumsum().searchsorted(
                        np.random.sample(Total_Population))
```
Synthetic populations (Ye *et al.*, 2009; Antoni *et al.*, 2017) are often used in mobility and transportation studies (Barthelemy and Toint, 2013; Moeckel *et al.*, 2003) but are seldom implemented in social sciences. In this sense, this approach depicts an innovation that brings validated computational methods of other fields to social research. Figure 14.2 shows a screenshot of the final code generated to create these artificial populations.

Finally, we extrapolated from the individual level to the regional level by computing the probability of acceptance for each individual using six predictive models (LR, DT, RF, SVM, SVM2, KNN) and for each of the periods (November 2015,

---

[5] A synthetic population is an artificial and simplified representation of a real population regarding some specific sociodemographic factors. The synthetic population is not identical to the actual population and does not represent all residents faithfully. Instead, the synthetic population matches various statistical distributions of the real one, and therefore is close enough to the true population to be used statistically and in modelling.

```
#type_community
#0= NO, 1= YES
type_community_Large_town = np.array([1,0]).cumsum().searchsorted(np.random.sample(Total_Population))
type_community_Rural_area_village = np.array([1,0]).cumsum().searchsorted(np.random.sample(Total_Population))
type_community_Small_middle_town = np.array([0,1]).cumsum().searchsorted(np.random.sample(Total_Population))

#occupation
#0= NO, 1= YES
occupation_Employed = np.array([.50,.50]).cumsum().searchsorted(np.random.sample(Total_Population))
occupation_Not_active = np.array([.52,.48]).cumsum().searchsorted(np.random.sample(Total_Population))
occupation_Unemployed = np.array([.98,.02]).cumsum().searchsorted(np.random.sample(Total_Population))

#GENDER
#0= NO, 1= YES
gender_Man = np.array([.51,.49]).cumsum().searchsorted(np.random.sample(Total_Population))
gender_Woman = np.array([.49,.51]).cumsum().searchsorted(np.random.sample(Total_Population))

#marital_status
#0= NO, 1= YES
marital_status_Divorced_Separated = np.array([.94,.06]).cumsum().searchsorted(np.random.sample(Total_Population))
marital_status_Married = np.array([.53,.47]).cumsum().searchsorted(np.random.sample(Total_Population))
marital_status_Partnership = np.array([1,0]).cumsum().searchsorted(np.random.sample(Total_Population))
marital_status_Single = np.array([.60,.40]).cumsum().searchsorted(np.random.sample(Total_Population))
marital_status_Widow = np.array([.93,.07]).cumsum().searchsorted(np.random.sample(Total_Population))

#generation of synthetic population
features = [native, educational, age, household_composition, country_BALGARIJA, country_BELGIQUE, country_CESKA_REPUB
df = pd.DataFrame(features)
df = df.T
population = df.as_matrix()
```

Figure 14.2 Jupyter notebook to create synthetic populations.

```
prob_lr_models_nov_2017 = lr_models_nov_2017.predict_proba(population_std)
prob_lr_models_nov_2017 = prob_lr_models_nov_2017[:, 0]
prob_lr_models_nov_2017 = np.average(prob_lr_models_nov_2017)
prob_tree_models_nov_2017 = tree_models_nov_2017.predict_proba(population)
prob_tree_models_nov_2017 = prob_tree_models_nov_2017[:, 0]
prob_tree_models_nov_2017 = np.average(prob_tree_models_nov_2017)
prob_forest_models_nov_2017 = forest_models_nov_2017.predict_proba(population)
prob_forest_models_nov_2017 = prob_forest_models_nov_2017[:, 0]
prob_forest_models_nov_2017 = np.average(prob_forest_models_nov_2017)
prob_svm_models_nov_2017 = svm_models_nov_2017.predict_proba(population_std)
prob_svm_models_nov_2017 = prob_svm_models_nov_2017[:, 0]
prob_svm_models_nov_2017 = np.average(prob_svm_models_nov_2017)
prob_svm2_models_nov_2017 = svm2_models_nov_2017.predict_proba(population_std)
prob_svm2_models_nov_2017 = prob_svm2_models_nov_2017[:, 0]
prob_svm2_models_nov_2017 = np.average(prob_svm2_models_nov_2017)
prob_knn_models_nov_2017 = knn_models_nov_2017.predict_proba(population)
prob_knn_models_nov_2017 = prob_knn_models_nov_2017[:, 0]
prob_knn_models_nov_2017 = np.average(prob_knn_models_nov_2017)

print([Code_of_nuts2, prob_lr, prob_tree, prob_forest, prob_svm, prob_svm2, prob_knn,
       prob_lr_models_nov_2015, prob_tree_models_nov_2015, prob_forest_models_nov_2015, prob_svm_models_nov_2015,
       prob_svm2_models_nov_2015, prob_knn_models_nov_2015, prob_lr_models_may_2016, prob_tree_models_may_2016,
       prob_forest_models_may_2016, prob_svm_models_may_2016, prob_svm2_models_may_2016, prob_knn_models_may_2016,
       prob_lr_models_nov_2016, prob_tree_models_nov_2016, prob_forest_models_nov_2016, prob_svm_models_nov_2016,
       prob_svm2_models_nov_2016, prob_knn_models_nov_2016, prob_lr_models_may_2017, prob_tree_models_may_2017,
       prob_forest_models_may_2017, prob_svm_models_may_2017, prob_svm2_models_may_2017, prob_knn_models_may_2017,
       prob_lr_models_nov_2017, prob_tree_models_nov_2017, prob_forest_models_nov_2017, prob_svm_models_nov_2017,
       prob_svm2_models_nov_2017, prob_knn_models_nov_2017])
```

Figure 14.3 Jupyter notebook to estimate the probability of acceptance of refugees for each region.

May 2016, November 2016, May 2017, November 2017, and total), and later estimated the average probability for all the 271 regions. Additionally, we created an average variable that summarised the six predictive models. In sum, we set up a database with 271 cases (all NUTS 2 regions in Europe) and 42 estimated probabilities of acceptance of refugees. Figure 14.3 shows a screenshot of the code we generated to estimate the probability of acceptance of refugees for each region.

Results

Based on the predictions for all regions of Europe from the model that summarises the five surveys, an online interactive map was created with the Tableau platform, which is available online for consultation, updating, and reproducibility.[6] In this map, it is possible to visualise, explore, and compare the estimates of support for refugees in each of the basic regions offered by each of the models. The links to these interactive maps, in addition to the Jupyter Notebooks for the generated synthetic populations and predictive models, and a longitudinal database with the estimates for each of the surveys, are available on the author's GitHub repository.[7]

Figure 14.4 shows the comparative maps, where we can visualise the regional predictions with each model for the aggregated data and notice that there are some differences between them, from the more homogeneous predictions in decision trees to the more heterogeneous in logistic regression or KNN (the darker the region, the more support for refugees). Responding to RQ1, based on the performance that is reflected in the evaluation metrics shown in Table 14.2, we can confirm that the prediction model that seems most suitable for estimating support to help refugees using the synthetic populations is the one generated with logistic regression, followed by the one generated with SVM.

Secondly, responding to RQ2, when looking at the maps at the highest level we can clearly observe that *country* is a strong predictor of the social support for refugees because we see apparent homogeneity within the regions of each country. However, depending on the model, there are other variables that have an important weight in predicting refugee support in synthetic populations for each region. Thus, next to *country*, determining in most cases, other variables with a relevant weight are *age*, *education*, or *household composition*, as can be seen in Figure 14.1, which shows the representation of weights in the model generated with a random forest.

In order to summarise the models, we computed the average of the six predictions for each region and replotted the map. In Figure 14.5 we can visualise this average estimate, where it is clearly seen which countries are most likely to socially support refugees. The countries that seem to offer the most support for refugees are Sweden, Spain, the United Kingdom, or Germany, and those that seem to offer the least acceptance are the Czech Republic, Bulgaria, Hungary, or Romania, precisely the same countries that opposed adopting a mandatory temporary relocation system from the outset.

Comparing the countries at a statistical level through the non-parametric Kruskal–Wallis test and using the average estimates of the regions by country, we confirm that there are significant differences in the level of support for refugees that

---

[6] The interactive map is directly accessible at https://public.tableau.com/profile/carlos.arcila#!/vizhome/visualization_32/Historia2

[7] The repository with the notebooks, the longitudinal database, and the interactive maps is available at https://github.com/carlosarcila/mlrefugees

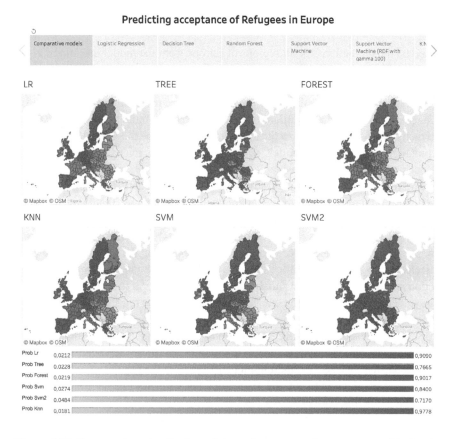

Figure 14.4 Comparative visualisation of the estimates on refugee support with the six predictive models in all regions of Europe. Colour version printed as Plate 11.

the models estimate from the synthetic populations for each of the countries at a general level [$H(28) = 270.999$; $p < 0.01$, $\eta^2 = 0.98$]. Specifically, as expected from the visualisation of the maps, the pairwise comparisons indicate that there are differences between the Czech Republic, the country with the lowest level of support for refugees ($Mdn = 0.32$), and the countries that register the highest level, which are Great Britain ($Mdn = 0.77$) [$H(28) = -180.900$; $p < 0.01$], Netherlands ($Mdn = 0.78$) [$H(28) = -212.417$; $p < 0.01$, Spain ($Mdn = 0.78$) [$H(28) = -220.263$; $p < 0.01$], Germany ($Mdn = 0.79$), [$H(28) = -248.767$; $p < 0.01$], and Sweden ($Mdn = 0.80$), [$H(28) = -265.625$; $p < 0.01$]. There are also differences between the second country with the lowest level of acceptance, Hungary ($Mdn = 0.34$), and Great Britain [$H(28) = -175.757$; $p < 0.01$], Netherlands [$H(28) = -207.274$; $p < 0.01$], Spain [$H(28) = 215.120$; $p < 0.01$], Germany [$H(28) = 243.624$; $p < 0.01$], and Sweden [$H(28) = -260.482$; $p < 0.01$]. Similarly, there are differences between the third country with the lowest acceptance, Bulgaria ($Mdn = $

Figure 14.5 Summarised visualisation with the average probability of acceptance for the six models and all the analysed periods (2015–2017).

0.37), and once again Great Britain [$H(28) = -169.400$; $p < 0.01$], Netherlands [$H(28) = -200.917$; $p < 0.01$], Spain [$H(28) = -280.173$; $p < 0.01$], Germany [$H(28) = -237.167$; $p < 0.01$], and Sweden [$H(28) = -254.125$; $p < 0.01$].

These differences can be seen more clearly in Figure 14.6, where we have represented through a bar graph the average level of support for refugees that each of the European countries has, based on the estimates of the models for each of their regions, except for countries with only one or two regions (such as Malta or Luxembourg), where no means could be drawn or compared. In this graph, in addition to the average estimate by country, highlighting countries with a significantly higher or lower extent of support for refugees, the total mean of all the countries, the total median, as well as the quartiles and the maximum and minimum values can be seen.

These estimates fully coincide with comparative European surveys, something that shows the reliability of the strategy and the models. Nevertheless, these results still offer little relevant contribution, except for the method used for their generation.

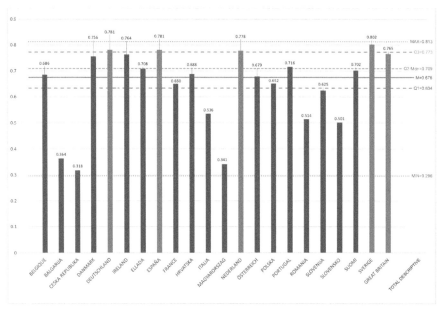

Figure 14.6 Average level of support for refugees by country and total descriptive statistics.

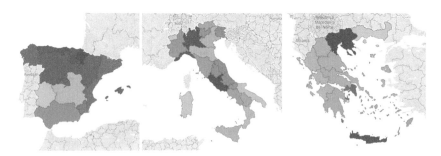

Figure 14.7 Estimated refugee support in regions of Spain, Italy, and Greece.

If we focus on each country we see more interesting internal differences (although the ranges of the estimates are narrower), responding to RQ3 and fulfilling an existing gap in the EU surveys and empirical studies. For example, in the case of Italy, Greece, and Spain (Figure 14.7) we observe that populated regions are the most likely to support and accept refugees, which can be explained by their previous experience with massive arrivals of migrants and their multicultural and cosmopolitan societies. Some of these regions are Athens, Thessaloniki, Rome, Milan, Madrid, or Catalonia.

As an example of statistical comparison by regions, an intermediate level (between countries and basic regions) has been used, in which we have several estimates with which to compare medians. Thus, we have compared the two large German regions, East and West, whose division is possible thanks to the structuring of the 2016 NUTS 2, using the non-parametric *Mann–Whitney test*. The results indicate that, indeed, in Germany there are statistically significant internal differences with respect to the level of acceptance estimated by synthetic populations, with West Germany being the area with the highest support for refugees ($Mdn = 0.79$) compared to East Germany, with significantly less support ($Mdn = 0.74$) [$U(n_1 = 30, n_2 = 8) = 0.00; z = -4.297, p < 0.01, \eta^2 = 0.486$].

Finally, regarding the longitudinal dataset, in order to respond to RQ4 the repeated measures analysis of variance test was used to compare the mean level of support for refugees in European countries, using the mean estimate of all models. The statistical test revealed that indeed there are significant differences between the mean acceptance offered by the models with the data from each of the surveys of the five time periods. In this way, it can be confirmed that there are temporary differences in the level of acceptance of refugees and asylum seekers that predictive models estimate [$F(3.04, 838.68) = 55.462; p < 0.01; \eta_p^2 = 0.17$]. The pairwise comparisons show that there are no statistically significant differences between the estimates for the survey of November 2015 ($M = 0.687; SD = 0.121$) and the two of 2017, both in May ($M = 0.680; SD = 0.143$) and November ($M = 0.684; SD = 0.121$), the three moments in which a higher level of acceptance is estimated. But there are differences between the one of November 2015 and the two of 2016, where the level of acceptance seems to decrease, both in the one of May ($M = 0.656; SD = 0.132$) [$t(9) = 103.33; p < 0.01; d = 0.24$] and in the one of November ($M = 0.672; SD = 0.144$) [$t(9) = 50; p < 0.01; d = 0.11$]. Similarly, differences were detected between the mean estimate for the data of the May 2017 survey and the one of May 2016 [$t(9) = 120; p < 0.01; d = 0.17$], and that of November 2016 [$t(9) = 4; p < .01; d = 0.06$], and between the mean estimate for the last survey collected, that of November 2017, and also those of both 2016 surveys, both the one of May [$t(9) = 145; p < 0.01; d = 0.22$], and the one of November [$t(9) = 43.33; p < 0.01; d = 0.09$]. Finally, these multiple comparisons also highlighted a statistically significant difference between the level of acceptance found for both surveys in 2016, this being lower in May than in November [$t(9) = 80; p < 0.01; d = 0.12$]. All the differences detected between the mean estimates for the different periods have a small effect size.

Thus, according to the mean estimates of the predictive models based on the synthetic populations generated, the period with the highest acceptance within the data collected would be November 2015, followed by the moment of the survey of November 2017. Meanwhile, we can conclude that 2016 was the worst year for social integration in Europe, with May 2016 being the period with the lowest estimated acceptance, when a significant decrease is perceived compared to the other surveys. These longitudinal differences can be seen in Figure 14.8. From our dataset can also be make these longitudinal estimates for each of the regions, and our interactive map can visualise differences over time.

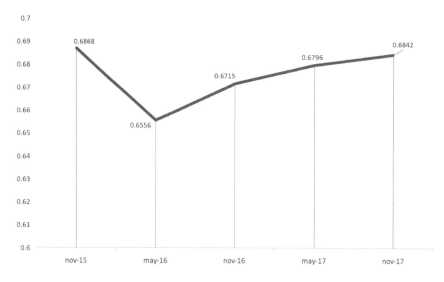

Figure 14.8 Longitudinal estimates of support for refugees in Europe by period.

Discussion and conclusions

With this work we have confirmed that it is possible to develop a computational strategy that integrates machine learning and synthetic populations to make predictions on social issues, in this case on the level of support for refugees, based on sociodemographic data and data from European surveys launched by countries. Of the six algorithms used to generate the predictive models, we have concluded that the ones with the best performance were logistic regression and support vector machines. In all the models, in addition, the factors with the most important weights that influenced the estimates were the country, but also age, education, and household composition, among others. When comparing the level of support for refugees at the country level, it was confirmed that the models show reliable estimates, since they coincide with the results obtained by Eurobarometer surveys, with countries such as Sweden, Germany, the Netherlands, Spain, or Great Britain showing a higher level of support, with Czech Republic, Bulgaria, Hungary, or Romania showing a lower level. It should also be remembered that these countries where a lower level of support was detected were the ones that refused to adopt the Temporary Relocation Scheme, as mentioned at the beginning of the chapter. At the regional level, statistical differences have been found in the mean estimated support for the two main areas of Germany, with the level of West Germany being significantly higher than that of East Germany. This statistical comparison can be applied to any of the geographical areas within the countries. At the level of basic regions, without entering into specific comparisons, it has been confirmed that large capitals, with the largest population and most multiculturalism, are those that show a higher level of support for refugees, such as Athens and Thessaloniki in Greece, Rome and Milan in Italy, or Madrid and Catalonia in Spain. Finally, we have detected longitudinal differences in the average European estimate produced by the mean of all models, confirming that 2016 was the worst year in terms of social acceptance, and for the integration of refugees and asylum seekers, on the European continent.

In this way, to the best of our knowledge we have generated the first articulated data that estimate the social integration of refugees in all basic regions of Europe from sociodemographic data. The dataset (available online for reproducibility) was produced using the above-mentioned computational approach, joining machine learning and synthetic populations, something innovative in the field of social sciences. In addition, since the sociodemographic characteristics, such as the contexts that influence attitudes towards refugees and migration, are changing, this database, used to generate the models that estimate the level of support for refugees, can be updated and adapted to other regions and contexts. Thus, we conclude that these machine learning models can improve our understanding of the possible variables that affect the attitudes of Europeans towards refugees and migrants in general, and that synthetic populations can help us to extrapolate individual data to a geographical level, using innovative computational methods in social research. Also, we consider that this data-driven approach might help scholars, governmental institutions, NGOs, and other stakeholders to anticipate which populations might have more resistance to the future arrivals of new asylum seekers, and particularly which ones might be more likely to accept and contribute to the integration of those forcibly displaced people. This innovative approach can make a significant contribution to a longstanding debate on criteria of efficient fair distribution of refugees between EU countries (Holtug, 2016; Jones and Teytelboym, 2017). In particular, this computational approach can be useful for the resettlement programmes of the UNHCR. These models are not intended to stigmatise citizens or regions with certain features. Instead, this predictive analytic approach can help to mitigate exclusion risks at an aggregate level through the planning of integration policies, including education strategies, based on existing data. Furthermore, the dataset that trains and generates the models can be updated with new inputs and labelled data (e.g., from any other public survey) and with data at a local level (NUTS 3), providing the flexibility needed to adapt to changing contexts. It was known that focusing on the NUTS 2 level could be risky and could limit the potential for analysis, as there is an overall lack of harmonised comparative data. Nevertheless, this level was used in order to simplify the work, since the objetive of this chapter was only to provide and evaluate a method that would serve to disaggregate any survey, thus being able to reach NUTS 3 level, as well as being applied using other new dimensions or variables.

Apart from what has been mentioned, it is important to highlight a series of limitations in this work. In the first place, we are aware that support for refugees is just one of the variables that can and should be taken into account for the integration of asylum seekers and, ultimately, for decision-making in migration management or the resettlement processes. Along with this dimension, others should be considered, as already mentioned in this chapter, which may be employability, housing opportunities, or schooling opportunities, among others. Second, we are also aware that survey data that measure perceptions have different biases, such as social desirability, as citizens seldom respond faithfully. Citizens often answer these types of surveys in a politically correct manner, or as they are expected to answer. Furthermore, a person who shows a positive attitude towards refugees will not necessarily take an active behaviour and mobilise to support and facilitate the integration of these displaced people in their country, and conversely, a person who expresses a negative attitude or a low level of support for refugees will not necessarily be opposed in a practical way and through behaviour to the integration of asylum seekers or make their integration more difficult, although it is more probable. Also, the perceptions collected in this type of survey are often volatile and changing, so it would be convenient to be attentive to the constant evolution of public opinion in different countries. Finally, it should be noted that the machine learning and big data approaches serve to generalise, but sometimes they do not have to be fully representative. In addition, these techniques have certain shortcomings when it comes to focusing on analysing and responding to specific cases in depth, for which preferably qualitative studies would be required.

Considering these limitations, we propose to advance this line of research to improve the strategy in different ways. On the one hand, the models that we have presented should be evaluated and validated at the applied level, making comparisons with new real data. On the other hand, in future research it would be convenient to also use deep learning algorithms, which could offer better performance and greater reliability, but also the construction of more complex prediction models, with multidimensional approaches. Along this line, we raise the possibility of generating a more sophisticated multi-level prediction strategy that includes, in addition to the support for refugees perceived through surveys, other variables that can collect the attitudes of citizens towards refugees and migrants in an observed way, such as perhaps the latent sentiment in messages published on social media; but also other dimensions that can be detected, both from existing data and theoretical variables, such as the tradition of migration in the city, the ideological line of the government in force in each country, or the economic conditions of the regions for the reception of refugees.

Acknowledgements

This work was carried out at the EUROLAB at GESIS – Leibniz Institute for the Social Sciences, and was financially supported by the GESIS visiting research grant EL-2017-152 awarded to Dr. Carlos Arcila Calderón.

References

Ahmed, M. N., Barlacchi, G., Braghin, S., Calabrese, F., Ferretti, M., Lonij, V. P., Nair, R., Novack, R., Paraszczak, J., and Toor, A. S. (2016), 'A multi-scale approach to data-driven mass migration analysis', *in* R. Gavaldà, I. Zliobaite, and J. Gama, *Proceedings of the First Workshop on Data Science for Social Good co-located with the European Conference on Machine Learning and Principles and Practice of Knowledge Discovery in Databases*, CEUR Workshop Proceedings 1831.

Alpaydin, E. (2020), *Introduction to Machine Learning*, MIT Press, Cambridge, MA.

Antoni, J.-P., Vuidel, G., and Klein, O. (2017), 'Generating a located synthetic population of individuals, households, and dwellings', Luxembourg Institute of Socio-Economic Research (LISER) Working Paper (2017-07).

Bansak, K., Ferwerda, J., Hainmueller, J., Dillon, A., Hangartner, D., Lawrence, D., and Weinstein, J. (2018), 'Improving refugee integration through data-driven algorithmic assignment', *Science* 359(6373), 325–9.

Bansak, K., Hainmueller, J., and Hangartner, D. (2016), 'How economic, humanitarian, and religious concerns shape European attitudes toward asylum seekers', *Science* 354(6309), 217–22.

Barthelemy, J. and Toint, P. L. (2013), 'Synthetic population generation without a sample', *Transportation Science* 47(2), 266–79.

Bolin, N. and Lidén, G. (2015), 'The non-receivers. Explanations as to why some Swedish municipalities resist refugee reception', *in Proceedings of the Second International Conference on Public Policy*.

Callens, M.-S. and Meuleman, B. (2017), 'Do integration policies relate to economic and cultural threat perceptions? A comparative study in Europe', *International Journal of Comparative Sociology* 58(5), 367–91.

Cameron, L., Rutland, A., Brown, R., and Douch, R. (2006), 'Changing children's intergroup attitudes toward refugees: Testing different models of extended contact', *Child Development* 77(5), 1208–19.

Campillo, F. M. (2017), 'El reasentamiento y la reubicación de refugiados y su aplicación en la actual crisis humanitaria', *bie3: Boletín IEEE* (5), 717–32.

Coletto, M., Esuli, A., Lucchese, C., Muntean, C. I., Nardini, F. M., Perego, R., and Renso, C. (2016), 'Sentiment-enhanced multidimensional analysis of online social networks: Perception of the Mediterranean refugees crisis', *in Proceedings of the 2016 IEEE/ACM International Conference on Advances in Social Networks Analysis and Mining (ASONAM)*, 1270–77.

Colic-Peisker, V. and Tilbury, F. (2003), '"Active" and "passive" resettlement: The influence of support services and refugees' own resources on resettlement style', *International Migration* 41(5), 61–91.

De Coninck, D. (2020), 'Migrant categorizations and European public opinion: Diverging attitudes towards immigrants and refugees', *Journal of Ethnic and Migration Studies* 46(9), 1667–86.

De Coninck, D. and Matthijs, K. (2020), 'Who is allowed to stay? Settlement deservingness preferences towards migrants in four European countries', *International Journal of Intercultural Relations* 77, 25–37.

Drinkwater, S., *et al.* (2013), 'Regional variations in attitudes towards refugees: Evidence from Great Britain', Technical report, Centre for Research and Analysis of Migration (CReAM).

Escalona-Orcao, A. I. (1995), 'El estudio de las migraciones de refugiados: Cuestiones teóricas y metodológicas', *Geographicalia* (32), 63–82.

Esses, V. M., Hamilton, L. K., and Gaucher, D. (2017), 'The global refugee crisis: Empirical evidence and policy implications for improving public attitudes and facilitating refugee resettlement', *Social Issues and Policy Review* 11(1), 78–123.

Finney, N. and Peach, E. (2004), 'Attitudes towards asylum seekers, refugees and other immigrants: A literature review for the Commission for Racial Equality', Technical report, Commission for Racial Equality, London.

Han, J. and Kamber, M. (2001), *Data Mining Concepts and Techniques*, Morgan Kaufmann, San Francisco.

Hand, D. J. (2007), 'Principles of data mining', *Drug Safety* 30(7), 621–2.

Hawelka, B., Sitko, I., Beinat, E., Sobolevsky, S., Kazakopoulos, P., and Ratti, C. (2014), 'Geo-located Twitter as proxy for global mobility patterns', *Cartography and Geographic Information Science* 41(3), 260–71.

Holtug, N. (2016), 'A fair distribution of refugees in the European Union', *Journal of Global Ethics* 12(3), 279–88.

Jones, W. and Teytelboym, A. (2017), 'The international refugee match: A system that respects refugees' preferences and the priorities of states', *Refugee Survey Quarterly* 36(2), 84–109.

Kelleher, J. D., Mac Namee, B., and D'Arcy, A. (2015) *Fundamentals of Machine Learning for Predictive Data Analytics*, MIT Press, Cambridge, MA.

Lamanna, F., Lenormand, M., Salas-Olmedo, M. H., Romanillos, G., Gonçalves, B., and Ramasco, J. J. (2018), 'Immigrant community integration in world cities', *PLOS One* 13(3), e0191612.

Mitchell, T. (1997), *Machine Learning*, McGraw-Hill Inc, New York.

Moeckel, R., Spiekermann, K., and Wegener, M. (2003), 'Creating a synthetic population', *in Proceedings of the Eighth International Conference on Computers in Urban Planning and Urban Management (CUPUM)*.

Molodikova, I. N. and Lyalina, A. V. (2017), 'Territorial differences in the attitudes to the migration crisis in Germany: The political aspect', *Baltic Region* 9(2), 60–75.

Murphy, K. P. (2012), *Machine Learning: A Probabilistic Perspective*, MIT Press, Cambridge, MA.

Niemann, A. and Zaun, N. (2018), 'EU refugee policies and politics in times of crisis: Theoretical and empirical perspectives', *JCMS: Journal of Common Market Studies* 56(1), 3–22.

Schweitzer, R., Perkoulidis, S., Krome, S., Ludlow, C., and Ryan, M. (2005), 'Attitudes towards refugees: The dark side of prejudice in Australia', *Australian Journal of Psychology* 57(3), 170–79.

Singer, J. D. (1988), 'Reconstructing the correlates of war dataset on material capabilities of states, 1816–1985', *International Interactions* 14(2), 115–32.

Song, J. H.-L. (1992), 'Attitudes of Chinese immigrants and Vietnamese refugees toward law enforcement in the United States', *Justice Quarterly* 9(4), 703–19.

Wike, R., Stokes, B., and Simmons, K. (2016), 'Europeans fear wave of refugees will mean more terrorism, fewer jobs', Pew Research Center.

Wolffhardt, A., Joki, A.-L., and Solano, G. (2019), 'Facilitating evidence-based integration policies in cities'. Options report of the Stakeholder Working Group, Technical report, Migration Policy Group, European Commission.

Ye, X., Konduri, K., Pendyala, R. M., Sana, B., and Waddell, P. (2009), 'A methodology to match distributions of both household and person attributes in the generation of synthetic populations', *in Proceedings of the 88th Annual Meeting of the Transportation Research Board*, Washington DC.

Zagheni, E., Garimella, V. R. K., Weber, I., and State, B. (2014), 'Inferring international and internal migration patterns from Twitter data', *in Proceedings of the 23rd International Conference on World Wide Web*, 439–44.

Zorlu, A. (2017), 'Attitudes toward asylum seekers in small local communities', *International Migration* 55(6), 14–36.

15

Issues about Analysing Multilingual Communication in Immigrant Contexts

A. SEZA DOĞRUÖZ

Introduction

HUMAN MOBILITY BRINGS people with diverse backgrounds, languages, and cultures together and is a key feature of immigration. With the availability of computational tools and methods, it is possible to harness large-scale digital data and make predictions about diverse research topics related to immigration. However, analysing language use through text-based datasets in immigrant communities is a complex issue. It involves analyses of multiple languages as well as cultural and social factors. Ignoring this amalgam of factors operating in the immigrant context and just focusing on the automatic analysis of multilingual textual data from the data science perspective will lead to a partial understanding of the community dynamics that lacks useful insights for making policies targeting these communities (cf. Doğruöz et al., 2021).

In order to avoid these pitfalls, this chapter aims to inform the reader about the (socio)linguistic issues operating in immigrant contexts, clarify the terminology about multilingualism, present findings of relevant studies, and make comparisons (e.g., research questions, types of datasets, methods of analyses) across academic fields (e.g., sociolinguistics and computational areas of research) to address the challenges and opportunities for interdisciplinary research in this area.

Clarification of terminology about language use in immigrant contexts

Meaningful analysis of language use is useful for understanding the dynamics of social interaction in immigrant communities. In order to address the relevant research questions in this context, there is a need to clarify the terminology as follows.

Sociolinguistics investigates language in relation to society (Hudson, 1996). Bilingualism/multilingualism is commonly observed in immigrant contexts, and it is one of the sub-areas of Sociolinguistics. Duration, intensity of contact, and social factors (and their interaction with each other) determine the outcomes of linguistic contact between languages (Thomason, 2001). Initially, speakers of immigrant languages start borrowing lexical items from the host languages and become bilingual/multilingual at later stages of contact (Winford, 2003). However, host languages may also borrow lexical items (e.g., food-related words) from the immigrant languages as well (Winford, 2003). Immigrant community members may use diverse languages in their daily lives depending on the interlocutors and communication contexts. Linguistic competencies of the speakers, their attitudes toward languages (e.g., immigrant vs host language), generation of immigration, formality of communication environment, social rules and conventions may influence the communication patterns in multilingual contexts (Thomason, 2001; Winford, 2003). A heritage language refers to the language/s and/or dialect/s spoken by the immigrant community members. It is usually different than the language of the non-immigrant (i.e., local and/or host) community. Some scholars (e.g., Winford, 2003) associate immigrant languages with the minority groups and the host language with the dominant groups in society. Due to the variation in the backgrounds of the speakers, their immigration histories, minority status, and linguistic proficiencies, the definition of a heritage language and terminology (e.g., 'heritage', 'ancestral', 'immigrant') may vary across immigration contexts.

In the Canadian context, Cummins (1991) excluded English and French from the definition of heritage languages and included languages of the indigenous people and/or immigrants. Fishman (2001; as reported in King and Ennser-Kananen, 2012) defines heritage languages as ancestral languages, which may be indigenous (e.g., Navajo in the US), colonial (e.g., early immigrants of European descent in the US), or may have roots in immigration (e.g., Hmong, Mexican communities in the US). However, these definitions do not necessarily entail or guarantee that the heritage languages are spoken at home or in the community regularly. This view is in line with Kondo-Brown (2003), who stated that a heritage language can be related to the identification with a certain group rather than the linguistic proficiency. For example, new generations may not speak the heritage language of the immigrant community anymore, but they may still use the heritage language to identify themselves with their family roots.

Rothman (2009, p. 156) defined a heritage language as 'a language spoken at home or otherwise readily available to young children and crucially this language is not a dominant language of the larger (national) society'. Similar to Valdés (2001), Rothman expects heritage speakers to obtain some command of heritage language naturalistically along with the majority language spoken in the wider community. On the other hand, Aalberse and Muysken (2013) emphasised the link between language and cultural heritage of the speakers. More specifically, they highlighted the heritage speakers who are familiar with the language/s spoken in their community but did not hear or speak these languages within their family environment while growing up (e.g., Amboy Malay is spoken mostly by first-generation Indonesian immigrants in the Netherlands but it is not necessarily used for raising children).

Analysing heritage languages of immigrant communities is one of the key areas of research in immigrant contexts. More specifically, linguistic structures (e.g., word order, morphology, vocabulary, phonology) are analysed either in terms of how they change through the influence of the host language or how they resist change and remain intact (maintained) despite the influence of the host language. Heritage languages of Spanish (Silva-Corvalán, 1994) and Russian (Polinsky, 2018a) immigrant communities in the US and Germany, the Turkish immigrant community in the Netherlands (Doğruöz and Backus, 2007, 2009) and Germany (Treffers-Daller *et al.*, 2007), and the Chinese community in immigrant contexts (He, 2008) have already been investigated in terms of changing and maintained linguistic structures. Not all immigrant contexts are the same, and there are controversial findings about the changing vs maintained linguistic structures in relation to the social factors and duration of contact operating in the respective contexts. For example, word order in a heritage language is expected to change due to contact with the host language. However, Doğruöz and Backus (2007) revealed that the basic word order of the Turkish spoken in the Netherlands (heritage language) does not change significantly due to Dutch (host language) influence.

In addition to analysing linguistic changes in heritage languages, some researchers focus on analysing the mixed language communication in immigrant contexts. Example (1) illustrates language mixing between German and Turkish (in bold) at the phrase/sentence level (Karakoç and Herkenrath, 2019).

Example (1)
Hat sie dir was abgegeben? ... **Öyle dedin.**
*Did she share anything with you? ... **You said so.***

Although first-generation immigrants may or may not learn the language of the host community, the second and third generations (usually) grow up learning the language of the host community. In addition, some immigrant families speak more than one heritage language/dialect at home as well (e.g., French, Lingala, and Swahili spoken by the Zairian immigrant community in Belgium, as reported by Meeuwis and Blommaert, 1998). In these multilingual contexts, switching across languages is very common and it is not merely a linguistic phenomenon. It is influenced by social factors and contexts as well. For example, Ting *et al.* (2020) analysed multilingual communication in business negotiations in Malaysia, which hosts a major Chinese immigrant community. According to their findings, English was the preferred language of negotiation for more expensive products whereas Hokkien (a dialect of Chinese) and Malay (host community language) were used for cheaper products. In other words, being aware of the language dynamics of the target group could also be useful for successful business interactions in the particular immigrant context.

Code-switching and language mixing in immigrant communities have been studied extensively across languages and contexts, e.g., Chinese–English switches in the UK by Wei and Milroy (1995) and Wei (2013), Spanish–Moroccan Arabic switches in Spain by Vicente (2007), Greek–English switches in Australia by Alvanoudi (2018), Turkish–Dutch switches in the Netherlands (Backus and van der Heijden, 2002; Papalexakis *et al.*, 2014), Spanish–English switches within the Mexican community in Los Angeles (Silva-Corvalán, 1994) and the Puerto Rican community in New York (Poplack, 1980), and Persian–English switches in Canada (Samar and Meechan, 1998).

From a developmental point of view, it is not always easy to measure the linguistic development of children in immigrant settings while they acquire multiple languages simultaneously or sequentially (Håkansson *et al.*, 2003). If their linguistic abilities are not measured properly, it may not be possible to decide whether or not there is a need for intervention (e.g., extra learning activities, treatment for speech disorders). This concern is also shared by Grimm and Schulz (2014), who drew attention to the need for more research about the misdiagnosis (e.g., under or overdiagnosis) concerning specific language impairment in children who acquire a second language. Their claim is directly relevant for children growing up with multiple languages in immigrant settings, since they may be misdiagnosed for language impairments due to their multilingual skills.

Learning the language of the host community is often considered to be useful for adult immigrants to lead an independent life and take part in the host society. However, adults usually need explicit instruction to learn foreign languages and there is a variation among members of the immigrant communities in terms of educational means, motivations, and resources to learn the language of the host community. According to van Tubergen and Wierenga (2011), age of immigration, proficiency in mother tongue, participation in voluntary activities in the host society, and years of education within the education system of the host community are factors that influence second language learning among male Turkish and Moroccan immigrants in Belgium.

In terms of gender differences, van der Slik *et al.* (2015) reported a study carried out among immigrants learning Dutch as a second language in the Netherlands. Analyses of the test scores in a language proficiency test (27,199 participants with 49 different language backgrounds) indicated that females perform better than males in spoken and written proficiency tests but there were no significant differences in reading and listening skills.

Janko *et al.* (2019) compared the level of education vs length of residence for acquisition of the host community language (Greek) by Albanian immigrants. Their findings indicate that the level of education has some influence on grammar-related tasks, whereas length of residence has more influence on the fluency in the host language. Mocciaro (2019) claimed that the literacy level of an immigrant community member in his/her native language has an influence on learning Italian as a second language. Similarly, Ćatibušić et al. (2021) analysed the needs of Syrian refugees while learning English in Ireland and intercultural support mechanisms. Their findings highlight the importance of learning the language of the host community for the personal well-being, autonomy, and dignity of the participants with an immigrant background in addition to other well-known effects (e.g., employment prospects and social interaction). Similarly, Abou-Khalil et al. (2019) investigated the language learning needs of Syrian refugees who settle down in Lebanon and Germany through participatory design. Through interacting with the participants, the authors found that refugees have different needs (e.g., family reunion, finding jobs) and styles of learning foreign languages. Although they may have access to digital language learning tools and apps (e.g., mobile phones), they also express the need for social learning (e.g., practising German with native German speakers), guidance for self-motivation, discipline, and time-management skills.

Attitudes and policies regarding language use have also been studied in immigrant contexts. From a theoretical point of view, Chick and Hannagan-Lewis (2019) discussed the policies for Syrian refugees in the UK, and Gándara and Rumberger (2009) explained the educational policies toward immigrant students in the US. Following a survey-based method, Utych (2018) studied the influence of using dehumanising words towards immigrants, Zhang and Slaughter-Defoe (2009) investigated the attitudes toward heritage language use among Chinese immigrant families, Hopkins (2015) explained the link between the perception of immigrant community members and their accent in the host community languages, and Ibarraran et al. (2008) studied the perceptions and attitudes of students with immigrant backgrounds toward multilingual communities.

Analysing language use in immigrant contexts through spoken data

Traditionally, linguistic performances of immigrant community members are mostly evaluated through spoken data since their literacy skills and language proficiencies may not be adequate for eliciting written data. Spoken data could be elicited through controlled (e.g., task-based and experimental methods) or less controlled methods (e.g., informal and unstructured conversations). Polinsky (2018b) offered a detailed description of tasks and methods for assessing linguistic proficiencies of heritage speakers and eliciting production data from them. In addition to the scientific descriptions of such tasks, there are also practical issues and challenges about conducting linguistic research in immigrant settings.

In controlled experiments, there is a need for a homogeneous group of participants to measure the influence of social variables (e.g., age, gender, educational and linguistic background) on linguistic variation. However, it is often challenging to find a balanced set of speakers within the immigrant community with similar background characteristics and who are willing to take part in a scientific study. Therefore, researchers may be limited to relatively small sample sizes of participants for their experimental studies. When the study involves an experimental task, participants are invited to the experimental location (e.g., a university lab) where the researchers have access to the technical equipment. This type of setup protects the participants from external distractions and enables them to focus solely on the experimental task. On the other hand, this safe option may also inhibit the participants from taking part in the study, since it means more time and effort for them to travel to the experimental location. In addition, an isolated experimental environment may also lead to divergences from the usual linguistic practices of the participants in their daily lives.

In the case of conversational data collection, the researcher is not limited to a certain location which could be convenient for the participants. However, s/he still needs to make sure that the recordings (audio and/or video) are of good quality without external distractions and noise (cf. Eppler and Codó, 2016). For example, multiple participants and interruptions during the conversation lead to difficulties in transcription and linguistic analyses later.

Similar to the controlled tasks, it is time-consuming to find and convince participants within the immigrant community to assist in conversational data collection. Unless the researcher is familiar with the community, s/he needs to invest time and create a network to gain the trust of the community members. Once that trust is established, the researcher allocates time and resources to meet with the participants from the immigrant community. Similar to studies in other research domains, the participants could change their minds and decide not to take part in the study as well. In these cases, the researcher needs to secure a large pool of participants who may replace each other in the case of a drop out. However, this practice could be challenging due to relatively small participant pools in immigrant settings.

Participants may vary and accommodate their linguistic performance depending on the context, the topic of conversation, their mood, or the conversation partners they interact with. It is not uncommon to encounter situations in multilingual settings where speakers adapt their linguistic performance in line with what they assume the researcher needs to hear (Thomason, 2007). As a result, the collected data may not reflect the actual language practices in the immigrant community.

In order to analyse the conversational spoken data, transcription is the first step. Although there are some automatic speech-to-text tools, they may not be available for the languages spoken in immigrant contexts. Even when they are available, transcribing conversational data involving multiple participants is rather hard for most automatic tools (Aoki *et al.*, 2006). There is often a need for additional manual error correction. However, this additional correction could be more time-consuming than the manual transcription in the first place. The process of manual transcription is also time-consuming (approximately four hours of transcription for one hour of spoken data) and requires special training depending on the research goals and protocols of the study.

As an alternative to collecting spoken data from immigrant community members, some researchers conduct surveys to assess spoken language use to reach out to a wider participant pool in a shorter time. However, language use reported in surveys may not always mirror the findings in spoken data (Doğruöz and Gries, 2012).

In addition, education level, literacy rate, and linguistic competency (both in the heritage and host languages) among immigrant community members may influence their participation in surveys as well. For example, younger generations in immigrant communities often receive education and schooling in the language of the host community. Although they may speak and understand heritage languages spoken in the community, they may lack literacy skills in these languages (Benmamoun *et al.*, 2013). Therefore, conducting surveys about heritage languages presents a challenge for these groups of speakers. In addition, there are also criticisms about the predictability of replies in surveys as well (Arnulf *et al.*, 2014).

The discussion about the difficulties of finding participants and collecting and analysing spoken data brings us to the question of searching for alternative data sources for linguistic research in immigrant communities. Which other data sources are available? What are the pros and cons of such data sources? The next section explores the answers to these questions.

Analysing language use in online environments for immigrant communities

Qualitative methods of analysis

Androutsopoulos (2007) was one of the early researchers to investigate communication between users with a Persian immigrant background on a digital discussion platform in Germany. His linguistic analyses suggest a link between language and the topic choices of the users. More specifically, the users in his study preferred using Persian for topics related to the traditional culture and entertainment in comparison to other topics of discussion. However, the amount of data, the duration of data collection, and methods of analyses were not explained in detail.

On a similar topic, Androutsopoulos (2015) analysed the online communication among Facebook users in Germany with a Greek immigrant background. With the permission of these users, he collected data (90 pages) from their Facebook accounts over a period of one year and reported one week's communication of this dataset in his study. Although there are descriptions of language switches (Greek–German) within the same post and across posts (e.g., users replying to each other's messages), he does not mention any patterns regarding the reasons why and how these speakers switch across languages.

Dorleijn (2017) analysed the code-switching (Turkish–Dutch) on a dataset (17,000 words) obtained from a digital platform dominated by users with immigrant backgrounds in the Netherlands. Through qualitative methods of analyses, she analysed the complexity of code-switching through the interplay of different grammatical units (e.g., phonology, syntax, morphosyntax). However, it was not possible to make any generalisations due to the small-scale and ongoing data analyses.

In addition to linguistic analyses, there have also been studies investigating the language preferences of immigrant users and their reported experiences in online environments through surveys. For example, Velázquez (2017) analysed how Spanish immigrant speakers in the US utilise Spanish with respect to their reported literacy, media consumption, and social media use (as a digital resource) through ethnographic interviews and an online survey. The analyses of her data revealed that Spanish was highly (83%) relevant for the reading and writing activities of the heritage speakers in daily life. In terms of social media use, 61% of immigrant speakers reported using Spanish frequently in their online communication. Similarly, 89% of the immigrant speakers reported using Spanish for texting messages. The lower use of Spanish (the heritage language) in social media is linked to the fact that the speakers with an immigrant background in this study attended US colleges where English was the dominant language.

The studies above investigated the language practices of immigrant speakers in online environments using qualitative methods of analyses. However, making comparisons across these studies is challenging. First of all, communication style, text size, and types of media for sharing (e.g., text, photos, videos) differ across social media platforms (e.g., Facebook and Twitter) in online environments. Users may select or limit the audience for their posts and accommodate their language accordingly (Nguyen et al., 2016). These inherent differences across online media services and platforms may influence the linguistic performance of immigrant language users and qualitative studies may not capture this variation systematically.

Secondly, there is no consensus on how to report the size and duration of the online data for immigrant language analyses in qualitative studies. For example, Androutsopoulos (2015) reported his data size in terms of page numbers, whereas Dorleijn (2017) reported hers in number of words. This difference in measurement of data size leads to difficulties for systematic comparisons across online immigrant communities and their language use practices.

Thirdly, there are not always detailed explanations about the procedures and methods that are followed to extract and compile data from online environments for qualitative studies. Without these explanations, it is hard to carry out similar studies in the future.

Despite these drawbacks, qualitative studies provide insights and prepare the ground for new research questions in online environments using computational methods of analyses in larger and longitudinal datasets. The next subsection focuses on the computational approaches to studying language use and communication in immigrant contexts and digital environments.

Computational methods of analysis

Computational methods are useful for analysing language use on digital platforms with immense data sizes and variation in data sources. To start with multilingual data analyses, there is a need to automatically identify the language of the digital post/message content. However, automatic language identification is a challenging task for multilingual digital posts. Examples (2) and (3) illustrate language switches between Turkish and Dutch (in bold) as they were observed on an online discussion platform used by immigrant community members in the Netherlands (Nguyen and Doğruöz, 2013). Although Turkish and Dutch languages dominate the discussions on the platform, the use of English and/or Moroccan Arabic (another minority population in the Netherlands) is occasionally observed as well (Papalexakis and Doğruöz, 2015). Since these posts also contain creative use of social media language (e.g., unconventional spellings of Turkish characters), it is hard for automatic tools to make meaningful linguistic identification and segmentation.

Example (2)
Mijn dag kan niet stuk :) Cok guzel bir haber aldim.
This made my day:) I received good news.

Example (3)
Kahvalti **met vriendinnen by mij thuis.**
Breakfast with friends at my home.

Off-the shelf automatic methods for language identification and processing are usually developed after training on monolingual and standard written language data (Nguyen et al., 2016). These methods are useful for language identification of text-based documents (e.g., web pages). However, automatic language identification is more challenging for shorter texts (e.g., social media messages) and multilingual digital posts which contain multiple languages and unconventional forms. Nguyen and Doğruöz (2013) was one of the first to tackle this challenge for automatic language identification of multilingual digital posts written by users within an immigrant community. After the initial steps of cleaning the data (e.g., smileys, URLs, links, user names, images), annotation, and normalisation, they developed automatic language identification methods to recognise the language of digital posts at various levels (e.g., word, phrase, and/or post levels) with relatively high accuracy. Considering the difficulty of manual language identification for such large and online datasets, automatic methods save time in classifying the multilingual digital posts (e.g., per language) accurately and preparing the data for further research.

Social and linguistic factors influencing code-switching (i.e., language mixing) in multilingual communication have been described earlier in sociolinguistic studies (e.g., Thomason, 2001; Gardner-Chloros and Edwards, 2004). However, it has not been possible to predict when users/speakers switch across languages automatically. Using the linguistic and non-linguistic features from earlier studies, Papalexakis et al. (2014) were one of the first to develop computational methods to predict code-switching in multilingual communication of immigrant community members on an online platform.

Even when there is no trace of code-switching in communication, linguistic changes could still take place at the underlying linguistic levels in immigrant contexts. If the host language has an influence on these changes, they will not be observed in the non-immigrant variety. Although it may sound simple, it is not easy to detect these underlying linguistic differences between the varieties of the same language immediately. For example, Turkish spoken by the immigrant community in the Netherlands is quite similar to Turkish spoken in Turkey in terms of basic word order (Doğruöz and Backus, 2007). However, there are ongoing changes in multi-word expressions that are translated literally from Dutch into Turkish (Doğruöz and Backus, 2009). Using these changing linguistic cues as features in computational experiments, it has been possible to automatically differentiate between the immigrant (e.g., Turkish spoken in the Netherlands) and non-immigrant varieties (e.g., Turkish spoken in Turkey) of the same language (Doğruöz and Nakov, 2014).

Language use in immigrant contexts has also been used for automatic author identification. From a historical and digital humanities perspective, Müller *et al.* (2020) trained neural networks for automatic author identification in texts written by the Czech immigrants to Berlin (Germany) in the 18th century.

In addition to focusing on language use by immigrant community members, computational methods are also used to analyse the language use toward immigrant communities and/or minorities. As a collective initiative, Basile *et al.* (2019) organised a shared task for automatic identification of hate speech against immigrants and women on Twitter in English and Spanish. Along similar lines, Capozzi *et al.* (2019) introduced a platform to detect and monitor hate speech against immigrants, Roma, and minorities in Italian social media. In a separate paper, Pontiki *et al.* (2020) automatically analysed verbal aggression and xenophobic attitudes about immigrants in Greek on Twitter.

From a computational social science perspective, Lapesa *et al.* (2020) introduced a manually annotated (e.g., claim identification, claim classification, actor identification, claim attributes, date, and polarity) dataset to follow the immigration debate on German media. Similarly, Fokkens *et al.* (2018) developed a tool to automatically detect stereotypes about Muslims in Dutch media in the Netherlands. Through combining questions from social sciences with textual data and computational methods of analyses, the outputs of these projects reflect the attitudes toward immigrants and minorities across contexts and societies.

Depending on the particular context and social factors, members of the immigrant communities are often expected to learn the language of the host community. In addition to the traditional methods of language learning in classroom settings, there are also studies about using computer-assisted tools and services for language learning for members of the immigrant communities. However, these tools should not be mistaken for commercial language learning products, which are not necessarily developed according to the needs and preferences of immigrant community members. In other words, the commercial success or wide availability of a digital language learning tool does not guarantee the desired results for language learning in immigrant communities. Instead, there is a need for research-based language learning tools that are specifically designed for the specific immigrant context (e.g., a computer-assisted vocabulary learning tool, SweLLex, for learners of Swedish with an immigrant background in Sweden (Volodina *et al.*, 2016)).

As the studies in this section illustrate, the availability of computational tools to harness very large and longitudinal datasets makes online data attractive for analysing communication and language use among immigrant community members. However, analysing online communication data in immigrant contexts introduces new challenges from computational, linguistic, and social sciences perspectives as well.

First of all, not all members of the immigrant community may have access to the internet. For example, older generations of the immigrant communities often lack the resources and digital skills to use internet-based devices and services (Chen et al., 2020). In addition, purchasing smart devices and paying for internet-based services could be financially cumbersome for immigrant community members with restricted income. Therefore, analysing language use in online environments for immigrant communities faces challenges about representativeness.

Second, analysing large-scale communication data among immigrant community members in online environments has several linguistic challenges. In order to analyse the content of the multilingual communication, there is a need for an automatic language identification process (Nguyen and Doğruöz, 2013; Frey et al., 2019). However, creative language use in social media communication and language mixing lead to difficulties for automatic language identification processes. Although off-the shelf computational tools are available, these tools are usually developed through training on monolingual and standard written language data. If the training data is in the standard and written language, it may not capture the dynamic, creative, and ever-changing aspects of multilingual language used by immigrant community members in digital environments. In addition, most of these tools are developed for major languages (e.g., English) and may not be available for processing the less spoken and/or low resource languages in immigrant contexts.

Third, unless the data services are publicly accessible and/or immigrant community members provide their consent, it is not easy to collect social media data. Even in publicly accessible cases, there may be quota restrictions that may prohibit extensive research about language use in immigrant communities.

Finally, the background (e.g., age, education, gender) and socioeconomic status of the users are difficult to verify in digital environments (Nguyen et al., 2016). Although some background information about users may be available, these data are often incomplete and/or filled in randomly to hide the true identity of the users. Lack of personal information about the users prevents researchers form making links between language use and social factors to analyse communication in online communication for immigrant communities.

Discussion and conclusion

The goal of this study was to inform the reader about the scientific discussion around language use by and about immigrant communities through making comparisons across academic fields, research questions, datasets, and methodologies.

There is no unique remedy to avoid the pitfalls and carry out a 'perfect' study that reflects and captures multilingual language use with all its diversity in immigrant contexts. For example, qualitative studies investigating multilingual language use within immigrant communities usually focus on small datasets (e.g., the datasets described in the 'Qualitative methods of analysis' section) in depth. Although their results may not be generalisable across all users or contexts, the descriptions of the data or reported results could serve as starting points for hypothesis testing in larger and longitudinal datasets for research on immigrant languages using computational methods of analysis.

Online sources offer larger and longitudinal datasets for immigrant language research in comparison to traditional data collection and analysis methods. However, extracting adequate and representative datasets from online sources requires certain computational skills (e.g., programming skills, web crawling, database management systems), time, and expertise (e.g., cleaning and classifying data into meaningful categories). In addition, systematic analysis of these datasets requires expertise in computational methods (e.g., machine learning and natural language processing) which may not be the main focus of research training in many humanities and/or social sciences programmes. Similarly, data scientists may have the computational skills and tools to harness large-scale online data, but lack the theoretical background to interpret the interwoven linguistic and social factors operating in multilingual immigrant contexts. Therefore, there is a need for collaboration across academic fields for research on language use in immigrant communities.

Finally, big data is not very meaningful on its own. Only after extensive cleaning and restructuring can one look for patterns and analyse the data to make it more meaningful for research purposes. In order for textual data to be processed automatically, the data are often cleaned and normalised (see Box 8.1, this volume). However, valuable information about multilingualism and language variation (e.g., unique linguistic styles associated with certain speakers and contexts) within immigrant communities could be lost during the cleaning and normalisation stages (Nguyen *et al.*, 2016; Eisenstein, 2013).

References

Aalberse, S. and Muysken, P. (2013), 'Language contact in heritage languages in the Netherlands', *in* J. Duarte and I. Gogolin, eds, *Linguistic Superdiversity in Urban Areas: Research Approaches*, Vol. 2, John Benjamins Publishing, Amsterdam, 253–74.

Abou-Khalil, V., Helou, S., Flanagan, B., Pinkwart, N., and Ogata, H. (2019), 'Language learning tool for refugees: Identifying the language learning needs of Syrian refugees through participatory design', *Languages* 4(3), 71.

Alvanoudi, A. (2018), 'Language contact, borrowing and code switching: A case study of Australian Greek', *Journal of Greek Linguistics* 18(1), 3–44.

Androutsopoulos, J. (2007), 'Language choice and code-switching in German-based diasporic web forums', *in* B. Danet and S. C. Herring, eds, *The Multilingual Internet: Language, Culture, and Communication Online*, Oxford University Press, Oxford, 340–61.

Androutsopoulos, J. (2015), 'Networked multilingualism: Some language practices on Facebook and their implications', *International Journal of Bilingualism* 19(2), 185–205.

Aoki, P. M., Szymanski, M. H., Plurkowski, L., Thornton, J. D., Woodruff, A., and Yi, W. (2006), 'Where's the "party" in "multi-party"? Analyzing the structure of small-group sociable talk', *in Proceedings of the 20th Anniversary Conference on Computer Supported Cooperative Work*, 393–402.

Arnulf, J. K., Larsen, K. R., Martinsen, Ø. L., and Bong, C. H. (2014), 'Predicting survey responses: How and why semantics shape survey statistics on organizational behaviour', *PLOS One* 9(9), e106361.

Backus, A. and van der Heijden, H. (2002), 'Language mixing by young Turkish children in the Netherlands', *Psychology of Language and Communication* 6(1), 55–73.

Basile, V., *et al.* (2019), 'Semeval-2019 task 5: Multilingual detection of hate speech against immigrants and women in Twitter', *in Proceedings of the 13th International Workshop on Semantic Evaluation*, Association for Computational Linguistics, 54–63.

Benmamoun, E., Montrul, S., and Polinsky, M. (2013), 'Heritage languages and their speakers: Opportunities and challenges for linguistics', *Theoretical Linguistics* 39(3–4), 129–81.

Capozzi, A. T., *et al.* (2019), 'Computational linguistics against hate: Hate speech detection and visualization on social media in the "Contro L'Odio" project', *in Proceedings of the Sixth Italian Conference on Computational Linguistics, CLiC-it 2019*, 2481.

Ćatibušić, B., Gallagher, F., and Karazi, S. (2021), 'Syrian voices: An exploration of the language learning needs and integration supports for adult Syrian refugees in Ireland', *International Journal of Inclusive Education* 25(1), 22–39.

Chen, X., Östlund, B., and Frennert, S. (2020), 'Digital inclusion or digital divide for older immigrants? A scoping review', *in* Q. Gao and J. Zhou, eds, *Proceedings of the International Conference on Human–Computer Interaction*, Springer, New York, 176–90.

Chick, M. and Hannagan-Lewis, I. (2019), 'Language education for forced migrants: Governance and approach', *Languages* 4(3), 74.

Cummins, J. (1991), 'Introduction', *The Canadian Modern Review* 47(4), 601–5.

Doğruöz, A. S. and Backus, A. (2007), 'Postverbal elements in immigrant Turkish: Evidence of change?', *International Journal of Bilingualism* 11(2), 185–220.

Doğruöz, A. S. and Backus, A. (2009), 'Innovative constructions in Dutch Turkish: An assessment of ongoing contact-induced change', *Bilingualism: Language and Cognition* 12(1), 41–63.

Doğruöz, A. S. and Gries, S. T. (2012), 'Spread of on-going changes in an immigrant language', *Review of Cognitive Linguistics* (published under the auspices of the Spanish Cognitive Linguistics Association) 10(2), 401–26.

Doğruöz, A. S. and Nakov, P. (2014), 'Predicting dialect variation in immigrant contexts using light verb constructions', *in Proceedings of the 2014 Conference on Empirical Methods in Natural Language Processing (EMNLP)*, 1391–5.

Doğruöz, A. S., Sitaram, S., Bullock, B. E., and Toribio, A. J. (2021), 'A survey of code-switching: Linguistic and social perspectives for language technologies', *in Proceedings of the Joint Conference of the 59th Annual Meeting of the Association for Computational Linguistics and the 11th International Joint Conference on Natural Language Processing (ACL-IJCNLP 2021)*, Association for Computational Linguistics, 1654–66.

Dorleijn, M. (2017), 'Is dense codeswitching complex?', *Language Sciences* 60, 11–25.

Eisenstein, J. (2013), 'What to do about bad language on the internet?', *in Proceedings of the 2013 Conference of the North American Chapter of the Association for Computational Linguistics: Human language technologies*, 359–69.

Eppler, E. D. and Codó, E. (2016), 'Challenges for language and identity researchers in the collection and transcription of spoken interaction', *in* S. Preece, ed., *The Routledge Handbook of Language and Identity*, Routledge, London, 304–19.

Fokkens, A., Ruigrok, N., Beukeboom, C., Sarah, G., and Van Atteveldt, W. (2018), 'Studying Muslim stereotyping through microportrait extraction', *in Proceedings of the 11th International Conference on Language Resources and Evaluation (LREC 2018)*.

Frey, J.-C., Stemle, E. W., and Doğruöz, A. S. (2019), 'Comparison of automatic vs. manual language identification in multilingual social media texts', *in* C. R. Wigham and E. W. Stemle, eds, *Building Computer-Mediated Communication Corpora for Socio-Linguistic Analysis*, University of Clermont Publications, France, 47–69.

Gándara, P. and Rumberger, R. (2009), 'Immigration, language, and education: How does language policy structure opportunity?', *Teachers College Record* 111(3), 750–82.

Gardner-Chloros, P. and Edwards, M. (2004), 'Assumptions behind grammatical approaches to code-switching: When the blueprint is a red herring', *Transactions of the Philological Society* 102(1), 103–29.

Grimm, A. and Schulz, P. (2014), 'Specific language impairment and early second language acquisition: The risk of over- and underdiagnosis', *Child Indicators Research* 7(4), 821–41.

Håkansson, G., Salameh, E.-K., and Nettelbladt, U. (2003), 'Measuring language development in bilingual children: Swedish-Arabic children with and without language impairment', *Linguistics* 41(2), 255–88.

He, A. W. (2008), 'Chinese as a heritage language', *in* W. S.-Y. Wang and C. Sun, eds, *The Oxford Handbook of Chinese Linguistics*, Oxford University Press, New York, 578–90.

Hopkins, D. J. (2015), 'The upside of accents: Language, inter-group difference, and attitudes toward immigration', *British Journal of Political Science* 45(3), 531–57.

Hudson, R. A. (1996), *Sociolinguistics*, Cambridge University Press, Cambridge.

Ibarraran, A., Lasagabaster, D., and Sierra, J. M. (2008), 'Multilingualism and language attitudes: Local versus immigrant students' perceptions', *Language Awareness* 17(4), 326–41.

Janko, E., Dąbrowska, E., and Street, J. A. (2019), 'Education and input as predictors of second language attainment in naturalistic contexts', *Languages* 4(3), 70.

Karakoç, B. and Herkenrath, A. (2019), 'Understanding retold stories: The marking of unwitnessed events in bilingual Turkish', *Turkic Languages* 23(1), 81–121.

Kim, J., Pollacci, L., Rossetti, G., Sîrbu, A., Giannotti, F., and Pedreschi, D. (2022), 'Twitter data for migration studies', *in* A. A. Salah, E. E. Korkmaz, and T. Bircan, eds, *Data Science for Migration and Mobility*, Proceedings of the British Academy, British Academy / Oxford University Press, London.

King, K. A. and Ennser-Kananen, J. (2012), 'Heritage languages and language policy', *in* C. A. Chapelle, ed, *The Encyclopedia of Applied Linguistics*, Wiley, Chichester.

Kondo-Brown, K. (2003), 'Heritage language instruction for post-secondary students from immigrant backgrounds', *Heritage Language Journal* 1(1), 1–25.

Lapesa, G., Blessing, A., Blokker, N., Dayanık, E., Haunss, S., Kuhn, J., and Padó, S. (2020), 'DEbateNet-mig15: Tracing the 2015 immigration debate in Germany over time', *in Proceedings of the 12th Language Resources and Evaluation Conference*, 919–27.

Meeuwis, M. and Blommaert, J. (1998), 'A monolectal view of code-switching: Layered code-switching among Zairians in Belgium', *in* P. Auer, ed, *Code-Switching in Conversation: Language, Interaction and Identity*, Routledge, Abingdon, 76–98.

Mocciaro, E. (2019), 'Emerging constructions in the L2 Italian spoken by low literate migrants', *Languages* 4(4), 86.

Müller, K., Tikhonov, A., and Meyer, R. (2020), 'LiViTo: Linguistic and visual features tool for assisted analysis of historic manuscripts', *in Proceedings of the 12th Language Resources and Evaluation Conference*, 885–90.

Nguyen, D. and Doğruöz, A. S. (2013), 'Word-level language identification in online multilingual communication', *in Proceedings of the 2013 Conference on Empirical Methods in Natural Language Processing*, 857–62.

Nguyen, D., Doğruöz, A. S., Rosé, C. P., and De Jong, F. (2016), 'Computational sociolinguistics: A survey', *Computational Linguistics* 42(3), 537–93.

Papalexakis, E. and Doğruöz, A. S. (2015), 'Understanding multilingual social networks in online immigrant communities', *in Proceedings of the 24th International Conference on World Wide Web*, 865–70.

Papalexakis, E., Nguyen, D., and Doğruöz, A. S. (2014), 'Predicting code-switching in multilingual communication for immigrant communities', *in Proceedings of the First Workshop on Computational Approaches to Code Switching (EMNLP 2014)*, Association for Computational Linguistics, 42–50.

Polinsky, M. (2018a), 'Bilingual children and adult heritage speakers: The range of comparison', *International Journal of Bilingualism* 22(5), 547–63.

Polinsky, M. (2018b), *Heritage Languages and their Speakers*, Cambridge University Press, Cambridge.

Pontiki, M., Gavriilidou, M., Gkoumas, D., and Piperidis, S. (2020), 'Verbal aggression as an indicator of xenophobic attitudes in Greek Twitter during and after the financial crisis', *in Proceedings of the Workshop about Language Resources for the SSH Cloud*, 19–26.

Poplack, S. (1980), 'Sometimes I'll start a sentence in Spanish y termino en espagñol: Toward a typology of code-switching', *Linguistics* 18, 581–618.

Rothman, J. (2009), 'Understanding the nature and outcomes of early bilingualism: Romance languages as heritage languages', *International Journal of Bilingualism* 13(2), 155–63.

Samar, R. G. and Meechan, M. (1998), 'The null theory of code-switching versus the nonce borrowing hypothesis: Testing the fit in Persian–English bilingual discourse', *International Journal of Bilingualism* 2(2), 203–19.

Silva-Corvalán, C. (1994), *Language Contact and Change: Spanish in Los Angeles*, Clarendon Press, Oxford.

Thomason, S. (2007), 'Language contact and deliberate change', *Journal of Language Contact* 1(1), 41–62.

Thomason, S. G. (2001), *Language Contact*, Edinburgh University Press, Edinburgh.

Ting, S.-H., Then, D. C.-O., and Ong, O. G.-B. (2020), 'Prestige of products and code-switching in retail encounters', *International Journal of Multilingualism* 17(2), 215–31.

Treffers-Daller, J., Özsoy, A. S., and Van Hout, R. (2007), '(In)-complete acquisition of Turkish among Turkish–German bilinguals in Germany and Turkey: An analysis of complex embeddings in narratives', *International Journal of Bilingual Education and Bilingualism* 10(3), 248–76.

Utych, S. M. (2018), 'How dehumanization influences attitudes toward immigrants', *Political Research Quarterly* 71(2), 440–52.

Valdés, G. (2001), 'Heritage language students: Profiles and possibilities', *in* J. Peyton, D. Ranard, and S. McGinnis, eds, *Heritage Languages in America: Preserving a National Resource*, Delta Systems Company Inc., McHenry, IL.

van der Slik, F. W., van Hout, R. W., and Schepens, J. J. (2015), 'The gender gap in second language acquisition: Gender differences in the acquisition of Dutch among immigrants from 88 countries with 49 mother tongues', *PLOS One* 10(11), e0142056.

van Tubergen, F. and Wierenga, M. (2011), 'The language acquisition of male immigrants in a multilingual destination: Turks and Moroccans in Belgium', *Journal of Ethnic and Migration Studies* 37(7), 1039–57.

Velázquez, I. (2017), 'Reported literacy, media consumption and social media use as measures of relevance of Spanish as a heritage language', *International Journal of Bilingualism* 21(1), 21–33.

Vicente, Á. (2007), *Two Cases of Moroccan Arabic in the Diaspora*, Routledge, Abingdon.

Volodina, E., Pilán, I., Llozhi, L., Degryse, B., and François, T. (2016), 'Swellex: Second language learners' productive vocabulary', *in Proceedings of the Joint Workshop on NLP for Computer Assisted Language Learning and NLP for Language Acquisition*, 76–84.

Wei, L. (2013), 'Codeswitching', *in* R. Bayley, R. Cameron, and C. Lucas, eds, *The Oxford Handbook of Sociolinguistics*, Oxford University Press, New York, 360–78.

Wei, L. and Milroy, L. (1995), 'Conversational code-switching in a Chinese community in Britain: A sequential analysis', *Journal of Pragmatics* 23(3), 281–99.

Winford, D. (2003), *An Introduction to Contact Linguistics*, Wiley-Blackwell, Oxford.

Zhang, D. and Slaughter-Defoe, D. T. (2009), 'Language attitudes and heritage language maintenance among Chinese immigrant families in the USA', *Language, Culture and Curriculum* 22(2), 77–93.

16

Applying Computational Linguistic and Text Analysis to Media Content about Migration

WILLIAM L. ALLEN

Introduction

WITHIN THE DOMAIN of migration studies, itself a multi- and interdisciplinary field concerned with a broad array of questions spanning scales of geography and analysis (Gamlen *et al.*, 2013; Pisarevskaya *et al.*, 2020), researchers have regularly addressed issues surrounding how migrants and migration are represented in different settings such as media. Documenting these patterns of representations is important for several reasons. First, media analysis is a form of knowledge production that enables comparison with other epistemological viewpoints, such as migrants' own understandings and journalistic expressions (Shumow, 2014). Second, these patterns serve as inputs for other phenomena of interest to social scientists, including immigration attitude formation (see Dinesen and Hjorth, 2020 for a review), elections and voting behaviour (e.g., Hobolt *et al.*, 2021), integration in host communities (e.g., Bos *et al.*, 2016), policy-making (e.g., Allen and Blinder, 2018), and migrant decision-making (e.g., Crawley and Hagen-Zanker, 2019).[1] Third, analyses of media texts can serve as (part of) the evidence base which facilitates a range of interventions aiming to either inform audiences, itself a worthy goal (Schudson, 2010), or affect their behaviours, such as taking a stand on issues and talking about politics among their networks (King *et al.*, 2017).

Thanks to advances in computational and digital methods, social scientists are increasingly able to collect and make sense of larger and more varied sets of texts, whether they involve digitised or digital-native sources. Meanwhile, communicating the results of these analyses in visual and graphical ways is becoming more

---

[1] For a comprehensive review of major themes in recent scholarship on media and migration, see Allen *et al.* (2017).

important as a growing number of visualisation tools has placed relatively high-quality outputs within the reach of non-specialist users. On the one hand, these developments have spurred tremendous uptake of these approaches to analyse textual data across a range of domains. On the other hand, the rise in work claiming to use textual analysis has attracted a degree of scepticism, particularly on grounds of validity and reliability when measured against humans' performance (e.g., Brookes and McEnery, 2019; van Atteveldt et al., 2021). Therefore, a key problem confronting social scientists is how to think through the opportunities and limitations of computational text analysis methods as applied to their specific projects.

In this chapter I aim to provide such a guide for researchers by drawing together several strands of my research into mass media portrayals of migrants and migration. While the examples from my own work mainly draw from the domains of newspapers and journalism, the lessons and observations about computational methods apply to other forms of digital textual data that researchers increasingly access (Allen and Easton-Calabria, 2022). My approach has been motivated by the sentiment expressed by Tony McEnery, a prominent linguist who has sought to apply knowledge about how languages operate to social scientific questions. In short, he has urged linguists (as well as humanities and social science researchers using texts) to find what is 'distinctive and good' (McEnery, 2015, p. 2) about the interface of expertise and data, rather than abandon this effort in favour of purely algorithmic solutions that are divorced from either theory or practice. This echoes parallel trends in critical data studies examining how quantitative data (as well as the people, methods, and processes which generate them) both shape and are shaped by politics (Amoore and Piotukh, 2015; Bigo et al., 2019).

I have organised this chapter around four key verbs as both a nod to the linguistic content and to walk through the discrete steps involved in doing textual analysis. The first section, 'orienting', sets out the main approaches to text analysis that I will focus on, including some reflection on their limitations. The second section, 'collecting', focuses on the ways that researchers gather and organise media data. Third, in the section 'analysing', I explain how I identify patterns in texts (e.g., frequencies of words) and how these link to substantive concepts of interest to social scientists (e.g., agendas). Finally, the fourth section, 'communicating', explores different ways of sharing both the outputs of and procedures involved in analysis. This is an important step that is often overlooked yet is increasingly consequential for enhancing the impact of research, which is often publicly funded in the first place, and for taking an ethical stance towards Open Science principles that emphasise how researchers should be transparent about how they reached their conclusions (Lewis Jr, 2020). These are summarised in Box 15.1.

Orienting: Approaches and limitations

In response to the shift towards quantitative methods across the social sciences, as well as broader interest in making sense of the growing volume and varieties of data

> **Box 15.1** Open Science principles
>
> Open Science is a movement to improve access to scientific content worldwide, as well as collaborative research and wide-scale research replication, which can subsequently improve verification of scientific results (see, for instance, OECD's recommendations on this subject, available at https://www.oecd.org/sti/inno/open-science.htm). We briefly summarise the main points here from a communication science perspective, based on Lewis Jr (2020). There are three sets of good practices recommended in Lewis Jr (2020) for getting started with Open Science.
>
> *Preregistration* is the practice of 'creating a public record of what the researchers' questions were, what method(s) they planned to use, and how they planned to analyse their data'. It is a spreading practice in clinical science, and a search for 'Clinical Trials Register' shows several sites around the world, including one managed by the World Health Organization. This practice helps with the publication of negative results as well, and deals with bias in reporting. In computing science, cherry-picking models that perform well on a certain problem to report high accuracy is a well-known issue, and preregistration is not a common practice.
>
> *Open Materials* aims at making the research publications available to a wider public (e.g., via open access publishing and open repositories of publications maintained by institutions) and by providing study materials that are important in helping readers understand the research findings. Since most publication venues limit the amount of material, linked resources (such as appendices, supplementaries, and web resources) are used.
>
> *Open Data* is about publishing the data that are necessary to replicate the research along with the publication. This is more challenging, because of data protection and privacy considerations that dictate limited use of potentially sensitive data, from both legal and ethical perspectives (Salah *et al.*, Chapter 2, this volume). Similar concerns exist for sharing code, which may additionally have commercial implications.
>
> Open Science practices are seen as particularly important in Europe, and we see institutions taking steps to help researchers with these goals, incorporating practices in their strategic plans. For example, the University of Oxford started the Reproducible Research Oxford (RROx) initiative (see https://www.ox.ac.uk/research/support-researchers/open-research), and Utrecht University recently launched the Utrecht University Open Science Programme (see https://www.uu.nl/en/research/open-science).

now available (Mayer-Schönberger and Cukier, 2013), researchers increasingly turn to solutions that rely on various computational tools. This is particularly true when it comes to texts and other forms of content which are digitised or digitisable. Given the range of possible methods, as well as the potential complexity of the task, getting to grips with this fast-growing field may seem overwhelming.[2]

---

[2] Compare, for example, the methodological development with respect to analysing political texts in just 10 years between the advisory pieces of Quinn *et al.* (2010) and Barberá *et al.* (2021), both of which are excellent guides to the field.

My broader body of work draws upon two distinct yet related approaches to analysing large amounts of textual content. The first, typically called 'text as data', comprises statistical techniques that aim to identify patterns within texts while making minimal assumptions about how those texts were produced or how they may relate to one another (Laver *et al.*, 2003; Grimmer and Stewart, 2013). The second, under the labels of corpus and computational linguistics, incorporates models of language use into modes of annotating and analysing texts (McEnery and Hardie, 2011; Biber and Reppen, 2015). This is related to natural language processing, which harnesses advances in computing power to effectively organise and make sense of language appearing in 'the real world' through written or spoken forms (Jurafsky and Martin, 2009; see also Box 8.1, this volume). These techniques have clear benefits in terms of efficiency and reliability: algorithms, unlike humans, do not tire or become bored when faced with large numbers of repetitive tasks. Moreover, they offer ways by which researchers can test, share, and replicate their analyses, which are important dimensions of Open Science principles.

However, like all methods, they attract concerns on several grounds; see Baden *et al.* (2022) for a comprehensive review. First, do these methods provide valid measures of patterns in texts that are of interest to social scientists? Empirical evaluations of how well computational approaches perform compared to human judgement suggest that there are significant gaps, particularly when categories derived from one set of texts are applied to a different set of texts which has different characteristics (Brookes and McEnery, 2019). On this front, there is growing consensus around (and evidence for) the value of subjecting computational analyses to diverse forms of validation (Barberá *et al.*, 2021; van Atteveldt *et al.*, 2021).

Second, since computational approaches to text analysis rely upon and prioritise the quantification of features including sentiment, topics, and populations, do they generate, rather than merely reflect, perspectives in ways that have political implications? This is connected to broader concerns about the assumptions made by researchers who are fixated on harnessing growing amounts of data without considering the impacts of their work (boyd and Crawford, 2012). Specifically to modes of computational text analysis, there is a risk that these techniques produce outputs which outwardly give impressions of being objective, coherent, and comprehensive, features which may obscure how they necessarily involve choices and trade-offs that aim to simplify complex realities as manifested through texts (Marciniak, 2016). This is especially important to consider when using these approaches to study texts about migration and refugee issues: high levels of abstraction may inhibit public understanding of, and action towards, these potentially vulnerable groups. Here, having a clear self-awareness of one's stance and objectives for doing research is crucial.

Third, can these techniques adequately account for the varied ways in which messengers create and express meaning beyond text? This is relevant for considering portrayals of migration in media that comprise both textual and visual modes; see Smets *et al.* (2020) for an overview. In various settings, from social media platforms (Hameleers *et al.*, 2020) to websites about salient issues (Engebretsen, 2020), visual elements often accompany text. To be sure, parallel developments in computational image analysis now afford researchers greater flexibility and power in responsibly handling these forms of data (e.g., Byrne *et al.*, 2019). While this chapter does not focus on visual methods, it is worth highlighting how the realities of digital media present their own challenges to textual analysis.

Collecting: Media data and the politics of their origins

Having outlined some of the main contours of contemporary computational text analysis, I now turn attention to the next step of collecting textual data. This stage is often overlooked, yet it has important implications for the analysis which follows, though see Kim *et al.* (Chapter 8, this volume) and Doğruöz (Chapter 15, this volume), respectively, for further discussion involving specific datasets. Where can researchers access media content? Within the context of digital research, two broad avenues are available: use established repositories, possibly third-party archival services, or collect it using webscraping techniques. Both approaches present opportunities and limitations.

A growing number of platforms and services make media data available to researchers who possess varying levels of computing proficiency.[3] These intermediaries provide valuable services for different audiences. Some of the most well known, Factiva and LexisNexis, aim their services at businesses for market research purposes. One advantage of these kinds of services is that they generally have good coverage of international, national, and regional media outlets. Another relates to the ease with which users can search, filter, and download media texts (within some limits). Yet gains in accessibility and convenience come with losses in understanding precisely how and to what extent these texts are stored, labelled, and eventually delivered. For instance, ready-made categories and classification systems built into these platforms may reflect the broader interests in more generalised audiences rather than the needs of social scientists (e.g., Akdag Salah *et al.*, 2012). What is more, the terms that generated these typologies may not be transparent or even published at all, preventing replication by other researchers or by the same researcher at a later point in time. Even the total number of documents in these archives, an important feature for making conclusions about the proportion of coverage dedicated to a topic such as migration, may not be available, as this could be considered proprietary information. Therefore, current guidance advises developing and using one's own search terms to identify relevant texts in these databases (Gabrielatos, 2007; Barberá *et al.*, 2021).

Given these limitations, collecting media data at their sources (known as 'scraping' data when it involves computational approaches) is appealing. Not only does

---

[3] Here, I use 'media' in its widest sense to include textual content as conveyed through a variety of communication modes, not just mass media.

this expand the universe of potential media beyond those sources which have already been collected, but also it promises researchers more control over the scope, organisation, and reporting of the content. There are many off-the-shelf tools available for webscraping, developed by academics and for-profit companies alike: for example, the Digital Methods Initiative (Rogers, 2013) of the University of Amsterdam offers several scrapers for Google Images and other online sources. For those who possess more coding skills, the Python programming language remains the preferred way of quickly and effectively collecting textual data from online sources. Using packages such as BeautifulSoup and pandas, which offer powerful ways of parsing and organising webscraped data, researchers can assemble their own datasets and publish their methods for doing so.[4] This can be made even more effective by using application programming interfaces (APIs) provided by major media sources, allowing access to large and growing portions of their databases for research purposes.[5]

Yet, as in the case of using existing repositories, these solutions also involve engaging with intermediaries, whether they are companies providing APIs or the tools themselves which are doing the webscraping. Moreover, it is not always clear which data are being scraped, and whether this will remain consistent in the future. For example, Kim *et al.* (2022) consider the specific affordances of Twitter's modes of API access, and how this has changed over time, with consequences for academic research. Some critical scholarship observes how this creates a situation where researchers are actually studying a 'black box' (Driscoll and Walker, 2014). Moreover, all of these platforms and code are part of digital infrastructures that generate their own sets of politics and privileges around knowledge creation and sharing (Bigo *et al.*, 2019; Allen, 2020). For example, comparative research shows how Google search queries in developing countries tend to show results from US or Europe-based sites rather than local sources, contributing to further digital inequalities (Ballatore *et al.*, 2017). Finally, the growth of webscraping as a technique raises questions about researchers' fixation on 'freshness' and how this may affect what kinds of research questions receive priority (Marres and Weltevrede, 2013). These aspects of digital data collection bear some similarities to curation: factors both internal and external to the research process, including algorithms, potentially affect the eventual contents of media datasets.

My own research on media portrayals of migrants and migration has engaged with both avenues of data collection. One study into British press coverage relied on national newspaper data collected from NexisUK (Blinder and Allen, 2016; Allen *et al.*, 2017). In the process of assembling the dataset, it became apparent that NexisUK did not hold several years' worth of data from a particular publication. Yet this period was available using the Factiva service. Qualitative examination of the output from Factiva did not reveal any obvious systematic differences or gaps compared

---

[4] For more practical guidance on these topics, see McKinney (2018) and Mitchell (2018).
[5] For example, Twitter provided an academic API; see Chapter 8 in this volume and https://twittercommunity.com/t/introducing-the-new-academic-research-product-track/148632

to what was otherwise available in the NexisUK database, so I merged the results. What is more, between stages of the study, an entire publication (*The Independent*) was removed from the NexisUK database when it ceased publishing printed copies in 2016. These examples demonstrate how commercial archival services present challenges for data collection.

In other projects, I have turned to variations of webscraping to collect media data from online sources. For example, to study the dominant features of migration data visualisations (Allen, 2021), I used the Google Image Scraper[6] to identify and download sets of highly ranked results for subsequent content analysis. Although the tool allows a high degree of control over different search parameters, it nevertheless reflects what Google's algorithm reports. To check the sensitivity of the tool to different search environments, I used a virtual private network to simulate what users in several countries would see, while also deleting browser histories between searches. Fortunately, most of the results were consistent across searches. The broader point of this example is to highlight how, despite the potential convenience and comprehensiveness that computational tools offer for social science, they do not absolve researchers from asking critical questions about the scope, provenance, and veracity of the data at hand.[7]

Analysing: Linking textual patterns and mental schemas

Having collected media data, how can social scientists analyse that data to generate meaningful insights? The key word here, of course, is 'meaningful'. On the one hand, meaning might arise or emerge from patterns identified in textual data. For example, topics comprising clusters of related words might be a form of meaning that could tell researchers something about a set of documents as demonstrated through unsupervised learning methods (see Barberá *et al.*, 2021). On the other hand, meaning might come from a theory-driven view of which characteristics or aspects of texts are more relevant or important: in this mode, a researcher might be looking for evidence of a mechanism or property. Both approaches display their own susceptibilities. Results from 'data-driven' modes can be sensitive to parameters and settings which are set by researchers, opening concerns about the risk of generating and interpreting spurious relationships. Meanwhile, theory-driven modes of enquiry may overlook newer concepts that are not well captured by existing models or categories but nevertheless are significant.

In my own practice, I have mainly used text analysis as a means of generating results that serve as evidence of theoretical mechanisms or outcomes. For example, a long tradition of political communication scholarship has developed the concepts of

---

[6] Available from the Digital Methods Initiative website, https://wiki.digitalmethods.net/Dmi/ToolDatabase

[7] This point is equally applicable to those who use more conventional quantitative datasets such as observational surveys (Gray *et al.*, 2015).

'agendas' and 'media agenda-setting' (McCombs and Shaw, 1972; Boydstun, 2013) as ways of linking changes in media content with subsequent changes in public attitudes. Broadly, media can make some issues seem more important by mentioning them more frequently ('first-level agenda-setting') or by linking them with other issues that are also perceived to be important ('second-level agenda-setting'). These second-level agendas are sometimes seen as attributes of issues (Soroka, 2002): for example, media might link the issue of asylum seekers with attributes relating to security and terrorism rather than economic development. Therefore, security might be considered a second-level agenda of asylum that makes people think the issue is more important. If found, this result would be evidence of an agenda-setting effect.

But how does this precisely happen via media content? Here is where I have used the theory of 'lexical priming' proposed by the linguist Michael Hoey (2005). Essentially, lexical priming proposes a way by which some words are more strongly associated with a target word such as 'immigrant' or 'refugee'. When considering the word 'pitch', for example, you might think of related words like 'football' (if you are inclined toward sports) or possibly 'music' if you have an arts background. These words, called 'primes', become related to target words through repeated use or familiarity: if certain primes are more readily available and top-of-mind than others, they will become more strongly related to the target word. Of course, the strength of these relations may change through use.

Linking this theorised mechanism with the concept of a second-level agenda led me to a particular kind of textual feature: collocation with key migration terms. The best candidates for strong primes of 'immigration' or 'refugees' would likely be those words which were frequently linked with those target words in the dataset. In this case, those links took the form of a grammatical association: adjectives referring to nouns. By noting the adjectives most frequently linked with nouns of interest (e.g., *asylum-seeker*, *refugee*, *immigrant*), I began generating second-level agendas associated with migration. Clustering these terms using prior qualitative work on similar topics in the British press (Baker *et al.*, 2013) revealed six sets of issue attributes that I later interpreted as representing second-level agendas of migration in British newspapers: the economy; legal status; policymaking; sociocultural dimensions; geographic origins; and the scale and pace of immigration.

To be clear, there are multiple ways of identifying and measuring agendas in media texts, some of which can include computationally inducing topics or patterns from content. Moreover, I could also have used these techniques at a later stage of my analysis to sort and make sense of the lists of collocates for each target word. My point, however, is to demonstrate how the analytical choices that researchers must make about handling text can be driven by theoretical goals as well as technical concerns about efficiency. In this case, my goal was to measure a theoretically useful concept (i.e., second-level agendas) using a computational technique (i.e., collocational analysis deriving from grammatical rules). Whichever approaches social scientists use, they should be mindful of the needs to clearly justify their choices and make explicit links to their research questions or objectives.

Communicating: Sharing results and decision-making processes for public impact and replicable science

Analysing texts, while obviously important to do correctly, is not the end point. Rather, communicating the results to different audiences, whether they are other scholars, members of the interested public, or decision-makers in policy and civil society domains, is a crucial step that is closely linked to analysis. This is becoming even more true as researchers are increasingly expected to demonstrate how their work has public relevance or impact, especially when that work is funded by public sources.

Scholars using computational text analysis need to be attuned to this question of how to effectively communicate their research for at least two reasons. First, specific to the domain of media analysis, large-scale text analysis offers valuable avenues for making sense of these communication forms in ways that can inform decisions or change public perceptions. Those shifts, in turn, might have profound impacts on the lives of migrants. For example, in a report that analysed British media content on migration, Crawley *et al.* (2016) showed how migrant voices tend to be missing from mainstream reporting. This presents implications for journalism practice: it is possible that greater migrant representation in news, especially through the means of direct quotation, may change public perceptions. Second, speaking to other researchers, textual datasets and methodologies are important artefacts of the scientific process that potentially enable future replication and reuse, in the tradition of 'open science' principles. Therefore, clear documentation that explains the steps taken to produce a given output is vital.

In my own work, I have experimented with visualising textual analyses for and among public users. Visualisation, or the visual representation of data to enhance understanding (Kirk, 2019), is a potentially powerful way of communicating quantitative information; see also Telea and Behrisch (Chapter 11, this volume) and Loaiza *et al.* (Chapter 12, this volume), respectively. The kinds of quantities and patterns that computational analyses of text produce (frequencies, clusters, changes over time or among subsets of documents) lend themselves to visual representation. Yet there are multiple choices involved in creating effective visualisations, which in turn involve several sets of 'hands' through which the analysis runs (Allen, 2018). For example, there are potentially several ways of showing the strength of a relationship between a target word and its primes: intensity of colour, widths of connecting lines, or varying sizes of symbols (Allen, 2017). Each approach presents advantages and limitations depending on the intended purpose and audience. The point here is not to recommend any particular approach, but rather to draw attention to the need for social scientists using computational approaches to also consider how they communicate their results, and whether these are the most appropriate for their objectives and key stakeholders.

Conclusion: Towards an agenda for social scientific, and socially responsible, text analysis

In this chapter I have outlined what I think are four key steps in doing computational text analysis: orienting oneself in the field, collecting textual materials, analysing those texts with respect to given research goals (such as testing theories), and communicating the results in effective ways. Here, it is important to note that tools and techniques, while important in their own rights, are parts of the wider process involved in using computational methods. Other chapters in this volume provide more detailed examples of specific datasets and methods for identifying, assembling, and analysing data at scale. Instead, my goal has been to draw attention to the ways that these aspects are linked to broader questions of research design.

Indeed, computational approaches to text analysis like the ones I have illustrated through my own work on media representations of migrants and migration are neither value neutral nor divorced from deeply political questions involving human mobility, data, or media (Hovy and Spruit, 2016). Rather, they raise important ethical and normative questions about *how* and *for what purposes* social scientists use these methods to say things about the world. For example, the practice of media monitoring, particularly for the purposes of gathering data on and about flows of asylum seekers, has been restricted by the European Union on several grounds including potential misuse, privacy concerns, and the questionable veracity of the collected data (European Data Protection Supervisor, 2019). Meanwhile, there is a growing body of work showing how algorithms and computational methods can reproduce their creators' own prejudices (Leese, 2014; Amoore and Piotukh, 2015; Koenecke *et al.*, 2020). This is not merely a theoretical problem: as more aspects of everyday life become quantified and algorithmically informed, the risk of reinforcing latent or unnoticed biases looms large; see Escalante *et al.* (2020) for an example involving job hiring procedures. More broadly, the large-scale processing of many types of data, including text, enable and disable different forms of data politics (boyd and Crawford, 2012; Bigo *et al.*, 2019). In the context of mobility, answers to these questions have real-world consequences for the lives of migrants.

Given this reality, what would a socially responsible computational approach to media and text analysis look like? Recognising how notions of 'responsibility' are themselves context- and time-specific, I cautiously advance a few suggestions. First, it would be attuned to issues of power and inequality by acknowledging how researchers' choices throughout the life cycle of designing, implementing, and communicating textual analyses are the products of particular contexts and characteristics. Second, it would consider how the research would be used, or could be used, for different objectives, and whether these objectives correspond with researchers' ethical stances. Third, it would adhere to Open Science principles of transparency and replicability, as far as the data and materials allow; see Lewis Jr (2020) in the field of communication studies. Yet, building on the first two points, it would also be mindful of how the implementation of these principles relate to broader societal values and objectives, such as justice and public benefit, that are particularly salient when working with marginalised populations (Fox *et al.*, 2021). Together, these aspects represent an emerging agenda for socially responsible computational text analysis. Developing and revisiting such an agenda will undoubtedly remain important as greater volumes and forms of data continue to come within the grasp of researchers, while issues such as migration and the movement of people remain visible in the collective consciousness of the public, policy-makers, and media.

References

Akdag Salah, A., Gao, C., Suchecki, K., and Scharnhorst, A. (2012), 'Need to categorize: A comparative look at the categories of Universal Decimal Classification System and Wikipedia', *Leonardo* 45(1), 84–5.

Allen, W. (2017), 'Making corpus data visible: Visualising text with research intermediaries', *Corpora* 12(3), 459–82.

Allen, W. (2020), 'Mobility, media, and data politics', *in* K. Smets, K. Leurs, M. Georgiou, S. Witteborn, and R. Gajjala, eds, *The SAGE Handbook of Media and Migration*, Sage, Thousand Oaks, CA, 180–91.

Allen, W., Blinder, S., and McNeil, R. (2017), 'Media reporting of migrants and migration', Technical report, International Organization for Migration, available at https://publications.iom.int/system/files/pdf/wmr_2018_en_chapter8.pdf

Allen, W. L. (2018), 'Visual brokerage: Communicating data and research through visualisation', *Public Understanding of Science* 27(8), 906–22.

Allen, W. L. (2021), 'The conventions and politics of migration data visualizations', *New Media & Society*, https://doi.org/10.1177/14614448211019300.

Allen, W. L. and Blinder, S. (2018), 'Media independence through routine press–state relations: Immigration and government statistics in the British press', *The International Journal of Press/Politics* 23(2), 202–26.

Allen, W. L. and Easton-Calabria, E. (2022), 'Combining computational and archival methods to study international organizations: Refugees and the International Labour Organization, 1919–2015', *International Studies Quarterly* 66(3), sqac044.

Amoore, L. and Piotukh, V. (2015), *Algorithmic Life: Calculative Devices in the Age of Big Data*, Routledge, Abingdon.

Baden, C., Pipal, C., Schoonvelde, M., and van der Velden, M. (2022), 'Three gaps in computational text analysis methods for social sciences: A research agenda', *Communication Methods and Measures* 16(1), 1–18.

Baker, P., Gabrielatos, C., and McEnery, T. (2013), 'Sketching Muslims: A corpus driven analysis of representations around the word 'Muslim' in the British press 1998–2009', *Applied Linguistics* 34(3), 255–78.

Ballatore, A., Graham, M., and Sen, S. (2017), 'Digital hegemonies: The localness of search engine results', *Annals of the American Association of Geographers* 107(5), 1194–215.

Barberá, P., Boydstun, A. E., Linn, S., McMahon, R., and Nagler, J. (2021), 'Automated text classification of news articles: A practical guide', *Political Analysis* 29(1), 19–42.

Biber, D. and Reppen, R. (2015), *The Cambridge Handbook of English Corpus Linguistics*, Cambridge University Press, Cambridge.

Bigo, D., Isin, E., and Ruppert, E., eds (2019), *Data Politics: Worlds, Subjects, Rights*, Routledge, London.

Blinder, S. and Allen, W. (2016), 'UK public opinion toward immigration: Overall attitudes and level of concern', Migration Observatory briefing, COMPAS, University of Oxford.

Bos, L., Lecheler, S., Mewafi, M., and Vliegenthart, R. (2016), 'It's the frame that matters: Immigrant integration and media framing effects in the Netherlands', *International Journal of Intercultural Relations* 55, 97–108.

boyd, d. and Crawford, K. (2012), 'Critical questions for big data: Provocations for a cultural, technological, and scholarly phenomenon', *Information, Communication & Society* 15(5), 662–79.

Boydstun, A. E. (2013), *Making the News: Politics, the Media, and Agenda Setting*, University of Chicago Press, Chicago, IL.

Brookes, G. and McEnery, T. (2019), 'The utility of topic modelling for discourse studies: A critical evaluation', *Discourse Studies* 21(1), 3–21.

Byrne, L., Angus, D., and Wiles, J. (2019), 'Figurative frames: A critical vocabulary for images in information visualization', *Information Visualization* 18(1), 45–67.

Crawley, H. and Hagen-Zanker, J. (2019), 'Deciding where to go: Policies, people and perceptions shaping destination preferences', *International Migration* 57(1), 20–35.

Crawley, H., McMahon, S., and Jones, K. (2016), 'Victims and villains: Migrant voices in the British media', Technical report, Centre for Trust, Peace and Social Relations, Coventry University, available at http://www.migrantsrights.org.uk/files/news/Victims_and_Villains_Digital.pdf

Dinesen, P. T. and Hjorth, F. (2020), 'Attitudes toward immigration: Theories, settings, and approaches', *in* A. Mintz and L. Terris, eds, *The Oxford Handbook of Behavioral Political Science*, Oxford University Press, Oxford, 1–30.

Doğruöz, A. S. (2022), 'Issues about analyzing multilingual communication in immigrant contexts', *in* A. A. Salah, E. E. Korkmaz, and T. Bircan, eds, *Data Science for Migration and Mobility*, Proceedings of the British Academy, British Academy / Oxford University Press, London.

Driscoll, K. and Walker, S. (2014), 'Big data, big questions| Working within a black box: Transparency in the collection and production of big Twitter data', *International Journal of Communication* 8, 20.

Engebretsen, M. (2020), 'From decoding a graph to processing a multimodal message: Interacting with data visualization in the news media', *Nordicom Review* 41(1), 33–50.

Escalante, H. J., Kaya, H., Salah, A. A., Escalera, S., Güçlütürk, Y., Güçlü, U., Baró, X., Guyon, I., Jacques, J. C., Madadi, M., Ayache, S., Viegas, E., Gurpinar, F., Wicaksana, A. S., Liem, C., van Gerven, M. A. J., and van Lier, R. (2020), 'Modeling, recognizing, and explaining apparent personality from videos', *IEEE Transactions on Affective Computing* 13(2), 894–911.

European Data Protection Supervisor (2019), 'Social media monitoring reports', Technical report, European Data Protection Supervisor, available at https://edps.europa.eu/sites/default/files/publication/19-11-12_reply_easo_ssm_final_reply_en.pdf

Fox, J., *et al.* (2021), 'Open science, closed doors? Countering marginalization through an agenda for ethical, inclusive research in communication', *Journal of Communication* 71(5), 764–84.

Gabrielatos, C. (2007), 'Selecting query terms to build a specialised corpus from a restricted-access database', *International Computer Archive of Modern and Medieval English (ICAME) Journal* 31, 5–44.

Gamlen, A., Betts, A., Delano, A., Lacroix, T., Paoletti, E., Sigona, N., and Vargas-Silva, C. (2013), 'Faultlines and contact zones: A new forum for migration studies', *Migration Studies* 1(1), 1–3.

Gray, E., Jennings, W., Farrall, S., and Hay, C. (2015), 'Small big data: Using multiple data-sets to explore unfolding social and economic change', *Big Data & Society* 2(1), https://doi.org/10.1177/2053951715589418.

Grimmer, J. and Stewart, B. M. (2013), 'Text as data: The promise and pitfalls of automatic content analysis methods for political texts', *Political Analysis* 21(3), 267–97.

Hameleers, M., Powell, T. E., Van Der Meer, T. G., and Bos, L. (2020), 'A picture paints a thousand lies? The effects and mechanisms of multimodal disinformation and rebuttals disseminated via social media', *Political Communication* 37(2), 281–301.

Hobolt, S. B., Leeper, T. J., and Tilley, J. (2021), 'Divided by the vote: Affective polarization in the wake of the Brexit referendum', *British Journal of Political Science* 51(4), 1476–93.

Hoey, M. (2005), *Lexical Priming: A New Theory of Words and Language*, Routledge, London.

Hovy, D. and Spruit, S. L. (2016), 'The social impact of natural language processing', in *Proceedings of the 54th Annual Meeting of the Association for Computational Linguistics*, Vol. 2, 591–8.

Jurafsky, D. and Martin, J. H. (2009), *Speech and Language Processing: An Introduction to Natural Language Processing, Computational Linguistics, and Speech Recognition*, Pearson/Prentice Hall, London.

Kim, J., Pollacci, L., Rossetti, G., Sîrbu, A., Giannotti, F., and Pedreschi, D. (2022), 'Twitter data for migration studies', in A. A. Salah, E. E. Korkmaz, and T. Bircan, eds, *Data Science for Migration and Mobility*, Proceedings of the British Academy, British Academy / Oxford University Press, London.

King, G., Schneer, B., and White, A. (2017), 'How the news media activate public expression and influence national agendas', *Science* 358(6364), 776–80.

Kirk, A. (2019), *Data Visualisation: A Handbook for Data Driven Design*, 2nd edn. Sage, London.

Koenecke, A., Nam, A., Lake, E., Nudell, J., Quartey, M., Mengesha, Z., Toups, C., Rickford, J. R., Jurafsky, D., and Goel, S. (2020), 'Racial disparities in automated speech recognition', *Proceedings of the National Academy of Sciences* 117(14), 7684–9.

Laver, M., Benoit, K., and Garry, J. (2003), 'Extracting policy positions from political texts using words as data', *American Political Science Review* 97(2), 311–31.

Leese, M. (2014), 'The new profiling: Algorithms, black boxes, and the failure of anti-discriminatory safeguards in the European Union', *Security Dialogue* 45(5), 494–511.

Lewis Jr, N. A. (2020), 'Open communication science: A primer on why and some recommendations for how', *Communication Methods and Measures* 14(2), 71–82.

Loaiza, I., Sánchez, G., Chan, S., Montes Jiménez, F., Bahrami, M., and Pentland, A. (2022), 'Voyage viewer: A multivariate visualisation tool for migration analysis', in A. A. Salah, E. E. Korkmaz, and T. Bircan, eds, *Data Science for Migration and Mobility*, Proceedings of the British Academy, British Academy / Oxford University Press, London.

Marciniak, D. (2016), 'Computational text analysis: Thoughts on the contingencies of an evolving method', *Big Data & Society* 3(2), https://doi.org/10.1177/2053951716670190

Marres, N. and Weltevrede, E. (2013), 'Scraping the social? Issues in live social research', *Journal of Cultural Economy* 6(3), 313–35.

Mayer-Schönberger, V. and Cukier, K. (2013), *Big Data: A Revolution that will Transform How We Live, Work, and Think*, Houghton Mifflin Harcourt, Boston, MA.

McCombs, M. E. and Shaw, D. L. (1972), 'The agenda-setting function of mass media', *Public Opinion Quarterly* 36(2), 176–87.

McEnery, T. (2015), 'Editorial', *Corpora* 10(1), 1–3.

McEnery, T. and Hardie, A. (2011), *Corpus Linguistics: Method, Theory and Practice*, Cambridge University Press, Cambridge.

McKinney, W. (2018), *Python for Data Analysis: Data Wrangling with Pandas, NumPy, and IPython*, O'Reilly Media, Inc., Newton, MA.

Mitchell, R. (2018), *Web Scraping with Python: Collecting More Data from the Modern Web*, O'Reilly Media, Inc., Newton, MA.

Pisarevskaya, A., Levy, N., Scholten, P., and Jansen, J. (2020), 'Mapping migration studies: An empirical analysis of the coming of age of a research field', *Migration Studies* 8(3), 455–81.

Quinn, K. M., Monroe, B. L., Colaresi, M., Crespin, M. H., and Radev, D. R. (2010), 'How to analyze political attention with minimal assumptions and costs', *American Journal of Political Science* 54(1), 209–28.

Rogers, R. (2013), *Digital Methods*, MIT Press, Cambridge, MA.

Salah, A. A., Canca, C., and Erman, B. (2022), 'Ethical and legal concerns on data science for large scale human mobility', *in* A. A. Salah, E. E. Korkmaz, and T. Bircan, eds, *Data Science for Migration and Mobility*, Proceedings of the British Academy, British Academy / Oxford University Press, London.

Schudson, M. (2010), 'Political observatories, databases & news in the emerging ecology of public information', *Daedalus* 139(2), 100–109.

Shumow, M. (2014), 'Media production in a transnational setting: Three models of immigrant journalism', *Journalism* 15(8), 1076–93.

Smets, K., Leurs, K., Georgiou, M., Witteborn, S., and Gajjala, R., eds (2020), *The Sage Handbook of Media and Migration*, SAGE Publications Ltd, London.

Soroka, S. N. (2002), 'Issue attributes and agenda-setting by media, the public, and policy-makers in Canada', *International Journal of Public Opinion Research* 14(3), 264–85.

Telea, A. and Behrisch, M. (2022), 'Visual exploration of large multidimensional trajectory data', *in* A. A. Salah, E. E. Korkmaz, and T. Bircan, eds, *Data Science for Migration and Mobility*, Proceedings of the British Academy, British Academy / Oxford University Press, London.

van Atteveldt, W., van der Velden, M. A., and Boukes, M. (2021), 'The validity of sentiment analysis: Comparing manual annotation, crowd-coding, dictionary approaches, and machine learning algorithms', *Communication Methods and Measures* 15(2), 121–40.

17

Exploring Digital Connectivities in Forced Migration Contexts: 'Digital Making-Do' Practices

AMANDA ALENCAR AND MARIE GODIN[*]

Introduction

IN RESPONSE TO the so-called 'European refugee crisis' beginning in 2015, the amount of research exploring the use of new technologies by refugees has increased rapidly. Initial studies focused on single aspects of the use of new technologies, such as how they are used to access information, or how they influence which routes migrants choose to take, what methods of travel they use, and their final destinations (Gillespie *et al*., 2016; Dekker *et al*., 2018; Zijlstra and van Liempt, 2017). The research primarily highlighted how mobile phones were supporting migrants in their day-to-day survival ('technologies for survival') as well as how phones allowed them to maintain transnational contact with people in their country of origin as well as with people they met while travelling ('technologies for belonging') (Donà and Godin, 2019). Over time, more comprehensive approaches to the study of mobile phone usage by refugees developed, examining refugees' material, psychological, and social needs and how these needs can be met by mobile technologies. For instance, the research of Alencar *et al.* (2019) shows that for refugees, a smartphone is simultaneously a companion (family and refugee community), an organisational hub (localisation and administration), and a lifeline, but also a (meaningful) diversion. These studies also recognise barriers faced by refugees, such as a lack of resources and available credit, which could influence the type of phone they must rely on, and the technological disruption they may experience on their journeys (Gillespie *et al*., 2018; Kaufmann, 2018).

However, unstable information and communication environments that can limit refugees' agency reveal the negative aspects of the use of digital technologies

[*] The authors have contributed equally to the chapter.

among refugees. Recent evidence suggests that increased digital consumption by refugees and the related possibilities of generating 'digital traces' may exacerbate their vulnerability due to surveillance and privacy issues (Latonero and Kift, 2018; Metcalfe and Dencik, 2019). In addition, the so-called 'European refugee crisis' that has unfolded over the last few years has generated a dynamic response from a diverse representation of social groups, including humanitarian organisations, local authorities, international and local NGOs, private individuals (such as software developers, entrepreneurs, and technology experts), and grassroots actors, including citizens and refugees. By connecting with one other through digital technologies, new types of social actors have come to play more prominent roles in providing various forms of aid, assistance, and protection to migratory people (Godin and Donà, 2021). As argued by Godin and Donà (2021, p. 3279):

> The smartphone revolution has shaped not only how states operate but also the responses of other social actors with relief workers increasingly reliant on digital mobile devices to deliver aid to migrants while on the move. This emergence of 'digital humanitarianism' has extended the delivery of conventional aid to digital packages and e-infrastructures.

While there has been significant research on the links between humanitarian aid and digital innovation when that innovation is provided by standard humanitarian organisations, large corporations, and multinationals (Madianou, 2019), less is known about the work of small-scale social actors in the field in relation to refugees. These include (but are not limited to) humanitarian actors, tech-for-good community, volunteer, or grassroots organisations, as well as refugee-led organisations. For instance, in 2016 in Germany, a group of Syrian refugee tech entrepreneurs developed an app called *Bureaucrazy*, an innovative, tech-driven application for helping new refugees navigate the maze of German bureaucracy (Oltermann, 2016). It was designed by Syrian refugee entrepreneurs living in Berlin who came up with the idea after struggling to find their way through German immigration bureaucracy. Currently, there is little data on how complex webs of collaboration affect the development of both mediated solidarity and governance in the context of refugee movement and settlement in Europe and beyond. This chapter discusses the emerging and expanding digital initiatives put in place by multiple groups, including humanitarian agencies of varying sizes, grassroots organisations including refugee-led organisations, and technology developers, in order to provide care and services in forced migration contexts in both the Global North and Global South.

Development of digital innovations in forced migration contexts: A critique

The importance of access to information and communication technology and the skills to utilise these technologies for shaping social and economic inclusion of refugees have become much-debated topics over the past decade, with media and migration scholars emphasising the need to foster conditions that will provide refugees with more inclusive digital solutions as pathways for accessing their rights as new citizens of their host countries (Georgiou, 2019; Leurs and Smets, 2018). A common critique of the development of digital innovations in forced migration contexts is that they often rely on a needs-based approach (Awad and Tossell, 2021), wherein large humanitarian agencies and organisations in the Global North tend to decide what constitutes the needs of refugees and the digital initiatives to best address the challenges of refugee protection and (re)settlement. Top-down technology solutions can therefore potentially reinforce power imbalances in refugee settings, as they may clash with social imaginaries, cultures, traditions, and literacies of refugee populations (United Nations High Commissioner for Refugees, 2020).

Alongside disconnections related to digital imaginaries of diverse stakeholders, concerns over the critical mass of data that is produced around and collected from refugees through digital initiatives and applications have become more prevalent over the past few years (Madianou, 2019). This becomes evident in several technology projects involving a set of ethically questionable data practices that, rather than facilitating inclusion and enabling empowerment for migrants and refugees, tend to create relationships of dependency and exploitation, even in outspokenly humanitarian projects. These challenges inevitably lead to questions of collaboration and inclusion, and, more specifically, to debates on ethical technology and data transparency (Marino, 2021; Molnar, 2020).

Moreover, very little is currently known about approaches that take into consideration the 'human right to communication', which accounts for the context and policies where the digital initiatives are implemented. Following Uppal *et al.* (2019, p. 324), 'a rights-based approach' to digital connectivity acknowledges individuals as citizens rather than simply consumers, and aims to enhance the rights of access to communication in unequal and diverse societies. Similarly, the work of Isin and Ruppert (2020) within critical citizenship studies highlights the importance of digital spaces for citizens to perform digital rights in the context of existing sociocultural and political structures. Hence, the rights-based approach focuses on facilitating structural changes that can foster representation and social participation of marginalised populations in and through digital technologies (see also Leurs, 2017; Hamelink and Hagan, 2020). Applying the rights-based approach to the context of digital initiatives, developed by private actors and the technology sector through partnerships with government and humanitarian organisations, reveals a tendency among these actors to support the view that refugees can improve their social and economic participation only if they have access to information and resources through apps supported by tech companies, platforms, hackathons, and other similar technologies (Georgiou, 2019). As stated by Uppal *et al.* (2019), the needs-based discourse surrounding technological development serves to legitimise a neoliberal agenda and public–private partnerships, while creating dependencies on technology solutions that, in many cases, are not sustainable and that bypass the priorities of refugees as competent citizens with unique voices (Leung, 2018).

Over the past few years, multiple initiatives led by a range of new actors have used 'new technologies' in order to solve some of the challenges specific to refugees, mainly related to protection, assistance, access to information, and connectivity. Although these actors likely harboured good intentions, technologies, such as smartphone apps, often went unused by refugees or quickly became defunct. Leurs and Smets (2018) recalled that at the peak of the 'crisis', 1500 apps for migrants and refugees were developed as a result of hundreds of hackathons that were organised around the world. However, some studies have shown that migrating people often stick to basic websites and social media applications and services, such as Facebook, YouTube, Instagram, LinkedIn, Twitter, Snapchat, Skype, WhatsApp, and Viber, because they are reliable, easily accessible, and widely used (Dekker *et al.*, 2018; Kaufmann, 2018; Merisalo and Jauhiainen, 2020). Refugees are also aware of digital surveillance and monitoring practices and often use some 'digital tactics', as discussed below, to avoid being tracked. As such, in many cases refugees prefer existing tools over complex, customised, and new English-only apps. This raises questions concerning the realities of the local context as well as the impact of a colonial legacy on social development and innovation initiatives targeted toward refugees. Through digital tools, 'power asymmetries of humanitarianism, data, and innovation practices' are being reproduced and 'colonial relationships of dependency' are being reshaped; they also 'are not sustainable in refugee contexts' (Madianou, 2019).

However, not all digital initiatives fall under this framework, and some of them have taken a hybrid shape or have attempted to implement new forms of humanitarian assistance in acknowledging the role of local contexts for refugees. One example is the organisation *Techfugees*, which was created in 2015 by Mike Butcher, the editor-at-large for TechCrunch in Europe. He put out a call to action on Facebook after seeing the picture of Alan Kurdi, a three-year-old Syrian boy whose body was found on a Turkish beach on 2 September 2015, along with his mother and brother, after drowning in the Mediterranean Sea. A few days later, one of the first hackathons took place in London and subsequently spread to other European cities, including Oslo, Paris, and Turin. The organisation then expanded beyond Europe, recruiting volunteers in over 10 countries and attracting more than 50,000 online members. In April 2019, an African hackathon for refugees was held in Nairobi by *Techfugees Kenya*. With the aim of supporting refugees in the Kakuma and Kalobeyei settlements, the event was sponsored by the Kenya Red Cross Society (KRCS), Google Kenya, Oracle Kenya, and the iHub, the event's host and Kenya's then leading technology incubator. This type of initiative is similar to others that took place in many parts of the world during that period, with hybrid forms of mobilisation combining humanitarian actors, the private sector, and small technology entrepreneurs. The Nairobi hackathon included the participation of refugees from the Kakuma refugee camp, as well as students from Kibera (an extremely poor neighbourhood of Nairobi). During the event, a competition was held to determine the 'best app' for refugees; the group *The Faceless Hackers* won for their e-health project in Kakuma refugee camp. The project intended to improve emergency response and to assist KRCS community health volunteers and community leaders supporting refugees in need of medication or medical care (Braune, 2020). This project, which includes both young refugees and Kenyan students, constitutes a new type of initiative with refugee voices included in the different phases of development (conceptualisation, design, implementation, and use). The participation of both young refugees and Kenyan students from deprived neighbourhoods shows new forms of humanitarian and civic initiatives among refugee youth as well as the youth living in the host community. The connections between refugees and their host communities are often overlooked in the literature, focusing only on the costs and benefits to either population. However, as the Kenyan event shows, this type of partnership opens the way to new forms of collaboration and social networking among the youth in both communities. Whether or not these new forms of collaborations will be able to shift power imbalance between 'donors' and 'refugees' will have to be examined in the future.

Departing from a needs-based approach, which often characterises the activities implemented by a plurality of social actors involved in refugee assistance through digital innovation, this chapter shows how these top-down initiatives can not only fail to improve the realities of refugees, they can also create dependencies on technologies and initiatives that are not sustainable in many forced migration contexts. Building on critical discussions of digital connectivity and developments from a rights-based approach, we put forward the concept of 'digital making-do' as a way in which refugees mobilise and negotiate their rights. We will do so based on a series of examples taken from distinct forced migration contexts in which the two authors conducted research in Brazil, looking in particular at the case of Venezuelan refugees, and with people on the move at the transit space of Calais, at the France–UK border.

'Digital making-do' practices

In this section we suggest the concept of 'digital making-do' to define refugees' tactical engagements with technology in order to navigate everyday uncertainties of life after displacement in situations where digital media transcends basic survival needs ('safety nets') and serves as more than a simple practical purpose (Gillespie *et al.*, 2016). Moreover, these tactical engagements are defined as acts of agency and resistance to the tech used by states and corporations. That is, the concept of 'digital making-do' refers not only to acts of survival but also acts of self-governance that transform a refugee's conditions. Greene (2020) argued that mediated practices of 'making-do' constitute emotive tactics that refugee women develop to cope with protracted experiences of displacement in Greek camps. While the author situates the notion of 'making-do' in the context of transnational digital intimacy practices by refugee women, we expand on this concept by analysing the ways in which refugees engage in digital tactics to circumvent power through top-down technology projects in particular places. In this chapter we argue that 'digital making-do' practices by refugees have the potential to shape digital initiatives put in place by governance actors to support, control, and manage refugee populations.

Digital technologies are critical for helping refugees maintain and expand social relationships and access the resources and support needed to improve their participation in the activities of their new communities (Alencar, 2018). Recent studies suggest that in some ways refugees are becoming active agents of their own narratives on social media platforms, with several important initiatives being implemented to highlight migrants' diverse stories (Georgiou, 2019). The aspirational nature of refugees' digital experiences and practices reflect the new situations of refugees, which directly challenge assumptions that are widely held in the humanitarian, policy-making, and academic fields that see refugees as helpless victims in need of care from outsiders (Pincock *et al.*, 2020).

Against this background, there are also forms of subversion among refugees to 'make do' with top-down digital initiatives that are adopted as strategic mechanisms by governance actors to control refugees. A critical relational perspective is proposed by the French philosopher Michel de Certeau (1984) when dealing with questions of 'strategies' and 'tactics', two relational concepts which are used to further explain power relations between 'urban planners' and 'city dwellers' in negotiations of city spaces. According to de Certeau (1984), strategies stand as possibilities of action for dominant actors, capable of establishing a field of operation under which they have a certain degree of more or less control and predictability. Tactics, on the other hand, can be defined as calculated actions which are determined by the absence of one's own action. 'A tactic has no place other than that of the other' (de Certeau, 1984, p. 94). In short, 'the tactic is determined by the absence of power, just as the strategy is organised by the postulate of a power' (de Certeau, 1984, p. 96). We pay attention, however, to the meaning of the 'absence of power' as the power to establish the conditions of circumscription; there is, digital 'making-do' practices as a force of subversion are put into the uses made in the domain of top-down digital strategies.

Before examining some examples taken from two case studies, the next section demonstrates that in each context, conditions of connectivity and digital media landscapes prompted the development and implementation of certain digital initiatives. Distinctive national and local policies towards refugees play a crucial role in promoting or discouraging formal digital support for and by refugees. This geographical breadth is important because, despite the recognition of the benefits of conducting comparative research in the field of refugee studies, comparison between field sites remains scarce. Looking at the case of Venezuelan refugees in the city of Boa Vista, Northwestern Brazil, located in the border region with Venezuela, and refugees at the France–UK border, these two contexts present the opportunity to examine 'digital making-do' practices. Inspired by the call of Robinson (2016) for comparative imagination, we will adopt a comparative tactic of 'thinking of cities/the urban' through elsewhere in order to better understand the different urban outcomes and to contribute to broader conceptualisations and conversations about (aspects of) the urban, the place of refugees, and the role played by new technologies in these different contexts.

Research contexts

We will now briefly introduce the two different contexts from which the empirical examples are taken. Since 2015, according to UNHCR, approximately four million Venezuelans have fled hunger, violence, and hyperinflation in their country. Official statistics estimate that, by the end of 2020, 285,000 migrants from Venezuela have applied for asylum in Brazil (United Nations High Commissioner for Refugees, 2020). While Venezuelans wait for their asylum request to be resolved, they are allowed to work and can live in the shelters that function as reception centres for refugees in the border city of Pacaraima, or Boa Vista, capital of the state of Roraima in Northwestern Brazil. International, regional, and local humanitarian assistance in these contexts has been crucial to providing refugees with food, shelter, relevant information, and medical support (de Oliveira, 2019), especially considering the lack of employment opportunities and precarious conditions in the country.

The so-called 'Calais jungle' refers to an informal refugee camp that was located at the France–UK border which had reached an estimated 6000–8000 residents over the summer 2016. The camp was dismantled by the French authorities with refugees being dispersed across France in October 2016. However, informal settlements have never stopped. Today, refugees in Northern France face extremely harsh conditions, especially given the authorities' policy of fighting against fixation points that prevent grassroots initiatives from providing food and drink to displaced communities. They also deprive migrants of the right to shelter and decent housing, and people are evicted daily from their informal living sites (Human Rights Observer, 2020). In the context of Calais, a series of grassroots digital initiatives were developed and implemented at the time of the so-called 'Calais jungle'. While many of these initiatives ended after the camp was dismantled, others have continued their activities on the ground.

The next section expands on the concept of 'making-do' by discussing the conditions through which digital initiatives have been developed for and by refugees, as well as how social media platforms and apps have been reappropriated by refugees from two different localities in both northern and southern nations.

Digital initiatives for/with refugees: Facilitating access to refugee's rights

In forced migration contexts in Boa Vista, a significant number of Venezuelans do not own a smartphone or other digital devices due to their severe economic constraints (Alencar, 2020). In their accounts of the events, some Venezuelans mentioned they often owned mobile phones and computers in Venezuela, while others commented that they had to sell their phones to be able to afford their trip to Brazil

(Alencar and Camargo, 2022). For those who brought a smartphone or a simple mobile phone with them, it was difficult to purchase a SIM card, since telephone companies require a valid national identification in Brazil and many lacked (or were still waiting for) a valid identity document at the time fieldwork was conducted. This results in the use of workarounds, such as having SIM cards registered in others' names, or sharing mobile devices (Alencar, 2020). In response to communication policy barriers, these 'digital making-do' practices by refugees can also create other layers of vulnerability to refugees. For instance, by relying on others' names to register a SIM card, refugees can become responsible for anything wrong others can do, including receiving calls about crimes that people have committed. In the case of sharing mobile phone practices, refugees are also subjected to personal data breach, such as passwords of social media accounts, and personal information online. Despite awareness of some of these risks, Venezuelan refugees depend greatly on 'digital making-do' practices to access devices and internet connections in order to obtain relevant information about their rights, health assistance, and job opportunities, as well as for supporting their families who stayed put.

Although there have been several local initiatives put in place by humanitarian actors in partnership with local organisations and agencies to provide (digital) communication services (such as the case of the Technology Reference Center at the Federal University of Roraima, and the provision of phone calls in the shelters by Red Cross, among others), digital precarity among Venezuelans remains a predominant obstacle to their engagement in the economic, social, and cultural fabric of their new society (Wall *et al.*, 2017). Many reported not being aware that internet services or apps were available in their city, or that they could have access to free phone calls in the Technology Reference Center. Similarly, issues of connectivity and usability of digital systems posed barriers to Venezuelans when it comes to obtaining information and other resources available through platforms developed by mainstream organisations, such as the case of the platform *Help* developed by UNHCR. The platform *Help*, for instance, was designed by tech developers with a focus on techno-solutionism, reinforcing digital infrastructures that do not fully acknowledge the socioeconomic and legal problems of refugee settings, while prompting more data collection from refugees (Madianou, 2019). According to Venezuelans, the platform included information and resources that were not accessible for refugee populations with limited or no connectivity. For the most part, it can be observed that refugees engaged in unpaid digital labour, as they were actively asked to contribute data that helped improve the work of humanitarian actors and their services (Casilli, 2017).

More recently, and in response to the problem of fake news in refugee shelters during the Covid-19 pandemic, there has been the development of community-based initiatives with the support of UNHCR and IOM to co-create an online radio programme called *The Voice of Refugees*. In this initiative, Venezuelans receive adequate training to produce podcasts about the issues affecting the community and help debunk false rumours and raise awareness about the risks and appropriate measures to avoid the spread of the virus, functioning as spaces of support for

Venezuelans. The informative podcasts are transmitted through the sound infrastructures of the shelters. Venezuelans stated that being involved in this project represents an opportunity to shape the radio production process in order to provide the Venezuelan community in the shelters with quality information as a fundamental right. The topics addressed in *The Voice of Refugees* episodes are also determined by Venezuelan voluntary members, reflecting the interests of the communities who also produce the daily contents. The episodes tend to be short to facilitate their dissemination via WhatsApp messages among refugees in and outside the shelters.

Examples from the transit space in Calais at the France–UK border serve to illustrate contexts where refugees experience obstacles to sustaining continuous, stable, and reliable digital connectivity. During 2015 and 2016, digital connectivity and access to Wi-Fi became recognised as a fundamental need and right of refugees. Indeed, connectivity is now recognised as a right no different from shelter, health, and food (United Nations High Commissioner for Refugees, 2020). Similar to other locations, new technologies and digital initiatives have been implemented in the so-called 'Calais jungle'. For instance, one of the first initiatives introduced in Calais was *Refugee Phones* with the aim of donating unwanted smartphones to refugees in need of connectivity. The grassroots organisation mobilised citizens around the globe via its social media platforms, including its Twitter account, *RefugeePhone*. Currently, their official UK website (http://refugeephones.co.uk) and Swedish website (http://refugeephones.com) have both been deactivated and are for sale. These broken internet links and out-of-date websites are often identified as 'digital litter' (Benton, 2019) that can confuse and frustrate refugees looking for information on the labour market, education, and migration routes.

Although countless digital initiatives put in place by 'new' humanitarian actors often become defunct just a few months later, not all of them did. Among these, the *Refugee Info Bus* and *Phone Credit for Refugees and Displaced People (PC4R)* initiatives emerged. One is still active at the local level, whereas the other has expanded its activities beyond the border of Calais to other parts of France as well as in other refugee contexts across Europe, Asia, Africa, and the Middle East.

To overcome barriers to accessing mobile technology for refugees on the move, *Refugee Info Bus* provides smartphones and access to mobile infrastructure, such as 3G and Wi-Fi. With its mobile bus, the organisation offers a range of services including phone charging, repair, and local and mobile digital infrastructure for refugees on the move in order to ensure their right to connectivity. The organisation targets refugees who have just arrived in Northern France, providing them with up-to-date practical information and assistance, along with access to the internet and phone charging. It also provides legal information and support, as well as practical information on available services for food, clothing, and access to education or employment. The organisation is active online through Facebook and Instagram. It has a strong following of service users on Facebook who request information in different languages, and it provides online videos and services to increase the organisation's reach. Fulfilling another connectivity need for refugees, *PC4R* was created in 2015 by a British volunteer who began adding credit to residents' phones on UK networks. Subsequently, he created a Facebook page where he asked friends to support him so he could help more residents in the camp. The page evolved into a matchmaking service through which individual donors were matched with refugees who needed phone credit. Over time, the group expanded to provide support to refugees with insecure accommodation, refugees making unsafe journeys, and refugees who had been detained and had not received credit from the organisation for the last 30 days. Overall, the organisation has topped up the credit of 97,000 users' cell phones and raised over one million pounds.

Every week, members of *PC4R* join 'the Friday Conga' to try and hack the mysteries of the 'Facebook algorithm'. These online campaigns, gathering more than 60,000 members, are meant to encourage people to donate, comment, and interact with one another to attract more donations to *PC4R*. The organisation also uses these events to reach more people in need of phone credits, providing the digital infrastructure for a matchmaking service between individual donors and refugees who need credit. To this end, the organisation screens and monitors applicants via chatbots. For instance, when a potential donation recipient joins the Facebook page, they are asked to input certain information (i.e., phone number, IMEI number, and Google map location with location sharing) to ensure that they meet the organisation's criteria. They can only request credit after sharing a series of photographs that show their hands but not their face, known as 'hand photos'. In these photos, they reveal their sleeping place, the roof over their head, and the door of their room. This process takes some time; once completed, the refugee's request for credit is either approved or denied. For approved requests, credit is manually applied to the applicant's phone. The *PC4R* programme therefore holds a position of power, as administrators are responsible for storing sensitive information about refugees' asylum process and location. Some of the volunteers are aware of the potential risks associated with this data collection, and they recognise the need to safely and securely store data to ensure refugees' right to privacy. In addition, to reduce the arbitrary nature of the selection process, the organisation relies heavily on referrals from grassroots organisations such as *Refugee Info Bus* in order to provide phone credit to those who are deemed most in need. While the *Refugee Info Bus* initiative in Calais is an on-the-ground initiative to equip refugees in hostile environments with smartphones and access to Wi-Fi, the *PC4R* initiative is taking place mainly remotely to cover phone credits for refugees.

In the different examples discussed above, each organisation takes both needs- and rights-based approaches to different degrees. In the case of the platform *Help* developed by UNHCR, an only-need-based approach was put in place leading to an extremely extractive process that relies on the refugee's use of the platform in order

---

[1] Phone Credit for Refugees tweet, https://twitter.com/credit4refugees/status/1480247041179762689
[2] Tech solutions to help refugees, from Calais to the UK, by Louise Brosset, 17 November 2021, retrieved from https://techfugees.com/all_news/tech-solutions-to-help-refugees-from-calais-to-the-uk/

to generate data, instead of enhancing the availability and quality of information and resources for refugees.

In the case of *The Voice of Refugees* the process was different, with more ownership given to refugees, combining both a needs- and a rights-based approach. In the Calais context, the two organisations (the *Refugee Info Bus* and the *PC4R*) have developed services that primarily aim to facilitate refugee access to their rights to communication and information, having developed new ways to collaborate and mobilise both online and offline. However, as described, hierarchical power relationships are still taking place with both initiatives not directly led by refugees; that is, refugees often remain dependent on the organisations, which can raise ethical concerns about their right to privacy and consent. However, refugee-led initiatives are also making use of digital technologies to share information, provide assistance and protection for refugees.

Digital initiatives by refugees: Enabling refugees to exercise their rights

In Calais, at the time of the 'jungle', social media platforms, and in particular Facebook, became an opportunity for refugees to organise themselves. Having observed how volunteers were organised through social media, this prompted some refugees to create their own Facebook pages such as 'RefugeesVoice2015'. The initiative was driven not only by the fact that refugees have a better understanding of the needs within their respective communities but also, as argued by a previous resident, by the right to human dignity. Through the Facebook page, they could raise awareness of the conditions and needs of migrants, amplifying their voices and providing first-hand information about how to enable safer crossings (Godin and Donà, 2021). This grassroot initiative continued after the closure of the camp in the form of *Hopetowns*, an organisation established in the UK by ex-residents who had crossed the channel and by ex-volunteers who had supported refugees in the camp. This refugee-led organisation informs refugees about their rights, acting as a bridge between the different refugee organisations and the refugees themselves and providing services directly to refugees (i.e., providing support with asylum claims, helping to make GP appointments, providing language support, and providing information on their rights in general). These services were provided face-to-face until the Covid-19 pandemic. During the successive lockdowns, the organisation had to adapt. The mission shifted to organising food banks, distributing food to refugees directly at their doorsteps, organising English classes online via Zoom, and providing mental health support via WhatsApp. As one of the leaders mentioned, he is now administering more than 15 WhatsApp groups based on the different services the organisation provides but also based on national groups, age, and the hotels where people live. Since the pandemic, thousands of asylum seekers were accommodated in hotels in England, in London in particular, often for weeks and months in dehumanising conditions with inadequate support (see The Refugee Council

2021 Report). While *Hopetowns* leaders would like to have more online visibility to express their voices and concerns, the lack of time and resources is often a challenge. In addition, the use of social media platforms by humanitarian organisations can sometimes contribute to reducing the visibility of refugee initiatives on the ground. The extensive use of social media by pro-refugee organisations can paradoxically make refugee-led initiatives less visible. Online participation of refugees can also be problematic. Not only are they often less connected but also they do not have access to laptops, relying on their smartphones to manage their online presence. Digital traces left by refugees on social media platforms can threaten refugees as well as jeopardise their journeys by allowing them to be monitored and located (Alinejad *et al.*, 2019; Gillespie *et al.*, 2016). 'Opting out' from social media platforms can therefore be a 'digital making-do' tactic to avoid causing more harm to refugees in preserving their right to privacy. Preventing themselves from accessing digital spaces in response to state surveillance can also affect refugees' right to communication and information, as well as the development of more inclusive and sustainable digital initiatives. In some cases, refugee leaders can also deploy more visible 'digital making-do' tactics by 'opting-in' other organisations' social media platforms in order to amplify their message so they can reach out to more people while protecting refugees' anonymity.

In another forced migration context, Lucia, a former architecture student from Venezuela, based on her frustration at not receiving useful information but also at being misrepresented, decided to create her own YouTube channel highlighting her refugee experience in Boa Vista. She regularly posts stories of fellow Venezuelans and videos about the opportunities and challenges of living in Boa Vista. Collaborators in Lucia's YouTube channel also share their city experiences in interviews, accompanied by relevant information and photos of themselves at different locations. Similarly, Juan, a 65-year-old Venezuelan, started recording a series of videos in the shelters. He used metaphors and narratives to highlight the stories of struggle and his hopes for a new life in Brazil. One of the defining features of Venezuelans' migration experiences is their great dependence on informal social networks (both online and offline) to navigate the complex infrastructures and systems of support as well as obstacles of adaptation into their host community. In this sense, the temporality of migrants' experiences and uncertainties can be linked to the predominance of informal channels of communication and information provision among the community. In contrast to more established migrant populations in Brazil, such as the case of the Haitian diaspora with solid migration networks and significant experiences of activism and participation in the production of digital media initiatives (Cogo, 2019), Venezuelans' digital networks of support upon arrival can be characterised as survival 'making-do' tactics shaped by individual actions of everyday resistance and solidarity (de Certeau, 1984). This is evident in the case of groups on Facebook (e.g., the Facebook group 'Venezuelans in Boa Vista') and WhatsApp which are mainly created to share information about a variety of topics without a clear and reliable structure that affirms the goals of the digital networks put in place as well as the veracity of information sources. These informal networks on Facebook remain active despite the risks that sharing information online about smuggling networks, suspicious commercial ads, or job posts can pose to their asylum applications or settlement trajectories, while at the same time actively contributing to generating data which can potentially be used by government actors to develop and implement policies on borders tha restrict refugees' mobility and agency in both Global North and South countries (Latonero and Kift, 2018; Molnar, 2020).

As mentioned above, the spread of false information is recurrent across Venezuelan social networks online, exacerbating refugees' vulnerabilities and existing uncertainties (Alencar, 2020). Interviews with Venezuelans revealed the negative consequences brought on by the dissemination of false and fractured information in different social media platforms. Many reported that being exposed to unverifiable sources made them more vulnerable to financial loss, discrimination, and aggressive behaviour from locals in the streets and public transportation, leading to the deterioration of their mental health (Alencar and Camargo, 2022). Despite these limitations, the creation of support/help groups in WhatsApp did facilitate language translation of government measures for Covid-19 and assistance, as well as other relevant information about asylum applications and access to public services. These informal survival 'digital making-do' practices became essential to fill the gaps in the state's asylum and integration systems during the pandemic and beyond.

Through these empirical examples, a series of both informal as well as formal 'digital making-do' practices were described showing the importance of taking into consideration the local context. This reveals a persistent gap between idealised views of what digital connectivity can achieve globally and evidence about how new connections are used in specific contexts (Smart *et al.*, 2016). In introducing the concept of 'digital making-do', we argue for the importance of reaching beyond the 'empowerment–control nexus' (Nedelcu and Soysüren, 2020) when looking at the use of new technologies in refugee settings. By using the concept of both 'tactics' and 'strategies', as developed by de Certeau (1984), we show that digital initiatives developed by social actors, including civil society organisations, or actors within the so-called tech-for-good community, can create the conditions for both empowerment and control, regardless of their positive intentions. Refugees are navigating these digital infrastructures and have developed a set of 'digital making-do' practices as a result. In doing so, they not only regain ownership of their trajectories and lives but also retain some control over the data they produce when using the services provided for them. They also reclaim their rights.

Conclusion

While not losing sight of top-down 'digital infrastructures for movement' (Latonero and Kift, 2018) that affect refugees' everyday lives, this chapter focuses on how refugees' creative and effective adoptions of technologies include the ways in which they deal with datafication processes that are often undertaken 'for their good' but often without their consent and knowledge. The deployment of digital technologies has been consistently emphasised by government and humanitarian organisations as crucial to promoting refugees' self-reliance and well-being, as well as in implementing innovative solutions to address the challenges of refugees (Easton-Calabria, 2019). Despite the importance of digital media to support and implement innovative forms of refugee assistance in different contexts (Sandvik et al., 2017), these technologies are also increasingly being used as instruments of power that instil new inequalities and undermine the real needs of displaced people and refugees on the ground (Maitland, 2018). As mobile technologies become more widely distributed among migrants and refugees, they also facilitate new kinds of inequality. Differential access to mobile technologies can create new forms of social stratification (Gillespie et al., 2016). This chapter highlighted how some applications and social media platforms can potentially create a usage-related imbalance and reinforce existing inequalities. In many instances, digital interventions through international humanitarian agencies and local NGOs do not take the lived realities of refugees into consideration (Leurs and Smets, 2018). Even in cases where refugees participate in the testing of digital tools, pre-established mechanisms underpinning the development and implementation of platforms and other digital solutions can contribute to reinforcing discrepancies and power imbalances in refugee contexts (Maitland, 2018).

Although significant efforts have been directed toward improving communication channels in different refugee contexts, broader barriers to digital infrastructure investment still need to be overcome to facilitate equal rights to connectivity and representation of refugee voices. This chapter has highlighted a few issues that data scientists need to understand before designing digital initiatives for refugees. It has discussed how refugee voices should be at the centre of such initiatives and how issues related to sustainability, accountability, and maintenance must be thoroughly explored before implementation.

Up to now, a critical mapping of existing 'refugee-tech digital initiatives' designed for, by, and/or with refugees in different contexts has not yet been undertaken in different contexts of forced migration. At the time of the so-called 'refugee crisis', Hounsell (2017) commented:

> While 30 percent of the global refugee population lives in sub-Saharan Africa, compared to 14 percent in Europe, four out of the top seven countries building tech solutions for refugees are in Europe, with Germany, Greece, the UK and France leading the way.

Examining the state of the refugee digital divide, Hounsell highlighted how innovation for Africa's displaced fell behind, pushing for more initiatives to take place. However, colonial footprints of migration in and through digital spaces are critical to identify and study. More and more, a shift toward new digital initiatives is being developed and tested in refugee communities in Europe, its borderlands, and beyond. Critical data mapping could be built upon criteria such as: the programme's scale of action (local, national, transnational, global); the target audience (refugees, host communities, both); the type of actors who initiated the project (refugee-led initiatives, private/third sector initiatives, public sector / civil society initiatives); the relevant field of action (health, education, employment); the promoted human rights; and how refugees' voices and agency are included in the entire process. This typology would contribute critically to the discussion about the usefulness of digital initiatives for, with, and by refugees, and will allow more space to capture refugees' everyday social practices in relation to digital technologies.

In this chapter, drawing on the theorisation of 'making-do' (Greene, 2020), we used the concepts of 'strategies' and 'tactics' (de Certeau, 1984) to relate them to the 'digital making-do' practices of refugees, situated in a social constructionist configuration of the rights-based approach. Specifically, the uses that refugees make of technologies in the strategic space (of top-down digital infrastructures, exploitative data practices, and digital labour), operating in their gaps, producing deviated, clandestine digital practices may be experienced as opportunities for resistance. With the term 'digital making-do', we were able to discuss context-dependent methods of appropriating new technologies by refugees as acts that go beyond survival, constituting acts of self-determination and making claims for their rights.

References

Alencar, A. (2018), 'Refugee integration and social media: A local and experiential perspective', *Information, Communication & Society* 21(11), 1588–603.

Alencar, A. (2020), 'Mobile communication and refugees: An analytical review of academic literature', *Sociology Compass* 14(8), e12802.

Alencar, A. and Camargo, J. (2022), 'Stories of migration: Exploring the links between emotions and technologies in the narratives of Venezuelan refugees in Brazil', *in* P. Tsatsou, ed, *Digital Inclusion: Enhancing Vulnerable People's Social Inclusion and Welfare*, Palgrave, London.

Alencar, A., Kondova, K., and Ribbens, W. (2019), 'The smartphone as a lifeline: An exploration of refugees' use of mobile communication technologies during their flight', *Media, Culture & Society* 41(6), 828–44.

Alinejad, D., Candidatu, L., Mevsimler, M., Minchilli, C., Ponzanesi, S., and Van der Vlist, F. N. (2019), 'Diaspora and mapping methodologies: Tracing transnational digital connections with "mattering maps"', *Global Networks* 19(1), 21–43.

Awad, I. and Tossell, J. (2021), 'Is the smartphone always a smart choice? Against the utilitarian view of the "connected migrant"', *Information, Communication & Society* 24(4), 611–26.

Benton, M. (2019), 'Digital litter: The downside of using technology to help refugees', Migration Information Source, available at https://www.migrationpolicy.org/article/digitallitter-downside-using-technology-help-refugees

Braune, L. (2020), 'Faceless Hackers improves Kakuma's refugees access to healthcare', 6 November, *Techfugees*, available at https://techfugees.com/all_news/community/faceless-hackers-kakuma-refugees-healthcare/

Casilli, A. A. (2017), 'Global digital culture| Digital labor studies go global: Toward a digital decolonial turn', *International Journal of Communication* 11, 3934–54.

Cogo, D. (2019), 'Communication, migrant activism and counter-hegemonic narratives of Haitian diaspora in Brazil', *Journal of Alternative & Community Media* 4(3), 71–85.

de Certeau, M. (1984), *The Practice of Everyday Life*, S. Rendall, trans, University of California Press, Berkeley, CA.
de Oliveira, M. G. A. G. (2019), 'Use of the Brazilian military component in the face of Venezuela's migration crisis', *Military Review* 1, 94–108.
Dekker, R., Engbersen, G., Klaver, J., and Vonk, H. (2018), 'Smart refugees: How Syrian asylum migrants use social media information in migration decision-making', *Social Media + Society* 4(1), 2056305118764439.
Donà, G. and Godin, M. (2019), 'Mobile technologies and forced migration', *in* A. Bloch and G. Dona, eds, *Forced Migration: Current Issues and Debates*, Routledge, Abingdon, 126–44.
Easton-Calabria, E. (2019), 'Digital livelihoods for people on the move', Technical report, UNDP, available at https://www.undp.org/content/dam/undp/library/prosperity/economic-recoverymobility/MASTER
Georgiou, M. (2019), 'City of refuge or digital order? Refugee recognition and the digital governmentality of migration in the city', *Television & New Media* 20(6), 600–16.
Gillespie, M., Lawrence, A., Cheesman, M., Faith, B., Illiou, E., Issa, A., Osseiran, S., and Skleparis, D. (2016), 'Mapping refugee media journeys: Smartphones and social media networks', Technical report, The Open University and France Médias Monde.
Gillespie, M., Osseiran, S., and Cheesman, M. (2018), 'Syrian refugees and the digital passage to Europe: Smartphone infrastructures and affordances', *Social Media + Society* 4(1), 2056305118764440.
Godin, M. and Donà, G. (2021), 'Rethinking transit zones: Migrant trajectories and transnational networks in techno-borderscapes', *Journal of Ethnic and Migration Studies* 47(14), 3276–92.
Greene, A. (2020), 'Mobiles and "making do": Exploring the affective, digital practices of refugee women waiting in Greece', *European Journal of Cultural Studies* 23(5), 731–48.
Hamelink, C. and Hagan, M. (2020), 'Communication rights for migrants', *in* K. Smets, K. Leurs, M. Georgiou, S. Witteborn, and R. Gajjala, eds, *The SAGE Handbook of Media and Migration*, Sage, Thousand Oaks, CA, 373–84.
Hounsell, B. (2017), 'Refugee digital divide: Innovation for Africa's displaced falls behind', The New Humanitarian, available at https://deeply.thenewhumanitarian.org/refugees/community/2017/02/22/refugee-digital-divide-innovation-for-africas-displaced-falls-behind
Human Rights Observer (2020), 'Observations of state violence at the French–UK border: Calais and Grande-Synthe', Technical report, Human Rights Observer (HRO) Annual Report, available at http://www.laubergedesmigrants.fr/wp-content/uploads/2021/05/HRO-2020-Annual-Report_All.pdf
Isin, E. and Ruppert, E. (2020), *Being Digital Citizens*, 2nd edn, Rowman & Littlefield Publishers, Lanham, MA.
Kaufmann, K. (2018), 'Navigating a new life: Syrian refugees and their smartphones in Vienna', *Information, Communication & Society* 21(6), 882–98.
Latonero, M. and Kift, P. (2018), 'On digital passages and borders: Refugees and the new infrastructure for movement and control', *Social Media + Society* 4(1), 2056305118764432.
Leung, L. (2018), *Technologies of Refuge and Displacement: Rethinking Digital Divides*, Lexington Books, Lanham, MA.
Leurs, K. (2017), 'Communication rights from the margins: Politicising young refugees' smartphone pocket archives', *International Communication Gazette* 79(6–7), 674–98.

Leurs, K. and Smets, K. (2018), 'Five questions for digital migration studies: Learning from digital connectivity and forced migration in (to) Europe', *Social Media + Society* 4(1), 2056305118764425.

Madianou, M. (2019), 'Technocolonialism: Digital innovation and data practices in the humanitarian response to refugee crises', *Social Media + Society* 5(3), 2056305119863146.

Maitland, C. (2018), *Digital Lifeline?: ICTs for Refugees and Displaced Persons*, MIT Press, Cambridge, MA.

Marino, S. (2021), *Mediating the Refugee Crisis*, Springer, New York, 171–8.

Merisalo, M. and Jauhiainen, J. S. (2020), 'Digital divides among asylum-related migrants: Comparing internet use and smartphone ownership', *Tijdschrift voor economische en sociale geografie* 111(5), 689–704.

Metcalfe, P. and Dencik, L. (2019), 'The politics of big borders: Data (in) justice and the governance of refugees', *First Monday* 24(4).

Molnar, P. (2020), 'Technological testing grounds: Migration management experiments and reflections from the ground up', Technical report, EDRi and the Refugee Law Lab.

Nedelcu, M. and Soysüren, I. (2020), 'Precarious migrants, migration regimes and digital technologies: The empowerment–control nexus', *Journal of Ethnic and Migration Studies* 48, 1821–37.

Oltermann, P. (2016), 'Syrian refugees design app for navigating German bureaucracy', 5 August, *The Guardian*, available at https://www.theguardian.com/world/2016/aug/05/syrian-refugees-app-navigating-german-bureacracy-bureacrazy

Pincock, K., Betts, A., and Easton-Calabria, E. (2020), *The Global Governed?: Refugees as Providers of Protection and Assistance*, Cambridge University Press, Cambridge.

Robinson, J. (2016), 'Comparative urbanism: New geographies and cultures of theorizing the urban', *International Journal of Urban and Regional Research* 40(1), 187–99.

Sandvik, K. B., Jacobsen, K. L., and McDonald, S. M. (2017), 'Do no harm: A taxonomy of the challenges of humanitarian experimentation', *International Review of the Red Cross* 99(904), 319–44.

Smart, C., Donner, J., and Graham, M. (2016), 'Connecting the world from the sky: Spatial discourses around Internet access in the developing world', *in Proceedings of the Eighth International Conference on Information and Communication Technologies and Development*, 1–11.

The Refugee Council (2021), ' "I sat watching life go by my window for so long", The experiences of people seeking asylum living in hotel accommodation', Technical report, The Refugee Council, available at https://media.refugeecouncil.org.uk/wp-content/uploads/2021/04/22152856/I-sat-watching-my-life-go-by-my-window-for-so-long-23rd-April-2021.pdf

United Nations High Commissioner for Refugees (2020), 'Connecting with confidence: Managing digital risks to refugee connectivity', Technical report, United Nations High Commissioner for Refugees (UNHCR).

Uppal, C., Sartoretto, P., and Cheruiyot, D. (2019), 'The case for communication rights: A rights-based approach to media development', *Global Media and Communication* 15(3), 323–43.

Wall, M., Otis Campbell, M., and Janbek, D. (2017), 'Syrian refugees and information precarity', *New Media & Society* 19(2), 240–54.

Zijlstra, J. and van Liempt, I. (2017), 'Smart (phone) travelling: Understanding the use and impact of mobile technology on irregular migration journeys', *International Journal of Migration and Border Studies* 3(2–3), 174–91.

18

Conflict and Forced Migration: Social Media as Event Data

H. AKIN UNVER AND AHMET KURNAZ

Introduction: Defining the Violence-Migration Nexus

WAR HAS ALWAYS been synonymous with large-scale human displacement. Although inter-state wars and large-scale global conflicts have been the main culprits of forced migration in history, more recent cases of human displacement have been triggered either by environmental problems (famine, drought, floods) or by civil wars and subnational violence, or an interaction of both. Since civil wars are increasingly being fought over the control of civilian populations, their impact on forced migration is often more pronounced compared to inter-state military disputes. Perhaps the worst such calamity of modern times, the Syrian Civil War, has produced upwards of 5.6 million refugees and 6.2 million internally displaced people.

Conflicts generate population displacement both because of their immediate violent effect, and due to their secondary after-effects that generate infrastructure destruction, homelessness, poverty, and lack of access to food, water, and security. Contemporary responses to mitigate forced migration have taken on two major forms. The first of those is the 'root causes' literature that explores social, political, and economic drivers of forced migration and seeks to build more sustainable and long-term improvements in target societies to minimise the likelihood of mass migration (Schmeidl, 2001). The second line of response is the protection, assistance, and aid camp, which seeks to create emergency response mechanisms to protect populations from violence, and deploy safeguards and urgent aid to prevent displacement. This second 'urgent response' camp, namely peacekeepers, aid workers, and emergency assistance professionals, have increasingly relied on situational awareness data, which would supply them with patterns of violence (Thobane *et al.*, 2007; Harrington, 2005).

Although not all conflict-exposed populations migrate (Ibáñez and Vélez, 2008), organised violence, especially recurring violence that incurs sustained damage to the livelihood of inhabitants, is among the primary predictors of forced migration (Czaika and Kis-Katos, 2009). Although war and sustained conflict, without direct violence, may also generate the groundwork for forced migration due to its aftershock effects on poverty, displacement, and grievances, acute violence often serves as a substantial variable that affects the locals' calculus to stay or leave (Moore and Shellman, 2004). In the presence of indiscriminate violence, and exchange of territory where the replacing power has no immediate plans to establish law and order, incentives to leave towards an unknown outcome may outweigh the more explicit benefits of staying (De Mesquita et al., 2005). Earlier studies have demonstrated that conflict-related forced migration creates an outflow towards regions with better security, law and order, as well as better access to employment, social networks, and pre-existing contacts (Dustmann and Kirchkamp, 2002; Pellegrini and Fotheringham, 2002; Klabunde and Willekens, 2016).

However, conflict and violence serve as a more important variable in the study of forced migration than simply being a cause of it. Such violence may not only affect the migration route and tempo of the migrants but may also significantly affect the level of further violence that the migrants suffer at the hands of the warring parties (Salt and Stein, 1997). The tendency to migrate is more significant with populations that have a longer planning horizon, as younger people may become a particular target for combatants when a particular area changes from the jurisdiction of one side to another (Stark and Levhari, 1982; Katz and Stark, 1986; Todaro, 1969). In other words, direct violence or threat of violence both mitigates the effect of uncertainty on populations making a migration choice and strengthens the risk-taking behaviour of populations living close to flashpoint areas.

Because armed conflicts significantly influence not only the decision to migrate, but also the trajectory, direction, tempo, and volume of migration, conflict monitoring and data collection are important tools that assist in the study of force migration (Schon, 2019). Organised violence can also lead to further cases of secondary violence such as deliberate migrant targeting, massacres, and other atrocities, which is why the empirical study of the conflict–migration nexus is important both to understand some of the causes of forced migration and also to develop mechanisms to protect displaced persons during their mobility (Kaiser and Hagan, 2015). This growing need to study more detailed mechanisms and patterns of violence has brought about the need for more granular data of 'events', namely who creates violence, who receives violence, and how the act of violence is being transmitted across actors.

Out of both ground operatives' and policy-makers' need for greater situational awareness came the idea of event datasets. While earlier examples of event datasets relied on aggregated data that provided a higher-level view of disputes and crises, over time, event datasets evolved into highly disaggregated, granular, and daily collections of important conflict events (Chojnacki et al., 2012). As conflict event datasets became more granular, they yielded higher-quality data to undertake forecasting, and also enabled researchers to cross-utilise them with other forms of social, econometric, and political data to explain the onset of armed disputes better (Weidmann, 2013). As a result, a very rich and rigorous field emerged that leveraged conflict event datasets to explore the relationship between poverty, environmental degradation, social hostilities, government quality, and level of repression, and the main drivers of armed conflict.

This chapter explores some of the current debates on conflict event data creation and analysis, how to use social media data as a form of conflict data, and how both rapidly emerging fields can assist forced migration scholars. It starts out with a comparison of the most commonly used conflict event datasets in the field, including their comparative advantages and disadvantages in forced migration research. Then, it explores the methodological advances in harvesting both conventional and social media data as conflict event data sources, paying specific attention to media and availability biases that limit the extent to which we can rely on them. Finally, the chapter ends with a demonstration of how to harvest Twitter data to study a violent conflict (Operation Olive Branch in northern Syria), paying specific attention to how this method compares to the leading datasets, ACLED and UCDP/PRIO.

Problems with social media as data: A brief warning about availability bias

Although traditionally scientists worked with data provided by the state security agencies (Kalyvas and Kocher, 2009; Berman *et al.*, 2011) or local security forces (Bowsher *et al.*, 2018), with the increasing presence of aid organisations and reporters, their frontline workers and even civilian reports have turned into valuable sources of event data (Lyall, 2010; Nettelfield, 2010). The multiplicity of data sources that come from different phases of a conflict (combat, aid, reconstruction), as well as different parties (combatants, workers, reporters, civilians), cause data availability asymmetries. Such asymmetries have been a chronic flaw of conflict event datasets, rendering micro-level comparative analyses of multiple conflicts difficult from an availability bias point of view.

In order to remedy some of this mismatch, major dataset projects have been using newspaper reports along with official or journalistic field reports in order to bring some uniformity to different conflict event data collection efforts. Weidmann (2015, 2016) discussed the benefits and pitfalls of such media-based data creation processes by focusing on three dynamics. First, that often media outlets are more interested in furthering political or ideological interests than objectively reporting on violent events, and as a result, some events may be methodically omitted while others are represented exclusively. Second, media outlets usually focus on large events, which forces them to leave out 'smaller' events due to editorial concerns. Third, most media corporations report on events that are relevant to their readership; for example, media companies in the US may be more interested in covering events that affect American troops or assets nearby, while disregarding those that have no direct relevance.

The advent of social media was initially thought to be a positive development to bridge the above gaps. After all, social media not only contains reports and narratives from a broad range of news sources, but it also contains messages, videos, and images from the frontline combatants and civilians themselves. Such forms of data have no filter, no editorial oversight or immediate government censorship, and flow at a higher volume than regular media-based data. To that end, harvesting and logging social media event data has the potential to mitigate the data availability gap between various event datasets and conflicts. However, precisely because of the unmediated nature of social media event data, it has also fallen prey to disinformation, redundant reports, and reporting bias. For example, one of the most frequently recurring bias problems in social media data availability is the proximity to cell phone or 3G towers. Pierskalla and Hollenbach (2013) particularly demonstrated how cell phone coverage significantly affects the volume and quality of the event data we extract from ICT-based reports (see also Hollenbach and Pierskalla, 2017). Such distortions and biases between event datasets have a direct impact on conflict analysis as well as more practical applications such as aid distribution or peacekeeping (Duursma, 2018).

A more interesting point is that conflict events may often be non-violent events. The traditional method of measuring conflict intensity via the number of casualties is a practice that is being increasingly questioned in the literature for this very reason (Gleditsch, 2020). This is because literature definitions of 'peace' often stray into the 'absence of violence' territory, which is misleading because not all absences of death and violence constitute peace (Diehl, 2016). Sometimes frozen conflicts may record zero casualties, but the armed dispute (frontlines, mobilised fighters, clashes) may endure and cause forced migration. In other cases, sides may not be able to mobilise resources to fight a war, but may be in direct hostilities nonetheless. A very robust new sub-field on 'rebel governance' aims to address this problem by establishing new conflict datasets that include diplomacy, administration, and social work-related events (Arjona *et al.*, 2015). While these new datasets and their research focus undoubtedly enrich conflict research, it also brings in new challenges with regard to measurement, generalisability, and reporting bias, as the micro-analysis of such event types are often less clear and harder to quantify in relation to casualties (Galtung *et al.*, 2013).

'Off-the-shelf' conflict event datasets: A comparison

The origins of conflict event data go back to the 1960s, to Charles McClelland's 'The acute international crisis', and David Singer's 'Correlates of War project' (McClelland, 1961; Singer, 1988). Both of these earliest attempts to generate event data for the quantitative study of international diplomatic and violent events establish some of the most important benchmarks on the classification of conflict types, periodisation, and the coding of event actors. Today, the publicly available conflict-related data ecosystem is quite robust, with generalised 'broad event datasets' such as the Uppsala Conflict Data Program – Peace Research Institute of Oslo (UCDP/PRIO) datasets, Armed Conflict Location and Events Dataset (ACLED) or Integrated Crisis Early Warning System (ICEWS), as well as more specialised datasets such as the Global Terrorism Database (START-GTD), TRAC (Terrorism Research and Analysis Consortium), International Crisis Behavior (ICB), or the Mass Mobilization (MM) Data Project. These datasets are used by governments, civil society, and NGO analysts, as much as serving as the basis of scientific research on the micro-dynamics of violent events.

Today, 'conflict event data' is widely defined as any observable information related to the interaction between violent parties. This may take the form of actual violent events such as deaths, bombings, airstrikes, drone strikes, terrorist attacks, or infrastructure targeting, or non-violent events researchers measure or observe because they have a direct impact on the course of a conflict. These may be threats, public declarations, alliance formations or break-ups, merging or splitting of organisations, and so on. ACLED's definition of an 'event' is any violent event that occurs between two designated actors that can be narrowed down into a specific time frame; these designated actors are coded as organised political groups, including militant organisations or rebel groups (Raleigh et al., 2010). UCDP's definition of an event, on the other hand, is more specific and has clear criteria for them to be coded as events:

> the incidence of the use of armed force by an organised actor against another organised actor, or against civilians, resulting in at least one direct death in either the best, low or high estimate categories at a specific location and for a specific temporal duration. (Sundberg and Melander, 2013)

These definitional variances (i.e., whether an 'event' constitutes fatality, injury, strategic action, or a threat) across datasets and over what constitutes a 'conflict event' are often so broad that they determine the selection rationale of one dataset over others, as it fits a research question or measurement method better. After all, a terrorist organisation blowing up a pipeline, which forces a nearby village to evacuate, a split within a militant group that leads to higher taxation of a particular network of towns under new leadership, and a verbal threat of a state military force to attack a rebel stronghold that is dug-in within civilian areas all constitute 'events' that directly cause forced migration and population movements (Wood, 1994).

For any newcomer to the field, choosing which dataset to use can be a daunting task. For researchers of forced migration, the most important criterion has to be disaggregation. For a very long time, aggregated datasets that were structured on a 'country/year level' coding format dominated the field. The 'disaggregation revolution' increased pace in the wake of the September 11 attacks in the US, and the growing need for more granular and detailed conflict and violence event datasets. Disaggregation in conflict event data implies separating 'event metadata' into constitutive actors, date, time, location, and type. In exploring causal mechanisms of conflict that affect forced migration, disaggregation is critical in determining the effect of each variable (date, actor, location) on migration intensity, direction, and target (Shellman, 2008; Hegre et al., 2009). This provides a much better data architecture that enables researchers to explore deeper causes of conflict, via either surveys in conflict areas or geolocated spatiotemporal events.

Here are some of the most frequently used 'off-the-shelf' conflict event datasets popular in the scientific and policy community alike:

UCDP/PRIO: As one of the 'industry standard' conflict event datasets, both the joint UCDP/PRIO Armed Conflict Dataset and UCDP's other datasets such as the Georeferenced Disaggregated Event Dataset, one-sided, non-state, or the battle-related death datasets have been among the most frequently used in both policy and scientific analysis (Kreutz, 2010; Croicu and Kreutz, 2017; Sundberg et al., 2012; Sundberg and Melander, 2013; Gleditsch et al., 2002). Various levels of detail in these individual datasets relate to the granularity of spatial data (specific coordinates, village-, town-, and city-level), as well as temporality (hour, day, month, year). The UCDP/PRIO Armed Conflict Dataset and other UCDP datasets contain a unique conflict identifier (*conflict_id/integer*), location of event (*location/string*), parties to the conflict (*side_a, side_b, side_b_id, side_b_2nd/string*), source of disagreement (*incompatibility/integer*), conflict area (*territory_name/string*), along with a large selection of disaggregated variables related to the violent dispute that go back to either 1946 or 1989. Uppsala University has a related side project called ViEWS, a political Violence Early-Warning System, that forecasts violence through UCDP data (Hegre et al., 2019). This project is of particular importance to the researchers of forced migration.

ACLED: Another frequently used dataset, ACLED, is separated into regions: Africa, Middle East, Eastern and Southeastern Europe/Balkans, and so on (Raleigh et al., 2010). This is great for carrying out research on a specific region, but cross-regional historical analysis gets complicated as different regions start from different years. For example, while the Africa dataset starts from 1997, most Central Asia and Caucasus events start from 2016 or 2017. Likewise, Latin America data collection has begun very recently, in 2019. The temporal limitations of this dataset are formidable, but ACLED is also a better dataset for researchers of recent conflicts, as they update their dataset more frequently (weekly) than, say, UCDP/PRIO (annually). The events are coded by a unique API key, date range, event type, sub-event type (if the type of event can be categorised in two ways; for example, an act that can both be logged as 'violence against civilians' and 'excessive use of force against protestors' at the same time), type of actor, and location/region.

START-GTD: The University of Maryland's Study of Terrorism and National Responses to Terrorism Global Terrorism Database is a specialised dataset that only logs events that are defined as terrorist incidents. These incidents are defined as '[t]he threatened or actual use of illegal force and violence by a non-state actor to attain a political, economic, religious, or social goal through fear, coercion, or intimidation' (LaFree and Dugan, 2007, p. 10). However, the dataset only contains actual use of force and does not log any threats. Additional problems originate from the fact that it becomes very difficult to distinguish most crisis events that include non-state violence against civilians as a terrorist tactic, or a threat of violence by states that targets populations indiscriminately as a battle tactic. Regardless, GTD has been a cornerstone of quantitative terrorism research since 1970, although newer datasets like ACLED and UCDP/PRIO have refined their event definitions and operationalisations to a greater degree. GTD variables include target country, type of attack (assassination, armed assault, bombing, hijacking, hostage-taking, infrastructure targeting, unarmed assault), target type (police, citizens/property, government, utilities-transportation, etc.), weapon type, perpetrator, and casualties (fatalities and injuries).

GDELT: The Global Database of Events, Language, and Tone project is among the earliest attempts to harvest large, multi-language, global media reports and log them into a unified event dataset. It monitors and scrapes web news media sources (both national and local) from around the world with a 15-minute regular update tempo (Leetaru and Schrodt, 2013). Recently, GDELT has begun feeding real-time, multi-language, machine-translated social media data into its monitoring systems to provide a broader coverage of events. GDELT has an event database of around 250 million data nodes collected since 1979. GDELT is not confined to conflict events, and includes a far broader repertoire of event types but, regardless of the type of protest, crisis, violence, economic, legal, events it logs are directly relevant to researchers of population movements and forced migration. The GDELT dataset does not attempt to provide the 'most accurate' form of event reporting, and rather focuses on collecting a trove of media narratives and perspectives. To that end, it is a dataset of 'reports about events', rather than events themselves, which is a crucial difference when it comes to using GDELT for migration research. More specifically, the GDELT dataset is more vulnerable to false reporting and misinformation in the form of false positives, both because of its very large data harvesting capacity, and the fact that the harvesting and coding are conducted by algorithms.

ICEWS: The Integrated Crisis Early Warning System is a more US-focused 'dataset of datasets', as its primary goal has been to assist American government analysts to predict and respond to crises that are relevant to its political objectives (Hammond and Weidmann, 2014). It is structured upon four components: iData, which is the underlying raw data of around 50 million stories from around the globe in four languages (English, Spanish, Portuguese, and Arabic) with 25 million geocoded events; iTrace, which converts iData events into index-based structured datasets that demonstrate interactions between actors, groups, and countries; iCast, which is a forecasting module that produces projects for up to six months ahead on political crisis, international crisis, religious violence, and rebellion event types; and finally, iSent, which provides a more real-time analysis of social-media-heavy content to provide more recent situational awareness. The main problem with ICEWS is that it is not publicly available. As it is a product designed for US government use, it is accessed through specialised servers, although the scientists in charge of the project upload past versions of it on Dataverse.[1] This is still very useful for analyses of past events (for example, the relationship between conflict, crisis, and forced migration in previous years), but unlike GDELT, most up-to-date ICEWS data are not open for public use.

xSUB: As another attempt to create an integrated database, xSub merges more than 25,000 event datasets and organises them into easily navigable variables related to spatial (coordinates, grid, town/city name), temporal (dd.mm.yy format), and actor-specific conditionals that go back to 1969 (Zhukov *et al.*, 2019). xSub is a very important project for researchers who seek to understand the comparative advantages of various datasets and test hypotheses using datasets with different measurement, periodisation and actor focus types. The need for xSub originated from the observation that 'grand' datasets like ACLED and UCDP/PRIO are often not detailed enough for micro-level analyses of very clearly defined crises, especially at the spatial level. In order to remedy this gap, most studies end up creating their own specialised, dedicated datasets, leading to a proliferation of very detailed but disconnected subnational event datasets. In addition, multiple datasets that cover the same (period, actor) dyad or events use different definitions and operationalisations, leading to important incompatibilities that impair replicability. xSub's data sources include ACLED, Empirical Studies of Conflict's Worldwide Incidents Tracking System, the US government's Iraq Significant Acts (SIGACTS) database, the Social Conflict Analysis Database (SCAD), and other major 'off-the-shelf', as well as donated, research data. These data sources are integrated with a dedicated R package called MELTT (Matching Event Data by Location, Time, and Type), which dictates the fundamental aggregation principle of the xSub project.

The conflict event data ecosystem goes beyond these usual suspects. Although these datasets are some of the most frequently used in both more established and more recent scholarly works, there are important additional datasets that would enable researchers to cross-validate data sources. Some of those important supplementary datasets are:

Social Conflict Analysis Database (SCAD): covers protests, intra-state conflicts, strikes/riots, and one-sided violence across the African continent, Latin America, and the Caribbean through 1990–2017 (Salehyan *et al.*, 2012);

Mass Mobilization Data Project:[2] logs anti-government protests and demonstrations across 162 countries through 1990–2018, and includes protester demands, government reactions, location, and mobilisation identity variables;

---

[1] Harvard Dataverse: Integrated Crisis Early Warning System (ICEWS) Dataverse, https://dataverse.harvard.edu/dataverse/icews

[2] Mass Mobilization Project: An Effort to Understand Citizen Movements Against Governments, https://massmobilization.github.io/

Integrated Network for Societal Conflict Research (INSCR):[3] supported by the US government to create a policy-relevant 'master database' of forcibly displaced populations, major episodes of political violence, state failure, high-casualty terrorist bombings, and state fragility markers in 167 countries from 1946 to date;

Sexual Violence in Armed Conflict (SVAC): an ambitious attempt to identify and log one of the most difficult-to-measure indicators in civil wars. It systematically lists all conflict-related sexual violence committed by government militaries, pro- and anti-government militias as well as terrorist/insurgent groups, and contains data about perpetrators, victims, time, and location of sexual violence events (Cohen and Nordås, 2014).

Extracting social media as conflict event data: a sample workflow

Depending on the research question or the scope of the study, 'off-the-shelf' data solutions may not be sufficient. This may be due to the recency of the event that is being studied: prominent datasets may have been late to log them into their data pool. Or the event may be taking place in a region that is not covered by any of the datasets. Equally likely is the possibility that a study may be focusing on a different level of analysis compared to what other datasets are offering. In such cases, researchers may have to create their own event datasets, and social media offers an excellent data source to establish those tailored event data pools.

This section demonstrates a sample workflow (see Figure 18.1) that is intended to serve as an inspiration for conflict researchers and a way for newcomers to the

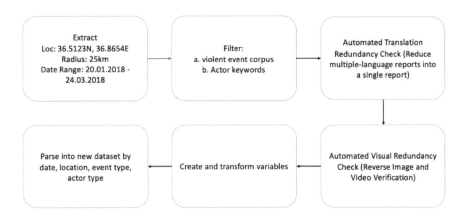

Figure 18.1 A sample workflow for automated violent event data extraction and processing.

---

[3] Centre for Systemic Peace: INSCR Data Page, http://www.systemicpeace.org/inscrdata.html

field to gauge how to build their own workflows. Although most of the specific techniques mentioned here will inevitably become obsolete with time, the underlying principle of the workflow should have some methodological shelf-life. Most importantly, social media sites continually update their scraping and data extraction policies, so the method outlined here may not be fully available in this form at a future date.

There are two prominent ways of extracting violent event data from social media: manually, and automatically. Manual extraction, such as those based on the Textual Analysis By Augmented Replacement Instructions (TABARI) coding system (Best *et al.*, 2013), involves employing coders (read: armies of assistants) that scroll through social media feeds on Twitter, Facebook, or any other platform to identify and log events one by one, by hand. This method is feasible for the study of short-lived isolated incidents with a moderate amount of data, such as small-scale clashes or incidents. Manual extraction has a lower likelihood of producing redundant or faulty data, due to the fact that the coder extracts such information one by one, checking for such errors in real time (King and Lowe, 2003). Automatic extraction, on the other hand, uses one extraction algorithm (or a combination of several) to set extraction criteria (such as named-entity recognition) to fish for data within a larger pool of social media feeds. Box 18.1 provides an overview of reliability in content analysis and annotation quality assessment, which is particularly important for large-scale data annotation.

The first decision a researcher will have to make will inevitably depend on the research question: is the study focusing on a particular event (i.e., armed clash, threats against energy infrastructure, suicide bombing), a group (a militant organisation, or members of a particular tribe, ethnic/sectarian populace), or a region (town/village, pipeline network, migration route)? This is crucial because a study that tests whether violence against a particular ethnic or a religious group, or violence in a region close to border areas, creates a greater magnitude of forced migration will have to follow different entity extraction protocols. Similarly, a study that focuses on whether a certain threshold of violence against civilians in areas under peacekeeper control triggers greater mistrust towards peacekeeping, and hence, greater likelihood of migration, will require different named entities.

For the sake of demonstration, this section will focus on Operation Olive Branch, the cross-border incursion by the Turkish Armed Forces into northern Syria to push the People's Protection Units (YPG) out of the town of Afrin (20 January to 24 March 2018) using Twitter data only. As mentioned earlier, the extraction criteria for social media data largely depend on the research question. Here we will apply a two-tier methodology: first, we'll extract all data from a 25 km radius of Afrin (36.5123°N, 36.8654°E), then omit irrelevant data based on a corpus of keywords. These keywords can either be fed into a corpus via pre-extraction from newspaper sources or user-generated word combinations, or simply can be extracted through machine-learning algorithms that are trained on datasets like UCDP/PRIO, ACLED, and others. A sample violent event type list could be listed as follows. Given space constraints it is impractical to create a sub-list of keywords that belong to these

> **Box 18.1** Reliability in content analysis
>
> Scraping or collecting large datasets from the internet is possible, but annotation of these datasets can be tedious and expensive. Manual annotation can be subjective and occasionally erroneous. Subsequently, using multiple annotators for the same data item and looking at their agreement is a typical solution to ensure annotation quality.
>
> Amazon's *Mechanical Turk* service made large-scale, distributed, and cheap human annotation possible, and other initiatives followed suit. Approaches to improve the quality of annotations include specifying qualification levels (i.e., filtering the annotators), inserting items with known labels (i.e., *implicit screening questions*) to perform quality assessment, analysis of correlations between annotations, IP address analysis, attention checks, outlier analysis, anomalous pattern detection, response time checks, and such. Providing good instructions to annotators, randomising items, and constraining task completion times are other recommendations.
>
> For two annotators annotating nominal data, *Cohen's kappa* is used as an inter-annotator agreement measure, where the probability of chance agreement is also taken into account (Cohen, 1960). In this and other agreement coefficients, the general form is:
>
> $$Agreement = 1 - \frac{Observed\ disagreement}{Expected\ disagreement}.$$
>
> Accordingly, Cohen's kappa is written as:
>
> $$\kappa = 1 - \frac{1 - p_o}{1 - p_e},$$
>
> where p_o is the relative observed agreement among raters, and p_e is the hypothetical probability of chance agreement. In practice, p_e is also estimated from the data of the annotators, and not assumed via problem structure. It is taken as a squared geometric mean of proportions. In a similar measure, called *Scott's pi* (Scott, 1955), the main formula is the same, but p_e is calculated by the squared arithmetic means of the marginal proportions. For more annotators, *Fleiss' kappa* can be used, which generalises Scott's pi (Fleiss et al., 2013).
>
> Krippendorff (2004) discussed reliability in content analysis, and noted that 'agreement is what we measure; reliability is what we wish to infer from it'. According to him, an agreement coefficient can become an index of reliability only if (1) it is applied to proper reliability data, resulting from duplicating the process of coding, categorising, or measuring a sample; (2) it treats units of analysis as separately describable or categorisable, whereby a coding procedure is used and coders are treated as interchangeable, and observable coder idiosyncrasies are counted as disagreement; (3) its values indicate, and correlate with, the conditions under which one is willing to rely on imperfect data, which means it should produce meaningful and interpretable values.

event lists, but further information on this could be found in (Atkinson et al., 2017; Alhelbawy et al., 2016). Depending on the research question, researchers could use automated translation API services or human translators to create Arabic, Farsi, or Kurdish versions of these lists, as required (see Table 18.1). Then, optionally, a

Table 18.1 A sample meta-keyword list containing macro-level violent event types

aerial_attack, armed_clash, border_incident, chemical_attack, drone_strike, espionage, explosion, military_exercise, military_operation, sabotage, shelling, shooting, curfew, protest, riots, road_blockade, assassination, bomb_defusal, kidnapping, security_incident, security_operation, smuggling, pipeline_damage, pipeline_shutdown

Table 18.2 Actor-specific entity recognition list for Kurdish groups in, or relevant to, northern Syria

Partiya Karkerên Kurdistanê, PKK (Kurdistan Workers' Party) – Hêzên Parastina Gel, HPG (People's Defence Forces) – Yekîneyên Jinên Azad ên Star, YJA STAR (Free Women's Units) – Koma Civakên Kurdistan, KCK (Group of Communities in Kurdistan) – Teyrênbazê Azadiya Kurdistan, TAK (Kurdistan Freedom Falcons) – Partiya Yekîtiya Demokrat, PYD (Democratic Union Party, Syria) – Tevgera Ciwanen Welatparêz Yên Şoreşger, YDG-H (Patriotic Revolutionary Youth Movement) – Yekîneyên Parastina Gel, YPG (People's Protection Units) – Yekîneyên Parastina Jin, YPJ (Women's Protection Units) – Yekîtiya Nîştimanî ya Kurdistanê, PUK (The Patriotic Union of Kurdistan) – Partiya Demokrat a Kurdistanê, KDP (Kurdistan Democratic Party) – Encûmena Niştimanî ya Kurdî li Sûriyê, KNC (Kurdish National Council) – Peshmerga (Pêşmerge) – Partiya Jiyana Azad a Kurdistanê, PJAK or HRK (Party of Free Life of Kurdistan) – Hêzên Parastina Jinê, HPJ (Women's Defence Forces) – Yekîneyên Parastina Rojhilatê Kurdistan, YRK (East Kurdistan Defense Units) – Yekîneyên Berxwedana Şengalê, YPŞ (Sinjar Resistance Units) – Parastin u Zanyari (Protection and Information, KRG official intelligence) – Quwwāt Sūriyā al-Dīmuqrāṭīya, SDF (Syrian Democratic Forces)

second layer of keyword filter can be introduced to sort violent event data according to actors (groups, individuals). A sample collection of Kurdish-specific group keywords (Kurdish and English-only) relevant during Operation Olive Branch are given in Table 18.2.

It is important to expect data redundancy in social media data extracted from war zones. Often a violent event may have multiple reports in the same language or across different languages, so it is imperative to build precautions that will reduce multiple reports of the same events into a single event at the level required by the research question. Most automated translation API services like Google Translate or Microsoft Translate work fine, at least in recognising simple violent events that do not contain sarcasm. While they are imperfect at this time, they omit quite a significant amount of redundancy, leaving a more manageable set of data cleaning tasks for human coders.

Similarly, the heavy presence of disinformation and information manipulation in war zones continue to be one of the most problematic hurdles against automated conflict event data generation from social media feeds. Often, videos and images taken earlier in a different location are reshared as if they are happening recently, either as a propaganda technique or as a form of deterring the other side. One way of dealing with this is to conduct reverse image or video checks of extracted content

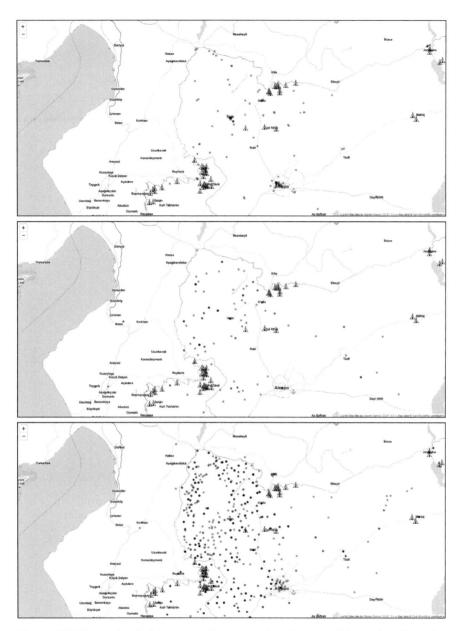

Figure 18.2 Region-level violent event data comparison in geographic relationship to the nearest refugee camps. Top: Twitter extraction output (authors' work); middle: UCDP/PRIO; bottom: ACLED. Each dot represents a single logged violent event. Tent icons indicate The Assistance Coordination Unit (ACU) IDP camps (data: The Syrian IDP Camps Monitoring Study, Northern Syria Camps: https://data.humdata.org/dataset/idp-camps-monitoring-november-of-2018). While Twitter data yields more events compared to UCDP/PRIO, ACLED offers the largest set of events.

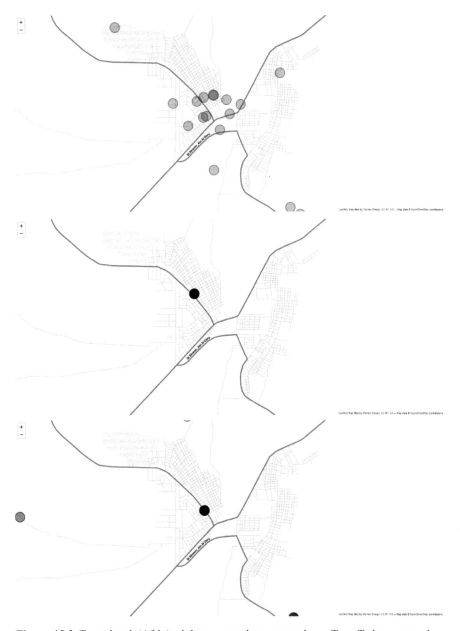

Figure 18.3 Town-level (Afrin) violent event data comparison. Top: Twitter extraction output (authors' work); middle: UCDP/PRIO; bottom: ACLED. Each dot represents a single logged violent event. Twitter data yields more events at this level compared to both UCDP/PRIO and ACLED.

SOCIAL MEDIA AS EVENT DATA 397

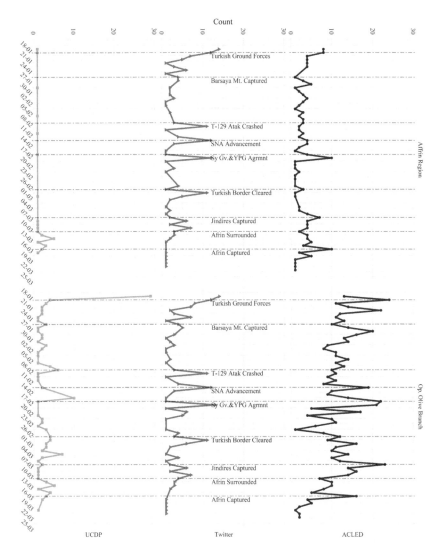

Figure 18.4 Time-series graph showing ACLED, Twitter, and UCDP data frequencies corresponding to major violent events (18 January to 25 March 2018). Top: Afrin town and immediate vicinity ([latitude ≥ 36.49 & $latitude$ ≤ 36.52 & longitude < 37 & longitude > 36.8, geo_code := 'Afrin Region']); bottom: wider Operation Olive Branch area ([latitude ≥ 36.49 & latitude ≤ 39 & longitude < 37 & longitude > 35, geo_code := 'Op. Olive Branch']).

via TinyEye[4] or Berify,[5] which can be integrated with the researcher's event data extraction algorithm to verify media data in real time. Once event data are extracted, they can be parsed into variables required by the researchers. For the purposes of

---

[4] TinEye, https://tineye.com/
[5] Berify, https://berify.com/

this study we have parsed it into date, location, event type, and actor type variables. We have tested whether our Twitter-focused data extraction can offer us any advantages against two giants: the UCDP/PRIO georeferenced event dataset and ACLED. In this test, we have assessed both the spatial validity and granularity of social media data against UCDP/PRIO and ACLED, as well as their size (volume) advantages. The spatial test was conducted at both region (see Figure 18.2) and town level (see Figure 18.3).

At the broader Operation Olive Branch area, we see that ACLED data has better coverage compared to both Twitter data and UCDP/PRO data. This superiority is apparent both at the spatial level and time-series interpretation (see Figure 18.4). However, zooming into the more specific Afrin town area, ACLED and Twitter data become almost comparable in terms of granularity and volume. In some cases, such as the crash of the Turkish T-129 attack helicopter, the territorial gains of the Syrian National Army (SNA) and Turkish forces' control of the entire border area are better represented in the Twitter data. This means that at the micro level, Twitter data extraction does catch quite important and relevant violent events that are not covered by ACLED. In contrast, ACLED does better in terms of logging rural violent events. Surprisingly, Twitter data are less impressive in logging the conflict termination phase (the capture of Afrin by the Turkish forces), which is better represented by ACLED and UCDP/PRIO.

Overall, in this test the advantage of automated social media violent event data was its better performance in monitoring inner-settlement dynamics (control of streets, capture of buildings) compared to ACLED, which did better in logging violence in areas outside cities. ACLED also had an overall higher volume of violent event data, although it did miss a number of very relevant events that had a direct impact on the outcome and course of the 2.5-month operation.

Conclusion

Scholars of forced migration have begun using conflict event datasets more frequently over the last decade. Part of this rising popularity is due to the datasets' rapidly increasing quality and granularity, enabling observers to predict, monitor, and explain forced migration events with greater accuracy and causal validity. Since the 1970s, various such datasets emerged testing different data extraction and recording techniques and various levels of analysis. However, with the advent of social media and computational research tools that allow us to harness such data, a new methodological thrust emerged that tries to build more 'bespoke' and 'research-specific' datasets from social media streams.

This chapter aimed to introduce current debates, datasets, and measurements that are involved in conflict research, and to provide an insight into how researchers can leverage a social media stream to produce tailor-made event datasets for their own work. In our study, Twitter-based conflict event data was more advantageous to ACLED and UCDP/PRIO at the local level, but fell short against ACLED in a wider operational area. Yet despite its numerical advantages, ACLED did miss a number of significant events in our case study, Operation Olive Branch, that had a direct impact on the outcome of the war. Overall, extracting violent event data from social media is still a labour-intensive, often frustrating, but nonetheless rewarding endeavour that will certainly become more relevant to scientific research in the coming years. Especially as social media membership proliferates and smartphone ownership expands well into war zones, we can predict that more and higher-quality conflict data will be available within the next few years.

That said, social-media-based event data suffer from two major biases that affect data quality, and thus research findings. The first is the access to physical infrastructure, such as smartphones, cell phone towers, and data coverage. In areas that lack any of these prerequisites, extracting event data is still difficult, which leads to biased data that omit information from low-access regions. Although in the last few years this issue has been remedied by makeshift routers and satellite up-link facilities, it is still a major problem in war zones. The second major problem is the proliferation of disinformation and information manipulation. Conflict areas are rife with misleading content, either for deterrence purposes, or with the aim of pursuing propaganda efforts. These misleading claims can be cleaned by human coders if the data volume is low, but in a major crisis that produces a very large volume of social media data, cleaning it manually becomes impossible. Automated disinformation-recognition tools are still in their infancy, as most machine learning fact-checking systems can be easily misled. As a result, there is currently no working automated model to accurately identify disinformation in war zones, causing significant data validity problems.

We expect these problems to be less relevant in the future, given the quality of research dedicated to remedying both problems. Along with the rapidly increasing usage of smartphones and social media among refugee and combatant groups alike, the volume and quality of the data that we extract from them will be significantly improved in the near future.

Acknowledgements

This work was supported by The Scientific and Technological Research Institution of Turkey (TUBITAK), ARDEB 1001 Program, Project Number: 120K986, Title: 'Silahlı Örgütlerin Dijital Kamu Diplomasisi – Suriye Ve Irak Örnekleri [Digital Public Diplomacy of Armed Organizations – Syria and Iraq Cases]'.

References

Alhelbawy, A., Massimo, P., and Kruschwitz, U. (2016), 'Towards a corpus of violence acts in Arabic social media', *in Proceedings of the Tenth International Conference on Language Resources and Evaluation (LREC'16)*, 1627–31.

Arjona, A., Kasfir, N., and Mampilly, Z. (2015), *Rebel Governance in Civil War*, Cambridge University Press, Cambridge.

Atkinson, M., Piskorski, J., Tanev, H., and Zavarella, V. (2017), 'On the creation of a security-related event corpus', *in Proceedings of the Events and Stories in the News Workshop*, 59–65.

Berman, E., Shapiro, J. N., and Felter, J. H. (2011), 'Can hearts and minds be bought? The economics of counterinsurgency in Iraq', *Journal of Political Economy* 119(4), 766–819.

Best, R. H., Carpino, C., and Crescenzi, M. J. (2013), 'An analysis of the TABARI coding system', *Conflict Management and Peace Science* 30(4), 335–48.

Bowsher, G., Bogue, P., Patel, P., Boyle, P., and Sullivan, R. (2018), 'Small and light arms violence reduction as a public health measure: The case of Libya', *Conflict and Health* 12(1), 1–9.

Chojnacki, S., Ickler, C., Spies, M., and Wiesel, J. (2012), 'Event data on armed conflict and security: New perspectives, old challenges, and some solutions', *International Interactions* 38(4), 382–401.

Cohen, D. K. and Nordås, R. (2014), 'Sexual violence in armed conflict: Introducing the SVAC dataset, 1989–2009', *Journal of Peace Research* 51(3), 418–28.

Cohen, J. (1960), 'A coefficient of agreement for nominal scales', *Educational and Psychological Measurement* 20(1), 37–46.

Croicu, M. and Kreutz, J. (2017), 'Communication technology and reports on political violence: Cross-national evidence using African events data', *Political Research Quarterly* 70(1), 19–31.

Czaika, M. and Kis-Katos, K. (2009), 'Civil conflict and displacement: Village-level determinants of forced migration in Aceh', *Journal of Peace Research* 46(3), 399–418.

De Mesquita, B. B., Smith, A., Siverson, R. M., and Morrow, J. D. (2005), *The Logic of Political Survival*, MIT Press, Cambridge, MA.

Diehl, P. F. (2016), 'Exploring peace: Looking beyond war and negative peace', *International Studies Quarterly* 60(1), 1–10.

Dustmann, C. and Kirchkamp, O. (2002), 'The optimal migration duration and activity choice after re-migration', *Journal of Development Economics* 67(2), 351–72.

Duursma, A. (2018), 'Information processing challenges in peacekeeping operations: A case study on peacekeeping information collection efforts in Mali', *International Peacekeeping* 25(3), 446–68.

Fleiss, J. L., Levin, B., and Paik, M. C. (2013), *Statistical Methods for Rates and Proportions*, John Wiley & Sons, Chichester.

Galtung, J., Fischer, D., and Fischer, D. (2013), *Johan Galtung: Pioneer of Peace Research*, Springer, New York.

Gleditsch, K. S. (2020), 'Advances in data on conflict and dissent', *in* E. Deutschmann, J. Lorenz, L. G. Nardin, D. Natalini, and A. F. X. Wilhelm, eds, *Computational Conflict Research*, Springer, Cham, 23–41.

Gleditsch, N. P., Wallensteen, P., Eriksson, M., Sollenberg, M., and Strand, H. (2002), 'Armed conflict 1946–2001: A new dataset', *Journal of Peace Research* 39(5), 615–37.

Hammond, J. and Weidmann, N. B. (2014), 'Using machine-coded event data for the micro-level study of political violence', *Research & Politics* 1(2), 1–8.

Harrington, C. (2005), 'The politics of rescue: Peacekeeping and anti-trafficking programmes in Bosnia-Herzegovina and Kosovo', *International Feminist Journal of Politics* 7(2), 175–206.

Hegre, H., et al. (2019), 'ViEWS: A political violence early-warning system', *Journal of Peace Research* 56(2), 155–74.

Hegre, H., Østby, G., and Raleigh, C. (2009), 'Poverty and civil war events: A disaggregated study of Liberia', *Journal of Conflict Resolution* 53(4), 598–623.

Hollenbach, F. M. and Pierskalla, J. H. (2017), 'A re-assessment of reporting bias in event-based violence data with respect to cell phone coverage', *Research & Politics* 4(3), 1–5.

Ibáñez, A. M. and Vélez, C. E. (2008), 'Civil conflict and forced migration: The micro determinants and welfare losses of displacement in Colombia', *World Development* 36(4), 659–76.

Kaiser, J. and Hagan, J. (2015), 'Gendered genocide: The socially destructive process of genocidal rape, killing, and displacement in Darfur', *Law & Society Review* 49(1), 69–107.

Kalyvas, S. N. and Kocher, M. A. (2009), 'The dynamics of violence in Vietnam: An analysis of the Hamlet Evaluation System (HES)', *Journal of Peace Research* 46(3), 335–55.

Katz, E. and Stark, O. (1986), 'Labor migration and risk aversion in less developed countries', *Journal of Labor Economics* 4(1), 134–49.

King, G. and Lowe, W. (2003), 'An automated information extraction tool for international conflict data with performance as good as human coders: A rare events evaluation design', *International Organization* 57(3), 617–42.

Klabunde, A. and Willekens, F. (2016), 'Decision-making in agent-based models of migration: State of the art and challenges', *European Journal of Population* 32(1), 73–97.

Kreutz, J. (2010), 'How and when armed conflicts end: Introducing the UCDP Conflict Termination dataset', *Journal of Peace Research* 47(2), 243–50.

Krippendorff, K. (2004), 'Reliability in content analysis: Some common misconceptions and recommendations', *Human Communication Research* 30(3), 411–33.

LaFree, G. and Dugan, L. (2007), 'Introducing the global terrorism database', *Terrorism and Political Violence* 19(2), 181–204.

Leetaru, K. and Schrodt, P. A. (2013), 'GDELT: Global data on events, location, and tone, 1979–2012', *in Proceedings of the ISA Annual Convention*, 1–49.

Lyall, J. (2010), 'Do democracies make inferior counterinsurgents? Reassessing democracy's impact on war outcomes and duration', *International Organization* 64(1), 167–192.

McClelland, C. A. (1961), 'The acute international crisis', *World Politics* 14(1), 182–204.

Moore, W. H. and Shellman, S. M. (2004), 'Fear of persecution: Forced migration, 1952–1995', *Journal of Conflict Resolution* 48(5), 723–45.

Nettelfield, L. J. (2010), 'From the battlefield to the barracks: The ICTY and the armed forces of Bosnia and Herzegovina', *International Journal of Transitional Justice* 4(1), 87–109.

Pellegrini, P. A. and Fotheringham, A. S. (2002), 'Modelling spatial choice: A review and synthesis in a migration context', *Progress in Human Geography* 26(4), 487–510.

Pierskalla, J. H. and Hollenbach, F. M. (2013), 'Technology and collective action: The effect of cell phone coverage on political violence in Africa', *American Political Science Review* 107(2), 207–24.

Raleigh, C., Linke, A., Hegre, H., and Karlsen, J. (2010), 'Introducing ACLED: An armed conflict location and event dataset: Special data feature', *Journal of Peace Research* 47(5), 651–60.

Salehyan, I., Hendrix, C. S., Hamner, J., Case, C., Linebarger, C., Stull, E., and Williams, J. (2012), 'Social conflict in Africa: A new database', *International Interactions* 38(4), 503–11.

Salt, J. and Stein, J. (1997), 'Migration as a business: The case of trafficking', *International Migration* 35(4), 467–94.

Schmeidl, S. (2001), 'Conflict and forced migration: A quantitative review, 1964–1995', in A. R. Zolberg and P. Benda, eds, *Global Migrants, Global Refugees: Problems and Solutions*, Berghahn, New York, 62–94.

Schon, J. (2019), 'Motivation and opportunity for conflict-induced migration: An analysis of Syrian migration timing', *Journal of Peace Research* 56(1), 12–27.

Scott, W. A. (1955), 'Reliability of content analysis: The case of nominal scale coding', *Public Opinion Quarterly* 19(3), 321–5.

Shellman, S. M. (2008), 'Coding disaggregated intrastate conflict: Machine processing the behavior of substate actors over time and space', *Political Analysis* 16(4), 464–77.

Singer, J. D. (1988), 'Reconstructing the Correlates of War dataset on material capabilities of states, 1816–1985', *International Interactions* 14(2), 115–32.

Stark, O. and Levhari, D. (1982), 'On migration and risk in LDCs', *Economic Development and Cultural Change* 31(1), 191–6.

Sundberg, R., Eck, K., and Kreutz, J. (2012), 'Introducing the UCDP non-state conflict dataset', *Journal of Peace Research* 49(2), 351–62.

Sundberg, R. and Melander, E. (2013), 'Introducing the UCDP georeferenced event dataset', *Journal of Peace Research* 50(4), 523–32.

Thobane, B., Neethling, T., and Vrey, F. (2007), 'Migration from the OAU to the AU: Exploring the quest for a more effective African peacekeeping capability', *Scientia Militaria: South African Journal of Military Studies*.

Todaro, M. P. (1969), 'A model of labor migration and urban unemployment in less developed countries', *The American Economic Review* 59(1), 138–48.

Weidmann, N. B. (2013), 'The higher the better? The limits of analytical resolution in conflict event datasets', *Cooperation and Conflict* 48(4), 567–576.

Weidmann, N. B. (2015), 'On the accuracy of media-based conflict event data', *Journal of Conflict Resolution* 59(6), 1129–49.

Weidmann, N. B. (2016), 'A closer look at reporting bias in conflict event data', *American Journal of Political Science* 60(1), 206–18.

Wood, W. B. (1994), 'Forced migration: Local conflicts and international dilemmas', *Annals of the Association of American Geographers* 84(4), 607–34.

Zhukov, Y. M., Davenport, C., and Kostyuk, N. (2019), 'Introducing xSub: A new portal for cross-national data on subnational violence', *Journal of Peace Research* 56(4), 604–14.

Part V

A Final Word

19

Eight Theses on Migration Studies and Big Data

EMRE EREN KORKMAZ

Technology and migrants/refugees as a field of political struggle

HUMANITY IS UNDERGOING a great technological transformation/revolution. This period is characterised by multiple technological advances, including in the fields of artificial intelligence algorithms, big data, robotics, and blockchain, and people's daily lives as well as social, economic, political, and cultural relationships are affected by this transformation. Social media platforms, smart phones, and technological products that smarten up everything in our homes and workplaces and make them talk to one another have now become an ordinary part of our daily lives, giving rise to fears and worries about the future. Worries are fed by the potential for the reproduction of structural inequalities and social problems as a result of the new instruments now available to the rich and the powerful for social manipulation, from the future of jobs to the fear of mass unemployment due to widespread automation, and from big advances in military technologies to the deepening of surveillance society.

This transformation affects all areas of life, and migration is no exception. Tools such as social media platforms, street mapping, and translation applications on smartphones offer migrants and refugees great new opportunities, beginning with making the decision to migrate and going all the way to building a new life in their host societies, but they also make it easy for states and global corporations to monitor, direct, manipulate, and prevent migration movements (Beduschi, 2017; Bigo, 2002; Gillespie *et al.*, 2016; Latonero *et al.*, 2018). This is why critical academic studies in the field of migration are now more valuable than ever.

Technological products do not have a will or power of their own. They are serving the owners of these means of production. Although a translation application can empower refugees, independent of the commercial interests behind the application, many mostly speculative pilot projects in migration management to predict migration, automate asylum processes, or smarten borders could create the opposite illusion, leading people faced with the consequences of AI to believe that their outputs are objective decisions, and masking the powerful political and economic interests (Angwin *et al.*, 2016).

Yet, technology is just another field of political struggle. Advances in robotics and artificial intelligence can be used to establish a dystopic regime of oppression with mass unemployment, or to build a Utopian, egalitarian, democratic society where people work less and live in comfort. This is why we are witnessing, on the one hand, the concentration of technological production in the hands of a few global corporations with monopoly position, and on the other hand, the demilitarisation, popularisation, and democratisation of technological production as millions of people are easily able to learn these techniques, set up startups or social initiatives, and create alternative fields.

Serious debates and struggles are taking place in many countries concerning the effects of technological advances on individual and social life, as well as their political implications (Zuboff, 2019; Molnar and Gill, 2018). Depending on their visions of the future, individuals and a diverse set of organisations from business associations to labour unions and from concerned civil society organisations to academic institutions shape this process through their involvement. Parliaments and governments prepare strategic reports, make laws to protect the privacy of personal data and regulate the process, and provide funds and incentives to academia and businesses. Global technology companies, on the other hand, engage in lobbying, while reorienting themselves based on the demands from societies and states. The entire process indicates a dynamic political struggle being played out both at the global level and within unique national settings.

When we examine the field of migration, forced migration, and refugees, it is obvious that migrants have much less political power compared to citizens when it comes to challenging the adverse consequences of these technologies such as opposing biometrics, automated lie detectors and visa evaluations, or high-tech prison-style refugee camps. The process of acquiring a new identity as a result of the migration, traumas experienced by some, problems in adapting to a new country, and, in particular, the delay in acquiring citizenship rights and opportunities for democratic participation might prevent the emergence of a grassroots movement. Moreover, issues such as widespread anti-immigrant and anti-refugee feeling in many destination countries, and the denial, under the disguise of border security, of many of the rights granted by international law to refugees and asylum seekers, weaken the position of migrants, refugees, and their advocates. In short, compared to citizens, it is very difficult for migrants and refugees to make demands of host country governments on the deployment of advanced technological solutions, and make their voices heard in the face of corporations and states implementing a security-oriented approach to migration and border management.

Recognising this imbalance of power may allow academia, in particular, to avoid romanticising the use of technology by migrants and refugees, and instead focus on the arbitrary, uncontrolled, and unlawful behaviour of corporations and states that will be discussed in the following sections (Dave, 2017; Burns, 2015; Fussell, 2019; Latonero and Kift, 2018).

Big data and migrants/refugees

Machine learning related advances in the field of artificial intelligence, along with other advances in many fields from smartphones to social media platforms, has resulted in the generation of an unprecedented amount of data, and made it possible to process these datasets to make predictions. These enormous capabilities now make it possible to monitor social developments worldwide in real time, and better predict the potential trajectory of current events.

At this point, we face two basic problems. The first is that these advances strengthen surveillance capitalism (Zuboff, 2019). For example, the ability of social media companies to analyse data collected by their platforms, categorise users, and make predictions on this basis allows them to increase their profits. The business model based on serving personalised ads to users of platforms and services allowed a handful of corporations to establish global monopolies, and this enables not only companies in the business of selling goods and services, but also political parties and powers seeking political manipulation, to utilise this business model to better understand the political stances, fears, and yearnings of social media users and to serve messages designed to manipulate them (Zuboff, 2019). Such political manipulations, and incidents of hate speech and fake news, could be used to mobilise locals against migrants and refugees or could manipulate migrants and refugees to take certain actions.

The second basic problem is the realisation that the capabilities offered by the abundance of data might reproduce structural problems and inequality. Many academic studies have shown that algorithms used in courts, law enforcement, and human resources made suggestions against the interests of women, minorities, employees, and disadvantaged groups. This, in turn, adds fuel to the political struggle against the discrimination reproduced by algorithms (Molnar and Gill, 2018; ICRC and Privacy International, 2018). Here, there is a need to underline that these are an extremely small subset of AI algorithms in use; AI algorithms are virtually everywhere. When we argue that AI capabilities might reproduce structural problems, we do not mean the misuse, or the incorrect use, of these algorithms that creates these problems. Instead, as AI algorithms learn to mimic humans, their suggestions against the interests of women, minorities, employees, etc. demonstrate that the biases are already there, the AI just makes them easier to see. Therefore, automating an already broken system, or a 'a hostile environment' as mentioned by Theresa May, the former Prime Minister of the UK, the security-focused approach of Frontex or virtual walls of the US, would reproduce structural problems and would harm more refugees.

Hence, investigating the relationship between data and politics becomes ever more important. For example, it is well known that Blacks are significantly over-represented in the prison population in the United States, not because they have a greater tendency to commit crimes but because of the systemic racism and discrimination they face. Similarly, more illegal drugs are found in poor neighbourhoods because police conduct more searches in these areas, and act with more restraint in richer areas. This is a clear demonstration of the risks involved in making future predictions solely on the basis of current data. One aspect of this problem is that conventional data collection disregards current inequalities and discrimination. Another aspect is that when it comes to real-time data, different social groups have different levels of access to digital assets due to digital inequalities. Many factors including age, gender, class, and ethnicity affect access to the digital field and data generation. Hence, data and analysis are not objective or neutral, because the data collected are not independent of social conditions (Hernandez and Roberts, 2018).

Given this background, and when it comes to registered and unregistered migrants, refugees, asylum seekers, and forcible displaced people, it is critical to conduct big data analysis with the utmost care not to harm anyone (ICRC and Privacy International, 2018; Interaction, 2003). Attention must be paid, not only to data analysis, but to sources of data. Differences among refugees and migrants, access to digital tools, and different aspects of digital inequality and digital literacy should be taken into account.

With regards to the use of big data in migration studies, the quality and representativeness of datasets are one concern, and another topic worthy of study is the political manipulations mentioned above. During their journeys, migrants and refugees make heavy use of social media platforms, smartphone apps like translation and map apps, and video call apps to talk to their family and friends. Phone chargers are an important need in many refugee camps, and once they cross a border, refugees seek SIM cards and chargers in addition to food and water. However, these technological solutions can also create additional problems for vulnerable groups. Most of these preferred apps were not developed by taking the unique characteristics of migrants and refugees into account or in compliance with humanitarian principles. Because the business models of these companies, in line with surveillance capitalism, depend on serving ads on the basis of the data collected, they can serve as platforms for political and commercial manipulation targeting migrants and refugees. Moreover, states can monitor and prevent these journeys. Therefore, when it comes to migrants and refugees, the imbalance of power is much more pronounced compared to citizens, and the risk of harm from manipulative and unethical conduct should not be overlooked.

Who owns the data and who are the target audience of big data studies?

There has been an increase in the number of academic studies featuring big data analysis in the field of migration, refugees, and humanitarian aid. Many interdisciplinary research teams who gain access to a dataset of this sort make social, economic, and cultural analyses and predictions. These articles have good intentions, such as helping solve the problems of migrants and refugees and supporting their process of integration, stated as research aims. The findings of these articles, on the other hand, are addressed to states, humanitarian aid organisations, the United Nations, and civil society organisations. In short, when researches use big data analysis to identify the routes taken by forcibly displaced people out of a conflict zone, or to investigate the social and economic integration of migrants and refugees in a given country and make recommendations, the hope is that states and aid organisations would undertake planning and allocate their resources accordingly, facilitating migrants' and refugees' access to basic services.

The road to hell is paved with good intentions, and this approach has two main problems. The first is that in the world in general, and in the European Union, Australia, and North America (which are popular destinations among migrants and refugees) in particular, governments aim to control the arrival of migrants and refugees, severely limit the number of those admitted, and, if possible, have forcibly displaced people stay in neighbouring countries. Well-known examples of such policies include the EU's refugee readmission agreement with Turkey, and the deal to send migrants and refugees in the Mediterranean to camps in war-torn Libya (Bankston, 2021), as well as the US cooperation with Mexico for the latter to prevent arrivals at the US–Mexican border (Akhmetova and Harris, 2021). Other practices include making it illegal to provide aid to migrant boats in the Mediterranean, use of technological tools such as drones and sensors to control borders, building physical and virtual walls on borders, and prison-like refugee camps in many countries, all exemplifying governments' approach to the issue (d'Appollonia, 2012). Therefore, it would be a mistake to assume that states would respect the right of refugees to seek asylum when researchers have access to high-quality data. In short, researchers would be well advised to revisit the 'aims and significance' sections of their studies, usually presented at the outset, to the extent they involve informing governments.

The second issue concerns the privacy and security of personal data. Regulations and campaigns in many countries in the face of surveillance capitalism and the problems it causes made the protection of personal data a legal obligation. Although its efficacy is debated, user approval is requested for data sharing and cookies when visiting any website. Companies have the obligation to protect, anonymize, and, when the time comes, destroy digital data, and alternative approaches are emerging regarding data governance. Therefore, no research team or company should be able to collect citizens' data and present them to governments without obtaining these approvals and meeting legal obligations first.

However, when it comes to refugees, asylum seekers, forcibly displaced people, and illegal migrants, these legal requirements, civil society campaigns, and principles of academic research are sometimes disregarded. Even though the data in question are generated by migrants and refugees, a great majority of academic studies do not primarily address migrants and refugees, make them the focus of the study, or conduct analyses for them. The fact that the data were generated by refugees is disregarded, while complying with the permission and the limits set by the organisation that shares the dataset, for example a mobile network operator, and study findings are presented for use by governments and aid organisations. However, just as citizens' permission is sought and legal requirements and ethics- and privacy-related principles are followed in the case of data generated by citizens, analysis of big data concerning refugees should have refugees at the centre. The perspective should be one of developing the rights and freedoms granted to them by international law.

There is a large and growing literature in this field, and it is important for data scientists to work with experts and organisations specialising in diaspora and migrant issues. Governments and aid organisations can, of course, make use of studies by academics, but recommendations should take into account the fact that the real risk they face comes from governments that do not respect their rights.

Smart borders and their relationship with big data

In recent years, the US, Canada, and members of the European Union have made big investments in smart borders. Academic criticism of these investments focuses on how these investments represent the securitisation of migration policies and violate the basic rights of migrants, asylum seekers, and refugees. Reports also note that most of the companies that develop these technologies operate in the military/intelligence industry (Akkerman, 2016; Bankston, 2021; Akhmetova and Harris, 2021). This is why it is worth studying the relationship between smart borders and big data analysis. Yet, smart borders are the manifestation of the expectation, mentioned in the previous section, that analysis of refugee data would help governments make necessary preparations.

Smart border technologies deployed by the US on its border with Mexico and by the EU in the Mediterranean are based on analysis of data from unmanned aerial vehicles (drones), satellites, and cameras and sensors placed on the border, as well as from mobile phones and social media. The investment in drones, sensors, and cameras is focused on collecting as much cross-border data as possible and using these data to monitor, predict, and take measures to prevent migration flows (Benson, 2015; Franco, 2019).

The goal is to stop migrants before they arrive at the border and apply for asylum. An important consequence of deploying these technological means force irregular migrants to take the most dangerous parts of the desert in Mexico, and in the case of the European Union, to choose passages at the most dangerous times and through the most dangerous waters in the Mediterranean, which risk their lives and even cause many migrant deaths. Another method is to inform Mexico in the case of the United States and countries like Libya in the case of the European Union so that they would stem the flow of migrants (Bankston, 2021; Ghaffery, 2019; Rohrlich, 2020).

Smart border 'solutions' also include efforts, currently at the testing stage in many countries, to use artificial intelligence algorithms in order to automate asylum applications and the process of granting refugee status, so that would-be refugees would not talk to a border official but to a kiosk that also acts as a lie detector, trying to explain their problems and register their application (Akhmetova and Harris, 2021; Keung, 2017). These kiosks analyse a range of data from the attitudes and behaviours of applicants to their life stories, compare them to data from other applicants, and make a decision or transfer the file to a human worker.

Solutions such as smart borders and virtual walls are presented as a more humane and modern alternative to Trump's physical wall and are defended by the Democratic Party in the US, but their consequences are not more humane (Franco, 2019). Moreover, many of the smart border technologies are against migrants and refugees, represent a denial of their rights under international law, and result in a higher death toll among refugees (Franco, 2019). Data scientists and academics working on big data projects in the field of migration and refugees should take this connection into account in their work. One visible outcome of big data analysis used by states has been smart borders, and so far it has been a negative outcome.

The business models of technology companies and the issue of big data on refugees

Another issue that needs to be taken into account in big data studies on refugees is the growing interest in the field of refugees and humanitarian aid among global technology companies, data mining companies, mobile phone operators, and financial companies due to their business models discussed above in the context of surveillance capitalism.

For example, Palantir, a leading data-mining company in Silicon Valley that offers surveillance services and works with security agencies such as the CIA, made an agreement with the World Food Programme in 2019 to provide the technological infrastructure for the food aid provided by this UN agency to more than 90 million people worldwide (ResponsibleData, 2019). Another example is the humanitarian aid provided to refugees and forced migrants. In recent years, the idea that providing cash support instead of aid in kind would be more appropriate for refugees and forced migrants took hold among donor countries. Arguably, because refugee crises are long-term crises spanning multiple years, providing cash support instead of aid in kind allows refugees to choose the products they prefer, save money, and invest. However, it is very risky to send cash to war and conflict zones. One risk concerns security during the transport of money, and another risk is the danger that gangs or local authorities can appropriate the money to be distributed (Kaurin, 2019; Madianou, 2019). Hence, banks and mobile phone operators cooperate with NGOs and UN agencies to operate in the field of humanitarian aid, and mobile banking apps and digital platforms are used in many countries to send cash support to aid recipients, who can spend the money in designated stores.

With the significant increase in the number of humanitarian aid recipients worldwide, three issues come to the fore regarding big data analysis. First, UN agencies and humanitarian aid organisations must follow certain principles when interacting with refugees and communities at risk. The first principle, in this regard, is to do no harm. As humanitarian aid operations are digitised, migrants and refugees leave more digital traces than ever, and it becomes critical to prevent warring sides or anti-immigrant political groups from obtaining these data. This is why many humanitarian organisations have created rules and guides regarding data collection and storage. However, sending cash support via digital platforms requires sharing these data with banks and mobile phone operators. Many of these organisations, however, have little or no experience working in the field of humanitarian aid and refugees, no protective measures in place, and few, if any, experts in these issues. Sharing the collected data with unqualified organisations may end up harming refugees (Bansak et al., 2018; UNCTAD, 2018).

The second issue is that by investing in the field of humanitarian aid, technology companies, financial organisations, and mobile phone operators access a large new market and millions of new customers. Acting with a profit motive and not viewing this work as an issue of corporate social responsibility, companies reinforce the perception that humanitarian aid and refugee issues are not a matter of provision of public services, while accessing two types of customers: first, refugees and migrants, and second, humanitarian aid organisations that support them. Hence, researchers should be aware of this issue and take necessary precautions when working with datasets on refugees obtained from financial organisations and mobile phone operators.

The third issue, from the perspective of companies that implement the business model of surveillance capitalism, is that companies operating in the field of data mining and artificial intelligence, in particular, gain access to raw and unprocessed data collected from millions of refugees, migrants, forcibly displaced persons, and asylum seekers. Because refugees usually live in developing countries, which tend to regulate the privacy and protection of personal data lightly if at all, it is possible to access and process big data to train algorithms without worrying about regulation. Supporting humanitarian aid in this field allows these companies to reap public relations benefits while collecting data for themselves in large and difficult localities. This is yet another issue that needs to be taken into account in big data studies on migrants and refugees.

Storage of big data and digital identity solutions

Collecting some data is necessary for refugees, forcibly displaced persons, asylum seekers, and registered and unregistered migrants to have access to basic rights such as education and health in their destination countries and receive humanitarian aid. This can be done by host countries or UN agencies, or in some cases undertaken by Red Crescent/Red Cross and other humanitarian aid organisations. The first step is to provide identity documents to new arrivals (Korkmaz, 2021; Brinham, 2019).

The importance of identity documents is not limited to enjoying basic rights. They are also important for obtaining the cash support discussed in the previous section, and having access to certain services required for integrating into their new countries. For example, ID cards are required for purchasing a SIM card and opening a bank account. Businesses in these fields are required to comply with international 'know your customer' rules. No bank can open an account for a customer whose identity they don't know, and no mobile phone operator can sell a SIM card without identification. Therefore, obtaining identity documentation is the first step. However, refugees and unregistered migrants face serious problems in many countries because they do not have identity documents. Hence, initiatives led by the UN and supported by some global fintech companies and mobile operators advocate for digital identity solutions (Korkmaz, 2021).

Digital identities, of course, would allow storing a large amount of data. Information registered on plastic ID cards is limited; they may, for example, record date and place of birth, but a digital identity can hold a wide range of data. Looking at the example of Turkey, ID cards issued to refugees allow them to access basic services, purchase SIM cards, and open bank accounts. The government also offers a wide range of services online through the e-government system. However, issuing digital identities remains on the agenda. When it comes to issues such as financial integration, entrepreneurship, and calculating credit scores, in particular, it is argued that data accumulated on digital identities can play a role in credit assessment by financial organisations.

In addition to financial integration, pilot projects undertaken in many countries use digital identities to store a wide range of information from diplomas and training certificates to vaccination records and aid received. These solutions often utilise biometrics (see Box 19.1) and blockchain-based technologies based on strong cryptography, mainly to protect data on groups at risk and prevent third parties that may cause harm to them from accessing these data.

This has two important consequences for big data analysis. The first is that when identities are digitised and used to store a lot of data, each digital identity becomes a valuable source of data, and so does the totality of the digital identities issued in a community. These datasets become an important source for UN agencies, humanitarian aid organisations, and technology companies that provide the infrastructure, as well as banks and mobile phone operators that offer services on the basis of these identities. The second is that in a blockchain-based digital identity, refugees themselves must have the private keys to ensure they have full control over

> **Box 19.1** Biometrics
>
> *Biometrics* are digital identity solutions, where a person is identified with 'what they are, instead of what they have or what they know'. ID cards, passports, passwords, keys can be stolen, misplaced, or lost. Biometrics can also be lost, but under more severe circumstances. Considering that about a billion people in the world do not have an ID card (according to the World Bank's Identification For Development (ID4D) Global Dataset, see https://datacatalog.worldbank.org/search/dataset/0040787), biometrics has a considerable potential for ID management.
>
> Commercial biometric modalities include physical characteristics like fingerprint, iris and retina, face, hand, and behavioural characteristics like voice, signature, and gait. For more forensic purposes, DNA analysis can also be used for identification. These modalities offer a range of possibilities in terms of *convenience* and *security*, which usually are at the two ends of this range: high convenience means ease of access, and hence lower security.
>
> There are a few modes of operation in biometric systems. *Biometric authentication* (also called verification) is the comparison of a biometric sample with an existing template from a claimed identity. It is thus a one-to-one matching, which results in a similarity score. If the score is high enough (typically based on a threshold), the claim is validated. A high threshold will result in more secure systems, and a low threshold will produce more convenient systems. The possible errors have different implications. A *false positive* in this context means verifying a person and granting access rights to someone incorrectly. A *false negative* means denying access to someone incorrectly. Depending on the system, multiple attempts may be possible. But obviously, in a smart border scenario, these two errors have very different implications.
>
> The second major mode of operation is *recognition*, where a person is matched in a database of stored templates from a number of people, called the *gallery*. This scenario can be used to identify people on a small wanted list in an airport, or by identifying a person from a camera taken by a border surveillance system. With unlawful practices of collecting images from the internet and social media, it becomes possible to identify billions of people via face images.
>
> Biometrics is a growing market, and the technology is improving each year, getting more accurate and more accessible. See https://www.thalesgroup.com/en/markets/digital-identity-and-security/government/inspired/biometrics for an accessible and broader introduction.

their data. A blockchain is an online trust system, where instead of a single trusted authority, a distributed set of blockchain users collectively store copies of a public ledger, and transactions are stored on this ledger for verification and bookkeeping. In blockchain applications, everyone has a public key (which potentially everybody can know) and a private key (which is secret, and only known by the user); the public key is shared when making a money or document transfer, and the private key is used to access a transfer received. However, in many pilot projects, the private keys of parties are stored by the technology company involved in the project, which then performs all transactions on behalf of stakeholders, because refugees tend to have low digital literacy and sometimes are not literate at all, and the aid organisations and local companies involved in the project do not have technical experts on blockchains. This, in turn, means that refugees have zero control over their identity and their data.

Given that digital identity applications are likely to gain widespread use in the near future, they could be used as another source of data for big data analysis projects, in which case these risks would need to be taken into account.

Use of refugees as test subjects in the development of technological products

The above examples give rise to the criticism that refugees and migrants are used as test subjects in pilot projects concerning the latest technologies and access to new sources of data. Use of artificial intelligence algorithms that also serve as lie detectors in the case of asylum applications, an example of smart border solutions, and the use of blockchain-based identity projects without the knowledge or consent of refugees or other stakeholders are examples of refugees being used as test subjects for emerging technologies.

Another example is Frontex, the border security organisation of the European Union, which used cutting-edge technologies to build refugee camps on Greek islands, criticised as being modern prisons and testing grounds for new technologies (Molnar, 2021). Through cameras, sensors, and products such as face recognition and movement tracking systems, refugees in these camps are kept under constant surveillance and data are collected.

It is now possible, because of the Covid-19 pandemic, to use these technologies on masses, but under normal conditions it is difficult to put citizens through lie detectors, monitor and collect data on their movements, and use novel technologies for financial transactions. However, it becomes difficult to resist or expose such practices in the case of refugees and unregistered migrants.

Data-driven decision-making and qualitative studies

The notion of data-driven decision-making gained huge popularity in recent years. After the start of the Covid-19 pandemic, in particular, making political decisions in a data-driven manner has been a commonly made argument. In this approach, data is treated as constituting an objective, irrefutable piece of evidence, and whatever data analysis generates is taken to be the neutral, objective reality.

The argument so far is that it is wrong to treat data as being objective in itself. However, this does not mean that all datasets are problematic. This is not a rejection of data analysis, either; the amount of data generated by people and machines increases on a daily basis, and processing and analysing these data makes it possible to investigate issues in more depth and detail. Data from social media, cell phones, satellites, and sensors allow understanding developments and changes in these fields in real time or almost real time (Maxmen, 2019).

Analysis of these datasets can prove very valuable, but it should be kept in mind that these datasets can be biased, reproducing structural inequalities in society, and there are class, status, gender, and age differences among the people who generate these data, as well as between them and people who do not generate any data (Hernandez and Roberts, 2018).

Moreover, if a study involves vulnerable groups or groups at risk, such refugees, unregistered migrants, forcibly displaced people, or asylum seekers, it would be best to exercise extra caution. This is first because findings of big data studies can be used against refugees by governments that do not recognise their rights and freedoms, and can lead, as seen in the example of smart borders, in a larger death toll among refugees. Second, it should be kept in mind that there are deep inequalities among refugees, many of whom have experienced traumas, legal problems, and fears, and do not have sufficient knowledge of the language, culture, and socioeconomic structure of their host societies. Analysis of data collected from the cell phones or social media accounts of migrants and refugees might represent a smaller community within all migrants.

Among the new data sources and methodologies employed in migration studies, big data analysis provides important insights, but two caveats should be kept in mind. First, big data analysis should be supported and triangulated with qualitative research to expose the risks and problems created by large-scale data analysis approaches. Face-to-face interviews, sociological and ethnographic research, and evaluation of the historical background remain valuable tools in understanding the sociological, psychological, and economic realities of communities at risk. The second issue is that data analysis should be conducted with an ethical approach that avoids doing harm to refugees. Migrants and refugees themselves should be at the centre of the study, and care should be taken to avoid serving refugees' data to governments and thus supporting their anti-refugee policies. This, in turn, requires undertaking mixed methods research with a multidisciplinary research team.

References

Akhmetova, R. and Harris, E. (2021), 'Politics of technology: The use of artificial intelligence by US and Canadian immigration agencies and their impacts on human rights, *in* E. E. Korkmaz, ed, *Digital Identity, Virtual Borders and Social Media*, Edward Elgar Publishing, Cheltenham.

Akkerman, M. (2016), 'Border wars: The arms dealers profiting from Europe's refugee tragedy', Transnational Institute and Stop Wapenhandel.

Angwin, J., Larson, J., Mattu, S., and Kirchner, L. (2016), 'Machine bias', ProPublica, available at https://www.propublica.org/article/machine-bias-risk-assessments-in-criminal-sentencing

Bankston, J. (2021), 'Migration and smuggling across virtual borders: A European Union case study of internet governance and immigration politics', *in* E. E. Korkmaz, ed, *Digital Identity, Virtual Borders and Social Media*, Edward Elgar Publishing, Cheltenham.

Bansak, K., Ferwerda, J., Hainmueller, J., Dillon, A., Hangartner, D., Lawrence, D., and Weinstein, J. (2018), 'Improving refugee integration through data-driven algorithmic assignment', *Science* 359(6373), 325–9.

Beduschi, A. (2017), 'The big data of international migration: Opportunities and challenges for states under international human rights law', *Georgetown Journal of International Law* 49(3), 981–1017.

Benson, T. (2015), '5 ways we must regulate drones at the US border', *Wired*, available at http://www.wired.com/2015/05/drones-at-the-border

Bigo, D. (2002), 'Security and immigration: Toward a critique of the governmentality of unease', *Alternatives* 27(1_suppl), 63–92.

Brinham, N. (2019), 'When identity documents and registration produce exclusion: Lessons from Rohingya experiences in Myanmar', Middle East Centre Blog, available at https://blogs.lse.ac.uk/mec/2019/05/10/when-identity-documents-and-registration-produce-exclusion-lessons-from-rohingya-experiences-in-myanmar/

Burns, R. (2015), 'Rethinking big data in digital humanitarianism: Practices, epistemologies, and social relations', *GeoJournal* 80(4), 477–90.

Dave, A. (2017), 'Digital humanitarians: How big data is changing the face of humanitarian response: Patrick Meier, 2015, CRC Press', *Journal of Bioethical Inquiry* 14(4), 567–9.

d'Appollonia, A. C. (2012), *Frontiers of Fear: Immigration and Insecurity in the United States and Europe*, Cornell University Press, Ithaca, NY.

Franco, M. (2019), 'Democrats want a "smart wall". That's Trump's wall by another name', *The Guardian*, available at www.theguardian.com/commentisfree/2019/feb/14/democrats-wall-border-trump-security

Fussell, S. (2019), 'The increase in drones used for border surveillance', *The Atlantic*, available at www.theatlantic.com/technology/archive/2019/10/increase-drones-used-border-surveillance/599077/

Ghaffery, S. (2019), 'The "smarter" wall: How drones, sensors, and AI are patrolling the border', *Vox*, available at https://www.vox.com/recode/2019/5/16/18511583/smart-border-walldrones-sensors-ai

Gillespie, M., Ampofo, L., Cheesman, M., Faith, B., Iliadou, E., Issa, A., Osseiran, S., and Skleparis, D. (2016), 'Mapping refugee media journeys: Smartphones and social media networks', Technical report, The Open University and France Médias Monde.

Hernandez, K. and Roberts, T. (2018), 'Leaving no one behind in a digital world', Technical report, The K4D Emerging Issues Report Series, Institute of Development Studies.

ICRC and Privacy International (2018), 'The humanitarian metadata problem: "Doing no harm" in the digital era', Technical report, ICRC and Privacy International, available at https://privacyinternational.org/report/2509/humanitarian-metadata-problem-doing-no-harm-digital-era

Interaction (2003), 'Data collection in humanitarian response: A guide for incorporating protection', Technical report, Global Protection Cluster, available at https://www.globalprotectioncluster.org/

Kaurin, D. (2019), 'Data protection and digital agency for refugees', Technical Report 12, World Refugee Council Research Paper, available at https://www.cigionline.org/sites/default/files/documents/WRCResearchPaperno.12.pdf

Keung, N. (2017), 'Canadian immigration applications could soon be assessed by computers', *Toronto Star*, available at https://www.thestar.com/news/immigration/2017/01/05/immigration-applications-could-soon-be-assessed-by-computers.html

Korkmaz, E. E. (2021), 'Introduction to digital identity, virtual borders and social media', in E. E. Korkmaz, ed, *Digital Identity, Virtual Borders and Social Media*, Edward Elgar Publishing, Cheltenham.

Latonero, M. and Kift, P. (2018), 'On digital passages and borders: Refugees and the new infrastructure for movement and control', *Social Media + Society* 4(1), 1–11.

Latonero, M., Poole, D., and Berens, J. (2018), 'Refugee connectivity: A survey of mobile phones, mental health, and privacy at a Syrian refugee camp in Greece', Harvard Humanitarian Initiative, available at https://hhi.harvard.edu/publications/refugee-connectivity-survey-mobile-phones-mental-health-and

Madianou, M. (2019), 'Technocolonialism: Digital innovation and data practices in the humanitarian response to refugee crises', *Social Media + Society* 5(3), 1–13.

Maxmen, A. (2019), 'Can tracking people through phone-call data improve lives?', *Nature* 569(7758), 614–17.

Molnar, P. (2021), 'Technological testing grounds and surveillance sandboxes: Migration and border technology at the frontiers', *Fletcher Forum of World Affairs* 45, 109.

Molnar, P. and Gill, L. (2018), 'Bots at the gate: A human rights analysis of automated decision-making in Canada's immigration and refugee system', Citizen Lab and International Human Rights Program, available at https://citizenlab.ca/wp-content/uploads/2018/09/IHRP-Automated-Systems-Report-Web-V2.pdf

ResponsibleData (2019), 'Open letter to WFP re: Palantir Agreement', ResponsibleData, available at https://responsibledata.io/2019/02/08/open-letter-to-wfp-re-palantir-agreement/

Rohrlich, J. (2020), 'Court document shows US troops surveilling migrants at the Mexico border', *Quartz*, available at https://qz.com/1815249/us-troops-are-surveilling-migrants-along-the-border-with-mexico/

UNCTAD (2018), 'Technology and innovation report 2018. Harnessing frontier technologies for sustainable development', Technical report, United Nations Conference on Trade and Development.

Zuboff, S. (2019), *The Age of Surveillance Capitalism: The Fight for a Human Future at the New Frontier of Power*, Profile Books, London.

Glossary

Anonymisation A process by which personal data is modified such that a data subject can no longer be identified directly or indirectly. Using additional data sources may reveal the identities in an anonymised dataset, and such scenarios must be considered for proper anonymisation.

Bias Errors in modelling due to systematic differences between the target variables and the predictions. Sampling bias will result from improper sampling from a population, where the target variable's distribution in the sample does not coincide with the distribution in the whole population. Algorithmic bias, on the other hand, is a systematic difference caused by the algorithm directly. For instance, if the shape of the actual distribution is different than what the algorithm can fit, this may cause a bias.

Black-box algorithms Black-box algorithms are those which can be viewed in terms of their inputs and outputs, without any knowledge of their internal workings (as opposed to white-box algorithms).

Emigration From the perspective of the country of departure, the act of moving from one's country of nationality or usual residence to another country, so that the country of destination effectively becomes his or her new country of usual residence (IOM, 2019). Similar to immigration, the EU defines emigration by a projected residence change of at least 12 months.

Gini coefficient A number that is used to evaluate the degree of equality of income and wealth distribution in a country. A value of zero means complete equality, whereas a value of one means complete inequality, where a single person holds all the wealth. Also called the Gini index.

Global North and Global South The concepts of Global North and South were developed by Emmanuel Wallerstein, where the Global North denotes the economically strong regions of North America, Europe, and Australia, and the Global South refers to the economically weaker countries of Latin America, Asia, Africa, and Oceania.

Group privacy The claim of groups of people to determine for themselves when, how, and to what extent information about them is communicated to others. Defining privacy over individual identity is not sufficient to protect groups of people. Subsequently, group privacy is defined to address the privacy of a named group of people, where the group concept is broadly defined and can encompass any boundary of interest.

Immigration From the perspective of the country of arrival, the act of moving into a country other than one's country of nationality or usual residence, so that the country of destination effectively becomes his or her new country of usual residence (IOM, 2019). The EU's definition for immigration is the action by which a person establishes his or her usual residence in the territory of a Member State for a period that is, or is expected to be, of at least 12 months, having previously been usually resident in another Member State or a third country.[11]

Integration outcomes The integration situation of migrants in different areas of social life (e.g., employment, education, and health). Examples of integration outcomes are employment rates and educational attainments of migrants.

Internal migration The movement of people between different residences within the same country (Bartram *et al.*, 2014; Rees, 2011).

Internal mobility The temporary (either short- or long-term) mobility of the residents within the country borders.

International migration Following the UN recommended definitions (2012), we define (long-term) international migration as the movement to a country other than that of the migrant's usual residence for a period of at least a year (12 months), so that the country of destination effectively becomes the new country of usual residence.

International mobility Unlike international migration, which emphasises the aim of a change in residence between countries, international mobility is defined as cross-border, but temporary, movements of the residents of a given country.

Machine learning The study of computer algorithms that can improve a performance measure, such as an error count or prediction accuracy, through experience, which typically comes in the form of data collected from a specific domain.

Migrant As defined by the IOM (2019), migrant is an umbrella term, not defined under international law, reflecting the common lay understanding of a person who moves away from his or her place of usual residence, whether within a country or across an international border, temporarily or permanently, and for a variety of reasons. The term includes a number of well-defined legal categories of people, such as migrant workers; persons whose particular types of movements are legally defined, such as irregular migrants; as well as those whose status or means of movement are not specifically defined under international law, such as international students.

Migration The most widely adopted definition of the IOM (IOM, 2019) is also based on the UN definition from 2012 and defines migration as the movement of persons away from their place of usual residence, either across an international border or within a State.

---

[1] Regulation (EC) No 862/2007 on Migration and international protection.

Glossary 421

Migration flows The number of international migrants arriving in a country (immigrants) or the number of international migrants departing from a country (emigrants) over the course of a specific period (UN, 2012; IOM, 2019).

Migration policies All policies that relate to the selection, admission, integration, and settlement of migrants in a country.

Migration trends The volume and characteristics of both the migrants arriving in a country (migration flows) and the migrant population already in the country (migration stocks).

Mobility Generally, human mobility studies make reference to movements rather than the groups that made them and the places where they occurred. We define human mobility as the temporary movement of persons without the aim of changing their residence, unlike migration.

NUTS The NUTS classification (Nomenclature of Territorial Units for Statistics) is a coherent and hierarchical system set up by Eurostat for dividing up the economic territory of the EU and the UK in order to produce regional statistics. Specifically, NUTS 1 refers to major socioeconomic regions, NUTS 2 to basic regions for the application of regional policies, and NUTS 3 to small regions for specific diagnoses.

OECD The Organisation for Economic Co-operation and Development defines itself as 'an international organisation that works to build better policies for better lives'. OECD has about 300 committees, expert and working groups which cover many areas of policy-making.

Outlier Values distant from most other values. As they can be caused by measurement noise, outlier detection and removal are used both in statistics and machine learning to reduce their effect on the results. Some models are more sensitive to outliers, and it is important to pay attention to their presence during model selection.

Parameter A variable in a model that is adjusted during the modelling process. In machine learning, most parameters are learned from training data. Hyperparameters refer to structural parameters that are set before a single model is trained with data. For example, the number of clusters in a k-means clustering algorithm, or the learning rate in a neural network algorithm, can be set as hyperparameters. The individual weight matrices of the neural network are learned parameters of the model.

Policy Index A set of indicators that are eventually aggregated to provide a concise measure of the nature of policy.

Policy outcomes The impact that policies might have (e.g., immigration stock and flows), i.e., the result of the implementation of those laws and policies. Policy outcomes on migration refer to migration trends (e.g., immigration flows) and integration outcomes of migrants. For example, on the integration of refugees in the labour market a possible policy outcome is the number of self-employed refugees.

Policy outputs The formulation of laws and policies. They are policy measures, such as the adoption of a law/policy by government entities on topics related to migration. For example, on the integration of refugees in the labour market, a possible policy output is the set of laws regulating refugees' access to self-employment.

Refugees and asylum seekers Migrants who have left their countries and request international protection on account of persecution, war, or other factors that put their lives or security at risk (Bartram et al., 2014). In countries with individualised procedures, an asylum seeker is someone whose claim has not yet been finally decided on by the country in which he or she has submitted it. Not every asylum seeker will ultimately be recognised as a refugee, but every recognised refugee is initially an asylum seeker (IOM, 2019).

Social network advertising The process of matching social network users by their profile data available on the social network to target groups specified by the advertiser to deliver advertisements.

Stock migration For statistical purposes, the total number (at a particular point in time) of international migrants present in a given country, who have ever changed their country of usual residence (UN, 2012; IOM, 2019).

Variance As opposed to bias, which is a systematic shift in the measurements, variance refers to the spread of values around the true target. In a predictive model, a low variance is desired.

References

Bartram, D., Poros, M., and Monforte, P. (2014), *Key Concepts in Migration*, Sage, Thousand Oaks, CA.

IOM (2019), 'Glossary on migration', number 34 *in International Migration Law*, International Organization for Migration.

Rees, P. (2011), 'The dynamics of populations large and small: Processes, models and futures, *in* J. Stillwell and M. Clarke, eds, *Population Dynamics and Projection Methods*, Springer, New York, 1–28.

UN (2012), 'Toolkit on international migration', United Nations Department of Economic and Social Affairs.

Index

accountability 41
admission policies 189
Afghanistan 244
AI Ethics Lab 36
algorithmic bias 407
American Community Survey (ACS) 145
anonymisation 28, 168, 419
application programming interfaces (APIs) 15, 66, 143, 153, 162, 357, 393
armed conflict 130
Association of South-East Asian Nations (ASEAN) 81
asylum 199, 411
asylum seeker 313, 359; definition 422
audience estimates 142
Australia 315, 339

Bangladesh 29, 79, 80
base transmission station 72
Bayesian inference 216
Belgium 338, 339
bias 45, 419; algorithmic 28, 31, 152, 361; mitigation 155; sampling 152; selection 175, 213; self-report 152; self-selection 152; social desirability 332; unbiased estimator 101
big data 6, 10, 159
biometric authentication 414
biometric recognition 414
biometrics *see* digital identity
black-box algorithms 30, 153, 357, 419
blockchain 413
Brazil 259, 371, 377
Bulgaria 325
Burkina Faso 8, 79

Canada 337, 339
causality 216, 301
CCPA 86
census data 130, 275
CESSDA Data Catalogue (CDC) 52, 54
China 276
circular migration 104
citizenship 199
clustering; k-means 251
code-switching 339, 342
Colombia 78, 79, 130, 144
computational linguistics 355
computational social science 4

conflict analysis 386
conflict event data 385
consent 28, 29, 38, 97, 154
Consortium of European Social Science Data Archives (CESSDA) 51
control creep 98
controlled vocabularies 69
coverage 83
Covid-19 3, 269, 373, 376, 415
critical citizenship studies 368
cross-country comparative analysis 184
cultural diversity 159
cultural integration 161
Czech Republic 313, 325
Côte d'Ivoire 86

DARIAH project 44
data augmentation 101
data broker 154
data collaboratives 15, 84
Data Documentation Initiative (DDI) 54
Data Ethics Canvas 36
Data Ethics Decision Aid (DEDA) 37
Data for Development (D4D) Challenge 30
Data for Integration (D4I) 174
Data for Refugees (D4R) Challenge 10, 76, 96, 283, 293, 296
data gaps 9
data imputation 101, 257
Data Management Expert Guide 67
data management plan (DMP) 44, 67
data model 242
data normalisation 257; min–max normalisation 101; z-normalisation 101, 257
data owners 12
data politics 361
data privacy 39
data protection 39; by design and default 33
data science; definition 5
data scraping 356
data security 98
data sharing models 14
data steward 15
DataFrame 75
Dataverse 390
de-identification 28
Deadly Voyages Project 273
demographic research 152

424   Index

Determinants of International Migration (DEMIG) 185
differential privacy 15
digital humanitarianism 367
digital identity 16, 413
digital image processing 124
digital making-do 370
Digital Methods Initiative 357
digital traces 367
direct discrimination 32
Directorate General of Migration Management in Turkey 78, 291
Displacement Tracking Matrix (DTM) 41
district attractiveness 77
do no harm principle 27, 98, 408, 412
dual loyalty 38
Dublin regulation 199

early warning systems (EWS) 115
Earth observation (EO); definition 117
Earth Observing System (EOS) 122
Ecuador 82
electromagnetic (EM) radiation 117
EM-DAT dataset 81
emigration; definition 419; policy 189
endogenous variable 216, 301
Enhanced Vegetation Index (EVI) 125
environmental migration 79
Estonia 96
ethics 166
Ethiopia 79, 131
Ethnic and Migrant Minorities (EMM) Survey Registry 64
EU28 189
Euclidean distance 252, 320
EUCROSS Survey 7
Eurobarometer 59, 196, 201, 311, 330
European Centre for Medium-Range Weather Forecasts (ECMWF) 123
European Language Social Science Thesaurus (ELSST) 52, 56
European Open Science Cloud (EOSC) 54, 62
European Organisation for the Exploitation of Meteorological Satellites (EUMETSAT) 123
European Research Area (ERA) 63
European Research Infrastructure Consortium (ERIC) 52
European Resettlement Scheme 314
European Social Survey (ESS) 59, 196, 200, 311
European Space Agency (ESA) 123
European Strategic Forum for Research Infrastructures (ESFRI) 52
European Union Framework Programmes (FPs) 63
Eurostat 195, 196, 199, 200, 311, 323
event data; Armed Conflict Location and Events Dataset (ACLED) 387, 388; conflict events 387; Global Database of Events, Language, and Tone (GDELT) 7, 77, 389; Global Terrorism Database (GTD) 388; Integrated Crisis Early Warning System (ICEWS) 387, 389; Sexual Violence in Armed Conflict (SVAC) 391; Significant Acts Database (SIGACTS) 390; Social Conflict Analysis Database (SCAD) 390; Uppsala Conflict Data Program – Peace Research Institute of Oslo Dataset (UCDP/PRIO) 387, 388; xSUB 390
exogenous variable 216, 301
explainability 28, 31
explanation-based models 6
extended detail records (XDR) 83

Facebook 142, 153
Facebook Advertising Platform 141
Factiva 356, 357
FAIR principles 51, 67
fairness 32
fake news 373, 399, 407
false negative 414
false positive 414
feature extraction 258
feature selection 257
federated learning 15
field work 9
financial data 212; spending behaviours 223; transactional records 212
findability 65
Finnish Data Service 68
fixed effects model 294, 301
Flowminder Foundation 85, 95, 111
found data *see* secondary data
France 276, 371
freemium model 141
Frobenius norm 76
Frontex 41, 408, 415

General Data Protection Regulation (GDPR) 38, 86, 154
Geneva Convention 45, 312
Geocoded Disasters dataset (GDIS) 81
geocoding 173
GeoJSON 75
geolocation 173
geotagging 173
Germany 325, 328, 338, 342, 367
GESIS data catalogue 196

Index

Gini coefficient 76, 419
Global Compact for Safe, Orderly and Regular Migration (GCM) 42
Global Monitoring for Environment and Security (GMES) 123
Global Refugee Populations 273
gold standard dataset 160
Google trends 11
government censorship 386
GovLab 44
Granger causality 216
graphs 247
gravity model 11, 77, 78, 215
Greece 313, 314, 328, 370, 415

Haiti 80
hate speech 407
Hausdorff distance 252
heatmap 219
heritage language 337
high-risk AI systems 40
home location 103, 163, 297
homogeneous flux 224
homophily 77
Human Costs of Border Control Project 276
human mobility 160
human rights 43
Human Rights Watch (HRW) 30
humanitarian causes 269, 383, 413
HumMingBird Project 63
Hungary 313, 325
Hurricane Maria 146, 155
hydrating 164

identity documents 413
image processing; Gaussian filter 251; kernel density estimation (KDE) 251
image recognition 125
immigration; definition 420; policy 189
Immigration Policies in Comparison (IMPIC) 184–186
in situ data 123
indirect discrimination 32
Integrated Network for Societal Conflict Research (INSCR) 391
Integrated Public Use Microdata Series Project 275
integration 159; economic 217, 409; labour market 188; outcomes 420; policy 188; survey data 200
Intercultural Cities Index (ICC) 190
International Ethnic and Immigrant Minorities' survey data Network (ETHMIGSURVEYDATA) Project 64
International Labor Organization 81
International Monetary Fund (IMF) 217

International Organization for Migration (IOM) 3, 8, 186, 275, 373; Data Portal 186, 241; Missing Migrant Project 276
International Social Survey Programme 59
International Survey Data Network 63
International Telecommunication Union (ITU) 71
Iran 244
Iraq 11
isolation 77
Istanbul 76
Italy 42, 313, 328

Japan 79
Jetson Project 8
JSON 164
justice 32

Kalman filter 216
Kenya 369

labour market 292
language mixing 339
Leaf Area Index (LAI) 126
Leibniz Institute for Social Science (GESIS) 59; Historical Statistics Database 61
lexical priming 359
LexisNexis 356
Libya 42, 409
light detection and ranging (LiDAR) 117
LinkedIn 11, 142
LinkedIn Advertising Platform 141
Lucify; The Flow Towards Europe 272

machine learning 5, 125, 155, 216, 311, 317, 420; convolutional neural network (CNN) 320; decision tree 320, 325; deep learning 5, 11; deep neural network 320; k-means clustering 251; k-nearest neighbours (KNN) 320, 325; linear discriminant analysis (LDA) 320; neural network (NN) 320, 345; one-hot encoding 320; one-hot learning 172; random forest 320, 322, 325; support vector machine (SVM) 320, 325; transfer learning 172; zero-shot learning 172
MACIMIDE Global Expatriate Dual Citizenship Database 190
MADIERA Project 56
Malaysia 338
Mass Mobilization Data Project 390
measles 8
Mechanical Turk 393
media agenda-setting 359
media and migration 352
media monitoring 361

methods creep 107
Mexico 80, 130, 212, 409
microdata 196
migrant 13; definition 420; nowcasting migrant stocks 10, 156
Migrant Integration Policy Index (MIPEX) 190, 192
migration 4; child 271; climate induced 127; definition 420; displacement 383; ethnic 128; family 189; flows 421; forced 4, 130, 383; forced displacement 268; forecasting 161; humanitarian 189; integration 183, 279, 284, 292, 311; internal 161, 212, 222, 276, 292, 420; internally displaced persons 116; international 161, 276, 420; irregular 4, 189; labour 81, 82, 189; management 14, 41; policies 183, 312, 421; policy indicators 184; rural–urban 130; seasonality 216, 302; stock 156, 422; trends 421
mixed effects model 294
mixed methods research 129
mobile call detail record (CDR) 10, 72, 95, 212, 277, 294
mobile call metadata 296
mobility 3, 4; definition 421; internal 420; international 420; matrix 76, 105; seasonal 107
Mobility and Migration Research Platform 62
modelling pandemics 78
Modified Soil Adjusted Vegetation Index (MSAVI) 125
Médecins sans Frontières (MSF) 33, 131

named entity recognition 173
Namibia 82
National Administrative Department of Statistics of Colombia (DANE) 78
national household survey 10
National Institute of Health (NIH) 69
National Integration Evaluation Mechanism (NIEM) 190
National Oceanic and Atmospheric Administration (NOAA) 120, 122, 126
nationality 160
natural language processing (NLP) 170, 171, 355; author identification 345; automatic language identification 343; hate speech detection 345
Nepal 80
Netherlands Data Archiving and Networked Services (DANS) 58
Netherlands, the 338, 339, 342
NexisUK 357
Nigeria 11, 82

Nomenclature of Territorial Units for Statistics (NUTS) 173; definition 421
non-disclosure agreement (NDA) 15
non-refoulement principle 42
Normalised Difference Vegetation Index (NDVI) 125
Northern Ireland 323
Norwegian Centre for Research Data (NSD) 58, 59

Oaxaca earthquake 79
open access 67, 204, 354
Open Algorithms (OPAL) 85
Open Archives Initiative Protocol for Metadata Harvesting (OAI-PMH) 68
Open Data Institute (ODI) 36
open science 360
OpenAIRE 54
Operation Olive Branch 392
orbital period 117
Organisation for Economic Co-operation and Development (OECD) 8, 58, 189, 421; countries 189; Family Database 66
organised violence 384
origin–destination matrix 231, 245, 254
origin–destination paths 247
outliers 101, 260, 393, 421

Pakistan 244
Palantir 411
period-based methods 222
persistent identifier 66
personal data 39, 409
point of interest (POI) 77, 218
policy 154; educational 340; index 421; indicator 192; outcomes 421; outputs 422
population density mapping 131
Portugal 276
predictive models 6
principlism 27
privacy 27, 28, 166, 284, 367, 375, 409; group privacy 15, 34, 36, 98, 153, 419
protected attribute 32
proxy indicators 5, 216, 300
pseudonymisation 74, 168
Puerto Rico 146, 155
purpose limitation 38
pushback of migrants 42
Python 174

qualitative methods 3

radar 117
radiation model 79
re-identification 30, 97, 168

rebel governance 386
Red Cross Climate Centre (RCCC) 131
refugee; definition 422; settlements 131, 292, 305, 372
Refugee Movements Visualiser Project 273
Refugee Processing Center (RPC) 241
remittances 215
remote sensing 115; active 117; agricultural drought indicator 131; anthropogenic change 130; CORINE Land Cover 295, 299; data products 124; data sources 119; definition 117; Earth observation (EO) 116; Earth observation sensors 117; Google Earth Engine 130; land cover and land use 125, 295, 306; night-lights 125, 302; passive 118; satellite imagery 6, 11, 125, 295; very high resolution (VHR) 132
remotely piloted aircraft systems (RPAS) 117
Reproducible Research Oxford (RROx) 354
residence 160
residential inclusion 77
results creep 107
reverse geocoding 173
Rohingya 18, 29
Romania 313, 325
Rwanda 10, 82–84

satellite data 115, 293
Scopus 11
secondary data 14, 101
secondary mobility 97
segregation 77
sentiment analysis 162
shapefile 75
Simpson's paradox 32
Slovakia 313
smart border technology 410, 416
smartphone refugee 95
SoBigData Project 74
social good 13
social integration 77
social media data 385; extraction 392; TABARI coding system 392
social network 159; advertising 142, 422
Social Sciences and Humanities Open Cloud (SSHOC) Project 61
sociolinguistics 337
software; Amazon Web Services 277; ArcGIS 301; BeautifulSoup 357; Berify 397; Bureaucrazy 367; CARMEN 174; CUBu xxxi, 248, 252, 260, 261; FlowKit 80; GapMinder 244; GeoPandas 75; Geopy 174; Google Charts 243; Google Earth 8; Google Image Scraper 358; Google Maps Geocoding API 174; Google Search API 174; Google Translate 172, 394; GraphViz 261; Hunspell 172; Hydrator 164; JFlowMap xxix, 244; KDEEB 261; LGC 258; MapTrix 255; MediaWiki 174; MELTT 390; Microsoft Translate 394; MongoDB 277; MovingPandas 75; NLTK 172; OpenStreetMap 274, 276; PAISA 172; pandas 75, 357; Particles 261; Polyglot 172; pySocialWatcher 145; R 100, 301; ReactJS 277; scikit-mobility 75; Spacy 172; Stanza 172; SweLLex 345; Tableau 243, 258, 261, 325; TextBlob 172; TinyEye 397; TreeTagger 172; Tulip 258, 261; Twitter Firehose 176; Twitter Streaming API 176; Voyage Viewer 267
Soil Adjusted Vegetation Index (SAVI) 125
Somalia 8
Spain 325, 328, 339
spatial join operation 75
statistical testing; analysis of variance (ANOVA) 128, 329; Kruskal–Wallis test 325; Mann–Whitney test 329; Tukey–Kramer honest significant difference test 128
straight-line paths 246, 247
structural equation model 216
Sudan 11
superdiversity index 160
surveillance 29, 33, 367, 369, 405, 415
surveillance capitalism 407, 412
survey data 59, 156, 195, 197
Sustainable Development Goals (SDGs) 5, 16
Sweden 325
Switzerland 190
synthetic populations 323
synthetic-aperture radar (SAR) 118
Syria 96, 211, 273, 385, 392
Syria Visualised Project 273
Syrian National Army (SNA) 398

Techfugees 369
Telecom Italia Challenge 74
terms of service 165
text as data 355
The Human Costs of Border Control Project 273
The Refugee Project 274
time series 125
tokenisation 171
trails 247
transparency 18, 27, 28, 368
trend analysis 216
triangulation 129, 416
Turkey 7, 8, 10, 76, 96, 212, 283, 291, 314

Turkish Statistical Institute (TURKSTAT) 78, 231
Twitter 11, 77, 385

Uganda 128
UK Data Archive (UKDA) 58
UNICEF 271
United Kingdom 325, 339, 371, 375
United Nations (UN) 8, 18, 271
United Nations High Commissioner for Refugees (UNHCR) 8, 312, 373; The World in Numbers 271
United Nations Office for the Coordination of Humanitarian Affairs (OCHA); Centre for Humanitarian Data 269
United States 83, 156, 338, 343, 387, 408
United States Geological Survey (USGS) 119
UNSTATS 111
urbanisation 130
Utrecht University Open Science Programme 354

variance 422
Venezuela 78, 146, 371, 377
verification *see* biometric authentication
Vietnam 115
ViEWS project 388
virtual private network (VPN) 358
virtual research environments (VRE) 69
visual analytics 259
visual encoding 242
visualisation 268, 360; adjacency matrix 254; animation 254; bar chart 245; bubble chart 244; bundling xxx, 251, 252; chord diagram 272; choropleth map 230, 279; density map xxx, 251; flow map 249; heat map 251, 269, 281; interactive 268; Kernel Density Estimation Edge Bundling (KDEEB) 252; Sankey diagram 249, 261, 272, 273, 284; scalability 262; small multiples 253; treemap 281, 282; zoomability 271
Visualising Palestine 273
Voyage Viewer 267

webscraping *see* data scraping
World Bank 217; Identification For Development (ID4D) Global Dataset 414
World Food Programme 411
World Health Organisation (WHO); Natural Disasters Mortality Dashboard 269
World Health Organization (WHO) 354

Zaragoza declaration 199
Zenodo 66